**1 YEAR UPGRADE**

BUYER PROTECTION PLAN

# C# .NET

## Web Developer's Guide

Adrian Turtschi

DotThatCom.com

Jason Werry

Greg Hack

Joseph Albahari

**Saurabh Nandu** Technical Editor

**Wei Meng Lee** Series Editor

| KEY | SERIAL NUMBER |
| --- | --- |
| 001 | CDFE48952P |
| 002 | NHBN9436KH |
| 003 | BAEN24P7BV |
| 004 | HY9W84UJTA |
| 005 | RTW9B39RE4 |
| 006 | JSE4FAHT82 |
| 007 | VTS8TYCGF2 |
| 008 | AUTGFLDCWR |
| 009 | 833K74SLAF |
| 010 | VFR4MHY3XW |

PUBLISHED BY
Syngress Publishing, Inc.
800 Hingham Street
Rockland, MA 02370

**C# .NET Web Developer's Guide**

Printed in the United States of America

1 2 3 4 5 6 7 8 9 0

ISBN: 1-928994-50-4

Technical Editor: Saurabh Nandu  
Co-Publisher: Richard Kristof  
Acquisitions Editor: Catherine B. Nolan  
Developmental Editor: Kate Glennon  
CD Production: Michael Donovan  

Freelance Editorial Manager: Maribeth Corona-Evans  
Cover Designer: Michael Kavish  
Page Layout and Art by: Shannon Tozier  
Copy Editor: Darren Meiss  
Indexer: Rich Carlson  

Distributed by Publishers Group West in the United States and Jaguar Book Group in Canada.

# Acknowledgments

We would like to acknowledge the following people for their kindness and support in making this book possible:

Richard Kristof and Duncan Anderson of Global Knowledge, for their generous access to the IT industry's best courses, instructors, and training facilities.

Ralph Troupe, Rhonda St. John, and the team at Callisma for their invaluable insight into the challenges of designing, deploying and supporting world-class enterprise networks.

Karen Cross, Lance Tilford, Meaghan Cunningham, Kim Wylie, Harry Kirchner, Kevin Votel, Kent Anderson, and Frida Yara of Publishers Group West for sharing their incredible marketing experience and expertise.

Mary Ging, Caroline Hird, Simon Beale, Caroline Wheeler, Victoria Fuller, Jonathan Bunkell, and Klaus Beran of Harcourt International for making certain that our vision remains worldwide in scope.

Annabel Dent of Harcourt Australia for all her help.

David Buckland, Wendi Wong, Marie Chieng, Lucy Chong, Leslie Lim, Audrey Gan, and Joseph Chan of Transquest Publishers for the enthusiasm with which they receive our books.

Kwon Sung June at Acorn Publishing for his support.

Ethan Atkin at Cranbury International for his help in expanding the Syngress program.

Jackie Gross, Gayle Vocey, Alexia Penny, Anik Robitaille, Craig Siddall, Darlene Morrow, Iolanda Miller, Jane Mackay, and Marie Skelly at Jackie Gross & Associates for all their help and enthusiasm representing our product in Canada.

Lois Fraser, Connie McMenemy, and the rest of the great folks at Jaguar Book Group for their help with distribution of Syngress books in Canada.

# Contributors

**Todd Carrico** (MCDBA, MCSE) is a Senior Database Engineer for Match.com. Match.com is a singles portal for the digital age. In addition to its primary Web site, Match.com provides back-end services to AOL, MSN, and many other Web sites in its affiliate program. Todd specializes in design and development of high-performance, high-availability data architectures primarily on the Microsoft technology. His background includes designing, developing, consulting, and project management for companies such as Fujitsu, Accenture, International Paper, and GroceryWorks.com. In addition to his contribution to *C# .NET Web Developer's Guide*, Todd has also contributed chapters to other books in the Syngress .NET Series including the *ASP .NET Web Developer's Guide*, and the *VB .NET Developer's Guide*. Todd resides in Sachse, TX, with his wife and two children.

**Mark Tutt** is a Senior Software Engineer with MICROS Systems. MICROS provides complete information management solutions for the hospitality industry, including software, hardware, enterprise systems integration, consulting, and support. Mark is the principle designer of a number of software packages, including Guest Service Solution, a customer relationship management system for the MICROS Restaurant Enterprise Series platform. In addition to his product development duties, Mark is a key contributor to the design and development of system integration software and customer-specific product extensions that allow MICROS clients to fully integrate MICROS products into their overall technology plans. Mark currently resides in Baltimore, Maryland with his wife Malinda and their twin sons, Fred and Jackson.

**Jason Werry** (MCSD) runs a consulting firm, Synergy Data Solutions, in Australia. He currently provides strategic and technical consulting to his clients and specializes in Windows-based enterprise systems development. Jason has an extensive background using Microsoft technologies and is currently developing state-of-the-art, Web-based applications on the .NET platform. His clients have ranged from a Taiwanese multimedia company to various government departments and local startups. A natural born programmer, Jason started coding Z80 processors in Assembly at age 13. Since then he has used most popular programming languages and presently enjoys working with SQL Server, MTS, IIS, Visual Basic, and C#. Jason holds a bachelor's degree in Mathematics/ Computer Science from The University of Queensland. He dedicates his writing to his loving wife, LiHsing.

**Patrick Coelho** (MCP) is an Instructor at The University of Washington Extension, North Seattle Community College, Puget Sound Center, and Seattle Vocational Institute, where he teaches courses in Web Development (DHTML, ASP, XML, XSLT, C#, and ASP .NET). Patrick is a Co-Founder of DotThatCom.com, a company that provides consulting, online development resources, and internships for students. He is currently working on a .NET solution with contributing author David Jorgensen and nLogix. Patrick holds a Bachelor's of Science degree from the University of Washington, Bothell. Patrick lives in Puyallup, WA with his wife Angela.

**David Jorgensen** (MCP) is an Instructor at North Seattle Community College, University of Washington extension campus, and Puget Sound Centers. He is also developing courses for Seattle Vocational Institute, which teaches .NET and Web development to the underprivileged in the Seattle area. David also provides internship opportunities through his company DotThatCom.com, which does online sample classes and chapters of books. David holds a bachelor's degree in Computer Science from St. Martin's College and resides in Puyallup, WA with his wife Lisa and their two sons Scott and Jacob.

**Greg Hack** is a Senior Software Engineer with Allscripts Healthcare Solutions. Greg has over 15 years experience developing software on platforms ranging from the mainframe to the desktop using a wide variety of languages and technologies. Recent work includes a Web-based application that allows patients to view their medical records and a Pocket PC application that delivers clinical information to physicians at the point of care.

**Axel Goldbach** is a Senior Consultant with modulo3 GmbH, a consulting company based in Germany and specializing in project management consulting throughout Europe. modulo3 is a process implementation specialist for the major networking frameworks, including eXtreme Programming, MSF and V Modell. Axel currently provides senior-level strategic and technical consulting to all modulo3 clients in Germany and Central Europe. His duties include analysis and development of multi-tiered applications in heterogeneous environments.

Axel also works as a technical scout and trainer for modulo3. His training specialties include programming languages, networking, and academic fields such as development methodology, parser- and interpreter-technology, theory of complexity, and provable correct software.

**Joseph Albahari** is a freelance consultant and developer with over 10 years experience in designing networked systems. He has led a string of successful projects, from custom application frameworks for start-up companies, to high-performance OLAP and data warehousing systems for telecommunications giants. His knowledge in object-oriented user interface design has been called upon in the planning or production of many large and complex systems, where well-balanced abstractions are of key importance. Joseph is also experienced in SQL Server database administration, and has developed high-performance solutions for clients with specialized requirements—such as a replication system providing field level synchronization, or a high-throughput bulk-copying agent. Joseph holds a Bachelor's degree in computer science and physics.

**Adrian Turtschi** (MCSE, MCSD) is Lead Architect Solution Development with Avanade (Germany), where he is responsible for the solution offering in the mobile computing space. He has been working on the Microsoft .NET platform since fall 2000, specializing in developing enterprise systems using Web Services. He is particularly interested in using Web Services to bridge platform and system boundaries. Prior to joining Avanade, Adrian worked for KPMG's Global Knowledge Exchange in Boston, where he helped design and develop KPMG's global knowledge management and collaboration solution, used by its 100,000 professionals world-wide. Adrian has work experience in Switzerland, the Netherlands, and the US. He has degrees in Mathematics and Computer Science. He currently lives in Berlin, Germany.

# Technical Editor and Reviewer

**Saurabh Nandu** is the Founder of www.MasterCSharp.com which concentrates on teaching C# and .NET. He worked with HTML, JavaScript, Flash 5.0 before he started programming in Java. Saurabh has been impressed by the power and flexibility of .NET. He is currently employed by YesSoftware Inc. as Technical Evangelist.

## Technical Editor's Acknowledgements

I would like to thank my friend Nanu Jogi without whose direction I would have never got into working on the .NET Platform. I would also like to thank my family, especially my brother Pritesh, for their support.

# Series Editor

**Wei Meng Lee** is Series Editor for Syngress Publishing's .NET Developer Series. He is currently lecturing at The Center for Computer Studies, Ngee Ann Polytechnic, Singapore. Wei Meng is actively involved in Web development work and conducts training for Web developers and Visual Basic programmers. He has co-authored two books on WAP. He holds a Bachelor's degree in Information Systems and Computer Science from the National University of Singapore. The first and second books of the .NET series, *VB .NET Developer's Guide* (ISBN: 1-928994-48-2), and *ASP .NET Developer's Guide* (ISBN: 1-928994-51-2) are currently available from Syngress Publishing.

# About the CD

This CD-ROM contains the code files that are used in each chapter of this book. The code files for each chapter are located in a *chXX* directory (for example, the files for Chapter 8 are in the *ch08* directory). Any further directory structure depends on the projects that are presented within the chapter.

To work with the examples provided, you will need at least the Windows 2000 or Windows XP Professional operating system with the latest service packs, IIS 5.*x*, and IE 6.0, since ASP.NET and Web Services (a part of ASP.NET) are *not* supported on earlier operating systems such as Windows 9*x*/WindowsME/WindowsNT. Also needed is the .NET SDK Beta2 (the latest public release available while writing this book) and the Visual Studio.NET Beta2 IDE.

*The C# .NET Web Developer's Guide* provides you with extensive examples that will help solve the problems you might face while developing applications for the .NET Platform rather than concentrating on the theory of C# and .NET programming. Therefore code is the main feature of this book.

The chapters contain both code snippets and sample programs that illustrate the principles discussed. Chapter 2 presents a series of sample programs that introduce concepts in C# that are different from other object-oriented languages. Chapter 4 helps you understand the basics of building Graphical User Interface (GUI)-rich Windows Forms applications; the examples presented in this chapter are the launch pad for Windows Forms applications used in other chapters. Similarly, code presented in Chapter 8 helps you to interact with various databases using ADO.NET; again, this chapter acts as a foundation for further chapters' database coverage. Chapter 9 will acquaint you with using .NET Class Libraries to interact with XML and its related technologies.

Chapters 5, 6, and 11 discuss technologies and Application Program Interfaces (APIs) that help two applications to communicate and interact with each other. Chapter 5 focuses on enabling applications to communicate over the TCP and UDP protocols and provides an overview of the techniques used to interact with Web pages programmatically. Code examples in Chapter 6 and Chapter 11 concentrate on using Simple Object Access Protocol (SOAP) and object serialization and deserialization.

Chapter 7 examples examine message delivery in distributed applications using Microsoft Message Queuing (MSMQ). Chapter 10 takes a comprehensive look at ASP.NET and helps you build various applications of increasing complexity and functionality, starting with an XML Poll, progressing to a SQL-powered Message Board, and ending with a Shopping Cart.

Lastly, to end on a lighter note, Chapter 12 takes you through building a Jokes Web Service. The code in this chapter helps you build both the Jokes Web Service as well as the Windows Forms Client for the service.

 **Look for this CD icon to obtain files used in the book demonstrations.**

# From the Series Editor

For many years, C and C++ programmers have been searching for alternative programming languages that offer the same kind of flexibility and power of C and C++, but without the complexities and steep learning curve required for mastery of the language. What many programmers desired was a language that would allow applications to be built rapidly, but at the same time giving them the ability to code at low level. The search has finally ended with Microsoft's new language—C#, a member of the .NET Framework.

C# is the revolutionary new language from Microsoft, designed solely to run on the .NET framework. Drawing experiences from C, C++, and Visual Basic, C# was designed to be a simple and modern object oriented programming language.

But why learn C#? With the integration of C# and the Visual Studio.NET (known as Visual C#), developing Windows and Web applications has been radically simplified. With full access to the .NET Class Libraries, C# includes built-in support for developing robust Web services and ASP.NET applications. (It was reportedly said that Visual Studio.NET was built entirely using C# and that most of the examples in MSDN were coded in C#. That in and of itself is a very good reason to learn C#!) Besides this, C# enhances the productivity of programmers by eliminating common errors often associated with C and C++.

While many of the earlier C# books have primarily focused on the language syntax, *The C# .NET Web Developer's Guide* illustrates the uses of C# for Web developers looking to harness the new functionality and ease of this powerful programming language. The best way to learn a new language is by trying out the examples while you are reading this book. Within many chapters, you will find numerous code examples used in various practical situations; this hands-on, code-intensive approach allows you to have a deeper understanding of issues involved in C# Web development, and at the same time allows you to cut and paste portions of applicable code into your current projects, thereby shortening development time.

We are constantly working hard to produce the best technical books needed by professional programmers like you. I sincerely hope you will enjoy reading this book as much as the authors did writing it!

*Wei Meng Lee, Series Editor*
*Syngress .NET Developer Series*

# Contents

# Foreword

Seldom in the history of computer software has any technology received such a positive response from developers and the industry, even while the technology is still in its nascent beta stage. The .NET Beta2 SDK from Microsoft has already been downloaded by millions of developers all over the world. There have been dozens of published books, Web sites and newsgroups devoted to the .NET platform, its related technologies and languages.

Microsoft has invested billions of dollars and years of research in the creation of .NET. .NET is a comprehensive strategy ,consisting of operating systems, database servers, application servers, and the .NET Runtime, as well as managed languages that operate over the .NET platform.

Many people see the .NET platform as the practical implementation of the previously formulated Windows DNA. Others see it as a response to developer woes from working with previous technologies and languages. However, the common opinion simply offers that .NET is a significant improvement over previous Microsoft technologies. The .NET platform has been built from the ground up with numerous goals in mind, including security, scalability, reliability, flexibility, and interoperability—these goals have all been dealt with from the start to help to make the .NET platform enterprise ready and developer-friendly.

The .NET platform displays a significant shift in Microsoft's thinking. While building the .NET platform, Microsoft has shown strong support for open standards like XML, SOAP, and UDDI, rather than building its own proprietary standards and technologies. Even the core part of the .NET platform—the Common Language Infrastructure (CLI)—and the C# specifications have been placed before ECMA for standardization.

C# is defined as a simple, modern, object-oriented, and type-safe programming language derived from C and C++. Developed by Anders Hejlsberg of Microsoft especially for the .NET platform, C# derives its features from a number of languages like C, C++, and Java. Specifically written to offer the simplicity of Visual Basic and power of C++ as an object-oriented language, C# makes it easier for developers to create, debug, and deploy enterprise applications. It has also been predicted that C# will become the favored language for developing applications on the .NET platform.

Visual Studio.NET, the next version of Visual Studio IDE, is also a key component of the .NET strategy. The Visual Studio.NET IDE has also been given a facelift and packed with a wide variety of new functionalities. A bitmap editor, debugger, Web Forms designer, Windows Forms designer, Web Services designer, XML editor, HTML editor, Web browser, Server Resources Explorer, and multi-language support have all been packed into one single IDE.

The focus of *The C#.NET Web Developer's Guide* is not on teaching you the core C# language, but rather providing you with code examples that will help you leverage the functionalities of the .NET Framework Class Libraries. The .NET Framework collection of base classes cover many of the multiple APIs. Although impossible for one book to cover all the features, in this book we have covered the key concepts, libraries, and APIs of the .NET Framework that we feel will help you easily create new applications using C#.

You have a whole host of features to learn and master, so why wait? Let's get started!!

*—Saurabh Nandu, Technical Editor*
*Founder, www.MasterCSharp.com*

# Chapter 1

# Introducing the Microsoft .NET Platform

## Solutions in this chapter:

- **Introducing the .NET Platform**
- **Features of the .NET Platform**
- **Components of the .NET Architecture**
- **Exploring the Code Cycle**
- **The Pursuit of Standardization**

- ☑ **Summary**
- ☑ **Solutions Fast Track**
- ☑ **Frequently Asked Questions**

# Introduction

The .NET platform is the foundation upon which the next generation of software will be built. Microsoft has invested a lot of capital in its development, and is putting its considerable weight behind its adoption as a new standard. A long list of Microsoft partners have also announced support for .NET tools and components—you can check http://msdn.microsoft.com/vstudio/partners for a current list of vendors who have .NET offerings.

The .NET platform is much more than a new language, software development kit (SDK), or even an operating system. It offers powerful new services, a new processor-independent binary format, new managed languages, managed language extensions to existing languages, and the list goes on. Effectively using these new tools is not possible without a firm background of the platform that will empower your applications.

In this chapter, we take a look at the various components of the .NET platform. We introduce not only the concepts and their technology, but explain the terminology used to describe them. This will enable you to have a strong understanding of the internal workings of the .NET platform, and get the full benefit of the information in the following chapters.

# Introducing the .NET Platform

The precept behind the .NET platform is that the world of computing is changing from one of PCs connected to servers through networks such as the Internet, to one where all manner of smart devices, computers, and services work together to provide a richer user experience. The .NET platform is Microsoft's answer to the challenges this change will provide for software developers.

The .NET platform has several components—however, who you ask will probably affect the answer you receive. Servers such as BizTalk and SQL Server, as well as services such as .NET My Services and its first visible component, .NET Passport, are being described by some as integral parts of the .NET platform. However, for many of us, the .NET Framework is what we think of when .NET is mentioned. It includes Visual Studio.NET (VS.NET), the .NET Common Language Runtime (CLR), and the .NET Base Class Libraries (BCL). The other components may be required by specific applications, but they are not a necessary part of all .NET applications.

Looking at the overall architecture, .NET consists of three primary components:

- **The .NET Framework** A completely new application development platform.

- **Several .NET products** Various applications from Microsoft based on the .NET Framework, including new versions of Exchange and SQL Server, which are Extensible Markup Language (XML)–enabled and integrated into the .NET platform.

- **Several .NET services** Provided by Microsoft for use in developing applications running under the .NET Framework. Microsoft's Hailstorm project is actually an attempt to package some of the most crucial Web Services under the Microsoft brand name.

The .NET Framework itself can be divided into three parts:

- **The CLR** A managed execution environment that handles memory allocation, error trapping, and interacting with the operating-system services.

- **The Base Class Library** An extensive collection of programming components and application program interfaces (APIs).

- **Two top-level development targets** One for Web applications (ASP.NET) and another for regular Windows applications (Windows Forms).

The advantages offered by the .NET Framework include shorter development cycles (code reuse, fewer programming surprises, support for multiple programming languages), easier deployment, fewer data type–related bugs due to integral type safety, reduced memory leaks thanks to the garbage collector, and, in general more scalable, reliable applications.

# Microsoft .NET and Windows DNA

If some of the marketing speak surrounding .NET sounds familiar, there's a good reason: The .NET platform is the next generation of what was called Windows DNA. However, although Windows DNA did offer some of the building blocks for creating robust, scalable, distributed systems, it generally had little substance in and of itself.

Windows DNA was a technical specification that focused on building software based on Microsoft server products, utilizing numerous technologies and languages (ASP, HTML, JavaScript, MTS, COM, and so on), many of which are quite unrelated from a developer's point of view. The servers and languages involved all have varying APIs and type systems, making interoperability a challenge at best. Herein lies the big difference: .NET is much more than a specification. A product in its own right, it includes the tools and languages required to make developing these types of *n*-tiered applications easier, neatly packaged as a single coherent and comprehensive API.

# Microsoft .NET Architecture Hierarchy

The diagram in Figure 1.1 shows the .NET platform architecture. Essentially, the .NET families of languages are each compiled into Microsoft Intermediate Language (MSIL, or just IL) output according to the Common Language Specification. The primary types of application development are Web Forms, Web Services, and Windows Forms applications. These applications communicate using XML and Simple Object Access Protocol (SOAP), getting their functionality from the Base Class Library and run within the Common Language Runtime environment. Visual Studio.NET is not required in order to develop .NET Framework applications, however it does offer an extensible architecture that makes it an ideal choice for developing .NET software.

**Figure 1.1** The .NET Platform Architecture

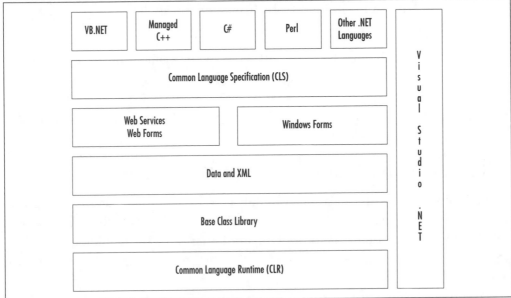

# Features of the .NET Platform

The core of the .NET platform is found in the Common Language Runtime, Base Class Library, and the Common Language Specification. The .NET Base Class Library exposes the features of the Common Language Runtime in much the same way that the Windows API allows you to utilize the features of the Windows operating system; however, it also provides many higher-level features that facilitate code reuse.

This architecture gives a great number of benefits, not the least of which is a consistent API. By writing to the Common Language Runtime and using the .NET Base Class library, all application services are available via a common object-oriented programming model. Today some OS functions are accessed via DLL calls using the C-based API and other facilities are accessed via COM objects, making the developer do the necessary legwork to make everything work together smoothly. Some features are available only to developers working in low-level languages, forcing design decisions.

This new programming model greatly simplifies the efforts that were required when writing Windows DNA applications, or for that matter, almost any Win32 and COM project. Developers no longer need to be a Windows or COM architecture guru with an in-depth understanding of GUIDs, IUnknown, AddRef, Release, HRESULTS, and so on. .NET doesn't just hide these from the developer; in the new .NET platform, these concepts simply do not exist at all.

Another great benefit for .NET developers is its model for error handling via exceptions. Developing software for the Windows platform has always meant you were pulled into its own inconsistencies; particularly in the ways errors were returned. Some functions would return Win32 error codes, some return HRESULTS, and some raise exceptions, all requiring the programmer to write different types of error-handling code. In .NET, all errors are reported via exceptions, which greatly simplifies writing, reading, and maintaining code. Thanks to the Common Language Specification and Common Type System, .NET exceptions work across module and language boundaries as well.

## Multilanguage Development

Because many languages target the .NET Common Language Runtime, it is now much easier to implement portions of your application using the language that's best suited for it. Older methods of allowing different programming languages to interoperate, such as COM or CORBA did so through the use of an Interface Definition Language (IDL). The .NET platform allows languages to be integrated with one another through the use of the MSIL. Although it contains instructions that appear similar to assembly code, such as pushing and popping values and moving variables in and out of registers, it also contains instructions for managing objects and invoking their methods, manipulating arrays, and raising and catching exceptions.

The Microsoft Common Language Specification describes what other development tool authors must do in order for their compilers to output IL code that will allow them to integrate well with other .NET languages. Microsoft currently provides several compilers that produce IL code targeting the .NET Common Language Runtime: C++ with managed extensions, C#, Jscript, and Visual Basic. In addition, several companies other than Microsoft are producing compilers for languages that also target the .NET Common Language Runtime. Currently support for COBOL, Eiffle, Fortran, Perl, Python, Scheme, and many more have been announced by various vendors. For a current list check http://msdn .microsoft.com/vstudio/partners/language/default.asp.

Why should you care about the details of IL? Because this is how .NET manages many of its cross-language features. No Interface Definition Language is required to enable cross-language functionality because IL metadata handles the entire translation overhead. For instance, with an exception object defined by IL, the same object can be caught regardless of the .NET language used. Your component written in C# can raise an exception that can be caught by the Fortran application using it. No more worries about different calling conventions or data types, just seamless interoperability.

Cross-language inheritance is another feature made possible by the use of IL. You can now create new classes based on components written in other languages, without needing the source code to the base component. For example, you can create a class in C++ that derives from a class implemented in Visual Basic. .NET can enable this because it defines and provides a type system common to all .NET languages.

One of the great challenges of developing applications under the Windows DNA specification was in debugging applications developed in a variety of languages. Thanks to the unified development environment of Visual Studio.NET and the use of IL as the output of all .NET languages, cross-language debugging is possible without resorting to assembly language. The .NET Common Language Runtime fully supports debugging applications that cross language boundaries. The runtime also provides built-in stack-walking facilities, making it much easier to locate bugs and errors.

# Platform and Processor Independence

The intermediate language is CPU-independent, and it's much higher level than most machine languages. Once written and built, a managed .NET application can execute on any platform that supports the .NET Common Language Runtime. Because the .NET Common Type System defines the size of the base data types that are available to .NET applications, and applications run within the Common Language Runtime environment, the application developer is insulated from the specifics of any hardware or operating system that supports the .NET platform.

Although at the time of this writing .NET applications run only on Windows platforms, on June 27th, 2001 Microsoft announced that it had reached an agreement with Corel to develop a shared-source implementation of a C# compiler and the .NET Framework infrastructure components for the FreeBSD version of Unix. This is currently expected to be available in a beta version sometime in the first half of 2002.

A few weeks later, on July 10, 2001 Microsoft gave the go-ahead to an open-source version of .NET being planned by Ximian, the developer the popular GNOME user interface for Linux. You can find the project, called Mono, at www.go-mono.net. The group is developing a C# language compiler, along with the .NET Common Language Runtime. Work has also begun on the Base Class Library. The release of the first usable Project Mono code is planned for the end of 2001.

# Automatic Memory Management

The mere mention of a memory leak problem brings forth images of endless hours of debugging for developers who've come from a development environment that did not offer automatic memory management. Even for those fortunate enough to work with this in some form have likely spent some time trying to hunt down obscure bugs caused by tricky code that circumvented the resource management methodology.

Developers coming from Visual Basic or COM backgrounds are familiar with the reference counting technique. This technique recovers the memory used by an object when no other object has a reference to it, essentially when it's no longer needed. Although this sounds perfect in theory, in practice it has a few problems. One of the most common is a circular reference problem where one object contains a reference to another object which itself contains a reference back to the first object. When the memory manager looks for objects that are not in use, these objects will always have a reference count greater than zero, so unless they are implicitly deconstructed, their memory may never be recovered.

For a C or C++ programmer—accustomed to ensuring that objects are properly destroyed, essentially managing memory on their own—this sounds perfectly normal, and a good reason for not trusting anyone else to take care of managing resources. However, in the .NET environment, Microsoft is striving to make developing software easier. Later in this chapter, we cover a how .NET garbage collection works, and the improvements that have been made over strict reference counting or manual memory management approaches.

# Versioning Support

Anyone who doesn't understand the phrase "DLL Hell" hasn't been developing (or at least supporting) software for Windows very long. For the uninitiated, you'll find yourself in DLL Hell someday when a customer installs a software package that uses one of the same DLLs as your application. However, your application used version 1.0 of this DLL, and the new software replaces it with version 1.1. We developers all always make sure everything is 100% backwards-compatible, right? The new DLL makes your application exhibit some strange problem or perhaps just stop working altogether. After a lot of investigation, you figure out what the offending DLL is and have the customer replace the new one with the version that works with your software. Now their new software doesn't work… welcome to DLL Hell. Many developers resort to simply installing every DLL their application requires in the application directory so that it will be found first when the application loads the libraries. This defeats the purpose of shared libraries, but it is one way around the problem.

COM was going to change this; one of its primary tenants was that you never changed a methods interface you simply add new methods. Unfortunately, software developers are frequently perfectionists, and leaving a "broken" function alone just chafes some people. Problem is, changing a components interface once it's in use can have adverse affects on the client software that expected the old behavior. Because COM objects are loaded using information in the Registry, simply placing the DLL or control in the application directory doesn't work for this problem.

The .NET architecture now separates application components so that an application always loads the components with which it was built and tested. If the application runs after installation, the application should always run. This is done with *assemblies*, which are .NET-packaged components. Although current DLLs and COM objects do contain version information, the OS does not use this information for any real purpose. Assemblies contain version information that the

.NET Common Language Runtime uses to ensure that an application will load the components it was built with. We cover more of the specifics of how assemblies and versioning works later in the chapter.

## Support for Open Standards

In today's world, not every device you may want to work with is going to be running a Microsoft OS or using an Intel CPU. Realizing this, the architects of .NET are relying on XML and its most visible descendant, SOAP, an emerging standard for sending messages across the Internet that activates programs or applications regardless of their underlying infrastructure. SOAP will provide the means for disparate systems to exchange information easily, but even more, SOAP allows you to invoke methods on remote systems and return the results. Because SOAP is a simple text-based protocol similar to HTTP, it can easily pass through firewalls, unlike DCOM or CORBA objects.

Other standards employed by the .NET platform include Universal Description, Discovery, and Integration (UDDI), a directory of companies and their XML interfaces and the Web Services Description Language (WSDL), which describes what a piece of application code can do. By basing much of .NET on open standards and by submitting the proposed draft standards for C# and the .NET Common Language Infrastructure to ECMA, an international standards organization, Microsoft hopes to see its version of the future of software adopted beyond its own domain.

## Easy Deployment

Today, developing installations for Windows-based applications can be incredibly difficult, to the point that most companies use third party tools for developing their installation programs, and even then it's not pleasant. There are usually a large number of files to be installed in several directories, various Registry settings, installation of required COM components, and shortcuts that need to be created, and so on. Completely uninstalling an application is nearly impossible, most leave bits and pieces of themselves around even if they provide an uninstall feature. With the release of Windows 2000, Microsoft introduced a new installation engine that helps with some of these issues, but it is still possible that the author of a Microsoft Installer Package may fail to do everything correctly. Even with those third party tools specifically designed to make developing installation programs easier, it is still frequently a monumental task to correctly install a retrievial application.

The .NET design team must have felt the same way about this problem, because .NET plans to do away with these issues for good. .NET components are not referenced in the Registry, thanks to the use of metadata and reflection, components are self describing. In fact, installing many .NET applications will require no more than copying their files to a directory, and uninstalling an application will be as easy as deleting those files.

### Developing & Deploying...

## Using the Visual Studio.NET Setup Tools

Realizing that deploying applications and authoring installation packages is frequently a monumental task, the Visual Studio.NET team integrated a number of setup tools into the Visual Studio.NET environment.

After you have completed your Visual Studio.NET project development, start a new project from the File menu. Choose **Setup and Deployment Projects** from the selection list. You'll see a number of setup project options listed:

- Cab Project
- Deploy Wizard
- Merge Module Project
- Setup Project
- Setup Wizard
- Web Setup Project

Using the wizards, you can select the Visual Studio project you want to use and have a setup or deployment project created automatically. If the defaults are not sufficient for your needs, you can use the new setup project as a basis for creating your custom setup or deployment.

# Distributed Architecture

Today's distributed applications are much different than those we will see in the future. Microsoft certainly believes this; they say they are betting the company on the concept of distributed Web services.

For example, today when a user is interacting with a portal site, it appears to them that they are working with one remote server. Most of us know that is normally not the case, at least for a site of any significant size. There are various servers and applications behind the scenes are accessing information on several remote sites, combining it with information from their user database and merging it all into an integrated product that is delivered to the user via their browser.

As useful as these types of applications are, they are all very complex to develop and maintain. Each provider of information has developed different interfaces to access data and processes on their servers. This redundant development is grossly inefficient and for the most part fairly boring, so there has been a great deal of activity around three standards to streamline the process: XML, SOAP, and UDDI. As we discussed earlier, these are used in .NET and also in competing, less well known initiatives from IBM and Sun.

# Interoperability with Unmanaged Code

As you can probably guess, unmanaged code is code that isn't managed by the .NET Common Language Runtime. However, this code is still run by the CLR, it just doesn't get the advantages that it offers, such as the Common Type System and Automatic Memory Management. You will probably end up using unmanaged code in a couple of different situations:

- **Calling DLL functions** There is a lot of functionality locked inside DLLs today. Not every company is going to rush to deliver a .NET component version of their products, so if you need to interface with them, you'll be calling unmanaged code.

- **Using COM components** This is likely to be for pretty much the same reasons you might be required to call DLL functions.

- **Calling .NET services from COM components** Although this sounds a little odd, it is possible. A COM client can be made to call a .NET component as though it was a COM server.

Here's a little more information on the COM interoperability issue. Microsoft didn't want to force companies to abandon their existing COM components; especially because many of Microsoft's own products are COM-based today. COM components interoperate with the .NET runtime through an *interop* layer that handles all the work required when translating messages that pass back and forth between the managed runtime and the COM components operating as unmanaged code.

On the other side of the coin, companies with a vested interest in COM technology might want to use a few bits and pieces from the .NET platform, sticking a toe in before taking the plunge. COM clients can easily interface with .NET components through the COM *interop* layer.

# Security

Distributed component-based applications require security, and thus far Microsoft hasn't had a lot of positive feedback about its products' security features. Fortunately, the .NET designers decided to take a new approach, different than traditional OS security, which provides isolation and access control based on user accounts, and also unlike the model used by Java, where code that is not trusted is run in a "sandbox," with no access to critical resources. The .NET Framework provides a fine-grained control of application security.

Security for .NET applications starts as soon as a class is loaded by the CLR. Before the class loader instantiates a class, security information—such as accessibility rules and self-consistency requirements—are checked. Calls to class methods are checked for type safety. If you've ever heard of a security vulnerability caused by a "buffer overrun," you can understand why this is important. With verified code, a method that is declared as taking a 4-byte integer parameter will reject an attempt to call it with an 8-byte integer parameter. Verification also prevents applications from executing code at a random location in memory, a common tactic in buffer overflow exploits.

Additionally, as code requests access to certain resources, the class credentials are verified. .NET security crosses process boundaries and even machine boundaries to prevent access to sensitive data or resources in a distributed application environment. The following are some of the basic elements of the .NET security system:

- **Evidence-based security is a new concept introduced by the .NET Framework.** An assembly contains several important pieces of information that can be used to decide what level of access to grant the component. Some of the information used includes what site the component was downloaded from, what *zone* that site was in, (Internet, intranet, local machine, and so on) and the *strong name* of the assembly. The strong name refers to an encrypted identifier that uniquely defines the assembly and ensures that it has not been tampered with.

- **The .NET Common Language Runtime further provides security using a Policy-Driven Trust Model Using Code Evidence.**

It sounds worse than it really is. Essentially this is a system of security policies that can be set by an administrator to allow certain levels of access based on the component's assembly information. The policies are set at three levels: the enterprise, the individual machine, and the user.

- **Calling .NET Framework methods from the Base Class Library get the benefits of built in security.** That is, the developer doesn't have to make explicit security calls to access system resources. However, if your components expose interfaces to protected resources, you will be expected to take the appropriate security measures.

- **Role-based security plays a part in the .NET security scheme.** Many applications need to restrict access to certain functions or resources based on the user, and .NET introduces the concepts of identities and principals to incorporate these functions.

- **Authentication and authorization functions are accessed through a single API.** It can easily be extended to incorporate application-specific logic as required. Authentication methods include basic operating system user identification, basic HTTP, ASP.NET forms, Digest and Kerberos, as well as the new .NET service, Microsoft .NET Passport.

- **Isolated storage is a special area on disk assigned to a specific assembly by the security system.** No access to other files or data is allowed, and each assembly using isolated storage is separated from each other. Isolated storage can be used for a saving a components state, or saving settings, and can be used by components that do not have access to read and write files on the system.

- **A robust set of cryptographic functions that support encryption, digital signatures, hashing, and random-number generation are included in the .NET Framework.** These are implemented using well-known algorithms, such as RSA, DSA, Rijndael/AES, Triple DES, DES, and RC2, as well as the MD5, SHA1, SHA-256, SHA-384, and SHA-512 hash algorithms. Additionally, the XML Digital Signature specification, under development by the Internet Engineering Task Force (IETF) and the World Wide Web Consortium (W3C), is also available. The .NET Framework uses these cryptographic functions to support various internal services. The cryptographic objects are also available in the Base Class Library for developers who require this functionality.

# Performance and Scalability

Let's face it—there is no magic bullet that will allow a poorly designed application to scale well. What the .NET Framework is giving you are tools to make it easier to design better performing software. One big gain for Web development will come from ASP.NET's improved support for keeping code, data, and presentation separate. .NET offers features for transaction handling and component pooling, but makes them easier to use than they were in previous incarnations, so more development will be likely to take advantage of them. The .NET Base Class Library has an enormous set of functionality, which means that you will have to write less basic code and spend more time refining the features and performance of your applications.

New versions of Microsoft software christened with the .NET emblem offer improved performance over earlier versions. SQL Server.NET offers quite an enhancement over earlier versions of the database engine, and other server products offer enhanced scalability as well. When you redesign an application around the .NET Framework, take advantage of the latest advances all around and see what the results are.

# Components of the .NET Architecture

As we mentioned earlier, there is a lot to the .NET Framework. In this section, we identify the individual components and describe their features and how they fit into the overall picture.

## .NET Runtime

The heart of the .NET Framework is the CLR. Similar in concept to the Java Virtual Machine, it is a runtime environment that executes MSIL code. Unlike the Java environment, which is the concept of one language for all purposes, the .NET platform supports multiple programming languages through the use of the Common Language Specification, which defines the output required of compilers that want to target the CLR.

## Managed/Unmanaged Code

Because all code targeted at the .NET platform runs with the CLR environment, it is referred to as managed code. This simply means that the execution of the code and its behavior is managed by the CLR. The metadata available with managed code contains the information required to allow the CLR to manage its safe execution. By *safe execution* we mean memory and security management, type safety, and interlanguage interoperability. Unmanaged code can write to areas of memory it does not own, execute instructions at arbitrary locations in memory, and exhibit any number of other bad behaviors that cannot be managed or prevented by the CLR. Most of the applications running on Windows today are unmanaged.

## Intermediate Language

The .NET intermediate language, MSIL, is defined in the Common Language Specification. It is an amalgam of a low-level language similar in many ways to a machine language and a higher object language. You can write applications directly in MSIL, much as you can write directly in assembly language. Thankfully, this is not necessary for most purposes.

## Common Type System

.NET applications, regardless of their source languages all share a common type system. What this means is that you no longer have to worry when doing development in multiple languages about how a data type declared in one language needs to be declared in another. Any .NET type has the same attributes regardless of the language it is used in. Furthermore, all .NET data types are objects, derived from *System.Object*.

Because all data types derive from a common base class, they all share some basic functionality, for example the ability to be converted to a string, serialized, or stored in a collection.

## .NET Base Class Library (BCL)

If I could have bought a library that offered everything the .NET Base Class Library offers when I started programming, a year's salary would have seemed reasonable—there really is that much to it. Almost everything in the .NET environment is contained within the BCL. Let's look at a "Hello World" example:

```
using System;


class Hello
{
    public static void Main()
    {
```

```
                    Console.WriteLine("Hello World");

        }

}
```

The only function contained in this simple program is a call to the *WriteLine* method of the *Console* class. What is really unique about the .NET environment is that .NET languages don't have to implement even the most basic functions; they are available in the BCL. Because all .NET languages share the same common set of libraries, the code being executed by your C# program is the same code being executed by a program written in another language. This means that all languages that target the .NET environment essentially share the same capabilities, except they have different syntax.

Some people will wonder why we even have different languages if they all have the same capabilities. A few reasons immediately spring to mind:

- Programmers don't like change.

- Programmers usually have a favorite language.

- Programmers don't like change…

Imagine if Microsoft had come out with all the good things in .NET, but said that in order to use it, we all had to learn a new language. Lots of people might have never even given it an honest look unless forced by their employers. Making it available for all languages makes it seem less like the chore of learning a new language and more like the excitement of receiving a new library with tens of thousands of functions that will make your life as a developer easier.

# Assemblies

Assemblies are the means of packaging and deploying applications and components in .NET. Just like a compiled application or component today, assemblies can be made up of either single or multiple files. An assembly contains metadata information (covered in the next section), which is used by the CLR for everything from type checking and security to actually invoking the components methods. All of this means that you don't need to register .NET components, unlike COM objects.

# Metadata

Metadata is the feature that lets the CLR know the details about a particular component. The metadata for an object is persisted at compile time and then queried at runtime so that the CLR knows how to instantiate objects, call their methods, and access their properties. Through a process called *reflection*, an application can interrogate this metadata and learn what an object exposes. This is similar to the way *IDispatch* and type libraries work in COM.

Unlike COM, where the information about a component can be found in type libraries and the Registry, where it is only associated with the actual component, .NET metadata is stored within the component itself in a binary format packaged inside the assembly. The metadata contains a declaration for every type and a declaration, including names and types, for all of its members (methods, fields, properties, and events). For every method implemented by the component, the metadata contains information that the loader uses to locate the method body. It is also possible (but not required) for the creator of a class type to associate help text and comments with a method or parameter in the metadata, similar to the way that information can be associated with a component using information within the IDL in the COM world.

Besides the low-level information described in this section, a component also includes information regarding its version and any culture information specific to the component. The culture information can be queried at runtime and used in developing localized applications. Look at the *System.Reflection.AssemblyName* class as a place to get started, and check out the *CultureInfo* class to see how extensive the culture support of .NET components can be. You can also use reflection to determine a components version, which might be useful if your application is dynamically loading components and needs to make adjustments for different versions.

## Assemblies and Modules

.NET applications are deployed as assemblies, which can be a single executable or a collection of components. When you create a .NET application, you are actually creating an assembly, which contains a manifest that describes the assembly. This manifest data contains the assembly name, its versioning information, any assemblies referenced by this assembly and their versions, a listing of types in the assembly, security permissions, its product information (company, trademark, and so on), and any custom attribute.

An assembly that is shared between multiple applications also has a *shared name* (also known as a *strong name*). This is a key pair containing a globally unique name (think GUID from COM) as well as an encrypted digital signature to prevent tampering. This information is optional and may not be in a component's manifest if it was not intended as a shared component.

Creating .NET modules that do not contain assembly manifest data is also possible. These modules can then be added to an assembly, by including it in the Visual Studio project. An example of why you might want to do this would be if you had a component that was logically divided into several subcomponents that would be best distributed and versioned as a single unit.

## Debugging...

### Finally, a Complete Debugging Solution

Some old-school programmers eschew today's fancy Integrated Development Environments (IDEs) as a mere toy for the weak. (Giving away my age, it's mostly us crusty old Unix programmers) However, the debugging capabilities offered by the new Visual Studio.NET IDE may finally change their minds. The new IDE provides end-to-end debugging of applications across languages, projects, processes, and stored procedures. This is a monumental achievement on the part of the Visual Studio development team.

Using the integrated debugger, developers can step between HTML, script, and code written in any of the .NET supported languages complete with integrated call stacks offering a total solution for end-to-end development.

## Assembly Cache

The *assembly cache* is a directory normally found in the \WinNT\Assembly directory. When an assembly is installed on the machine, it can be merged into the assembly cache, depending upon the installation author or the source of the assembly. The assembly cache has two separate caches: a global assembly cache and a transient assembly cache. When assemblies are downloaded to the local machine using Internet Explorer, the assembly is automatically installed in the transient assembly cache. Keeping these assemblies separated prevents a downloaded component from impacting the operation of an installed application.

Now for what may be a great feature that you won't think of until your project is finished. The assembly cache will hold multiple versions of an assembly, and if your installation programs are written correctly, they cannot overwrite a previous version of an assembly that may be needed by another application. You read that right, the .NET Framework is making a solid effort to banish DLL Hell.

Just to clarify what this means, the assembly cache can contain multiple versions of a component, as an example, we'll say we've installed versions 1.0 and 1.1 of MyComponent.dll on a system. If an application was built and tested using Version 1.0 of MyComponent.dll, the CLR will see this when it reads the application's metadata and will load Version 1.0 of MyComponent.dll, even though a later version of the assembly exists in the cache. The application will continue to function normally because the code that it is executing is the same code that it was built and tested with. Thanks to this feature, you also don't have to maintain compatibility with earlier versions of your components. This feature alone is enough to make the .NET architecture great.

# Reflection

*Reflection* is the means by which .NET applications can access an assembly's metadata information and discover its methods and data types at runtime. You can also dynamically invoke methods and use type information through late binding through the Reflection API.

The *System.Type* class is the core of the reflection system. *System.Type* is an abstract class that is used to represent a Common Type System type. It includes methods that allow you to determine the type's name, what module it is contained in, and its namespace, as well as if it is a value or reference type.

For example, using the *System.Reflection.Assembly* class you can retrieve all of the types in an assembly, and all of the modules contained in the assembly. To invoke a method of a class loaded at runtime, you would use a combination of the *Activator* class to create an instance of the type you had obtained through the *Assembly* class. Then you can use the type's *GetMethod* method to create a *MethodInfo* object by specifying the method name that you wish to invoke. At this point, you can use the *MethodInfo* object's *Invoke* method, passing it the instance of the type you created with the *Activator* class.

It sounds a lot like some of the nasty bits of COM programming, but the Reflection API genuinely makes it a lot easier.

# Just In Time Compilation

The .NET CLR utilizes Just In Time (JIT) compilation technology to convert the IL code back to a platform/device–specific code. In .NET, you currently have three types of JIT compilers:

- **Pre-JIT** This JIT compiles an assembly's entire code into native code at one stretch. You would normally use this at installation time.

- **Econo-JIT** You would use this JIT on devices with limited resources. It compiles the IL code bit-by-bit, freeing resources used by the cached native code when required.

- **Normal JIT** The default JIT compiles code only as it is called and places the resulting native code in the cache.

In essence, the purpose of a JIT compiler is to bring higher performance to interpreted code by placing the compiled native code in a cache, so that when the next call is made to the same method/procedure, the cached code is executed, resulting in an increase in application speed.

# Garbage Collection

Memory management is one of those housekeeping duties that takes a lot of programming time away from developing new code while you track down memory leaks. A day spent hunting for an elusive memory problem usually isn't a productive day.

.NET hopes to do away with all of that within the managed environment with the garbage collection system. Garbage collection runs when your application is apparently out of free memory, or when it is implicitly called but its exact time of execution cannot be determined. Let's examine how the system works.

When your application requests more memory, and the memory allocator reports that there is no more memory on the managed heap, garbage collection is called. The garbage collector starts by assuming everything in memory is trash that can be freed. It then walks though your application's memory, building a graph of all memory that is currently referenced by the application. Once it has a complete graph, it compacts the heap by moving all the memory that is genuinely in use together at the start of the free memory heap. After this is complete, it moves the pointer that the memory allocator uses to determine where to start allocating memory from the top of this new heap. It also updates all of your application's references to point to their new locations in memory. This approach is commonly called a *mark and sweep* implementation.

The exception to this is with individual objects over 20,000 bytes. Very large objects are allocated from a different heap, and when this heap is garbage collected, they are not moved, because moving memory in this size chunks would have an adverse effect on application performance.

As you can see, garbage collection involves a lot of work, and it does take some time. A number of performance optimizations involved in the .NET garbage collection mechanism make it much more than the simple description given here.

Normally you will just let the CLR take care of running garbage collection when it is required. However, at times you may want to force the garbage collector to run, perhaps before starting an operation that is going to require a large amount of memory. To do this, just call *GC.Collect()*. And if you want to report on your memory use at various points during your application's execution to help you determine when might be a good time to force collection, you can use *GC.GetTotalMemory(bool forceFullCollection)*.

As you can probably guess, the parameter *forceFullCollection* determines if garbage collection is run before returning the amount of memory in use.

## NOTE

For those of you who may want to know more about how the .NET garbage collector actually works its magic, Jeffery Richter wrote two articles for MSDN magazine in the November and December 2000 issues that describe the system architecture in some depth. You can find them online at msdn.microsoft.com/msdnmag/issues/1100/GCI/GCI.asp and msdn.microsoft.com/msdnmag/issues/1200/GCI2/GCI2.asp.

# Exploring the Code Cycle

Let's take a look at what's really going on with a .NET application from code to execution. We've already covered that the compiler is going to transform your source code into IL, but what else is happening from code to running application? Here's an example:

1.  You write your "Hello World" application in Visual Studio .NET using the C# Console Application project.

2.  The compiler outputs the MSIL code and a manifest into an exe file that has a standard Win32 executable header.

Let's stop here and take a look at the output using ildasm.exe, a MSIL disassembly tool provided with the .NET SDK. Here is the Hello.exe manifest:

```
.assembly extern mscorlib
{
  .publickeytoken = (B7 7A 5C 56 19 34 E0 89 )          // .z\V.4..
  .ver 1:0:2411:0
}
.assembly Hello
{
  .custom instance void [mscorlib]System.Reflection.
AssemblyKeyNameAttribute::.ctor(string) = ( 01 00 00 00 00 )
  .custom instance void [mscorlib]System.Reflection.
AssemblyKeyFileAttribute::.ctor(string) = ( 01 00 00 00 00 )
  .custom instance void [mscorlib]System.Reflection.
AssemblyDelaySignAttribute::.ctor(bool) = ( 01 00 00 00 00 )
  .custom instance void [mscorlib]System.Reflection.
AssemblyTrademarkAttribute::.ctor(string) = ( 01 00 00 00 00 )
  .custom instance void [mscorlib]System.Reflection.
AssemblyCopyrightAttribute::.ctor(string) = ( 01 00 00 00 00 )
  .custom instance void [mscorlib]System.Reflection.
AssemblyProductAttribute::.ctor(string) = ( 01 00 00 00 00 )
  .custom instance void [mscorlib]System.Reflection.
AssemblyCompanyAttribute::.ctor(string) = ( 01 00 00 00 00 )
  .custom instance void [mscorlib]System.Reflection.
AssemblyConfigurationAttribute::.ctor(string) = ( 01 00 00 00 00 )
  .custom instance void [mscorlib]System.Reflection.
AssemblyDescriptionAttribute::.ctor(string) = ( 01 00 00 00 00 )
  .custom instance void [mscorlib]System.Reflection.
AssemblyTitleAttribute::.ctor(string) = ( 01 00 00 00 00 )
 //--The following custom attribute is added automatically, do not
 // uncomment--
 // .custom instance void
 // [mscorlib]System.Diagnostics.DebuggableAttribute::.ctor(bool,
 //                                    bool) = ( 01 00 01 01 00 00 )
  .hash algorithm 0x00008004
  .ver 1:0:628:38203
}
```

```
.module Hello.exe
// MVID: {D840F359-1315-4B70-8238-0D77358D57D0}
.imagebase 0x00400000
.subsystem 0x00000003
.file alignment 512
.corflags 0x00000001
// Image base: 0x032c0000
```

You can see that the manifest references the assembly *mscorlib* that contains the *System.Console.WriteLine* method. It also contains the version of this assembly that the application was built with, so that the correct one can be loaded when the application is executed. And here is the MSIL output for the *Main()* function:

```
.method public hidebysig static void  Main() cil managed
{
  .entrypoint
  // Code size       11 (0xb)
  .maxstack  8
  IL_0000:  ldstr      "Hello World"
  IL_0005:  call       void [mscorlib]System.Console::WriteLine(string)
  IL_000a:  ret
} // end of method Hello::Main
```

Pretty basic stuff—the CLR is doing all the work. What you can't see is that behind the scenes the compiler added a call to a function in the .NET Runtime named *_CorExeMain*. If you examine the EXE using the depends.exe utility that installs with VS .NET, you will see that it is bound to mscoree.dll for this function, but you won't see any of the DLLs containing the .NET Base Class Library Functions. This is because those functions are invoked through the CLR, not through the normal Windows operating system functions. Figure 1.2 illustrates the process by which your application's source code is eventually executed as native code.

1.  When the application is executed, it first behaves just like a normal Win32 application, loading any required libraries, including mscoree.dll, which exports the *_CorExeMain* function.

2.  The loader then jumps to the EXE's entry point. Because the Windows operating system itself cannot execute the MSIL code, the C# compiler placed the *_CorExeMain* function at the entry point.

3. When the _CorExeMain_ function is invoked, it begins the execution of the MSIL code.

4. The CLR compiles the MSIL code into the native machine format as it processes the MSIL code by using a JIT compiler. The JIT compiles code as it is executed, it does not process the entire application before beginning execution. Once a given function is compiled, the resulting machine code is cached so that it does not have to be recompiled at a later point.

5. The native code is then executed by the system.

**Figure 1.2** Code Cycle Diagram

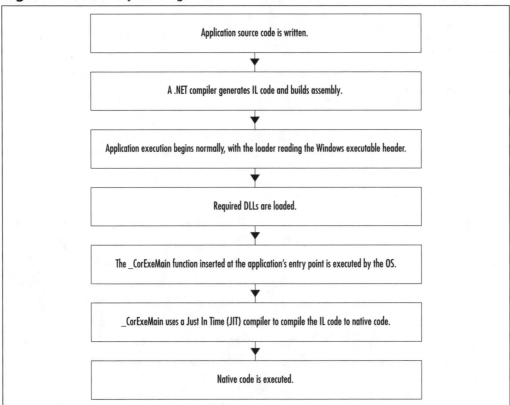

# The Pursuit of Standardization

Microsoft is actively pursuing a process whereby the Common Language Infrastructure and C# Programming Language can be standardized so that any company or individual can create applications based on a recognized standard. On October 31, 2000, Hewlett-Packard, Intel, and Microsoft jointly submitted proposed draft standards to ECMA for use in defining the C# Programming Language (ECMA TC39/TG2) and the Common Language Infrastructure (ECMA TC39/TG3) standards. The official submissions are available from the ECMA Web site at www.ecma.ch.

Since submission, the original documents have been reviewed and edited by the participants of ECMA TC39/TG2 and TC39/TG3. However, little information is available about the group's progress, other than the availability of updated documentation once or twice a month. Given that the standards process for platforms and languages that have already been released and are in widespread use is generally measured in years, it is probably premature at this point to say much about the progress that is being made.

Fujitsu Software, Hewlett-Packard, Intel Corporation, International Business Machines, ISE, Microsoft Corporation, Monash University, Netscape, Openwave, Plum Hall, and Sun Microsystems are all participants in the standards process.

# Summary

The .NET platform is a great leap forward in the evolution of computing from PCs connected to servers through networks such as the Internet, to one where all manner of smart devices, computers, and services work together to provide a richer user experience. The .NET platform is Microsoft's vision of how the developers of this new breed of software will approach the challenges this change will provide.

If some of the .NET concepts sound familiar, there's a good reason: The .NET platform is the next generation of what was called Windows DNA. Although Windows DNA did offer some of the building blocks for creating robust, scalable, distributed systems, it generally had little substance in and of itself, where .NET actually has an integrated, comprehensive design and well conceived, usable tools.

The components at the heart of the .NET platform are the Common Language Runtime, the Base Class Library, and the Common Language Specification. The .NET Base Class Library exposes the features of the Common Language Runtime in much the same way that the Windows API allows you to utilize the features of the Windows operating system. However, it also provides many higher-level features that facilitate code reuse. The Common Language Specification gives language vendors and compiler developers the base requirements for creating code that targets the .NET Common Language Runtime, making it much easier to implement portions of your application using the language that's best suited for it. The .NET platform allows languages to be integrated with one another by specifying the use of the Microsoft Intermediate Language (MSIL, or just IL) as the output for all programming languages targeting the platform. This intermediate language is CPU-independent, and much higher level than most machine languages.

Automatic resource management is one of the most discussed features of the .NET platform, and for good reason. Countless man-hours have been spent chasing problems introduced by poor memory management. Thanks to the managed heap memory allocator and automatic garbage collection, the developer is now relieved of this tedious task and can concentrate on the problem to be solved, rather than on housekeeping. When an allocated object is no longer needed by the program, it will be automatically be cleaned up and the memory placed back in the managed heap as available for use.

Once written and built, a managed .NET application can execute on any platform that supports the .NET Common Language Runtime. Because the

.NET Common Type System defines the size of the base data types that are available to .NET applications, and applications run within the Common Language Runtime environment, the application developer is insulated from the specifics of any hardware or operating system that supports the .NET platform. Although currently this means only Microsoft Windows family of operating systems, work is underway to make the .NET core components available on FreeBSD and Linux.

The .NET architecture now separates application components so that an application always loads the components with which it was built and tested. If the application runs after installation, the application should always run. This is done with assemblies, which are .NET-packaged components. Assemblies contain version information that the .NET Common Language Runtime uses to ensure that an application will load the components it was built with. Installing a new version of an assembly does not overwrite the previous version, thanks to the assembly cache, a specialized container (directory) that store system-installed .NET components.

Given the massive amount of legacy code in use, it was necessary to allow .NET applications to interact with unmanaged code. As you can probably guess, unmanaged code is code that isn't managed by the .NET Common Language Runtime. However, this code is still run by the CLR, it just doesn't get the advantages that it offers, such as the Common Type System and Automatic Memory Management. There are a couple of times when you will probably end up using unmanaged code, making API or other DLL calls, interfacing with COM components or allowing COM components to utilize .NET components. However, realize that by calling unmanaged code, you may be giving up portability.

Developing software using .NET technology is a big change; the technology has a lot of pieces to the puzzle and more than a few new ideas. Hopefully, we have given you a solid introduction into the basics, and you now have a foundation upon which to build your skills using the information found in the rest of the book. If you want more detail on a particular feature of the platform, the MSDN Web site contains a vast amount of reference material that covers the features of the .NET platform at a much more technical level than we attempted here.

# Solutions Fast Track

## Introducing the .NET Platform

☑ Software is changing from a closed to a connected world, much like personal computers themselves are. The .NET Framework is designed to make it easier to create distributed applications that leverage this new paradigm.

☑ There are multiple pieces to the .NET Framework, starting from a shared Common Language Infrastructure and extended to various Microsoft servers and services.

☑ The .NET Framework is designed as a single consistent development environment offering shorter development cycles, improved scalability, and better behaved programs.

## Features of the .NET Platform

☑ The .NET platform hides the gory details of interfacing with the underlying operating system functions and lets you concentrate on the solution at hand.

☑ Multilanguage development is greatly simplified thanks to the use of the intermediate language and Common Language Runtime.

☑ Automatic memory management reduces the level of effort required to manage resources; you can simply let the garbage collector take care of cleaning up and preventing memory leaks.

☑ It includes a new versioning system designed to end DLL Hell.

☑ Much of the platform is built on open standards, such as XML and SOAP.

☑ You are not forced to rewrite everything to use .NET—interoperability with existing code and components is maintained.

☑ It includes an improved security model, which allows a fine-grained control as well as integrated safety from security flaws caused by problems related to buffer overruns.

## Components of the .NET Architecture

☑ The Common Language Runtime is a managed execution environment offering many advantages over the traditional native code development methods.

☑ All languages compile to the same intermediate language. The IL is platform- and processor-independent, potentially allowing .NET applications someday to run on non-Windows operating systems.

☑ The Common Type System allows all languages to share data types without requiring that the developer deal with interpreting different languages conventions.

☑ It includes a large Base Class Library shared by all .NET languages, offering a wide range of functionality intended to improve developer functionality.

☑ Assemblies and metadata are designed to improve on some of the weaknesses of the COM model, by including information about the versions of required components a given component was built with.

☑ The assembly cache is a new facility designed to contain shared .NET components. The assembly cache can contain multiple versions of a given assembly, helping to put an end to DLL Hell.

☑ Through a process called reflection, an application can interrogate this metadata and learn what an object exposes.

## Exploring the Code Cycle

☑ Compiling your source code, regardless of the language used, results in IL code output.

☑ Behind the scenes, the compiler inserts a stub function to load the CLR, which then runs the Just In Time Compiler to transform the IL code into native code.

## The Pursuit of Standardization

☑ Microsoft is making an active effort to see that the technologies on which the .NET platform is based are accepted as standards by a recognized standards organization.

☑ The draft standards for the CLI and C# language have been submitted to ECMA.

☑ The current versions of the standards are available online. They are updated once or twice a month at the current time.

# Frequently Asked Questions

The following Frequently Asked Questions, answered by the authors of this book, are designed to both measure your understanding of the concepts presented in this chapter and to assist you with real-life implementation of these concepts. To have your questions about this chapter answered by the author, browse to **www.syngress.com/solutions** and click on the **"Ask the Author"** form.

**Q:** If any .NET language has access to everything in the Base Class Library, why is there so much talk about C#?

**A:** Although in theory all .NET languages have equal access to the BCL, in reality it was left up to the language teams to determine what level of support they wanted to offer, at least beyond the minimums needed for basic compliance. In our opinion, C#, because it was developed as a new language specifically for the .NET platform, has the best support for .NET applications.

**Q:** I'm a C/C++ developer. Why on earth would I give up all the power and control I have now? And what about speed—native code is always better.

**A:** The .NET platform is all about a new way of developing applications. Many of the enhancements are there for increased productivity. For example, today a C++ application for the desktop and PocketPC are vastly different pieces of code. In the .NET world, they can be the same. Additionally, there are a lot of prebuilt classes available in the BCL that have a lot to offer any developer. As to the native code issue, that is debatable. In a perfect model, you might be right, but for the majority of applications developed today, it's just not a significant factor. The improvements in versioning support and automatic memory management alone make a good argument for the managed environment.

**Q:** Is everything in the Win32 API exposed through the BCL?

**A:** Not through the BCL, but you can make API calls directly through most languages.

**Q:** Why not just switch to Java?

**A:** I'm going to preface this answer by saying that I like Java, I've written several successful commercial projects in Java, and it met the requirements of those projects well. However, Java as a platform requires the developer to buy into the idea of a single language for all things, which goes against my philosophy of "use the right tool for the job." The .NET design allows and encourages cross-language development, letting programmers make use of language skills already developed as well as leverage the various strengths of each .NET language. As to the cross-platform features, my experience and that of many others is summarized by the often-heard phrase "write once, test everywhere," rather than the advertised "Write once, run everywhere." In my opinion, Java also suffers from some earlier design oversights that .NET appears to have learned from. Look at the difference in the Streams implementation on both platforms for an example; the initial Java design did not accommodate Unicode character streams. When this was corrected in JDK 1.1, Java ended up with four base stream classes.

**Q:** Isn't the fact that .NET applications aren't native code going to increase PC requirements?

**A:** This depends on what type of application you're developing, but it's a pretty safe bet. The managed environment introduces additional memory requirements, but they will be negligible in practice. Every new development in software engineering has required more horsepower, and we're really not taxing today's processors with most software. Buying more memory, if it is required, should be a simple sale; developer man-hours are generally a lot more expensive than more memory.

# Chapter 2

# Introducing C# Programming

## Solutions in this chapter:

- **Getting Started**

- **Creating Your First C# Program**

- **Introducing Data Types**

- **Explaining Control Structures**

- **Understanding Properties and Indexers**

- **Using Delegates and Events**

- **Using Exception Handling**

- **Understanding Inheritance**

☑ **Summary**

☑ **Solutions Fast Track**

☑ **Frequently Asked Questions**

# Introduction

Let's start with your first look into the C# language. This chapter teaches you to write, build, and execute console applications. This provides the groundwork for developing applications that use more advanced features of .NET in later chapters.

The C# language is a modern object-oriented language. In some ways, it can be seen as an extension of other languages that came before it. C# is most often compared with Java and C++. If you are not familiar with C# programming, this chapter gets you started. If you are familiar with Java or C++, you may want to just skim this chapter because the concepts presented will look very familiar to you. If you already know C#, feel free to skip this chapter entirely. We assume you have a basic understanding of at least one object-oriented language.

We've mentioned that C# is a modern object-oriented language. Let's take a little time to explain what we mean by that. C# is a modern language. It supports the notion of data types, flow of control statements, operators, arrays, properties, and exceptions. Depending on the language(s) you are accustomed to programming in, most of these concepts should be familiar to you. Throughout the chapter, you will see examples and/or discussions of most of these features of C#.

C# is an object-oriented language. It supports the notion of classes and the object-oriented nature of classes including encapsulation, inheritance, and polymorphism. C# also supports interfaces in conjunction with the .NET Common Language Runtime (CLR) garbage collection, which some feel is necessary in an object-oriented language. It also supports the notion of indexers, which in simplified terms lets you manipulate objects as arrays and delegates, which you can think of as method callbacks on steroids.

The .NET Framework supports console applications, graphical user interface (GUI) applications (Windows Forms), browser-based applications (Web Forms and ASP.NET), and Web Services. This chapter will focus on command line applications, which are known as *console applications*. Console applications have a text-only user interface. In later chapters, you will learn how to create other types of applications. The focus of this chapter is to explain the concepts that are new and/or different in C# from other object-oriented languages. Concepts that are familiar to object-oriented programmers are covered in brief.

Throughout the chapter, a series of sample programs are presented that illustrate the concepts introduced in each section. The sample programs are available on the CD included with this book. Although there are separate sample programs for each section, each sample builds on concepts covered in earlier sections of this chapter.

# Getting Started

Microsoft supplies a full-blown development environment—Visual Studio .NET—for building .NET applications. But, you don't need to buy anything to get started writing C# programs. The Microsoft.NET Framework software development kit (SDK) is available for download from Microsoft's Web site for free (http://msdn.microsoft.com/net). It contains a command line C# compiler that we use to compile the examples in this chapter. This chapter assumes you have already installed the Microsoft.NET Framework SDK. The only other thing you need to get started is a text editor. Because you are writing C# programs for the Microsoft.NET Framework on Microsoft Windows platforms, you have several choices freely available in the Windows operating system. We will stick with the old reliable Notepad as our source code editor of choice.

For users that may be new to the Windows operating system, we run through some explicit instructions on using the command line and Notepad. If you are familiar with Windows, or if you aren't interested in typing the programs in yourself, you can skip ahead to the next section.

The first things you need to do are start a command line session and create some directories to store your sample programs in. To start a new command line session, click **Start** on the lower-left corner of the screen. Select the **Run** menu option from the pop-up menu. The Run dialog box will appear. Type **cmd** in the edit box and click **OK**. You should now see a command line window similar to Figure 2.1.

**Figure 2.1** A Command Line Window

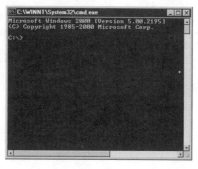

Now you will create directories to save your C# programs in. You can set up any directory structure you like, but for purposes of this example, we use a structure that uses an abbreviated book title as the root directory, the chapter as a subdirectory, and the program name as the lowest level directory:

1. Type **md C#.NET** at the command prompt and press **Enter**.

2. Type **cd C#.NET** and press **Enter** to navigate to the C# .NET directory.

3. Type **md chap1** and press **Enter** to create a subdirectory called chap1.

4. Type **cd chap1** and press **Enter** to navigate to the chap1 directory.

5. Type **md FirstCSharpProgram** and press **Enter**.

6. Type **cd FirstCSharpProgram**.

You have now created the directory to store your first C# program, which will be called **FirstCSharpProgram**. Leave the command-line window open. You will use it to compile your first program a little later.

As previously mentioned, Notepad is our preferred source code editor. To start Notepad, click **Start | Programs | Accessories | Notepad**. You should now see the Notepad application. You will now create an empty source code file in the directory you previously created for your first C# program:

1. Click **File | Save**.

2. In the **Save** dialog box, use the Save In drop-down list to select the **FirstCSharpProgram** folder you just created.

3. C# programs typically use the file extension .cs, which is the convention we will follow. Type **FirstCSharpProgram.cs** in the File name edit area. The dialog box should look like Figure 2.2.

4. Click **Save**.

**Figure 2.2** Saving a File in Notepad

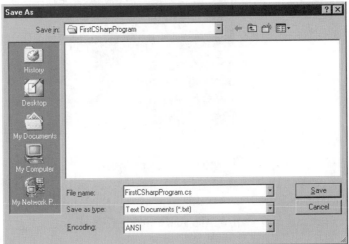

You now have an empty source file available for your first C# program. As you type C# source code into Notepad, you can save your source at any time by clicking **File | Save**. You are finally done with the preliminaries and are ready to start writing code.

# Creating Your First C# Program

The first C# program we look at is a very simple program that writes a couple of lines of text to the console. The program source code is shown in Figure 2.3. If you are following along, type in the program using Notepad and save it. We examine the code in the following sections to get a general feel for the structure of a C# console application. The source code is included on the CD that accompanies this book in a file named FirstCSharpProgram.cs.

**Figure 2.3** The FirstCSharpProgram.cs Listing

```
using System;

namespace FirstCSharpProgram
{
  /// <summary>
  /// My first C# class. Contains the program entry point.
  /// </summary>
  class FirstCSharpClass
  {
    static void Main( string[] args )
    {

      try
      {
        /*
         *   Show when we wrote our first program on screen.
         */
        DateTime today = DateTime.Now;
        Console.WriteLine( "I wrote my first C# program at: " +
          today.ToString() );
```

**Figure 2.3** Continued

```
        if ( args.Length > 0 )
        {
            // Show an optional message on screen.
            string msg = "You wanted to say: " + args[0];
            Console.WriteLine( msg );
        }
    }
    catch ( Exception exception )
    {
        // Display any errors on screen
        Console.WriteLine( exception.Message );
    }

    }
  }
}
```

# Compiling and Executing

The command line compiler included in the Microsoft.NET Framework SDK is named csc.exe. To compile the application, type **csc.exe /out: FirstCSharpProgram.exe FirstCSharpProgram.cs** on the command line and press **Enter**. If you typed the program correctly, no errors should display.

Taking a look at the command line, the first part of the statement, *csc.exe*, invokes the C# compiler. The compiler takes two arguments in this case. The first is */out:FirstCSharpProgram.exe*. The */out* compiler switch indicates that the following text will be the name of the compiled file that will be created, in our case *FirstCSharpProgram.exe*. The final argument is the name of the source code file to compile, *FirstCSharpProgram.cs*. The compiler takes many other optional arguments. But for simple programs, you should be able to use the same command-line text and just replace the name of the output file and the name of the source code file.

*FirstCSharpProgram* takes one optional command-line argument when it executes, that is, the message to display. To execute the program with an optional message, type the following at the command line prompt: **FirstCSharpProgram "C#, I like it!"** Be sure to include the quotes. You should see output very similar to Figure 2.4 after compiling and running the program.

**Figure 2.4** Compiling and Executing the FirstCSharpProgram

Now that you've written, compiled, and executed your first C# program, let's take a look in the next sections at some of the features of C#.

## Debugging...

## Compiling C# Programs/Environment Variables

Your environment variables may not be properly set up if you get the following error message when compiling your program:

```
'csc.exe' is not recognized as an internal or external command,
operable program or batch file.
```

When you installed the Framework SDK, your environment variables should have been set up correctly for you to compile programs. If you get the error just shown, your environment variables have not been set correctly. To fix this problem, execute the batch file corvars.bat located in the bin directory of the SDK. Change directories to the Framework SDK root directory, normally installed in the directory \Program Files\ Microsoft.NET\FrameworkSDK\bin. Execute the batch file by typing **corvars** on the command line. Now change directories back to where your program is saved and compilation should be successful.

# Defining a Class

Classes are the basic ingredients of object-oriented languages. Classes are declared in C# by using the *class* keyword followed by the class name and brackets surrounding the body of the class. The *FirstCSharpProgram* sample has one class, named *FirstCSharpClass*.

C#, like most object-oriented classes, supports member variables and methods. Here is another class that contains some methods and member variables:

```
class Employee
{
    // Member variables
    private string m_FirstName;
    private string m_LastName;

    // Constructor
    public Employee( string FirstName, string LastName )
    {
        m_FirstName = FirstName;
        m_LastName = LastName;
    }

    // Public methods
    public string getFirstName() { return m_FirstName; }
    public string getLastName() { return m_LastName; }
}
```

This class has three methods, the constructor *Employee* and two other methods, *getFirstName* and *getLastName*. It has two member variables, *m_FirstName* and *m_LastName*. Classes and class members (methods and variables) can have access modifiers associated with them that define their level of visibility. Table 2.1 lists the class and class member visibility access modifiers. Some restrictions apply to use of the access modifiers—consult the .NET SDK documentation for details.

**Table 2.1** Class and Class Member Visibility Access Modifiers

| Access Modifier | Visibility |
| --- | --- |
| public | Accessible from anywhere |
| protected | Accessible from this class or any class derived from this class |
| internal | Accessible within current program (assembly) only |
| protected internal | Accessible within current program (assembly) or any class derived from this class |
| private (default) | Accessible only within current class |

You can see some of these access modifiers applied to the *Employee* class and its members. Classes can also support interfaces. You can think of interfaces as contracts with a class to supply methods defined in the interface. Interfaces supply class methods and signatures but no implementations. Classes that support a given interface must supply the implementation of the methods defined by the interface. Here is the previous *Employee* class extended to support an interface:

```
// IXmlRepresentation interface signature
interface IXmlRepresentation
{
    string getXML();
}


// Employee class implements IXmlRepresentation
class Employee : IXmlRepresentation
{
    private string m_FirstName;
    private string m_LastName;

    public Employee( string FirstName, string LastName )
    {
        m_FirstName = FirstName;
        m_LastName = LastName;
    }


    public string getFirstName() { return m_FirstName; }
```

```
public string getLastName() { return m_LastName; }


// getXML method implements a method in IXmlRepresentation interface
public string getXML()
{
    string xmlEmployee = "<Employee>";
    xmlEmployee += "<FirstName>" + m_FirstName + "</FirstName>";
    xmlEmployee += "<LastName>" + m_LastName + "</LastName>";
    xmlEmployee += "</Employee>";
    return xmlEmployee;
}
}
```

An interface named *IXmlRepresentation*, which has one method *getXML*, returns a string. The definition of the interface supplies no implementation. The declaration of the *Employee* now looks like this:

```
class Employee : IXmlRepresentation
```

You can see the interface *IXmlRepresentation* after the class name and a colon. This signifies that the *Employee* class must supply an implementation for all the methods declared in an interface. As you can see, the *Employee* class does supply an implementation for the *getXML* method. The compiler would generate an error if the *getXML* method were missing from the Employee class. Interfaces are often used to supply functionality to a class that really is not part of the class's core functionality. In the case of the *Employee* class, getting an XML representation of the employee really is not related to being an employee at all. But, it may be useful for another class that outputs XML to call the *getXML* method on *Employee*. We show other examples of interfaces later in this chapter.

**WARNING**

C# does not have deterministic destructors like C++ does. The .NET Common Language Runtime (CLR) uses garbage collection to clean up memory and other resources. Long time C++ programmers have a hard time getting used to this idea. This is a topic that is hotly debated on newsgroups and bulletin boards devoted to C# programming.

# Declaring the *Main* Method

Every C# program must have a *Main* method. Here is the declaration of the *Main* method of the *FirstCSharpProgram*:

```
static void Main( string[] args )
```

Execution of the program starts at the *Main* method. The *Main* method is always declared *static*, which indicates that it is a method of the class and not of a particular class instance. Also note that the *Main* method is declared as a method of the class *FirstCSharpClass*. In other languages, such as C/C++, the entry point is often a global function. Global functions are not supported in C#. Also note that the letter *M* is capitalized in the keyword *Main*.

The *Main* method can take command-line arguments in the form of a string array. In *FirstCSharpProgram*, we check to see if at least one command-line argument exists. If yes, we print a message to the screen. Here is the relevant code from *FirstCSharpProgram* to accomplish this:

```
if ( args.Length > 0 )
{
    string msg = "You wanted to say: " + args[0];
    Console.WriteLine( msg );
}
```

Program flow of control starts at the beginning of the *Main* method and continues executing all statements within the *Main* method, or until a *return* statement is encountered. When all statements have been executed, the program terminates.

# Organizing Libraries with Namespaces

Namespaces are used in.NET to organize class libraries into a hierarchical structure. One reason to do this is to help organize classes in a meaningful way that is understood by consumers of the class library. For instance, the .NET Framework SDK has many namespaces, such as *System*, *System.Windows.Forms*, *System.IO*, and *System.XML*. You get a good idea of the types of classes that are contained within the namespace from just the namespace name itself. The fully qualified name of a class is the class name prefixed with the namespace name. The period character is used to separate namespaces nested within other namespaces. It is also used to separate the class name from the innermost namespace. For example, within the

*System.IO* namespace is a class named *File*. Here is some C# code to create an instance of the class—observe how we wrote the fully qualified name of the class *File* by prefixing the namespace name *System.IO*. Also note that *System* is the top namespace and *IO* is the nested namespace within which the *File* class resides:

```
System.IO.File file = new System.IO.File();
```

Another reason to use namespaces is to reduce naming conflicts. For example, if your company name is Synergistic Corporation, you could have all of your namespaces contained with a root namespace named *Synergistic*. One namespace might be *Synergistic.Tools*, and a typical class within the namespace might be *Logger*. The full name of the class would be *Synergistic.Tools.Logger*. It is unlikely that you will find another class with the same name anywhere, thus eliminating naming conflicts.

Here is a snippet of the *FirstCSharpProgram* source code:

```
namespace FirstCSharpProgram
{
    /// <summary>
    /// My first C# class.
    /// </summary>
    class FirstCSharpClass
    {
        ...
    }
}
```

The *namespace* keyword indicates that the class *FirstCSharpClass* is contained within the namespace *FirstCSharpProgram*. Therefore, to create an instance of *FirstCSharpClass*, use the following code:

```
FirstCSharpProgram.FirstCSharpClass myInstance =
    new FirstCSharpProgram.FirstCSharpClass();
```

# Using the *using* Keyword

You might be thinking this namespace thing is all right, but you sure do have to type a lot code to create a new instance of a class. Fortunately, a shortcut exists: the *using* keyword.

In *FirstCSharpProgram*, we call the static method *WriteLine* of the *Console* class to write text to the screen. The *Console* class is actually part of the *System* namespace in the .NET Framework class library, so you would expect to see *System.Console.WriteLine()* instead of *Console.WriteLine()*. Take a look at the following line code at the top of the program:

```
using System;
```

The *using* keyword allows you to reference classes in the *System* namespace without having to include *System* prior to the class name. This works equally well with nested namespaces as in our example of the *File* class. You can now create a new instance of a file object by using the following statements:

```
using System.IO;
File file = new File();
```

# Adding Comments

C# supports three different types of source code comments, single-line comments, multiline comments, and source code documentation comments. Single-line comments begin with **//**. Multiline comments begin with **/\*** and end with **\*/** and can span multiple lines. Text between them constitutes the comment. Source code documentation comments begin with **///**. Examples of all three types of comments from *FirstCSharpProgram* are shown here:

```
// Show an optional message on screen.


/*
 *   Show when we wrote our first program on screen.
 */


/// <summary>
/// My first C# class.
/// </summary>
```

Source code documentation comments deserve further explanation. You can supply an additional argument to the C# compiler to parse the source code documentation comments and emit XML as documentation. The additional argument takes the form */doc:filename*. Here is the command line to build *FirstCSharpProgram* modified to create the documentation file:

```
csc.exe /out:FirstCSharpProgram.exe FirstCSharpProgram.cs /
    doc:FirstCSharpProgram.xml
```

Here is the XML that is generated by the compiler.

```
<?xml version="1.0"?>
<doc>
    <assembly>
        <name>FirstCSharpProgram</name>
    </assembly>
    <members>
        <member name="T:FirstCSharpProgram.FirstCSharpClass">
            <summary>
            My first C# class.
            </summary>
        </member>
    </members>
</doc>
```

## Debugging...

### Debugging Console Applications: Cordbg.exe

The .NET Framework SDK includes a command-line debugger that you can use at runtime to debug your applications. A simple example follows:

```
cordbg FirstCSharpProgram.exe  !b FirstCSharpProgram.cs:100
```

The example starts execution of FirstCSharpProgram.exe and sets a breakpoint at line 100 of the file FirstCSharpProgram.cs. The debugger allows you to set and display the value of variables in your program to aid in debugging your application. You can find more information on *cordbg* in the .NET Framework SDK documentation.

*FirstCSharpProgram* uses the <summary> tag, which is recognized by the compiler as a source code documentation tag. You can use many other tags to document other parts of your code, including parameters, return codes, and so on. In effect, you can self-document your classes and methods for other program-mers using source code documentation comments. The XML emitted can be converted into other formats, such as HTML, and then be published so that other programmers can learn the classes and methods available in your program. You can learn more about XML in Chapter 9.

# Introducing Data Types

A programming language wouldn't be able to do much if it didn't have data to work with. C# supports two data types: value types and reference types. *Value types* are the typical primitive types available in most programming languages and are allocated on the stack. *Reference types* are typically class instances and are allo-cated on the heap. Both are discussed in further detail in the following sections.

## Value Types

Value types encompass the data types you would traditionally encounter in nonobject-oriented programming languages. This includes numeric, strings, bytes, and Booleans. Value types in C# are implemented in the form of Structures and Enums. Value types are allocated on the stack and therefore have little overhead associated with them.

### Primitive Data Types

Primitive data types include all value types except structures. The primitive data types are shown in Table 2.2.

**Table 2.2** Primitive Data Types, Sizes, and Descriptions

| Data Type | Size in Bytes | Description |
| --- | --- | --- |
| sbyte | 1 | Signed byte |
| byte | 1 | Unsigned byte |
| short | 2 | Signed short |
| ushort | 2 | Unsigned short |
| int | 4 | Signed integer |
| uint | 4 | Unsigned integer |
| long | 8 | Signed long integer |
| ulong | 8 | Unsigned long integer |
| float | 4 | Floating point |

*Continued*

**Table 2.2** Continued

| Data Type | Size in Bytes | Description |
|-----------|---------------|-------------|
| double | 8 | Double-precision floating point |
| decimal | 8 | 96-bit signed number |
| string | n/a | Unicode string |
| char | 2 | Unicode character |
| bool | n/a | True or false |

# Reference Types

Instances of classes are reference types. Reference types are allocated on the heap. In C#, all classes are derived from the .NET Framework class *Object* within the *System* namespace. C# does not support pointers, but classes, being reference data types, act like pointers. If you copy a pointer to another pointer, they both still reference the same object. You can modify the contents of the original object from either pointer. In C#, if you instantiate a class object and then make a copy of it, changes made to either instance of the class change the original object. If you pass an instance of a class to a class method, changes made to the object passed in will persist upon returning from the method call.

As we mentioned previously, reference types are allocated on the heap. The *new* keyword is used to allocate a new instance of a reference type (class). You don't need to free an instance of a class in C#, however. The CLR does garbage collection on object instances that are no longer referenced. Here is a simple example of instantiating an object of a class:

```
using System;

class TestSomeClass
{
    static void Main(string[] args)
    {
        // Class is instantiated here using the new keyword. A new object
        // of type SomeClass will be allocated on the heap.
        SomeClass instance = new SomeClass();
        instance.showMessage( "Here is the message" );
    }
```

```
}

class SomeClass
{
    public void showMessage( string message )
    {
        Console.WriteLine( message );
    }
}
```

Sometimes class methods require class instances derived from the .NET Framework class *object*. The odd thing is that you can pass a primitive data type, such as an *int*, to the method. How can this be? C# has a feature called *boxing*, which will automatically convert a value type to a reference type when a reference type is required. Upon return from the method, the reverse process, called *unboxing*, will convert back to a value type. As a programmer, you don't need to do anything special to take advantage of boxing. You should note, however, that some overhead is involved in the boxing/unboxing process.

# Explaining Control Structures

The C# language supports all of the flow-of-control statements you would normally expect. This section gives you a very brief look at them. We point out a few of the problem areas (especially for C/C++ programmers).

## Using the *if* Statement

The *if* statement executes a series of statements if a test Boolean expression evaluates to true. The test expression to evaluate must be Boolean. You cannot use a test numeric expression as in C/C++:

```
int i = 3;
int j = 0;

if ( i > 2 )
{
    j = 3;
}
```

# Using the *if-else* Statement

The *if-else* statement adds a path for the false evaluation of the Boolean expression.

```
int i = 3;
int j = 0;
int k = 0;

if ( i > 2 )
{
    j = 3;
}
else
{
    j = 4;
    k = 5;
}
```

# Using the *switch case* Statement

The *switch* statement chooses flow of control based on the evaluation of a numeric or string comparison. The *switch* statement does not allow control to fall through to the next case as in C/C++ unless the *case* statement is followed immediately by another *case* statement. In other words, you must use a *break* statement with every case statement. You can also use a *goto* statement, although most programmers frown on using them. Here are two examples:

```
int j = 0;
int i = 1;

switch ( i )
{
    case 1:
        j = 7;
        break;

    case 2:
    case 3:
```

```
        j = 22;

        break;


    default:

        j = 33;

        break;

}


string lastName = "";

string text = "fred";


switch ( text )

{

    case "fred":

        lastName = "Flinstone";

        break;


    case "barney":

        lastName = "Rubble";

        break;


    default:

        lastName = "Slate";

        break;

}
```

# Using the *for* Statement

The *for* statement is used to loop through a series of statements until a test Boolean expression evaluated at the beginning of the loop is false. In the following example, the *WriteLine* method will execute five times:

```
for ( int i = 0; i < 5; i++ )

{

    Console.WriteLine( "I will not talk in class" );

}
```

# Using the *while* Statement

The *while* statement is also used to loop through a series of statements until a test Boolean expression evaluated at the beginning of the loop is false. The following code has the same result as the previous *for* statement example:

```
int i = 0;
while ( i < 5 )
{
    Console.WriteLine( "I will not talk in class" );
    i++;
}
```

# Using the *do while* Statement

The *do while* statement is also used to loop through a series of until a test Boolean expression evaluated at the end of the loop is false. Therefore, the series of statements contained within the *do while* loop will always execute at least once:

```
int i = 6;
do
{
    Console.WriteLine( "I will not talk in class" );
    i++;
}
while ( i < 5 );
```

# Using the *break* Statement

The *break* statement exits the loop of a *for*, *while*, or *do while* statement regardless of value of the test Boolean expression. In each of the following examples, the *WriteLine* method will execute two times:

```
int j = 0;
for ( int i = 0; i < 5; i++ )
{
    Console.WriteLine( "I will not talk in class" );
    j++;
    if ( j == 2 )
```

```
        break;
}

int i = 0;
int j = 0;
while ( i < 5 )
{
    Console.WriteLine( "I will not talk in class" );
    i++;
    j++;
    if ( j == 2 )
        break;
}

int i = 0;
int j = 0;
do
{
    Console.WriteLine( "I will not talk in class" );
    i++;
    j++;
    if ( j == 2 )
        break;
}
while ( i < 5 );
```

# Using the *continue* Statement

The *continue* statement will pass flow of control immediately to the start of a loop
when encountered. In the following example, "I will not talk in class" will display
twice and "At least I'll try not to talk in class" will display three times:

```
int j = 0;
for ( int i = 0; i < 5; i++ )
{
    j++;
```

```
    if ( j > 2 )
    {
        Console.WriteLine( "At least I'll try not to talk in class" );
        continue;
    }


    Console.WriteLine( "I will not talk in class" );
}
```

# Using the *return* Statement

The *return* statement returns flow of control from a method to the caller, optionally passing back a return value. Here is a complete example:

```
using System;

class TestDivision
{
    static void Main(string[] args)
    {
        int dividend = 2;
        int divisor = 0;

        Divider divider = new Divider();
        bool ret = divider.divide( dividend, divisor );
        if ( ret == true )
            Console.WriteLine( "I divided!" );
        else
            Console.WriteLine( "Something went horribly wrong!" );
    }
}

class Divider
{
    public bool divide( int dividend, int divisor )
    {
```

```
    if ( divisor == 0 )

        return false;


    int result = dividend / divisor;


    return true;

}

}
```

**NOTE**

A better way to handle this case would have been to throw an exception when the divisor is zero. We cover exceptions in a later section.

## Using the *goto* Statement

The *goto* statement has been the bain of structured programming for many years. C# supports the *goto* statement, although as previously stated, we wouldn't recommend using it. The *goto* statement immediately transfers flow of control to the statement following a label. If you must use *goto*, here is an example:

```
int i = 0;
int j = 0;
while ( i < 5 )
{
   Console.WriteLine( "I will not talk in class" );
   i++;
   j++;
   if ( j == 2 )
       goto jumpeddoutofloop;
}


jumpeddoutofloop:
   Console.WriteLine( "I jumped out" );
```

# Understanding Properties and Indexers

Two of the more interesting features of C# are properties and indexers. *Properties* allow you to call methods on a class using syntax that indicates you are accessing member variables. *Indexers* allow you to access collections within a class using array syntax. You will see examples of each in the following sections.

## Using Properties

If you come from a C++ background, you have probably written many *get* and *set* methods for classes you have created. A typical pattern used by C++ programmers is to make member variables of a class private and provide public accessor methods to assign and retrieve the values of the member variables. A public *set* method is written to assign a value to a member variable, and a *get* method is written to retrieve the value assigned to a member variable. An alternate solution is to make the member variables themselves public. The advantage of using *get* and *set* methods is that if the underlying data type ever changes, the consumer of the class does not have to change his code. Only the *get* and *set* methods need to be rewritten. This is often referred to as *data hiding*.

Using *get* and *set* methods has a couple of disadvantages. First, it seems a little more intuitive to just assign a value to a data member or retrieve its value rather than having to use accessor methods. Also, slightly less typing is involved in accessing the data member directly.

C# provides the best of both methods. It supports the idea of properties. *Properties* are method calls that look like direct access to member data. Figure 2.5 is a complete listing that shows properties in action. The program is included on the CD in the file Properties.cs.

---

**NOTE**

Throughout the rest of the chapter, we expand on this example of an employee list.

---

**Figure 2.5** The Properties.cs Program Listing

```
using System;
```

```
/// <summary>
```

**Continued**

**Figure 2.5** Continued

```csharp
/// Contains the program entry point for the Properties Sample.
/// </summary>
class PropertySample
{
    static void Main( string[] args )
    {
        try
        {
            // Create a new employee
            Employee employee = new Employee();

            // Set some properties
            employee.FirstName = "Timothy";
            employee.MiddleName = "Arthur";
            employee.LastName = "Tucker";
            employee.SSN = "555-55-5555";

            // Show the results on screen
            string name = employee.FirstName + " " + employee.MiddleName +
                " " + employee.LastName;
            string ssn = employee.SSN;

            Console.WriteLine( "Name: {0}, SSN: {1}", name, ssn );
        }
        catch ( Exception exception )
        {
            // Display any errors on screen
            Console.WriteLine( exception.Message );
        }
    }
}
```

**Continued**

## Figure 2.5 Continued

```csharp
/// <summary>
/// Represents a single employee
/// </summary>
class Employee
{
    private string m_firstName;
    private string m_middleName;
    private string m_lastName;
    private string m_SSN;

    // FirstName property
    public string FirstName
    {
        get { return m_firstName; }
        set { m_firstName = value; }
    }

    // MiddleName property
    public string MiddleName
    {
        get { return m_middleName; }
        set { m_middleName = value; }
    }

    // LastName property
    public string LastName
    {
        get { return m_lastName; }
        set { m_lastName = value; }
    }

    // SSN property
```

**Continued**

**Figure 2.5** Continued

```
public string SSN
{
    get { return m_SSN; }
    set { m_SSN = value; }
}
}
```

# Get Accessor

Let's take a look at the source code for the *get* accessor of the *SSN* property (SSN being the employee's social security number). Consider the following source code for the *SSN* property:

```
public string SSN
{
    get { return m_SSN; }
    set { m_SSN = value; }
}
```

First, let's take a look at the property declaration. The *public* keyword of the property indicates its visibility. Normally you will make a property public because the purpose is to allow consumers to have access to the data associated with the property. Next, this property works with string data as indicated by the *string* keyword. Finally, the name of the property is *SSN*.

The *get* accessor method is relatively simple. It just returns the value of the private data member *m_SSN*. In the program, you can see the *SSN* property is accessed using syntax usually reserved for accessing member data:

```
string ssn = employee.SSN;
```

# Set Accessor

Here are code snippets that show invocation of the set property of *SSN* and the implementation of the *set* property itself:

```
employee.SSN = "555-55-5555";
set { m_SSN = value; }
```

The *set* accessor assigns a value to the member variable *m_SSN*. The *value* keyword contains the value of the right side of the equal sign when invoking the *set* property. The data type of *value* will be the type in the declaration of the property. In this case, it is a *string*.

One thing to note about the *set* accessor is that it can do more than just set the value of a data member. For instance, you could add code to validate the value and not do the assignment if validation fails.

**NOTE**

Throughout the samples in this chapter, you will see a lot of string operations that use the overloaded concatenation operators such as "+" and "+=" as in the following code:

```
string string1 = "a" + "b" + "c";

string1 += "e" + "f";
```

In C#, strings are *immutable*, which means they cannot be changed once they have a value assigned to them. In the previous example, each time the string is modified, a new copy of the string is created. This can lead to performance problems in code that does a large amount of string operations. The .NET Framework supplies the *System.Text.StringBuilder* class, which allows you to create and manipulate a string using a single buffer in memory for cases where you do a lot of string processing.

## Accessing Lists with Indexers

The need to create and manipulate lists is a common programming task. Let's extend our employee example from the last section. Let's say you need to display a list of employees. The most logical thing to do would be to create a new *Employees* class, which contains all of the individual *Employee* instances. You would then iterate through all of the employees displaying each one until there are no further employees. One way to solve this would be to create a property that returns the number of employees and a method that returns a given employee given its position in the list, such as the following:

```
for ( i = 0; i < employees.Length; i++ )
{
```

```
        Employee employee = employees.getEmployee( i );
        Console.WriteLine( employee.LastName );
}
```

However, it would be more intuitive if we could just treat the list of employees as an array contained with the *Employee* object. Here is what that might look like:

```
for ( i = 0; i < employees.Length; i++ )
{
        Console.WriteLine( employees.[i].LastName );
}
```

This is precisely what indexers do. They let you use array syntax to access a list of objects contained inside another class. Indexers do not imply a specific implementation for the list, however. The list within the containing class could be a static array, a file on disk, one of the collection classes supplied by the .NET Framework, or some other implementation. If the underlying implementation is changed from a static array to a collection class, for example, a programmer using the *Employees* class would not need to change her code. This is highly desirable and analogous to the same situation described in the section discussing properties in this chapter. Figure 2.6 extends the code listing in Figure 2.5 to make use of an indexer to iterate through a list of employees. The program is included on the CD in the file Indexers.cs.

**Figure 2.6** The Indexers.cs Program Listing

```
using System;
using System.Collections;


/// <summary>
/// Contains the program entry point for the Indexers Sample.
/// </summary>
class IndexersSample
{
    static void Main( string[] args )
    {
        try
        {
```

**Continued**

**Figure 2.6** Continued

```csharp
// Create a container to hold employees
Employees employees = new Employees(4);

// Add some employees
employees[0] = new Employee ( "Timothy", "Arthur",
    "Tucker", "555-55-5555" );

employees[1] = new Employee ( "Sally", "Bess",
    "Jones", "666-66-6666" );

employees[2] = new Employee ( "Jeff", "Michael",
    "Simms", "777-77-7777" );

employees[3] = new Employee ( "Janice", "Anne",
    "Best", "888-88-8888" );

// Display the employee list on screen
for ( int i = 0; i < employees.Length; i++ )
{
    string name = employees[i].FirstName + " " +
        employees[i].MiddleName + " " +
        employees[i].LastName;

    string ssn = employees[i].SSN;

    Console.WriteLine( "Name: {0}, SSN: {1}", name, ssn );
}

Employee employee = employees["777-77-7777"];
if ( employee != null )
{
    string name = employee.FirstName + " " +
        employee.MiddleName + " " + employee.LastName;
```

**Continued**

**Figure 2.6** Continued

```
                string ssn = employee.SSN;

                Console.WriteLine( "Found by SSN, Name: {0}, SSN: {1}",
                    name, ssn );
            }
            else
            {
                Console.WriteLine(
                    "Could not find employee with SSN: 777-77-7777" );
            }
        }
        catch ( Exception exception )
        {
            // Display any errors on screen
            Console.WriteLine( exception.Message );
        }
    }
}


/// <summary>
/// Container class for employees. This class implements two
/// indexers
/// </summary>
class Employees
{
    private ArrayList m_Employees;
    private int m_MaxEmployees;

    public Employees( int MaxEmployees )
    {
        m_MaxEmployees = MaxEmployees;
        m_Employees = new ArrayList( MaxEmployees );
```

**Continued**

**Figure 2.6** Continued

```csharp
}

// Here is the implementation of the indexer by array index
public Employee this[int index]
{
    get
    {
        // Check for out of bounds condition
        if ( index < 0 || index > m_Employees.Count - 1 )
            return null;

        // Return employee based on index passed in
        return (Employee) m_Employees[index];
    }

    set
    {
        // Check for out of bounds condition
        if ( index < 0 || index > m_MaxEmployees-1 )
            return;

        // Add new employee
        m_Employees.Insert( index, value );
    }
}

// Here is the implementation of the indexer by SSN
public Employee this[string SSN]
{
    get
    {
        Employee empReturned = null;
```

**Continued**

**Figure 2.6** Continued

```csharp
        foreach ( Employee employee in m_Employees )
        {
            // Return employee based on index passed in
            if ( employee.SSN == SSN )
            {
                empReturned = employee;
                break;
            }
        }

        return empReturned;
    }
}


// Return the total number of employees.
public int Length
{
    get
    {
        return m_Employees.Count;
    }
}
}


/// <summary>
/// Represents a single employee
/// </summary>
class Employee
{
    private string m_firstName;
    private string m_middleName;
    private string m_lastName;
    private string m_SSN;
```

**Continued**

**Figure 2.6** Continued

```csharp
// Constructor
public Employee( string FirstName, string LastName, string
    MiddleName, string SSN )
{
    m_firstName = FirstName;
    m_middleName = MiddleName;
    m_lastName = LastName;
    m_SSN = SSN;
}

// FirstName property
public string FirstName
{
    get { return m_firstName; }
    set { m_firstName = value; }
}

// MiddleName property
public string MiddleName
{
    get { return m_middleName; }
    set { m_middleName = value; }
}

// LastName property
public string LastName
{
    get { return m_lastName; }
    set { m_lastName = value; }
}

// SSN property
```

**Continued**

**Figure 2.6** Continued

```
public string SSN
{
    get { return m_SSN; }
    set { m_SSN = value; }
}
}
```

You can see how this sets the value of an item in the list and get the value of an item in the list using arraylike syntax such as this:

```
employees[0] = new Employee ( "Timothy", "Arthur",
    "Tucker", "555-55-5555" );


string ssn = employees[i].SSN;
```

The portion of the code that implements an Indexer follows:

```
public Employee this[int index]
{
    get
    {
        if ( index < 0 || index > 4 )
            return null;

        return m_Employees[index];
    }

    set
    {
        if ( index < 0 || index > 4 )
            return;

        m_Employees[index] = value;
        updateCount();
    }
}
```

This sample code implements two indexers, one based on an index entry in the list and the second based on the SSN of an employee. The code to implement an indexer is just a property on the containing class. The only real difference is that now the property takes the index within the list as a parameter. This example uses an *ArrayList*, which is part of the *System.Collections* namespace of the .NET Framework. So, the code to get an item in the list via an index entry just returns the item in the *ArrayList* based on the index entry requested. Similarly, the code to set an item in the list just sets the item in the *ArrayList*. A check is also done to validate that the index entry passed in is within bounds based on the maximum size of the list passed to the constructor of the *Employees* class. Our implementation is relatively simple in that it returns if the index is out of bounds. A better implementation would be to throw an exception. We cover exceptions later in this chapter.

The code also implements a second read-only indexer based on *SSN*. This illustrates that an indexer can be implemented using more than just the index of an entry in the list. In the *Main* method of the program, you can see the following statement:

```
Employee employee = employees["777-77-7777"];
```

This code calls our *SSN* indexer implementation. The *SSN* indexer loops through the *Employee* instances contained in the m_*Employees ArrayList*. If it finds an *Employee* instance that has the SSN requested, it returns that *Employee* instance. If it doesn't find it, it returns null.

In C#, the *foreach* keyword is used to iterate through a list of objects contained within another object. Here is what our sample program would look like using *foreach*:

```
foreach ( Employee employee in employees )
{
    string name = employee.FirstName + " " +
        employee.MiddleName + " " + employee.LastName;

    string ssn = employee.SSN;
    Console.WriteLine( "Name: {0}, SSN: {1}", name, ssn );
}
```

To use the *foreach* keyword, the class that contains the list must implement the *IEnumerable* interface contained within the *System.Collections* namespace. The

*IEnumerable* interface has one responsibility: return an instance of an object that implements the *IEnumerator* interface also from the *System.Collections* namespace.

The class that implements the *IEnumerator* interface is responsible for maintaining the current position in the list and knowing when the end of the list has been reached. Although this seems overly complex, it allows the flexibility of having the implementation of *IEnumerator* be in the class containing the list or in a separate class.

The complete sample that implements the *IEnumerable* interface is on the CD in the Enumerable.cs file. Because the *ArrayList* class already implements the *IEnumerable* interface, all that is necessary in the *Employees* class is to declare the class as implementing the *IEnumerable* interface and then provide the implementation of the *GetEnumerator* method of the *IEnumerable* interface. The *GetEnumerator* method simply returns the *ArrayList* implementation. The relevant code from the sample on the CD that accomplishes this is shown here:

```
/// <summary>
/// Container class for employees. This class implements
/// IEnumerable allowing use of foreach sytax
/// </summary>
class Employees : IEnumerator
{
    // IEnumerable implementation, delegates IEnumerator to
    // the ArrayList
    public IEnumerator GetEnumerator()
    {
        return m_Employees.GetEnumerator();
    }
}
```

At first glance, indexers seem somewhat complex, and talking about them in the abstract can be a bit confusing. However, when you see the code, it is relatively simple and provides a clean and simple syntax to iterate though a list of objects.

# Using Delegates and Events

If you are familiar with Windows programming, you've most likely dealt with callbacks. *Callbacks* are method calls that are executed when some event happens during processing. For instance, a callback can be established to handle the processing of an incoming message on a communications port. Another part of the communications program can wait for messages on a communications port and invoke the callback whenever a new message arrives. Function pointers perform the same sort of tasks in straight C/C++ programs.

*Delegates* in C# improve on method callbacks in two areas. Delegates are type safe, unlike callbacks in Windows programming. In addition, delegates can call more than one callback when an event occurs. This is termed *multicasting*.

# Delegates

Let's extend our employees sample to use delegates. This sample simulates a background process that receives messages to add new employees to the employee list. Our queue will be a static array, but in the real world it could be a message queue (Microsoft Message Queue [MSMQ]), a socket, or some other type of queue. The source code in Figure 2.7 shows the relevant portions of the sample pertaining to delegates. The full source code for this sample is on the CD in the file Delegates.cs.

**Figure 2.7** Relevant Portions of the Delegates.cs Program Listing

```
using System;
using System.Collections;


/// <summary>
/// Contains the program entry point for the Delegates Sample.
/// </summary>
class DelegatesSample
{
    static void Main( string[] args )
    {
        try
        {
            // Create a container to hold employees
            Employees employees = new Employees(4);

            // Create and drain our simulated message queue
            EmployeeQueueMonitor monitor =
```

**Continued**

**Figure 2.7** Continued

```
                new EmployeeQueueMonitor( employees );


        monitor.start();
        monitor.stop();


        // Display the employee list on screen
        Console.WriteLine(
            "List of employees added via delegate:" );


        foreach ( Employee employee in employees )
        {
            string name = employee.FirstName + " " +
                employee.MiddleName + " " + employee.LastName;


            string ssn = employee.SSN;


            Console.WriteLine( "Name: {0}, SSN: {1}", name, ssn );
        }
    }
    catch ( Exception exception )
    {
        // Display any errors on screen
        Console.WriteLine( exception.Message );
    }
    }
}


/// <summary>
/// Simulates our message queue.
/// </summary>
class EmployeeQueueMonitor
{
    // Delegate signature
```

**Figure 2.7** Continued

```
public delegate void AddEventCallback( string FirstName,
    string LastName, string MiddleName, string SSN );

// Instance of the delegate
private AddEventCallback m_addEventCallback;

private Employees m_employees;
private int m_lengthQueue;

private string[, ] m_msgQueue =
{
    {"Timothy", "Arthur", "Tucker", "555-55-5555"},
    {"Sally", "Bess", "Jones", "666-66-6666" },
    {"Jeff", "Michael", "Simms", "777-77-7777"},
    {"Janice", "Anne", "Best", "888-88-8888" }
};

public EmployeeQueueMonitor( Employees employees )
{
    m_employees = employees;
    m_lengthQueue = 4;

    // Create an instace of the delegate and register the
    // addEmployee method of this class as a callback.
    m_addEventCallback = new AddEventCallback(
        this.addEmployee );
}

// Drain the queue.
public void start()
{
    if ( m_employees == null )
        return;
```

Continued

**Figure 2.7** Continued

```
    for ( int i = 0; i < m_lengthQueue; i++ )
    {
        string FirstName = m_msgQueue[i,0];
        string MiddleName = m_msgQueue[i,1];
        string LastName = m_msgQueue[i,2];
        string SSN = m_msgQueue[i,3];

        // Invoke the callback registered with the delegate
        Console.WriteLine( "Invoking delegate" );
        m_addEventCallback( FirstName, LastName, MiddleName,
            SSN );
    }
}


public void stop()
{
    // In a real communications program you would shut down
    // gracefully.
}


// Called by the delegate when a message to add an employee
// is read from the message queue.
public void addEmployee( string FirstName, string MiddleName,
    string LastName, string SSN )
{
    Console.WriteLine( "In delegate, adding employee\r\n" );

    int index = m_employees.Length;
    m_employees[index] = new Employee ( FirstName, MiddleName,
        LastName, SSN );
}
}
```

# Single Cast

The source code in the previous section is an example of a single cast delegate. A *single cast* delegate invokes only one callback method. Let's examine our previous sample to see this.

The *EmployeeQueueMonitor* class simulates a message queue. It contains a static array that holds the current messages. At the top of *EmployeeQueueMonitor* are the following lines:

```
public delegate void AddEventCallback( string FirstName,
    string LastName, string MiddleName, string SSN );


private AddEventCallback m_addEventCallback;
```

The first statement defines a delegate and the parameters an object instance of the delegate takes. In this case, we callback to a method that takes first name, last name, middle name, and SSN. We do this whenever a request to add a new employee appears in the message queue.

The second statement declares a member variable to hold our delegate. It is initially set to null. A new object instance must be created prior to making method calls through the delegate. An object instance is instantiated in the constructor of *EmployeeQueueMonitor*.

```
m_addEventCallback = new AddEventCallback( this.addEmployee );
```

This statement creates a new object instance of the delegate. The delegate takes as an argument the method to call when the delegate is invoked. In this case, whenever the delegate is invoked, the method that will execute is *EmployeeQueueMonitor.addEmployee*.

In the *start* method of *EmployeeQueueMonitor* is the following code:

```
for ( int i = 0; i < m_lengthQueue; i++ )
{
    string FirstName = m_msgQueue[i,0];
    string MiddleName = m_msgQueue[i,1];
    string LastName = m_msgQueue[i,2];
    string SSN = m_msgQueue[i,3];

    // Invoke the callback registered with the delegate
    Console.WriteLine( "Invoking delegate" );
```

```
    m_addEventCallback( FirstName, LastName, MiddleName, SSN );
}
```

This code simulates draining the message queue of any waiting messages. The callback function is invoked by treating the *m_addEventCallback* member variable as if it were a method call passing it our four parameters. Note that you do not specify the callback itself when making the call. The delegate maintains the address of the callback internally and therefore knows the method to call. The following example shows what *not* to do:

```
// Incorrect

m_addEventCallback.addEmployee( FirstName, LastName, MiddleName, SSN );
```

## Multicast

The true power of delegates becomes apparent when discussing multicast delegates. Let's extend our previous example a bit further. Because background processes do not usually have a user interface for human interaction, they typically log incoming events for later review. Let's add a second callback to our sample to log incoming add employee requests. The relevant snippets of code are shown in Figure 2.8. The full source code is for this sample is on the CD in the file Multicasting.cs.

**Figure 2.8** Relevant Portions of the Multicasting.cs Program Listing

```
class EmployeeQueueMonitor
{
    // Delegate signature for add employee event callback
    public delegate void AddEventCallback( string FirstName,
        string LastName, string MiddleName, string SSN );

    // Instance of the delegate
    private AddEventCallback m_addEventCallback;

    private EmployeeQueueLogger m_logger;

    public EmployeeQueueMonitor( Employees employees )
    {
```

**Continued**

**Figure 2.8** Continued

```
    m_employees = employees;
    m_lengthQueue = 4;


    m_logger = new EmployeeQueueLogger( "log.txt" );


    // Register the methods that the delegate will invoke when an
    // add employee message is read from the message queue
    m_addEventCallback =
        new AddEventCallback( this.addEmployee );


    m_addEventCallback +=
        new AddEventCallback( m_logger.logAddRequest );
}


// Drain the queue.
public void start()
{
    if ( m_employees == null )
        return;


    for ( int i = 0; i < m_lengthQueue; i++ )
    {
        string FirstName = m_msgQueue[i,0];
        string MiddleName = m_msgQueue[i,1];
        string LastName = m_msgQueue[i,2];
        string SSN = m_msgQueue[i,3];


        Console.WriteLine( "Invoking delegate" );


        // Invoke the delegate passing the data associated with
        // adding a new employee resulting in the subscribed
        // callbacks methods being executed, namely
        // Employees.this.addEmployee()
```

**Continued**

**Figure 2.8** Continued

```
            // and EmployeeQueueLogger.logAddRequest()
            m_addEventCallback( FirstName, LastName, MiddleName,
                SSN );
        }
    }


    // Called by delegate whenever a new add employee message
    // appears in the message queue. Notice the signature matches
    // that requried by AddEventCallback
    public void addEmployee( string FirstName, string MiddleName,
        string LastName, string SSN )
    {
        Console.WriteLine( "In delegate, adding employee\r\n" );

        int index = m_employees.Length;
        m_employees[index] = new Employee ( FirstName, MiddleName,
            LastName, SSN );
    }
}


/// <summary>
/// Writes add employee events to a log file.
/// </summary>
class EmployeeQueueLogger
{
    string m_fileName;

    public EmployeeQueueLogger( string fileName )
    {
        m_fileName = fileName;
    }

    // Called by delegate whenever a new add employee message
```

*Continued*

**Figure 2.8** Continued

```
// appears in the message queue. Notice the signature matches
// that requried by AddEventCallback
public void logAddRequest( string FirstName, string LastName,
    string MiddleName, string SSN )
{
    string name = FirstName + " " + MiddleName + " " + LastName;

    FileStream stream = new FileStream( m_fileName,
        FileMode.OpenOrCreate, FileAccess.ReadWrite);

    StreamWriter writer = new StreamWriter( stream );
    writer.BaseStream.Seek( 0, SeekOrigin.End );

    writer.Write("{0} {1} \n", DateTime.Now.ToLongTimeString(),
        DateTime.Now.ToLongDateString());

    writer.Write( "Adding employee - Name: {0}, SSN: {1}",
        name, SSN );
    writer.Write("\n-------------------------------------\n\n");
    writer.Flush();
    writer.Close();
    }

}
```

A new class, *EmployeeQueueLogger*, has been added. It has a method *logAddRequest*, which logs requests to add employees to a log file. The important thing to note is that the *logAddRequest* method has a signature that matches the *AddEventCallback* delegate signature. An instance of the logger is created in the constructor of *EmployeeQueueMonitor*. The code that wires up the delegates is also in the constructor and is shown here:

```
m_logger = new EmployeeQueueLogger( "log.txt" );
m_addEventCallback = new AddEventCallback( this.addEmployee );
m_addEventCallback += new AddEventCallback(
    m_logger.logAddRequest );
```

First, a new logger instance is created. Next, the delegate is initialized with a first callback function to the *addEmployee* method of *EmployeeQueueMonitor*. Finally, a second callback is added to the delegate, which will invoke the *logAddRequest* of the *EmployeeQueueLogger* class. Notice that the plus sign is used to add the second callback to the delegate. The plus sign (addition operator) has been overloaded in the *System.Delegate* class of the .NET Framework to call the *Combine* method of that class. The *Combine* method adds the callback to the list of methods the delegate maintains. The minus sign (subtraction operator) is also overloaded to call the *Remove* method, which removes a callback from the list of methods the delegate maintains. The rest of the source code remains unchanged. When the delegate is invoked in the *start* method of *EmployeeQueueMonitor*, both *EmployeeQueueMonitor.addEmployee* and *EmployeeQueueLogger.logAddRequest* are executed.

# Events

The event model is often referred to as the *publish/subscribe model* or the *listener pattern*. The idea behind the event model is that a class publishes the events that it can raise. Consumers of the class object subscribe to the events they are interested in. When the event occurs, the object that monitors the event notifies all subscribers that the event has been raised. The subscribers then take some action.

The event model is often used in GUI programs. Handlers are set up for common events, such as pressing a button. When the button press event occurs, all subscribers registered for the button press event are invoked. The .NET Framework uses the event model and in particular the *System.Event* delegate for Windows Forms–based applications.

The .NET Framework supplies a built in delegate of type *System.Event*. The idea of events in the .NET Framework is to supply a single signature for the delegate regardless of the data that is passed to the subscribed callback. One of the arguments for the Event delegate is an object derived from the .NET Framework class *System.EventArgs*, which contains the data the callback needs. You declare a class derived from *System.EventArgs* with the data your callback needs. When the event takes place, you instantiate your derived *EventArgs* object and invoke the event. Callback functions subscribed to the event are called passing the object derived from *EventArgs*. Changes to the multicast delegate code sample that implement events are shown in Figure 2.9. The full source code for this sample is on the CD in the file Events.cs.

**Figure 2.9** Relevant Portions of the Events.cs Program Listing

```csharp
/// <summary>
/// Defines the data that will be passed from the event delegate to
/// the callback method when the event is raised
/// </summary>
class AddEmployeEventArgs : EventArgs
{
    string m_FirstName;
    string m_LastName;
    string m_MiddleName;
    string m_SSN;

    public AddEmployeEventArgs( string FirstName,
        string LastName, string MiddleName, string SSN )
    {
        m_FirstName = FirstName;
        m_LastName = LastName;
        m_MiddleName = MiddleName;
        m_SSN = SSN;
    }


    // Event argument properties contain the data to pass to the
    // callback methods subscribed to the event.
    public string FirstName { get { return m_FirstName; } }
    public string LastName { get { return m_LastName; } }
    public string MiddleName {get { return m_MiddleName; } }
    public string SSN { get { return m_SSN; } }
}


/// <summary>
/// Simulates monitoring a message queue. When a message appears
/// the event is raised and methods subscribed to the event
//  are invoked.
/// </summary>
```

**Continued**

**Figure 2.9** Continued

```
class EmployeeQueueMonitor
{
    // Event signature for AddEmployeeEvent
    public delegate void AddEmployeeEvent( object sender,
        AddEmployeEventArgs e );


    // Instance of the AddEmployeeEvent
    public event AddEmployeeEvent OnAddEmployee;


    private EmployeeQueueLogger m_logger;


    private Employees m_employees;
    private int m_lengthQueue;


    private string[, ] m_msgQueue =
    {
        {"Timothy", "Arthur", "Tucker", "555-55-5555"},
        {"Sally", "Bess", "Jones", "666-66-6666" },
        {"Jeff", "Michael", "Simms", "777-77-7777"},
        {"Janice", "Anne", "Best", "888-88-8888" }
    };


    public EmployeeQueueMonitor( Employees employees )
    {
        m_employees = employees;
        m_lengthQueue = 4;


        m_logger = new EmployeeQueueLogger( "log.txt" );


        // Register the methods that the Event will invoke when an add
        // employee message is read from the message queue
        OnAddEmployee +=
            new AddEmployeeEvent( this.addEmployee );
```

**Continued**

**Figure 2.9** Continued

```
    OnAddEmployee +=
        new AddEmployeeEvent( m_logger.logAddRequest );
}


// Drain the queue.
public void start()
{
    if ( m_employees == null )
        return;

    for ( int i = 0; i < m_lengthQueue; i++ )
    {
        // Pop an add employee request off the queue
        string FirstName = m_msgQueue[i,0];
        string MiddleName = m_msgQueue[i,1];
        string LastName = m_msgQueue[i,2];
        string SSN = m_msgQueue[i,3];

        Console.WriteLine( "Invoking delegate" );

        // Create the event arguments to pass to the methods
        // subscribed to the event and then invoke event resulting
        // in the callbacks methods being executed, namely
        // Employees.this.addEmployee() and
        // EmployeeQueueLogger.logAddRequest()
        AddEmployeEventArgs args = new AddEmployeEventArgs( FirstName,
            LastName, MiddleName, SSN );
        OnAddEmployee( this, args );
    }
}


public void stop()
{
```

**Continued**

**Figure 2.9** Continued

```
        // In a real communications program you would shut down
        // gracefully.
    }


    // Called by event whenever a new add employee message appears
    // in the message queue. Notice the signature matches that required
    // by System.Event
    public void addEmployee( object sender, AddEmployeeEventArgs e )
    {
        Console.WriteLine( "In delegate, adding employee\r\n" );

        int index = m_employees.Length;
        m_employees[index] = new Employee ( e.FirstName, e.MiddleName,
            e.LastName, e.SSN );
    }
}


/// <summary>
/// Writes add employee events to a log file.
/// </summary>
class EmployeeQueueLogger
{
    string m_fileName;

    public EmployeeQueueLogger( string fileName )
    {
        m_fileName = fileName;
    }

    // Called by event whenever a new add employee message appears
    // in the message queue. Notice the signature matches that required
    // by System.Event
    public void logAddRequest( object sender, AddEmployeeEventArgs e )
```

**Continued**

## Figure 2.9 Continued

```
    {
        string name = e.FirstName + " " + e.MiddleName + " " +
            e.LastName;

        FileStream stream = new FileStream( m_fileName,
            FileMode.OpenOrCreate, FileAccess.ReadWrite);

        StreamWriter writer = new StreamWriter( stream );
        writer.BaseStream.Seek( 0, SeekOrigin.End );

        writer.Write("{0} {1} \n", DateTime.Now.ToLongTimeString(),
            DateTime.Now.ToLongDateString());

        writer.Write( "Adding employee - Name: {0}, SSN: {1}",
            name, e.SSN );
        writer.Write("\n------------------------------------\n\n");
        writer.Flush();
        writer.Close();
    }

}
```

A new class, *AddEmployeeEventArgs*, has been added. It contains the information that will be passed to callback methods subscribed to the event. Notice the data members of the *AddEmployeeEventArgs* class are the same as the signature for the *AddEventCallback* delegate in our previous sample. Instead of invoking the callback with individual arguments, when using events, you pass a class object, which contains the arguments instead.

Just as with the delegates samples, we declare the signature and create a member variable for the delegate in *EmployeeQueueMonitor* class. The only difference is that the signature matches the signature necessary for events. The first parameter is the object that raised the event, and the second is the object instance that contains the arguments passed to subscribed callback methods. This is shown here:

```
public delegate void AddEmployeeEvent( object sender,
```

```
      AddEmployeeEventArgs e );
public event AddEmployeeEvent OnAddEmployee;
```

In the constructor of the class, we subscribe the callback methods to the event as shown here:

```
OnAddEmployee +=
    new AddEmployeeEvent( this.addEmployee );
OnAddEmployee +=
    new AddEmployeeEvent( m_logger.logAddRequest );
```

The callback methods have the correct signature for event callbacks. Here are the callback method's signatures:

```
public void addEmployee( object sender, AddEmployeeEventArgs e )
public void logAddRequest( object sender, AddEmployeeEventArgs e )
```

When an add employee message is popped off the queue in the start method of *EmployeeQueueMonitor*, an instance of the *AddEmployeeEventArgs* is created and the event is invoked. Here is the code that accomplishes this:

```
AddEmployeeEventArgs args = new AddEmployeeEventArgs( FirstName,
    LastName, MiddleName, SSN );
OnAddEmployee( this, args );
```

As you can see, using events instead of delegates is really just a syntactic difference. The code is nearly identical. The main benefit is that you don't have a different delegate signature for every delegate you create based on the data that is passed to subscribed callbacks. Instead, the standard event delegate signature will suffice.

# Using Exception Handling

If you look through the .NET Framework SDK documentation, you won't find an error code returned from any method calls in the library. Instead, the Framework uses exceptions to indicate errors that occur. To illustrate exceptions, consider the code snippet in Figure 2.10 that builds upon the Enumerable sample from the Indexers section of this chapter. The complete sample is included on the CD in the file Exceptions.cs.

**Figure 2.10** Relevant Portions of the Exceptions.cs Program Listing

```csharp
using System;
using System.Collections;


/// <summary>
/// Contains the program entry point for the Exceptions Sample.
/// </summary>
class ExceptionsSample
{
    static void Main( string[] args )
    {
        try
        {
            // Create a container to hold employees
            Employees employees = new Employees(4);

            // Add some employees
            addOneEmployee ( employees, "Timothy", "Arthur",
                "Tucker", "555-55-5555" );

            addOneEmployee ( employees, "Sally", "Bess",
                "Jones", null );

            addOneEmployee ( employees, "Jeff", "Michael",
                "Simms", "777-77-7777" );

            addOneEmployee ( employees, "Janice", "Anne",
                "Best", "9888-88-88889" );

            // Display the employee list on screen
            foreach ( Employee employee in employees )
            {
                string name = employee.FirstName + " " +
                    employee.MiddleName + " " + employee.LastName;
```

**Continued**

**Figure 2.10** Continued

```
            string ssn = employee.SSN;

            Console.WriteLine( "Name: {0}, SSN: {1}", name, ssn );
        }
    }
    catch ( Exception exception )
    {
        // Display any errors on screen
        Console.WriteLine( exception.Message );
    }
}


// Helper method to add an employee to the list
static void addOneEmployee( Employees employees,
    string FirstName, string MiddleName, string LastName,
    string SSN )
{
    bool addedEmployee = false;

    try
    {
        Console.WriteLine( "Adding an employee" );

        // SSN cannot be NULL, throw exception
        if ( SSN == null )
            throw new ArgumentNullException( "SSN is null!" );

        // SSN length must be 11, throw exception
        if ( SSN.Length != 11 )
            throw new ArgumentOutOfRangeException(
                "SSN length invalid!" );
```

**Continued**

**Figure 2.10** Continued

```csharp
        // Add the employee
        employees[employees.Length] = new Employee ( FirstName,
            MiddleName, LastName, SSN );

        addedEmployee = true;
    }
    catch ( ArgumentOutOfRangeException exception )
    {
        Console.WriteLine( "We caught ArgumentOutOfRangeException" );
        Console.WriteLine( exception.Message );
    }
    catch ( ArgumentNullException exception )
    {
        Console.WriteLine( "We caught ArgumentNullException" );
        Console.WriteLine( exception.Message );
    }
    catch ( Exception exception )
    {
        Console.WriteLine( "We caught a base exception" );
        Console.WriteLine( exception.Message );
    }
    catch
    {
        Console.WriteLine( "We caught an unknown exception" );
        Console.WriteLine( "Unknown exception caught!" );
    }
    finally
    {
        if ( addedEmployee == true )
            Console.WriteLine( "Add was successful\r\n" );
        else
            Console.WriteLine( "Add failed\r\n" );
    }
```

**Continued**

**Figure 2.10** Continued

```
    }
}
```

## Using the *try* Block

Code that may throw an exception is placed inside a *try* block. In this example, the *addOneEmployee* method has a *try* block surrounding the code that will add a new employee to the list of employees. If an exception is thrown in a *try* block, control is passed to the *catch* block.

## Using the *catch* Block

The *catch* block is where you handle exceptions that are thrown. The first exception type that matches the exception thrown has control passed to its block of source code. In our example, if SSN length is not 11, an *ArgumentOutOfRangeException* exception is thrown. This results in execution of the *catch* block of *ArgumentOutOfRangeException*.

You should order your catch blocks so that the most general exceptions come last. If you put the general exceptions at the top of your *catch* blocks, they will always catch the exception. This can cause problems if you need to do special processing based on the exception type. Because all exceptions in the .NET Framework derive from *System.Exception*, the last two catch blocks in our sample are equivalent. They will catch any exceptions that are not caught by a more specific exception above. They are both shown in Figure 2.10 for completeness.

## Using the *finally* Block

The *finally* block is the last part of a *try-catch-finally* block for handling exceptions. The *finally* block is always executed regardless of whether an exception was thrown. Typically, *finally* blocks include cleanup code, such as closing files or databases. You do not have to include a *finally* block if you have no need to do special processing. In our example, the *finally* block prints a different message based on whether an exception was thrown.

## Using the *throw* Statement

You can throw exceptions to indicate errors that occur in your programs by using the *throw* keyword. To throw an exception, you create a new instance of a

*System.Exception* class that indicates the type of exception encountered. Exceptions derived from the *System.Exception* class take a message, which you can set as one of the parameters. The code that catches the exception can retrieve the message for display or logging purposes. In the previous sample code, an exception is thrown when SSN is null or is not eleven characters in length. Here is the relevant code:

```
// SSN cannot be NULL, throw exception
if ( SSN == null )
    throw new ArgumentNullException( "SSN is null!" );


// SSN length must be 11, throw exception
if ( SSN.Length != 11 )
    throw new ArgumentOutOfRangeException( "SSN length invalid!" );
```

The CLR will also throw exceptions if it encounters errors. For instance, it will throw an error if a divide-by-zero operation is attempted. If an exception is thrown, and the method it is thrown in doesn't contain a *catch* block, the CLR will look for a *catch* block in the calling method, if one exists. It will keep looking for a *catch* block up the call chain until it finds one that matches or until it has reached the top-level method call. If it still doesn't find a match, the system will handle the exception. This typically results in an error message being displayed and the program being aborted. You need to understand that even though you may not throw any exceptions, the runtime may. So, if you have a program that needs to keep running indefinitely, you should catch exceptions somewhere in the call chain and then continue executing your application.

All of the exceptions in the sample are ones defined by the .NET Framework. You can define your own exceptions as well. Typically, you just need to derive your own exception from the *System.Exception* class provided by the Framework and implement any behavior specific to your custom exception. Before you can do that however, you need to understand inheritance in C#—we cover that next.

# Understanding Inheritance

Inheritance and polymorphism are the two characteristics that make object-oriented programming languages so powerful. Many books, articles, and Web sites have been written explaining the subjects with flowing prose. We distill it down to a couple of short sentences. *Inheritance* means you can create a new type of object B that inherits all of the characteristics of an existing object A. *Polymorphism* means that this new object B can choose to inherit some characteristics and supply its own implementation for others.

Just in case it needs a bit more explanation, here is an example. Throughout this chapter, you have seen examples that use the *Employee* class. An employee in our case has a first name, middle name, last name, and SSN. What happens when we add in wage information? Now we have two different types of employees: salaried and hourly. They both still have the original characteristics of an employee but one now has an hourly wage and the other a yearly salary. When you need to run payroll for the employees, each type of employee's pay is calculated differently.

One way to solve this would be to put a flag in the *Employee* class indicating hourly or salaried. Then whenever you need to do something that requires knowledge of the type of employee, you have to check the flag and do the appropriate thing. This works fine for our simple example, but what if there are 20 kinds of things? Suddenly, a lot of code is spent just checking what type of thing it is before doing further processing.

Fortunately we have inheritance to help us solve this problem. Inheritance lets you create two new types of employees—hourly and salaried—that inherit all of the characteristics of the Employee class. Here are the declarations of the two new classes. We get to the implementations in a moment.

```
class SalariedEmployee : Employee
{
}


class HourlyEmployee : Employee
{
}
```

The text to the right of the colon indicates the base class of the new class. Therefore, both *SalariedEmployee* and *HourlyEmployee* each have *Employee* as their base class, or you can say they are derived from *Employee*. This means that they inherit all of the characteristics of the *Employee* class. For instance, you can instantiate a new *SalariedEmployee* object and write code like this:

```
string LastName = salariedEmployee.LastName;
```

That solves our first problem. You now have two types of employees to manipulate. But you still don't have a way to calculate payroll. Derived classes can override methods defined in the base class. So one way to solve this is to create a new base class method named *getPayroll* and have both classes write their own implementation of the method. Portions of the class implementations are shown here to demonstrate this:

```csharp
class Employee

{

    virtual public double getPayroll()

    {

        return 0.0;

    }

}


class SalariedEmployee : Employee

{

    private double m_Salary;

    public SalariedEmployee( double Salary )

    {

        m_Salary = Salary;

    }

    override public double getPayroll()

    {

        return m_Salary / 12;

    }

}


class HourlyEmployee : Employee

{

    private double m_HourlyRate;
    private double m_HoursWorked;

    public HourlyEmployee ( double HourlyRate )
```

```
    {
        m_HourlyRate = HourlyRate;
    }


    public double HoursWorked
    {
        get { return m_HoursWorked; }
        set { m_HoursWorked = value; }
    }


    override public double getPayroll()
    {
        return m_HoursWorked * m_HourlyRate;
    }
}
```

Notice that all three classes have a *getPayroll* method. The *SalariedEmployee* class calculates monthly payroll by dividing yearly salary by 12. The *HourlyEmployee* class calculates payroll by multiplying pay rate by the number of hours worked. This is exactly what we want. Each type of employee calculates payroll the appropriate way. Notice the *getPayroll* method of the *Employee* class is prefaced with the keyword *virtual*. Also notice that the *SalariedEmployee* and *HourlyEmployee* classes are prefaced with the keyword *override*. The *virtual* keyword indicates that if a derived class provides the same method with the same signature and is prefaced with the *override* keyword, call the derived classes implementation instead of the base classes. The best way to explain is with a simple example:

```
Employee employee = new Employee();
SalariedEmployee salariedEmployee = new SalariedEmployee( 600000 );
HourlyEmployee hourlyEmployee = new HourlyEmployee( 10.00 );
hourlyEmployee.HoursWorked = 10;

Console.WriteLine( employee.getPayroll() );
Console.WriteLine( salariedEmployee.getPayroll() );
Console.WriteLine( hourlyEmployee.getPayroll() );
```

The resulting output would be as follows:

0

5000

100

This is just what you would expect. Each type of employee returns the correctly calculated payroll amount. This is polymorphism at work. We can choose to inherit those things that are common and implement those things that aren't in derived classes.

Let's take a further look at polymorphism. The true power of polymorphism allows you to use a derived class when an object of the base class is specified. The following code demonstrates this:

```
Employee employee = new Employee();
SalariedEmployee salariedEmployee = new SalariedEmployee( 600000 );
HourlyEmployee hourlyEmployee = new HourlyEmployee( 10.00 );
hourlyEmployee.HoursWorked = 10;

displayPayrollAmount( employee );
displayPayrollAmount( salariedEmployee );
displayPayrollAmount( hourlyEmployee );

public void displayPayrollAmount( Employee employee )
{
    Console.WriteLine( employee.getPayroll() );
}
```

The resulting output would once again be as follows:

0

5000

100

Notice that the *displayPayrollAmount* method takes an *Employee* object as a parameter. But it is passed an instance of both *SalariedEmployee* and *HourlyEmployee*. The *displayPayrollAmount* method also displays the payroll amount appropriate to the class type passed in. This is polymorphism at work. A *SalariedEmployee* is an *Employee*, and an *HourlyEmployee* is an *Employee* as far as the

CLR is concerned. So any method that expects an object of class type *Employee* will also take an object of class types *SalariedEmployee* or *HourlyEmployee*.

There is still one odd thing about the code. The class *Employee* returns zero if *displayPayrollAmount* is called. In truth, it doesn't make any sense to create an object of type *Employee*. All employees must be salaried employees or hourly employees. But with the current code, nothing is stopping a programmer from instantiating a class object of type *Employee*.

Fortunately, in C# you can make the *Employee* class an abstract class, and the compiler will generate an error if an object of type *Employee* is created. Here are the changes necessary to the enable this:

```
abstract class Employee
{
    abstract public double getPayroll();
}
```

If you now try to create an instance of *Employee*, such as

```
Employee employee = new Employee();
```

the compiler will generate an error saying it cannot create an abstract class *Employee*.

Notice that the *Employee* class declaration uses the keyword *abstract*. This indicates to the compiler that an object of this class type can never be created. Another change is that the *getPayroll()* method is also prefixed by the keyword *abstract*. Notice that we supply only the signature for the method and no implementation. The *abstract* keyword indicates that a derived class must implement the method. Note the distinction between the *virtual* and *abstract* keywords applied to a base class method. The *virtual* keyword says the derived class is free to implement its own version of a method. If the derived class does not implement the method, the base classes method will execute when called. The *abstract* keyword says that the derived class must implement the method.

You can apply one other keyword to classes. The *sealed* keyword indicates that the class cannot be used as a base class. Use the *sealed* keyword if you never want other classes to derive from a class.

The *getPayroll* method shown in the examples in this section could also be written as a property. Let's take a look at how the code would change to support this. The full source code for the three classes is shown here (the code is also included on the CD in a sample program in the file Payroll.cs):

```csharp
/// <summary>
/// Base class for an employee. Note that this is an abstract class
/// and therefore cannot be instantiated.
/// </summary>
abstract class Employee
{
    private int m_ID;
    private string m_firstName;
    private string m_middleName;
    private string m_lastName;
    private string m_SSN;

    public Employee( int ID, string FirstName, string LastName,
        string MiddleName, string SSN )
    {
        m_ID = ID;
        m_firstName = FirstName;
        m_middleName = MiddleName;
        m_lastName = LastName;
        m_SSN = SSN;
    }

    abstract public double Payroll
    {
        get;
    }

    public int ID
    {
        get { return m_ID; }
    }

    public string FirstName
    {
```

```
        get { return m_firstName; }

        set { m_firstName = value; }

    }

    public string MiddleName

    {

        get { return m_middleName; }

        set { m_middleName = value; }

    }

    public string LastName

    {

        get { return m_lastName; }

        set { m_lastName = value; }

    }

    public string SSN

    {

        get { return m_SSN; }

        set { m_SSN = value; }

    }

}


/// <summary>

/// Salaried employee class. Implements the abstract method Payroll

/// defined in the base class.

/// </summary>

class SalariedEmployee : Employee

{

    private double m_Salary;

    public SalariedEmployee( int ID, string FirstName,

        string LastName, string MiddleName,string SSN,

        double Salary ) :
```

```csharp
            base( ID, FirstName, LastName, MiddleName, SSN )
    {

        m_Salary = Salary;

    }


    override public double Payroll
    {

        get { return m_Salary / 12; }

    }

}


/// <summary>
/// Hourly employee class. Implements the abstract method Payroll
/// defined in the base class. Also implements some class
/// specific methods
/// </summary>
class HourlyEmployee : Employee
{
    private double m_HourlyRate;
    private double m_HoursWorked;

    public HourlyEmployee( int ID, string FirstName,
        string LastName, string MiddleName, string SSN,
        double HourlyRate ):
        base( ID, FirstName, LastName, MiddleName, SSN )
    {
        m_HourlyRate = HourlyRate;
        m_HoursWorked = 0;
    }


    public double HoursWorked
    {
        get { return m_HoursWorked; }
        set { m_HoursWorked = value; }
```

```
    }


    override public double Payroll

    {

        get { return m_HoursWorked * m_HourlyRate; }

    }

}
```

The *Employee* class now has a *Payroll* property that is declared as abstract:

```
abstract public double Payroll

{

    get;

}
```

Notice that the *get* method has no implementation. The *SalariedEmployee* and *HourlyEmployee* classes supply the following implementations of the property:

```
// SalariedEmployee implementation

override public double Payroll

{

    get { return m_Salary / 12; }

}


// HourlyEmployee implementation

override public double Payroll

{

    get { return m_HoursWorked * m_HourlyRate; }

}
```

The payroll sample program included on the CD in the file payroll.cs incorporates most of the concepts we have covered in this chapter. It extends the employee message queue we have seen throughout this chapter. In particular, it highlights the power and practical use of inheritance and polymorphism in C#. The sample extends the messages received in the message queue to include messages that indicate hours worked for hourly employees as well as supporting the add new employee message. After processing all of the messages in the queue, the program lists each employee and the amount of their paycheck for the month.

Along with the *Employee*, *SalariedEmployee*, and *HourlyEmployee* classes just shown, it illustrates inheritance and polymorphism in a few other classes. As mentioned earlier in the chapter when discussing exceptions, you can derive custom exceptions. We have derived a new custom exception from *System.Exception* that is thrown when an attempt is made to read past the end of the message queue. Here is the declaration of the class:

```
/// <summary>
/// Custom exception which is thrown when an attempt is made to
/// read past the end of the queue.
/// </summary>
class EndOfMessageQueueException : Exception
{
    public EndOfMessageQueueException( string Message ) :
      base( Message )
    {
    }
}
```

The sample also derives the *Employees* message queue class directly from *ArrayList* instead of including an *ArrayList* as a member of the class. Because *ArrayList* already supports *IEnumerable*, there is little we need to implement ourselves. Here is the *Employees* class code:

```
/// <summary>
/// Container class for employees derived from ArrayList
/// </summary>
class Employees : ArrayList
{
    public int Length
    {
        get { return this.Count; }
    }
}
```

We've also created a new *Logger* base class and have derived the *EmployeeLogger* class and a new *ErrorLogger* class from it. You can see from the following code that the Logger class performs the actual writing of text to a disk file while the other two classes implement methods specific to the type of logging they perform:

```
/// <summary>
/// General logging class to a file. Base class for other more
/// specific loggers.
/// </summary>
class Logger
{
    string m_fileName;

    public Logger( string fileName )
    {
        m_fileName = fileName;
    }

    protected void log( string text )
    {
        FileStream stream = new FileStream( m_fileName,
            FileMode.OpenOrCreate, FileAccess.ReadWrite);

        StreamWriter writer = new StreamWriter( stream );
        writer.BaseStream.Seek( 0, SeekOrigin.End );

        writer.Write("{0} {1} \n", DateTime.Now.ToLongTimeString(),
            DateTime.Now.ToLongDateString());

        writer.Write( text );
        writer.Write("\n-------------------------------------\n\n");
        writer.Flush();
        writer.Close();
    }
}


/// <summary>
```

```csharp
/// Writes add employee events to a log file.
/// </summary>
class EmployeeQueueLogger : Logger
{
    public EmployeeQueueLogger( string filename ) :
        base( filename )
    {
    }

    public void logAddRequest( object sender,
        AddEmployeeEventArgs e )
    {
        string name = e.FirstName + " " + e.MiddleName + " " +
            e.LastName;

        string text = "Adding Employee\n";
        text += "EmployeeID: " + e.ID.ToString();
        text += ", Name: " + name;
        log( text );
    }

    public void logHoursWorked( object sender,
        HoursWorkedEventArgs e )
    {
        string text = "Adding Hours Worked\n";
        text += "EmployeeID: " + e.ID.ToString();
        text += ", Hours Worked: " + e.Hours.ToString();
        log( text );
    }
}

/// <summary>
/// Logs error meessage to a log file.
/// </summary>
```

```
class ErrorLogger : Logger
{
    public ErrorLogger( string filename ) :
        base( filename )
    {
    }


    public void logError( Exception exception )
    {
        log( exception.Message );
        log( exception.StackTrace );
    }
}
```

The payroll sample should provide you with several good examples of inheritance and polymorphism. With the other samples you have seen and the concepts discussed in this chapter, you should have a solid foundation to start creating your own C# programs.

# Summary

C# is a modern object-oriented language. The Microsoft.NET Framework software development kit (SDK) and a text editor are all you need to get started programming in C#. In conjunction with the Common Language Runtime (CLR), you can develop console applications, graphical user interface (GUI) applications, and Web-based applications using C# and the .NET Framework.

C# includes all of the features you would expect in a modern object-oriented language. It supports the notion of classes and the object-oriented nature of classes, including inheritance and polymorphism. Classes are one of two data types in C#, reference types, which are allocated on the heap. Value types, which are allocated on the stack, are also supported including the usual primitive numeric and string data types. The looping and conditional statements available in most modern languages are part of C#, including *if-else* statements, *switch* statements, *for* loops, *while* loops, and *do-while* loops.

C# also includes advanced features such a properties and indexers which provide intuitive syntax for accessing data members while promoting data hiding. Delegates and events allow you to define events in your programs and set up callbacks to subscribed class methods when the event is raised. Exception handling is supported, which moves the clutter of error-checking outside of your main processing, resulting in clearly defined business logic.

# Solutions Fast Track

## Getting Started

- ☑ C# is a modern object-oriented language.

- ☑ The Microsoft .NET Framework software development kit (SDK) and a text editor are all you need to begin programming in C#. The Windows family of operating systems supplies several adequate editors including Notepad.

- ☑ Microsoft sells a feature rich development environment for developing .NET applications: Visual Studio .NET.

- ☑ You can use C# in development of console applications, graphical user interface (GUI) applications, and Web-based applications.

# Creating Your First C# Program

☑ A command-line compiler, csc.exe, is supplied with the .NET Framework SDK. You use it to compile console applications.

☑ Every C# program must have a static *Main* method, which is the entry point of the program. C# does not support global functions, so *Main* must be a class method.

☑ You can use namespaces to group related classes together. The *using* keyword allows you to reference a class object without prefixing it with the full namespace.

☑ You can also use source code control comments to document your program classes and methods for other programmers that may call your code.

# Introducing Data Types

☑ C# supports two data types: value types and reference types.

☑ Value types are allocated on the stack and include primitive types such as numerics, Booleans, characters, and strings. Structures and Enums are also value types.

☑ Reference types are allocated on the stack and are typically instances of class objects.

☑ C# does not support pointers.

# Explaining Control Structures

☑ C# supports the control structures you normally find in a modern language: *if-else* conditional, *for* loop, *do while* loop, *while* loop, and the *switch* statement.

☑ The test expression in an *if-else* statement must evaluate to a Boolean value. Numeric test expressions are not supported as they are in C/C++.

☑ The *switch* statement does not support falling through to the next *case* statement as it does in C/C++.

# Understanding Properties and Indexers

☑ Properties are method calls that appear to be member variables. Properties hide the underlying data type allowing you to change the implementation without the need to change code that uses the property.

☑ Indexers allow you to use array syntax to access a list of objects contained inside another class. Like properties, indexers hide the underlying implementation allowing you to change it without the need to change code that uses the indexer.

☑ Implementing indexers that support the *IEnumerator* interface allows you to use the *for-each* looping syntax to access the list objects of the indexer.

# Using Delegates and Events

☑ You can use delegates to call subscribed method calls when a triggering event happens. Delegates are similar to callback functions in Microsoft Windows programs or function pointers in C++.

☑ A single cast delegate invokes a single subscribed method. A multicast delegate invokes more than one subscribed method.

☑ Events are a type of a delegate that is provided for you in the .NET Framework. Methods subscribing to an event always provide the same set of arguments. This differs from delegates in that each delegate provides a unique signature for its subscribed methods.

# Using Exception Handling

☑ You use exception handling return and trap errors in C# programs.

☑ Exception handling uses the *try-catch-finally* syntax. *Try* blocks define the code that may throw exceptions. One or more *catch* blocks trap and handle exceptions of various types. The *finally* block is always executed regardless of whether an exception was thrown and is typically used to free resources.

☑ Because the .NET Common Language Runtime (CLR) may throw exceptions even if you don't, you should catch exceptions somewhere near the top of your call chain to be sure you program will continue running.

# Understanding Inheritance

☑ C# is an object-oriented language and as such supports inheritance and polymorphism. Inheritance means you can create a new type of object B that inherits all of the characteristics of an existing object A. Polymorphism means that this new object B can choose to inherit some characteristics and supply its own implementation for others.

☑ The *virtual* keyword is used to define methods in a base class that a derived class supplies its own implementation of. The *override* keyword is used by a method with the same signature in the derived class to provide a different implementation than the base class.

☑ The *abstract* keyword applied to a class definition indicates that the class is abstract and cannot be instantiated.

☑ The *abstract* keyword applied to a method call of an abstract class means the method has no implementation in the base class and must be implemented in the derived class.

# Frequently Asked Questions

The following Frequently Asked Questions, answered by the authors of this book, are designed to both measure your understanding of the concepts presented in this chapter and to assist you with real-life implementation of these concepts. To have your questions about this chapter answered by the author, browse to **www.syngress.com/solutions** and click on the **"Ask the Author"** form.

**Q:** Does C# support *friend* classes like in C++?

**A:** No. About the closest you can come is using the *internal* keyword, which allows access within the current assembly. But, there is no way to specify specific a class that knows about another class's private implementation.

**Q:** I thought destructors didn't exist in C#. Why can I declare one?

**A:** You can declare a method that looks like a C++ destructor such as *~Employee()*. But it really becomes a shorthand way to define *System.Object.Finalize*. The *Finalize* method is not the same as a C++ destructor. A short explanation is that C++ destructors are called when the call stack unwinds. The *Finalize* method will be called when the garbage collector of the CLR is ready to destroy the object.

**Q:** How do I convert a numeric type to a string?

**A:** Call *Sytem.Object.ToString()*. For example, if the variable *count* is an integer, write the following:

```
string text = count.ToString();
```

**Q:** How do I call a member method and pass a primitive type (Value Type) by reference?

**A:** Use the *ref* keyword when declaring the parameter of the method, for example:

```
public bool GetValue( ref int returnValue );
```

This will pass the numeric by reference. You can modify the value of *returnValue* within the body of *GetValue* and it will persist when the method call returns.

**Q:** Can I call a Win32 API function from a C# program?

**A:** Yes, you can. The .NET Framework provides a set of services called Platform Invoke, also known as PInvoke. Refer to the .NET Framework documentation for examples of using PInvoke services.

# Chapter 3

# Visual Studio.NET IDE

## Solutions in this chapter:

- **Introducing Visual Studio.NET**
- **Components of VS.NET**
- **Features of VS.NET**
- **Customizing the IDE**
- **Creating a Project**

☑ **Summary**

☑ **Solutions Fast Track**

☑ **Frequently Asked Questions**

# Introduction

In addition to the powerful .NET platform, Microsoft has introduced a new version of its Visual Studio Suite, called Visual Studio.NET (VS.NET). Even in its Beta stages, VS.NET provides the developer with powerful visual tools for developing all kinds of applications on the .NET platform.

VS.NET helps in the speedy creation and deployment of applications coded in any of the managed languages, including C#. This chapter gets you familiar with the new features of VS.NET and teaches you to customize it according to your needs. We cover the many new features of VS.NET, including the .NET Framework, Web Services, XML support, and the Integrated Development Environment (IDE).

Also, we cover the XML editor, which has tag completion for Extensible Stylesheet Language Transformations (XSLTs). We go over the IntelliSense feature and how it is used in the different windows. Finally, we cover how to customize your settings within the IDE.

VS.NET is a complete development environment. The components stay the same regardless of language, making it very easy to switch projects and languages and have the same features in the same place. Also, with the expanded IntelliSense with tag completion, routine code writing is faster.

# Introducing Visual Studio.NET

The Start pages deliver a great many resources for the development environment. The Start page is the default home page for the browser inside of the IDE. You can tap all aspects of the IDE from these pages. We go over the three most useful Start pages, starting out with the "What's New" page and the "My Profile" page, and ending with the "Get Started" page. We show you what is new with VS.NET, set up your profile, and get started using the tool.

Let's open up VS.NET and take a look at the first of the Start pages (see Figure 3.1).

You can filter the "What's New" Start page to whatever topic you are interested in—we have chosen to filter by .NET Framework. All content in the "What's New" Start page will be rendered based on the filter, so you can save some time by not looking up new features for VB, for example. You can also select **Check availability of Visual Studio.NET service packs** from this Start page and check to see if you need the latest download for VS.NET. Let's look at the "My Profile" page next, shown in Figure 3.2.

**Figure 3.1** VS.NET Start Page: What's New

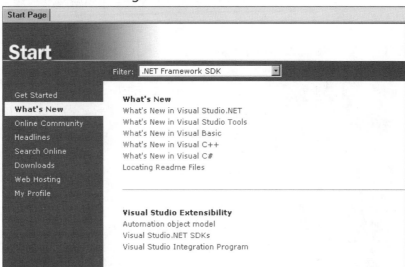

**Figure 3.2** VS.NET Start Page: My Profile

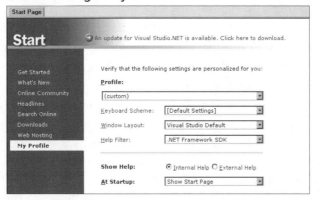

The "My Profile" section of the Start page lets you create your own (custom) profile or select from any of the options listed. If you happen to come from a VB background, using the VB profile would be beneficial so that you could be familiar with the tools from VS 6. Likewise, a C++ or Interdev user from VS 6 will benefit from the same environment. This will help you to learn the tool by showing a familiar layout. You can also select to have only external help, which will open the Help documentation in a new window outside of the IDE. You can filter the Help topics; in our case, we've selected **.NET Framework SDK** in the **What's New** section Start page. You can also select the window layout that you want to use. You then can select the **Get Started** Start page, shown in Figure 3.3.

**Figure 3.3** VS.NET Start Page: Get Started

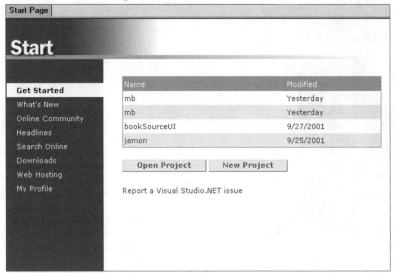

Here you can select projects you worked on previously, and you can also see where they are located on the machine by dragging the mouse over the name of the file. This is a nice feature that you can use where you have two projects named the same but at different locations.

The Start page is the default page for the Web browser window in VS.NET, so if you close it and want to get it back, simply hit the home icon on the Web toolbar and the page will load in the design window.

# Components of VS.NET

The Visual Studio.NET IDE is made up of many components that interact with one another. You can use each of them separately or at the same time. This feature lets the user decide which set of components he wishes to use. All of the components together create an intuitive graphical user interface (GUI).

## Design Window

The design window is used when you are graphically creating an application using the Toolbox to drag and drop objects onto the window. Much like the code window and browser, the design window cannot be docked or set to Auto Hide. You can split the design view or have tab groups added to it. Splitting the window helps when you need to compare code from two separate files (see Figure 3.4).

**Figure 3.4** Split Window View

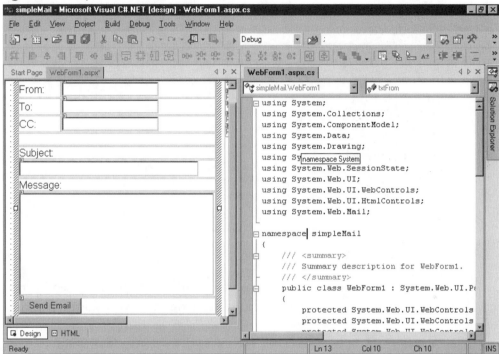

Here you can see windows for both design and code. This is a C# Web application, but the functionality is the same for any project.

# Code Window

As we mentioned, the code window is much like the design window. There is no toolbox functionality within the code view, however—you cannot drag and drop objects from the toolbox into the code view. If you create objects in the code view and then switch back to the design view, the objects that you added would persist in design view. Again you cannot dock this window nor allow it to float. You can, however, split it and add new tab groups to the display. Figure 3.5 shows the code window split and a tab vertical tab order added.

If you look at Figure 3.5 a little more closely, you can see a collapsible menu tree on the left-hand side. This is created every time you create a class or function, enabling you to collapse each section independently to save space for viewing other code present within the window. Note that you must have the default option Outlining Mode checked for this to work. If you want to have line numbers show for your code, you will have to choose **Tools | Options**. In the Options dialog box, select **Text/Editors**. Select **C#** and then choose the option to have line numbers added.

**Figure 3.5** Code View

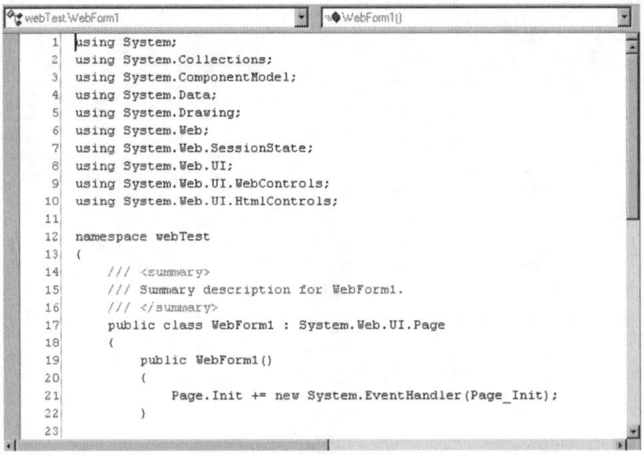

You may also define your own regions of code that may be collapsed. To do this simply add the following code to your class or function you want to make into a region:

```
#region

        ///Comments and code

#endregion
```

# Server Explorer

The Server Explorer is by far one of the best features in VS.NET. From this window you can connect to a server on the network and have full access to that server or servers. You can also link to any database servers on the network. Let's see how to do that. Click the **Connect to Database** icon in the title bar of the window (see Figure 3.6). You will be prompted to give all information required for a Universal Data Link (UDL).

Fill out the UDL Wizard and test the connection. After this is done, you can access everything within that database that the user has rights to. Let's take a look at that in Figure 3.7.

**Figure 3.6** Add Database to Server Explorer

**Figure 3.7** Expanded Database View

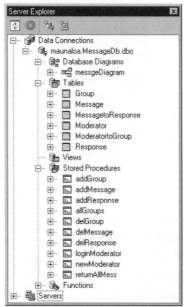

You can now click on any object within the Server Explorer and edit it within VS.NET. This is a timesaver from having to have both the Query Analyzer and VS.NET open at the same time and going back and forth between the two just to switch a data type of one stored procedure input parameter.

# Toolbox

The Toolbox, shown in Figure 3.8, includes Data, Components, Web Forms, and Window Forms tabs. As stated earlier in the chapter, you can use the Toolbox with the Design View window. You can drag and drop each component or control onto the design window. Also, you may customize the Toolbox by adding in your own code fragments and renaming them to something meaningful.

**Figure 3.8** The Toolbox Window

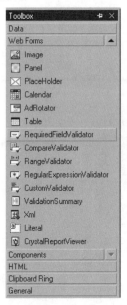

To do this, simply right-click on the Toolbox and select **Add Tab**. Give it a name that is different than the existing tabs, and you are ready to add your own tools. To add a new tool, highlight a block of code that you want to make into a tool and drag it onto the Toolbox label you just created.

The Clipboard Ring stores all the items that you have copied in code view automatically. You can then double-click these and add them to the source code.

# Docking Windows

One of the new features for VS.NET is that you can dock or expand or collapse all the windows within the IDE. To add windows to your IDE, navigate to the standard toolbar and select **View**; here you can select all the windows that you want to have immediately available in your environment. One drawback to this is that you will not have much room left to work in if you select a lot of windows to show, but the Auto Hide feature of each window makes them slide off the screen and embed in the side when not needed. This enables you to have max-imum code view but still have all windows present. To see a window that has Auto Hide enabled, simply position your mouse over the window icon on either side of the IDE. You can dock each window into place by clicking on the pin or by navigating to the standard toolbar and choosing the **Window** menu option. Once a window is docked, it is there permanently; you can, however, make the window float by selecting **Window | Floating** (see Figure 3.9).

**Figure 3.9** Floating Window

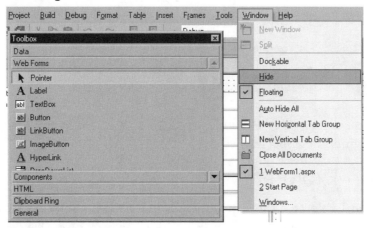

# Properties Explorer

The Properties Explorer is much as it was in VS 6 and the Visual Basic IDE and Visual Interdev IDE. Select an object from the design window, and in the Properties Explorer, you will see available attributes for that object listed, as shown in Figure 3.10. The right-hand column lists the property names, and the left-hand column stores the attribute's value. The Properties window enables Rapid Application Development (RAD) by allowing you to quickly create a graphical representation of the application you are building without doing any coding whatsoever. Some options are available in the Properties Explorer. You can select from the drop-down list the actual object you want to view. You can also select the **Events** option and have the event available to that object displayed. You can organize the Properties Explorer either by categories or alphabetically.

**Figure 3.10** Properties Explorer

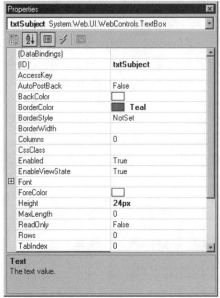

Any changes made in this window will be propagated to the design view and code view windows, respectively.

# Solution Explorer

The Solution Explorer is the same as it was in VS 6. The Solution Explorer is a look at all the files in your solution. In the title menu bar, you have four options: Refresh, Copy Web, Show All Files, and Properties. The Properties option lets you set all of your solutions' properties, including debug parameters options. The .NET IDE has two different types of containers available for holding items: *solutions* and *projects*. The main difference between the two is that you can have multiple projects within a solution, whereas the project container keeps only files and items within files. To view a project's properties, right-click the project and select **Properties**. Let's look at project properties in more detail in Figure 3.11.

Here, you need to make two changes. Set the target schema to **Internet Explorer 3.2 & Navigator 3.0**. Also, change the page layout from Grid to

**Flow**. These two changes will make all the JavaScript comply with the selected browsers. This will enable you to code without having to check to make sure if your scripts will work in older browsers. By making the change to "flow layout," you prevent your code from using absolute positioning within span tags so that it will be safe for Netscape users. These two changes are useful for any ASP.NET development you may do inside of the VS.NET IDE.

**Figure 3.11** Project Properties

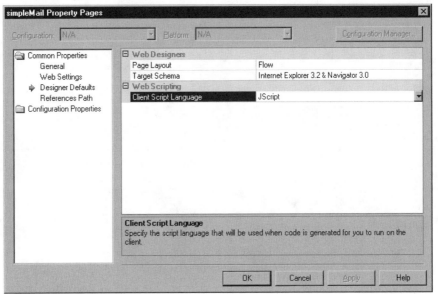

## Object Browser

The Object browser will give you a complete list of all classes' methods and properties in your solution. Everything is listed, and it is quite in depth. If you want to, you can look up parents of classes that you are using and list out the methods and properties you might need. By double-clicking on an external class in your solution, the Object browser will load and have all parent and child nodes of the class listed with each of their methods and properties included. This comes in handy when you are in need of finding a suitable substitute class to handle some part of your application. Like in Java, .NET has an incredible quantity of built-in classes that can accomplish just about everything you may need—the trouble is finding their location and how to access their methods and properties. Using the Object Browser enables you to achieve this in a timely fashion (see Figure 3.12).

**Figure 3.12** Object Browser

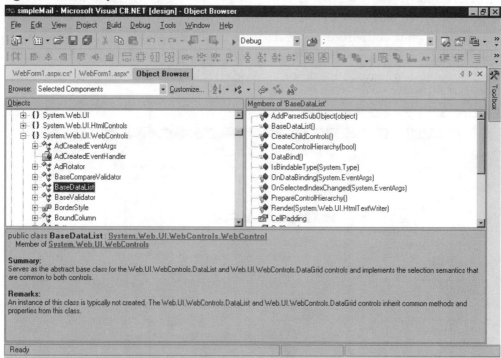

From this window, you can quickly drill through a class that is not your own and see what methods and properties it has; you also will get a summary of what it does and how it is instantiated.

# Dynamic Help

Dynamic Help is a dockable window just like the previous windows we have discussed. To get Dynamic Help to appear, simply choose **Help | Dynamic Help**. You can then make the window float or Auto Hide. One thing to note is that each part of Help (Index, Contents, Search, Index Results, and Search Results), are all separate windows, so if you undock them and make them all float you will have quite a few windows appearing on the screen. One thing you may do is load all the Help windows into themselves and a bottom tab order will appear inside the main Help window; you can then access all parts of Help from the same window (see Figure 3.13).

To customize the Dynamic Help window, choose **Tools | Options**. In the Options dialog box, select **Environment** and then select **Dynamic Help**.

Here you can specify what topics you want to have available and in what order. You may also specify how many links are displayed per topic. You may also create a custom Help file on your own for your project, by following the XML schema named vsdh.xsd. Create your XML file based off of that schema list and place the file where you want your Help topics to be displayed.

**Figure 3.13** Docked Help Windows

Tabbing through the many different Help options and getting to the information you need is now easy. If you have the hard drive space, loading all the MSDN Help files from the disks that come with VS.NET would be beneficial. To do this, simply check the option on the installation sequence that will run from the computer and not the CD. This will prevent you from constantly having to load another disk every time you want to look up a particular topic. This gets quite annoying when you need one disk to open the tree view and another to access the topic within.

## Task List Explorer

The Task List (see Figure 3.14) enables you to add tasks that need to be done and organize them in a number of different ways and with priority. It is very simple to use. If you are using Source Safe, a group of developers can quickly see what needs to be done and what has been done by viewing the Task List for each file in the project.

**Figure 3.14** Task List

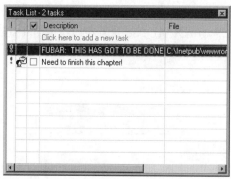

Another feature of the Task List is that it will create tasks on the fly as you debug your application by marking down any errors. You can then go back and fix each task and have it removed. You can organize the task list on Build errors. Also you can create your own custom *token*, which is a unique key that tells the Task List that a comment needs to be added to the list, to appear in your Task List from your code. You can map out your function or method or whatever you are coding with your own custom tokens and have them appear in the Task List.

To create your own custom token to add to the default tokens available (HACK, TODO, UNDONE), choose **Tools | Options | Task List**. Give the token name and priority. To use the token, simply add something like the following in your code window (use the comment tag "//" and then the token name followed by the instruction for the task):

```
// FUBAR what I want in the task list to appear.
```

# Features of VS.NET

VS.NET has a combination of new and old features built into the IDE. We discuss the additions to IntelliSense, the new features of XML support, and the many different ways you can now customize the IDE. Let's begin with IntelliSense.

## IntelliSense

IntelliSense is a form of code completion that has been part of most Microsoft developer tools for many years now. Code completion technology assists when you start to type a tag, attribute, or property by providing the resulting ending so that you will not have to write out the whole item. You will notice this right away.

VS.NET has IntelliSense support for all of the primary programming languages: VB.NET, C#, and C++. IntelliSense even exists for Cascading Style Sheets and HTML. Unfortunately, VS.NET doesn't include IntelliSense for XSLT in the Beta2 version—we may have to wait for the release version. Currently ActiveState does make an XSLT plug-in for VS.NET that provides this functionality; you can obtain a free trial version at http://aspn.activestate.com/ASPN/Downloads/VisualXSLT.

While developing, you will notice that IntelliSense provides information about active classes only, meaning those that you have created in your project or those referenced in your page with the *using* Directive (for code-behind pages: pagename.aspx.cs). If you are trying to use an object or method, and no IntelliSense appears for it, you may have forgotten to include the reference.

For example, if you attempt to do data operations using the *SqlCommand* object, no IntelliSense will appear until you reference the appropriate data class (see Figure 3.15):

```
using System.Data.SqlClient;
```

**Figure 3.15** Using IntelliSense

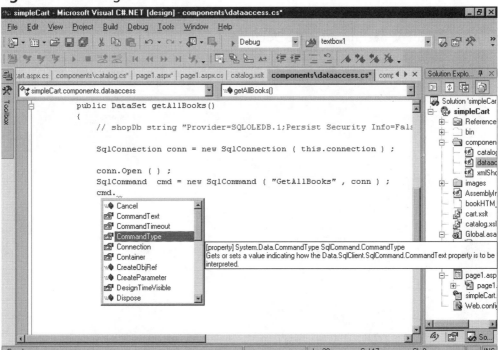

For C#, IntelliSense is available only in the code-behind page and not in the ASPX page itself. This may change in the release version. To disable IntelliSense, choose **Tools | Options | Text/Editor** and select the editor you are using, which should be C#. In the Statement Completion section, uncheck all the options, which will disable IntelliSense for the editor.

# XML Editor

When working with XML, VS.NET has some interesting features. If you create a well-formed XML document of your own, you can easily generate a corresponding XSD schema that conforms to the 2001 W3C XML schema. Once this is done, your XML document will have code completion based on this new schema. To test creating a schema, let's open poll.xml and generate a schema for it:

- Choose **File | Open**. Navigate to your CD-ROM drive and locate the file poll.xml.

- Click **Open**. This should load the page into the IDE.

- If the XML is one continuous line, simply click the **Format the Whole Document** icon (see Figure 3.16).

**Figure 3.16** Formatting an XML Document

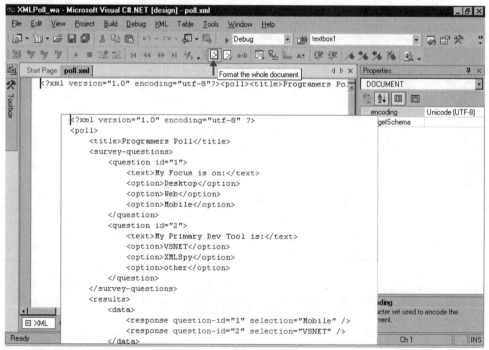

Now, let's create a schema for this file. Right-click anywhere in the text editor and select **Create Schema**. You can see these resulting changes in Figure 3.17:

- A new file called poll.xsd was auto-generated by VS.NET.

- In the Properties window, the new schema is set as the file's target schema.

- An XML namespace attribute is added.

- IntelliSense based on the schema is now available for this document.

**Figure 3.17** Generating a Schema for a Well-Formed XML Document

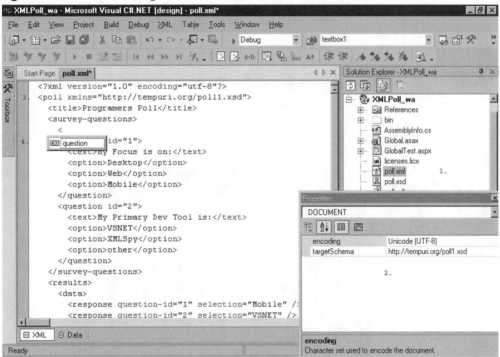

You can also select a different schema to base the XML file on by selecting a new schema from the *targetSchema* drop-down (see Figure 3.18). This would then provide IntelliSense based on the schema selected.

You can also view XML documents from the Data mode. This presents the document in a hierarchical structure. From this view, you can also add new nodes and data to the document (see Figure 3.19).

**Figure 3.18** Selecting a Target Schema

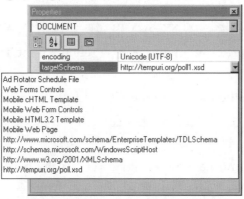

**Figure 3.19** Viewing an XML Document in Data Mode

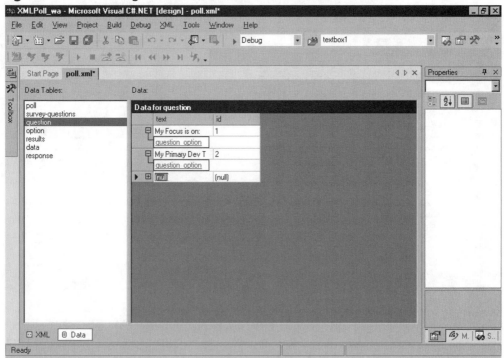

# Documentation Generation (XML Embedded Commenting)

This feature enables you to comment your code with an embedded XML tagging structure. When XML documentation is enabled, an XML documentation file will be created during the build process. In the Solutions Explorer, right-click on the project name, then select **Properties**. The Project Properties dialog appears. Click the **Configuration Properties** folder and select **Build**.

Find the item called **XML Documentation File** in the textbox next to this, provide a relative path to the file location you would like the Documentation written to, and click **Apply** (see Figure 3.20).

**Figure 3.20** Setting the XML Documentation File Source in the Project Properties Dialog

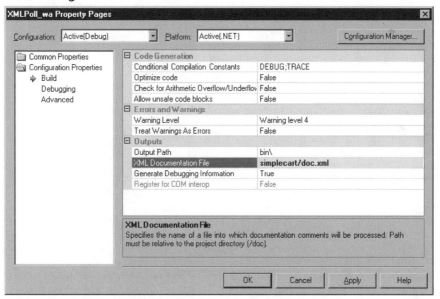

Now let's look at how to add XML comments to the code.

## Adding XML Document Comments to C# Pages

The file used in this example is from a sample application built in Chapter 10 and is on the CD (See catalog.cs in the components folder.) To add XML documentation comments to your code, simply type three slashes above any class, method, or variable.

```
public DataSet catalogItemDetails( string book_isbn )
{
return catalogRangeByCategory( -1, -1, book_isbn);
}
```

An XML representation of its inputs and outputs will be generated:

```
/// <summary>
///
/// </summary>
/// <param name="book_isbn"></param>
/// <returns></returns>
public DataSet catalogItemDetails( string book_isbn )
{
      return catalogRangeByCategory( -1, -1, book_isbn);
}
```

Simply add appropriate notes and build the project:

```
/// <summary>
/// Specialized interface to catalogRangeByCategory.
/// This Method returns all the data for only the given book
/// </summary>
/// <param name="book_isbn">string</param>
/// <returns>DataSet</returns>
public DataSet catalogItemDetails( string book_isbn )
{
return catalogRangeByCategory( -1, -1, book_isbn);
}
```

When you build the project, you will receive a list of warnings corresponding to every *Public* variable, property, method, and class that is not commented. Figure 3.21 shows what happens when you tell it to create comments; this is how it tells you what variable isn't commented. This will not prevent program execution, nor the writing of the documentation file. Figure 3.22 contains the XML generated on build.

**Figure 3.21** Warning for Uncommented Public Variables, Properties, Methods, and Classes

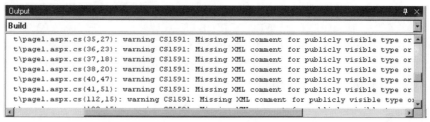

**Figure 3.22** Generated XML Documentation

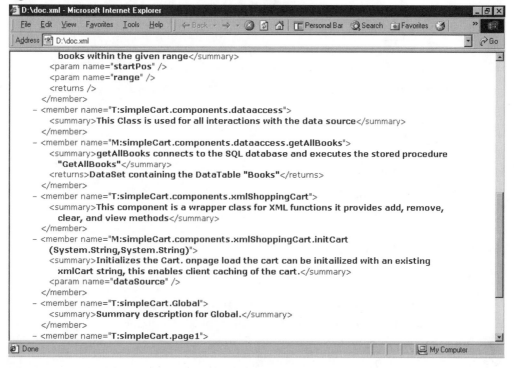

# Customizing the IDE

The VS.NET IDE is fully customizable. All windows can be set to *dockable*, *hide*, *auto hide*, and *floating*. You can display different toolbars for each different type of file, and you can create customizable toolbars. You can set font, tab, and text layout properties for each type of file. You can set the default Start page to open the last project, or even set it to a user-created page. If you mess up the layout, you can easily set it back to several predefined layouts.

# Creating a Project

Now that we have covered all the different aspects of the IDE, let's create a test project. We cover the different type of projects available, show how to add a Web reference to the project, and briefly go over some of the debugging tools available to the IDE. This should give a well-rounded tour of the complete IDE. Now let's go over the projects available.

## Projects

We cover the projects available to C# development:

- Windows application
- Class Library
- Windows Control Library
- ASP.NET Web application
- ASP.NET Web service
- Web Control Library
- Console application
- Windows Service
- Empty project
- Empty Web project
- New project in existing folder

Most of these are self-explanatory. Users new to .NET will see that three Web projects are added into the project listing for all languages. These are the ASP. NET, Application, Web Service, and Control Library. The other projects will be familiar to all VS 6 users (see Figure 3.23).

## Creating a Project

For this example, we will build an ASP.NET Web application (see Figure 3.23). You may keep the name as the default or select a new name. The location should be localhost if you are developing on the same box as the IIS server; if not, you will have to place the location of the server in that text box, either through IP or the name of server. The next option is to either close any open solutions and open this new, or add it to the existing solution. We recommend that you choose to have it close all open solutions and open new, so as not to task your machine with having multiple solutions in the same IDE. Click **OK**, and VS.NET will create the project for you.

**Figure 3.23** Project Listing in the IDE

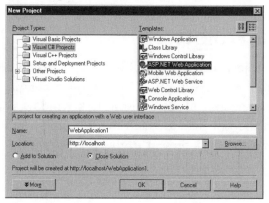

## Add Reference

One of the great benefits of working within the IDE of VS.NET is that you can add references to your project with ease. Try it out: In this project, select the project name in the Solutions Explorer. Right-click and select **Add Web Reference**. Now you will have to have a location to a WSDL file from which to locate and add in the Web Service to the project. This is covered later in the book.

You may also add a reference to a DLL to your project. This will be done much the same way as the Web Reference. Instead of selecting Add Web Reference as we just did, select **Add Reference**, then choose from all the available references on your machine.

## Build the Project

To build a project, simply press **F5** or click the **Start icon** on the main window menu bar. The project will be compiled. You must also set a Start page before this takes place. To do that, right-click on the file you want to have be the Start page or window and set it to **Start page**. This will launch this page first after the project has been compiled and run (see Figure 3.24).

**Figure 3.24** Compiling a Project

# Debugging a Project

While building the project, any errors will bring up a dialog box, which will ask you to continue with the errors in place, or to strop debugging and correct any errors displayed. These errors will show in the Task window. You may double-click on any error in the Task window, and the IDE will take you to that location in the code. As you fix the bugs present in the task list, they will be removed. You can also set breakpoints and step over and step into options.

# Summary

In this chapter, we've taken a tour of the VS.NET IDE. We've seen an overview of the interface, some of its component windows and some of its built-in features. The design window and the code window are graphical tools used in creating an application. You can split the windows or have tab groups added to them; you can use the Toolbox (which includes Data, Components, Web Forms, and Window Forms) to drag and drop objects onto the design window. The Server Explorer window allows you to connect to a server on the network and have full access to that server, and to link to any database servers on the network.

One of the new features for VS.NET is that you can dock all the windows, or expand and collapse them within the view of the IDE. The Auto Hide feature of each window makes them slide off the screen and embed in the side when not needed; this enables you to have maximum code view but still have all windows present.

The Properties Explorer (similar to the one in VS 6 and the Visual Basic IDE and Visual Interdev IDE) allows you to select an object from the design window to see available attributes for that object listed. Any changes made in this window will be propagated to the design view and code view windows respectively.

The Solution Explorer (the same as in VS 6) is a look at all the files in your solution via the four options: Refresh, Copy Web, Show All Files, and Properties. The VS.NET IDE has two different types of containers available for holding items, solutions and projects (you can have multiple projects within a solution, whereas the project container keeps only files and items within files). The Object browser will give you a complete list of all classes' methods and properties in your solution.

Other windows include Dynamic Help and the Task List. Dynamic Help is a dockable window that you can fully customize to make it easy to tab to whatever information you are interested in. You can use the Task List for collaborative projects and in debugging; it lets you add and prioritize tasks.

IntelliSense, the code-completion technology Microsoft uses, is supported in VS.NET for VB.NET, C#, and C++, but not yet for XSLT. IntelliSense provides information about active classes. For C#, IntelliSense is available only in the code-behind page and not in the ASPX page itself.

Another important feature is XML Documentation. This feature enables you to comment your code with an embedded XML tagging structure. When XML documentation is enabled, an XML documentation file will be created during the build process.

We've looked at some issues like the customizable, dockable, hide, auto hide, and float settings for many of the component windows along with the profile setting on the Start page. VS.NET is a collection of integrated developer tools that you should definitely familiarize yourself with.

# Solutions Fast Track

## Introducing Visual Studio.NET

- ☑ Visual Studio.NET (VS.NET) provides a consistent interface across the primary development languages.

- ☑ VS.NET provides easy to use tools for Windows and WebForms rapid prototyping across languages (including C# and Managed C++).

## Components of VS.NET

- ☑ Enhanced window manipulation for user preferences within the Integrated Development Environment (IDE) gives the developer the ability to dock, auto hide, hide, or float all component windows.

- ☑ Task List has the ability to create custom tokens to map out and prioritize your code via the Task List.

- ☑ Server Explorer allows the developer to quickly connect and access any database server on the network, enabling direct access to all database objects, including stored procedures, functions, and user settings.

## Features of VS.NET

- ☑ IntelliSense is one of the best tools at your disposal when learning a new language or technology. VS.NET has built IntelliSense into almost every aspect of the development process.

- ☑ Dynamically generated XML Documentation provides a fast and easy way to comment your code and generate a separate XML formatted documentation file. This tool makes code more self-documenting, and it should save developers time and ensure that some documentation is provided.

☑ Generating XML schemas from well-formed XML is now a breeze with .NET. You can also create new XML documents that conform to popular standards by selecting a *targetSchema* and using the IntelliSense feature to create valid XML documents.

## Customizing the IDE

☑ The VS.NET IDE is fully customizable. All windows can be set to dockable, hide, auto hide, and floating. You can display different toolbars for each different type of file and create customizable toolbars. You can set font, tabbing, and text layout properties for each type of file.

☑ You can set the default Start page to open the last project, or even set it to a user-created page.

☑ The IDE also includes several common default settings in case you mess up while customizing your interface, settings like the default VB 6 interface or Visual InterDev.

## Creating a Project

☑ One of the great benefits of working within the IDE of VS.NET is that you can add references to your project with ease.

☑ To build a project, simply press **F5** or click the **Start icon** on the main window menu bar.

☑ While building the project, any errors will bring up a dialog box, which will ask you to continue with the errors in place, or to strop debugging and correct any errors displayed.

# Frequently Asked Questions

The following Frequently Asked Questions, answered by the authors of this book, are designed to both measure your understanding of the concepts presented in this chapter and to assist you with real-life implementation of these concepts. To have your questions about this chapter answered by the author, browse to **www.syngress.com/solutions** and click on the **"Ask the Author"** form.

**Q:** How can I look up a parent class method or property of any System-level object?

**A:** Use the Class View window, accessed from the standard toolbar by clicking **View | Class View**.

**Q:** Does VS.NET support line numbering in its text editor?

**A:** Yes, from the standard toolbar select **Tools | Options**. This will open the Options dialog; select the **Text Editor** folder, pick the language, and click on the check box for line numbering under the display section.

**Q:** Is there a way to set the tab size in the text editor?

**A:** Yes, from the standard tool bar select **Tools | Options**. This will open the Options dialog; select the **Text Editor** folder, choose a language folder, select **Tabs**, and set them to your desired setting.

# Chapter 4

# Windows Forms

## Solutions in this chapter:

- **Introducing Windows Forms**

- **Writing a Simple Windows Forms Application**

- **Writing a Simple Text Editor**

- **Using the ListView and TreeView Controls**

- **Creating Controls**

☑ **Summary**

☑ **Solutions Fast Track**

☑ **Frequently Asked Questions**

# Introduction

With so much focus on Web-based user interfaces, it's easy to dismiss the traditional Windows architecture when developing for the Internet. The recent popularity, however, of peer-to-peer file sharing and online chat programs demonstrates that the "rich client" can work extremely well over the Internet, and provide features unavailable in thin client model. The .NET platform provides a modern solution for developing Windows applications, with the following key features:

- A revamped object-oriented model, with a focus on consistency and extensibility

- A rapid application development environment in Visual Studio

- Easy access to the Internet through .NET networking libraries and Web Services

- Managed execution environment that allows custom controls to be hosted in a Web page

- Compilation to a small executable

And, of course, you no longer have any installation worries—you just need to copy a small executable to the target machine and run it. Rich client has become thin.

The components provided in the .NET library for writing Windows applications can broadly be divided into two groups: Windows Forms (the components that manage windows and controls) and the graphics device interface known as GDI+ (the classes that encapsulate the lower-level graphics functions). This chapter covers Windows Forms in some detail, also touching upon GDI+, and it takes you step by step through the process of creating typical rich client applications.

# Introducing Windows Forms

In essence, Windows Forms is a collection of classes and types that encapsulate and extend the Win32 API in a tidy object model. In other words, the components used to create Windows GUI applications are provided as .NET classes and types that form part of an orderly hierarchy.

This hierarchy is defined by inheritance: Simple reusable classes such as *Component* are provided, and then used as a base from which more sophisticated classes are derived. We can draw a useful overview by representing the inheritance hierarchy in a treelike diagram. Figure 4.1 summarizes at a high level the classes that comprise Windows Forms and GDI+.

**Figure 4.1** A Summary of Window Forms and GDI+ Classes

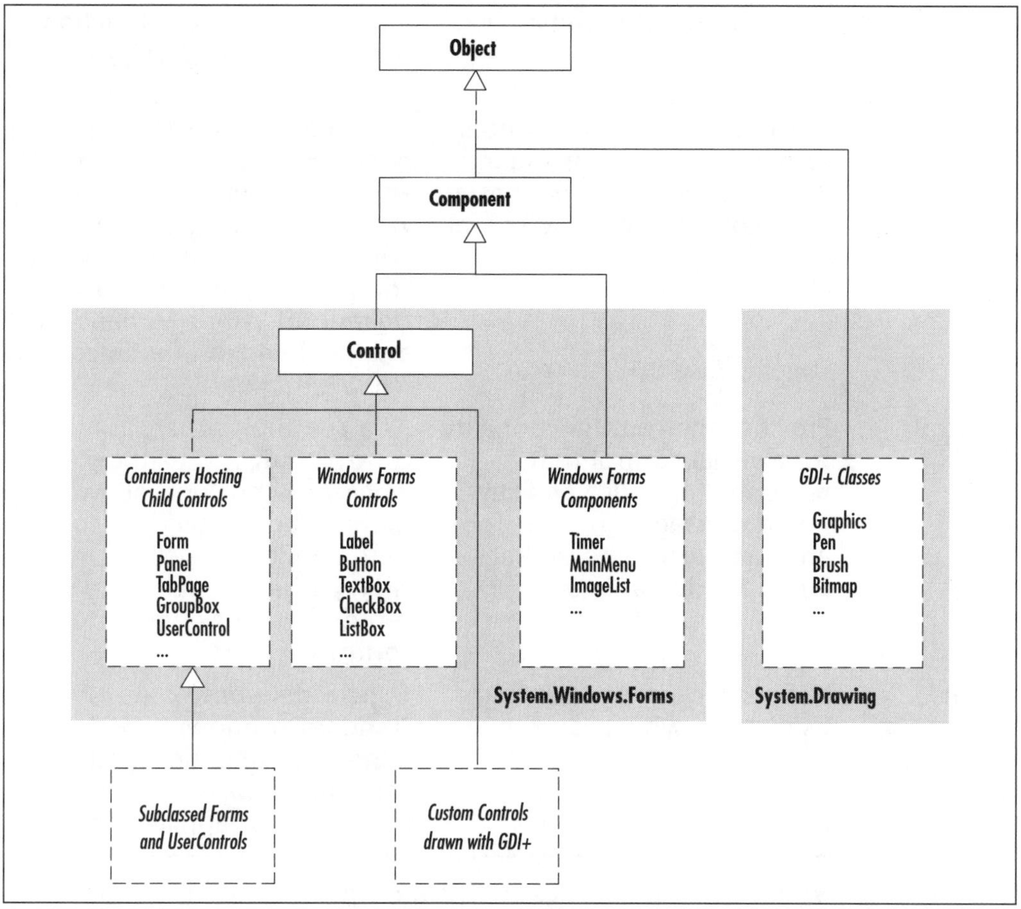

The arrows represent inheritance: *Control* assumes all the functionality of *Component*, which assumes all the functionality of *Object*. Table 4.1 provides a quick and pragmatic summary of the four essential classes on which the Windows Forms types are based.

**Table 4.1** Core Classes

| Class | What It Does | Why We Need It |
|---|---|---|
| Object | Acts as a base class for all types in the .NET Framework. | For a tidy unified type system, and to provide core functionality available to all types (such as *ToString*). |
| Component | Provides the basics of containership, facilitates hosting in a visual designer, and defines a protocol for resource disposal. | So Visual Studio's Designer can host a wide variety of controls and components in a generic way, to provide a base from which you can write nonvisual components, and to allow the cleanup of Windows handles and file handles in a timely and reliable manner. |
| Control | Provides the core functionality for a visual control that responds to mouse and keyboard messages, accepts focus, and can participate in drag-and-drop operations. | As a common superclass for all controls, such as textboxes, labels, and buttons, allowing them to be treated in a consistent manner, as well as providing a base from which you can derive your own custom controls. |
| Form | Defines a class representing a window to which you can add controls. | To provide a base class with standard windowing and containership functionality that you can subclass to create forms in your application. |

Creating a Windows Forms application is largely just a matter of instantiating and extending the Windows Forms and GDI+ classes. In a nutshell, you typically complete the following steps:

1. Create a new project defining the structure of a Windows Forms application.

2. Define one or more Forms (classes derived from the *Form* class) for the windows in your application.

3. Use the Designer to add controls to your forms (such as textboxes and checkboxes), and then configure the controls by setting their properties and attaching event handlers.

4.  Add other Designer-managed components, such as menus or image lists.

5.  Add code to your form classes to provide functionality.

6.  Write custom controls to meet special requirements, using GDI+ classes to handle low-level graphics.

In this chapter, we cover each of these steps through a series of walkthroughs. Starting with a new Windows Forms project, we visually add controls to a simple form, add an event handler, and then demonstrate how controls can be added at runtime. In the next walkthrough, we write a simple text editor, illustrating menus, single and multiple-document interfaces, dialog forms, and visual inheritance. In the following example, we introduce the *ListView* and *TreeView* controls, going step-by-step through the process of setting up a splitter, adding a context menu, and enabling drag and drop between the controls. In the final walkthrough, we write our own controls—starting with a simple address container and finishing with a scrolling text banner. We then show how custom controls can be hosted on an HTML page—demonstrating how C# and Windows Forms can be used to write Java-like Internet applets.

# Writing a Simple Windows Forms Application

The first step to building a Windows Forms application is creating a project. A Windows Forms project is just like any other type of project in that it consists of a grouping of source code files, a list of references to required .NET code libraries, and an appropriate configuration of compilation and debugging options. When you use Visual Studio to create a project from a template, it sets all of this up for you, providing a "skeleton" appropriate to the template you've selected. In the case of Windows Forms, this consists of the following:

- A project of Output Type *Windows Application*. You can view or change this in the **Project | Properties** dialog box.

- References to the .NET assemblies required for typical Windows Forms applications (covering most of the types in the *Windows Forms* namespace). You can see a list of the project references in the Solution Explorer.

- A blank form, called *Form1* (a C# class with the structure required for a visually editable form).

- A *Main* method in *Form1* that instantiates and displays the form.

Let's start the walkthrough by creating a new Windows Forms project. From the main menu, choose **File | New | Project**, click **Visual C# Projects**, and choose the **Windows Application** template (see Figure 4.2). Change the project name to **SimpleApp** and click **OK**.

**Figure 4.2** Creating a New Windows Forms Project

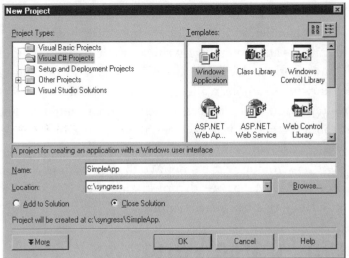

## Adding Controls

Once we've created the project, Visual Studio opens the main form (*Form1*) in the Designer—the visual editor for our C# form class. Basically, a form created in Visual Studio is just a C# file, defining a class based on *System.Windows.Forms.Form*, containing code to add and configure the controls created visually. Visual Studio is a "two-way tool" meaning that we can work with the same code either visually (using the Designer) or programmatically (in the Code Editor).

Let's use the Designer to add a few controls to *Form1*. We can add controls and components from the toolbox window and then configure them using the Properties window.

1. From the toolbox, add a Label control to the form. By default, Visual Studio will name the control *Label1*.

2. From the Properties Window (F4) change *label1's Text* property to **Favorite CD**, and change its *AutoSize* property to **True** (see Figure 4.3). This tells the control to size itself according to the metrics of the font and width of the text.

**Figure 4.3** Adding and Configuring a Label Control

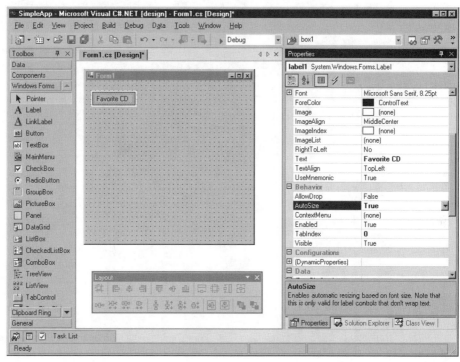

3. Now add a **TextBox** from the toolbox onto the form, and position it below the label. Enlarge it horizontally and clear its *Text* property.

4. Add another label to the form, setting its *Text* property to **Favorite Style**, and *AutoSize* property to **True**.

5. Add a **ComboBox** and position it below the *Favorite Style* label. Clear its *Text* property.

6. Select the combo's *Items* property, and then click the ellipses on the right to open the String Collection Editor. Type in a few styles of music— each on a separate line, as shown in Figure 4.4.

7. Click **OK**, and then press **F5** to save, compile, and run the application.

**Figure 4.4** Populating a ComboBox Items Collection

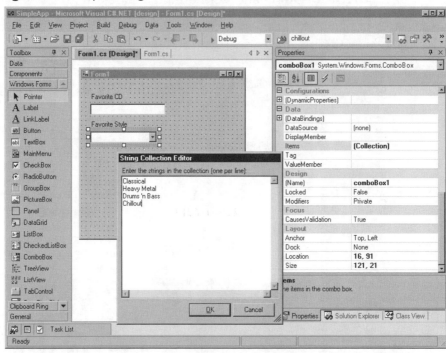

### Developing & Deploying…

## Working with Controls: Using TextBoxes

To create and work with textboxes having more than one line:

1. Set *MultiLine* to **True** and *AutoSize* to **False**.

2. Set *AcceptsTab* and *AcceptsReturn* to **True** to allow tabs and new lines to be entered via the keyboard.

3. Set the *ScrollBars* property to Vertical (or Both if *WordWrap* is false).

4. Use the *Lines* property to access the control's text one line at a time.

5. Use \r\n for a new line, for example, Flat 18\r\nQueen St.

To use the control for entering a password, set the *PasswordChar* property to *. To read or update selected text, use the *SelectionStart*, *SelectionLength*, and *SelectedText* properties.

# Adding an Event Handler

Let's add some functionality to the form.

1. Add a **Button** and **ListBox** to the form.

2. Select the button, and change its *Text* property to **Update**. Then click the **lightning icon** in the Properties window to switch to the Events View (see Figure 4.5).

**Figure 4.5** Properties Window Events View

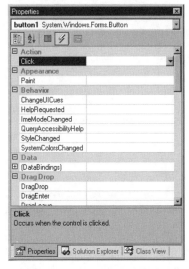

Think of these events as "hooks" into which we can attach our own methods. You can either double-click on an event to create a new event-handling method, or use the drop-down list to connect into an existing compatible method.

3. Double-click on the **Click** event. Visual Studio will write a skeleton event-handling method, wiring it to the event. It will then place you in the Code Editor, inside the empty method definition:

```
private void button1_Click(object sender, System.EventArgs e)
{


}
```

The .NET convention for event handling requires two parameters: a sender parameter of type *object*, and an event arguments parameter of type *EventArgs*—or a descendant of *EventArgs*. The sender parameter tells us which control fired the event (this is useful when many controls have been wired to the same event-handling method). The second parameter is designed to supply special data about the event. In the case of *Click*, we have a standard *EventArgs* object, and this contains no useful information—it's just there to meet the protocol required to support more sophisticated events (such as *KeyPress* or *MouseDown*).

The actual name for this method (*button1_Click*) is just a convenient identifier generated by Visual Studio; Windows Forms doesn't impose any particular naming convention.

4.  Add the following code to the event handler:

```
private void button1_Click(object sender, System.EventArgs e)
{
    listBox1.Items.Clear();
    listBox1.Items.Add ("Fav CD: " + textBox1.Text);
    listBox1.Items.Add ("Fav Style: " + comboBox1.Text);
}
```

Here we're manipulating our list box through its *Items* property. *Items* returns a collection object, having methods to add and remove items from its list. Note how we access each control through its name—this is possible because the Designer creates class fields matching the names of each control. You can see these declarations at the top of the class definition.

5.  Press **F5** to compile and run the program (see Figure 4.6).

**Figure 4.6** Running a Simple Windows Forms Application

> ### Developing & Deploying...
>
> ### Working with Controls: Using the ComboBox and ListBox Controls
>
> To add items to the controls' selection lists programmatically:
>
> 1. Call the *Item* property's *Add* method to append to the end of the list, for example:
>
> ```
> myControl.Items.Add ("My New Item");
> ```
>
> 2. Use the *Item* property's *Insert* method to insert within the list.
>
> 3. Because these methods expect an *Object* type, the item you add can be of any class, including your own (this is *polymorphism* in action—one of the benefits of a working in an object-oriented language). The control simply calls the item's *ToString* method to determine what to display.
>
> To get the currently selected item:
>
> 1. Use the *Text* property to return a string.
>
> 2. Use *SelectedIndex* to get a numeric position within the list.
>
> 3. Use *SelectedItem* to get an object reference. If the item is of your own custom class, you'll need to explicitly cast the returned value back to your type.
>
> To allow the user to select only from items in a *ComboBox* list, set the *DropDownStyle* property to *DropDownList*.

# Adding Controls at Runtime

Sometimes it's necessary to add controls without the help of the Designer. For instance, you might want some controls to appear on a form only when a particular button is clicked.

In learning how to programmatically add controls, it's very helpful to examine a visually created form in the Code Editor. If you expand the Designer Generated Code region, you'll see a method called *InitializeComponent* containing all the code that creates and configures each of the form's visual components.

---

**W**ARNING

Although reading Designer-generated code is useful in understanding how components are instantiated and configured, you shouldn't make manual changes to this code without exercising some caution. In particular, you should check that the control renders as expected in the Designer before saving the form. You should also check your code after making some visual change—Visual Studio completely rewrites the Designer-generated code section, so your modifications may not appear as originally entered.

---

Here are the four steps to programmatically adding a control or component:

1.  Add a class field declaration for the new control.

2.  Instantiate the control.

3.  Configure the control by setting its properties and adding event handlers, if required.

4.  Add the control to the form's *Controls* collection (or alternatively, to the Controls collection of a container control, such as a *GroupBox*).

Let's work through an example: we'll create a new form, add a button, and then have a textbox appear when the user clicks the button:

1.  Create a new Windows Forms project called *SimpleApp2* and add a *Button* control from the toolbox onto the new form.

2.  Press **F7** to open the Code Editor, and locate *button1*'s declaration. Below this, add a similar declaration for our new textbox, as follows (you can exclude the *System.Windows.Forms* prefix if your form has the appropriate *using* statement):

```
private System.Windows.Forms.Button button1;
private System.Windows.Forms.TextBox myTextBox;
```

You need to understand that this declaration doesn't actually create a textbox. All it does is instruct the compiler, once our form is instantiated, to create a field that can *reference* (point to) a textbox object—one that does not yet exist. This declaration exists so as to provide a convenient way to refer to the control throughout the lifetime of the form. In the cases where we don't need to explicitly reference the control after its been created, we can do away with this declaration.

3. Return to the Designer, and double-click on the button. This is a quick way to attach an event handler to the button's default event (Click).

4. Add the following code to the button's event handler:

```
private void button1_Click(object sender, System.EventArgs e)
{
    // Create the actual textbox and assign its reference to
        myTextBox
    this.myTextBox = new TextBox();

    // Position the control
    myTextBox.Location = new Point (30, 20);

    // Put the control on the form.
    this.Controls.Add (myTextBox);
}
```

5. Press **F5** to test the application (illustrated in Figure 4.7).

**Figure 4.7** Adding Controls at Runtime

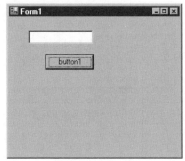

You might have noticed that we created a *Point* object to position the control. *Point, Size,* and *Rectangle* are three "helper types" defined in the *System.Drawing* namespace, and are used extensively in Windows Forms—as well as other parts of the .NET Framework. Table 4.2 illustrates how these types are most commonly applied in Windows Forms.

**Table 4.2** Helper Types for Positioning and Sizing

| Type | Example | Notes |
|------|---------|-------|
| *Point* struct | `button1.Location = new Point (100, 80);` | Sets *button1*'s position 100 pixels across and 80 pixels down. |
| | `button1.Left = 100;` `button1.Top = 80;` | Equivalent to the above. |
| | `Console.WriteLine (button1.Location.X);` | Equivalent to outputting *button1.Left*. |
| | `button1.Location.X = 100;` | Not permitted because of the way structs are marshaled in C#. |
| *Size* struct | `button1.Size = new Size (75, 25);` | Resizes *button1* to 75 by 25 pixels. |
| | `button1.Width = 75;` `button1.Height = 25;` | Equivalent to the above. |
| | `// Assuming "this" is our form` `this.Size = new Size (button1.Right,` `button1.Bottom);` | Attempts to resize the form so it just fits *button1*. However, the form's Size property includes the title bar and borders—its usable space is less, and *button1* won't quite fit. |
| | `this.ClientSize = new Size` `(button1.Right, button1.Bottom);` | *ClientSize* excludes title bars and borders so this works correctly. |
| *Rectangle* struct | `button1.Bounds = new Rectangle` `(100, 80, 50, 20);` | Rectangle combines *Point* and *Size*. |
| | `button1.Bounds = new Rectangle` `(0, 0, this.ClientSize.Width,` `this.ClientSize.Height);` | Moves and sizes *button1* to fill the whole client area of our form (later we'll see that docking provides a better solution to achieving this). |

Developing & Deploying…

## Working with Controls: Using Controls Collections

The *form* class is an example of a control that hosts other controls. Windows Forms manages this containership by providing a *Controls* property, returning a *ControlCollection* object that has methods to add, remove, and access the child controls. Like other .NET collections, it implements standard interfaces such as *ICollection* and *IList*—and this means we can work with them all in a similar way.

To access an individual control by its position in the collection, use its Indexer—for example:

```
Controls[0].Hide()  // hide the first control in the collection
```

To iterate through every control, use the *foreach* structure—for example:

```
// Write the Text property of each control on the form
foreach (Control c in Controls)
    Console.WriteLine (c.Text);
```

To remove a control from the collection, use the *Remove* method—for example:

```
Controls.Remove (txtMiddleName);
```

To reparent a control to another collection:

- Change the control's *Parent* property.

- A control's position in the collection determines its z-order (front-to-back order), where position 0 is at the front. When you use *Bring To Front* and *Send To Back* in the Designer, you're actually changing the control's position in its parent's *Controls* collection. You can also achieve the same thing at runtime by calling the object's *BringToFront* and *SendToBack* methods, or by using the parent collection's *SetChildIndex* method.

Here are some other commonly used container-style controls that offer the same property:

**Continued**

- **Panel**  A simple container for other controls.

- **GroupBox**  A container with a border and caption text, used for visually grouping controls on a form. It's also often used to host *RadioButton* controls (only one radio button can be checked at a time inside each group box).

- **TabPage**  A *TabControl* contains a collection of *TabPage* controls—each of which acts as a container for child controls, with its own *Controls* property.

# Attaching an Event Handler at Runtime

Let's suppose we want to set up our newly created textbox so that when it's right-clicked, a message box appears. We need to add an event handler to the textbox at runtime, and there are two steps to this:

- Writing the event-handling method.

- Attaching the method to the control's event.

In our case, we'll need to attach to the textbox's *MouseDown* event (because there's no specific right-click event). First, we need to write the event-handling method, with parameters of the correct type for a *MouseDown* event. You can determine an event's signature in two ways:

- Look for the event in the Microsoft documentation, and then click on its delegate (in our case, *MouseEventHandler*).

- Using the Designer, add a dummy control of the type we're attaching to, create an appropriate event handler, and then delete the dummy control. The event-handling method will still be there—with the correct signature. All we need to do is rename it.

Here's how we do it:

1. Using either approach, add a method to our form, as follows:

```
void myTextBox_MouseDown (object sender, MouseEventArgs e)
{
    if (e.Buttons == MouseButtons.Right)
        // Show is a static method of System.Windows.Forms.MessageBox
        MessageBox.Show ("Right Click!");
}
```

2. Next, we attach this method to *myTextBox*'s *MouseDown* event. Return to the *button1_Click* method and add the following line of code:

```
myTextBox.MouseDown += new MouseEventHandler (myTextBox_MouseDown)
```

On the left-hand side, **myTextBox.MouseDown** is the event to which we're attaching, using the += operator. On the right-hand side, we're creating a new *MouseEventHandler* delegate instance: in other words, an object containing a pointer to a method (*myTextBox_MouseDown*) conforming to *MouseEventHandler*'s signature.

3. Test the application.

### Developing & Deploying...

## Why We Need Delegates

It's often asked, "why can't we simply assign a target method (for example, *myTextBox_MouseDown*) directly to an event?" C# doesn't allow this because the language is strongly typed, and the event needs to pass parameters to the target method. If we could assign a method directly to an event, there would be no place to formalize the number and types of these parameters (the method signature). We need a way of describing an agreed method signature, and for this we have delegates. The easiest way to think of a delegate is in two parts:

- **The delegate definition** This simply describes a method signature.
- **A delegate instance** This is an object containing a pointer to a method conforming to the signature.

Most of the delegate definitions you'll come across are part of the .NET Framework—although sometimes you define your own—usually when writing custom controls. Delegate instances, however, are created whenever you hook up to an event.

Here's an example of a complete delegate definition:

```
public delegate void EventHandler (object sender, EventArgs e)
```

As you can see, all this does is set out a signature: two parameters, one of type object, and the other of type *EventArgs*, and a *void* return type. *EventHandler* is the "plain vanilla" delegate used extensively in the

*Continued*

> .NET Framework. Events are declared of this type if they don't require any special information sent to the target.
>
> Here's an example of a delegate instance:
>
> ```
> EventHandler eh = new EventHandler (textBox1_Click);
> ```
>
> This simply contains a reference (pointer) to *textBox1_Click*. The compiler will check that the target method's signature agrees with the delegate definition (*EventHandler*). The following line of code attaches *eh* to *myTextBox*'s click event:
>
> ```
> myTextBox.Click += eh;
> ```
>
> Review Chapter 2 for more information on delegates and events.

# Writing a Simple Text Editor

This walkthrough will take you through developing a simple Notepad–style text editor, demonstrating the following:

- Adding a menu

- Creating and activating a new form

- Creating a Multiple Document Interface

- Creating a dialog form

- Using form inheritance

- Adding a tab control

- Anchoring controls

- Connecting the dialog form

The code for this walkthrough is on the accompanying CD-ROM, in folder the TextEditor directory.

## Starting the Project

First, we'll create a new project. We'll then rename the main form Visual Studio creates for us to something more meaningful:

1. Create a new Windows Forms Project, naming the project *TextEditor*.

2. From the Solution Explorer, rename Form1.cs to MainForm.cs (press **F2** or right-click and choose **Rename**). Also, from within the Properties

window, change the form's name to *MainForm* (this changes its class name), and change its *Text* property to *Simple Editor*.

3. In the Code Editor, check that the class's *Main* method references *MainForm* rather than *Form1*, changing it if necessary.

## Creating a Menu

Next, we'll create the main menu:

1. From the toolbox, drag a **MainMenu** component onto the form. The Designer provides a *WYSIWYG* interface for populating the menu. In other words, it's just a question of typing directly into the menu.

2. Type in menu items for **File**, **New**, and **Exit**, as in Figure 4.8.

**Figure 4.8** Creating a Main Menu

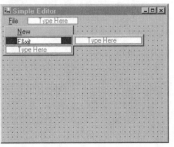

To enter the underlined accelerator keys, put an ampersand (&) before the desired character (the same principle works with label controls). To enter the separator between New and Exit, type a single hyphen (-).

3. Click on the **New** menu item, and from the Properties window, set its shortcut to **Ctrl+N**.

4. Right-click on one of the menu items, select **Edit Names**, and enter meaningful menu item names such as **miFile**, **miNew**, and **miExit**. This will help later on with coding and debugging. Right-click again and uncheck **Edit Names**.

5. Double-click on the **Exit** menu item. This will create and attach an event handler (to *Click*, the default event for the *MenuItem* class) and place you in the code window. Add the following line:

```
private void miExit_Click(object sender, System.EventArgs e)
{
```

```
        Close();
    }
```

Because we're in the application's startup form, closing the form is sufficient to close the application (and any other forms that are open). If we wanted to exit the application from another form, we could instead call *Application.Exit()*.

6. Run the application. There's our menu!

## Developing & Deploying...

### Working with Controls: Using Menus

Menus are not strictly controls—in fact, they're based on *Component*—because menus and menu items don't exhibit the normal behavior of a control. Each menu is encapsulated by a *MainMenu* component, comprised of a collection of *MenuItem* components. Although you can have any number of main menus on a single form, only one can be active at a time (this is determined by the form's *Menu* property). A context menu (right-click pop-up menu) is encapsulated by the *ContextMenu* component, and this also comprises a collection of *MenuItems*.

To add a menu item at runtime:

1. Define an appropriate event-handling method for the menu item's *Click* event, such as the following:

```
void miNew_Click (object sender, EventArgs e)
{
    MessageBox.Show ("New Item Clicked!");
}
```

2. Create and configure a *MenuItem* object, and then add it to the main menu's *MenuItem* collection. For example:

```
MenuItem mi = new MenuItem
    ("New", new EventHandler (miNew_Click));
mi.Shortcut = Shortcut.CtrlN;
mainMenu1.MenuItems.Add (mi);
```

**Continued**

> To add subitems at runtime:
>
> 1. Define an event-handling method, then create and configure a **MenuItem** object as in the previous bullet item.
> 2. Add the new object to the parent menu item's *MenuItem* collection, as follows:
>
> ```
> miFile.MenuItems.Add (mi);
> ```
>
> To enable and disable menu items, set the menu item's *Enabled* property to **True** or **False** (the parent menu item's *Popup* event is a convenient place in which to do this). To check and uncheck menu items, set the menu item's *Checked* property to **True** or **False**.

## Adding a New Form

Let's create a new form for editing text documents:

1. Go to **Project | Add Windows Form**, name the class **EditForm.cs**, and then change the form's *Text* property to **Untitled**.

2. Drag a **TextBox** control from the toolbox to the form, and from the Properties windows, change its name to **txtEdit**.

3. Clear the textbox's *Text* property and change its font's point size to **10**.

4. Set *AutoSize* to **False** and *MultiLine* to **True**. This allows us to vertically enlarge the textbox.

5. Change the *Dock* property to **Fill** (from the drop-down, click the box in the center). This expands the textbox so that it fills the entire client area (inside area) of the form. If you subsequently resize the form, the textbox will still fill the entire area.

6. Set *AcceptsReturn* and *AcceptsTab* to **True**.

7. Drag a **MainMenu** control onto the form, and create a **View | Options** menu structure, as in Figure 4.9.
   Let's now hook this up to our main form.

8. Return to the main form, and double-click on the menu item for **New**. Add the following code to its event handler:

```
private void miNew_Click(object sender, System.EventArgs e)
{
    EditForm ef = new EditForm();  // Create new instance of form
```

```
    ef.Show();                                // Display form modelessly
}
```

**Figure 4.9** *EditForm* Menu structure

Now run the application, and click **New** a few times to open up several text editor windows. Notice how each of the forms is *modeless* (you can click randomly on any form) and *top-level* (each window floats independently on the desktop). If we moved the **File** menu to the child form itself, and did away with the main form entirely, we'd have a *Single Document Interface* (SDI) application. Internet Explorer is an example of an SDI (see Figure 4.10).

**Figure 4.10** Single Document Interface

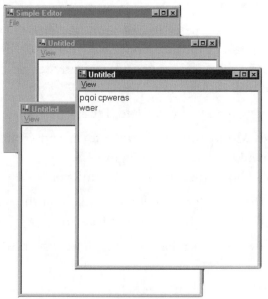

# Creating a Multiple Document Interface

In the example in the preceding section, we would prefer the editor forms to be physically constrained to the main parent window, and to have only one menu, with the View menu items merged into the main menu. This describes a *Multiple Document Interface* (MDI) style. Let's turn our interface into an MDI:

1. Enlarge the main form, and change its *IsMdiContainer* property to **True**.

2. Click on our main menu component and add a new menu item for a **Window** menu. Set its *MdiList* property to **True** (this instructs Windows to add items for child forms automatically) and set its *MergeOrder* to a large value such as 20 (so that the Window menu item appears at the right-hand side, when merged with child menus).

3. Press **F7** to return to the Code Editor, and enhance the event handler for *miNew* as follows:

```
private void miNew_Click(object sender, System.EventArgs e)
{
    EditForm ef = new EditForm();
    ef.MdiParent = this;                    // this makes ef an MDI
                                            // child form
    ef.Show();
}
```

4. Run the application. We now have an MDI (see Figure 4.11).

**Figure 4.11** Multiple Document Interface

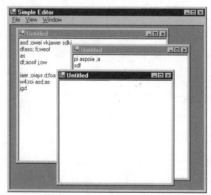

Let's now enhance this by adding "Tile" and "Cascade" menu items:

1. Add menu items to the Window menu, titled **Tile Vertical**, **Tile Horizontal**, and **Cascade**.

2. Double-click each of the menu items to create event handlers. In each method, call the form's *LayoutMdi* method with an appropriate member of the *MdiLayout* enumeration, such as in the example below:

```
private void miTileVertical_Click(object sender,
    System.EventArgs e)
{
    LayoutMdi (MdiLayout.TileVertical);
}
```

# Creating a Dialog Form

A form with OK and Cancel buttons is usually described as a dialog. In most cases, dialog forms are *modal* rather than *modeless*, meaning the user must accept or cancel before clicking on another form. Making and displaying a dialog form involves three parts:

- Creating a form that has the "look and feel" of a dialog
- Displaying the form modally—using *ShowDialog()* instead of *Show()*
- Disposing of the form when we're finished

Let's first create a basic dialog form. Later we'll use this as a base for creating an Options Form within our text editor:

1. Add a new form to the project called **DialogForm**.

2. Put two buttons onto the form. Name one **btnOK** and the other **btnCancel**. Change their *Text* properties to **OK** and **Cancel**.

3. Set the *DialogResult* property of the OK button to **OK** and the Cancel button to **Cancel**. This instructs the form to automatically close when the button is pressed (and to return an appropriate *DialogResult* to the calling program).

4. Click directly on the form, and change its *FormBorderStyle* property to **FixedDialog**. This will prevent the user from resizing the form. Of course, you can still resize it from within the Designer.

5. Set *MaximizeBox* and *MinimizeBox* properties to **False** and the *StartPosition* to **CenterScreen**.

6. Set the *AcceptButton* property to **btnOK** and the *CancelButton* property to **btnCancel**. This will hook up the Enter and Escape keys to the OK and Cancel buttons (see Figure 4.12).

**Figure 4.12** Basic Dialog Form

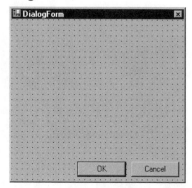

7. Finally, we need to remove the form's icon and associated menu. This is not possible with the Designer, however, it can be done programmatically. In the form's constructor, after the call to *InitializeComponent*, add the following:

```
this.Icon = null;
```

8. Next, we need to activate and test the dialog. We'll do this from the Options menu item in *EditForm*. Return to *EditForm* and double-click on the **Options** menu item. Add the following code:

```
private void miOptions_Click(object sender, System.EventArgs e)
{
    DialogForm df = new DialogForm();
    if (df.ShowDialog() == DialogResult.OK)
        MessageBox.Show ("OK Pressed!");

    df.Dispose();       // modal forms don't dispose automatically!
}
```

The *ShowDialog* method returns a *DialogResult* enumeration, and this tells us how the form was closed. You can also query the form's *DialogResult* property to the same effect. The call to *Dispose* is required because a form activated with *ShowDialog* does automatically clean up when it's closed. This is a useful feature because it allows us to query the state of its controls after the form's been closed. But once we're done, we must remember to call *Dispose*—otherwise the form will continue to consume operating system resources—even after the garbage collector has released its memory. This completes the skeleton dialog form. You can run the application as it is, to ensure that the form works as expected.

## Debugging...

### Remembering to Call Dispose

As a rule, if a .NET object has a *Dispose* or *Close* method, it must be called once the object is no longer required. But in practice, we rarely dispose Windows Forms components explicitly because most components are parented to a container collection that handles disposal automatically. For instance, a control object is normally parented to a form's *Controls* collection (or some other *Controls* collection), and this is programmed to dispose all child controls automatically with the parent.

In a couple of situations, however, you do need to explicitly dispose—when you've programmatically instantiated an object having a *Dispose* method that's *not* managed through a component collection (such as a *Bitmap*), and when you've instantiated a form modally (by calling *ShowDialog*).

Disposing is about releasing resources—such as Windows handles and file handles. It's not about releasing memory: The CLR's garbage collector does this automatically (some time) after an object is no longer referenced. Calling *Dispose* does not influence garbage collection, and conversely, the garbage collector knows nothing about *Dispose*.

It's sometimes asked, "why doesn't the class's destructor handle disposal?" The answer is that inherent limitations are associated with destructors activated via automatic garbage collection, and disposal is considered too important to be subject to these limitations.

## Using Form Inheritance

The dialog form we've just designed is an example of a template that could be utilized in many places within an application. We could keep this form as it is (our "skeleton" dialog), and then whenever we need a real dialog, we could create a copy to which we add controls.

But this approach is inflexible in that if we later enhance the base dialog form, we'd have to manually update each of the forms we've already created. By using inheritance, we get around this problem: Forms that have been *subclassed* from the base dialog form will automatically assume its functionality—even if the base class is later modified.

Let's turn our *DialogForm* into a reusable base class. We need to make only one small change. Select the OK button and change its *Modifiers* property to **Protected** (sometimes called Family), and likewise with the Cancel button.

This allows subclasses to access the buttons—and change their properties. Subclassed dialogs will need to modify the buttons' *Location* properties, otherwise they'll be stuck in one position on the form.

---

### WARNING

Once you've created a reusable form, such as a dialog, it's quite tempting to subclass it again to create another reusable form—such as a tabbed dialog, which in turn is subclassed into a sizable tabbed dialog, then a dialog with an Apply button, and so on. This leads to a messy and inflexible hierarchy, causing many more problems than the designer set out to solve. It's usually best to keep (implementation) inheritance as simple as possible—the best object-oriented designs often employ *component reuse* and *interface inheritance* as alternatives to keep complexity and coupling to a minimum. It's worth reading a book or two on object-oriented design before diving into a big project—if these concepts are unfamiliar.

---

Now we can subclass and create the options form. First, rebuild the project (**Shift+Ctrl+B**). Then select **Project | Add Inherited Form**, name the class **OptionsForm**, and select **DialogForm** from the Inheritance Picker (see Figure 4.13).

To test this, modify the **miOptions_Click** method in **EditForm** so that it instantiates **OptionsForm** instead of **DialogForm** and run the application.

**Figure 4.13** Inheritance Picker

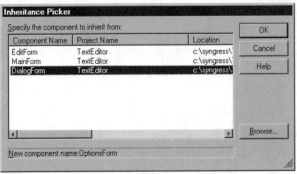

# Adding a *TabControl*

When designing a form, it's a good idea to start with a *TabControl* if you plan to have a lot of controls—or if you anticipate a lot of controls in the future. It discourages future developers from cluttering the form, as well as giving dialog forms a tidy presentation.

Let's add a tab control to *OptionsForm*:

1. Drag a **TabControl** onto the options form, and align it with the OK and Cancel buttons, as shown in Figure 4.14. (The easiest way to align the Cancel button is to select it together with the tab control by using the **Ctrl** key, and then choosing **Align Rights** from the Layout toolbar or Format menu.)

**Figure 4.14** Options Form with *TabControl*

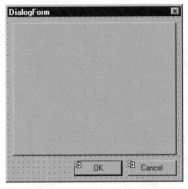

2. Select the tab control and then click **Add Tab** at the bottom of the Properties window.

3. Click inside the dashed rectangle on the tab control to select a *TabPage,* and then set its *Text* property to **Editor**.

Note that you can also add and configure tab pages by clicking the ellipses on the tab control's *TabPages* property. Now we'll add controls to the tab page.

4. Put a couple of checkboxes, a *NumericUpDown* control, and a label onto the tab page, as in Figure 4.15. Name the controls **chkWordWrap**, **chkApplyAll**, and **nudFontSize**.

**Figure 4.15** Adding Controls to the *TabPage*

5. Choose **View | Tab Order** and click each control in sequence, from top to bottom. This sets the order of focus when the **Tab** and **Shift+Tab** keys are used.

## Developing & Deploying…

### Working with Controls: Using TabControls

A *TabControl* consists of a collection of *TabPages*, each of which hosts a collection of controls.

To determine the active tab page:

1. Use the *SelectedTab* property to get a *TabPage* object.

2. Use the *SelectedIndex* property to get its position.

To add a page at runtime:

**Continued**

1. Create a new *TabPage* control:

```
TabPage tp = new TabPage ("Advanced Properties");
```

2. Add the new *TabPage* control to the tab control's *TabPages* collection:

```
tabControl1.TabPages.Add (tp);
```

To programmatically add controls to a tab page:

1. Declare, create, and configure the control as if it were to go directly on the form.
2. Add the control to the tab page's *Controls* collection instead of the form's *Controls* collection:

```
tabPage4.Controls.Add (myTextBox);
/*or*/ tabControl1.TabPages[3].Controls.Add (myTextBox);
```

# Anchoring Controls

Next, we'll make the form sizable. This is a useful feature in forms that have controls with a lot of information to display—such as the TabPage Collection Editor in Visual Studio. Of course in our case, we have only two checkboxes and an up-down control, but we'll gloss over that for now:

1. Change the tab control's *Anchor* property to **all four sides** (from the drop-down, click on the bottom and right rectangles so that all four rectangles are selected). Selecting two opposite sides instructs a control to expand or shrink in that direction. Our tab control will expand or shrink both vertically and horizontally.

2. Change the OK and Cancel button's *Anchor* properties to **Bottom** and **Right** (from the drop-down, uncheck the rectangles at the top and left, and check those at the bottom and right). This instructs the buttons to maintain their alignment to the bottom and right of their parent container (in this case the form).

3. Change the Form's *FormBorderStyle* to **Sizable**.

Now try resizing the form. You can test this better by adding a dummy list box to the tab page (placing it the area at the right), and anchoring it to all four sides. Anchoring works in the same way at runtime.

Developing & Deploying…

## Navigating in the Designer and Code Editor

- To select the parent of the control you're on, press **Escape**. For example, if you have a *TabPage* selected, pressing **Escape** will select its *TabControl*, and pressing **Escape** again will select the form.

- In the Code Editor, press **Ctrl+spacebar** to redisplay an object's list of members. Press **Shift+Ctrl+spacebar** to redisplay its parameters.

- Use the **F12** shortcut to jump to a class or member's definition.

- Enable *Auto Hide* on the Output and Task List windows to see more form and code.

## Changing the Startup Form

Once you have several forms in your application, you might want to change the form used for startup. This is simply a matter of moving the *Main* method:

1. Cut and paste the *Main* method from the old startup form to the new startup form.

2. Update this method so that it instantiates the new form class instead.

As long as you have only one *Main* method in your project, the compiler will find it, and make that class the startup object. If you have more than one method in your project with this name, you need to specify which should be the startup object in the **Project | Properties** dialog.

## Connecting the Dialog

Let's now write the code to make the Options form function. We'll need to pass data to and from the dialog form—in our case, the editing form's textbox. To do this, the first thing we'll need is a field in the Options form to hold a reference to textbox it's controlling:

1. Add the following declaration to the *OptionsForm* class:

```
public class OptionsForm : TextEditor.DialogForm
{
    private TextBox hostControl;
```

   Next, we'll need some way to get the textbox in, so we can save it to the class field. The easiest way is through its constructor. Once we have the textbox, we can also set the initial values for the word wrap and font size controls.

2. Modify the form's constructor, as follows:

```
public OptionsForm (TextBox hostControl)
{
    InitializeComponent();


    // Save hostControl parameter to class field
    this.hostControl = hostControl;
    chkWordWrap.Checked = hostControl.WordWrap;
    nudFontSize.Value = (decimal) hostControl.Font.Size;
}
```

   When the user clicks OK, we need to update the textbox's word wrap and font properties.

3. Double-click on the **OK** button to attach a *Click* event handler, and enter the following:

```
private void btnOK_Click(object sender, System.EventArgs e)
{
    hostControl.WordWrap = chkWordWrap.Checked ;
    hostControl.Font = new Font
      (hostControl.Font.Name, (float) nudFontSize.Value);
}
```

   The method that displays this form is going to be responsible for propagating the settings to all other open windows, if the Apply All checkbox is checked. This means we need to provide a way in which this checkbox can be queried from outside the class.

4. Add a property definition inside the *OptionsForm* class as follows:

```
public bool ShouldApplyAll
{
    get {return chkApplyAll.Checked;}
}
```

Finally, we need to make a couple of modifications to *EditForm*. We require a property to expose the textbox, and *miOptions_Click* needs to be updated so that it passes in the form's textbox to *OptionsForm*, and then checks and handles the "Apply All" scenario. The following below illustrates how to iterate through MDI child forms. Note that because the *MdiChildren* collection consists of plain Form objects, we need to cast each child into the expected class, so we access its specific properties (in this case, *EditControl*).

5. Make the following changes to EditForm.cs:

```
public TextBox EditControl
{
    get {return txtEdit;}
}
private void miOptions_Click(object sender, System.EventArgs e)
{
    OptionsForm of = new OptionsForm (txtEdit);
    if (of.ShowDialog() == DialogResult.OK && of.ShouldApplyAll)
        foreach (Form child in MdiParent.MdiChildren)
        {
            TextBox childEdit = ((EditForm) child).EditControl;
            childEdit.WordWrap = txtEdit.WordWrap;
            childEdit.Font = txtEdit.Font;
        }
    of.Dispose();
}
```

This completes the simple text editor.

Debugging...

### Using the Console Class

You'll remember from the second chapter that the *Console* class provides **Write** and **WriteLine** methods that send output to the screen in command-line applications. You can call the same methods from a Windows Forms application, and the text will be diverted to Visual Studio's Output window—providing a quick and easy mechanism for generating debugging output.

# Using the ListView and TreeView Controls

Most people are very familiar with Windows Explorer: On the left is a tree view displaying folders hierarchically; on the right is a list view offering four modes of display (Large Icons, Small Icons, List, and Detail). In this walkthrough, we'll create a *ListView* and *TreeView* control, add images and items, and then attach a context menu to allow the user to switch between each of the four views. Then we'll insert an Explorer-style splitter and enable a simple drag–and–drop facility between the controls. The code for this walkthrough is on the accompanying CD-ROM, in the WeatherView folder.

## Building an *ImageList*

Before we can set up a list or tree view capable of displaying icons, we need to create an *ImageList* component. An image list is just a convenient repository, into which we can load a collection of same-sized images, and then use in any number of controls on the form.

In this example, we'll create two image lists: one suitable for a *TreeView* and a *ListView*'s Small Icons view and another suitable for a *ListView*'s Large Icons view:

1. Create a new Windows Forms project called **WeatherView**, and drag an **ImageList** from the toolbox to the form. Because it's a component rather than a control, its icon appears in the bottom section of the Designer.

2. Change its *Name* property to **ilSmall**, and its *ImageSize* to 16x16 pixels—this is the size of the small icons we'll be loading.

3. Next we need to find some images to load in. Search your hard drive for the Elements folder (this is usually in Program Files\Microsoft Visual Studio.NET\Common7\Graphics\Icons).

4. Expand the component's *Images* collection property, and add four icons appropriate for **Sun**, **Snow**, **Clouds**, and **Rain** (see Figure 4.16).

**Figure 4.16** Populating an *ImageList*

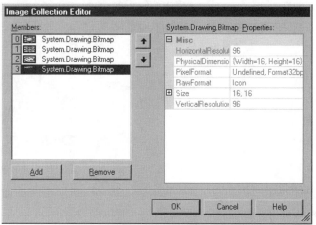

Note that while we've loaded images from ICO files, the image list control stores the data in ordinary bitmap format.

5. Add a new **ImageList** called **ilLarge**, change its *ImageSize* to 32x32 pixels, and repeat the previous steps (using the same icons).

6. Check that the images in the two lists appear in the same order. If not, use the up and down arrow buttons in the Collection Editor to rearrange the images.

**NOTE**

When designing custom graphics for use in an *ImageList* control, saving into the GIF format is a good idea, because it provides transparency in an easy and reliable manner. If you're using Microsoft Paint in Windows 2000, you can select the transparency color from **Image | Attributes** (this option is only enabled once the file's been saved as a GIF).

## Adding a *ListView*

Now that we have the image lists set up, creating a list view is easy:

1. Add a **ListView** control to the form, setting its *LargeImageList* property to **ilLarge** and its *SmallImageList* property to **ilSmall**.

2. Expand its **Items** property and add four items with text properties: **Sun**, **Snow**, **Clouds**, and **Rain**. Set the *ImageIndex* on each to the corresponding icon (see Figure 4.17).

**Figure 4.17** *ListViewItem* Collection Editor

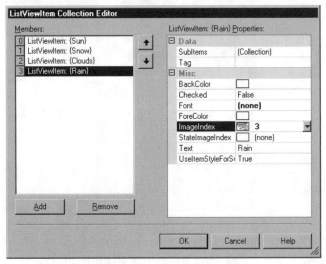

The control defaults to the Large Icons view. You can see the Small Icons view by changing the control's *View* property in the Designer.

3. Attach a handler to the control's *ItemActivate* event, and add the following code:

```
MessageBox.Show (listView1.SelectedItems[0].Text);
```

Because list views allow multiple items to be selected, the control has a collection property for this purpose. In this case, we're interested only in the first selected item.

4. Run the application and double-click on a list item to test the event handler.

# Using the Details View

The Details view allows us to add columns. This is often used in Windows Forms to provide simple grid control, without with the need for a dataset. In this example, we're going to enhance our list view by defining two columns:

1. Change the list view's *View* property to **Details**, and then expand its *Columns* collection property. Add two columns, and set their *Text* properties to **Outlook** and **Probability**.

   Once you close the dialog, you can visually resize the columns by dragging their headers in the Designer.

2. Return to the *Items* Collection Editor, and for each member, open its *SubItems* collection. Add a subitem, and set its *Text* property to some random value, such as in Figure 4.18.

**Figure 4.18** Adding SubItems to a *ListViewItem*

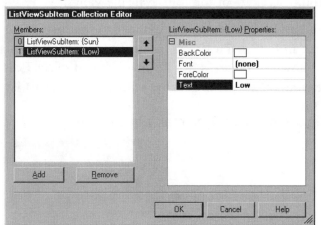

We'll also add an item programmatically.

3. In the form's constructor, after the call to *InitializeComponent*, add the following:

```
ListViewItem lvi = new ListViewItem
    (new string[] { "Hail", "Possible" } );


listView1.Items.Add (lvi);
```

4. Run the form (see Figure 4.19).

**Figure 4.19** Details View at Runtime

# Attaching a Context Menu

It would be nice if the user could right-click on the list view control, and then from a menu, select one of the four available views:

1.  Add a **ContextMenu** component to the form, naming it **cmView**, and type in four menu items: **Large Icons**, **Small Icons**, **List**, and **Details**, as shown in Figure 4.20. Right-click and select **Edit Names**, and rename them **miLargeIcon**, **miSmallIcon**, **miList**, and **miDetails**.

**Figure 4.20** Designing a Context Menu

2.  Double-click each of the menu items, to create handlers for their *Click* events. Code each method as follows (where *XXXX* is **LargeIcon**, **SmallIcon**, **List**, or **Details**):

```
private void miXXXX_Click(object sender, System.EventArgs e)
{
```

```
listView1.View = View.XXXX;
}
```

3. Select the **cmView** component, and in the Properties window, switch to the Events view and then double-click its *Popup* event. Here's where we'll tick the selected view:

```
private void contextMenu1_Popup(object sender,
    System.EventArgs e)
{
    miLargeIcon.Checked = (listView1.View == View.LargeIcon);
    miSmallIcon.Checked = (listView1.View == View.SmallIcon);
    miList.Checked = (listView1.View == View.List);
    miDetails.Checked = (listView1.View == View.Details);
}
```

4. Finally, select the list view control, set its *ContextMenu* property to **cmView**, and then test the form.

## Adding a *TreeView*

Setting up a tree view control is rather similar to setting up a list view. First you create and attach an image list (if icons are required), and then add items to the tree—either visually or programmatically. In this example, we'll use one of the image lists we created earlier:

1. Put a **TreeView** control on the form, set its *ImageList* property to **ilSmall**. With this control, there's only one image list, equivalent to the list view's Small Icons view.

2. Expand the tree view's *Nodes* collection, and add three root nodes for **Sun**, **Snow**, and **Clouds**. Then add a child node for **Rain**, below Clouds. Set their *Label*, *Image*, and *Selected Image* properties as in Figure 4.21.
   Now we'll add an item programmatically. The tree view's items are managed through *Nodes*—a property returning a collection—rather like with the list view control's *Items* property, except that in this case it's hierarchical. *Nodes* itself has itself a *Nodes* property, returning another tree node collection. Adding nodes is largely just a question of finding the right place in the containership tree.

**Figure 4.21** *TreeNode* Editor

Let's insert a node as a child to **Snow**. First, we need to know its numeric position. Because it's second in the list, and the list is zero-indexed, its position is 1. We'll also give the new node an *ImageIndex*—in this case, we'll use Snow's image (also position 1).

3. Add the following to the form's constructor:

```
// Use snow's ImageIndex (1) for image & selected image
TreeNode tn = new TreeNode ("Sleet", 1, 1);


// treeView1.Nodes[1] is the Snow Node.
// We want to add to *its* node collection.
treeView1.Nodes[1].Nodes.Add (tn);
```

4. Test the form.

**NOTE**

Sometimes you need to add custom information to list view items or tree nodes. The easiest solution is to use the *Tag* property. This property is of type *Object* (allowing data of any class to be stored)—and this works in the same way as the *Tag* property in the *Control* class. As an alternative you can subclass *ListViewItem* or *TreeNode*, adding your own fields and methods, and then instantiating the subclassed versions instead to create items or nodes. Note that with the latter approach, you cannot then add your subclassed items or nodes through the Designer.

# Adding a Splitter

Let's now add an Explorer-style splitter bar between the tree view and list view controls. Getting a splitter to work is largely about getting all the controls in the correct front-to-back order (z-order). In a nutshell, we need the following:

- A side-docked control, at the *back* of the z-order
- A splitter control, docked to the same side, in the *middle* of the z-order
- A fill-docked control, at the *front* of the z-order

We already have the two controls we want to split—all that's required is the splitter control, and of course, everything in the right z-order.

1. Set the tree view's *Dock* property to **Left** (click the leftmost rectangle in the drop-down). This pushes it up hard against the left-hand side of the form.

2. Add a **Splitter** control from the toolbox, and change its *Dock* property to **Left** (if not already docked left). Because we've just put it on the form, it'll be in front of the tree view, and will appear to its right.

3. Set the list view's *Dock* property to **Fill** (click the center rectangle in the drop-down) and then right-click the control and select **Bring to Front**. Now it'll be at the front, with the splitter in the middle, and the side-docked tree view at the back.

4. Test the application. The controls will automatically resize as you drag the splitter (and also when you resize the form), as shown in Figure 4.22.

**Figure 4.22** Splitter Control at Runtime

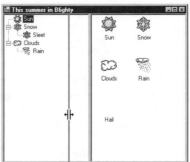

# Implementing Drag and Drop

When demonstrating the list view and tree view controls, it's hard to put them side-by-side without someone asking about drag and drop. The good news is that dragging between these controls is reasonably easy to implement in Windows Forms.

---

**W**ARNING
_____

When you create a Windows Forms project, Visual Studio adds the *[STAThread]* attribute to the startup form's *Main* method. This tells the compiler to apply the Single Threaded Apartment threading model, allowing your application to interoperate with other Windows and COM services. If you remove this attribute, features such as drag and drop will not work—even between controls within your own application.

---

Let's take a look at drag and drop in general. As you might guess, it consists of two parts. In the first part, you need to identify when the user starts dragging the mouse, and then ask Windows to start the operation, supplying data necessary for the recipient when processing the drop. In Windows Forms, this is done as follows:

1. Decide from which event to start the operation. If you're dragging from a list view or tree view control, it'll be the special event called *ItemDrag*. With other controls, it will usually be the *MouseDown* or *MouseMove* event.

2. Package information to be sent to the target in a *DataObject*. If you want to interoperate with another Windows application, you must use one or more of the standardized formats listed in the *DataFormats* class, such as *Text* or *HTML*.

3. Decide on what actions (such as Move or Copy) are permitted. You can't always be sure at this point on what will end up happening, because it could depend on where the item is dropped.

4. Call *DoDragDrop* to start the operation.

The second part is about enabling a target control to accept a drop. In Windows Forms, this is done as follows:

1. Set the target's *AllowDrop* property to **True**.

2. Handle the *DragEnter* or *DragMove* event. *DragEnter* fires just once when the cursor enters the control; *DragMove* fires continually as the cursor moves through the control. In the event handler, you need to decide if the drop is allowable—and this is done by checking that the packaged data is of an expected type. If so, you set the *DragEventArg* parameter's *Effect* property to one of the permitted actions, and this enables the drop (changing the cursor accordingly).

3. Handle the *DragDrop* event. To get at the packaged data, you first need to extract it and cast it back into its original type.

## NOTE

The advantage of passing a *DataObject* to *DoDragDrop* is that you can include data in multiple formats, allowing external applications, such as Microsoft Word, to function as drop targets. Standard formats are defined (as *static public* field) in the *DataFormats* class.

In our example, we're going to allow dragging from the tree view to the list view:

1. Double-click the tree view's *ItemDrag* event, and type the following:

```
treeView1.DoDragDrop (e.Item, DragDropEffects.Move);
```

The first parameter is our package of information. Because we've not wrapped it in a *DataObject*, Windows Forms does this for us automatically, as if we did the following:

```
treeView1.DoDragDrop (new DataObject (e.Item),
    DragDropEffects.Move);
```

*e.Item* is the actual data we want to send to the target: in this case the *TreeNode* we're dragging. The second parameter describes the allowed actions: In this example, we're going to allow only moving.

2. Set the list view's *AllowDrop* property to **True**.

3. Double-click the list view's *DragEnter* method, and type the following:

```
private void listView1_DragEnter(object sender,
    System.Windows.Forms.DragEventArgs e)
{
```

```
if (e.Data.GetDataPresent (typeof (TreeNode)))

    e.Effect = DragDropEffects.Move;

}
```

*e.Data* returns the packaged information, as a *DataObject*. Regardless of how the data went in when we called *DoDragDrop*, we always get back a *DataObject*. This class is designed to hold information in multiple formats, and we call its *GetDataPresent* method to find out if a particular type of data is supported.

4. Double-click the list view's *DragDrop* event, and type the following:

```
private void listView1_DragDrop(object sender, DragEventArgs e)

{

    if (e.Data.GetDataPresent (typeof (TreeNode)))

    {

        TreeNode tn = (TreeNode) e.Data.GetData
            (typeof (TreeNode));
        listView1.Items.Add (tn.Text, tn.ImageIndex);
        treeView1.Nodes.Remove (tn);

    }

}
```

We use the data object's *GetData* method to retrieve our original data, and then cast it back to the original type. Once this is done, we can treat it again as a normal *TreeNode*.

5. Test the application. You'll now be able to drag items from the tree view to the list view.

**Developing & Deploying…**

**Dragging Into a Tree View**

If setting up to drag *into* a tree view, you might want the dropped item to be inserted into the tree at the position under the mouse pointer. For this, you first need to determine which tree node is positioned under the mouse, as follows:

Continued

```
void treeView1_DragDrop(object sender, DragEventArgs e)
{
    Point pos = treeView1.PointToClient (new Point (e.X, e.Y));
    TreeNode tn = treeView1.GetNodeAt (pos);
    ...
```

# Creating Controls

Sometimes your requirements demand extending or replacing standard Windows Forms controls. It could be that your requirements are specific to a particular application—or they could warrant developing a general-purpose component for use in thousands of applications. Writing and deploying custom components is easy, because .NET components are self-describing, they don't require registration, and are not accidentally overwritten by subsequent software installations. Let's look at the three most common scenarios:

- You have a recurring group of controls that you would like to make into a reusable component (a *UserControl*).

- You need a control that cannot be assembled or adapted from existing components (a custom control).

- You want to extend a standard control—in order to modify or enhance its appearance or behavior (an inherited control).

In the following sections, we'll walk through solutions to each of the scenarios.

## Creating a User Control

Suppose your application contains several forms with a group of controls for entering an address. Assembling these controls into a reusable class would be nice—both for visual consistency, and so that common functionality can be added, such as postcode lookup. In this walkthrough, we'll create a user control to show how to do this:

1. Create a new Windows Forms project, and then choose **Project | Add User Control**, naming the file **Address.cs**.

2. Add a group of controls suitable for entering an address, such as in the example in Figure 4.23.

**Figure 4.23** *UserControl* in Designer

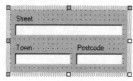

3.  Build the project (**Shift+Ctrl+B**) and return to *Form1*. At the bottom of the toolbox, in the Windows Forms tab, will be a new control called *Address*. Add this to *Form1* and then run the application.

# Adding a Property

Our address control is not much use because there's no way for the form to determine what the user typed in. For this, we need to add properties to our control. Here's how we add a property to allow access the contents of the Street textbox:

1.  Add the following declaration to the *Address* class:

```
[Category ("Data"), Description ("Contents of Street Control")]
public string Street
{
    get {return txtStreet.Text;}
    set {txtStreet.Text = value;}
}
```

The first line is optional—it specifies *Category* and *Description* attributes, to enhance the control's presentation in the Designer. Without the *Category* attribute, the property would appear in the "Misc" section in the Properties window.

2.  Rebuild the project, and return to *Form1*. The address control now has a *Street* property into which you can type. Of course, it can also be accessed programmatically as with any other control property.

# Adding Functionality

Once the control has been set up, it's fairly easy to modify its class so as to add reusable functionality, such as postcode lookup. It's just a matter of capturing events such as *TextChanged* or *Validating* and then updating the properties of other controls accordingly. We don't provide an example, because it doesn't introduce aspects of Windows Forms we haven't already covered. However, it's worth mentioning that in a real situation you would consider good object-oriented design, and abstract the postcode-lookup functionality into a class separate from the user interface. You could also consider basing this class on a (C#) interface—to which the user control would be programmed. This would allow the control to plug in to different implementations (to facilitate internationalization, for instance).

# Writing a Custom Control

If your needs are more specialized, you can paint a control from scratch with GDI+. In principle, this is fairly simple: You subclass *Control*, and then override its *OnPaint* method, where you render the graphics. You can also capture mouse and keyboard events by overriding methods such as *OnMouseDown* and *OnKeyPress*.

---

**N**OTE

Every event had a corresponding protected method, prefixed with the word *On*. Some people have asked about the difference between handling the event (such as Paint) and overriding the protected *OnXXXX* method (such as *OnPaint*). There are a number of differences:

- Overriding the protected method is faster because the CLR doesn't have to traverse an event chain.
- Because the protected method *fires* the event, you can effectively snuff the event simply by failing to call *base.OnXXXX*.
- Events can be attached and detached at runtime; code in overridden *OnXXXX* methods always runs.
- When subclassing a control, you generally override protected methods rather than handling events.

---

GDI+ is accessed through a *Graphics* object—a representation of a drawing surface, with methods to draw lines, shapes, and text. GDI+ is stateless, meaning that a graphics object doesn't hold properties to determine how the next object will be drawn (the "current" color, pen, or brush)—these details are supplied with each call to a GDI+ drawing method. Tables 4.3 and 4.4 summarize the most common GDI+ helper types.

**Table 4.3** Commonly Used GDI+ Helper Types

| Type | Description |
|---|---|
| *Color* struct | Represents an RGB or ARGB color (where *A* represents alpha, or transparency). Also used in Windows Forms. |
| *Font* class | Represents a font consisting of a name (referred to as the font "family"), a size, and a combination of styles (such as bold or italic). Also used in Windows Forms. |
| *Brush* class | Describes a fill color and style for areas and shapes. A brush can consist of solid color, graded color, a bitmap, or hatching. |
| *Pen* class | Describes a line color and style. A pen has a color, thickness, dash-style, and can itself contain a brush describing how the line should be rendered. |

**Table 4.4** Instantiating GDI+ Helper Types

| Type | Example | Notes |
|---|---|---|
| *Color* | `Color gray = Color.FromArgb (192, 192, 192);` | Creates a color from its red, blue, and green intensities (0 to 255). |
| | `Color blueWash = Color.FromArgb (80, 0, 0, 128);` <br> `Color grayWash = Color.FromArgb (80, gray);` | The *alpha* component is optional and specifies opacity: 0 is totally transparent; 255 is totally opaque. *gray* is defined above. |
| | `Color green = Color.Green;` | *Green* is a static property of the *Color* struct. |
| | `Color background = SystemColors.Control;` <br> `Color foreground = SystemColors.ControlText;` | Use this class if the color you need is part of the Windows color scheme. |
| *Font* | `Font f1 = new Font ("Verdana", 10);` <br> `Font f2 = new Font ("Arial", 12, FontStyle.Bold | FontStyle.Italic);` <br> `Font f3 = new Font (f2, FontStyle.Regular);` | When specifying font styles, use the bitwise *OR* operator (|) to combine members of the enumeration. There are 13 ways to call *Font*'s constructor. |

*Continued*

**Table 4.4** Continued

| Type | Example | Notes |
|------|---------|-------|
| *Brush* | `Brush blueBrush = Brushes.Blue;` | Returns a solid blue brush. |
| | `Brush border =`<br>`SystemBrushes.ActiveBorder;` | The preferred way to obtain brushes consistent with the Windows color scheme. |
| | `Brush grayBrush = new SolidBrush`<br>`(this.BackColor);`<br>`Brush crisscross = new HatchBrush`<br>`(HatchStyle.Cross, Color.Red);` | The *Brush* class itself is abstract; however, you can instantiate its subclasses such as *SolidBrush* or *HatchBrush*. |
| *Pen* | `Pen p = Pens.Violet;` | Creates a violet pen with thickness of one pixel. |
| | `Pen ht = SystemPens.HighlightText;` | The preferred way to obtain pens consistent with the Windows color scheme. |
| | `Pen thick = new Pen (Color.Beige, 30);` | A beige pen 30 pixels wide. |
| | `Pen ccPen = new Pen (crisscross, 20);` | A pen 20 pixels wide drawn with the *crisscross* brush (defined earlier in this table). |

In this walkthrough, rather than defining our control as part of a Windows Forms project, we'll make a class library—so our control can be used in a number of different applications:

1. From **File | New Project**, choose the **Windows Control Library** template, calling the library **FunStuff**. Visual Studio assumes we'll start with a user control. However in this case we want a custom control.

2. From the Solution Explorer, delete *UserControl1*. The project should now be empty.

3. From **Project | Add New Item**, select **Custom Control**. Name the file **ScrollingText.cs**.

4. Switch to the Code View. Notice that Visual Studio has based our class on *Control*, and that it has added code to overwrite the *OnPaint* method. This is where we use GDI+ to draw the control—for now, we'll just fill the control's area with red, and then draw a green ellipse in the middle.

5. Enter the following code into the overridden *OnPaint* method:

```
protected override void OnPaint(PaintEventArgs pe)
{
    pe.Graphics.Clear (Color.Red);
    Brush b = Brushes.Green;
    pe.Graphics.FillEllipse (b, ClientRectangle);
    b.Dispose();
    base.OnPaint (pe);
}
```

The *PaintEventArgs* parameter contains a *Graphics* object used to access GDI+ methods—such as *Clear* and *FillEllipse*. We use static properties of the *Color* and *Brushes* types as shortcuts to creating *Color* and *SolidBrush* objects. *ClientRectangle* describes the inside bounds of the control based on a (0, 0) origin. (In this case, the inside and outside areas are equivalent because there are no Windows-imposed borders or scroll-bars). We call *base.OnPaint* so that the *Paint* event still fires—in case the end user of our control wants to attach to this event for any reason.

6. Build the project. We now have a custom control (*ScrollingText*) as part of a reusable library (*FunStuff*).

---

Developing & Deploying…

## Using GDI+ to Draw Custom Controls

To obtain a *Graphics* object:

■ From within a subclassed *OnPaint* method, use *PaintEventArgs* parameter's *Graphics* property.

**Continued**

■ From outside an *OnPaint* method, use *Control.CreateGraphics* or *Graphics.FromImage*. It's not often that you should need to access GDI from outside *OnPaint*—an example is the use of *MeasureString* to calculate how many pixels are required to display a string in a given font. Remember to call *Dispose* when you're finished.

To draw a bitmap, create an image using the *Bitmap* class's constructor, and call *DrawImage*, for example:

```
Image im = new Bitmap (@"c:\docs\pics\mypic.bmp");

pe.Graphics.DrawImage (im, ClientRectangle);

im.Dispose();
```

To repaint the control, call *Invalidate*.
To draw 3D borders, sizing handles, selection frames, disabled text, and images, use static methods provided in the *ControlPaint* class.

## Testing the Control

Now that we've built the custom control, we can use it two different ways:

■ From a new Windows Forms project, we can add the compiled custom control to the toolbox. We do this by right-clicking the toolbox, selecting **Customize Toolbox**, and from the .NET Framework Components tab, clicking **Browse** and locating the Control Library DLL (in our case, FunStuff\bin\debug\FunStuff.dll). The component (*ScrollingText*) will then appear in the list, and if checked, will be added to the toolbox.

■ We can create a solution containing two projects: both the Control Library and a new Windows Forms project.

Normally, you opt for the second approach if you are still developing the control (and have access to its project file and source code), because it means you can more easily make any necessary changes. This is what we'll do in our example:

1. From the Solution Explorer, right-click on the solution and select **Add | New Project**. Then choose the **Windows Application** template, naming the project **TestFunStuff**.

2.  Locate the *Scrolling Text* control in the toolbox, and drag it to *Form1*. If the control is not in the toolbox, rebuild the project and look again. If it still doesn't appear, right-click the toolbox, select **Customize ToolBox**, and from the .NET Framework Components tab, click **Browse** and locate the Control Library DLL (try FunStuff\bin\debug\FunStuff.dll), and then check the **ScrollingText** component in the list.

    You'll notice that as you resize the control in the Designer, it won't render properly because the control doesn't assume it needs to be redrawn when resized. We can resolve this in two ways: We can override its *OnResize* method, calling *Invalidate* (marking the control "dirty" so that it gets redrawn), or in the control's constructor we can set a special flag to have this happen automatically. Let's take the latter approach:

3.  Modify the control's constructor as follows:

```
public ScrollingText()
{
    SetStyle (ControlStyles.ResizeRedraw, true);
}
```

4.  Rebuild the project and return to *Form1*. It will now render properly in the Designer when resized (see Figure 4.24).

**Figure 4.24** Custom Control in Designer

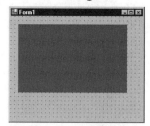

5.  Finally, we should test the form at runtime. Because we started out creating a control library, the startup project will be a DLL—which can only compile and not run. We can change this from the Solution Explorer: Right-click the **TestFunStuff** project, select **Set as Startup Project**, and then run the application.

# Enhancing the Control

Let's turn this custom control into a real-world example: a scrolling text banner. This is easier than it sounds: it's simply a matter of maintaining a text string, to which with a *Timer*, we periodically remove a character from the left—and add to the right. The text is rendered using *DrawString* in the *Graphics* class, using a graded brush for effect. We can also allow the user to start and stop the animation by overriding the control's *OnClick* method. The code for the *ScrollingText* control is on the accompanying CD-ROM, in the FunStuff folder. Here's the complete code listing:

```
using System;

using System.Collections;

using System.ComponentModel;

using System.Drawing;

using System.Data;

using System.Windows.Forms;


namespace FunStuff

{

    public class ScrollingText : System.Windows.Forms.Control

    {

        Timer timer;              // this will animate the text

        string scroll = null;    // the text we're going to animate


        public ScrollingText()

        {

            timer = new Timer();

            timer.Interval = 200;

            timer.Enabled = true;

            timer.Tick += new EventHandler (Animate);

        }


        void Animate (object sender, EventArgs e)

        {

            // Create scroll string field from Text property
```

```
        if (scroll == null) scroll = Text + "    ";


        // Trim one character from the left, and add it to the right.
        scroll = scroll.Substring (1, scroll.Length-1)
          + scroll.Substring (0, 1);


        // This tells Windows Forms our control needs repainting.
        Invalidate();
    }


    void StartStop (object sender, EventArgs e)
    { timer.Enabled = !timer.Enabled; }


    // When Text is changed, we must update the scroll string.
    protected override void OnTextChanged (EventArgs e)
    {
        scroll = null;
        base.OnTextChanged (e);
    }


    protected override void OnClick (EventArgs e)
    {
        timer.Enabled = !timer.Enabled;
        base.OnClick (e);
    }


    public override void Dispose()
    {
        // Since the timer hasn't been added to a collection (because
        // we don't have one!) we have to dispose it manually.
        timer.Dispose();
        base.Dispose();
    }
```

```
protected override void OnPaint(PaintEventArgs pe)
{
    // This is a fancy brush that does graded colors.
    Brush b = new System.Drawing.Drawing2D.LinearGradientBrush
        (ClientRectangle, Color.Blue, Color.Crimson, 10);

    // Use the control's font, resized to the height of the
    // control (actually slightly less to avoid truncation)
    Font f = new Font
        (Font.Name, Height*3/4, Font.Style, GraphicsUnit.Pixel);

    pe.Graphics.DrawString (scroll, f, b, 0, 0);
    base.OnPaint (pe);

    b.Dispose(); f.Dispose();
}
}
}
```

Figure 4.25 illustrates the control in the test form, at design time, with its *Text* and *Font* properties set. A nice touch in Visual Studio is that the control animates in the Designer.

**Figure 4.25** Completed *Scrolling Text* Control in Designer

# Subclassing Controls

Once we've designed a user control or custom control we can use inheritance to subclass it in the same way we did with our reusable dialog earlier in the chapter. You can also inherit from a standard control such as a *TextBox* or *Button*—in order to modify its appearance or behavior without going to the trouble of designing a new control from scratch.

Visual Studio distinguishes between inheriting user controls and custom controls. You can create an inherited user control directly—from **Project | Add Inherited Control**—whereas to create an inherited custom control (or to subclass a standard control) you need to write the class manually. The easiest way to go about this is to ask Visual Studio to create a custom control, and then in the Code Editor, to edit the control definition's base class.

To take an example, suppose your marketing department demands customizable "skins" in your Windows application. One approach (other than skinning the marketing department!) is to subclass some of the standard controls, such as *Button* and *Label*. The challenge would then be to decorate the controls without upsetting their existing graphics. Let's walk through this briefly:

1. From a new or existing Windows Forms project, go to **Project | Add New Item** and select **Custom Control**.

2. Switch to the Code Editor, and change the class definition so that we're subclassing *Button* instead:

   ```
   public class WashedButton : System.Windows.Forms.Button
   ```

   Now we need to override *OnPaint*. First, we'll have to invoke the base class's code so that it renders the button. Then we'll "wash" the control with a linear gradient brush—the same brush used in the scrolling text example, except that we'll use translucent colors so as not to erase the existing graphics. This is called *alpha blending* and activated simply by using a color with an alpha-value.

3. Update the *OnPaint* method as follows:

   ```
   protected override void OnPaint(PaintEventArgs pe)
   {
       base.OnPaint (pe);
       // Create two semi-transparent colors
       Color c1 = Color.FromArgb (64, Color.Blue);
       Color c2 = Color.FromArgb (64, Color.Yellow);
       Brush b = new System.Drawing.Drawing2D.LinearGradientBrush
           (ClientRectangle, c1, c2, 10);
       pe.Graphics.FillRectangle (b, ClientRectangle);
       b.Dispose();
   ```

```
}
```

4.  Build the project, and put the custom control onto a form as we did in the previous walkthrough (see Figure 4.26).

**Figure 4.26** Subclassed Buttons in Designer

# Custom Controls in Internet Explorer

The scrolling textbox we wrote in the "Writing a Custom Control" section is begging to be hosted on a Web page. Its compiled assembly is small enough to be downloaded over the Internet in a couple of seconds, and is secure because .NET code runs in a managed environment, rather like Java's virtual machine. In fact, both C# and Windows Forms have their roots in Java—their technical predecessors being J++ and its supplied Windows Foundation Classes. Of course, Windows Forms applets require that the client has a Windows operating system—with the .NET runtime installed. It also requires support at the server-end.

## Setting Up IIS

Before starting this walkthrough, you need to check that Internet Information Services is installed and running. IIS is shipped with Windows 2000 Professional—you can check that it's present and install it from the Control Panel (go to **Add/Remove Programs | Windows Components** and locate **Internet Information Services**). To check that it's running, choose **Administrative Tools | Services** from the Control Panel and locate the **World Wide Web Publishing Service**.

## Creating a Virtual Directory

We'll need a Virtual Directory to host the Web page and applet. This is done using the Internet Services Manager—in Windows 2000, we can access this through the Control Panel, under **Administrative Tools**.

1. From Internet Services Manager, expand your computer's icon and right-click **Default Web Site** choosing **New | Virtual Directory**. The Virtual Directory Wizard will then appear.

2. When prompted for an alias, type **FunStuff**.

3. It will then ask for a directory: When testing, it's easiest to specify the folder where Visual Studio compiles the component library's DLL (for example, **FunStuff\bin\debug**).

4. The wizard will then prompt for Access Permissions. Check **Read** and **Run Scripts** and uncheck everything else.

## Writing a Test Page

We'll need to create an HTML page to test the component. We can do this either in Visual Studio or with an independent HTML or text editor program such as Notepad. In this example, we'll use Visual Studio's editor. Note that the file will have to be in the folder specified when creating the virtual directory:

1. From Visual Studio, reopen the **FunStuff** solution. Click on the **FunStuff** project in the Solution Explorer, then click the **Show All Files** icon. Expand the folder containing the compiled DLL (for example, **bin\debug**), right-click the folder, and select **Add | Add New Item** and use the **HTML Page** template, naming the file **test.htm**.

2. Switch to the HTML view and add the following, inside the <BODY> section of the page:

```
<p> Testing our control! </p>
<object id="test"
  classid="http:funstuff.dll#FunStuff.ScrollingText"
  height="50" width="500">
  <param name="Text" value="The quick brown fox...">
</object>
```

This is rather like inserting a Java applet or ActiveX control. For the Class ID, we specify the DLL containing the custom control, followed by the class's full name, including its namespace (note that this is case-sensitive). The object size is specified in pixels—it's for this reason that when writing the control, we created a font matching the height of the control, rather than the other way round.

3. The final step is viewing the test page. Start Internet Explorer, and open **http://localhost/FunStuff/test.htm** (see Figure 4.27).

**Figure 4.27** Custom Control in Internet Explorer

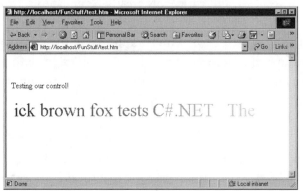

# Summary

Tools for writing Windows applications have come a long way since the early days of Visual Basic and C++; in this chapter we examined Windows Forms, Microsoft's modern object-oriented solution.

One of the benefits of an object-oriented framework is consistency: The same core classes, interfaces, and protocols are used repeatedly throughout the framework. And at the heart of consistency is inheritance: A combo box supports all the functionality of a control, which supports all the functionality of a component. This means that most of the objects we worked with here, were in effect, components, and it was by virtue of this we could manipulate them in the Designer, and know that they would be disposed automatically with the host control.

We dealt in this chapter with many components that hosted child objects: Forms that hosted controls, tab controls that hosted tab pages, menus that contained menu items, tree view controls that contained nodes. In all cases, the child objects were managed through a property returning a collection object—implementing consistent interfaces for adding, removing, and enumerating the members.

A Windows application is a consumer of events, and we saw in this chapter how this is modeled in Windows Forms through C# events and delegates. In adding an event handler programmatically, we saw how to instantiate a delegate object—a pointer to a method of an agreed signature, and then how it's attached to an event, using the += operator.

In writing a text editor, we discovered the default behavior of newly activated forms—modeless and top-level. But by changing a few properties, we created a multiple document interface (MDI) application, and later on we saw how we could use the *MdiChildren* collection property to enumerate the child forms. We also created a modal dialog, by building a form with the "look and feel" of a dialog, and then activating it with *ShowDialog*.

The anchoring and docking features make it easy to design forms that can be usefully resized. We found that anchoring was useful in creating a sizable dialog form, and docking was required when setting up a list view/tree view/splitter combination. Because docking space is allocated on a "first-come, first-served" basis—where controls at the back of the z-order are first—we needed to ensure the z-order of the participating controls was correct.

Windows Forms also provides access to operating system features such as drag and drop, and we looked briefly at a common scenario—calling *DoDragDrop* from a list view's *ItemDrag* event; seeing how a *DataObject* is marshaled to the recipient; and discussing how the *DragEnter* and *DragDrop* events on the target are handled to enable the operation.

The .NET Framework's object-oriented model is extensible, and by sub-classing the Windows Forms components and controls—as well as our own, we can start creating reusable classes. In the text editor example, we built a reusable dialog; later on we subclassed various Windows Forms classes to build custom controls. We derived from *UserControl* to create a composite of existing compo-nents, while we derived from *Control* to create a custom control on par with a label or textbox.

In our custom control, we used the stateless graphics device interface (GDI+) to render the graphics, through a *Graphics* object exposed in the *PaintEventArgs* parameter within the control's *OnPaint* method. Many of the GDI+ methods, such as *DrawLine* or *FillRectangle*, accept as parameters helper objects, such as pens, brushes, or images. These objects we created and disposed explicitly.

In the last walkthrough, we hosted a custom control in Internet Explorer. This raised the issue of C# and Windows Forms as an alternative to Java for Internet applets—this is currently limited by its requirement for the (less portable) .NET Common Language Runtime (CLR) on the client machine. However, it does illustrate how Windows Forms programs can compile to small executables that can run securely, requiring no special setup or deployment. These features—combined with other benefits provided by C# and the .NET CLR—make the platform a good choice for developing modern Internet-connected Windows applications.

# Solutions Fast Track

## Writing a Simple Windows Forms Application

- ☑ Use Visual Studio's Windows Forms project template to create the structure of a Windows application.

- ☑ Add controls and components visually using the Designer, and then use the Properties window to configure the objects and add event handlers.

- ☑ To add controls programmatically, first declare, instantiate, and configure the controls, then add them to the form or parent container's *Controls* collection.

☑ To attach an event handler at runtime, define a method matching the event delegate's signature, then attach a delegate instance wrapping the method to the event using the += operator.

# Writing a Simple Text Editor

☑ To add a main menu, use the *MainMenu* component—and then enter its items visually in the Designer.

☑ A new form is displayed by instantiating its class and calling *Show*. This results in a top-level modeless form.

☑ To implement a multiple document interface, set the parent window's *IsMdiContainer* property to **True**, and then assign each child's *MdiParent* property to the parent form.

☑ Use form inheritance to encapsulate common functionality. But keep the abstractions simple to minimize coupling and complexity.

☑ Use a *TabControl* to simplify forms with many controls.

☑ Use the anchoring and docking features to create resizable forms.

☑ Define public properties in a form's class to expose its controls to other forms or classes.

☑ Use the *MdiChildren* collection of an MDI parent to traverse its child forms.

# Using the *ListView* and *TreeView* Controls

☑ First set up one or more *ImageList* components if icons are required in the *ListView* or *TreeView*.

☑ Add items to a *ListView* control through its *Items* collection property.

☑ Use the *ListView*'s details view for a multicolumn grid-like control.

☑ Add items to a *TreeView* through its *Nodes* collection property. Subnodes can also be added to each node in the same way.

☑ To configure a splitter control, first set the docking properties of the participating controls, then arrange their z-order.

☑ Start a drag-and-drop operation by calling *DoDragDrop* from the *Itemdrag* event on the source control, passing any data required by the recipient.

☑ Enable a drop target by setting its *AllowDrop* property to **True**, and then handling its *DragEnter* and *DragDrop* methods.

## Creating Controls

☑ To encapsulate a reusable group of controls, build a *UserControl* and then add properties to enable access to its data.

☑ When you need to start from scratch, define a custom control—overriding the *Control* class's *OnPaint* method to render its graphics, using GDI+.

☑ When using GDI+, remember to dispose any *Pens* and *Brushes* that you create.

☑ Utilize inheritance to enhance existing controls, overriding their methods to add or change functionality.

☑ Use the object tag to insert controls from component libraries into HTML pages, specifying the assembly's DLL and the control's fully qualified name.

# Frequently Asked Questions

The following Frequently Asked Questions, answered by the authors of this book, are designed to both measure your understanding of the concepts presented in this chapter and to assist you with real-life implementation of these concepts. To have your questions about this chapter answered by the author, browse to **www.syngress.com/solutions** and click on the **"Ask the Author"** form.

**Q:** Can I easily rename a solution or project?

**A:** Yes—right-click from the Solution Explorer and choose **Rename**. You'll also have to edit the namespace declarations in any source code files you've created.

**Q:** How do I detach an event handler?

**A:** In the same way you attach an event handler, except using the -= operator. For example:

```
button1.Click -= new EventHandler (button1_Click);
```

**Q:** Where is image data loaded into *ImageList* controls actually stored in the project?

**A:** Each form has an associated resource file (with a .resx extension) where image data and localized strings are stored. You can see this by clicking the **Show All Files** icon in the Solution Explorer.

**Q:** Can a textbox control contain text in more than one color or font?

**A:** No. For this you need to use the *RichTextBox* control.

**Q:** How can I add icons to menu items?

**A:** Unfortunately there is no built-in feature for this. You need configure the menu items to be owner-drawn (set *OwnerDraw* to **True**) and then use GDI+ to draw both the text and graphics (handle the *MeasureItem* and *DrawItem* events). Microsoft's "Got Dot Net" site (www.gotdotnet.com) is a good place to start for information about implementing owner-drawn controls.

**Q:** What's the difference between tab-order and z-order?

**A:** Tab-order describes the order of focus as the user moves between controls using the **Tab** and **Shift+Tab** keys. This is determined by the control's *TabIndex* property—set either in the Properties window, or by selecting **View | Tab Order** and then clicking each control in order. Z-order describes the front-to-back order of controls, and this set in the Designer using the **Bring to Front** and **Send to Back** layout options. Z-order matters when controls visually overlap and also when docking: Those at the back of the z-order will be assigned docking space first.

**Q:** I need to determine the current mouse position and state of the **Shift**, **Control**, and **Alt** keys—but I'm not inside an event handler that provides this information. How can it be done?

**A:** Use the *MousePosition*, *MouseButtons*, and *ModifierKeys* static properties of the *Control* class.

**Q:** How can I screen input in a textbox?

**A:** For this, it's usually best to start by subclassing the *TextBox* control so that your solution is reusable within your project (or outside your project). Override *OnTextChanged,* or for more control, *OnKeyPress* and *OnKeyDown*.

*OnKeyPress* fires for printable characters; *OnKeyDown* fires for all key combinations. Both of these offer a *Handled* property in the event arguments parameter, which you can set to **True** to cancel the event.

**Q:** When designing an inherited or custom control, can I trap windows messages such as WM_PASTE?

**A:** Yes—by overriding the *WndProc* method.

**Q:** Is there a Windows Forms newsgroup where I can get help?

**A:** Microsoft provides a newsgroup: **microsoft.public.dotnet.framework .windowsforms**.

# Chapter 5

# Network Programming: Using TCP and UDP Protocols

## Solutions in this chapter:

- **Introducing Networking and Sockets**

- **Example TCP Command Transmission and Processing**

- **Example UDP Command Transmission and Processing**

- **Creating a News Ticker Using UDP Multicasting**

- **Creating a UDP Client Server Chat Application**

- **Creating a TCP P2P File Sharing Application**

- **Access to Web-Resources**

- ☑ **Summary**

- ☑ **Solutions Fast Track**

- ☑ **Frequently Asked Questions**

# Introduction

Networking can be defined, in a general sense, as *inter-process communication*. Two or more processes (such as applications) communicate with each other. The processes can run on the same or different computers or other physical devices. Connections between the network nodes are made mostly by a wire (such as local area network [LAN], wide area network [WAN], and Internet); by wireless via radio frequencies (such as cell phone, wireless appliances, wireless LAN, Internet, and Bluetooth); or by infrared (IR) light (such as a cell phone to a laptop).

In this chapter, we cover the basics of networking and how it is accomplished with C#. We start out with some theory, covering a little bit about the history of networking and the Internet and sockets; then we discuss commonly used protocols such as the Transmission Control Protocol (TCP) and User Datagram Protocol (UDP). Subsequently, we have a look at ports and their uses. The last point of theory is to get to know the .NET classes we use.

Keeping theory in mind, we then go into practice. First, we develop some very simple communication examples using TCP and UDP. Then we develop a multicast news ticker. We have a look at a chat server and client, where we combine the learned techniques. After all the client/server-applications, we develop a P2P file sharing system, and finally, we show how you can use special .NET classes that encapsulate the networking.

# Introducing Networking and Sockets

In the sixties, researchers of the Advanced Research Projects Agency (ARPA) in the U.S. were requested by the Department of Defense (DoD) to develop a system for saving information military important in case of a war. The result of their work was an electronic network—the ARPAnet. Military information was stored on all computers that were part of the network. The computers were installed in different places far away from each other and information was exchanged in several different ways. New or updated data on the computers was to be synchronized in a very short time so that in case of the destruction of one or more computers, no data would be lost.

In the 1970s, the DoD allowed nonmilitary research institutes to access the ARPAnet. The researchers were more interested in the connected computers than in synchronizing data. They used it for exchanging information, and students at these institutes used a part of the network as a blackboard for communicating with each other—this was the beginning of Usenet.

In the 1980s, the military and civil parts of the ARPAnet were divided. In other countries, similar activities led to national networks. At the end of the 1980s, most of the national networks became connected to each other. The Internet was born.

It was necessary to have a standardized way to communicate over different types of networks and with different kinds of computers. So TCP/Internet Protocol (TCP/IP), which was developed by ARPA, became a worldwide standard.

TCP/IP is a "protocol family" that allows connected computers to communicate and share resources across a network. (TCP and IP are only two of the protocols in this family, but they are the most widely recognized. Other protocols in this set include UDP.) For all protocols provided by .NET, have a look at the .NET reference documentation (class *System.Net.Sockets.Socket*).

To access IP-based networks from an application, we need *sockets*. A socket is a programming interface and communication endpoint that can be used for connecting to other computers, sending and receiving data from them. Sockets were introduced in Berkeley Unix, which is why sockets are often called Berkeley Sockets. Figure 5.1 shows the general architecture of IP-based communication.

**Figure 5.1** General Communication Architecture

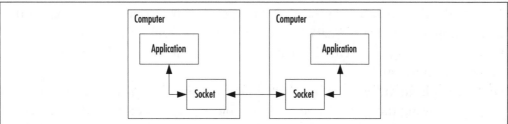

Generally, three types of sockets exist:

- **Raw sockets** This type is implemented on the network layer (see Figure 5.2). An example for a protocol on this layer is IP.

- **Datagram sockets** Datagrams are packets of data. This type of sockets is implemented on the transport layer (see Figure 5.2). However, the assignment to a layer is not strict, because, for instance, IP is also datagram-oriented. We go more in detail on this type of sockets later in this section.

- **Stream sockets** In contrast to datagram sockets, these sockets provide a stream of data. We go into more detail on this type of sockets later in this section.

**Figure 5.2** Communication Protocol Stack

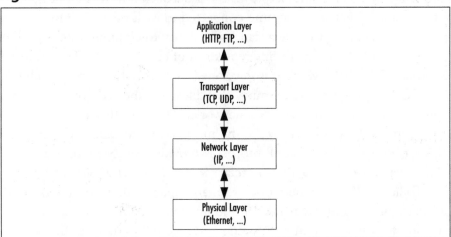

Modern communication architectures use a stack of different protocol layers where data is given to the top layer. Each layer is adding layer-specific protocol information to the data and then it is given to the next layer. The lowest layer is sending the data to another process running on another computer (or maybe the same computer) where the data goes up in the same stack of layers. Each layer removes the protocol-specific information until the application layer is reached. Figure 5.2 shows such a stack.

The application layer can be divided into sublayers. You may think of an application using the XML-based Simple Object Access Protocol (SOAP) using the Hypertext Transfer Protocol (HTTP) for sending SOAP commands in XML. This is called *HTTP tunneling* and is used especially with firewalls, so that the firewalls do not have to be reconfigured for passing through SOAP.

# Introduction to TCP

The Transmission Control Protocol is a connection- and stream-oriented, reliable point-to-point protocol. TCP communication is analogous to a phone call. You (the client) may want to talk with your aunt (the server). You establish a connection by dialing the number of your aunt's phone (point-to-point). This is shown in Figure 5.3.

If your aunt is at home, she will pick up her phone and talk to you (see Figure 5.4). The phone company guarantees that the words you and your aunt are speaking are sent to the other end and in the same order (reliability). As long as you are on the phone, you can speak continuously (stream-oriented).

**Figure 5.3** Calling Your Aunt (Point-to-Point Connection)

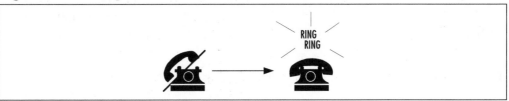

**Figure 5.4** Talking to Your Aunt (Reliability and Stream-Orientation)

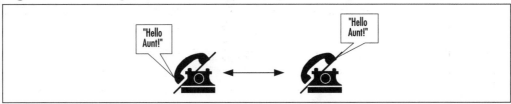

The connection will be established until you and your aunt are finished with your conversation (connection-oriented). See Figure 5.5 for an example of disconnecting.

**Figure 5.5** Aunt Hangs Up (Connection-Orientation)

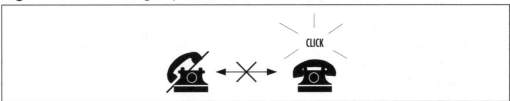

TCP uses IP as its network protocol. IP is datagram-oriented and a best-effort protocol. As mentioned before, datagrams are packets of data. *Best-effort* means that datagrams are sent without the guarantee of delivery and correct order.

As we have seen, TCP is stream-oriented. TCP must simulate the streaming of data. Therefore, it is necessary that TCP controls the order and correct occurrence of the datagrams. If a datagram is corrupt or lost, it must be resent. If this does not function, an error is reported. TCP also implements a number of protocol timers to ensure synchronized communication. These timers also can be used to produce timeouts, if needed.

The advantage of TCP is its reliability—TCP is the base of most reliable protocols such as HTTP, File Transfer Protocol (FTP), or Telnet. Those protocols are needed if delivery and order of packets is important. For instance, if you send an e-mail to your aunt starting with "Hello, Aunt," first it must be delivered, and second, it should not be delivered as "Hlnt Aeluo." The disadvantage to TCP is the loss of performance due to the administration overhead for handling the reliability. Figure 5.6 shows a sample stack of communication layers with HTTP.

**Figure 5.6** HTTP Communication Layers Stack

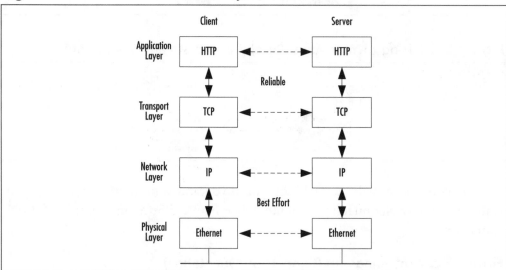

If reliability is not needed, you can choose the  protocol UDP. We discuss this protocol in the next section.

## Introduction to UDP

The User Datagram Protocol is a connection-less and datagram-oriented best-effort protocol. A UDP-communication is analogous to sending a letter. You (a peer) may want to send a letter to your aunt (another peer). You don't have to hand-deliver the letter to your aunt—the post office delivers the letter (a datagram), and it delivers it as a whole entity, rather than delivering page by page (see Figure 5.7).

Sending a letter is mostly, but not always, reliable. The post office offers a best-effort service. They don't guarantee an order in sending letters. If you send letter 1 today and send letter 2 tomorrow, your aunt may receive letter 2 before letter 1 arrives (see Figure 5.8).

On the other hand, one of your letters may get lost. The post office doesn't guarantee that a letter will be delivered (see Figure 5.9).

**Figure 5.7** Sending a Letter to Your Aunt (Whole Communication Delivery)

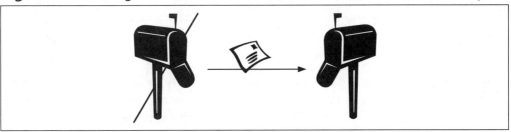

**Figure 5.8** No Delivery Order Guaranteed

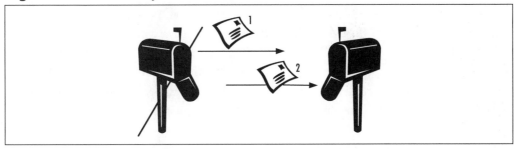

**Figure 5.9** Loss of a Communication Is Possible

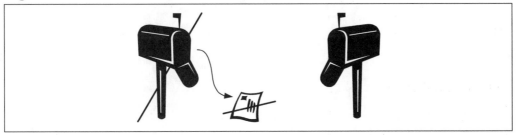

So why should you use such a protocol? For the following reasons:

- **Performance** UDP is faster than TCP because there is no administrative overhead to bring data in order or for resending lost packets. So it can be used for time-critical applications such as video- or audio-streaming.

- **If your application doesn't care about a lost packet.** Consider a time server: If the server sends a packet and the packet is lost, it doesn't make sense to resend it. The packet will be incorrect if the client receives it on the second try.

- **UDP causes less network traffic.**  UDP needs 8 bytes for protocol header information, whereas TCP needs 20 bytes. In times where we speak of gigabyte hard drives, 16 bytes doesn't seem like it should be a problem, but think of the sum of all packets sent in global communication—then 16 bytes becomes a very heavy weight.

- **If your application needs a best-effort protocol for analyzing the network.**  For instance, the *ping* command is used to test communication between two computers or processes. It needs to know about lost or corrupt packets to determine the quality of the connection. It doesn't make sense to use a reliable protocol for applications such as *ping*.

UDP is typically used for Domain Name System (DNS), Simple Network Management Protocol (SNMP), Internet telephony, or streaming multimedia.

Another advantage of UDP is in *multicasting*, which means that a number of processes can be grouped together by a special IP address (see Figure 5.10). The IP address must be in the range 224.0.0.1 to 239.255.255.255, inclusive. Every process contained in the group can send packets to all other processes of the group.

**Figure 5.10** UDP Multicasting

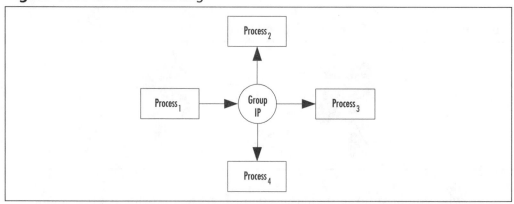

No process of the group knows how many other processes the group contains. If one application wants to send data to the others, it has to send the data to the IP address of the group. On the protocol layer, no process is a specialized server. Your job is to define clients and servers if needed. For more details, see the section "Creating a News Ticker Using UDP Multicasting" later in this chapter.

The next section introduces ports. Ports are important for identifying applications running on a computer.

Many firewalls are configured not to allow UDP. Firewalls are used to permit unauthorized access from outside the firewall. Using UDP, the firewall cannot determine if a packet comes from inside or outside because no connection is made explicitly. Remember that TCP is connection-oriented, as in a direction from the client to the server.

# Introduction to Ports

Generally, a computer has a single connection to the network. If all data arrives through one connection, how can it be determined which application running on the computer receives the data? The answer is through the use of ports.

A port is a 16-bit number in the range or 0 to 65535. The port numbers 0 to 1023 are reserved for special services such as HTTP (port 80), Mail (port 25), and Telnet (port 23).

A connected application must be bound to at least one port. *Binding* means that a port is assigned to a socket used by an application. The application is registered with the system. All incoming packets that contain the port number of the application in the packet header are given to the application socket (see Figure 5.11).

**Figure 5.11** Ports

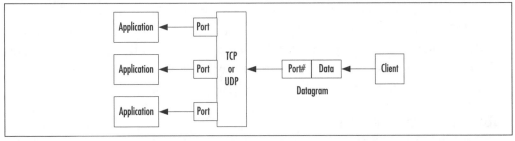

Please note that Figure 5.11 for TCP does not mean that only one socket can be bound to one port. If a socket is waiting on a port for an incoming connection, normally the port is blocked for other applications ("normally" means that this feature can be switched off—for more details, please have a look at the .NET reference documentation *System.Net.Sockets.Socket.SetSocketOption()* method). Let's call a socket waiting on a connection to a server socket. If a connection is accepted by a server socket, it creates a new socket representing the connection.

Then, the server socket can wait for a new connection request. So, multiple clients can communicate concurrently over the same port.

An example for an application using this feature is a Web server. For instance, while a Web page you requested is loaded by the browser, you can use a second browser to request another page from the same server. The next sections introduce the most important .NET classes we use for our examples.

---

**NOTE**

In this book, we focus more on real-life examples than on theory. Because classes like the .NET `Socket` class are complex in use, we show .NET classes that simplify the developing rather than the core networking classes.

---

## System.Net Namespace

Whereas the namespace *System.Net.Sockets* provide classes for more basic networking functionality, the *System.Net* namespace contains classes that encapsulate these basics for easier access. The classes of *System.Net* are a simple programming interface for some protocols used for networking.

At the core of this namespace are the classes *WebRequest* and *WebResponse*. These abstract classes are the base for protocol implementations. Two protocols are pre-implemented: HTTP with *HttpWebRequest* (with corresponding *HttpWebResponse*) and file system access (request-URIs starting with *file://*") with *FileWebRequest* (with corresponding *FileWebResponse*). The other classes are mostly helper-classes, such as IP addresses, authorization and permission classes, exceptions, and certificates. Table 5.1 shows the classes we use for our examples.

**Table 5.1** *System.Net* Classes

| Class | Description |
| --- | --- |
| *IPAddress* | Represents an IP address. |
| *IPEndPoint* | Identifies a network endpoint. A network endpoint is an IP address and a port. |
| *WebRequest* | Makes a request to a Uniform Resource Identifier (URI). This class is abstract and must be extended for the destination protocol. |

**Continued**

**Table 5.1** Continued

| Class | Description |
| --- | --- |
| *WebResponse* | Represents a response to a URI. This class is abstract and must be extended for the destination protocol. |
| *WebProxy* | Identifies an HTTP proxy. It contains all proxy settings used by *WebRequest*. |

# *System.Net.Sockets* Namespace

As mentioned earlier in the chapter, the *System.Net.Sockets* namespace contains classes that provide basic networking functionality. The central class is *Socket*. As mentioned, a socket is the most basic programming interface for networking. We use most of the classes of this namespace for our example. Table 5.2 shows the class we use.

**Table 5.2** *System.Net.Sockets* Classes

| Class | Description |
| --- | --- |
| *Socket* | Implements the Berkeley sockets programming interface. |
| *NetworkStream* | Allows easy access to data of stream sockets. |
| *TcpClient* | Provides a TCP client that can connect to a server socket. |
| *TcpListener* | Implements a TCP server socket listening for incoming connection-requests. |
| *UdpClient* | Provides a UDP peer with the possibility of multicasting. |

Enough theory—let's go into practice. The next section describes a simple command transmission and processing using TCP.

> **NOTE**
>
> For simplifying the code, all examples presented in this chapter do not contain any exception handling. (Refer to Chapter 2 for more information on exception handling.) Please have a look at the .NET class reference for each method which exceptions must be handled.

# Example TCP Command Transmission and Processing

The example in this section has a strict separation between the presentation layer and the functional layer. The presentation layer is the user interface (UI). In this example, you use a console application because you should focus first on communication and then concentrate on creating a good-looking UI. The functional layer is the part of the application that does all the work—for example, a business object for calculating something. Figure 5.12 shows the simplified architecture of the first example.

**Figure 5.12** Example Architecture

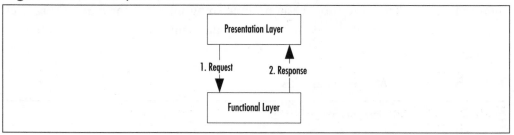

For the presentation layer, where the functionality is executed is unimportant. You can implement the functional layer within the same application, in another process on the same computer, or on another computer anywhere in a LAN or on the Internet. To make this architecture more flexible, you will add a command processor between the presentation and functional layers. The command processor is a standardized interface for the functional layer. The presentation layer is giving its requests in the form of commands to the processor. The processor is executing methods of the functional layer based on the commands. Finally, the command processor will take the results and give it back to the presentation layer. Figure 5.13 shows the extended architecture.

The command processor makes it simple to access the functional layer in various ways—either within the same application or via network communication on another computer. Figure 5.14 shows an example with a remote functional layer. The advantage of this model is that the presentation layer does not have to know where the functional layer is running. It just gives commands to the command processor and receives the result.

A typical example of such an architecture is a Web-browser-to-Web-server communication. You are typing in an URL in the address field of your browser.

The browser is converting the URL to a *GET* request for a Web server and is sending the request to the Web server. The Web server analyzes the request and returns an HTML page to the browser.

**Figure 5.13** Example Architecture with Command Processor

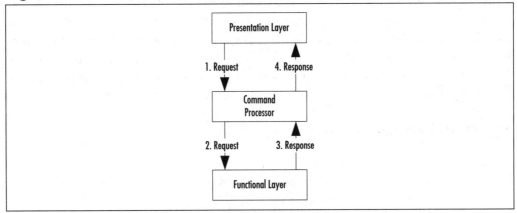

**Figure 5.14** Example Architecture with Communication

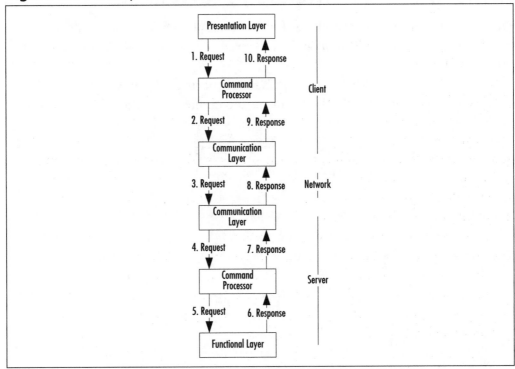

This example performs the same action in a very simplified form. A console client is sending a request to a server and the server returns "Hello World !" to the client. This example implements a simple communication protocol with two commands: *GET* and *EXIT*. A sample communication looks like this:

```
c: (establish tcp connection to the server)
s: (accept connection)
c: GET<CRLF>
s: "Hello World !"<CRLF>
c: EXIT<CRLF>
s: BYE<CRLF>
c: (close connection)
s: (close connection)
```

*c:* indicates the client and *s:* the server. <CRLF> means a carriage return followed by a line feed to indicate that the line is finished. This is commonly used with communication protocols such as HTTP or SMTP.

## General Usage of Needed .NET Classes

You need two main network classes for this example. On the client side, you use *System.Net.Sockets.TcpClient* and on the server side it is *System.Net.Sockets.TcpListener*.

Generally, on the client side a *TcpClient* connects to the server. Then you work with a stream given by the client on the connection. After all the work is done, you close the client:

```
// connect client to the server 127.0.0.1:8080
TcpClient client = new TcpClient ( "127.0.0.1", 8080 );


// get the network stream for reading and writing something
// to the network
NetworkStream ns = client.GetStream ();


// read/write something from/to the stream


// disconnect from server
client.Close ();
```

The server side involves one more step, but generally the code looks like the client code. You bind a *TcpListener* on a local port. Then, if a client connects to the listener, you get a socket. With this socket, you create a stream. From this point on, the code is the same as on the client side:

```
// create a listener for incoming TCP connections on port 8080
TcpListener listener = new TcpListener ( 8080 );
listener.Start ();


// wait for and accept an incoming connection
Socket server = listener.AcceptSocket ();


// create a network stream for easier use
NetworkStream ns = new NetworkStream ( server );


// read/write something from/to the stream


// disconnect from client
server.Close ();
```

After having a look at the general use of the networking classes, let's go further in our first example.

## The Server

Let's start with the server. The class is called *TCPHelloWorldServer*. The source code of Figures 5.15 to 5.18 is included on the CD in a file named TCPHelloWorldServer.cs. For simplification, only the client has a command processor component. Later, we show examples where the server also has a processor. For the server (see Figures 5.15 to 5.18), you need the following namespaces; again, for simplification, the class has a *Main()* method only.

**Figure 5.15** Needed Namespaces in TCPHelloWorldServer.cs

```
using System;
using System.IO;
using System.Net.Sockets;
```

The code in Figure 5.16 is a snippet of the *Main()* method in *TCPHelloWorldServer*. It shows the server initialization. For waiting for incoming connections on port 8080, use a *TcpListener* instance.

**Figure 5.16** Server Initialization in TCPHelloWorldServer.cs

```
Console.WriteLine ( "initializing server..." );


TcpListener listener = new TcpListener ( 8080 );
listener.Start ();


Console.WriteLine ( "server initialized, waiting for " +
   "incoming connections..." );


Socket s = listener.AcceptSocket ();
// create a NetworkStream for easier access
NetworkStream ns = new NetworkStream ( s );


// use a stream reader because of ReadLine() method
StreamReader r = new StreamReader ( ns );
```

The listener listens on port 8080 for incoming connections. The *AcceptSocket()* method returns a socket representing the connection to the client. This method blocks the program until a client opens a connection to the listener.

After a connection is established, the socket returned by *AcceptSocket()* is used for exchanging data with the connected client. The easiest way to do this is the use of a *NetworkStream*. This class is located in the namespace *System.Net.Sockets*. *NetworkStream* encapsulates the methods for reading and writing data with a socket. So, you can use this stream with code working only on streams.

The next step is creating a *StreamReader*. This class is part of the *System.IO* namespace. This class simplifies the access to a stream. Here, you use it because of its *ReadLine()* method. This method reads a single line of characters. The .NET reference documentation defines a line as follows: "A line is defined as a sequence of characters followed by a carriage return ("\r"), a line feed ("\n"), or a carriage return immediately followed by a line feed."

After the client establishes a connection, it sends a command to the connected server. Now the incoming commands must be parsed and executed by the server. The code is shown in Figure 5.17.

**Figure 5.17** Command Processing in TCPHelloWorldServer.cs

```csharp
bool loop = true;
while ( loop )
{

  // read a line until CRLF
  string command = r.ReadLine ();
  string result;

  Console.WriteLine ( "executing remote command: " +
    command );

  switch ( command )
  {
    case "GET":
      result = "Hello World !";
      break;

    // finish communication
    case "EXIT":
      result = "BYE";
      loop = false;
      break;

    // invalid command
    default:
      result = "ERROR";
      break;
  }

  if ( result != null )
  {
    Console.WriteLine ( "sending result: " + result );
```

**Continued**

**Figure 5.17** Continued

```
        // add a CRLF to the result
        result += "\r\n";

        // convert data string to byte array
        Byte[] res = System.Text.Encoding.ASCII.GetBytes (
          result.ToCharArray () );

        // send result to the client
        s.Send ( res, res.Length, 0 );
      }
    }
```

If the *GET* command is received, the server returns the string "Hello World !", and the loop continues. The loop also continues if an unknown command arrives. In that case, the string "ERROR" is returned. On the *EXIT* command, the server stops the loop. After that, the connection must be closed (see Figure 5.18). You can do this by simply calling the *Close()* method of the socket. Finally, the server waits for the pressing of the **Return** key.

**Figure 5.18** Server Shutdown in TCPHelloWorldServer.cs

```
Console.WriteLine ( "clearing up server..." );
s.Close ();

Console.Write ( "press return to exit" );
Console.ReadLine ();
```

That's all for the server. Let's move on to the client.

# The Client

The client is a bit more complex than the server. It has two parts: the UI (a simple console application), and the command processor, which contains the communication components.

Let's have a look at the command processor, named *TCPRemoteCommandProcessor*. The source code for Figures 5.19 to 5.25 is included on the CD in a file named Base.cs. This file is compiled to a library named Base.dll that is also contained on the CD. For the command processor, the needed namespaces are as shown in Figure 5.19.

**Figure 5.19** Used Namespaces in Base.cs

```
using System;
using System.IO;
using System.Net.Sockets;
```

First, you will write an interface. This interface gives you the flexibility to implement more than one type of command processor with different underlying network protocols, so a client gets only an object that implements the interface. This makes the client independent from the used network protocol (see Figure 5.20).

**Figure 5.20** *CommandProcessor* Interface in Base.cs

```
public interface CommandProcessor
{
  // execute a command and return the result
  // if the return value is false the command processing loop
  // should stop
  bool Execute ( string command, ref string result );
}
```

Now, create the *TCPRemoteCommandProcessor* class that implements the *CommandProcessor* interface. The class has three methods: a constructor, a *Close()* method, and the implementation of the *Execute()* method. The command processor has two different running modes. In the Hold Connection mode, the constructor establishes the connection to the server directly from the constructor. Disconnecting will be done at the moment the *Close()* method is called. In the Release Connection mode, every time the processor is requested to send a command to the server, the connection is established. After retrieving the result, the connection is closed. The first mode is for short-term or high-performance communication. The second mode is for long-term communication and can be used for saving money on the Internet or reducing use of network resources.

Let's start with the class fields. Figure 5.21 shows all the information and objects needed for running the communication process.

**Figure 5.21** Class Fields of *TCPRemoteCommandProcessor* in Base.cs

```
// remote host
private string host = null;
// remote port
private int port = -1;
// connection mode
private bool releaseConnection = false;
// communication interface
private TcpClient client = null;
// outgoing data stream
private NetworkStream outStream = null;
// ingoing data stream
private StreamReader inStream = null;
```

Now for the constructor (see Figure 5.22). It has three parameters: the name and port of the host to connect with and a Boolean flag determining the mode. If the flag is true, the command processor works in Release Connection mode. Otherwise, the Hold Connection mode is active. If the processor runs in the last mentioned mode, the constructor connects immediately to the server specified by the host name and port. Finally, it initializes the stream input and output stream fields.

**Figure 5.22** Constructor of *TCPRemoteCommandProcessor* in Base.cs

```
public TCPRemoteCommandProcessor ( string host, int port,
  bool releaseConnection )
{
  // add parameter checking here

  this.host = host;
  this.port = port;
  this.releaseConnection = releaseConnection;

  if ( !this.releaseConnection )
  {
    Console.WriteLine ( "connecting to " + this.host + ":" +
```

**Continued**

**Figure 5.22** Continued

```
      this.port + "..." );


   this.client = new TcpClient ( this.host, this.port );
   this.outStream = this.client.GetStream ();
   this.inStream = new StreamReader ( this.outStream );


   Console.WriteLine ( "connected to " + this.host + ":" +
      this.port );

   }

}
```

The *Close()* method is quite simple. It closes only the connection (see Figure 5.23). This will be done only in Release Connection mode. If the command processor is in Hold Connection mode, this method does nothing because the *client* field will be null.

**Figure 5.23** *Close()* Method of *TCPRemoteCommandProcessor* in Base.cs

```
public void Close ()
{
  if ( this.client != null )
  {
    this.client.Close ();


    Console.WriteLine ( "connection closed: " + this.host +
      ":" + this.port );

  }

}
```

**NOTE**

You do not have to flush the streams by using the *Flush()* methods of *NetworkStream* because these are not buffered streams. But if you develop classes that work only on streams *without* knowing which kind of streams it uses, you should always consider flushing them.

*Execute()* is more complex. If the command processor is in the Release Connection mode, it first must connect to the server and finally close the connection after sending the command (see Figure 5.24). For sending, the command is concatenated with a trailing carriage return and line feed. After that, it is converted to a byte array. This array is given to the output stream. Then the processor reads the response from the input stream. Finally, it checks if the response in the string is *"BYE"*. If so, false is returned; true otherwise.

**Figure 5.24** *Execute()* Method of *TCPRemoteCommandProcessor* in Base.cs

```
public bool Execute ( string command, ref string result )
{
  // add parameter checking here

  bool ret = true;

  if ( this.releaseConnection )
  {
    Console.WriteLine ( "connecting to " + this.host + ":" +
      this.port + "..." );

    // open connection to the server
    this.client = new TcpClient ( this.host, this.port );
    this.outStream = this.client.GetStream ();
    this.inStream = new StreamReader ( this.outStream );

    Console.WriteLine ( "connected to " + this.host + ":" +
      this.port );
  }

  // add a CRLF to command to indicate end
  command += "\r\n";

  // convert command string to byte array
  Byte[] cmd = System.Text.Encoding.ASCII.GetBytes (
    command.ToCharArray () );
```

**Continued**

**Figure 5.24** Continued

```
    // send request
    this.outStream.Write ( cmd, 0, cmd.Length );

    // get response
    result = this.inStream.ReadLine ();

    if ( this.releaseConnection )
    {
      // close connection
      this.client.Close ();

      Console.WriteLine ( "connection closed: " + host + ":"
        + port );
    }

    ret = !result.Equals ( "BYE" );

    return ret;
  }
}
```

Finally, you need a client using the command processor. Call it *TCPHelloWorldClient*. The source code for Figure 5.25 is included on the CD in the file TCPHelloWorldClient.cs. It creates a *TCPCommandProcessor* instance for communicating with the server. Then, it sends the *GET* command and displays the result on the console. After that, it sends the *EXIT* command and closes the connection.

**Figure 5.25** *TCPHelloWorldClient* Listing in TCPHelloWorldClient.cs

```
using System;
using System.IO;
using System.Net.Sockets;


public class TCPHelloWorldClient
```

**Continued**

**Figure 5.25** Continued

```
{
  public static void Main ()
  {
    Console.WriteLine ( "initializing client..." );

    TCPRemoteCommandProcessor proc = new
        TCPRemoteCommandProcessor ( "127.0.0.1", 8080, false );

    string result;
    Console.WriteLine ( "requesting..." );
    proc.Execute ( "GET", ref result );
    Console.WriteLine ( "result: " + result );

    Console.WriteLine ( "closing connection..." );
    proc.Execute ( "EXIT", ref result );

    proc.Close ();

    Console.Write ( "press return to exit" );
    Console.ReadLine ();
  }
}
```

Now you can compile and run the example.

# Compiling and Running the Example

Go to the directory where you can find the files TCPHelloWorldServer.cs and
TCPHelloWorldClient.cs. For compiling, batch file exists called compile.bat.
Because we are using TCP for this example, you must start the server before the
client is running.

Now you can start the client by double-clicking on **TCPHelloWorldServer
.exe**. A Console window like the one shown in Figure 5.26 will appear.

Now you can start the client by double-clicking on **TCPHelloWorldClient
.exe**. Another Console window like Figure 5.27 will appear.

**Figure 5.26** Server Waiting for Client Connection

**Figure 5.27** Running Client

The server window now looks like Figure 5.28. Now you can stop both applications by pressing any key. The next section uses the same example using UDP as underlying transport protocol.

**Figure 5.28** Server after Doing Its Work

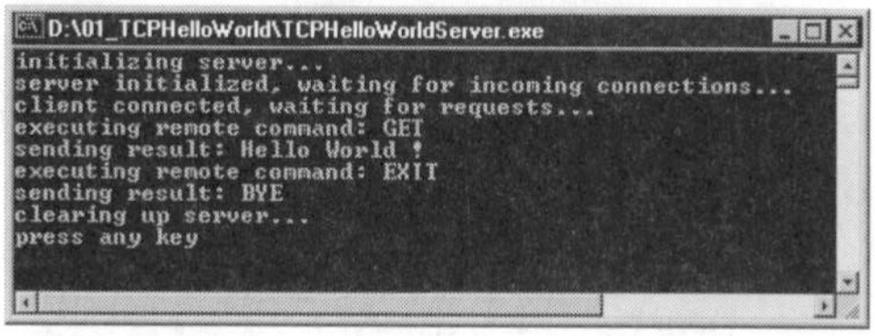

**NOTE**

Because you are using TCP, you must always start the server before the client begins trying to connect to the server.

# Example UDP Command Transmission and Processing

In this section, you rewrite the example from the section "Example TCP Command Transmission and Processing" for using UDP as the transport protocol.

Refer back to that section for the introduction to the architecture and the implemented communication protocol.

---

**NOTE**

As mentioned earlier, UDP is normally not used for request/response protocols like client/server command processing. This example is used for showing the differences in using UDP and TCP.

---

# General Usage of Needed .NET Classes

In contrast to TCP, in using UDP only one main network class is needed for this example. This is because the handling is like peer-to-peer (P2P). On both sides (client and server), we use **System.Net.Sockets.UdpClient**.

As a matter of principle, we can say a UDP client binds to a local port from which it receives data. Data is sent directly to another UDP client without connecting explicitly. That is what is meant by connection-less communication.

Generally, the code on both sides looks the same. A *UdpClient* is bound to a local port. Now it is ready to send and receive data. Because you bind the client to a local port only, you must use one *Send()* method that needs the remote host connection information. This information is used for sending the data to another UDP client. Because you bind the *UdpClient* to a local port, you receive data from this port, and you do not have to specify a receive point for the *Receive()* method. That is the reason why we use the *dummy* variable that is set to *null*.

```
// bind client to local port where it receives data
UdpClient client = new UdpClient ( 8081 );


// create a byte array containing the characters of
// the string "a request"
Byte[] request = System.Text.Encoding.ASCII.GetBytes (
  "a request".ToCharArray () );


// send request to the server
client.Send ( request, request.Length, "127.0.0.1", 8080 );
```

```
// create a dummy endpoint
IPEndPoint dummy = null;


// receive something from the server
byte[] response = client.Receive ( ref dummy );


// do something with the response


// unbind the client
client.Close ();
```

After having a look at the general use of the networking classes, let's move on to the second example.

## The Server

First, let's have a look at the server. The class is called *UDPHelloWorldServer* and is included on the CD in the file UDPHelloWorldServer.cs. The code does not differ very much from the code of the *TCPHelloWorldServer* class (see the section "Example TCP Command Transmission and Processing").

For simplification, the class also has a *Main()* method only. The initialization of the server is very simple. You just have to bind a *UdpClient* to a local port. The code of Figure 5.29 appears at the beginning of the *Main()* method.

**Figure 5.29** Server Initialization in UDPHelloWorldServer.cs

```
Console.WriteLine ( "initializing server" );


UdpClient server = new UdpClient ( 8080 );
```

Because UDP is a connection-less protocol, you cannot send back a response directly without the knowledge of where a request comes from. The header of a UDP datagram, among other things, contains the port where the sending socket is bound to (source port). On the IP layer, you can say the UDP datagram is embedded in an IP datagram. The header of the IP datagram contains the sender's IP address. But with C#, you cannot access this information with the simple API you use (at least with the Beta 2 of the .NET Framework). So the simplest way is to add the sender's information to a datagram if you want a receiver returning data. The syntax of command that will be sent to the server is as follows:

```
IP ADDRESS ":" PORT ":" COMMAND
```

where *IP ADDRESS* and *PORT* are the IP address and port of the sender. *COMMAND* is the command to execute. The server code for receiving a command is shown in Figure 5.30. After receiving the command string, it will be split into the parts described earlier.

**Figure 5.30** Receiving a Command in UDPHelloWorldServer.cs

```
// an endpoint is not needed the data will be sent
// to the port where the server is bound to
IPEndPoint dummy = null;


bool loop = true;
while ( loop )
{
  Console.WriteLine ( "waiting for request..." );


  byte[] tmp = server.Receive ( ref dummy );


  // split request string into parts, part1=client IP
  // address or DNS name, part2=client port, part3=command
  string dg =
    new System.Text.ASCIIEncoding ().GetString (
      datagram );
  string[] cmd = dg.Split ( new Char[] {':'} );
  string remoteClientHost = cmd[0];
  int remoteClientPort = Int32.Parse ( cmd[1] );
  string command = cmd[2];
  string result = null;


  // command execution
```

The command execution code is the same as in the *TCPHelloWorldServer* class. Also the result-sending code is similar to the code of the mentioned class (see Figure 5.31).

**Figure 5.31** Result Sending in UDPHelloWorldServer.cs

```
// convert data string to byte array
Byte[] d = System.Text.Encoding.ASCII.GetBytes (
  result.ToCharArray () );

// send result to the client
server.Send ( d, d.Length, remoteClientHost,
  remoteClientPort );
```

The shutdown code is also the same as the code you knew from *TCPHelloWorldServer*. Now let's have a look at the client.

## The Client

The client is called *UDPHelloWorldClient* and is included on the CD in the file UDPHelloWorldClient.cs. It is modified code from *TCPHelloWorldClient* with only one difference: the command processor and its instantiation. The command processor is called *UDPCommandProcessor*, and you can find it on the CD in the file Base.cs. Figure 5.32 shows the only different line of the code.

**Figure 5.32** Instantiation of the Command Processor in UDPHelloWorldClient.cs

```
UDPRemoteCommandProcessor proc = new
   UDPRemoteCommandProcessor ( 8081, "127.0.0.1", 8080 );
```

The parameter 8081 is the local port where the command processor is bound. The other two parameters of the constructor are the remote IP address and port of the server to which the command processor connects.

Now comes the command processor, called *UDPCommandProcessor*. Just like *TCPCommandProcessor*, this class has three methods: a constructor, a *Close()* method, and an *Execute()* method. First, let's have a look at the class fields (see Figure 5.33).

**Figure 5.33** Class Fields of *UDPCommandProcessor* in Base.cs

```
// the local port where the processor is bound to
private int localPort = -1;
```

**Continued**

**Figure 5.33** Continued

```
// the remote host
private string remoteHost = null;
// the remote port
private int remotePort = -1;
// communication interface
private UdpClient client = null;
```

The next stop is the constructor. It sets all class fields and binds the UDP client to a local port (see Figure 5.34).

**Figure 5.34** Constructor of *UDPRemoteCommandProcessor* in Base.cs

```
public UDPRemoteCommandProcessor ( int localPort,
   string remoteHost, int remotePort )
{
   // add parameter checking here

   this.localPort = localPort;
   this.remoteHost = remoteHost;
   this.remotePort = remotePort;

   this.client = new UdpClient ( localPort );
}
```

The *Close()* method is very simple. It calls the *Close()* method of the UDP client (see Figure 5.35).

**Figure 5.35** *Close()* Method of *UDPRemoteCommandProcessor* in Base.cs

```
public void Close ()
{
   this.client.Close ();
}
```

The *Execute()* method is very similar to the same named method of *TCPCommandProcessor*. You have a different handling in communication because of UDP. You need code for adding the local IP address and port to the command. Also, the sending and receiving of data is different. See Figure 5.36 for the UDP code.

**Figure 5.36** *Execute()* Method of *UDPRemoteCommandProcessor* in Base.cs

```
public bool Execute ( string command, ref string result )
{
  // add parameter checking here

  bool ret = true;

  Console.WriteLine ( "executing command: " + command );

  // build the request string
 string request = "127.0.0.1:" + this.localPort.ToString ()
   + ":" + command;

  Byte[] req = System.Text.Encoding.ASCII.GetBytes (
    request.ToCharArray () );

  client.Send ( req, req.Length, this.remoteHost,
    this.remotePort );

  // we don't need an endpoint
  IPEndPoint dummy = null;

  // receive datagram from server
  byte[] res = client.Receive ( ref dummy );
  result = System.Text.Encoding.ASCII.GetString ( res );

  ret = !result.Equals ( "BYE" );

  return ret;
}
```

# Compiling and Running the Example

Go to the directory where you can find the files UDPHelloWorldServer.cs and UDPHelloWorldClient.cs and start the compile.bat batch file.

Now, after successfully compiling all files, you are ready to run the example. Start the server by double-clicking on **UDPHelloWorldServer.exe** in Windows Explorer. A console window like the one shown in Figure 5.37 will appear.

**Figure 5.37** Server Waiting for Client Connection

Start the client by double-clicking on **UDPHelloWorldClient.exe**. Another console window like Figure 5.38 will appear.

**Figure 5.38** Running Client

The server window now looks like Figure 5.39.

**Figure 5.39** Server after Doing its Work

Now you can stop both applications by pressing any key. The next section discusses how to write a UDP multicasting application.

# Creating a News Ticker Using UDP Multicasting

A news ticker is an application where a news server sends messages to a number of clients. A client subscribes to the news server. From the moment of subscription, the client is allowed to receive new messages from the server.

You can implement implement such an architecture in several ways, but the easiest is using UDP multicasting. As described in the section "Introduction to UDP," with UDP, you can group applications (peers) together. An IP address together with a port is the alias for the group; that means a peer sends data to that IP address and port and all peers of that group will receive the data.

In this section, you will see how to develop a simple news ticker server and client. The server is a simple Windows Forms application with a text box and a button. The user types in the news in the text box. By clicking on the button, the server sends the news to the group (see Figure 5.40). The server must send news continuously so that a client can be started at any time for receiving the news.

**Figure 5.40** UDP Multicast News Server

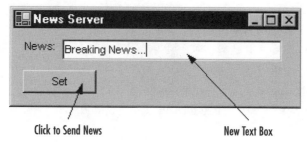

The client also is a simple Windows Forms application with only one text box. If news arrives, it will be displayed in the text box by shifting the text from the right to the left like a marquee (see Figure 5.41).

**Figure 5.41** UDP Multicast News Client

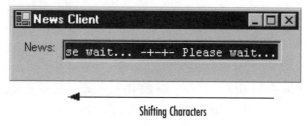

# General Usage of Needed .NET Classes

As you have seen with UDP, you need only one class: *System.Net.Sockets.UdpClient*. In addition to the methods discussed in the section "Example UDP Command Transmission and Processing," you can use the *UdpClient.JoinMulticastGroup()* method. This method registers a UDP peer to a multicast group.

The initialization of the news server and client is done by the same code. First, you bind a *UdpClient* to a local port. Then you register this client to a multicast group by calling its method *JoinMulticastGroup()*. This method gets the IP address of the group. Finally, you create an *IPEndPoint* to receive data from. As mentioned in the introduction, an *IPEndPoint* is the combination of an IP address and a port:

```
// create a peer bound to a local port
UdpClient peer = new UdpClient ( LOCAL_PORT );

// create the group IP address
IPAddress groupAddress = IPAddress.Parse ( GROUP_IP );

// add the peer to the group
peer.JoinMulticastGroup ( groupAddress );

// create an end point for sending data to the group
IPEndPoint groupEP = new IPEndPoint ( groupAddress,
  GROUP_PORT );
```

The code for sending and receiving is similar to the code in the section "Example UDP Command Transmission and Processing":

```
// send data to the group, d is a byte array
peer.Send ( d, d.Length, groupEP );

// receiving data from the group
IPEndPoint dummy = null;
byte[] d = peer.Receive ( ref dummy );
```

After having a look at the general use of the needed classes, let's go further into the news ticker example. Let's first have a look at a class that is used by the news client and news server. This class is called UDPPeer, and it is included on the CD in the file Base.cs. It represents a simplified interface to the *UdpClient* class.

The server can be driven in unicast or multicast mode. If the class is instantiated with the local port, only the unicast mode is active. If it is instantiated with an additional UDP multicast group IP address and port, multicast mode is used. The *Close()* method shuts down the server and the *Receive()* and *Send() methods* are used for receiving and sending data, respectively.

Let's now go more in detail and start with the class fields (see Figure 5.42).

**Figure 5.42** Class Fields of *UDPPeer* in Base.cs

```
// udp peer
private UdpClient server = null;
// multicast group IP address
private IPAddress groupAddress = null;
// multicast group endpoint (IP address and port)
private IPEndPoint group = null;
```

The *server* field is needed as a communication interface for unicasting and multicasting. The *groupAddress* and *group* fields are only needed in case of multicasting. The *groupAddress* field is the IP address of the UDP multicast group and *group* is the end point where the data is sent to.

The next is the unicast constructor (see Figure 5.43). It is very simple; it just binds the UDP peer to a local port.

**Figure 5.43** Unicast Constructor of *UDPPeer* in Base.cs

```
public UDPPeer ( int localPort )
{
  // add parameter checking here

  Console.WriteLine ( "initializing UDP server, port=" +
    localPort + "..." );

  this.server = new UdpClient ( localPort );

  Console.WriteLine ( "UDP server initialized" );
}
```

The multicast constructor calls the unicast constructor for binding the UDP peer to a local port and additionally registers the peer with the multicast group (see Figure 5.44). For registering an instance of *IPAddress* initialized with the group IP address is needed. This address is represented by the field *groupAddress*. The field *group* is an instance of the *IPEndPoint* class and is needed later for receiving data.

**Figure 5.44** Multicast Constructor of *UDPPeer* in Base.cs

```
public UDPPeer ( int localPort, string groupIP,
  int groupPort ) : this ( localPort )
{
  // add parameter checking here

  Console.WriteLine ( "adding UDP server to multicast " +
    "group, IP=" + groupIP + ", port=" + groupPort + "...");

  this.groupAddress = IPAddress.Parse ( groupIP );
  this.group = new IPEndPoint ( this.groupAddress,
    groupPort );

  this.server.JoinMulticastGroup ( this.groupAddress );

  Console.WriteLine ( "UDP server added to group" );
}
```

The *Close()* method is very simple. In case of multicasting, it deletes the peer from the multicast group. Finally, it calls the *Close()* method of *UdpClient* (see Figure 5.45).

**Figure 5.45** *Close()* Method of *UDPPeer* in Base.cs

```
public void Close ()
{
  if ( this.groupAddress != null )
    this.server.DropMulticastGroup ( this.groupAddress );

  this.server.Close ();
}
```

The *Receive()* method is a simple method that encapsulates the byte-array handling (see Figure 5.46). The received byte array is converted to a string, and it is returned to the caller of this method.

**Figure 5.46** *Receive()* Method of *UDPPeer* in Base.cs

```
public String Receive ()
{
   IPEndPoint dummy = null;

   // receive datagram
   byte[] data = this.peer.Receive ( ref dummy );

   return new System.Text.ASCIIEncoding ().GetString (
     data );
}
```

The *Send()* method is also simple. After converting the given string to a byte array, it calls the *Send()* method of the UDP peer (see Figure 5.47).

**Figure 5.47** *Send()* Method of *UDPPeer* in Base.cs

```
public void Send ( string message )
{
   // add parameter checking here

   Console.WriteLine ( "sending " + message + "..." );

   // convert news string to a byte array
   Byte[] d = System.Text.Encoding.ASCII.GetBytes (
     message.ToCharArray () );

   this.server.Send ( d, d.Length, this.group );

   Console.WriteLine ( "message sent" );
}
```

The next section discusses the UI of the news server.

# The Server

The *UDPPeer* class now makes it very easy to develop a simple user interface class for the news server. The class is named *UDPNewsServer* and is included on the CD in the file UDPNewsServer.cs.

The class has one constructor and three methods: an event handler for a window-closed event, an event handler for a button contained in the UI, and a method that is used by a thread for sending news continuously.

The news server class is derived from *System.Windows.Forms.Form*. Let's first have a look at the class fields, in Figure 5.48.

**Figure 5.48** Class fields of *UDPNewsServer* in UDPNewsServer.cs

```
// local port where the UDP server is bound to
private const int LOCAL_PORT = 8080;
// multicast group IP address
private const string GROUP_IP = "225.0.0.1";
// multicast group port
private const int GROUP_PORT = 8081;
// UDP server
private UDPPeer server = null;
// a thread for sending new continuously
private Thread serverThread = null;
// a data field for typing in a new message
private TextBox text = null;
// a button for setting the new message
private Button setButton = null;
// the news message
private string news = "";
```

Figure 5.49 shows the constructor code whereby the initialization of the UI components is not shown. If the Send button is clicked, the news server should update the news to be sent to the multicast group. In order to get notified by the button, register the *OnSet()* method with the button as a click event handler. The *OnClosed()* method is registered with the window for the *Closed* event. Finally, start a thread with the *Run()* method that continuously sends the news typed in the text field.

**Figure 5.49** Constructor of *UDPNewsServer* in UDPNewsServer.cs

```
public UDPNewsServer ()
{
  // UI components initialization

  // add an event listener for click-event
  this.setButton.Click += new System.EventHandler ( OnSet );

  // add an event listener for close-event
  this.Closed += new System.EventHandler ( OnClosed );

  // create communication components
  this.server = new UDPPeer ( LOCAL_PORT, GROUP_IP,
    GROUP_PORT );

  // start communication thread
  this.serverThread = new Thread (
    new ThreadStart ( Run ) );
  this.serverThread.Start ();

  Console.WriteLine ( "initialization complete" );
}
```

The thread is needed because the server must send the news continuously. Let's now have a look at the thread (see Figure 5.50). Every second it sends the content of the class field *news* to the multicast group and writes a message to the console that it is sending data. After sending, this method puts the thread to sleep for one second by calling the static method *Sleep()* of the *Thread* class. The value 1000 means one-thousand milliseconds—that is, one second. This call causes the current thread to sleep for the specified time.

**Figure 5.50** Sending Thread of *UDPNewsServer* in UDPNewsServer.cs

```
// sending thread
public void Run ()
{
  while ( true )
  {
    if ( !this.news.Equals ( "" ) )
    {
      Console.WriteLine ( "sending " + this.news );
      this.server.Send ( this.news );
    }

    // wait one second
    Thread.Sleep ( 1000 );
  }
}
```

The *news* field is set by the event handler that is registered for the click event of the Set button (see Figure 5.51).

**Figure 5.51** Button Event Handler of *UDPNewsHandler* in UDPNewsHandler.cs

```
// button click event handler
public void OnSet ( Object sender, EventArgs e )
{
  this.news = this.text.Text;
}
```

Finally, let's look at the shutdown code. It is placed in an event handler that is called if the form receives the *Closed* event. The method requests the sending thread to stop by calling its *Abort()* method and waits until it is dead. This is done with the call to the *Join()* method of the thread. After that, it calls the *Close()* method of the *UDPPeer* object. The code is shown in Figure 5.52.

**Figure 5.52** *OnClosed()* Method of *UDPNewsHandler* in UDPNewsHandler.cs

```
public void OnClosed ( Object sender, EventArgs e )
{
  Console.WriteLine ( "server shut down..." );

  // stop thread
  this.serverThread.Abort ();
  // wait until it's stopped
  this.serverThread.Join ();

  this.server.Close ();

  Application.Exit ();
}
```

# The Client

The client is also divided into two parts: a UDP multicast client class and a user interface. First, let's have a look at the client class. It is called *UDPMulticastClient* and is included on the CD in the file Base.cs.

In this example, you develop an asynchronous communication. An example for asynchronous communication is talking with a friend via e-mail or chat. You send a message to a friend and then you can do something else while you wait for the response. After a while, you receive your friend's answer and you are notified. Here in this example, *asynchronous* means that the client UI can be used while a thread in the background is waiting for incoming data. But the UI must be notified by the receiving thread if a message arrives. This is done by the thread calling a delegate that is implemented by the UI form. Figure 5.53 shows the architecture of the client.

The client is built of three main components; the UI, the ticker thread, and the receiving thread. The UI is a simple form with a text box. The ticker thread shifts the characters of the text box content by one position to left.

The receiving thread is implemented in *UDPMulticastClient* and is listening permanently for incoming messages. If a message arrives, it calls a *Notify()* delegate that is implemented as the *SetNews()* method in the UI. The *Notify()* delegate is shown in Figure 5.54. It is included on the CD in the file Base.cs. It acts a little bit like an event handler. If the thread receives a new message, it calls the delegate by passing the message to it. You will see this in the *UDPMulticastClient* class.

**Figure 5.53** Architecture of the News Client

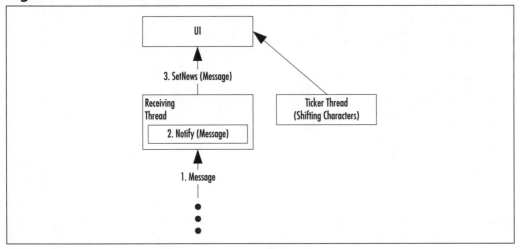

**Figure 5.54** The *Notify()* Delegate in Base.cs

```
public delegate void Notify ( string text );
```

**NOTE**

The *System.Net.Sockets.Socket* class implements an interface to the Windows sockets DLL. That means that not only the default Berkeley sockets are supported. You also find methods for asynchronous communication in this DLL and in the *Socket* class. For all methods like *Accept()* or *Receive()*, you'll find asynchronous methods like *BeginAccept()/ EndAccept()* or *BeginReceive()/EndReceive()*. For instance, *BeginAccept()* initiates the asynchronous wait for an incoming connection. Among others, this function takes a so-called *AsyncCallback*, which is a delegate that is called if a connection is accepted.

Now comes the *UDPMulticastClient* code. It has one constructor and two methods. The constructor initializes the UDP client that receives messages from the news server. The *Run()* method is used by a thread to listen for news, and the

*Close()* method shuts down the news client. We need at least three class fields: the notification delegate, the communication components, and a thread for asynchronous receiving of data (see Figure 5.55).

**Figure 5.55** Class Fields of *UDPMulticastClient* in Base.cs

```
// notification delegate
private Notify notify = null;
// communication interface
private UDPPeer peer = null;
// receiving thread
private Thread clientThread = null;
```

The constructor stores the notification delegate and initializes the UDP peer with the given group IP address and port. Finally, it starts the news receiving thread (see Figure 5.56).

**Figure 5.56** Constructor of *UDPMulticastClient* in Base.cs

```
public UDPMulticastClient ( string groupIP, int groupPort,
  Notify notify )
{
  // add parameter validation here

  Console.WriteLine ( "initializing UDP multicast " +
    "client, group=" + groupIP + ", port=" + groupPort +
    "..." );

  this.notify = notify;

  // create communication components
  this.client = new UDPPeer ( groupPort, groupIP,
    groupPort );

  // start listener thread
  this.clientThread = new Thread (
    new ThreadStart ( Run ) );
```

**Continued**

**Figure 5.56** Continued

```
    this.clientThread.Start ();

    Console.WriteLine ( "UDP multicast client initialized" );
}
```

The receiving thread is implemented by the *Run()* method. It is an endless loop that receives available data and gives it directly to the notification delegate (see Figure 5.57).

**Figure 5.57** Receiving Thread of *UDPMulticastClient* in Base.cs

```
public void Run ()
{
   while ( true )
      this.notify ( this.peer.Receive () );
}
```

The *Close()* method shuts down the client. It stops the receiving thread and calls the *Close()* method of its UDP peer (see Figure 5.58).

**Figure 5.58** *Close()* Method of *UDPMulticastClient* in Base.cs

```
public void Close ()
{
   this.clientThread.Abort ();
   this.clientThread.Join ();

   this.peer.Close ();
}
```

That's all there is to the UDP multicast client. Now let's look at the news client UI. The UI is a class derived from *System.Windows.Forms.Form*. It is called *UDPNewsClient* and contained on the CD in the file UDPNewsClient.cs. It simply contains a *TextBox*. The class also has one constructor and four methods. The constructor initializes the client application. Furthermore, it includes an event handler method called *OnClosed()* registered for the *Closed* event. Finally, there are the methods *RunTicker()* for shifting the characters in the text field and the *SetNews()* method. *SetNews()* implements the *Notify()* delegate and is used by the listener thread of *UDPMulticastClient* to update the news text field. First, consider the class fields shown in Figure 5.59.

**Figure 5.59** Class Fields of *UDPNewsClient* in UDPNewsClient.cs

```
// multicast group IP address
private const string GROUP_IP = "225.0.0.1";
// multicast group port
private const int GROUP_PORT = 8081;
// communication interface
private UDPMulticastClient client = null;
// ticker thread
private Thread tickerThread = null;
// new messages
private TextBox text = null;
// default news displayed at the beginning
private string news = "Please wait...";
```

The constructor initializes the *TextBox*, event handler, UDP peer, and ticker thread. Figure 5.60 shows the constructor without *TextBox* initialization.

**Figure 5.60** Constructor of *UDPNewsClient* in UDPNewsClient.cs

```
public UDPNewsClient ()
{
  // initialize UI


  // add an event listener for close-event
  this.Closed += new System.EventHandler ( OnClosed );


  // start communication thread
  this.client = new UDPMulticastClient ( GROUP_IP,
    GROUP_PORT, new Notify ( SetNews ) );


  // start ticker thread
```

*Continued*

**Figure 5.60** Continued

```
    this.tickerThread = new Thread (
       new ThreadStart ( RunTicker ) );
    this.tickerThread.Start ();


    Console.WriteLine ( "initialization complete" );
 }
```

The news client shutdown method called by the *Closed* event is shown in Figure 5.61. It closes the client and stops the ticker thread.

**Figure 5.61** Event Handler for *Closed* Event in UDPNewsClient.cs

```
public void OnClosed ( Object sender, EventArgs e )
{
   Console.WriteLine ( "client shut down" );


   this.client.Close ();


   this.tickerThread.Abort ();
   this.tickerThread.Join ();


   Application.Exit ();
 }
```

The ticker thread shifts—every 500 milliseconds—one character of the news string into the text box on the right and deletes one on the left. The implementation is not very smart, but for a simulation it is enough. Figure 5.62 also shows the notification method. It simply sets the message received by the multicast client to the news variable.

**Figure 5.62** Ticker Thread and Notification Method in UDPNewsClient.cs

```
public void RunTicker ()
{
   // initialze the textbox with the default text
   this.text.Text = " -+-+- " + this.news + " -+-+- " +
```

**Continued**

**Figure 5.62** Continued

```
    this.news + " -+-+- ";

  while ( true )
  {
    string data = this.news + " -+-+- ";

    // repeat as long as there are characters in the data string
    while ( !data.Equals ( "" ) )
    {
      // wait 500 milliseconds
      Thread.Sleep ( 500 );

      // remove the first character from the text field and add the
      // first character of the data string
      this.text.Text = this.text.Text.Substring ( 1 ) +
        data[0];

      // remove the first character from the data string
      data = data.Substring ( 1 );
    }
  }
}


// notification method, used by multicast client
public void SetNews ( string news )
{
  this.news = news;
}
```

You now have everything you need to compile and run the example.

# Compiling and Running the Example

Go to the directory where you can find the files UDPNewsClient.cs and UDPNewsClient.cs. Start the compile.bat batch file. After successful compiling, double-click UDPNewsClient.exe. A form like Figure 5.63 appears.

Note that the server must not be started first. This is because UDP is connection-less, that is, the client does not have to connect to the server. If the server sends data to the UDP multicast group, the clients simply receive the data.

**Figure 5.63** UDP News Client Form

To start the server, open a new console and type in **UDPNewsServer** or double-click on **UDPNewsServer.exe**. After typing in some news, the server form may looks like Figure 5.64.

**Figure 5.64** UDP New Server Form

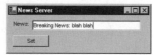

Now, click **Set**, and after a short period, your client looks like Figure 5.65.

**Figure 5.65** UDP News Client Receiving News

In the next section, you will develop a client/server chat application combining TCP and UDP technologies.

# Creating a UDP Client Server Chat Application

For users, a chat application seems to be a classic P2P application. You send a message to the chat room, and all users that take part at the chat receive the message. So far, you have learned something about the client/server protocol TCP, about the P2P (unicasting), and also peer-to-group (multicasting) protocol UDP.

So for a chat application, the UDP multicasting seems to be the best choice (okay, it is the simplest!). You can develop a UDP multicast peer, send this to your friends, and give them a common IP address to connect. You can send messages to this address and all friends that are connected receive these messages—a very simple but effective chat application.

Let's do something a little different to show a technique of other applications like Web servers. The result will be an application that guarantees a reliable delivery of the messages from a chat client to a chat server. The server will be a TCP server. You will see how the server can handle more than one client at the same time on the same port. This is like a Web server that responds to many requests at the same time on the standard HTTP port 80. Then, the server sends the messages via UDP to all connected chat clients.

Figure 5.66 shows the three phases from the client's connect request to client/ server communication:

- **Connect** The client connects to the server via TCP.
- **Create thread** The server creates a server thread for the client.
- **Communication/listen for new connection** The client communi- cates with the server thread. At the same time, the server listens for new connections.

**Figure 5.66** The Three Phases from Connection Request to Communication

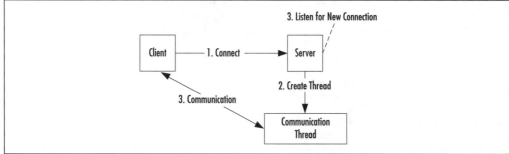

More interesting than listening for new connections while communicating is that the server can communicate with more than one client at the same time. This can happen at the same port. So a server is not restricted to "only" 65,536 connections. Theoretically the number of concurrent connections is unlimited. In reality, the number of concurrent connections depends on various conditions— for simplicity, this example focuses on the technique that builds the base for han- dling concurrent connections.

You will reuse most of the classes you developed until now. On the client side, you use *TCPCommandProcessor* for communicating with the chat server and *UDPMulticastClient* for receiving messages from the server that were sent by other clients. On the server side, you use *UDPPeer* for sending chat messages received from the clients.

For handling multiple client connections, you will develop two new classes. The *TCPServer* class will be the class that listens for incoming client connections. If a connection is accepted, *TCPServer* creates an instance of *TCPServerSession* that handles the communication with the client. This instance will be driven by a thread. *TCPServerSession* will receive the chat protocol commands from the *TCPCommandProcessor* on the client side. The commands will be given to a command processor object that implements the interface *CommandProcessor*, correspondingly, they are given to a method of this object that implements the delegate *ExecuteCommand*. This method interprets the commands and sends the containing message to the chat members. Figure 5.67 shows a UML-like sequence diagram that describes this behavior.

**Figure 5.67** UML-Like Sequence Diagram of the Chat Client/Server Behavior

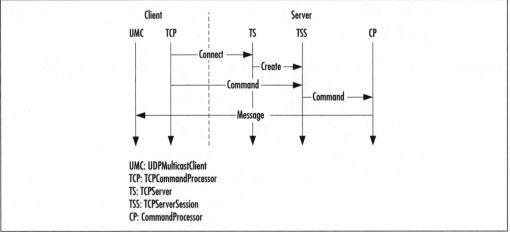

All mentioned classes, including the new ones, are contained on the CD in the file Base.cs. Let's start with the delegate *ExecuteCommand()* (see Figure 5.68). It has the same signature as the *Execute()* method of the interface *CommandProcessor* and is used to access this method of *CommandProcessor* implementing instances.

**Figure 5.68** The Delegate *ExecuteCommand()*

```
public delegate bool ExecuteCommand ( string command,
    ref string result );
```

## The *TCPServerSession* Class

This class has a constructor for initializing the server session and two methods. The *Close()* method shuts down the session and *Run()* listens for incoming commands. Let's start with the class fields of *TCPServerSession* (see Figure 5.69).

**Figure 5.69** Class Fields of *TCPServerSession* in Base.cs

```
// command processor
private ExecuteCommand executeCommand = null;
// communication interface
private Socket socket = null;
// open flag
private bool open = false;
```

The constructor gets a socket for listening for and responding to requests. It also gets an *ExecuteCommand()* delegate for executing incoming commands.

```
public TCPServerSession ( Socket socket,
    ExecuteCommand executeCommand )
{
    this.socket = socket;
    this.executeCommand = executeCommand;
    this.open = true;
}
public void Close ()
{
    // session closing
    ...
}
```

```
public void Run ()

{

  // command execution

  ...

}

}
```

The constructor gets the socket and an *ExecuteCommand* delegate. The socket represents the connection to the client. Behind the delegate is a command processor that executes the incoming commands.

Figure 5.70 shows the *Run()* method. It reads—in a loop—a command from the client. The command is given to the *ExecuteCommand* delegate that returns a result. The result is returned to the client. These steps are repeated as long as the delegate returns false or the *Close()* method was called.

**Figure 5.70** *Run()* Method of *TCPServerSession* in Base.cs

```
public void Run ()

{

  NetworkStream ns = new NetworkStream ( this.socket );

  StreamReader reader = new StreamReader ( ns );


  bool loop = this.open;

  while ( loop )

  {

    if ( ns.DataAvailable )

    {

      // read command from client

      string cmd = reader.ReadLine ();

      string result = "";


      // execute command

      loop = this.executeCommand ( cmd, ref result );


      Console.WriteLine ( "sending result, result=" + result );


      result += "\r\n";
```

**Continued**

**Figure 5.70** Continued

```
        Byte[] res = System.Text.Encoding.ASCII.GetBytes (
          result.ToCharArray () );

        // return result to client
        this.socket.Send ( res );

        Console.WriteLine ( "result sent" );
      }

      // repeat until executeCommand() returns false or
      // server session is closed
      loop = loop && this.open;
    }

  Close ();
}
```

The *Close()* method clears the open flag and closes the connection to the client (see Figure 5.71). If the thread is still running, the cleared open flag causes the *Run()* method to terminate.

**Figure 5.71** *Close()* Method of *TCPServerSession* in Base.cs

```
public void Close ()
{
  if ( this.open )
  {
    Console.WriteLine ( "TCP session is closing..." );

    this.open = false;

    this.socket.Close ();
```

**Continued**

**Figure 5.71** Continued

```
       Console.WriteLine ( "TCP session closed" );
   }
 }
```

# The *TCPServer* Class

The next class is *TCPServer*. As the name implies, it implements a simple TCP server. It can handle multiple clients by using a session for each client. The sessions are instances of *TCPServerSession*. *TCPServer* contains a constructor and two methods. The constructor initializes the server. The *Close()* method shuts down the server and *Run()* listens for incoming connection requests. Furthermore, *Run()* starts a session for each connected client. First, Figure 5.72 shows the class fields of *TCPServer*.

**Figure 5.72** Class Fields of *TCPServer* in Base.cs

```
// sessions list
private ArrayList sessions = null;
// session threads list
private ArrayList sessionThreads = null;
// command processor
private ExecuteCommand executeCommand = null;
// connection listener
private TcpListener listener = null;
// server thread
private Thread server = null;
// open flag
private bool open = false;
```

Figure 5.73 shows the constructor.

**Figure 5.73** Constructor of *TCPServer* in Base.cs

```
public TCPServer ( int port, ExecuteCommand executeCommand )
{
```

**Continued**

**Figure 5.73** Continued

```
    this.sessions = new ArrayList ();
    this.sessionThreads = new ArrayList ();

    this.executeCommand = executeCommand;

    Console.WriteLine ( "initializing TCP server..." );

    Console.WriteLine ( "creating listener..." );
    this.listener = new TcpListener ( port );

    Console.WriteLine ( "starting listener..." );
    this.listener.Start ();

    this.open = true;

    this.server = new Thread ( new ThreadStart ( Run ) );
    this.server.Start ();

    Console.WriteLine ( "TCP server initialization complete, port=" +
        port );
}
```

First, it creates two instances of *ArrayList*. The first is the class field *sessions* that contains all sessions. The second one is a list of the session threads and is represented by the class field *sessionThreads*. This list is needed for shutting down the session threads. This will be done by the *Close()* method. Furthermore, the constructor creates a listener that listens on the given port for incoming client connection requests. The other parameter is a delegate that implements a command processor. This delegate instance will be given to each started session for command execution. Finally, the constructor starts a thread for listening on incoming connections and starting a session for each connection. The thread runs the *Run()* method (see Figure 5.74).

**Figure 5.74** *Run()* Method of *TCPServer* in Base.cs

```
public void Run ()
{
  while ( this.open )
  {
    Console.WriteLine ( "listening for incomming connections..." );

    // wait for incoming client connection requests
    Socket s = this.listener.AcceptSocket ();
    if ( s.Connected )
    {
      Console.WriteLine ( "client connected, starting client " +
        "session..." );

      // create a client session
      TCPServerSession session = new TCPServerSession ( s,
        this.executeCommand );
      // add it to the session list
      this.sessions.Add ( session );

      // create a thread for the session
      Thread th = new Thread ( new ThreadStart ( session.Run ) );
      // start it
      th.Start ();
      // add it to the session thread list
      this.sessionThreads.Add ( th );
    }
  }
}
```

The *Run()* method listens for incoming connections. If the method receives a connection request, a session is started with the accepted socket and the command processor delegate. This is repeated as long as the open flag is set. If the open flag is cleared by the *Close()* method, the loop terminates (see Figure 5.75).

**Figure 5.75** *Close()* Method of *TCPServer* in Base.cs

```
public void Close ()
{
  Console.WriteLine ( "TCP server is closing..." );

  if ( this.open )
  {
    this.open = false;

    // stop listner
    this.listener.Stop ();

    // stop server thread
    this.server.Abort ();
    this.server.Join ();

    // stop all session threads and close the sessions
    while ( this.sessions.Count > 0 )
    {
      // stop session thread
      Thread th = (Thread)this.sessionThreads[0];
      th.Abort ();
      th.Join ();
      this.sessionThreads.Remove ( th );

      // close session
      TCPServerSession s = (TCPServerSession)this.sessions[0];
      s.Close ();
      this.sessions.Remove ( s );
    }
  }

  Console.WriteLine ( "TCP server closed" );
}
```

The *Close()* method stops the listener and the server thread that listens for incoming connections. Then, each session thread is stopped, and the suitable session is closed.

## The Chat Protocol

Here, you will implement three commands: *HELLO*, *SAY*, and *BYE*. The general syntax of a command line is as follows:

```
user_name ":" command [ ":" message ] CRLF
```

That syntax means a line contains the username that sends the command line followed by the actual command. An optional message may follow the command. The message is part of the command line if the command is *SAY*. A carriage return/linefeed terminates the line. The following is a sample communication between a client *c* and a server *s*:

```
c:  <user_name>:HELLO<CRLF>

s:  HELLO<CRLF>

    (sends via UDP multicast "<user_name> has joined the chat room")

c:  <user_name>:SAY:<message><CRLF>

s:  OK<CRLF>

    (sends via UDP multicast "<user_name>:  <message>")

c:  <user_name>:BYE<CRLF>

s:  BYE<CRLF>

    (sends via UDP multicast "<user_name> has left the chat room")
```

You now can describe the chat server class and client class. Let's start with the chat server.

## The *ChatServer* Class

This class is contained on the CD in the file ChatServer.cs. For simplification, the chat command processor is contained in the user interfaces classes. User interface is not a correct name; it is a simple console application without any user interaction. Because all functionality is contained in the classes described earlier, the server is very simple. It implements the *CommandProcessor* interface and has only three methods: a constructor, a *Close()*, and an *Execute()* method. Figure 5.76 shows the class fields of the *ChatServer* class.

**Figure 5.76** Class Fields of the *ChatServer* Class in ChatServer.cs

```
// listening port for incoming connection requests
private const int TCP_PORT = 8080;
// local port for the UDP peer for sending new messages
private const int UDP_LOCAL_PORT = 8081;
// multicast group IP address
private const string UDP_GROUP_IP = "224.0.0.1";
// multicast group port
private const int UDP_GROUP_PORT = 8082;
// TCP server for incoming connection requests
private TCPServer tcpServer = null;
// UDP peer for sending new messages
private UDPPeer udpPeer = null;
// list of currently connected users
private ArrayList users = null;
```

Now let's have a look at the constructor (see Figure 5.77). First, it creates the currently connected users list. Then the constructor starts the TCP server and the UDP peer.

**Figure 5.77** Constructor of *ChatServer* in ChatServer.cs

```
public ChatServer ()
{
  this.users = new ArrayList ();

  this.tcpServer = new TCPServer ( TCP_PORT,
    new ExecuteCommand ( Execute ) );
  this.udpPeer = new UDPPeer ( UDP_LOCAL_PORT, UDP_GROUP_IP,
    UDP_GROUP_PORT );
}
```

The next method is the *Close()* method (see Figure 5.78). It simply shuts down the UDP peer and TCP server by calling their *Close()* methods.

**Figure 5.78** *Close()* method of *ChatServer* in ChatServer.cs

```
public void Close ()
{
   this.udpPeer.Close ();
   this.tcpServer.Close ();
}
```

The command execution is determined by the chat protocol. A user can send messages to others only if the *HELLO* command was sent before. If the server receives that command, the username is added to the connected users list. Now if the server receives the *SAY* command from that user, it sends the message to the UDP multicast group. If a user wants to leave the chat room, it simply sends the *BYE* command. The server now removes the user form the user list and suppresses all possible *SAY* commands from that user. Figure 5.79 shows the *Execute()* method.

**Figure 5.79** *Execute()* Method of *ChatServer* in ChatServer.cs

```
public bool Execute ( string command, ref string result )
{
   bool ret = true;

   Console.WriteLine ( "executing command: " + command );

   // split the command into parts
   string[] cmd = command.Split ( new Char[] {':'} );
   string user = cmd[0];
   string operation = cmd[1];
   string message = null;

   // if the command string contains more than two ':' concatenate the
   // splitted rest, this may happen if the message contains ':'
   if ( cmd.Length > 2 )
   {
      message = cmd[2];
      for ( int i = 3; i < cmd.Length; i++ )
```

**Continued**

**Figure 5.79** Continued

```
      message += cmd[i];
}


// execute the command
switch ( operation )
{
  // user enters the chat room
  case "HELLO":
    if ( !this.users.Contains ( user ) )
    {
      result = "HELLO";


      // add user to currently connected users list
      this.users.Add ( user );


      // send message to all users
      this.udpPeer.Send ( user + " has joined the chat room" );
    }
    break;


  // user sent message to the chat room
  case "SAY":
    // execute only if user is currently connected
    if ( this.users.Contains ( user ) && ( message != null ) )
    {
      result = "OK";


      // send message to all users
      this.udpPeer.Send ( user + ": " + message );
    }
    break;


  // user disconnects from chat room
```

*Continued*

**Figure 5.79** Continued

```
        case "BYE":
          // execute only if user is currently connected
          if ( this.users.Contains ( user ) )
          {
            result = "BYE";

            // remove user from currently connected users list
            this.users.Remove ( user );

            // send message to all users
            this.udpPeer.Send ( user + " has left the chat room" );
          }
          break;

        // unknown command, return an error
        default:
          result = "ERROR";
          break;
    }

    return ret;
}
```

## SECURITY ALERT

A client can track all chat room messages if it knows the group IP address and port. It doesn't have to be connected with the *HELLO* command. The server's user administration takes care that unconnected users do not send messages to the chat room.

# The *ChatClient* Class

This class is contained on the CD in the file ChatClient.cs. For simplification, the client chat functionality is contained in the user interfaces classes. Here we have a Windows Forms application (see Figure 5.80).

**Figure 5.80** The Chat Client Form

Let's go through a small chat session. Assume that the chat server and client are still running. Type in a name to the **Name** data field. After clicking **Connect**, the code of its click event handler is executed (see Figure 5.81). This event handler is the *OnConnect()* method.

**Figure 5.81** *OnConnect()* Event Handler of the *ChatClient* Class in ChatClient.cs

```
public void OnConnect ( Object sender, EventArgs e )
{
    this.proc = new TCPRemoteCommandProcessor ( "127.0.0.1", TCP_PORT,
        true );


    string result = null;
    this.proc.Execute ( this.name.Text + ":HELLO", ref result );


    this.connected = result.Equals ( "HELLO" );


    // enable or disable controls on connection status
}
```

The class field *proc* is the command processor that sends commands to the chat server. After creating an instance of *TCPCommandProcessor*, the *HELLO* command is sent to the server. If the result of the command is *HELLO*, the connected flag is set. Now you can type a message into the **Message** data field. After clicking **Send**, the *OnSend()* method is called. This method is the click event handler of the Send button (see Figure 5.82).

**Figure 5.82** *OnSend()* Event Handler of the *ChatClient* Class in ChatClient.cs

```
public void OnSend ( Object sender, EventArgs e )
{
  string result = null;
  this.proc.Execute ( this.name.Text + ":SAY:" + this.message.Text,
    ref result );
}
```

The message is sent within a *SAY* command to the server. Before you get a look at the message-receiving code, let's discuss the disconnect code. The *OnDisconnect()* method is the click event handler of the Disconnect button (see Figure 5.83).

**Figure 5.83** *OnDisconnect()* Event Handler of the *ChatClient* Class in ChatClient.cs

```
public void OnDisconnect ( Object sender, EventArgs e )
{
  if ( this.connected )
  {
    string result = null;
    this.proc.Execute ( this.name.Text + ":BYE", ref result );

    this.proc.Close ();

    this.connected = false;

    // enable or disable controls on connection status
  }
}
```

For disconnecting, first the *BYE* command is sent. After that, the command processor will be closed and the connected flag will be cleared.

For receiving messages from the chat server, you use an instance of the *UDPMulticastClient* class. As you have seen in the section "Creating a News Ticker Using UDP Multicasting," the constructor of *UDPMulticastClient* needs a *Notify* delegate. This delegate will be initialized with the *SetMessage()* method of *ChatClient*. The instantiation of the multicast client is done by the constructor of the *ChatClient* class. (see Figure 5.84). A closed event handler for the form is registered here also.

**Figure 5.84** Constructor of *ChatClient* in ChatClient.cs

```
public ChatClient ()
{
  // create controls


  // add an event listener for close-event
  this.Closed += new EventHandler ( OnClosed );


  // create communication components
  this.group = new UDPMulticastClient ( UDP_GROUP_IP, UDP_GROUP_PORT,
    new Notify ( SetMessage ) );
}
```

As a result of receiving a message from the chat server, the *SetMessage()* method is called by the multicast client instance. The method simply concatenates the given string to the text in the multiline data field that shows the messages (see Figure 5.85).

**Figure 5.85** *SetMessage()* Method of *ChatClient* in ChatClient.cs

```
public void SetMessage ( string text )
{
  if ( !this.messages.Text.Equals ( "" ) )
    this.messages.Text += "\r\n";
  this.messages.Text += text;
}
```

Finally, we have a look at the *OnClosed()* method of the form. This method is registered to the form as a closed event handler. If the window is closed, the code is executed (see Figure 5.86).

**Figure 5.86** *OnClosed()* Method of *ChatClient* in ChatClient.cs

```
public void OnClosed ( Object sender, EventArgs e )
{
    OnDisconnect ( null, null );


    this.group.Close ();
}
```

First, the *OnDisconnect()* method is called for disconnecting the command processor if the Disconnect button wasn't clicked before. Then the multicast client is closed. Now you can compile and run your example.

# Compiling and Running the Example

Please go to the directory on the CD where you can find the files ChatServer.cs and ChatClient.cs. Start the batch file compile.bat to compile the example. After successful compiling, start the batch file run.bat. A server and a client is started. Now you can start a chat session as described in this section. Figure 5.87 shows the chat client after finishing a very short chat session. Figure 5.88 shows the chat server after the mentioned session.

**Figure 5.87** Chat Client after a Short Chat Session

**Figure 5.88** Chat Server after a Short Chat Session

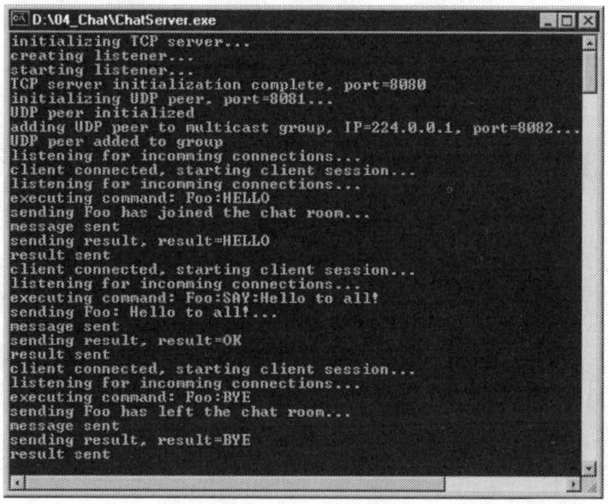

The next section shows one way you can implement a file sharing peer with .NET.

# Creating a TCP P2P File Sharing Application

The concept of peer-to-peer (P2P) is becoming more and more important in networks, and P2P Internet applications such as Napster and Gnutella are widely popular. But what exactly is a peer-to-peer application?

Well, first consider client/server applications, the most common model for communication today. A client requests or posts data to or from a server. The client knows how to request or post data and the server knows how to respond. For instance, a Web server listens for incoming connections until a browser requests a page. The Web server reacts only to browsers; it cannot arbitrarily contact a browser. Any communication is initiated by a client.

In P2P communication, on the other hand, all applications act as clients and servers at the same time. When peer A requests data from peer B, A acts like a client and B as a server. However, B can also request data from A, so B acts as a client and A as a server. Every peer adds a bigger amount of value to network. Furthermore, no centralized server is needed, which decreases the effort needed in administrating the data. Another advantage is that if a peer is down, only a small portion of data is unavailable.

This model does require additional functionality from the peer application. First, a peer must be able to find other peers. This is called *discovery*. There are different strategies for discovery. So-called pure P2P applications can discover other peers directly. Another approach is to have discovery servers where peers are registering if they are online. A peer searching for another peer requests the connection information from the discovery server.

Another key functionality of P2P networks is the so-called *content lookup*. A peer must be able to find data contained in the network. A pure P2P application can directly query the network for data. A second approach is the existence of a lookup server. Peers send information about their data to the lookup server. For instance, for file sharing peers, this information can be filename, length, type, and descriptions about file content. Another possible server is a content server. Peers upload their files to this server. Then a peer can download the files from this server.

In this section, you create a simplified P2P file sharing application with reduced functionality. The peer can upload or download files from another peer only. No discovery or lookup functionality is contained in this peer.

You may think that UDP is the best way to implement such a peer. Indeed this is how some remote file access systems are implemented. As mentioned, the advantage of UDP is the performance. However, you would have to implement a method that guarantees the correct order of the datagrams sent between the peers, so you'll use another way to implement the peer.

For the remote functionality, you develop a remote file stream that works in principle like CORBA, remoting, or RMI—because we're discussing .NET, we use the term *remoting*.

Generally speaking, all remote object architectures work in the same way. A remote object is divided into two parts. On the client side is a proxy object. The actual object functionality is implemented on the server side. For communication between the proxy and the server object, SOAP is used. Figure 5.89 shows this very simplified remoting architecture.

**Figure 5.89** Very Simplified Remoting Architecture

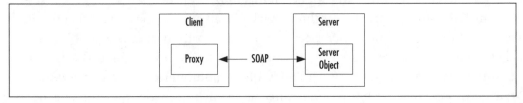

A proxy object acts like a normal object. The application using that object doesn't notice anything about the remote activity (except maybe a lower performance while executing object methods). Every method call to the proxy object leads to a protocol request to the server object. The parameters of the method must be serialized for sending. At the server side, the server object executes the called method with the deserialized data and returns a result as a response to the client request. This response also is serialized by the server object and deserialized at the client side. Now the client object returns the result as a normal object.

Based on this architecture, you develop a similar one. Your proxy server object is an instance of a class called *RemoteFileStreamProxy* and *RemoteFileStreamServer* respectively. Both classes are contained on the CD in the file Base.cs. Because a peer is both a client and a server, your peer class *FileSharingPeer* uses both remote file classes. The FileSharingPeer class is also contained on the CD in the file Base.cs. Figure 5.90 shows the architecture of our example.

**Figure 5.90** Architecture of File Sharing Peer Example

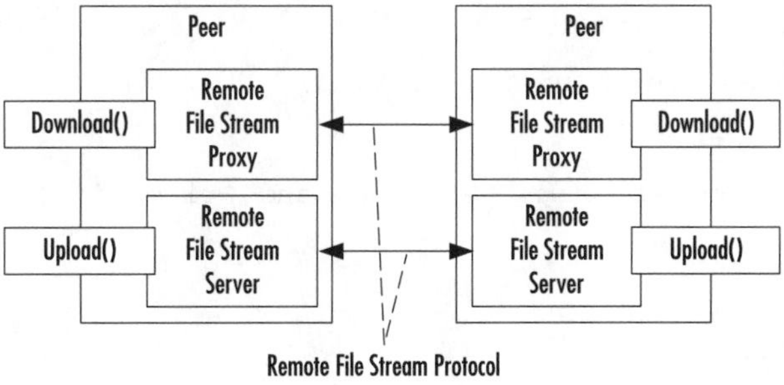

## The Remote File Stream Protocol

Let's start with the protocol between the proxy and the server. The commands of the protocol reflect the most important methods of a stream:

- **OPEN** Reflects the proxy object instantiating.
- **READ** Sent if the Read() method of the proxy is called.
- **WRITE** Sent if the Write() method of the proxy is called.
- **CLOSE** Sent if the *Close()* method of the proxy is called.

Now let's look at some example communications. Here we describe the communication between the proxy and the server class. The proxy requests are marked with *c:* and the server responses with *s:*.

Let's first have a look at a download scenario. The proxy calls the server for reading from a file:

```
c: OPEN:<file_name>:true<CRLF>
s: (opens the file <file_name> for reading and returns the file length
    of <file_name>)
c: READ:<count><CRLF>
s: (returns max. <count> bytes of the file <file_name>)
c: CLOSE<CRLF>
s: (closes connection)
```

If <count> is bigger than the file length, only the contained bytes of the file are sent. On the other hand, if <count> is less than the file length, the *READ* command will be repeated as long as the end of the file is reached.

The next example shows an upload scenario. The proxy calls the server for writing to a file:

```
c: OPEN:<file_name>:false<CRLF>
s: (opens the file <file_name> for writing)
c: WRITE:<count><CRLF>
s: (reads <count> bytes from the client and writes it to the file
    <file_name>)
c: CLOSE<CRLF>
s: (closes connection)
```

If <count> is less than the client's file length, the *WRITE* command will be repeated as long as the end of the file is reached.

## The *RemoteFileStreamServer* Class

This class is used by a thread and has only two methods: a constructor and the *Run()* method. Additionally, it has a private class field *client* of the type *System.Net.Sockets.NetworkStream*. The constructor initializes only the *client* field (see Figure 5.91).

**Figure 5.91** Constructor of *RemoteFileStreamServer* in Base.cs

```
public RemoteFileStreamServer ( Socket socket )
{
  Console.WriteLine ( "initializing remote filestream server..." );
```

**Continued**

**Figure 5.91** Continued

```
    this.client = new NetworkStream ( socket );

    Console.WriteLine ( "remote filestream server initialized" );
}
```

As you will see later, the socket comes from a connection request from a *RemoteFileStreamProxy* instance.

The *Run()* method is used by a thread that runs as long as the connected *RemoteFileStreamProxy* instance closes the connection. In a loop, all protocol request commands are handled. Figure 5.92 shows a snippet of the *Run()* method. For clarity, we first show the method frame without command processing.

First, a *StreamReader* is created for easier access to CRLF-terminated command lines from the proxy class. Then the method reads command lines in an endless loop. After reading a line, it is split into the parts described in the protocol section above. Now the parts are processed in the command processing.

**Figure 5.92** Snippet of the *Run()* Method of *RemoteFileStreamServer* in Base.cs

```
public void Run ()
{
    Console.WriteLine ( "starting remote filestream server..." );

    StreamReader cmdIn = new StreamReader ( this.client );

    FileStream f = null;

    int count = -1;
    byte[] buffer = null;

    bool loop = true;
    while ( loop )
    {
        // read the request line
        string[] buf = cmdIn.ReadLine ().Split ( new Char[] {':'} );
```

**Continued**

**Figure 5.92** Continued

```
    Console.WriteLine ( "request received, req=" + buf[0] );


    // buf[0] is the command
    switch ( buf[0] )
    {
        // command processing
        ...
    }


    Console.WriteLine ( "request executed, req=" + buf[0] );
}


Console.WriteLine ( "stopping remote filestream server..." );
}
```

Have a look at the *OPEN* command processing (see Figure 5.93). On the *OPEN* command, the server opens a local file. The file mode, reading or writing, depends on the read flag—true means reading and false means writing. If the file is opened for reading, the server returns the number of bytes of the file.

**Figure 5.93** *OPEN* Command Processing of *RemoteFileStreamServer* in *Base.cs*

```
    case "OPEN":
        // the name of the local file to open
        string file = buf[1];


        // open for reading or writing
        bool read = bool.Parse ( buf[2] );


        // open the local file
        f = new FileStream ( ".\\" +
            ( read ? "download" : "destination" ) + "\\" + file,
            ( read ? FileMode.Open : FileMode.Create ) );
```

**Continued**

**Figure 5.93** Continued

```
        // return the file length to client
        if ( read )
        {
          string length = f.Length.ToString () + "\r\n";
          Byte[] l = System.Text.Encoding.ASCII.GetBytes (
            length.ToCharArray () );
          this.client.Write ( l, 0, l.Length );
        }
        break;
```

On the *READ* command, the server reads the requested number of bytes from the local file and returns it to the client (see Figure 5.94).

**Figure 5.94** *READ* Command Processing of *RemoteFileStreamServer* in Base.cs

```
      case "READ":
        // number of bytes to read
        count = int.Parse ( buf[1] );

        // read/write buffer
        buffer = new byte[count];

        // read from the local file
        count = f.Read ( buffer, 0, count );

        // return the bytes to the client
        this.client.Write ( buffer, 0, count );
        break;
```

On the *WRITE* command, the server reads the requested number of bytes from the client and writes it to the local file (see Figure 5.95).

**Figure 5.95** *WRITE* Command Processing of *RemoteFileStreamServer* in Base.cs

```
case "WRITE":
  // number of bytes to write
  count = int.Parse ( buf[1] );

  // read/write buffer
  buffer = new byte[count];

  // read bytes from the client
  count = this.client.Read ( buffer, 0, count );

  // write bytes to the local file
  f.Write ( buffer, 0, count );
  break;
```

On the *CLOSE* command, the server closes the local file and the connection to the client. The loop terminates and the so does the thread (see Figure 5.96).

**Figure 5.96** *CLOSE* Command Processing of *RemoteFileStreamServer* in Base.cs

```
case "CLOSE":
  // close local file
  f.Close ();

  // close connection to the client
  this.client.Close ();

  // stop the loop
  loop = false;
  break;
```

# The *RemoteFileStreamProxy* Class

This class is derived from the abstract class *System.IO.Stream*. An instance of this class can be used as a normal stream. For instance, it can be given to a method that generally works on streams. Here we focus on the constructor and the *Read()*, *Write()*, and *Close()* methods. For all other methods and properties that must override abstract method's properties, refer to the class code in the file Base.cs on the CD.

First, the constructor (see Figure 5.97) opens the connection to the server, sends the *OPEN* command, and receives the remote file length if the open mode is read.

**Figure 5.97** Constructor of *RemoteFileStreamProxy* in Base.cs

```
public RemoteFileStreamProxy ( string host, int port, string file,
  bool read )
{
  this.read = read;

  this.remoteFile = new TcpClient ( host, port ).GetStream ();
  this.open = true;

  Send ( "OPEN:" + file + ":" + read );

  if ( read )
  {
    this.length = int.Parse (
      new StreamReader ( this.remoteFile ).ReadLine () );
  }
}
```

The next one is the *Read()* method (see Figure 5.98). It sends the *READ* command to the server and receives the bytes sent by the server.

**Figure 5.98** *Read()* Method of *RemoteFileStreamProxy* in Base.cs

```
public override int Read ( byte[] buffer, int offset, int count )
{
  // to do: implement exceptions here as described in .NET reference

  if ( !CanRead )
    throw new NotSupportedException ( "stream cannot read" );
```

**Continued**

**Figure 5.98** Continued

```
    Send ( "READ:" + count );

    return this.remoteFile.Read ( buffer, offset, count );
}
```

Now, let's look at the *Write()* method (see Figure 5.99). It sends the *WRITE* command and the bytes to write to the server.

**Figure 5.99** *Read()* Method of *RemoteFileStreamProxy* in Base.cs

```
public override void Write ( byte[] buffer, int offset, int count )
{
    // to do: implement exceptions here as described in .NET reference

    if ( !CanWrite )
        throw new NotSupportedException ( "stream cannot write" );

    Send ( "WRITE:" + count );

    this.remoteFile.Write ( buffer, offset, count );
}
```

Finally, the *Close()* method (see Figure 5.100). It sends the *CLOSE* command to the server and then it closes the connection.

**Figure 5.100** *Close()* Method of *RemoteFileStreamProxy* in Base.cs

```
public override void Close ()
{
    this.open = false;

    Send ( "CLOSE" );

    this.remoteFile.Close ();
}
```

As you have seen, the methods of the proxy are simpler than those of the server because the functionality is implemented in the server.

# The *FileSharingPeer* Class

*FileSharingPeer* has two main parts. The first part is a thread that accepts proxy connections. The thread creates for each connection request a *RemoteFileStreamServer* instance that handles the commands coming from the proxy. The second part contains two methods: *Download()* and *Upload()*. Both methods each create an instance of *RemoteFileStreamProxy* that communicates with the server for the requested functionality. Have a look at the class fields (see Figure 5.101).

**Figure 5.101** Class Fields of *FileSharingPeer* in Base.cs

```
// listener for incoming connections
private TcpListener listener = null;
// listening server thread
private Thread server = null;
```

Now, let's discuss the constructor (see Figure 5.102). It first initializes and starts a listener for incoming connection requests. Then it creates and starts a thread that uses the *Run()* method. This method is described later.

**Figure 5.102** Constructor of *FileSharingPeer* in Base.cs

```
public FileSharingPeer ( int localPort )
{
  Console.WriteLine ( "initializing file sharing peer, local port=" +
    localPort );

  // initialize proxy listener
  this.listener = new TcpListener ( localPort );
  this.listener.Start ();

  // start listening thread for incoming connection requests
  this.server = new Thread ( new ThreadStart ( Run ) );
  this.server.Start ();
```

**Continued**

**Figure 5.102** Continued

```
    Console.WriteLine ( "file sharing peer initialized" );
  }
```

In the constructor, you see the use of the *Run()* method for the server thread. This method handles the incoming connection requests (see Figure 5.103). After a proxy connects to the server, the resulting socket is given to the *RemoteFileStreamServer* instance. Then a thread for this instance is created and started. The *Run()* method of the *RemoteFileStreamServer* instance is used by this thread for handling the proxy requests.

**Figure 5.103** *Run()* Method of *FileSharingPeer* in Base.cs

```
public void Run ()
{
  while ( true )
  {
    Socket s = listener.AcceptSocket ();

    Console.WriteLine ( "client connected" );

    RemoteFileStreamServer srv = new RemoteFileStreamServer ( s );
    Thread th = new Thread ( new ThreadStart ( srv.Run ) );
    th.Start ();
  }
}
```

The *Close()* method stops the proxy listener and the server thread (see Figure 5.104).

**Figure 5.104** *Close()* Method of *FileSharingPeer* in Base.cs

```
public void Close ()
{
  // stop proxy listener
  this.listener.Stop ();
```

**Continued**

**Figure 5.104** Continued

```
// stop server
this.server.Abort ();
this.server.Join ();
}
```

As mentioned before, the proxy class is derived from *System.IO.Stream*. *System.IO.FileStream* is also derived from this class. So, downloading and uploading file is nothing else than reading data from one stream and writing this data to another stream. In other words, for downloading and uploading, you need only one method for a copy functionality. And now you have found a name for the method: *Copy()* (see Figure 5.105).

**Figure 5.105** *Copy()* Method of *FileSharingPeer* in Base.cs

```
protected void Copy ( Stream sin, Stream sout )
{
  byte[] buf = new byte[4096];
  long l = 0;
  while ( l < sin.Length )
  {
    int n = sin.Read ( buf, 0, 4096 );
    sout.Write ( buf, 0, n );

    l += n;
  }

  sout.Close ();
  sin.Close ();
}
```

The *Download()* and *Upload()* methods are opening a local file and a proxy stream. *Download()* reads from the proxy stream and writes to the local file. *Upload()* does the inverse. Figure 5.106 shows both methods.

**Figure 5.106** *Download()* and *Upload()* Methods of *FileSharingPeer* in Base.cs

```
public void Download ( string remoteHost, int remotePort,
   string file )
{
   Console.WriteLine ( "downloading file, host=" + remoteHost +
      ", port=" + remotePort + ", file=" + file + "..." );

   Stream sin = new RemoteFileStreamProxy ( remoteHost, remotePort,
      file, true );
   Stream sout = new FileStream ( ".\\destination\\" + file,
      FileMode.Create );

   Copy ( sin, sout );

   Console.WriteLine ( "file downloaded, host=" + remoteHost +
      ", port=" + remotePort + ", file=" + file   );
}

public void Upload ( string remoteHost, int remotePort, string file )
{
   Console.WriteLine ( "uploading file, host=" + remoteHost +
      ", port=" + remotePort + ", file=" + file + "..." );

   Stream sin = new FileStream ( ".\\upload\\" + file, FileMode.Open );
   Stream sout = new RemoteFileStreamProxy ( remoteHost, remotePort,
      file, false );

   Copy ( sin, sout );

   Console.WriteLine ( "file uploaded, host=" + remoteHost +
      ", port=" + remotePort + ", file=" + file   );
}
```

Now you can compile and run our example. You will learn something about the user interface in the next section.

## Compiling and Running the Example

Please go to the directory on the CD where you can find the file FileSharingPeer.cs. Start the compile.bat batch file. Start the resulting FileSharingPeer.exe two times. You can do this by simply starting the run.bat file in the same directory.

Two forms appear. Try the download or upload by choosing a file and pressing the button for the functionality you want to try. Also have a look at the two DOS consoles. Now the forms should be similar to Figure 5.107.

Note that this peer class just simulates a file sharing peer. It has a download and upload functionality only, and it knows which files can be found on the other peer.

**Figure 5.107** File Sharing Peers in Action

# Access to Web Resources

We've now investigated remote operating classes that encapsulate communication protocols and work like local classes; now we'll have a short look at some Web access classes of the .NET Framework. Three classes are of particular interest: *System.Net.WebRequest*, *System.Net.WebResponse*, and *System.Net.WebProxy*.

As mentioned in the introductory sections, the abstract classes *WebRequest* and *WebResponse* are general APIs to underlying protocol handlers like an HTTP handler. Your goal is to develop a small application that makes a request via an HTTP proxy to a Web server and receives the response. You could use such an application as a base for a Web browser or a crawler, for instance.

A *crawler* is an application that "walks" through the Web along the links in the HTML documents to track the structure behind. Crawlers are used by search engines to create a searchable database of documents. A search request to a search engine means that a query to the database of the engine is made. A crawler can also be useful for intranets to determine the structure, for example, for creating index pages.

## General Usage of Needed .NET Classes

Today many companies use proxies to channelize and control outgoing requests from the company to the Web (see Figure 108).

**Figure 5.108** Clients Access the Internet via Proxy

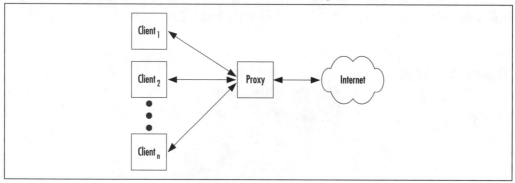

So, you can first define the parameters for the proxy to give them to the requesting class. This class then makes the request and receives the results page:

```
// create a request to the Syngress homepage
WebRequest request = WebRequest.Create (
  "http://www.syngress.com/" );


// set the proxy IP address an port
request.Proxy = new WebProxy ( proxyHost, proxyPort );


// set the proxy user and password
request.Proxy.Credentials = new NetworkCredential ( proxyUser,
  proxyPassword );


// get the reponse page
```

```
WebResponse response = request.GetResponse ();

// get the response stream
Stream s = response.GetResponseStream ();

// read from the stream

// close the stream
s.Close ();
```

*WebRequest.Create()* is a static method that creates a request object depending on the protocol defined in the URL parameter. The resulting object is of the type *System.Net.HttpWebRequest* because the protocol of the URL is HTTP. The string *proxyHost* and the *int proxyPort* are the IP address and port of your proxy. The *System.Net.NetworkCredential* class holds the authorization parameters for the proxy, that is, *proxyUser* and *proxyPassword* are the username and password needed to go through the proxy.

## A Web Access Client

Now, let's develop a small form that shows the HTML code of a Web page. It looks a little bit like a Web browser (see Figure 5.109).

**Figure 5.109** HTML Page Source Viewer

On the top of the form are fields for the proxy parameters. The URL field is for typing in the destination URL (for example, http://www.syngress.com/). The untitled field contains the source of the HTML page specified by the URL.

Before going into the form, you need to use a small class that allows easier handling of the Web access classes. It is called *WebAccessClient* and is included on the CD in the file Base.cs. The class has two constructors and the *Get()* method. One constructor is for initializing without using a proxy and one with a proxy. The constructor for initializing the client without a proxy simply does nothing. The *Get()* method returns a Web page based on a request URI. Figure 5.110 shows the class fields of *WebAccessClient*.

**Figure 5.110** Class Fields of *WebAccessClient* in Base.cs

```
// proxy parameters
private WebProxy proxy = null;
```

The *proxy* field holds the proxy parameters and is initialized by the constructor. The constructor code using a proxy looks like Figure 5.111.

**Figure 5.111** Constructor Using Proxy of *WebAccessClient* in Base.cs

```
// with proxy
public WebAccessClient ( string proxyHost, int proxyPort,
  string proxyUser, string proxyPassword )
{
  // create a proxy
  WebProxy proxy = new WebProxy ( proxyHost, proxyPort );

  // set user name and password for proxy
  proxy.Credentials = new NetworkCredential ( proxyUser,
    proxyPassword );

  // disable proxy use when the host is local
  proxy.BypassProxyOnLocal = true;

  // all new requests use this proxy info
  GlobalProxySelection.Select = proxy;
}
```

First, we create a proxy object as shown in the general usage section. But now comes something new—the property *BypassProxyOnLocal* is a flag that advises the request class not to try to connect through the proxy if a local URL such as localhost is requested (for example, a local Web server on the same computer). The other new element is the *GlobalProxySelection* class of the namespace *System.Net*. This class has a static property *Select*. This property is a proxy instance that *WebRequest* instances use to connect to the outside. You can set this once, and you don't have to set the *Proxy* property of *WebRequest*. (Note that this doesn't make a lot of sense in your class because there is only one constructor, but it's worth mentioning.)

The *Get()* method requests and returns a stream containing a Web page for a given URL (see Figure 5.112). It is a very simple method that does nothing too different from the example code in the general usage section.

**Figure 5.112** *Get()* Method of *WebAccessClient* in Base.cs

```
public Stream Get ( string url )
{
  // create a request based on the URL
  WebRequest req = WebRequest.Create ( url );

  // get the response
  WebResponse res = req.GetResponse ();

  // return a stream containing the response
  return res.GetResponseStream ();
}
```

Now we come to the form. The class is called *WebAccessClientForm* and is contained on the CD in the file WebAccessClient.cs. This class has only two methods: a constructor that initializes all controls, and a key event handler that is called if the URL field receives a *KeyUp* event. Let's focus here on the event handler (see Figure 5.113).

**Figure 5.113** *KeyUp* Event Handler of *WebAccessClientForm* in WebAccessClient.cs

```csharp
public void OnKeyUp ( Object sender, KeyEventArgs a )
{
  // read a page if the return key was pressed
  if ( a.KeyCode == Keys.Return )
  {
    // clear the result field
    this.text.Text = "";

    // create a Web access client
    WebAccessClient client = null;
    if ( this.proxyHost.Text.Equals ( "" ) )
      client = new WebAccessClient ();
    else
      client = new WebAccessClient ( this.proxyHost.Text,
        int.Parse ( this.proxyPort.Text ),
        this.proxyUser.Text, this.proxyPassword.Text );

    // get the response stream
    StreamReader s = new StreamReader (
      client.Get ( this.url.Text ) );

    // read the response and write it to the text field
    int BUFFER_SIZE = 4096;
    Char[] buf = new Char[BUFFER_SIZE];
    int n = s.Read ( buf, 0, BUFFER_SIZE );
    while ( n > 0 )
    {
      this.text.Text += new String ( buf, 0, n );

      n = s.Read ( buf, 0, BUFFER_SIZE );
    }
```

**Continued**

**Figure 5.113** Continued

```
    // close the stream
    s.Close ();
  }
}
```

The request should be made if the **Return** key was pressed in the URL field. This a little bit browser-like. First, you can create a *WebAccessClient* instance based on the proxy parameter fields. Then, you can make the request by calling the *Get()* method. The *StreamReader* is for your convenience because its *Read()* method reads into a char array that you can easily convert to a string. This string is simply concatenated with the content of your result text field. Finally, the stream is closed. Now you can compile and run the example.

## Compiling and Running the Example

Please go to the directory on the CD where you can find the file WebAccessClient.cs. Start the compile.bat batch file. After successful compiling, double-click on **WebAccessClient**.

Now a form appears. Please type in the proxy information and an URL. Finally press the **Return** key while the cursor resides in the URL field. Now the form should be similar to Figure 5.114.

**Figure 5.114** HTML Page Source Viewer after Doing a Request

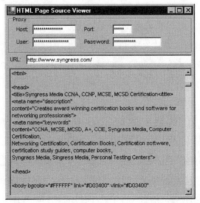

This example is only a start into Web access with .NET *WebRequest* classes. These classes offer many more features. Here you'll focus on *HttpWebRequest*. An

instance of this class is returned by the *Create()* method of *WebRequest* if the given URL starts with *http://*.

The *HttpWebRequest* class has a large number of properties to directly influence the HTTP request. Among others are properties for directly manipulating HTTP request header fields such as *Accept*, *Content-Length*, *Content-Type*, and so on. All headers can be accessed by the property *Headers*. This property is an instance of *WebHeaderCollection* and contains the headers exposed by the *HttpWebRequest* properties or unchangeable headers needed by the system. Please see the .NET reference documentation for mutable and immutable headers.

Some other functionality can be influenced directly by manipulating properties of *HttpWebRequest*. The following sections describe a part of it, especially the request method, redirection, authentication, and cookie handling.

# Request Method

By default, an *HttpWebRequest* instance created by the *Create()* method requests with the HTTP *GET*. If you want to use another method, such as *POST*, you can do this by setting the *Method* property of *HttpWebRequest*.

Other HTTP 1.1 methods are *HEAD*, *PUT*, *DELETE*, *TRACE*, or *OPTIONS*. If you want to use a version other than 1.1, you must set the *ProtocolVersion* property with the needed version. Please have a look at the .NET reference documentation for the *HttpVersion* class. The default HTTP version of *HttpWebRequest* is *HttpVersion.Version11*.

# Redirection

Normally, if you are implementing an HTTP client, you must react on the HTTP status codes starting with 301. These codes define redirection methods. To see which status code the response to your request has, have a look at the *StatusCode* property of the *HttpWebResponse* instance returned by the *GetResponse()* method of *HttpWebRequest*.

Mostly, *redirection* means that the requested page is not available anymore under the specified URL (see the W3C Web site for HTTP specifications, at www.w3.org). The response then contains the new URL of the requested page or another redirection page, so you then have to re-request with the new URL.

With the *HttpWebRequest* class you do not have to do this by hand if you do not want to. If the Boolean property *AllowAutoRedirect* is set to true the class does all the work for you. If this property is set to false, you must implement redirection by yourself. The default value of this property is true.

# Authentication

Sometimes a Web site requests an authentication from you for login. This is, if the response has the HTTP status *code 401 Unauthorized*. Normally, if you know what you need for authentication (for example, username and password) you re-request the page with these requirements contained in the *WWW-Authenticate* HTTP header. With the *HttpWebRequest* class, you can do this easily with the *PreAuthenticate* and *Credentials* properties.

The following procedure is the same whether you get a *401 Unauthorized* response or you know before for which Web site you need an authentication:

1. Set the *PreAuthenticate* property to true.

2. Create an instance of *NetworkCredential*. It is the same procedure as described for proxies in this section.

3. Set the *Credentials* property to the credential you created in Step 2.

4. Request or re-request the page.

# Cookies

Normally, cookies are used to store a state needed during long-term communication, such as revisiting a page. For instance, a Web site stores some customer information in a cookie on your computer. If you revisit the site it requests the cookie, in order to know immediately who you are, so that a page may be customized especially for you.

Because cookies are particular to the sites you request, we can only give you direction to get more detail about cookies:

- If you are new to cookies, please have a look at general documentation about cookies (RFC 2965, Proposed Standard for HTTP State Management Mechanism).

- In the .NET reference documentation, you will find the *System.Net .Cookie* class. As the name implies, this class represents an HTTP cookie.

- The *HttpWebRequest* class has a property named *CookieContainer*. This is an instance of the *System.Net.CookieContainer* class and contains all cookies for the request.

- The *HttpWebResponse* class has a property named *Cookies*. This is an instance of the *System.Net.CookieCollection* class and contains all cookies of the response.

# Summary

This chapter presents some examples of how to implement networking applications with the .NET Framework.

The most widely used protocols in networking are TCP and UDP. You can use TCP for reliable client/server applications because it is a reliable and connection-oriented protocol. On the other hand, you can use UDP for applications such as DNS, time servers, Internet telephony, and streaming multimedia in general because it is faster than TCP. The better performance is caused by the relative unreliability of the protocol. If a packet of data gets lost, no administrative overhead is needed to resend it. UDP also supports another option: multicasting. Multicasting means that one application sends data simultaneously to a group of applications without the knowledge of which kinds of applications are listening, or how many.

The chapter discussed the meaning of ports for developing networking applications—only if an application is registered with a port it can be reached by other processes.

As introductory examples, we developed simple remote command processing with TCP and UDP. These examples show how you can use the .NET networking classes for networking and what the differences are in using the TCP and UDP classes. These differences are caused by the different natures of the protocols. TCP is a connection- and stream-oriented client/server protocol. So, the .NET TCP classes reflect the client/server model by providing client and server classes. Clients have methods for connecting to and disconnecting from a remote host. Servers have methods for listening for and accepting incoming connections. Furthermore, after successful connection, TCP classes provide stream classes for accessing the data streams between client and server. The .NET UDP classes on the other hand have no connection establishment and stream functionality. Because UDP is connection-less and packet-oriented, these classes need send and receive methods only where network addresses and data are given directly. Data is sent and received without making a connection. UDP is peer-oriented, reflected in the absence of explicit client and server classes. The same class is used for sender and receiver applications.

The TCP and UDP examples are followed by a UDP multicasting example and a news ticker application. Multicasting is an option of UDP where a sender application sends data to an IP address. This address represents a group of applications. All these applications are able to receive the sent data. An application can take part in the group simply by registering with the group IP address.

The next example was a client/server chat application. It showed how you can use TCP and UDP in combination. You can use TCP to send messages to a server in a reliable way. You can use UDP multicasting for sending the chat messages to all clients that take part in the chat room. The most important technique shown with this example is how Web servers handle multiple client requests at the same time. If a TCP client establishes a connection to a server listener class, the server creates a socket for only this connection, then the server is ready for listening on its port for new clients.

A simple P2P file sharing application was the next example. Here we showed how to use the client/server-like protocol TCP for developing P2P applications. A peer must act like a TCP server and a TCP client simultaneously. Such a peer must be divided in two parts. First, a TCP client that connects to another peer for sending and receiving data (upload and download of files). Second, there must be a TCP server that accepts connection from another peer, so that this peer can download and upload files from the TCP server. The most important technique in this section is how to implement remote object access—such as remoting or CORBA—in a very simplified way. We developed a remote file stream. On the client side, we have a proxy, and on the server side a server class. The remote file stream on the client side is used similar to a "normal" file stream. But methods such as *Open()*, *Close()*, *Read()*, and *Write()* are working over a network using a simple communication protocol. The remote file stream class is derived from the .NET stream class and can be used in the same way as other stream classes. An application that works only on streams does not recognize a difference from other streams.

Finally, we show how to use special .NET classes for accessing Web resources. With the *System.Net.WebRequest* and *System.Net.WebResponse* classes, accessing a Web server is simple using only a few methods. These classes encapsulate HTTP or FTP handling. We also have shown how to request a Web page through a proxy. A proxy is an intermediate process between a Web client and server to channelize and control communication. Finally, we mentioned some other techniques in accessing Web resources by using .NET classes.

We described how to change request methods with the *System.Net .HttpWebRequest* class. The default method of this class is the HTTP *GET*, but for instance, some applications need the HTTP *POST* method.

Another point mentioned was redirection of Web pages. Sometimes it is necessary to change the URL of a Web page. Maybe this is caused by changing the host name of the Web server or other administrative work. But the page should still be accessible via the old URL. The Web server then returns a special redirection status code and a new URL for the page. The client then requests the page with the new URL. With .NET, we do not have to develop this by ourselves—the *HttpWebRequest* class does this work for us.

This class also does authentication handling. If a Web server requests authentication for accessing a page, we do not have to develop the HTTP authentication procedure. If authentication is requested by a Web server, it returns a special status code. The client now must re-request by adding the authentication information, for instance, username and password. This work is done by the *HttpWebRequest*.

Finally, we mentioned cookie handling. Cookies are small packets of information that bring states to the state-less HTTP. State-less means that every HTTP request/response pair is independent from former and further communication. State information on the client side can be stored with cookies. The Web server requests a cookie and knows in which state, for instance, a Web shop transaction is. Because of the special character of cookies depending on the application and their use, we showed only the .NET cookie class and where to find cookies in request and response classes.

# Solutions Fast Track

## Introducing Networking and Sockets

- ☑ Networking is inter-process communication. Two or more processes communicate with each other. The processes can run on the same or different computers or other technical devices.

- ☑ The most important networking API is the socket.

- ☑ Most networks today use the Internet Protocol (IP) as base protocol. The most widely used application protocols are the Transmission Control Protocol (TCP) and the User Datagram Protocol (UDP). TCP and UDP run on IP.

- ☑ TCP is a reliable connection- and stream-oriented point-to-point protocol. The communication is client/server–oriented. The delivery and order of data is guaranteed.

- ☑ UDP is a connection-less and datagram-oriented best-effort protocol. The delivery and order of data is not guaranteed. It can be used as a point-to-point protocol (unicasting) or as a point-to-group protocol (multicasting).

# Example TCP Command Transmission and Processing

- ☑ For TCP communication, the easiest way is to use the *System.Net .TcpListener* and *System.Net.TcpClient* classes.

- ☑ This section showed how a *TcpClient* on the client side connects to a *TcpListener* on the server side.

- ☑ The client sends a command and receives a result.

- ☑ This is similar to a browser making a request to a Web server and receiving a Web page.

# Example UDP Command Transmission and Processing

- ☑ For UDP communication, the easiest way is to use the *System.Net .UdpClient* classes.

- ☑ This section showed how a *UdpClient* on the client side communicates to another *UdpClient* on the server side. The client sends a command and receives a result.

- ☑ This example is similar to the example in the "Example TCP Command Transmission and Processing" section for showing the differences between TCP and UDP.

# Creating a News Ticker Using UDP Multicasting

- ☑ UDP can be used for sending data to a group of peers (multicasting).

- ☑ For multicasting, *System.Net.UdpClient* can also be used.

- ☑ This section showed how to develop multicasting between UDP peers.

# Creating a UDP Client Server Chat Application

- ☑ This example combined our TCP and UDP knowledge.

- ☑ TCP is used for transferring messages to the chat server; UDP is used for sending the messages to all connected chat clients.

## Creating a TCP P2P File Sharing Application

☑ This example showed how to develop TCP P2P applications.

☑ A TCP peer has one TCP server and one TCP client.

☑ This example showed in a very simplified way how remote object access such as remoting or CORBA is implemented. This is done by a so-called remote file stream.

## Access to Web-Resources

☑ You can easily create access to Web resources with the .NET classes *System.Net.WebRequest* and *System.Net.WebResponse*.

☑ *WebRequest* makes a request to a Web resource, such as a Web server. The result of the request is *WebResponse* instance that gives access to a stream, such as representing the requested Web page.

☑ Communicating through proxies is made with help of the *System.Net.WebProxy* class.

# Frequently Asked Questions

The following Frequently Asked Questions, answered by the authors of this book, are designed to both measure your understanding of the concepts presented in this chapter and to assist you with real-life implementation of these concepts. To have your questions about this chapter answered by the author, browse to **www.syngress.com/solutions** and click on the **"Ask the Author"** form.

**Q:** What is TCP and how does is work?

**A:** Today, most networks use the Internet Protocol (IP) on the network protocol layer. IP is an unreliable data packet (datagram) delivery service where the delivery and order of packets is not guaranteed (best-effort). The Transmission Control Protocol (TCP) is designed to address this problem—it guarantees reliability. If packets are lost, TCP can resend them. If the order of packets is not correct, TCP can put them in the right order. On the other hand, TCP is stream-oriented, that is, you can read your data byte-by-byte. Finally, TCP is connection-oriented, that is, a client opens a connection to a server, communicates with the server, and after finishing, it closes the connection.

**Q:** What is UDP and how does it work?

**A:** The User Datagram Protocol (UDP) provides an unreliable datagram-oriented protocol on top of IP. The delivery and order of datagrams are not guaranteed. It is connection-less, that is, a UDP application does not have to connect explicitly to another. Datagrams are simply sent or received.

**Q:** What is multicasting?

**A:** Multicasting means that a set of applications can be grouped together by an IP address. If an application sends data to that IP address, all members of the group receive the data. UDP provides this service.

**Q:** When do I use TCP, and when do I use UDP?

**A:** You should use TCP if a reliable connection is necessary. You can use UDP when you don't need reliability when or you need more performance.

**Q:** Why does UDP multicasting sometimes not work under the German version of Windows 2000?

**A:** We encountered problems with the German version of Windows 2000 Professional and Service Pack 2 using the Beta 2 of the .NET Framework. At the time of this writing, no solution has been found, either on the Microsoft Web site or from other sources. This problem seems to be deeper than the .NET Framework. Tests with Java applications also lead to negative results. At the time of this writing, we do not know if the problems also exist with other Windows 2000 versions.

**Q:** Why does the UDP unicast example sometimes not work under the German version of Windows NT 4?

**A:** We encountered a problem with the Beta 2 of the .NET Framework running under German Windows NT 4 Service Pack 6a. If the example is started with the run.bat file, UDP unicasting doesn't work. If the example is started directly, it works well. At press time, we do not know if the problems also exist with other Windows NT versions. With Windows 2000, the example works well when started directly or via batch file.

# Chapter 6

# Remoting

## Solutions in this chapter:

- **Introducing Remoting**

- **Creating a Simple Remoting Client Server**

- **Creating an Intranet Application**

- **Creating Service-Based Applications**

☑ **Summary**

☑ **Solutions Fast Track**

☑ **Frequently Asked Questions**

# Introduction

Ever since the early days of Windows programming, there has been a gradual improvement in operating system stability. Much of this is due to the separation of applications into distinct processes so that each has its own area of memory. Developers have had to use many tricks to get these applications to communicate with each other. Some of these methods included using the system clipboard, sending windows messages, using the Visual Basic (VB) *SendKeys* function or similar, transferring "message" files, or declaring an area of shared memory. Each of these methods had pros and cons and were generally "hacks" around the separation of processes. When Microsoft's Component Object Model (COM) arrived, the situation vastly improved, and such tricks were no longer needed, but COM did introduce a number of issues with versioning, registration, and administration that a generation of Windows developers has had to deal with. Now with the .NET platform, you get cross-application communication built-in, which provides you with an amazing amount of flexibility and control as to how you want your applications to communicate with each other.

Every application on the .NET platform exists in its own unique Application Domain. And every Application Domain is able to expose objects to the outside world from any type of application—from simple console applications to Windows Forms and Internet Information Server (IIS)–hosted applications. To enable applications running in one Application Domain to communicate with other applications in another Application Domain, you use *remoting*. Or you could say remoting allows you to call methods and pass objects across Application Domains.

The Remoting API on the .NET platform takes a different approach than the other application programming interfaces (APIs), such as Distributed COM (DCOM) and Remote Method Invocation (RMI) for communication and message format. Rather than relying on a proprietary message and protocol, the Remoting API uses well-established standards such as Simple Object Access Protocol (SOAP) for messaging and Hypertext Transfer Protocol/Transmission Control Protocol (HTTP/TCP) protocols for communication. This allows applications to communicate just as easily across the Internet as they do within the enterprise.

To understand how remoting works, imagine that you need to create your own method of cross-application communication. Imagine that you have an object that needs to accept calls from client applications across HTTP. First, you'd need to define your object's location as a URL of some kind. Then you would need to choose a port that the object should listen to. You would also need some way of publishing the interface of your object so that clients would know what methods are available to call, and you would need a method of describing the interface and handling the messaging between objects. The creators of the .NET Framework have done just that and have exposed the remoting functionality as a powerful way for programmers to start getting their applications to communicate.

This chapter introduces the remoting framework and provides many examples from real-world scenarios that occur during development. First, we get an overview of how remoting works and look at the variety of choices available to the developer as to how remoting is configured.

In the second part of the chapter, we produce a simple remoting example that is gradually extended to use a range of remoting services. We also take a look at how to deal with issues that developers face during the development lifecycle in regard to deployment, debugging, administration, documentation, and versioning while using the remoting framework.

# Introducing Remoting

*Remoting* provides you with a number of choices as to the method and configuration of communication used. Configuration areas are the choice of channel, type of hosting application, the activation model, the configuration method, and the method of exposing server metadata to the client application.

The channel is the means of communication used by an application to call to a remote object; the selection is between HTTP and TCP (SMTP doesn't appear to be ready in Beta 2). The HTTP channel is mostly used for Internet communication where firewalls need to be negotiated. The TCP channel has a performance gain by using direct socket connections over an arbitrary port selected by the developer. Both channels use SOAP for communication; the TCP channel defaults to use a faster (but proprietary) binary representation of the SOAP message, whereas the HTTP channel defaults to use the XML standard. The TCP channel can also use the normal XML-formatted SOAP messaging format.

The selection of the hosting application for the remote object is the next choice. A hosting application must be configured to listen on a channel and create the requested object in its own *AppDomain* when required. In Visual Basic 6, developers often used IIS or COM+ services to host remote objects—the mysterious dllhost.exe that you may see running in your Windows 2000 Task Manager is the hosting application used by COM+. With the .NET Framework, you can still use these hosting services, but you can gain more control by writing your own hosting applications. When creating your own hosting application, as we do in the first example, you may choose from a Console application, Windows Service, or Windows Forms application.

Choice number three is the activation model for the remote object. *SingleCall* objects are stateless in that they handle only single calls from clients and do not hold state between calls. After the call is handled, the object is discarded. *Singleton* objects can be shared between multiple clients. They are often used when the resources needed to initialize the object are large and the object's state needs to be preserved between method calls. You need to remember that *Singleton* objects do have a default lifetime and may be recycled—we'll see later how developers can control the object's lifetime to suit their needs. Client Activated Objects (CAOs) allows a client application to create a remote instance of the object for exclusive use and to preserve state between remote method calls.

Choice number four is the method of configuring the remote server. The host application can programmatically configure itself on startup or a configuration file can be used. Of course, using an external file to hold remoting configuration data enables changes to be made without a recompile of the source code. The configuration information contains the channel, port, activation model, type name, and assembly name of the object. A Uniform Resource Identifier (URI), which clients use to identify the object, is also specified.

The final choice is how the client obtains the remote object's metadata. Again comparing with Visual Basic 6, a server object's interface definition had to be on the client, either as a type library or an exported MTS package, to enable the client VB code to make the call over DCOM. With remoting, the situation is similar but improved by the .NET Framework's use of metadata. The first method is to set a reference to the remote object's DLL in the client project so that the compiler can extract the metadata. The second method, but only if using the HTTP channel, is to use the soapsuds.exe utility to generate a "proxy" class from the remote object's URI. This proxy class can then be included in the client project and used as if it is a local .NET type. Internally, the proxy class will route the call to the remote object.

# Remoting Architecture

An end-to-end picture of remoting is as follows. The host application is loaded and registers a channel and port on which to listen for incoming calls. The configuration file, if any, is read and an object's remoting information is loaded—the host application can now map a URI to the physical assembly and instantiate the object when required. The client application also registers the same channel and then attempts to create a new instance of the remote class. The remoting system handles the request for a new instance by providing a proxy object in place of the actual object on the server. The actual object is either created immediately for CAOs or on the first method call for *Singleton/Singlecall* objects—the remoting framework takes care of this for you automatically. When the client calls a method on the proxy object, the information is sent across the channel to the remote object. The remoting system will then pass back the results of the method across the channel in the same manner.

# Creating a Simple Remoting Client Server

We'll now create a simple client server application to demonstrate the usage of the remoting framework. The code for the server side is located in the ListServer directory of the CD—double-click on the solution file ListServer.sln so that you load both the server and the hosting application together. First, we'll create the remote class named *CompanyLists* that contains the functionality. All of the following code is on the CD.

> **NOTE**
>
> The code in this chapter uses localhost as the target server—this will self-reference your local computer so that you may use both the client and server code on the same PC. If you wish to place the server-side code on a remote server, you will need to replace localhost with the correct server name.

## Creating the Remote Server Object

The remote server object contains all the server-side functionality for our application:

1. Create a new Class Library application in Visual Studio named **ListServer**.

2. Right-click the **default Class1.cs** module in the Solution Explorer and choose **Delete**.

3. Right-click the **ListServer** project in the Solution Explorer, select **Add | Add Class**, and name your new class **CompanyLists.cs**.

4. Modify the class declaration to inherit from *MarshalByRefObject* so that a reference to the object can be passed remotely:

```
public class CompanyLists: MarshalByRefObject
{
}
```

5. Add a private variable to the *CompanyList* class that contains an array of strings:

```
private String[] Countries = {"Spain","France","Italy"};
```

6. Add a public method to *CompanyList* that returns the array of strings defined in the preceding step. The complete class should appear as:

```
public class CompanyLists: MarshalByRefObject
{
    private String[] Countries = {"Spain","France","Italy"};

    public String[] getCountryList()
    {
        return Countries;
    }
}
```

The *CompanyList* class can now be loaded by a hosting application for remoting. If you already have classes that you'd like to make remoting aware of, it's as simple as inheriting from *MarshalByRefObject* and then recompiling.

**NOTE**

If your class must receive and send objects during method calls, you will need to use the <Serializable> custom attribute to pass these objects by value or inherit from *MarshalByRefObject* to pass by reference. An example of this is shown later. If your class already inherits from another class, you'll need to make the parent class inherit from *MarshalByRefObject* because multiple inheritance is not allowed in C#.

# Creating the Hosting Application

Now we create the hosting application. This will be a console application initially, but in the real world, this would probably be a Windows Service application:

1. From the Visual Studio menu, choose **File | Add Project | New Project**. Select **Console Application** and name the new project **ListHost**.

2. Rename the default Class1.cs file to **CompanyListHost.cs**.

3. Add a reference to the *System.Runtime.Remoting* namespace and the *ListServer* project.

4. Add the following *using* statements at the top of the code window to reference the relevant namespaces:

```
using System.Runtime.Remoting;

using System.Runtime.Remoting.Channels;

using System.Runtim.Remoting.Channels.Http;
```

5. Add the following code to the *Main* method. This code creates an *HttpChannel* object that uses port 8080. The *RegisterChannel* method is then used to register the channel, after which the *RegisterWellKnownServiceType* method is called to register the class with the remoting framework. The *RegisterWellKnownServiceType* method contains three parameters that specify the type of the remoting class, the URI, and the object activation mode. After this method has been called, your class is then ready to accept requests from client applications.

```
static void Main(string[] args)

{

    HttpChannel myChannel = new HttpChannel (8080);


    ChannelServices.RegisterChannel(myChannel);


    RemotingConfiguration.RegisterWellKnownServiceType

    (typeof(ListServer.CompanyLists),

        "CompanyLists", WellKnownObjectMode.Singleton);

}
```

6. Build the console application to create the ListHost.exe console application.

The *CompanyList* class can now accept calls from remote clients. You'll notice that we have chosen port 8080 to listen to for client requests. The choice of port is rather arbitrary, although port 80 should be used to be firewall friendly. You need to remember that a port can only be registered once per machine. To see what happens when an attempt is made to register the same port twice, perform the following experiment:

1. In Windows Explorer, find and run the host application ListHost.exe.

2. While the console application is running, run the same host application from within the Visual Studio IDE. You may need to right-click the *ListHost* project in the Solution Explorer and select **Set as StartUp Project** to enable the IDE to do this.

3. Figure 6.1 shows the exception that occurs when the same port is reused.

**Figure 6.1** The Exception Generated after an Attempt to Reuse a Port

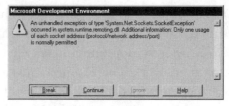

# Creating the Client Application

The client application will be a standard Windows Application with a main form, but it could also be any other type of .NET application. The source for this project is located under the ListClient directory of the CD:

1. From the Visual Studio menu choose **File | New | Project**. Select **Windows Application**, and name the new project **ListClient**.

2. Rename the Form1.cs file to **ListClient.cs**.

3. Add a reference to the *System.Runtime.Remoting* namespace and also to the ListServer.dll.

4. Add the following *using* statements at the top of the ListClient.cs code window to reference the relevant namespaces:

```
using ListServer;
using System.Runtime.Remoting;
using System.Runtime.Remoting Channels;
using System.Runtime.Remoting.Channels.Http;
```

5. Modify the code in the *Form1* constructor to appear as follows so that a new *HttpChannel* object is created and registered on application startup:

```
public Form1()
{
    InitializeComponent();


    HttpChannel c = new HttpChannel();
    ChannelServices.RegisterChannel(c);


}
```

6. Add a button and a textbox to the form. In the button's *click* event, add the following code. This code will create a reference to the remote object by using the *Activator.GetObject* method. Three parameters are used by this method to specify the type of the remote class, its URI, and the creation mode. The list of countries is then retrieved and used to populate the form's *ListBox* control:

```
private void button1_Click(object sender, System.EventArgs e)
{

    CompanyLists cLst = (CompanyLists)Activator.GetObject(typeof(
        CompanyLists),"http://localhost:8080/CompanyLists",
        WellKnownObjectMode.Singleton);

    listBox1.DataSource = cLst.getCountryList();


}
```

7. Run the host application ListHost.exe and leave the console window open. Figure 6.2 shows the host application.

**Figure 6.2** The Server Application Waiting for Clients

8.  Run the *ListClient* application. Click the button to retrieve the list country list from your server object. In Figure 6.3, you can see that the county list has been successfully obtained from the remote object.

**Figure 6.3** The Client Application

# Understanding the Remoting Code

The host application simply needs to register a channel and port using *RegisterChannel* and to register the remoting object using *RegisterWellKnownServiceType*. The *RegisterWellKnownServiceType* method takes three parameters—the type of the object, the object's URI as defined by the developer, and the creation mode. The first parameter provides the link between the hosting application and the remoting object—this is why having a reference to your class library's DLL is necessary. Developers that have used previous versions of Visual Basic may notice that we cannot magically determine the location of a DLL using *CreateObject*. We must explicitly tell the compiler the DLL's location. This is actually a major benefit of the .NET Framework because we no longer must trust that the Registry has accurate information to instantiate an object.

Another important point is that an object does not "own" a channel. You are free to register as many channels and objects in the hosting application as you like. Communication on the server side is multithreaded, so there is no need to worry about a request blocking a channel while processing is done. You may also want to use one channel for Internet clients and another for intranet clients and force this policy by screening ports on your proxy server.

The client application must also register a channel, but in this case the port does not need to be specified. This may seem strange at first—doesn't the client need to know which port to communicate with? The confusion lies in the double life of the *HttpChannel* class. Creating a *HttpChannel* object actually creates a *ClientChannel* and a *ServerChannel* object. The *ClientChannel* object does not need a port number because it can communicate with *any* port specified in the URL. You could replace *HttpChannel* with *ClientChannel* in the client code and everything would still work fine. The *ServerChannel* object is given to us for free by the remoting framework so that the server object can call back to the client if needed. By specifying a port when creating a *HttpChannel*, we are allowing our client app to "listen" on this port, but it has no influence on what port our app may talk to. Also, if you are a lazy programmer, you can actually forget about registering a channel altogether. The remoting framework will create one for you the first time you attempt to reference a remote object. Try commenting out the two lines of code that create and register a channel on the client (shown in Step 5 in the previous section) and then rerun the application.

The client application also needs a reference to ListServer.dll but for a different reason than the hosting application has a reference. The hosting application needs the reference so that it can create the remoting object to handle incoming requests. The client application needs the reference only so that it can access the DLL's metadata. As you will see soon, the SoapSuds.exe utility removes the need to reference the DLL by extracting the metadata and providing it to the client in the form of a proxy class.

To obtain a reference to the remote object, *Activator.GetObject* is used. This method takes two parameters—the type of the object and the remote object's URI. The reference returned by *GetObject* is actually a reference to a proxy object that routes messages to the remote server. The remote object is not created until the client makes the first method call. This explains why the first time the button is clicked in our example application that there is a delay—the remoting framework is instantiating the remote object. And for those developers that deleted the code to register the channel, there will be a slightly longer delay while the framework sets up a default channel for you to use.

Note that if you are using the HTTP channel then the host application can be tested by typing the remote object's URI into a browser. Try typing in **http://localhost:8080/CompanyLists?wsdl** into Internet Explorer. As long as the host application is running and configured correctly, you'll see the SOAP definition of the remote class as it appears in Figure 6.4.

**Figure 6.4** The SOAP Definition of the Remoting Class

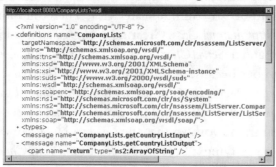

# Improving the Sample Application

Although the sample application is a good start and has shown how to execute calls to a remote object, some areas need improving in order to become a more real-world application. We introduce these improvements by adding to the sample code one step at a time.

# Adding Event Logging and Error Handling

A good coding standard would be to always have a hosting application write to the event log information regarding startup success or failure, the application name, server port number, and any other useful data. We now add event logging and error handling to the sample hosting application. This updated code is in the CompanyListHost2.cs file on the CD. The complete code for the host is shown in Figure 6.5.

**Figure 6.5** Adding Event Logging and Error Handling to the Hosting Application

```
using System;

using System.Runtime.Remoting;

using System.Runtime.Remoting.Channels;

using System.Runtime.Remoting.Channels.Http;

using System.Diagnostics;


namespace ListHost

{

    public class CompanyListHost
```

**Continued**

## Figure 6.5 Continued

```
    {
        EventLog myLog = new EventLog();
        myLog.Source = "ListHost";
        bool failed = false;

        try
        {
            HttpServerChannel myChannel = new HttpServerChannel (8080);
            ChannelServices.RegisterChannel(myChannel);
            myLog.WriteEntry("Registered HTTPChannel(8080)");
        }
        catch (Exception e)
        {
            myLog.WriteEntry("Failed to register HTTPChannel(8080) " +
    e.Message,System.Diagnostics.EventLogEntryType.Error);

            failed = true;
        }

        try
        {
            RemotingConfiguration.RegisterWellKnownServiceType(typeof(
                ListServer.CompanyLists), "CompanyLists",
                    WellKnownObjectMode.Singleton);

            myLog.WriteEntry("Registered ListServer.CompanyLists as
                Singleton");
        }

        catch (Exception e)
        {
            myLog.WriteEntry("Failed to register ListServer.CompanyLists
                " + e.Message);
```

**Continued**

**Figure 6.5** Continued

```
            failed = true;
        }


        if (failed)
        {
            System.Console.WriteLine("Errors at startup -
                see Event Log.");
        }


        System.Console.WriteLine("Press [Enter] to exit...");
        System.Console.ReadLine();

    }

}
```

The code that writes messages to the event log is quite straightforward. The *WriteEntry* method of the *EventLog* object is used to write error messages from within the *catch* blocks. Error handling has been added to trap exceptions caused while setting up the remoting configuration.

 # Using the soapsuds Tool

The need for every client application to have a reference to the remote assembly may be inconvenient for some third-party services. You use the soapsuds.exe tool to create a proxy object from the remote assembly's metadata so that a reference to the assembly is not needed. We now modify the sample application to use this proxy object by following the next few steps (The updated *ListClient* code is located in the ListClient2.cs file on the CD):

1. Open the **ListClient** project in Visual Studio.

2. From the command prompt, type **soapsuds –url:http://localhost:8080/CompanyLists?wsdl –gc**. This creates a proxy class named ListServer.cs.

3. Copy the ListServer.cs file to your source code directory.

4. Remove the project's reference to *ListServer* from the Solution Explorer window.

5. Right-click the **ListClient** project in the Solution Explorer window. Select **Add | Existing Item** and choose the **ListServer.cs** file to add it to your project.

6. Modify the *button1_click* method so that the code is as follows:

```
private void button1_Click(object sender, System.EventArgs e)
{
    CompanyLists cLst = new ListServer.CompanyLists();

    listBox1.DataSource = cLst.getCountryList();
}
```

7. Build the application.

Notice that the ListServer.cs file has taken the place of the reference to the remote assembly. Inspection of the ListServer.cs code reveals that this class is acting as a proxy by routing the remoting calls to the remote object's URI. This allows us to do away with the use of *Activator.GetObject* to obtain a remote reference—we can now program against *ListServer* as if it was a local class.

---

**NOTE**

The soapsuds utility has a range of command line options to aid client-side development—see the Microsoft documentation for details. When using this utility, it helps to remember that *wsdl* means Web Services Description Language and *-gc* means generate code. You'll then be able to amaze your friends and colleagues when you can type in soapsuds commands from memory.

---

# Using Configuration Files

Many settings to the configuration of .NET applications can be achieved not only inside code but with configuration files as well. All of these files use XML so that they are humanly readable and easily parsed by the .NET Framework. With remoting, you can use configuration files to handle all of the work necessary to expose and consume remoting objects.

You use the *Configure* method of the *RemotingConfiguration* class to configure the remoting framework by specifying the configuration file's location. We now modify the *ListHost* hosting application to read a configuration file at startup:

1.  Open the **ListHost** project in Visual Studio.

2.  Add a new file to the project called **ListHost.exe.config** (which is also located on the CD) with the following contents:

```
<configuration>
  <system.runtime.remoting>
   <application name="ListServer">
    <service>
     <wellknown mode="Singleton" type=
          "ListServer.CompanyLists,ListServer" objectUri="CompanyLists"/>
    </service>
    <channels>
     <channel type="System.Runtime.Remoting.Channels.Http.HttpChannel,
          System.Runtime.Remoting" port="8080"/>
    </channels>
   </application>
   <debug loadTypes="true" />
  </system.runtime.remoting>
</configuration>
```

3.  Modify the *Main()* method to use this configuration file on startup (CompanyListHost3.cs on the CD):

```
static void Main(string[] args)
{
    EventLog myLog = new EventLog();
    myLog.Source = "ListHost";
    bool failed = false;

    try
    {
        RemotingConfiguration.Configure(@"..\..\ListHost.exe.config");
        myLog.WriteEntry("Configuration from ListHost.exe.cfg
            successful");
```

```
    }

    catch (Exception e)
    {
        myLog.WriteEntry("Failed to configure host application: " +
        e.Message,System.Diagnostics.EventLogEntryType.Error);

        failed = true;
    }

    if (failed)
    {
        System.Console.WriteLine("Errors at startup - see Event Log.");
    }

    System.Console.WriteLine("Press [Enter] to exit...");
    System.Console.ReadLine();
}
```

Note that while running the host application in the Visual Studio IDE, the bin\debug directory will contain the executable. You'll therefore need to use the "..\..\" syntax in the file path to reach the configuration file in your source code directory. A further improvement would be to use a command line argument to specify the CFG file location. This would help during deployment, and you could test out a variety of configuration options easily without recompiling. Configuration files may also contain multiple channels definitions and object URI entries.

**NOTE**

The Microsoft standard for configuration files is that they should have the same name as the assembly, but with a .config extension. For example, myapp.exe will have the configuration file myapp.exe.config. This configuration file must be placed in the same directory as the assembly to enable utilities such as the .NET Framework Configuration tool to locate configuration information.

The type parameter is of the format *type="TypeName,AssemblyName"*. These parameters can be difficult to debug if they are wrong—no error message will be displayed during the call to *RemotingConfiguration.Configure*. To help with debugging, the *<debug loadTypes="true" />* attribute has been added, which causes the types specified in the configuration file to be loaded. Any errors in the spelling of a type name will then appear as a *FileNotFoundException* type exception.

On the client side a slightly different configuration file can be used:

```
<configuration>
  <system.runtime.remoting>
   <application name="ListClient">
    <client>
     <wellknown type="ListServer.CompanyLists, ListServer"
         url="http://localhost:8080/CompanyLists"/>
    </client>
    <channels>
     <channel type="System.Runtime.Remoting.Channels.Http.HttpChannel,
         System.Runtime.Remoting"/>
    </channels>
   </application>
  </system.runtime.remoting>
</configuration>
```

The client code also uses the *Configure* method of the *RemotingConfiguration* class to read the configuration file on startup. A client that uses a configuration file still needs a reference to the remoting application's DLL but can use the *new* keyword to instantiate the class. The client-side configuration actually redirects the object creation to the server and returns the remote reference. By using this method, it can be difficult to know if you are successfully creating the remote object. A mistake in the configuration file can cause the object to be instantiated locally instead of remotely. To avoid such subtle bugs, you can simply close down the remote hosting application and make sure that the object creation code causes an exception when running the client.

## Developing & Deploying…

### Remoting Applications

Remoting applications on the .NET platform have a great deal of flexibility as to how objects communicate with one another. It is even possible to "plug-in" your own (or a third party's) functionality to handle custom formatting, encryption, and more. This makes it all the more important for remoting issues to be considered up front in any design work. The areas that need to be examined include the following:

- Should objects be sent over the network by value or by reference?
- How large are these objects?
- How often will these objects need to be sent?
- For every remote method call, how many bytes of data would a typical call contain?
- How many client applications will a *Singleton* object need to handle?
- What are the lifetime issues with these objects? (that is, for how long must they maintain state?)
- Can a stateful object be used to increase performance?
- Will your firewalls allow your remoting calls through?
- Do your server-side objects need to call back to the clients? If so, will these clients have their own firewalls?
- If you need to shut down a hosting application to upgrade the server object, how will the clients handle this?

Deployment of remoting applications seems quite easy—and indeed it is. You could send the client-side executables with their configuration files via e-mail to a friend and he would only need to copy them to a directory and double-click the EXE to get started.

But wait, what happens if you want to move your server-side objects to another server? When version 2 of the server-side functionality is released, how do you let the client-side applications know? The solution to these issues is largely dependent on the type of applications you create, whether they are Internet- or intranet-based, and the number of clients that must be administered. One idea to get you started is to have

**Continued**

your client configuration files actually located on your Web server. This would need to be a server that is almost guaranteed not to have a domain name change. Instead of having thousands of client configuration files distributed around the globe—you now have only one. When client applications start up, they can get the configuration file via HTTP from your server and always have the latest version.

# Updating Configuration Files Using the .NET Framework Configuration Tool

Most developers are happy to use Notepad to update configuration files, but as the number of files increases, locating the necessary files in the directory tree can be troublesome. The .NET Framework provides you with a Microsoft Management Console (MMC) snap-in that serves as a central location for .NET configuration. Although in Beta 2 this snap-in appears to still need some improvement, it does hold promise of being a very useful tool. To start the snap-in, open a command prompt window and change the current directory to the installation directory of the .NET Framework, which will be *WINNT*\Microsoft.Net\Framework\v*x.y.z* (where *WINNT* is your windows directory and *x.y.z* is the version of the .NET Framework). Type **mscorcfg.msc** to start the .NET Framework Configuration tool. You will see a screen similar to Figure 6.6.

**Figure 6.6** The .NET Framework Configuration Tool

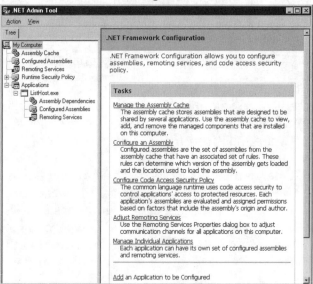

To add ListHost.exe to the Applications node, simply click the **Add an application to be configured** hyperlink and select the ListHost.exe file from the dialog. As long as your configuration file is named ListHost.exe.config and located in the same directory as the executable, you'll be able to modify the remoting configuration settings. To update the settings, right-click the **Remoting Services** node under ListHost.exe and select **Properties** from the context menu.

## Changing the Hosting Application to a Service

Hosting all of your remoting objects from console applications does appear strange at first sight. It's the 21st century and we still haven't completely got rid of those character-based applications! The fact is that console applications do provide a good environment for debugging applications that use remoting—you can immediately see if your hosting application is running, and you can easily send debug messages to the console window in real-time while you run your client-side app.

Once your server-side classes are ready for deployment, a Windows Service provides a better hosting environment. System administrators can easily start and stop your service, you can view your service from within Visual Studio's new Server Explorer, and you can guarantee that your service will be started after a reboot of the server. The service application we will create is located under the ListService directory on the CD. To create a new hosting service, follow these steps:

1. Load the **ListHost** project into Visual Studio.

2. Select and copy all the code from within the *Main()* method.

3. Select **File | New | Project**. Select the **Windows Service** template and type in **ListService** for the project name. Make sure that the **Add to Solution** option is set and then click **OK**.

4. While the Service1.cs file is in design view, use the Properties window to set the service name to **ListService**.

5. Switch to code view and paste the code you copied in Step 2 into the *OnStart()* method. Remove any code that was used to write to the console window. Replace any text within the code that refers to **ListHost** to be **ListService**.

6. Add the line **using System.Runtime.Remoting** to the start of Service1.cs.

7. Switch back to the Service1.cs design view. At the base of the Properties window, select the **Add Installer** link—see Figure 6.7.

**Figure 6.7** Setting the Properties of a Windows Service Application

8.  Select the **serviceProcessInstaller1** component (if this component is not visible, double-click the **ProjectInstaller.cs** file in the solution explorer) and set its *Account* property to **Local System**.

9.  Copy the ListHost.exe.config file to the winnt\system32 directory and rename as **ListService.exe.config**.

10. Change the method call that reads the configuration file to the following:

    ```
    RemotingConfiguration.Configure("ListService.exe.config")
    ```

11. Build the ListService project.

12. Open a command prompt window and change the current directory to the installation directory of the .NET Framework, which will be *WINNT*\Microsoft.Net\Framework\v*x.y.z* (where *WINNT* is your windows directory and *x.y.z* is the version of the .NET Framework).

13. Type **installutil** *appPath* where *appPath* is the directory path to ListService.exe. This will install your service.

14. The service is now installed. You can now start the service by using the Server Explorer from within Visual Studio.

You can also view the Event Log from the Server Explorer making Visual Studio the central hub of your development activities. Notice that the configuration file was placed in the winnt/system32 directory because this is a Windows Service application. If you need to keep the configuration file together with the executable, you will have to use the absolute path. Installing the service with the *installutil* tool has to be done only once. To update the executable, simply stop the service and rebuild the project.

# Using the TCP Channel with the Binary Formatter

Within a corporate intranet, you can gain more speed by using the TCP channel. To change the sample application to use the TCP channel all you need to do is do a search and replace of every "Http" with "Tcp" within the configuration files. The TCP channel uses binary formatting by default, whereas the HTTP channel defaults to SOAP formatting. Two downsides of using the TCP channel is that communication may be blocked by firewalls, and you cannot use your browser to examine the SOAP description of your hosting application.

# Summary of the Improved Sample Application

Your sample application now contains enough bells and whistles to provide a base for a real-world multitier application. You have seen how to host your remoting objects from within a Windows Service, how to write to the event log, how to handle exceptions on startup, and how clients can easily communicate with your remote objects. To further enhance the application you could connect to a database to obtain various lists of data that are in common use across all corporate applications—countries, clients, customers, languages, application settings, and so on. On the client side, you could then subclass a ComboBox control and add a property called *ListType*, which would load the corresponding list of items from your remote object on initialization. This control would save development time and provide a standardized user interface. ASP.NET applications could also use your remote objects in the same way.

# Creating an Intranet Application

The remoting framework provides fine control over how objects are sent to and from remote applications and also how objects are created and destroyed. We now look at an example of how you can use these features in a remoting application.

# Object Lifetime and Leasing

In the COM world, object lifetime was controlled by reference counting. As clients disconnected from the server object, the reference count was decremented until it reached zero. The server object was then unloaded immediately, and any hold on system resources was released. With the .NET Framework, no reference counting occurs. Instead, an object is marked to be garbage collected when no other object holds a reference to it. Because the garbage collector cannot detect remote references (because they are in another AppDomain), .NET uses another method for handling object lifetime called *leasing*.

Objects have a default lease time—when this time has passed, the object will be ready for garbage collection provided there are no references to the object from its own AppDomain. An object can change its own lease period on startup or even set it to infinity to maintain state forever (forever = until a server reboot!). Clients are able to renew this lease if they wish to keep communicating with the same object instance. Also, the client can register a sponsor for a lease. When the lease expires, the sponsor is given the opportunity to renew the lease.

We now create a sample application that uses the leasing features of the remoting framework. The source code for this project is in the CountServer directory—opening up the solution file CountServer.sln will make sure that both the server and the hosting application are loaded into Visual Studio.

## Creating the *CountServer* Project

This project contains the server-side functionality. The *Count* class implements a counter that can be incremented and decremented with the *inc* and *dec* methods respectively:

1. Create a new Class Library application in Visual Studio named **CountServer**.

2. Right-click the default **Class1.cs** module in the Solution Explorer and choose **Delete**.

3. Right-click the **ListServer** project in the Solution Explorer, select **Add | Add Class** and name your new class **Count.cs**.

4. Add the following code to Count.cs:

```
using System;
using System.Runtime.Remoting;
using System.Runtime.Remoting.Lifetime;


namespace CountServer
{
    public class Count: MarshalByRefObject
    {

        private int mVal;
```

```
        public Count()
        {
            mVal = 0;
        }


        public override Object InitializeLifetimeService()
        {
          ILease lease = (ILease)base.InitializeLifetimeService();
          if (lease.CurrentState == LeaseState.Initial)
            {
              lease.InitialLeaseTime = TimeSpan.FromSeconds(5);
              lease.RenewOnCallTime = TimeSpan.FromSeconds(1);
              lease.SponsorshipTimeout = TimeSpan.FromSeconds(5);
            }

            return lease;
        }

        public int inc()
        {
            mVal++;
            return mVal;
        }

        public int dec()
        {
            mVal—;
            return mVal;
        }
    }
}
```

This code is quite straightforward except for the *InitializeLifetimeService*
method. Every remoting object has this method because *InitializeLifetimeService* is

a method of the inherited *MarshalByRefObject* class. This method obtains the current lease for the object, and by overriding this method, an object can control/set its own lease properties. These lease properties can be set only before the object has been marshaled to the client—the *CurrentState* property is used to check that the lease is in its initial state and can therefore be modified. The three lease properties used in the code are the following:

- **InitialLeaseTime** The time of a lease. The object will be ready for garbage collection after this amount of time. Setting this property to *null* gives an infinite lease time.

- **RenewOnCallTime** Every call to the object will increase the lease time by this amount.

- **SponsorshipTimeout** When the lease has expired, the lease will contact any registered sponsors. The sponsor then has the opportunity of extending the lease. The *SponsorshipTimeout* value is the amount of time that the object will wait for a response from the sponsor. The sponsor class will be introduced shortly in the client-side code.

These default lease settings can also be placed within the configuration file as follows:

```
<application name="CountServer">
<lifetime leaseTime="5S" sponsorshipTimeOut="5S" renewOnCallTime="1S"/>
. . .
</application>
```

The units of time used in the configuration file are *D* for days, *M* for minutes, *S* for seconds, and *MS* for milliseconds.

**NOTE**

For a lease on the server to contact a sponsor on the client, the client must register a *ServerChannel* to listen on a port. If the lease attempts to contact your client-side sponsor and you do not have a *ServerChannel*, the contact will fail and the remoting object will be deactivated after the specified *SponsorshipTimeout* value. You will not receive an error in this situation.

# Creating the *CountHost* Project

This host application will configure the *Count* class for remoting as a *Singleton* object. Being a *Singleton* object, it is shared between all client applications:

1. Add a new Console Application project named **CountHost** to the current solution and add a reference to the CountServer project.

2. Add the call to *RemotingConfiguration* in the main method and reference the *System.Runtime.Remoting* namespace so that the complete console application code appears as follows:

```
using System;
using System.Runtime.Remoting;


namespace CountHost
{
    class Class1
    {
        static void Main(string[] args)
        {
            try
            {

RemotingConfiguration.Configure(@"..\..\CountHost.exe.config");
            }
            catch (Exception e)
            {
                System.Console.WriteLine("Failed to configure
hostapplication:
                "
+e.Message,System.Diagnostics.EventLogEntryType.Error);
            }


            System.Console.WriteLine("Press [Enter] to exit...");
            System.Console.ReadLine();
        }
    }
}
```

3.  Create the configuration file named **CountHost.exe.config** and place
    in the project directory:

```
<configuration>
  <system.runtime.remoting>
   <application name="CountServer">
    <channels>
      <channel displayName="MyChannel"
        type="System.Runtime.Remoting.Channels.Http.HttpChannel,
          System.Runtime.Remoting" port="8085" />
    </channels>
    <service>
      <wellknown displayName="MyService" mode="Singleton"
       type="CountServer.Count,CountServer"
       objectUri="CountServer" />
    </service>
   </application>
   <debug loadTypes="true" />
  </system.runtime.remoting>
</configuration>
```

4.  Build the project to produce the hosting application—CountHost.exe.

## Creating the *CountClient* Project

The *CountClient* project is a Windows Application that will remote to the server-side Count object and update the counter value. The app will also have two buttons that allow us to renew the lease and to also add a sponsor for the object. Follow the next steps to create the project or alternatively access the code from the CountClient directory on the CD:

1.  Create a new Windows Application for the client side called
    **CountClient**.

2.  Add four buttons to the form—**btnInc**, **btnDec**, **btnRenew**, and
    **btnSponsor** with the captions—"Inc", "Dec", "Renew Lease", and
    "Add Sponsor". Also add a textbox called **txtValue**.

3. Add click event handlers to each button and add the following code to the form:

```
using System;
using System.Drawing;
using System.Collections;
using System.ComponentModel;
using System.Windows.Forms;
using System.Data;
using System.Runtime.Remoting;
using System.Runtime.Remoting.Lifetime;


namespace CountClient
{
    public class Form1 : System.Windows.Forms.Form
    {
        private System.Windows.Forms.Button btnInc;
        private System.Windows.Forms.Button btnDec;
        private System.Windows.Forms.Button btnRenew;
        private System.Windows.Forms.Button btnSponsor;
        private System.Windows.Forms.TextBox txtValue;
        private System.ComponentModel.IContainer components;

        private CountServer.Count objCount;
        private ClientSponsor mSponsor;
        private ILease mLease;

        public Form1()
        {
            InitializeComponent();
            RemotingConfiguration.Configure(
                @"..\..\CountClient.exe.config");
            objCount = new CountServer.Count();
        }


        private void btnInc_Click(object sender, System.EventArgs e)
```

```
    {
        txtValue.Text = objCount.inc().ToString();
    }


private void btnDec_Click(object sender, System.EventArgs e)
{
        txtValue.Text = objCount.dec().ToString();
    }


private void btnRenew_Click(object sender, System.EventArgs e)
{
    mLease = (ILease)RemotingServices.
        GetLifetimeService(objCount);

    try
    {
        mLease.Renew(System.TimeSpan.FromSeconds(10));
        MessageBox.Show(this,"Lease renewed for 10 seconds");
    }
    catch
    {
        MessageBox.Show(this,"Lease has expired");
    }
}


private void btnSponsor_Click(object sender, System.EventArgs e)
{
    mLease = (ILease)RemotingServices.
        GetLifetimeService(objCount);
    mSponsor = new ClientSponsor();
    mSponsor.RenewalTime = TimeSpan.FromSeconds(15);
    try
    {
        mLease.Register(mSponsor);
    }
```

```
            catch

            {

                MessageBox.Show(this,"Lease has expired");

            }


            MessageBox.Show("Sponsor registered with object");

        }

    }

}
```

   4.   Create the client-side configuration file:

```xml
<configuration>
  <system.runtime.remoting>
   <application name="CountClient">
    <client>
      <wellknown type="CountServer.Count, CountServer"
       url="http://localhost:8085/CountServer"/>
    </client>
    <channels>
     <channel type="System.Runtime.Remoting.Channels.Tcp.TcpChannel,
      System.Runtime.Remoting" port="8011"/>
    </channels>
   </application>
  </system.runtime.remoting>
</configuration>
```

# Understanding the Leasing and Sponsorship Code

The increment and decrement buttons simply call the corresponding methods on the server-side *Count* object and display the result in the textbox. By observing the returned value, you can determine if you are still using the original class instance.

The Renew Lease button renews the lease of the current server-side *Count* object. To do this, the lease is obtained by calling *GetLifetimeService* on the remote object. A remote reference to the server-side lease is then returned and the *Renew* method is called on the lease. Note that the lease is also acting as a remote object in this scenario. The *Renew* method takes a *TimeSpan* parameter that specifies the new lease time.

The Add Sponsor button registers a sponsor so that you can receive a notification when the lease has expired. The code obtains a remote reference to the lease, creates a sponsor, and then registers the sponsor with the lease. In the preceding code, the sponsor will set the lease time to 15 seconds when notified by the server-side lease. By running the client-side application, you will see a form as shown in Figure 6.8.

**Figure 6.8** Controlling Object Lifetime with Leases and Sponsors

To test the object lifetime features of .NET remoting, click on the **Inc** button two times so that the value in the textbox is 2. The *InitialLeaseTime* set by the server-side *Count* object is 5 seconds—if you wait more than 5 seconds and then click on **Inc** again, you will notice that the counter has been reset. The remoting framework has destroyed the original instance after 5 seconds and has created a new object to handle the latest call.

The server-side lease property, *RenewOnCallTime*, has a value of 1 second. This will cause 1 second to be added to the lease time on every call to the remote object. You can test this by clicking on the **Inc** button quickly 20 times—you will notice that after waiting 20 seconds, and clicking **Inc** again, that the counter has not been reset.

Clicking **Renew Lease** will set the current lease time to 10 seconds. Again, by clicking on **Inc** a couple of times, waiting about 8 seconds, and then clicking **Renew Lease**, you will notice that the counter's life is extended. Clicking **Add Sponsor** has the effect of having a permanent *Singleton* object on the server. The sponsor will always set the lease time of the remote object to 15 seconds whenever it is notified by the server that the lease has expired. After the client application is closed, the server site lease will eventually attempt to notify the client of lease expiration. In our example, 15 seconds will pass while the server lease waits for an answer. When that answer doesn't arrive, the remote object will be shut down.

As a final experiment, start up two instances of the CountClient.exe and run them side-by-side. By clicking on the **Inc** and **Dec** buttons of each application, you will see that they both share the same *Singleton* instance of the server-side object. Also, if all client-side applications are shut down, the server-side component will still maintain its state if a new application calls the component before its lease expires.

## Debugging...

### Remoting Applications

Anyone that has started learning the .NET remoting framework will know how easy it is to accidentally stop an application from working. A wrong port number or a misspelled type name can take some time to track down. In a perfect world, you would get an error message like "You tried to communicate with server xyz on port 8050. There is nothing listening on that port but 8051 has something that may interest you." To help avoid these problems, a base application might help—this application would contain the three projects needed for a remoting app (server, host, and client) plus any boilerplate code and configuration files. This application could then serve as a starting point for all your remoting applications.

Another method to help (or avoid) debugging your applications is to start with the simplest case. A simple "test" method on each remote object could be used to test the communication channels between the tiers of your application. Such an approach is better than calling a complex method on an object that may contain other object references and serialized objects as parameters—there would just be too many places where something could go wrong. This "test" method would also help in the construction of a monitoring application that could ping your remote objects every few minutes and e-mail an administrator if an object does not respond.

## Client Activated Objects

The server-activated objects that we have been using so far in this chapter have been of two types, *Singleton* and *SingleCall*. The third type of remoting object is the CAO or Client Activated Object, which allows a client application to create a remote instance of the object for exclusive use, similar to the way that clients do in the COM world. These objects can maintain state without you having to worry about another client connecting to the remoting object and changing its state without your knowledge.

Making your objects ready for client activation is as easy as modifying the configuration file on the server. For example, the *CountClient*'s configuration file has the following section:

```
<service>
 <wellknown mode="Singleton" type="CountServer.Count,CountServer"
  objectUri="CountServer" />
</service>
```

To change this to a CAO, the *activated* attribute is used with only the *type* parameter instead of the *wellknown* attribute:

```
<service>
 <activated type="CountServer.Count,CountServer">
 </activated>
</service>
```

The client-side configuration file then requires a modified <client> specification that uses the same *activated* attribute parameters as the server-side configuration file:

```
<client url="http://localhost:8085">
  <activated type="CountServer.Count,CountServer"/>
</client>
```

When the client-side uses *new* to create a remote instance, the remote object is created immediately for the exclusive use of the client. Lifetime leasing and sponsorship need to be used in the same way as in the previous example—even though the object "belongs" to the client, it still has a lease that may expire, causing the object to lose state.

## Sending and Receiving Objects by Value

For more complex remoting applications, you may need to pass objects as parameters to remote method calls or receive such objects in return. For example, instead of passing a customer name and a customer ID in separate calls, it is more efficient to create a Customer object containing the required information and send the whole object to the server in one call. To achieve this, the remoting framework needs to be able to serialize your class so that it can be sent over a channel.

The *[serializable]* attribute is used to specify a class as being serializable and able to be remoted by value. Using the customer example, the class definition would appear as follows:

```
 [Serializable]
class Customer
{
    public Customer()
    {}

    int ID;
    String Name;
}
```

> **NOTE**
>
> It is important to consider the suitability of a class for remoting. If the class can hold large amounts of data and must be sent over a slow connection, application performance will suffer. Also, some types of data (for example, a file path) would have no meaning on a remote server.

## Sending and Receiving Objects by Reference

For overly large objects, passing them by reference to remote servers may be more efficient. This is roughly equivalent to simplified remoting—the remoting framework will create a proxy for your object on the server. As the server calls methods on your object, the proxy will route the calls to the real object on the client side. As you are controlling the creation of the object instance and handling the calls explicitly, you don't need to consider ports, channels, and object lifetime issues (although if you would like the server to call-back to your client object, keeping a reference to it would be a good idea to prevent it from being garbage collected).

For a class to be sent by reference, it is necessary for the class to inherit from *MarshalByRefObject*. The customer class would then appear as follows:

```
class Customer: MarshalByRefObject
{
```

```
    public Customer()
    {}

    int ID;
    String Name;
}
```

# Creating Service-Based Applications

A major improvement of .NET components compared to legacy COM components is the ability to use side-by-side deployment. Upgrading COM components
is an all-or-nothing affair, which can cause problems with client applications
relying on a specific version of a component. With the .NET Framework, you
can have different versions of the same component running at the same time. To
achieve this with your remoting applications, you need to give your server-side
assemblies what is known as a strong name.

## Building a Versioned Remoting Application

A *strong name* is a unique identifier for an assembly, which is generated by combining a text name, the version number, culture information (if it exists), a public
key, and a digital signature. This may sound complicated, but it is in fact quite
easy. We now create a remoting class and build the assembly with a strong name.
The following code is in the VersionServer directory on the CD:

1. Create a new Class Library application in Visual Studio named
   **VersionServer**.

2. Right-click the default **Class1.cs** module in the Solution Explorer and
   choose **Delete**.

3. Right-click the **ListServer** project in the Solution Explorer, select **Add
   | Add Class** and name your new class **Test.cs**.

4. Add the following code to Test.cs. The *getVersion* method will be used to
   return the current version string back to the client application:

   ```
   using System;
   using System.Windows.Forms;
   using System.Reflection;
   ```

```
namespace VersionServer
{
    public class Test:MarshalByRefObject
    {
        public Test()
        {
        }

        public String getVersion()
        {
            return Assembly.GetAssembly(this.GetType()).
            GetName().Version.ToString();
        }
    }
}
```

5. Now, use the strong name utility (sn.exe) to generate a new strong name key. To do this, use the *-k* parameter with the output file name. From the Visual Studio .NET Command Prompt type in **sn –k mykey.snk**. Copy the new key file to the source code area of the *VersionServer* project.

6. Now, add the key to the assembly manifest. Open the **AssemblyInfo.cs** file, which contains the assembly attributes, and find the *AssemblyKeyFile* attribute. Add the path to the key file to the *AssemblyKeyFile* attribute as shown here:

```
[assembly: AssemblyKeyFile("..\\..\\mykey.snk")]
```

7. Also, set the desired version number using the *AssemblyVersion* attribute as shown here:

```
[assembly: AssemblyVersion("1.0.0.99")]
```

8. After building the VersionServer.dll, you need to install the assembly into the Global Assembly Cache (GAC). The GAC is located in the Assembly directory under the Windows system directory. For example C:\WINNT\Assembly. To install the assembly, you can drag and drop the DLL into the GAC or you can use the gacutil.exe utility.

9. Now update the version to **2.0.0.0**. Rebuild the project and repeat Step 8. Update the version to **3.0.0.0** and repeat Step 8 again. You will now have three versions of the *VersionServer* in the GAC, as shown in Figure 6.9.

**Figure 6.9** Installing Multiple Versions in the GAC

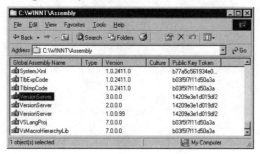

## Creating the *VersionHost* Project

The *VersionHost* project is a simple console application that will host the versioned components. The code for the project is located in the VersionHost directory on the CD. This code is the same as that used for the earlier examples except a slightly different configuration file is used (see Figure 6.10). In this configuration file, the required version has been added to the *wellknown* attribute. Even though you earlier created a version 3 of the assembly, you are able to choose version 2 (or any other version) by modifying this configuration file.

**Figure 6.10** Configuring a Versioned Remoting Application

```
<configuration>
  <system.runtime.remoting>
    <application name="CountServer">
      <channels>
        <channel type="System.Runtime.Remoting.
          Channels.Http.HttpChannel,System.Runtime.Remoting"
          port="8085"/>
      </channels>
      <service>
        <wellknown mode="SingleCall"
          type="VersionServer.Test,VersionServer,Version=2.0.0.0"
          objectUri="VersionServer2" />
```

**Continued**

**Figure 6.10** Continued

```
    </service>
  </application>
  <debug loadTypes="true" />
 </system.runtime.remoting>
</configuration>
```

This version setting will be used whenever a server activated *VersionServer* object is needed. This means that clients requesting a server activated object from a URI are not able to request a specific version—versioning is determined by the server. To enable client requests for different versions, you need to use a different URI for each version. You can do this by adding extra *wellknown* attributes to the configuration file, as shown in Figure 6.11.

**Figure 6.11** Including Multiple Versions in a Configuration File

```
<wellknown mode="SingleCall"
  type="VersionServer.Test,VersionServer,Version=2.0.0.0"
  objectUri="VersionServer2" />
<wellknown mode="SingleCall"
  type="VersionServer.Test,VersionServer,Version=3.0.0.0"
  objectUri="VersionServer3" />
```

**NOTE**

If the version is not specified in the server-side configuration file, the latest version available will always be loaded.

## Creating the *VersionClient* Project

The *VersionClient* project will be used to connect to a specific version of *VersionServer*. This will be done by specifying the corresponding URI in the client-side configuration file. Follow the next steps to create the project (or access the code from the VersionClient directory on the CD):

1. Create a new Windows Application called **VersionClient**.

2. Add a button to the form called **btnGetVersion**.

3. Add a click event handler to the button and add the following code to the form. The button will retrieve the version information from the remote object and display it within a message box:

```
using System;
using System.Drawing;
using System.ComponentModel;
using System.Windows.Forms;
using System.Runtime.Remoting;

namespace VersionClient
{

    public class Form1 : System.Windows.Forms.Form
    {
        private System.Windows.Forms.Button btnGetVersion;
        private System.ComponentModel.Container components = null;
        private VersionServer.Test objRemote;

        public Form1()
        {
            InitializeComponent();
            RemotingConfiguration.Configure(
                @"..\..\VersionClient.exe.config");
            objRemote = new VersionServer.Test();
        }

        private void btnGetVersion_Click(object sender,
            System.EventArgs e)
        {
            MessageBox.Show(objRemote.getVersion());
        }
```

```
      }
}
```

4. Create the client-side configuration file. The *VersionServer2* URI is used to connect to version 2 of the remote component:

```
<configuration>
 <system.runtime.remoting>
  <application name="VersionClient">
   <client>
    <wellknown type="VersionServer.Test, VersionServer"
      url="http://localhost:8085/VersionServer2"/>
   </client>
  </application>
 </system.runtime.remoting>
</configuration>
```

5. Start the VersionHost.exe console application and then build and run the *VersionClient* project. Clicking the button will display the version of the remote object—see Figure 6.12.

**Figure 6.12** Including Multiple Versions in a Configuration File

## Testing Side-By-Side Execution of Remote Objects

As a final experiment, we get two versions of the remote object running side by side. To do this, keep the *VersionClient* application running. Then open up the client-side configuration file and change the URI from *VersionServer2* to *VersionServer3*—this will not impact the running application because the configuration file is read only on startup. Now find the VersionClient.exe executable in Windows Explorer and run it. After clicking the button, you'll see that version 3 of the remote object is now being used. Click the button of the first application instance and version 2 is still available! Both application instances can run independently on the client, while multiple versions of the server-side objects can handle client requests at the same time.

# Summary

*Remoting* is used to allow .NET applications to communicate with each other across TCP or HTTP protocols. This communication takes place across a channel which uses SOAP to format message calls. These SOAP messages can either be XML formatted or sent as a binary stream. Although the HTTP channel is suitable for applications distributed on the Internet, the TCP channel is faster and is often used on corporate networks.

Server-side objects must be hosted in a hosting application to expose them to requests from client applications. A hosting application may be a Console, Windows Service, or Windows Forms application. When the hosting application starts, it must register a channel to listen for client requests by calling *ChannelServices.RegisterChannel*. The host will then register remoting configuration information with the remoting framework either in code (using the *RemotingConfiguration.RegisterWellKnownServiceType* method) or by using a configuration file (using the *RemotingConfiguration.Configure* method).

Remoting objects have three activation models—*SingleCall*, *Singleton*, and Client Activated Objects (CAO). *SingleCall* objects are stateless, whereas *Singleton* objects are stateful and able to be shared between client applications. CAO objects are created by a client application for exclusive use and they preserve state between remote method calls.

For a client application to be compiled in Visual Studio.NET, the remote server classes metadata is needed. The easiest method is to reference to the remote object's DLL in the client project. The other method is to use the soapsuds.exe utility to generate a proxy class from the remote object's URI.

For a client application to use remoting, a channel must be registered and the remoting framework configured in a similar manner to that used in the hosting application. If a configuration file is not used on the client and a proxy class is not available (from the soapsuds utility), the *Activator.GetObject* method must be used to create a reference to the remote object.

The lifetime of a remoting object is controlled by a lease. Objects have a default lease time after which they can be garbage collected. An object may change its default lease time on startup by overriding the *InitializeLifetimeService* method. Clients may also renew a lease to keep a remote object active. When a lease expires, the remoting framework will notify any registered sponsors so that a sponsor may renew the lease if required.

An assembly in which remoting classes reside may be versioned by using a strong name. A strong name allows the assembly to be placed in the Global

Assembly Cache (GAC) so that it may be located by the remoting framework. The server-side configuration file is used to expose a specific version of a component for remoting clients to access. It is possible for multiple versions of remoting objects to run side-by-side.

# Solution Fast Track

## Introducing Remoting

☑ Remoting allows cross-application communication, whether they are located on the same PC or across the Internet.

☑ Channels are used as the communications mechanism—HTTP and TCP channels may be used.

☑ Server-side objects need a hosting application to handle incoming requests. A hosting application may be in the form of a console application, Windows Service, forms-based app, IIS, or COM+ service.

## Creating a Simple Remoting Client Server

☑ All remoting objects must inherit from *MarshalByRefObject*.

☑ Hosting applications use the *RegisterWellKnownServiceType* method of the *RemotingConfiguration* class to register objects for remoting.

☑ *Singletons* objects only have a single instance and handle multiple client requests.

☑ *SingleCall* objects do not maintain state. They handle a single request and are then recycled by the remoting framework.

☑ Remoting applications that act as servers must listen on a port as specified by the developer.

☑ External XML configuration files may also be used to configure remoting on both the server and the client.

☑ Hosting remote objects in a Windows Service application eases the administration of server-side remoting objects.

# Creating an Intranet Application

☑ A lease controls object lifetime—the lease specifies the time-to-expire of the object.

☑ The default values of the lease may be specified by the remote object on startup.

☑ A client application may control the lease to keep a remote object active.

☑ A sponsor can be attached to a lease. When the lease has expired, the sponsor will be notified so that the lease may be extended if required.

# Creating Service-Based Applications

☑ Versioned assemblies require a strong name so that they can be uniquely identified by the .NET Framework.

☑ To generate a strong name, a strong name key is needed. The sn.exe utility is used to create key files.

☑ Versioned assemblies should be placed in the Global Assembly Cache (GAC)—the .NET Framework will search the GAC for strong-named (shared) assemblies.

☑ For server activated objects, the server configuration file is used to map a URI to the version of an assembly.

# Frequently Asked Questions

The following Frequently Asked Questions, answered by the authors of this book, are designed to both measure your understanding of the concepts presented in this chapter and to assist you with real-life implementation of these concepts. To have your questions about this chapter answered by the author, browse to **www.syngress.com/solutions** and click on the **"Ask the Author"** form.

**Q:** If I have a *Singleton* object to handle multiple clients and it only listens on a single port, doesn't this create a performance bottleneck?

**A:** Don't worry. Remoting objects are multithreaded so that one request does not block another.

**Q:** With .NET, it seems much easier to maintain state on the server. Will this change the way applications are developed?

**A:** The stateless model of development is often the most scalable and robust architecture. The lessons learned with Windows DNA multitier development still apply today.

**Q:** It is also easier now to have the server perform callbacks to the client side, in what situations can this be used?

**A:** Callbacks are easier with .NET as compared to VB in the past. They are also very interesting to program, but in a business setting, you should use them only when you have no other choice. For example, a callback to notify a user of a certain situation may be better handled with a generated e-mail instead. You could develop and debug the e-mail code a lot faster, and the end–user could then use her e-mail program to assign tasks, forward the e-mail, and so on.

**Q:** Where can I find out more about remoting?

**A:** The best newsgroup for this is the microsoft.public.dotnet.framework.remoting group. Also, the MSDN area on the Microsoft site often publishes articles on aspects of .NET remoting.

# Chapter 7

# Message Queuing Using MSMQ

### Solutions in this chapter:

- Introducing MSMQ

- Creating a Simple Application

- Creating a Complex Application

- Creating an Asynchronous Application

☑ Summary

☑ Solutions Fast Track

☑ Frequently Asked Questions

# Introduction

The connectivity of local area networks (LANs) and the Internet has made the concept of distributed applications a reality. Applications now routinely utilize remote machines to perform tasks and provide services. Unfortunately, a distributed application has many more points of failure than a nondistributed application—servers may be offline, the network may be overloaded, or the scheduled maintenance or upgrading of servers can also cause problems for distributed applications. What is needed is for an application to be able to continue running when distributed resources are unavailable—which is what the messaging infrastructure of Microsoft Message Queue (MSMQ) provides.

With MSMQ handling the communication between machines in a distributed application, it has a great deal of responsibility. All communication (messages) must have guaranteed delivery, security needs must be met, messages must be logged, and delivery confirmations must be sent, too. The MSMQ product provides all of these services and more—in fact, by using MSMQ technology, you can make your applications more robust and scalable. For a small increase in application complexity, you gain many rewards.

The .NET Framework provides added functionality during the development of .NET applications. Objects can be serialized to binary or XML and then sent as a message. By using .NET serialization you send any dataset, image, or file into a message with very little coding.

In this chapter, we look at how MSMQ uses queues to store messages that provide a communications mechanism between applications. You'll see the options that are available for the usage of queues and the variety of ways in which messages can be created, sent, and received. We develop a simple MSMQ example application, and we also discuss debugging and deployment issues. We then move on to the more advanced areas of MSMQ and develop some additional example applications to show how MSMQ can be of use in your own applications.

# Introducing MSMQ

MSMQ provides solutions to a range of problem scenarios that appear during application development. A common example is in client-server architecture where a direct connection to the server is needed to handle information updates. In this situation, any disruption to the server will cause all client applications to fail, possibly causing idle staff and lost productivity. Such a disruption may be caused by a hardware failure, power outage, or a server upgrade. The solution is to use message queuing to "uncouple" the client and the server by providing a storage point for communication between them. Now, if a connection to the server cannot be made, data entered in client application can be stored in a client-side message queue. Once a connection is reestablished, the messages are then automatically forwarded to the destination queue on a remote server. An application on the server will then read the messages from the message queue and perform the necessary database updates.

A similar situation to the client/server scenario is when it becomes quite common for client applications to be disconnected from the network. Sales staff often use notebook computers to run their sales applications while they are on the road. Some may type in information directly into the notebook, whereas others may wait until they arrive back at the office. Instead of writing code to handle the online and offline situations (and possibly an "upload to server" function), using message queuing to handle both cases is more efficient. In online mode, all messages will be sent directly to the server queue. In offline mode, the messages will be temporarily stored on the client, ready for forwarding to the server queue when the network connection is made.

MSMQ also provides the plumbing you need for true distributed processing. A good example of this is in the area of mathematical computation. If the work required to find a solution to a mathematical problem can be divided into pieces then such pieces could be placed on a queue. Each piece would constitute a message containing all the information required for an idle computer on a network to get started on the problem. These computers could take a piece of the mathematical puzzle, calculate their share of the solution, and send the result back to the queue. A central controlling application could then correlate the response messages with the request messages and combine these results into the total solution. You may also need MSMQ when you hear the following during conversations between IT personnel:

- "Not again!, This Web server always takes at least three minutes to respond on Monday morning, and my app slows to a crawl."

- "The application locks up when they back up the server every night. What can we do?"

- "How can we trace the communication between these applications?"

- "Last time our server was offline, we had 50 data entry operators idle for an hour. How can we avoid this in the future?"

A side effect of using MSMQ in your applications is that you can now easily trace the messages sent between your application tiers. This tracing can help with auditing and debugging your application. You can also authorize new applications to hook onto your messaging infrastructure to reuse the services that your message queuing applications provide.

The next time you participate in the planning phase of a software project, keep these scenarios in mind, and you may find areas where MSMQ can really save development time and increase application stability.

# MSMQ Architecture

In the world of MSMQ, you will be dealing with two main objects—queues and messages. A queue is a storage area for messages on a MSMQ server. A queue may be public or private. Private queues can only be used on a single machine, whereas public queues are replicated around the network for all machines to access. A message can be thought of as an envelope containing data plus information that describes the type of data being sent, its priority, security needs, acknowledgement, and timing information. Applications may send and receive messages from any queue that they have access to.

Computers running client applications must have MSMQ installed to be able to send messages. Within the MSMQ architecture are two types of clients:

- **Dependent clients**  Dependent clients must have direct access to a Message Queuing server. Client applications will then rely on the server to carry out all message queuing functions. When many dependent clients are connected to a Message Queuing server, a performance penalty can occur. Also, you cannot use the "store and forward" features of MSMQ with dependent clients—client apps will simply fail when disconnected from the network. For this and other reasons, independent clients are the recommended choice where possible.

- **Independent clients**  Independent clients do not need continuous access to a Message Queuing server to send messages. Any messages that are sent while disconnected from the network are stored locally in an outgoing queue. When a connection is reestablished, the messages in the outgoing queue will be sent to the destination queue.

# Installing MSMQ

To get started using MSMQ, you will need a computer running Windows 2000. Simply choose **Add/Remove Programs** from the Control Panel, select **Add/Remove Windows Components**, and select **Message Queuing Services** from the list of components, as shown in Figure 7.1. You may require your Windows 2000 installation CD to complete the install.

**Figure 7.1** Selecting Message Queuing Services for Installation

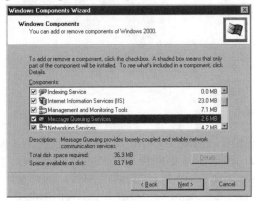

## Using Visual Studio to Manage Queues

Visual Studio.NET provides the Server Explorer to handle common server administration tasks, and you can use it to manage your MSMQ applications. If the Server Explorer is not visible, just use **Ctrl+Alt+S** to display it—you will see under the Servers node a list of computers that are available (see Figure 7.2). Your own computer will be listed here, but you can connect to other servers by using the **Connect To Server** toolbar button. Under a computer node is a list of application services including Message Queues, which allows you to create/delete queues and set various queue properties.

# Creating a Simple Application

We now create a simple application that will send a string message to a queue and receive it back. This application will be built upon later to demonstrate other aspects of Message Queue applications. The code for this application is located on the CD inside the MSMQapp1 project.

**Figure 7.2** The Server Explorer Showing Available Queues

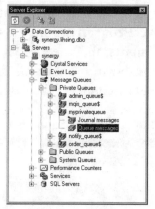

1. Create a new Windows Application type project in Visual Studio and name the project **MSMQapp1**.

2. From within the Server Explorer, right-click **Private Queues**, select **Create Queue**, and enter the name **Alpha** for the queue.

3. While *Form1* is in design mode, click and drag the **Alpha** queue from the Server Explorer to your form's design surface. This will create a queue component for your application to use.

4. Add two Buttons to the form called **btnSend** and **btnReceive**.

5. Add a private variable of type *int* to the class declaration of *Form1* as follows:

```
public class Form1 : System.Windows.Forms.Form
{
    private System.Windows.Forms.Button btnSend;
    private System.Windows.Forms.Button btnReceive;
```

```
private System.Messaging.MessageQueue MyMQ;
private System.ComponentModel.IContainer components;
private int iCount = 0;
```

. . .

6. Add the following code to the click events of the two buttons. A quick method of adding event handlers is to view the properties of a button, switch to event view by clicking the **Events** toolbar button at the top of the property window, and then double-click the *click* event from the event listing. This will create the event handler method for you and attach the new event handler to the button. It will also place the cursor at the correct location in the code for you to start coding the event handler. For those of you in more of a hurry, you can simply double-click the button on the form.

```
private void btnSend_Click(object sender, System.EventArgs e)
{
    iCount++;

    try
    {
        MyMQ.Send("message contents " + iCount.ToString());
    }
    catch(Exception ex)
    {
        MessageBox.Show(this,ex.Message);
    }
}


private void btnReceive_Click(object sender, System.EventArgs e)
{

    System.Messaging.Message m;
    String str;

    try
```

```
        {
                m = MyMQ.Receive(new TimeSpan(0, 0, 3));
                str = (String)m.Body;
        }
        catch
        {
                str = "No messages were receieved";
        }

        MessageBox.Show(this,str);
    }
```

7. Build and run the MSMQapp1 application.

You can now click **Send** to send some messages to the Alpha message queue. Now take a look at the Server Explorer and navigate to the Alpha node to see the messages that you have sent. If you are running the application from within Visual Studio, you will need to select **Debug | Break All** to pause execution so that you can use the Server Explorer. Notice that as you click on a message in Server Explorer, the Property window displays a large amount of information regarding the specific message.

To receive messages, click **Receive**. A message box will display the contents of the message received, as shown in Figure 7.3. Notice that the messages are received in the same order that they were sent—this cannot be relied upon. Messages that are sent with a higher priority can jump ahead of other messages on the queue while other applications may remove messages from the queue without your knowledge. A queue should be thought of as a "bag" of messages to emphasize that we cannot make assumptions as to the order of messages we will receive.

**Figure 7.3** A Simple Messaging Application

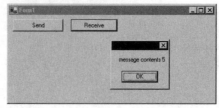

As a further experiment, try opening up two or more instances of the MSMQapp1 application by using Explorer to find and execute MSMQapp1.exe multiple times. Use one application instance to send messages and another instance to receive them. You can see that each application is completely independent and that they all share the same message queue.

# Understanding the Messaging Code

The MSMQ classes are contained within the *System.Messaging* namespace. Of the more than 20 classes contained within this namespace, the most important is *MessageQueue*. In Step 3 in the previous section, when the Alpha queue was dragged from Server Explorer to the form's design surface, four lines of code were automatically generated that will reference the *System.Messaging* namespace, declare and create a *MessageQueue* object, and set the *Path* property to the location of the Alpha queue. The format of the *Path* property is MachineName\\QueueName for public queues and MachineName\\$Private\\QueueName for private queues. Because the amount of generated code is quite small, manually adding similar code to your applications is quite easy.

To send a message to a queue, you use the *Send* method of the *MessageQueue* object. For the purposes of our example, a simple string was used as a message, but we will see later how more complex messages may be sent.

To receive a message from a queue, use the *Receive* method of the *MessageQueue* object. This method returns an object of type *Message* to the caller. The *Message* object contains a large amount of information in regard to the message itself—if you just want to know the content of the message, use the *Body* property. The *Body* is of type *object* and therefore must be cast to the correct type of the receiving variable, which in the example is type *(String)*. The *Receive* method accepts a *TimeSpan* parameter, which specifies how long we want to wait for the arrival of a message. If a message exists on the queue, *Receive* will return quickly, but if no messages exist, the application's thread of execution will be blocked while waiting for the next message. For this reason, keeping the wait time short is a good idea. An asynchronous (nonblocking) method of receiving messages is described later in this chapter in the section "Creating an Asynchronous Application."

## Sending Messages

Within the *System.Messaging* namespace is the *Message* class, which can be considered to be the "envelope" in which messages are sent. When you call the *Send* method of a queue and pass in an object as a parameter, the .NET Framework creates a new message and sets the *Body* property of the message to the object. For example, the following code fragment

```
MyMQ.Send("content");
```

is equivalent to

```
Message m = new Message();
m.Body = "Content";
MyMQ.Send(m);
```

Be aware, though, that in creating your own *Message* object that you must set the other properties of the *Message* object to suit your needs. When you send an object that is not a *Message*, the *Message* properties are set to those defined in the *DefaultPropertiesToSend* property of the queue.

You can test this method of sending messages by adding a button to *Form1* called *btnSend2* and adding the following code to the *click* event handler of the button:

```
private void btnSend2_Click(object sender, System.EventArgs e)
{
    System.Messaging.Message m = new System.Messaging.Message();
    m.Body = "Custom Message";
    MyMQ.Send(m);
}
```

**NOTE**

The code for this change is in the Form2.cs file on the CD. To update your project as you read the chapter, from within Visual Studio, right-click the Form1.cs file, choose **Exclude From Project**, then right-click the solution, choose **Add | Add Existing Item**, and select the Form2.cs file.

Then add code to set the queue's default properties for sending messages directly after the *InitializeComponent* call in the form's constructor:

```
public Form1()
{
```

```
    InitializeComponent();

    MyMQ.DefaultPropertiesToSend.Label = "Default Label";

    MyMQ.DefaultPropertiesToSend.Priority =

        MessagePriority.Highest ;

}
```

Now build and run the application. Clicking on the first Send button will now use the *DefaultProperties* for the queue because we are only passing a string to the *Send* method. After clicking this button, a few times you can use the Server Explorer to see the labels of the messages have been set to "Default Label". Using the second Send button will use the *Message* object that does not have a label set. Notice that we are also making all default messages to be of highest priority. This will cause the messages containing the words "message contents" to always be received before the custom messages that contain the text "Custom Message".

## Message Formats

All data that is sent to a remote server during Message Queue processing must be serialized into a stream. The method of serializing an object into a stream is called *formatting*. The *Message* class handles streaming automatically for you by applying a formatter to whatever object you set as the *Body* property. The output of the formatter appears in the *BodyStream* property of the message:

- **XMLMessageFormatter**  Streams objects and value types to human-readable XML.

- **BinaryMessageFormatter**  Streams objects to a binary stream.

- **ActiveXMessageFormatter**  Persists basic data types and enables a message queuing application to work together with previous versions of MSMQ.

You can also write a stream directly to the *BodyStream* property of the Message object, and we use this method later to send images to a queue.

To examine the contents of the *BodyStream* property, you can use the Server Explorer again to display the properties of a message. Click on the *BodyStream* property from within the Properties window and you will see a "..." button appear within the property value cell. Clicking on the button will display the Byte Array Property Editor, as shown in Figure 7.4.

**Figure 7.4** The *BodyStream* Contents—The Result of Streaming a Message to XML

To change the formatter that is used, you can use the property window of the MessageQueue component and select the formatter from the drop-down list. From within the code, you can do the same by setting a reference to the *System.Runtime.Serialization.Formatters* namespace and attaching a new formatter to the queue as follows:

```
MyMQ.Formatter = new BinaryMessageFormatter(FormatterAssemblyStyle.Full,
    FormatterTypeStyle.TypesAlways);
```

The *FormatterAssemblyStyle* and *FormatterTypeStyle* parameters determine how assembly and type names are sent to the stream. These choices handle all situations by using the most verbose method of describing the types—if a more compact stream is needed, you may want to experiment with the different options available.

# Sending and Receiving Messages with Complex Objects

Formatters provide a means of streaming not only single objects but also complex objects within a message. To test the sending of complex objects in a message, we now add two new classes to the example application, have one class contain a collection of the other class, instantiate the objects, and then pass them to a message queue. The updated code is within the Form3.cs file on the CD.

First, add the following assembly reference to the top of the form's code:

```
using System.Xml.Serialization;
```

Now, add two new classes to the application:

```
[XmlInclude(typeof(Student))]
public class Teacher
{
    public String name;
    public System.Collections.ArrayList students;
    public int salary;

    public Teacher()
    {
        students = new System.Collections.ArrayList();
    }
}


public class Student
{
    public String name;
    public int minutesInClass;
}
```

Don't forget the *[XmlInclude]* attribute! This is needed when you send an object of type *Teacher* to the XML formatter because the formatter will not recognize the *Student* objects within the *ArrayList.* This attribute allows the formatter to serialize the *Student* objects found nested within a *Teacher* object. If this attribute is not added, you will receive a runtime exception with the following message:

```
There was an error generating the XML document. The type
MSMQapp1.Student was not expected. Use the XmlInclude or SoapInclude
attribute to specify types that are not known statically.
```

Now add a new button to the form called *btnTeacher* and add the following code to the button's *click* event:

```
private void btnTeacher_Click(object sender, System.EventArgs e)
{
    Student s1 = new Student();
    Student s2 = new Student();
    Student s3 = new Student();
```

```
    Teacher t = new Teacher();

    s1.name = "Jason";
    s2.name = "Marlo";
    s3.name = "Jacky";

    s1.minutesInClass = 90;
    s2.minutesInClass = 5;
    s3.minutesInClass = 100;

    t.name = "Tom";
    t.salary = 50000;
    t.students.Add(s1);
    t.students.Add(s2);
    t.students.Add(s3);

    System.Messaging.Message m = new System.Messaging.Message();
    m.Body = t;

    try
    {
        MyMQ.Send(m);
    }
    catch (Exception ex)
    {
        MessageBox.Show(ex.Message + " " + ex.InnerException.Message);
    }
}
```

After building and running the application, click on the new button to send a *Teacher* object with its contained Students to a message queue. By using the Byte Array Property Editor to display the *BodyStream* property of the new message, you can see that the objects have been successfully streamed to human-readable XML, as shown in Figure 7.5.

**Figure 7.5** A Complex Object Streamed with the XML Formatter

```xml
<?xml version="1.0"?>
<Teacher xmlns:xsi="http://www.w3.org/2001/XMLSchema-instance"
    xmlns:xsd="http://www.w3.org/2001/XMLSchema">
  <name>Tom</name>
  <students>
    <Object xsi:type="Student">
      <name>Jason</name>
      <minutesInClass>90</minutesInClass>
    </Object>
    <Object xsi:type="Student">
      <name>Marlo</name>
      <minutesInClass>5</minutesInClass>
    </Object>
    <Object xsi:type="Student">
      <name>Jacky</name>
      <minutesInClass>100</minutesInClass>
    </Object>
  </students>
  <salary>50000</salary>
</Teacher>
```

Retrieving a complex object message from a queue is done using the familiar *Receive* method of the *MessageQueue* class. Once the message is received, you will need to use a formatter to obtain the original object from the *BodyStream*. This is done by creating a formatter and specifying the type of object that needs to be obtained. The *Body* property of the message can then be cast to the correct type. To try this, append the following code to the end of the code in the *btnTeacher_Click* event (this code is in Form4.cs on the CD):

```
System.Messaging.Message m2;
Teacher t2;

try
{
```

```
    m2 = MyMQ.Receive(new TimeSpan(0, 0, 3));
    m2.Formatter = new XmlMessageFormatter(new
        Type[]{typeof(Teacher),typeof(Student)});

    t2 = (Teacher)m2.Body;

    MessageBox.Show("Message received. " + t2.name + " has " +
        t2.students.Count + " students.");
}
catch (Exception ex)
{
    MessageBox.Show(ex.Message);
}
```

After building and running the application, click on the same button used earlier to send the *Teacher* object to the message queue. The preceding code will then immediately receive the message, define an XML formatter, and extract the *Teacher* object from the message. A dialog saying "Message received. Tom has 3 students." will then be displayed.

## Storing Files within Messages

The *BodyStream* property of the *Message* class contains the serialized form of the message contents and usually does not need to be directly accessed by the developer (although it can be handy during debugging). One situation in which we do need to use the *BodyStream* property is when we already have information in a stream and wish to send it directly to a message queue.

Streams are usually created during memory and file I/O operations—we use an image file to create a stream, pass the stream to a *Message* object, and then send it to a queue. This message will then be received and a *Bitmap* object created from the stream and displayed inside a *PictureBox* control.

The code for this example is in Form5.cs on the CD. First, add two new buttons to the simple messaging application called *btnSendImage* and *btnReceiveImage*. Add a picture box control named *picBox1* and also an *OpenFileDialog* component to the form. Then add a reference to the *System.IO* namespace as follows:

```
using System.IO;
```

Now add the following code to the *click* events of the two new buttons:

```csharp
private void btnSendImage_Click(object sender, System.EventArgs e)
{
    Stream imageStream;
    System.Messaging.Message mImage = new System.Messaging.Message();

    openFileDialog1.Filter = "image files (.bmp,.jpg,.gif)|
        *.bmp;*.jpg;*.gif;*.exe" ;
    openFileDialog1.FilterIndex = 1 ;

    if(openFileDialog1.ShowDialog() == DialogResult.OK)
    {
        if((imageStream = openFileDialog1.OpenFile())!= null)
        {
            mImage.BodyStream = imageStream;

            try
            {
                MyMQ.Send(mImage);
            }
            catch (Exception ex)
            {
                MessageBox.Show(ex.Message);
            }
            finally
            {
            imageStream.Close();
            }
        }
    }
}


private void btnReceiveImage_Click(object sender, System.EventArgs e)
{
    Bitmap bmp;
```

```
Stream imageStream;

System.Messaging.Message mImage = new System.Messaging.Message();

try

{

    mImage = MyMQ.Receive(new TimeSpan(0, 0, 3));

}

catch

{

    MessageBox.Show("No messages were received");

}


try

{

    imageStream = mImage.BodyStream;

    bmp = new Bitmap(imageStream);

    picBox1.Image = bmp;

}

catch(Exception ex)

{

    MessageBox.Show(ex.Message);

}

}
```

In the *btnSendImage_Click* event, the code obtains a file path from the user and a stream is opened from the file and passed to the *BodyStream* property of the message. The message is then sent in the usual manner using the *Send* method.

In the *btnReceiveImage_Click* event, a message is received, and a stream is obtained from the *BodyStream* property. A new bitmap is then created from the stream, and this bitmap is passed to a picture box object for display. The three lines of code to achieve this can be reduced to the following one line of code:

```
picBox1.Image = new Bitmap(mImage.BodyStream);
```

After building and running the application, click on the *btnSendImage* button and select a file from the dialog. Now click on the *btnReceiveImage* button, and the image will be displayed as shown in Figure 7.6.

**Figure 7.6** Sending and Receiving an Image from a Queue

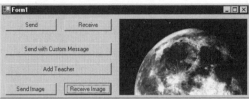

## Debugging…

### MSMQ Applications

During the development of MSMQ applications, many objects must act in unison to achieve the desired results. Problems can occur in the following areas:

- The *DefaultPropertiesToSend* property collection of a message queue can cause unexpected behavior during the sending of a primitive data type—make sure to check the settings of the default properties.

- The wrong formatter is used when sending a complex object.

- A complex object does not contain the required attributes to allow the serialization of the object's contents.

Developing the message queuing application using simple string messages can often be useful. Once the application has been debugged, you can use more complex messages and formatters. Remember that while debugging, you can always pause the execution of the code and examine the contents of the messages with the Server Explorer window.

Another useful debugging tool is the Performance Viewer located in the Administrative Tools area of the Control Panel. This tool displays performance information for a range of services and applications, one of them being MSMQ. To view the MSMQ performance statistics, click on the + icon and select **MSMQ Queue** from the Performance Object list. Choose one of the counters that displays either bytes or messages and then click **Add**. You will now see the activity of MSMQ in real time and can check that your queue is behaving as expected.

# Setting Queue Options

So far we have mostly accepted the default properties of a queue that the .NET Framework has provided. To improve the robustness of a message queuing application, you need to modify some of these properties. To do so, click on Message Queue component while your form is in design mode. The Property window will display the *DefaultPropertiesToSend* property with a **+** icon so that you can expand it. Some important properties to modify are the following:

- **AcknowledgeType**  Use this property to request acknowledgement on the success or failure of messages to reach a destination queue. Acknowledgements are sent as messages to the Administration queue defined by the developer.

- **AdministrationQueue**  This queue will receive acknowledgement messages that are generated on success or failure conditions as defined in the *AcknowledgeType* property.

- **Recoverable**  Setting this property to true will guarantee the delivery of a message even if a computer or network failure occurs. To achieve this, the message and its state are written to disk at all times in order to recover from such failures. Setting this option does degrade the throughput of the application.

- **TimeToBeReceived**  Sets the maximum amount of time for a message to wait on the destination queue. If the *UseDeadLetterQueue* property is set to true, the expired message will be sent to the dead-letter queue.

- **TimeToReachQueue**  Specifies the maximum amount of time for a message to arrive at the destination queue. If the *UseDeadLetterQueue* property is set to true, the expired message will be sent to the dead-letter queue.

**NOTE**

You can also specify the properties listed in this section on a per-message basis by setting the equivalent properties on a *Message* object.

We now use a couple of these properties to send expired messages to the dead-letter queue (the code for this is in the Form6.cs file on the CD):

1. Open the form of the simple messaging application in design mode.

2. Click on the message queue component under the form and bring up the Property window.

3. Expand the **DefaultProperties** property by clicking on the **+** icon.

4. Set the **TimeToBeReceived** property to 5 seconds.

5. Set the **UseDeadLetterQueue** property to true.

6. Build and start the project.

Now click Send (the very first button that was added to the project). You now have five seconds to click the Receive button to obtain the message before it expires and is sent to the dead-letter queue. Try this a few times and make sure to let a few messages expire! You can now view the dead-letter queue by using the Server Explorer, as shown in Figure 7.7.

**Figure 7.7** Examining the Dead-Letter Queue

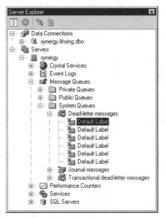

# Creating a Complex Application

We now create a more complex message queuing application. This application is composed of a form that allows the user to draw pictures using line segments. A *Drawing* object that contains a collection of *Line* objects will hold the drawing's information. The *Drawing* object will then be streamed to XML and sent to a queue. Another application will "listen" in on the queue and receive any new drawings that appear on the queue and then display them.

The application has three separate projects (the full source code is available on the CD):

- **MSMQGraphics** A class library application that contains the *Drawing* and *Line* classes. This DLL is used by the other two projects.

- **DrawingSender** A Windows application that allows the user to draw on the form and send the drawing as a message.

- **DrawingReceiver** A Windows application that listens for new drawings on the queue.

## Creating the *MSMQGraphics* Drawing Library

Figure 7.8 shows the code listing of the *MSMQGraphics* class library. This library contains all the functionality needed to draw a collection of line segments on a graphics surface.

**Figure 7.8** The Drawing Library Project

```
using System;
using System.Drawing;
using System.Xml.Serialization;
using System.Collections;

namespace MSMQGraphics
{
    [XmlInclude(typeof(Line))]
    public class Drawing
    {
        public ArrayList lines;

        public Drawing()
        {
            lines = new ArrayList();
        }

        public void clear()
        {
            lines.Clear();
        }
```

**Continued**

**Figure 7.8** Continued

```
        public void add(Line l)
        {
            lines.Add(l);
        }

        public void draw(Graphics g)
        {
            foreach (Line l in lines)
            {
                l.draw(g);
            }
        }
    }

public class Line
{
    public int x1;
    public int y1;
    public int x2;
    public int y2;
    public int Win32Color;

    public Line()
    {
    }

    public Line(int Win32Color,int x1,int y1,int x2,int y2)
    {
        this.x1 = x1;
        this.y1 = y1;
        this.x2 = x2;
        this.y2 = y2;
        this.Win32Color = Win32Color;
```

**Continued**

**Figure 7.8** Continued

```
        }

    public void draw(Graphics g)
    {
        g.DrawLine(newPen(ColorTranslator.FromWin32(Win32Color)),
            x1,y1,x2,y2);
    }
  }
}
```

This code should be straightforward for those that have spent some time with C# class definitions and collections, but some points must be noted. First, the *XmlInclude* attribute is necessary so that the XML formatter can recognize the *Line* objects within the *ArrayList*. Also, a default constructor for the *Line* class has been added because this is also required by the XML formatter. Finally, you will notice that we have used an integer value to determine the color instead of a *Color* object. This roundabout way is due to the XML formatter being unable to handle static classes. As you can see, it is important to design classes so that they may be easily handled by the XML formatter if you expect that they will be used within a MSMQ application.

---

### Developing & Deploying…

## MSMQ Applications

The development of message queuing applications can be aided by creating a class that hides many of the message queuing details from other areas. Such a class would have an event that was called when messages arrived allowing you to attach your own event handler. All formatting and streaming would be handled inside this class, too, and you could use extra methods to make development more efficient. For example, you could have a *Clear* method that would clear out all messages from your queue and a *Dump* method that could write the contents of all messages to a file. With some extra effort, this class could be reused in future message queue applications.

**Continued**

---

Message queuing code often has to depend on a queue having been already created by an administrator. By adding an installer for your queue, you can make sure that such queues are created during installation. To add an installer, click on the Message Queue component under your form while it is in design mode. View the properties for the component and click on the **Add Installer** hyperlink at the bottom of the Properties window. Visual Studio will create a new file named ProjectInstaller.cs and place the file in design mode so that the *messageQueueInstaller1* component is visible on the design surface. You can then click on the *messageQueueInstaller1* component and set the properties of the queue in the Property window. The executable built from this project will now contain a *ProjectInstaller* class that is detected by the installutil.exe tool. Running installutil.exe with the path to the project executable as a command-line parameter will then install the queue.

## Creating the *DrawingSender* Project

This project will use the *MSMQGraphics* library to allow the user to draw on a form. This form contains the following components:

- **pictureBox1**  The drawing surface.
- **btnColor**  This button is used to change the current color.
- **btnSend**  This button will send the drawing to the *drawings* message queue.
- **drawingMQ**  The message queue component that was created by dragging the *drawings* message queue from the Server Explorer window.
- **colorDialog1**  A color dialog window that allows the selection of a color.

The code that handles the drawing and sending of the message is shown in Figure 7.9.

**Figure 7.9** The *DrawingSender* Project

```
using System;
using System.Drawing;
using System.Collections;
using System.ComponentModel;
using System.Windows.Forms;
```

Continued

**Figure 7.9** Continued

```csharp
using System.Data;

using System.Messaging;

using System.Xml.Serialization;

using MSMQGraphics;


namespace DrawingSender

{
    public class Form1 : System.Windows.Forms.Form
    {
        private System.Windows.Forms.PictureBox pictureBox1;

        private System.Windows.Forms.Button btnSend;

        private System.Windows.Forms.ColorDialog colorDialog1;

        private System.Windows.Forms.Button btnColor;

        private System.Drawing.Color currentColor;

        private System.Drawing.Pen currentPen;

        private int startx;

        private int starty;

        private int endx;

        private int endy;

        private bool lineInProgress = false;

        private MSMQGraphics.Drawing thisDrawing =
            new MSMQGraphics.Drawing();

        private System.Messaging.MessageQueue drawingMQ;

        private System.ComponentModel.Container components = null;


        public Form1()
        {
            InitializeComponent();

            currentColor = Color.Black;

            currentPen = new Pen(currentColor);
        }


        private void btnSend_Click(object sender, System.EventArgs e)
```

**Continued**

**Figure 7.9** Continued

```csharp
    {
        System.Messaging.Message m = new System.Messaging.Message();
        m.Body = thisDrawing;

        try
        {
            drawingMQ.Send(m);
        }
        catch (Exception ex)
        {
            MessageBox.Show(ex.Message + " " +
                ex.InnerException.Message);
        }
    }

    private void btnColor_Click(object sender, System.EventArgs e)
    {
        colorDialog1.ShowDialog();
        currentColor = colorDialog1.Color;
        btnColor.BackColor = currentColor;
        currentPen = new System.Drawing.Pen(currentColor);
    }

    private void pictureBox1_MouseDown(object sender,
        System.Windows.Forms.MouseEventArgs e)
    {
        startx = e.X;
        starty = e.Y;
        lineInProgress = true;
    }

    private void pictureBox1_MouseMove(object sender,
        System.Windows.Forms.MouseEventArgs e)
    {
```

**Continued**

**Figure 7.9** Continued

```
            if (lineInProgress)
            {
                endx = e.X;
                endy = e.Y;
                pictureBox1.Invalidate();
            }
        }


    private void pictureBox1_MouseUp(object sender,
        System.Windows.Forms.MouseEventArgs e)
    {
        if (lineInProgress)
        {
            lineInProgress = false;
            Graphics g = pictureBox1.CreateGraphics();
            g.DrawLine(currentPen,startx,starty,e.X,e.Y);
            Line l = new Line(ColorTranslator.ToWin32(
                currentColor),startx,starty,e.X,e.Y);
            thisDrawing.add(l);
        }
    }


    private void pictureBox1_Paint(object sender,
        System.Windows.Forms.PaintEventArgs e)
    {
        thisDrawing.draw(e.Graphics);
        if (lineInProgress)
        {
            e.Graphics.DrawLine(currentPen,startx,starty,endx,endy);
        }
    }
    }
}
```

The form defined in this code has a private property that holds the current drawing, *thisDrawing*. As mouse events are detected, *Line* objects are created and then added to the line collection within the *Drawing* object. When the user is happy with the drawing, clicking the Send button sends the *Drawing* object together with its line objects to the message queue. Note that this project must have a reference to the *MSMQDrawing* project to enable the application to be compiled.

## Creating the *DrawingReceiver* Project

This project also uses the *MSMQGraphics* library and consists of the following components:

- **pictureBox1** The drawing surface.
- **timer1** A timer that attempts to receive messages every 5 seconds.
- **drawingMQ** The message queue component that was created by dragging the *drawings* message queue from the Server Explorer window.

The code that handles the receiving of the drawing message and displays it is shown in Figure 7.10.

**Figure 7.10** The *DrawingReceiver* Project

```
using System;
using System.Drawing;
using System.Collections;
using System.ComponentModel;
using System.Windows.Forms;
using System.Data;
using System.Messaging;
using System.Xml.Serialization;
using MSMQGraphics;


namespace DrawingReceiver
{
    public class Form1 : System.Windows.Forms.Form
    {
        private System.Windows.Forms.PictureBox pictureBox1;
```

*Continued*

## Figure 7.10 Continued

```
private MSMQGraphics.Drawing thisDrawing;
private System.Messaging.MessageQueue drawingMQ;
private System.Windows.Forms.Timer timer1;
private System.ComponentModel.IContainer components;

public Form1()
{
    InitializeComponent();

    thisDrawing = new MSMQGraphics.Drawing();
    timer1.Enabled = true;
}


private void checkForDrawing()
{
    System.Messaging.Message m;
    MSMQGraphics.Drawing d;

    try
    {
        m = drawingMQ.Receive(new TimeSpan(0, 0, 1));

        m.Formatter = new XmlMessageFormatter(new
            Type[]{typeof(MSMQGraphics.Drawing ),
            typeof(MSMQGraphics.Line )});

        d = (MSMQGraphics.Drawing )m.Body;

        thisDrawing = d;
        pictureBox1.Invalidate();
    }
    catch
```

**Continued**

**Figure 7.10** Continued

```
            {
                    // We don't want to display a message after
                        every 5 second poll if no messages are available
            }
        }


        private void pictureBox1_Paint(object sender,
            System.Windows.Forms.PaintEventArgs e)
        {

            thisDrawing.draw(e.Graphics);

        }


        private void timer1_Tick(object sender, System.EventArgs e)
        {

            checkForDrawing();

        }
    }
}
```

This form also has a reference to the *MSMQDrawing* project to give access to the *Drawing* and *Line* classes. After the queue is initialized, the timer control is enabled and polling of the queue at five-second intervals is started. When a message is received, the XML formatter is applied to the message to build the *Drawing* object together with the collection of *Line* objects. The *Invalidate* method is then called on the picture box control, which forces a *Paint* event and the subsequent display of the drawing.

After building the solution, two executables (DrawingSender.exe, DrawingReceiver.exe) will be created. By running the *DrawingSender* application, a form will be displayed, as shown in Figure 7.11.

By clicking and dragging on the form, you can draw line segments; you can change the current color selection by clicking the **Change Color** button. Clicking **Send** will send the drawing to the message queue. As you draw, you can send the latest version of the drawing to the queue at any time. By starting the drawing receiver application (DrawingReceiver.exe), you will see your drawing progressively appear as each drawing is received at five second intervals—see Figure 7.12.

**Figure 7.11** The *DrawingSender* Application

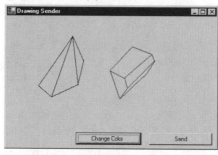

**Figure 7.12** The *DrawingReceiver* Application Receiving Images from a Message Queue

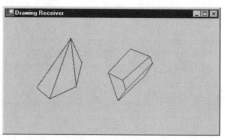

# Creating an Asynchronous Application

You may have noticed while working with the examples in this chapter that the application will stop responding while waiting to receive messages (especially if none are in the queue). In some situations, you may want the user or the application to perform some other task while waiting for a message. To make an asynchronous call, you use the *BeginReceive* method of the *MessageQueue* object.

The call to *BeginReceive* returns immediately, and a callback is made to the *ReceiveCompleted* method of the *MessageQueue* component when a message arrives. We will now modify the Drawing Receiver application to make asynchronous calls for receiving messages (this modified form is saved as *Form2* in the *DrawingReceiver* source code directory). This modified code is in the file Form2.cs in the *DrawingReceiver* directory on the CD:

- Remove the *timer1* control from the form.

- Remove the *timer1_Tick* method and the *timer1.Enabled* = *true* line of code from the form.

- While the form is in design-view, double-click the message queue component located under the form. This will create the *ReceiveCompleted* method.

- In the forms constructor, add a call to *checkForDrawing()*. The constructor will then have the following code:

```
public Form1()
{
    InitializeComponent();
    thisDrawing = new MSMQGraphics.Drawing();
    checkForDrawing();
}
```

- Modify the *checkForDrawing* method to call the *BeginReceive* method of the message queue and add code to the *ReceiveCompleted* method as shown here:

```
private void checkForDrawing()
{
    drawingMQ.BeginReceive(new TimeSpan(0, 0, 3));
}


private void drawingMQ_ReceiveCompleted(object sender,
    System.Messaging.ReceiveCompletedEventArgs e)
{
    System.Messaging.Message m;
    MSMQGraphics.Drawing d;

    try
    {
        if (e.Message != null)
        {
            m = e.Message;
            m.Formatter = new XmlMessageFormatter(new Type[]{typeof(
                MSMQGraphics.Drawing ),typeof(MSMQGraphics.Line )});

            d = (MSMQGraphics.Drawing )m.Body;
```

```
        thisDrawing = d;
        pictureBox1.Invalidate();
    }
}
catch
{ }


drawingMQ.BeginReceive(new TimeSpan(0, 0, 3));
}
```

The initial call to *checkForDrawing* simply initiates the asynchronous call. When the message is received (or the timeout has been reached), the *ReceiveCompleted* method is called, and it is here where the work is done to extract the message. After the message has been processed, the *BeginReceive* method is called again to restart the process.

# Using Public Queues While Disconnected from the Network

A useful feature of MSMQ applications is their ability to keep operating even when disconnected from the network. Once the client application is reconnected, the messages that have been stored on the client are then forwarded to the designation queue. To use this feature in your own applications, you need to modify the method of identifying the queue.

All of the examples in the chapter use the *Path* property to point to a queue. For example:

```
this.drawingMQ.Path = "synergy\\drawings";
```

If you attempt to send a message, and the queue specified in the *Path* can not be found, an exception is raised and the send fails. To avoid this problem, you can specify a path location in a second way, which uses the syntax *FormatName:[ format name ]*.

To obtain the *FormatName* for a queue, you use the Solution Explorer and click on the queue you want to use. The Property window will then show the *FormatName* property, which you can cut and paste into your code. The code to specify the message queue will then appear similar to this:

```
drawingMQ.Path="FormatName:Public={81c4c70d-71e7-4ec6-a910-
    9fcf16278f8b}";
```

# Summary

This chapter gave an introduction to the powerful services that Microsoft Message Queue (MSMQ) provides. Message queuing helps distributed applications in the following areas:

- Less reliance on permanent connections to servers
- Asynchronous requests capability
- Robustness in the face of hardware of network instability
- Communication encryption and authorization
- Tracing and failure notifications

A message queuing application sends and receives messages from queues. These queues may be located on the same machine or on a remote server. Examining the client tier of an application, there are two types of MSMQ clients—dependent and independent. A dependent client requires a direct connection to a Message Queuing server to send messages, whereas an independent client can operate with or without such a connection.

MSMQ is a Windows component. Therefore, you can install it from the Add/Remove Windows Components area of the Control Panel. During installation, you will be asked whether you require a dependent or independent client installation. After a successful installation, you can use Visual Studio.NET to manage your queues from the Server Explorer window.

The message queuing area of the .NET Framework is in the *System.Messaging* namespace. The most important class in this namespace, *MessageQueue*, allows you to send and receive messages and to manage your queues. The *Send* method of the *MessageQueue* class allows you to send messages; you use the *Receive* method to receive them. Although you can send simple strings as messages, you can also create and send a *Message* object. Using the *Message* object allows you to fine-tune the message settings on a per-message basis. The *Receive* method will block code execution while waiting for messages. To prevent this, you can use the asynchronous *BeginReceive* method—the method call will return immediately and the *ReceiveCompleted* method of the *MessageQueue* object will be called when a message arrives.

Messages that are sent to a queue must be serialized into a stream. The .NET Framework provides two serialization methods (formatters) for this purpose: *XMLMessageFormatter* and *BinaryMessageFormatter*, which are selected by using the *Formatter* property of the *MessageQueue* class. A third formatter type,

*ActiveXMessageFormatter*, is used when connecting to queues created with previous versions of MSMQ. By using formatters to stream message data, the .NET Framework allows the sending of complex nested objects as messages, too. It may be necessary to modify such classes so that they are "formatter friendly" before using them in a message queuing application. If an application is dealing with streams of data from files, memory, images, and so on, you can bypass the formatting process and send the stream directly into the message by using the *BodyStream* property of the *Message* class.

Message queues have a number of configuration settings that modify the way messages are handled. These settings are within the *DefaultPropertiesToSend* property collection of the *MessageQueue* class. The *TimeToBeReceived* and *TimeToReachQueue* properties specify the timeout settings of any messages sent to the queue—any messages that expire are sent to the dead-letter queue if *UseDeadLetterQueue* is set to *true*. The *Recoverable* property makes sure that all messages are written to disk so that you can recover them after an unexpected system shutdown. The *AcknowledgeType* property requests acknowledgement messages reporting on the success or failure of messages in reaching the destination queue—the *AdministrationQueue* specifies which queue will receive these acknowledgement messages. You can also set all of these properties for individual messages by setting the corresponding properties on a *Message* object.

When sending messages to a public queue on a remote server, you may need to handle the situation where a network connection is unavailable. In this case, you must use the *FormatName* of the queue. The *FormatName* is composed of a GUID string that uniquely identifies the queue on the network. All messages sent while disconnected from a network are stored temporarily in an outgoing queue, ready to be forwarded to the destination queue when a network connection is reestablished.

# Solutions Fast Track

## Introducing MSMQ

☑ Message queuing applications use queues and messages to communicate.

☑ Queues are storage areas for messages. Queues can be either public or private.

☑ Public queues can be shared by all computers on a network. Private queues can be used only by the machine where the queue resides.

☑ MSMQ client machines are either dependent or independent. A dependent client requires a connection to a remote queue to send messages, whereas an independent client does not.

# Creating a Simple Application

☑ Messages can be sent using two methods—by using a *Message* object or a simple data type.

☑ When sending a simple data type, the message queue's default properties are used.

☑ When using the *Message* object, you can set its properties to handle your messaging requirements instead of using the message queue's default properties.

# Creating a Complex Application

☑ You can send complex objects as messages by using a formatter to stream the message to XML.

☑ The class definitions of the complex object must contain attributes to help the formatter.

# Creating an Asynchronous Application

☑ An asynchronous message queuing application will immediately return control back to the user while waiting for messages to arrive.

☑ The asynchronous *receive* method will also return after a specified period of time if no messages were received.

☑ An asynchronous receive uses the *ReceiveCompleted* method of the *MessageQueue* object to notify an application when a message has been received.

# Frequently Asked Questions

The following Frequently Asked Questions, answered by the authors of this book, are designed to both measure your understanding of the concepts presented in this chapter and to assist you with real-life implementation of these concepts. To have your questions about this chapter answered by the author, browse to **www.syngress.com/solutions** and click on the **"Ask the Author"** form.

**Q:** In what ways can I improve the performance of my MSMQ applications?

**A:** With MSMQ, as in other software areas, a tradeoff exists between security/ stability and performance. Acknowledgement messages can lessen performance because they can effectively double the number of messages being handled. The *Recoverable* property, although useful in persisting messages to disk, can also cause performance problems with large numbers of messages. It is important to do performance testing under expected loads before the deployment of a new application.

**Q:** How can I programmatically list available queues?

**A:** The *GetPublicQueuesByLabel*, *GetPublicQueuesByCategory*, and *GetPublicQueuesByMachine* methods of the *MessageQueue* class provide access to queues on a network. To specify more exactly the type of queue you are looking for, the *GetPublicQueues* method has a *MessageQueueCriteria* parameter in which you can specify combinations of search criteria.

**Q:** I want to examine the contents of a message before actually removing it from the queue. How can I do that?

**A:** The *MessageQueue* class has *Peek* and *BeginPeek* methods that allow both synchronous and asynchronous retrieval of messages without removing them from the queue. These methods return a *Message* object that you can then examine, and you can store the ID of this message. Then, if your program logic decides to remove this message from the queue, it can use the *ReceiveById* method to remove the message. Using the ID for message removal is important because another application may also remove the message between your calls to *Peek* and *Receive*.

**Q:** How can I learn more about message queuing?

**A:** The microsoft.public.dotnet.general news group has some .NET-specific MSMQ information; the microsoft.public.msmq groups are the main areas of activity.

# Chapter 8

# ADO.NET

## Solutions in this chapter:

- **Introducing ADO.NET**
- **Working with System.Data.OleDb**
- **Working with SQL.NET**
- **Working with Odbc.NET**

- ☑ **Summary**
- ☑ **Solutions Fast Track**
- ☑ **Frequently Asked Questions**

# Introduction

ADO.NET is the latest implementation of Microsoft's Universal Data Access strategy. In the past few years, classic ActiveX Data Objects (ADO) has gone through many changes, bug fixes, and enhancements. These libraries have been the foundation for many Web sites and applications that are in place today. ADO.NET will be no different in this respect because Microsoft is positioning ADO.NET to be the primary data access technology for the .NET Framework. This will ensure that the Data Access Architecture is mature and robust because all the Common Language Runtime (CLR) languages will be using ADO.NET for their primary means of communicating with data providers.

Flexible and efficient data access technologies are at the heart of dynamic Web sites and Web applications. Classic ADO serialized data in a proprietary protocol that limited its reach, and it could have been made more efficient. ADO.NET serializes data using XML. This allows ADO.NET to take advantage of a standards-based approach to moving data back and forth in your applications. With rich support for any data source that can create or consume XML, ADO.NET is truly the data access technology for current and future applications. Through ADO.NET, you are able to connect to myriad data sources with the speed and flexibility that today's businesses require.

The goal for the developers of the ADO.NET architecture was to continue the tradition of ADO by further removing the complexities of interacting with different data providers and shielding you from the intricacies that would interfere with your primary mission: packing functionality and usefulness into your applications. After this chapter, you should feel comfortable with connecting, viewing, and editing data using ADO.NET in the .NET Framework.

# Introducing ADO.NET

To start with, let's talk about the foundation. ADO.NET is based on XML, so you have rich support for XML documents. Classic ADO had some support later on for XML, but the format was difficult to use unless you were exchanging it with another ADO client. The ADO.NET objects are consistent with the XML specification and are well-defined. It is possible to take a plain XML document with just a root node and open it in ADO.NET, add data to it, and save it back out. Pretty handy for persistence.

The ADO *Recordset* is dead. ADO.NET has a couple of new ways to serve data, which made the *Recordset* obsolete. In classic ADO, the *Recordset* object was a representation of a database cursor. You could open a *Recordset*, navigate forwards and backwards, change data, and leave it open. Leaving the *Recordset* open, however, would result in wasting resources on the database server. This was undesirable. In classic ADO, you could disconnect a *Recordset* and even save the *Recordset* to disk; however, updating a disconnected *Recordset* was difficult. ADO.NET has two options that work together to replace the *Recordset*: *DataSet* and the *DataReader*.

You can think of the *DataSet* as an in-memory relational database. It has provisions for multiple tables, relations within the *DataSet*, primary keys, views, sorting—the list goes on. Classic ADO has no counterpart to the *DataSet*. The *DataSet* is not connected to the data source and holds a copy of the data that is put into it from the data source. You can populate a *DataSet* from any .NET provider, and you can save the contents back to any .NET provider.

The *DataSet* requires a *DataAdapter*. The *DataAdapter* represents the connection and commands to "fill" the *DataSet*. After the user is finished adding or updating the *DataSet*, the *Update* method of the *DataAdapter* is called and the changes are committed back to the data source. A couple of notes here; changes are not required to be committed back to the original source, and you can transfer data to another data source as long as the schema's match. The other thing to keep in mind, especially when developing for ASP.NET, is that this is a disconnected copy of your data. It is suitable for a small subset of the data from your data source. For ASP.NET, a possible use would be for a small amount of data that needs to be retrieved more than once in the same page rendering, or that will not change in the course of a user's session. For example, consider a Web application that has a drop-down list that contains the 50 states in the United States of America. If more than one of these is used on a page, a *DataSet* could be filled and every instance of the drop-down list is bound to this *DataSet*. This way, a database connection is created and used once for all 50 states and the results can be reused.

You can think of the *DataReader* as a *fire hose recordset*. A fire hose recordset was a nickname given to a read-only, forward-only *Recordset* in classic ADO. So, a *DataReader* is a forward-only, non-updateable stream of data from the data provider. For ASP.NET work, this is the object that is most useful. Because Web development is stateless, fast access to the data is more important than scrolling and updating. Another noteworthy item is that the *DataAdapter* uses a *DataReader* to populate a *DataSet*.

The next item we want to discuss is the idea of Managed Providers. A Managed Provider is a namespace designed to connect to—and execute commands against—a data source. A good example is the SqlClient Managed Provider. This namespace is written specifically to connect to Microsoft SQL Server. ADO.NET can be separated into two fundamental architectures, the first being the data "containers," and the second being the Managed Providers. Data containers are the *DataSet*, *DataTable*, and *DataReader* objects. The objects are data-source-agnostic in that they do not contain any code specific to a data source. They do not really care where the data comes from—they are generic in nature.

Managed Providers, on the other hand, are specific to a data source. ADO.NET implements Managed Providers using different namespaces for the different data providers. In classic ADO, the Provider Property dictated the data source you were connecting to. For example, Microsoft Access would take a provider of "Microsoft.Jet.OLEDB.4.0". For SQL Server, it was "SQLOLEDB.1".

So, for example, this code:

```
Dim oConn as ADODB.Connection


SET oConn = New ADODB.Connection
oConn.Provider="SQLOLEDB.1"
```

becomes

```
SqlConnection oConn;


oConn = new SqlConnection(strConn);
```

More commonly, the *Provider* property was another parameter in the *Connection* string. The *Provider* property is still used in the OleDb, and the Open Database Connectivity (ODBC) namespaces, however, the *SqlClient* namespace does not use a *Provider* property, and if the *Provider* property is left in the *Connection* string for a *SqlConnection* object, the object will throw an exception. *Connection* strings are discussed in detail later in the chapter.

# ADO.NET Architecture

ADO.NET is the latest extension of the Universal Data Access technology. Its architecture is similar to classic ADO in some respects, but a great departure in others. ADO.NET is much simpler, less dependent on the data source, more flexible, and the format of data is textual instead of binary. Textual formatted data is more verbose than binary formatted data, and this makes it comparably larger. The tradeoff is ease of transportation through disconnected networks, flexibility, and speed.

Because data in ADO.NET is based on XML, Managed Providers are required to serve data in a proper XML format. Once a developer has written data access code, they only need to change a few parameters to connect to a different data source.

ADO.NET is based on a connection-less principle that is designed to ease the connection limitations that developers have traditionally had to deal with when creating distributed solutions. You no longer need to maintain a connection, or even worry about many of the connection options that developers had to deal with in the past.

Because the ADO.NET classes inherit from the same core of data access classes, switching data sources is much easier and less troublesome. Table 8.1 shows the core ADO.NET namespaces.

**Table 8.1** ADO.NET Core Namespaces

| Namespace | Description |
|---|---|
| *System.Data* | Makes up the core objects such as *DataTable*, *DataColumn*, *DataView*, and *Constraints*. This namespace forms the basis for the others. |
| *System.Data.Common* | Defines generic objects shared by the different data providers such as *DataAdapter*, *DataColumnMapping*, and *DataTableMapping*. This namespace is used by data providers and contains collections useful for accessing data sources. For the most part, you do not use this namespace unless you are creating your own data provider. |
| *System.Data.OleDb* | Defines objects that you use to connect to and modify data in various data sources. It is written as the generic data provider, and the implementation provided by the .NET Framework in Beta2 contained drivers for Microsoft SQL Server, the Microsoft OLE DB Provider for Oracle, and Microsoft Provider for Jet 4.0. This class is useful if your project connects to many different data sources, but you want more performance than the ODBC provider. |
| *System.Data.SqlClient* | A data provider namespace created specifically for Microsoft SQL Server version 7.0 and up. If you are using Microsoft SQL Server, this namespace is written to take advantage of the Microsoft SQL Server API directly and provides better performance than the more generic *System.Data.OleDb* namespace. |

**Continued**

**Table 8.1** Continued

| Namespace | Description |
|---|---|
| *System.Data.SqlTypes* | Provides classes for data types specific to Microsoft SQL Server. These classes are designed specifically for SQL Server and provide better performance. If you do not use these specifically, the *SQLClient* objects will do it for you, but may result in loss of precision or type-conversion errors. |
| *System.Data.Odbc* | This namespace is intended to work with all compliant ODBC drivers. It is available as a separate download from Microsoft. |

The *Command, Connection, DataReader*, and *DataAdapter* are the core objects in ADO.NET. They form the basis for all operations regarding data in .NET. These objects are created from the *System.Data.OleDb, System.Data.SqlClient*, and the *System.Data.Odbc* namespaces.

# Understanding the *Connection* Object

Making a database connection in ADO.NET is really very simple. The most difficult part of creating the connection is the *Connection* string. This is a semicolon-delimited string of name–value pairs. If you have worked with ODBC, or even OLE-DB, they are basically the same with a twist for the *SqlConnection* object. Because the only acceptable data source that the *SqlConnection* object can connect to is Microsoft SQL Server, you do not need to specify a provider, it is understood that SQL Server is the data provider.

It has become common to create what is referred to as the DAL, or Data Access Layer. This implies a multitiered approach to application architecture, and ADO.NET lends itself quite well for this purpose. Because the *System.Data* namespace doesn't really care about the data source or connection, the data container objects such as the *DataSet* can be populated from any provider that can understand how to connect between them and the data source. So, if a developer has a page level *DataSet*, it can be populated from an *OleDbDataReader* object, or the *SqlDataReader* object. The data source can be decided at runtime if the application requires it.

Each Managed Provider implements a connection object which is specific to the data sources it will connect to. The OleDb Managed Provider is specifically written to connect to a data source that understand the OLE-DB protocols. The same can be said for the ODBC, and SqlClient Managed Providers.

All of these Managed Providers are created specifically to interact with a particular database API. Microsoft released the ODBC Managed Provider well after the Beta 2 release of the .NET Framework. This demonstrates the extensibility of the .NET Framework. For instance, you can create a Managed Provider specifically for Oracle, or Exchange, and add them to the Framework.

---

### Developing & Deploying…

## Connection Pooling

Connection pooling for *SqlConnections* is handled in Windows 2000 Component services. Each connection pool is differentiated using a unique connection string. The uniqueness of the connection string is verified using an exact matching algorithm.

The *SqlConnection* is hosted in Windows 2000 Component services to take advantage of the resource management that Component Services provides. The .NET Framework SDK contains information on the parameters that can be included in the connection string to modify the default behavior of connection pooling for the *SqlConnection* object.

Connection pooling for the *OleDbConnection* object is handled using OLE DB session pooling, which is handled by each individual OLE DB provider if it supports connection pooling. Similar to *SqlConnection* pooling, connection pooling with the *OleDbConnection* object is modified with parameters in the connection string. These parameters are not documented in the Framework SDK, because they are specific to the OLE DB provider. Suffice to say that they are not the same as the *SqlConnection* options. Therefore, the connection strings are not portable across namespaces if they modify connection pooling.

---

# Building the *Connection* String

The first step in creating a connection is the *Connection* string. Depending on the namespace used, the *Connection* string will vary a little. Basically, the connection string for a SqlConnection does not have the *Provider* attribute, and a *Connection* string for ODBC must have the corresponding Data Source Name (DSN) Registry entries.

Connection to the SQL Server is done using the *System.Data.SqlClient* namespace. This namespace contains the classes for the *SqlConnection* object. As described above, the connection string is the hardest part of creating a connection. This is not to say that *Connection* strings are hard to create, but rather that connections in ADO.NET are not difficult to create. Table 8.2 lists some common keys, and the default values with some simple explanations.

**Table 8.2** Connection String Properties

| Name | Default | Description |
|------|---------|-------------|
| Connect Timeout -or- Connection Timeout | 15 | Seconds to try and make the connection. When these are up, an exception is thrown. |
| Data Source -or- Server -or- Address -or- Addr -or- Network Address | *<User Defined>* | The name or IP address of the SQL Server to make the connection with. For servers with multiple instances of SQL Server, this would be *<servername>\<instancename>*. |
| Initial Catalog -or- Database | *<User Defined>* | The name of the database. If you do not specify this, you will get a connection to the default database defined for the User ID. |
| Integrated Security -or- Trusted_Connection | 'false' | Whether SQL Server will use the NT user credentials or expect a SQL Server Username and password. |
| Password -or- Pwd | *<User Defined>* | The password for the SQL Server account logging on. For integrated security this is not specified. |
| Persist Security Info | 'false' | When set to 'false', security-sensitive information, such as the password, is not returned as part of the connection if the connection is open or has ever been in an open state. Resetting the connection string resets all connection string values including the password. |
| User ID | *<User Defined>* | The SQL Server login account. |

For example:

```
strConn = "Password=mypassword;User ID=admin;Initial
Catalog=northwind;Data Source=dbServer1";
```

This connection string would work for a *SqlConnection* because it lacks the *Provider* attribute. It would establish a connection to a Database named *northwind*, on the server named *dbServer1*. It would then log in with a user name of *admin*, using *mypassword* as a password.

A trick we have used in the past was to create a text file with *.udl* as the file extension. Executing this file would start the Connection Wizard and allow you to step through creating the connection string. When you are finished, open the file in Notepad and copy the completed connection string. For a *SqlConnection*, remove the *Provider* attribute.

# Understanding the *Command* Object

The command objects, *OleDbCommand*, *OdbcCommand*, and *SqlCommand* allow developers to execute statements directly against the database. They provide for a simple and direct route to data, regardless of where the data resides. They can have a collection of parameters that are used to pass variables in, and get variables out. If a developer needs to get the return value of a stored procedure, the *Command* object is the object they would use. *Command* objects are particularly useful for executing *INSERT*, *UPDATE*, and *DELETE* statements, but they can also generate *DataReader* and *XMLDataReader* objects for returning data:

```
string strSql = "SELECT * FROM Orders";
string sConn = "Provider=SQLOLEDB.1;" +
                "Password=password;" +
                "Persist Security Info=True;" +
                "User ID=sa;" +
                "Initial Catalog=Northwind;" +
                "Data Source=localhost";
OleDbConnection myConnection = new OleDbConnection(sConn);
OleDbCommand myCmd = new OleDbCommand(strSql, myOleDbConnection);
```

*Command* objects are the only means available in ADO.NET to execute commands against a data source. The *Command* objects are particularly suited for calling stored procedures, which are the preferred method for relational data access. Stored procedures allow some relational database management systems to precompile and take advantage of statistics that it has gathered on the source tables. Take this stored procedure as a simple example:

```
CREATE PROCEDURE getShippers AS
Select *
From shippers
Order By CompanyName
```

This stored procedure just returns an ordered list of records from the shippers table in the fictional Northwind database that installs with the .NET SDK. To call this procedure, you can use a couple of different syntaxes. You can just specify the name of the stored procedure instead of a SQL statement, or you can create a command object explicitly. Take this as an example of replacing a *SELECT* statement with the name of a stored procedure:

```
// strSql = "SELECT * FROM Shippers";
strSql = "getShippers";


objOleDbCommand = New OleDbCommand(strSql, myOleDbConnection);
```

Here, the line with the select statement in it is commented out, and the stored procedure name is inserted. For a better example, let's add an input parameter. By adding a parameter to this stored procedure, you can now limit the rows that the application uses and make it more efficient. For instance, say that you add a parameter to the stored procedure that is used to find a shipper with a particular *ShipperID*. To call it, just add the parameter in the order required by the stored procedure. In this case, with one parameter, it would look like this:

```
strSql = "getShippersByID 2";
```

This method is fine for instances when you are only trying to get some records back from a stored procedure, but not very useful if you are trying to get an output value or a return value. Here is where the parameter objects come into play. To implement the example with a parameter, the code would look like this:

```
string strSP;
OleDbCommand objOleDbCmd;
OleDbParameter objParam;
OleDbConnection objConnection;
OleDbDataAdapter objAdapter;
DataSet myDataSet;
```

```
try
{
strSP = "getShippersByID";
```

Get the new connection to the database. If you have a connection that is available, you could use it instead of creating a new one:

```
objConnection = new OleDbConnection(sConn);
objConnection.Open();
```

Instantiate a new command object and specify the new connection you just created. Set the type of command to stored procedure:

```
objOleDbCmd = new OleDbCommand(strSP, objConnection);
objOleDbCmd.CommandType = CommandType.StoredProcedure;
```

The line of code following this paragraph does several things. First, starting from the inner parenthesis, it creates a new *OleDbParameter* with a data type of unsigned integer and a size of 4. Then, it adds this new parameter to the *Parameters* collection of the *Command* object that you just created. Finally, it puts a reference to this newly created *Parameter* object in the variable *objParam*:

```
objParam = objOleDbCmd.Parameters.Add(New OleDbParameter("@ID", _
OleDbType.UnsignedInt, 4));
```

Here, you are setting the direction of the parameter and its value. The value is easy enough to explain, but the direction is a little more complicated. For an explanation of the different options you have for parameter direction, refer to Table 8.3.

**Table 8.3** Parameter Directions

| Member | Name Description |
|--------|------------------|
| *Input* | The parameter is an input parameter. This allows for data to be passed into the command, but not out. You may have more than one. |
| *Output* | The parameter is an output parameter. It is used to return variables, but you cannot use it to pass data into a command. You must write the command specifically to populate this variable as part of its routine. You may have more than one. |

**Continued**

**Table 8.3** Continued

| Member | Name Description |
| --- | --- |
| *InputOutput* | The parameter is capable of both input and output. Use it when you need to pass data into and out of a command in one object. It is exactly what the name says it is: It performs both the input and the output operations. You may have more than one. |
| *ReturnValue* | The parameter represents a return value. This is similar to the output parameter, except that you can have only one. |

```
objParam.Direction = ParameterDirection.Input;

objParam.Value = intShipperID;
```

This line of code sets the *SelectCommand* of the *DataAdapter* to the newly created *CommandObject objOleDbCmd*. You have the option of specifying *SelectCommand*, *InsertCommand*, *DeleteCommand*, and *UpdateCommand*:

```
objAdapter.SelectCommand = objOleDbCmd;
```

Here, you "fill" your *DataSet* by using the *SelectCommand* of the *Adapter* object:

```
objAdapter.Fill(myDataSet);
```

Now, all that is left is to set the data source of our *DataGrid* and complete the error handler:

```
DGorders.DataSource = myDataSet;

}

catch (Exception e)

{

        MessageBox.Show(e.ToString);

}

finally

{

        objConnection.Close();

}
```

This example demonstrated the use of an *OleDbCommand* object to populate a *DataSet*. You passed the *OleDbCommand* object you created into the

*SelectCommand* property of the *DataAdapter*. When you called the *Fill* method, ADO.NET used your *OleDbCommand* object to execute a *DataReader* and populate your *DataSet*.

You had to create a *Parameter* object, and set its *Direction* to *Input*, then its value. Note that in ADO you could make up your own names for the *Parameter* objects that you created. In ADO.NET, you must ensure that your parameters are named the same as they are in the definition of the stored procedure. ADO.NET uses them to implement named parameters and it will throw an exception if it doesn't find a match. Of course, data types and sizes must also match.

To get an output parameter, you can modify your stored procedure to return the current day of the server just as a demonstration of the output parameter. You can easily turn this into an example of returning the ID of a newly created record:

```
objParam = objOleDbCmd.Parameters.Add(New OleDbParameter("@CurrentDay",_
OleDbType.Date, 8));
objParam.Direction = ParameterDirection.Output;
```

To access this value after the *OleDbCommand.ExecuteNon Query* method had been called is simple:

```
dtServerDate = objSQLCmd.Parameters("@CurrentDay").Value;
```

Using the stored procedure in the SQL statement is simpler, but not as flexible, as you can see here. You can also access the return value using a similar technique. The only difference in using the return value is that you must declare a parameter with the name of *RETURN VALUE*, and a direction of type *return value*. After that, you access it just like any other output value. The return value from a SQL Server stored procedure can only be a data type of *Integer*. If the previous example were something like the number of days since an order date, you could use the following lines of code to get it. The stored procedure might look something like this:

```
CREATE PROCEDRUE GetDaysSinceLastOrder(@CustID nChar(5))
AS
DECLARE @iDays INT

Select @iDays = DATEDIFF(dd, Max(OrderDate), GETDATE())
From Orders
Where CustomerID = @CustID
Return @iDays
```

The code to create the parameter and get the return value should look something like this:

```
objParam = objOleDbCmd.Parameters.Add(New OleDbParameter("RETURN VALUE"_
, OleDbType.Char, 5));
objParam.Direction = ParameterDirection.ReturnValue;
```

Play around with this object. It is probably going to be one of the most used in your toolbox. Understanding how to use the output values and returning data from them will be essential to your high performance development.

## Understanding *DataReaders*

The *DataReader* is a read-only, forward scrolling data object that allows you to gain access to rows in a streaming fashion. You'll typically use it where you need read-only access to data because it is much faster than using a *DataSet*. A *DataSet* is populated behind the scenes using a *DataReader*, so if you don't need the features of a *DataSet*, you should not create one. A *DataReader* is created either from the OleDb libraries, or from the SqlClient libraries. This is a simple example of creating an *OleDbDataReader* from a *Command* object:

```
OleDbDataReader myReader = myCmd.ExecuteReader();
```

You now have a populated *DataReader* object that you can use like this:

```
while (myReader.Read())
{
    // do some row-level data manipulation here
}
```

The *DataReader* object allows for much greater speed, especially if you need to access a large amount of data. It does not allow you to update information, nor does it allows you to store information like the *DataSet* object does, but it does allow for very fast access to the data.

## Understanding *DataSets* and *DataAdapters*

A *DataSet* is an in-memory copy of a portion of one or more databases. This may be one table, or many tables. Imagine a small relational database residing in a variable. This is a complete copy of the requested data. It is completely disconnected from the original data source and doesn't know anything about where the data came from. You could populate the data from XML from your Microsoft BizTalk Server, save it to Microsoft SQL Server, and then write it out to an XML file.

When you are finished with your operations, the entire *DataSet* is submitted to the data source for processing. It takes care of standard data processing, such as updating, deleting, and inserting records. The *DataSet* object is a key player in the ADO.NET object model. Examine the object model in Figure 8.1 for the *DataSet* object and the collections it can contain. Due to the architecture of ADO.NET, several combinations of collections are possible. Take the *Columns* collection as an example. As you can see, the *DataTable* object has a *Columns* collection made up of *DataColumn* objects. The *PrimaryKey* property of the *DataTable* contains a collection of *DataColumns* as well. This is the same *DataColumn* object in the *DataTables.Columns* collection, but two different instances of them.

**Figure 8.1** DataSet Object Model and the Possible Collections It Can Contain

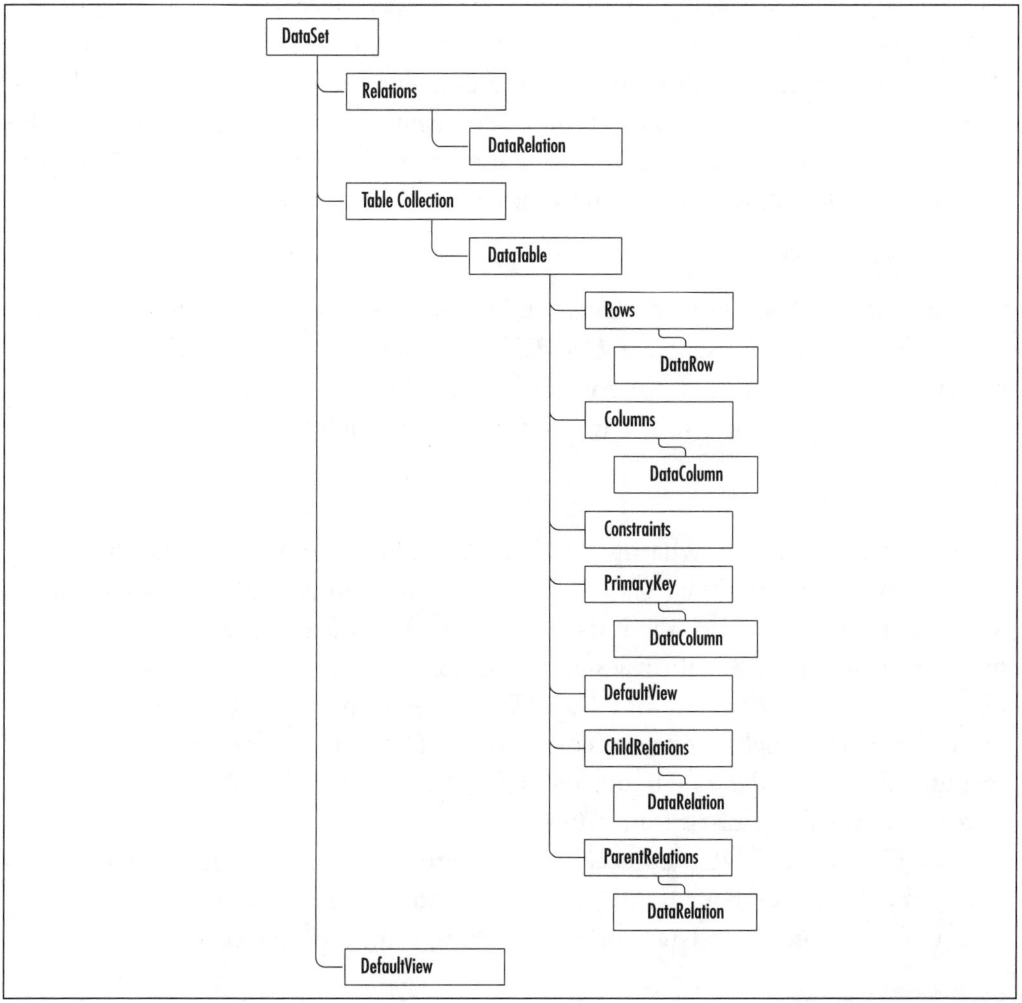

# DataTable

A *DataSet* contains a collection of *DataTables*. This collection is the key to the *DataSet*'s versatility. They are tabularized representations of your data. Essentially identical to the tables in your database, or other data source, they are added to our *DataSet* just like you add objects to other collections. Once they are in your *DataSet*, you can define properties, such as the *DataRelations*, *Primarykeys*, and so on. You can create *DataTables* programmatically, or retrieve them from a database through a *SqlDataAdapter/OleDbDataAdapter* object using the *Fill* method.

After you populate your *DataSet* with *DataTable* objects, you can access these tables by using an index or the name you gave the table when you add it to the *DataSet*.

The collection uses a zero-based index, so the first *DataTable* is at index 0:

```
ds.Tables[0];
```

The above mentioned method is more efficient, but harder to read, while the one below is easier to read, but a little less efficient. How inefficient has yet to be determined, but generally speaking your users won't be able to tell, so unless you have a compelling reason to use the index, this will be easier to maintain.

```
ds.Tables["Orders"];
```

The *Tables* collection is the basis for *DataSet* operations. From the collection, you can pull tables into separate *DataTable* variables and *DataView* objects. You can also bind them to bindable controls on Windows Forms and Web Forms, or act on them in the collection as in the previous examples.

# *DataColumn*

A *DataColumn* is exactly what it sounds like: a column of data. The *DataColumn* is the foundation of a *DataTable* and has very similar properties to a column in a relational database table. A relational database table is often represented in a spreadsheet-like format with rows and columns. The data in a *DataTable* is represented in the same manner. So, a *DataTable* is made up of *DataColumns* and *DataRows*. A *DataTable* contains a collection of *DataColumns*, and this could be considered the *DataTable*'s schema, or structure. This representation contains no data, but forms the basis or foundation to store and retrieve data.

*DataColumns* are .NET objects with properties and methods just like any other .NET object. Remember that unlike the column in a classic ADO *Recordset* object, a *DataColumn* is a true object, inheriting from the *System.Object* namespace.

This represents a huge shift forward in programming with data. In classic ADO, data was stored in a proprietary format, which consisted of a string of variant objects. These objects had all the overhead consistent with variants and resulted in a flexible container for any type of data. It also meant that that ADO had to do a lot of work behind the scenes sorting out data types and remembering the schema of the data.

Because a *DataColumn* is a true object, it has a complement of properties and methods that make interacting with it much more object-oriented in nature. Refer to Table 8.4 for a listing and description of the properties of a *DataColumn*, and Table 8.5 for the methods.

**Table 8.4** *DataColumn* Properties

| Property Name | Description |
| --- | --- |
| *AllowDBNull* | True or False, default is True. Determines whether the column will allow Null values. Null values represent the absence of a value and generally require special handling. |
| *AutoIncrement* | True or False, default is False. This indicates whether the *DataColumn* will automatically increment a counter. When this value is True, a numeric value will be placed in this column. If the column is not of a *Int16*, *Int32*, or *Int64*, it will be coerced to *Int32*. If the *DataTable* is to be populated by an array, a Null must be placed in the array position corresponding to the *AutoIncrement* column in the *DataTable*. If an expression is already present when this property is set, an exception of type *ArgumentException* is thrown. |
| *AutoIncrementSeed* | Default is 1. This is the starting value of the first row in the column if the *AutoIncrement* property is set to True. |
| *AutoIncrementStep* | Default is 1. This is the value that the counter is incremented by for each new row in the *DataColumn* is the *AutoIncrement* property is True. |
| *Caption* | Caption for the column. If a caption is not specified, the *ColumnName* is returned. |
| *ColumnMapping* | Determines the *MappingType* of the column, which is used during the *WriteXML* method of the parent *DataSet*. These are the *MappingTypes* and their descriptions:<br>■ *Attribute*  XML attribute |

**Continued**

**Table 8.4** Continued

| Property Name | Description |
|---|---|
| | ■ *Element* XML element<br>■ *Hidden* Internal structure<br>■ *SimpleContent* *XmlText* node |
| *ColumnName* | Name of the column in the *DataColumnCollection*. If a *ColumnName* is not specified before the column is added to the *DataColumnCollection*, the *DataColumnName* is set to the default (Column1, Column2, and so on). |
| *Container* | Returns the container of the component (inherited from *MarshalByValueComponent*). |
| *DataType* | Sets, or returns, the type of data in the column. These types are members of the *System.Type* class. Throws an exception of type *ArgumentException* if data is present in the *DataColumn* when the *DataType* is set. |
| *DefaultValue* | Determines the default value for a new row. |
| *DesignMode* | Returns a value indicating whether the component is in design mode (inherited from *MarshalByValueComponent*). |
| *Expression* | Defines an expression used to filter rows or create an aggregate column. |
| *ExtendedProperties* | Returns a collection of custom user information. |
| *MaxLength* | Defines the maximum length of a text column. |
| *Namespace* | Defines or returns the namespace of the *DataColumn*. |
| *Ordinal* | Returns the index or position of the column in the *DataColumnCollection* collection. |
| *Prefix* | Defines or returns an XML prefix used to alias the namespace of the *DataTable*. |
| *ReadOnly* | True or False, default is False. Indicates whether the column allows changes once a row has been added to the table. |
| *Site* | Returns a reference to the parent. If Null reference or nothing, the *DataColumn* does not reside in a container (inherited from *MarshalByValueComponent*). |
| *Table* | Returns a reference to the *DataTable* of which the column belongs. |
| *Unique* | True or False, default is false. Determines if the values in each row of the column must be unique. |

**Table 8.5** *DataColumn* Methods

| Method Names | Description |
| --- | --- |
| *Dispose* | Releases resources used by the component (inherited from *MarshalByValueComponent*). Overloaded. |
| *Equals* | Returns True if two instances of the *Object* are equal (inherited from *Object*). Overloaded. |
| *GetHashCode* | Hash function useful for hashing algorithms and data structures similar to hash tables (inherited from *Object*). |
| *GetService* | Returns the implementer of *iServiceProvider* interface (inherited from *MarshalByValueComponent*). |
| *GetType* | Returns the type of the current instance (inherited from *Object*). |
| *ToString* | Returns the existing column *Expression*. Overridden. |

Because *DataColumns* are proper .NET objects, you can create a *DataTable* at runtime, add *DataColumns* to the *DataColumnCollection* of the *DataTable* and populate this programmatically, or by binding the *DataTable* to an object that supports data binding, such as a *DataGrid*. Refer to Figure 8.2 for a simple example of creating a *DataTable* and adding two *DataColumns* to the *DataColumnCollection* (you can find the corresponding files on the CD that accompanies this book, in the folders DataColumn\AutoIncrementExample).

**Figure 8.2** Creating a Simple *DataTable* with Two *DataColumns* (DataColumn\AutoIncrementExample)

```
private DataTable AddAutoIncrementColumn()

{

    DataColumn myColumn = new DataColumn();

    DataColumn myData = new DataColumn();

    // Create an ID column

myColumn.DataType = System.Type.GetType("System.Int32");

myColumn.ColumnName = "PK_ID";

myColumn.AutoIncrement = true;

myColumn.ReadOnly = true;


// Create a data column

myData.DataType = System.Type.GetType("System.String");
```

Continued

**Figure 8.2** Continued

```
myData.ColumnName = "strData";

    // Add the columns to a new DataTable.
    DataTable myTable = new DataTable("MyTable");
    myTable.Columns.Add(myColumn);
    myTable.Columns.Add(myData);

    // Return the new DataTable to the caller
    return myTable;
}
```

This example demonstrated the creating of a *DataTable* and two *DataColumns*. It also demonstrated setting some of the properties to make the table a little more useful.

## DataRow

The *DataRow* object actually represents a single row of data in a *DataTable*. The *DataRow* is a fundamental part of a *DataTable*. *DataRows* are the objects that are used to interrogate, insert, or delete data in a *DataTable*. A *DataRow* is not a part of the *DataTable* definition or schema, but it represents the state of a *DataTable*. *DataRows* contain not only data, but also error information for the row, versions of the row, and of course, data.

As far as the *DataTable* is concerned, when you work with data you are manipulating the *DataRowCollection* of a *DataTable*. You need to realize that a *DataTable* contains a collection of *DataRows*. This becomes apparent when you review the methods for a *DataRow*. In a database, for example, you execute an *INSERT* statement to add rows to a table. Expecting an *INSERT* method of a *DataTable* to add new rows would not be unrealistic; after all, the *DataTable* looks and feels like a database table. Because the *DataRow* belongs in a collection, the *Add* method is used to insert data. When data is retrieved, the *Item* property is used to retrieve a specific column in the *DataRow*. You can place an entire row into an array with a single method call.

For a listing of properties and methods, refer to Tables 8.6 and 8.7, respectively. The *DataSet* object is a big reason the *Recordset* no longer exists in ADO.

**Table 8.6** *DataRow* Properties

| Property Name | Description |
|---|---|
| *HasErrors* | True or False, default is False. Indicates whether any column in the row contains an error. Use *GetColumnError* to return a single column in error, or *GetColumnsInError* to return an array of columns in error. |
| *Item* | An indexer for the *DataRow* class; sets or gets data in a particular column. Overloaded. |
| *ItemArray* | Allows all columns to be set or returned using an array. |
| *RowError* | Sets or returns a custom error description for a *DataRow*. |
| *RowState* | Used with the *GetChanges* and *HasChanges* method of the dataset, the *RowState* depends on two things: the changes that were made, and whether or not *AcceptChanges* has been called.<br>■ *Added*  The *DataRow* has been added to a *DataRowCollection*, and *AcceptChanges* has not been called.<br>■ *Deleted*  The *Delete* method of the *DataRow* has been called.<br>■ *Detached*  The *DataRow* is not part of a *DataRowCollection*. A *DataRow* in this state may have been removed from a *DataRowCollection* or just created.<br>■ *Modified*  Data has been modified and *AcceptChanges* has not been called.<br>■ *Unchanged*  Data has not changed since the last call to *AcceptChanges*. |
| *Table* | Returns a reference to the parent *DataTable*. |

**Table 8.7** *DataRow* Methods

| Method Name | Description |
|---|---|
| *AcceptChanges* | Commits changes made to the *DataRow* since the last time that *AcceptChanges* was called. When this method is called, the *EndEdit* method is implicitly called. The Current version of the data is discarded and the Proposed version of the data becomes the new Current version. If the *RowState* was deleted, the *DataRow* is removed from the *DataRowCollection*. Calling the *AcceptChanges* method does not update the data |

**Continued**

**Table 8.7** Continued

| Method Name | Description |
| --- | --- |
| | source; however, if the *Update* method of a *DataAdapter* is called to update the data source, and the *AcceptChanges* method of the *DataRow* or parent *DataTable* has not been called, the changes are not committed to the data source. The *AcceptChanges* method of the *DataTable* calls the *AcceptChanges* method for each *DataRow* in the *DataRowCollection*. |
| *BeginEdit* | Puts the *DataRow* into edit mode and suspends data validation events until the *EndEdit* method is called or the *AcceptChanges* method is called. Begins the storing of *DataRow* versions. |
| *CancelEdit* | Cancels the edit mode of the current row and discards the *DataRow* versions. |
| *ClearErrors* | Clears the errors for the row, including the *RowError* and errors set with *SetColumnError*. |
| *Delete* | Sets the *RowState* to Deleted. The row is not removed until the *AcceptChanges* method is called. Until the *AcceptChanges* method is called, the row can be "undeleted" by calling the *RejectChanges* method of the *DataRow*. |
| *EndEdit* | Ends the edit mode of the row, fires the *ValidationEvents*, commits the Proposed data to the Current data, and discards the versioned data. |
| *Equals* | Returns True or False, determines whether two *Object* instances are equal (inherited from *Object*). Overloaded. |
| *GetChildRows* | Returns the *DataRows* that are related to the current row using a *DataRelation*. Overloaded. |
| *GetColumnError* | Returns the error description for a column. Overloaded. |
| *GetColumnsInError* | Returns an array of columns that have errors. |
| *GetHashCode* | Hash function useful for hashing algorithms and data structures similar to hash tables (inherited from *Object*). |
| *GetParentRow* | Returns the parent *DataRow* of the current *DataRow* using the specified *DataRelation*. Overloaded. |
| *GetParentRows* | Returns the parent *DataRows* of the current *DataRow* using the specified *DataRelation*. Overloaded. |
| *GetType* | Returns the *Type* of the current instance (inherited from *Object*). |

**Continued**

**Table 8.7** Continued

| Method Name | Description |
|---|---|
| *HasVersion* | Returns True if the specific version exists. Possible versions are:<br>■ *Current*  *DataRow* contains current values.<br>■ *Default*  *DataRow* contains its default values.<br>■ *Original*  *DataRow* contains its original values.<br>■ *Proposed*  *DataRow* contains a proposed value. |
| *IsNull* | Returns True if the specified column contains a Null value. |
| *RejectChanges* | Rejects all changes made to the row since *AcceptChanges* was last called. |
| *SetColumnError* | Sets the error description for the current *DataRow*. Overloaded. |
| *SetParentRow* | Used in conjunction with a *DataRelation* to set the parent *DataRow* for the current *DataRow*. Overloaded. |
| *SetUnspecified* | Sets the value of a specified *DataColumn* to Unspecified. |
| *ToString* | Returns a string that represents the current *Object* (inherited from *Object*). |

Looking at the Table 8.6 and Table 8.7, you can see how powerful the *DataRow* object is and the possibilities it creates. For applications that need to work with disconnected data, the *DataRow* makes these applications easy to create, with some very powerful state management built in. Of course, when you populate a *DataTable* from a *DataSource*, ADO.NET creates the *DataColumns*, and then adds the *DataRows* to the *DataRowCollection* for you in one method call.

# Differences between *DataReader* Model and *DataSet* Model

Data in ADO.NET is disconnected for all practical purposes. Data access can be broken down into two methods, or models. The *DataSet* model involves reading the data into a local cache, interacting with it, and discarding, or synchronizing, the data back to the source. The *DataReader* model does not allow for updating data or reusing it. With a *DataReader*, data is read once and discarded when the next row is read.

When you populate a *DataSet* from the database, a connection is opened, the data is selected and returned into a *DataTable*, and then the connection is closed. The data is present in the *DataTable*, and an application is free to interact with it in any manner, however, the database is free to do whatever it needs to do. Resources are not being held on the database server while the application is being used.

When a *DataReader* is used for data access, a connection is opened, and the data is navigated using the *Read* method. It is not possible to "go back" and read data that has previously been read, or rather it is not possible to scroll backward in the data. Because a *DataReader* is forward-only and read-only, it is useful only for retrieving the data and is very efficient. You need to realize that during the scrolling process, resources are being held up on the server. This means that if an application allows a user to manually navigate in a forward-only manner, the database is serving the request and waiting. This may result in a resource problem at the database. It is best to use the *DataReader* when fast access to the data is needed, and the entire resultset is being consumed in a relatively short period of time. This, of course, depends on several variables, such as number of users, amount of data, hardware availability, and so on.

In both instances, the data is retrieved; however, with the *DataSet* it is persisted in a *DataTable*. As stated earlier, a *DataReader* is used to populate a *DataTable*, so in this regard if a developer needs to access the data once in a forward-only mode, the *DataReader* provides a faster mechanism. On the other hand, if this data is somewhat expensive to create, and it will be used repeatedly, using a *DataSet* makes more sense. These are the types of decisions that you will need to make during the course of designing the application.

The two models are similar in that they both provide data, but that is where the similarities end. The *DataReader* provides a stream of data, whereas the *DataSet* provides a rich object model with many methods and properties to interact with the data in any scrolling direction an application would need.

## Understanding the *DataView* Object

The *DataView* class is part of the *System.Data* namespace. The *DataView*'s main purpose is to provide data binding to forms and controls. Additionally you can use it to search, filter, sort, navigate, and edit the data. *DataView*s are based on *DataTable*s, therefore they do not stand on their own; however, they compliment the *DataTable* and provide a means to bind a *DataTable* to a Web Form or Windows Form.

You can use *DataView*s to present two views of the same data. For example, you may create a *DataView* to show only the current *DataRows* in a *DataTable*, and you could create another *DataView* to show only *DataRows* that have been deleted. This is made possible by a property of the *DataView* called *RowFilter*. Figure 8.3 contains an example of creating a *DataView* and setting some properties.

**Figure 8.3** Creating and Using a *DataView*

```
using System;
using System.Data;


namespace OrdersDataSet
{
    public class cDataView
    {
        public DataView filterCustomerByID(DataSet ds, string sCustID)
        {
            DataView dv = new DataView();

            dv.Table = ds.Tables("Orders");
            dv.AllowDelete = True;
            dv.AllowEdit = True;
            dv.AllowNew = True;
            dv.RowFilter = "CustomerID = '" + sCustID + "'";
            dv.RowStateFilter = DataViewRowState.ModifiedCurrent;
            dv.Sort = "OrderDate DESC";

            return dv;
        }
    }
}
```

The example creates a new *DataView* object, and then sets the *Table* property to the Orders *DataTable* in the *DataSet* that is passed in. This example also sorts the records by the *OrderDate* in descending order. This is an example that demonstrates the functionality; however, filtering the data in the *DataTable* when it was populated is more efficient, instead of loading all the records in the *DataTable* into memory and then choosing the records that needed viewing. Putting as little information into the *DataTable* and *DataSet* objects as possible is preferable. You don't need to transport this data if it is not needed.

# Working with System.Data.OleDb

The *System.Data.OleDb* namespace is the most flexible Managed Provider that ships with the .NET Framework. It provides a bridge from .NET to any data source that has implemented an OleDb provider. According to the Microsoft literature, the .NET Framework has been tested with MS SQL Server, Access, and Oracle—however, any existing OleDb provider should work. The examples that follow will use Access to demonstrate the functionality possible with ADO.NET, and specifically the *System.Data.OleDb* data provider. A simple application will be used with a *comboBox* and a *DataGrid*. This will allow you to focus on data access and manipulation, without having to worry about interface restrictions. Figure 8.4 is the final product; the source code for this is on the CD (Orders*DataSet*\ Orders*DataSet*.csproj).

**Figure 8.4** Completed *System.Data.OleDb* Example (OrdersDataSet\ OrdersDataSet.csproj)

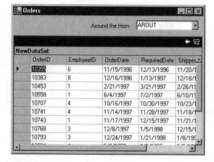

# Using *DataReaders*

As discussed earlier in the chapter, a *DataReader* is a read-only, forward-only stream of data. The project for the examples to follow is built around a DAL, or Data Access Layer. This is implemented in classes named *CDalOleDb*, *CDalSql*, and *CDalOdbc*. These will be used to demonstrate the similarities between the three namespaces.

The code in Figure 8.5 (the corresponding file on the CD is Orders*DataSet*\ CDalOleDb.cs) is the declaration of the *CDalOleDb* class, a constructor, and the *strConnection* property.

**Figure 8.5** *CDalOleDb* class declaration (OrdersDataSet\CDalOleDb.cs)

```
using System;
using System.Data;
using System.Data.OleDb;

namespace OrdersDataSet
{
    /// <summary>
    /// Summary description for CDalOleDb.
    /// </summary>
    public class CDalOleDb
    {
        string strConStr;
        private OleDbConnection cn;
        private OleDbDataAdapter adptr = new OleDbDataAdapter();

        public CDalOleDb(string sConn)
        {
            this.strConnection = sConn;
        }

        public string strConnection
        {
            get
            {
                return strConStr;
            }
            set
            {
                strConStr = value;
                try
                {
                    this.cn = new OleDbConnection(value);
                }
```

**Continued**

**Figure 8.5** Continued

```
                    catch (Exception e)
        {
                    throw e;
            }
        }
    }
```

These three lines declare some class-level variables that will be used to maintain some state in the Data Access Layer:

```
string strConStr;
private OleDbConnection cn;
private OleDbDataAdapter adptr = new OleDbDataAdapter();
```

If the constructor is fired, it simply calls the public property *strConnection* and forwards the connection string to the *Set* portion of the property procedure:

```
        public CDalOleDb(string sConn)
        {
            this.strConnection = sConn;
        }
```

The *strConnection* property sets the class-level variable *strConnStr*, and then proceeds to create a class-level connection. What this means is that when you instantiate an object based on this class, it will create a connection when it is initialized. This behavior may not be desirable depending on the application:

```
        public string strConnection
        {
            get
            {
                return strConStr;
            }
            set
            {
                strConStr = value;
                try
                {
```

```
                    this.cn = new OleDbConnection(value);
             }
         catch (Exception e)
         {
                throw e;
         }
      }
   }
```

The DAL now has a connection open and available during the life of the object. The code in Figure 8.6 (the corresponding file on the CD is Orders*DataSet*\CDalOleDb.cs) demonstrates several of the ADO.NET objects discussed earlier in the chapter, namely the *Command* object, *Connection* object, and the *DataReader*.

**Figure 8.6** The *GetCustomers()* Method (OrdersDataSet\CDalOleDb.cs)

```
public OleDbDataReader GetCustomers()
{
string sSQL = "SELECT CustomerID FROM Customers";
OleDbCommand cmd = new OleDbCommand(sSQL, cn);

    try
    {
if (cn.State != ConnectionState.Open)
        {
                cn.Open();
        }
        return cmd.ExecuteReader();
    }
    catch (Exception e)
    {
        throw e;
    }
}
```

Take a closer look at what the code is doing in Figure 8.6.

Create a variable to hold the simple *SELECT* statement, then create an instance of the *OleDbCommand* object, passing the newly created SQL statement and the class-level connection object.

```
string sSQL = "SELECT CustomerID FROM Customers";
OleDbCommand cmd = new OleDbCommand(sSQL, cn);
```

In a *try-catch* block, the connection is interrogated for its state; if the state is not open, open it. If a connection is already open and the *Open* method on the *cn* object is called, an exception is thrown halting execution. Next, the *ExecuteReader()* method is called to execute the command, and return a reference to a *DataReader* object. If an exception is thrown, the *catch* block bubbles the event back to the caller:

```
try
{
    if (cn.State != ConnectionState.Open)
    {
        cn.Open();
    }
    return cmd.ExecuteReader();
}
catch (Exception e)
{
    throw e;
}
}
```

This very simple DAL class now has one property, and a single method. It is capable of opening a connection to a database, and then returning the results in the form of a *DataReader*. Figure 8.7 demonstrates how you can use the object to populate a *ComboBox* on a Windows Form (the corresponding file on the CD is Orders*DataSet*\Form1.cs).

**Figure 8.7** Populate a *ComboBox* with an *OleDbDataReader* (OrdersDataSet\
Form1.cs)

```
public class Form1 : System.Windows.Forms.Form
{
    private System.Windows.Forms.ComboBox comboBox1;
    private string sConn = "<connection string>";
    private CDalOleDb db;

public Form1()
{
    // Required for Windows Form Designer support
    InitializeComponent();

    // TODO: Add any constructor code after InitializeComponent call
    db = new CDalOleDb(sConn);
    popCboCustomers();
}

private void popCboCustomers()
{
    OleDbDataReader dr;

    dr = db.GetCustomers();

    comboBox1.Items.Clear();
    comboBox1.BeginUpdate();
    while (dr.Read())
    {
        comboBox1.Items.Add(dr.GetString(0));
    }
    comboBox1.EndUpdate();

    // always call Close when done reading, this frees up the
    // connection to service other requests.
```

**Continued**

**Figure 8.7** Continued

```
        dr.Close();


}
```

The code in Figure 8.7 begins with declaring a variable named *db* that is derived from the *CDalOleDb* class. In the Form1 method, the db object is set to a new instance of the *CDalOleDb* class, and the connection string is passed to the constructor. This fires the *strConnection* method, and a connection is created (note that the connection is not open, and therefore is not taking up resources on the database server).

The next step is a call to the private method to populate *comboBox1*. This method declares a variable of type *OleDbDataReader* and sets the instance of the *DataReader* to the output of the *GetCustomers* method of the DAL. The next step in the method is to loop through the data and populate the *ComboBox* with the *CustomerID*'s using the *Read()* method of the *DataReader*.

The *Read()* method of a *DataReader* object returns True if a row was successfully retrieved, False if a row was not found signaling the end of the data. This allows you to set up a simple looping construct with a *while* statement. The *GetString* method of the *OleDbDataReader* allows a programmer to retrieve a result from the *DataReader* of type *string*. Because .NET is a strongly typed environment, this saves you the hassle of having to cast the data to a type *string*. Calling the *BeginUpdate* and *EndUpdate* methods of the *ComboBox* object will keep the screen from flickering while the data is added to the *ComboBox*.

# Using *DataSets*

As we discussed earlier in the chapter, a *DataSet* is basically an in-memory relational database. The sample application uses a *DataGrid* populated with some order information from the Northwind database that comes with Access and SQL 2000. To continue creating the DAL, the next method is the *GetOrders* method. The code in Figure 8.8 contains the implementation of the *GetOrders* method (which you can find on the accompanying CD as OrdersDataSet\ CDalOleDb.cs). This method returns a *DataSet* that is used to populate the *DataGrid* on the form.

**Figure 8.8** *GetOrder* Method of the DAL (OrdersDataSet\CDalOleDb.cs)

```csharp
// Class-level DataAdapter, and CommandBuilder. These lines are
// included in the class declaration
private OleDbDataAdapter adptr = new OleDbDataAdapter();
private OleDbCommandBuilder cmdBldr;

public DataSet GetOrders(string sCustID)
{
    DataSet ds = new DataSet();
    string sSQL = "SELECT OrderID, EmployeeID, " +
        " OrderDate, RequiredDate, " +
        " ShippedDate, ShipVia " +
        " FROM Orders " +
        " WHERE CustomerID = '" + sCustID + "'";

    try
    {
        if (cn.State == ConnectionState.Closed)
        {
            cn.Open();
        }

        cmdBldr = new OleDbCommandBuilder(adptr);
        adptr.SelectCommand = new OleDbCommand(sSQL, cn);
        adptr.Fill(ds, "Orders");
    }
    catch (Exception e)
    {
        throw e;
    }

    return ds;

}
```

*Continued*

**Figure 8.8** Continued

```
public void SaveRecords(string sTable)
{
      try
      {
          adptr.Update(ds, sTable);
      }
      catch (Exception e)
      {
          throw e;
      }

}
```

Notice the input parameter, and how it is used to build the *SELECT* state-ment for the variable named *sSQL*. You could have just as easily used a stored procedure if the data source supported it.

Again, the code is using the class-level *Connection* object. It also uses the class-level *DataAdapter*, which we discussed as representing the *Connection* and *Command* objects for connecting a *DataSet* to a data source. The *DataAdapter* is specific to the Managed Provider; such as the *OleDbDataAdapter*, or the *SqlDataAdapter*. The code in Figure 8.8 ensures that the connection is open, cre-ates a *Command* object, and sets it as the *SelectCommand* for the *DataAdapter*. The code then populates the *DataSet* using the *DataAdapters Fill()* method. Again, the code bubbles any *Exceptions* back to the caller or returns the *DataSet*.

In addition to setting the *SelectCommand* of the *DataAdapter*, the code in Figure 8.8 instantiates the class-level *OleDbCommandBuilder*. The *CommandBuilder* will take the syntax from the *SelectCommand* and synthesize the corresponding *UpdateCommand*, *InsertCommand*, and *DeleteCommand* objects for the *DataAdapter*. These commands are used during the *DataAdapter.Update* method. Again, the *CommandBuilder* must be created before the *DataAdapter.SelectCommand* is speci-fied. The *CommandBuilder* "listens" for the *SelectCommand* property to be set, and then builds the corresponding commands for the developer.

The *SaveRecords* method in Figure 8.8 demonstrates the *Update* method of the *DataAdapter* class. This method fails if the correct *UpdateCommand*, *InsertCommand*,

and *DeleteCommands* are not specified explicitly, or by using the *CommandBuilder*. The implementation of the *GetOrders* method is shown in Figure 8.9 (Orders*DataSet*\Form1.cs on the accompanying CD).

**Figure 8.9** *GetOrders* Implementation. (OrdersDataSet\Form1.cs)

```csharp
private void comboBox1_SelectedIndexChanged(object sender,
    System.EventArgs e)
{
    string sCustID = comboBox1.SelectedItem.ToString();
    Cursor.Current = Cursors.WaitCursor;
    label1.Text = GetCustomerName(sCustID);
    popGrdOrders(sCustID);
    Cursor.Current = Cursors.Default;
}


private void popGrdOrders(string sCustID)
{
    if (ds != null)
    {
        ds.Clear();
    }
    ds = db.GetOrders(sCustID);
    dataGrid1.DataSource = ds;
}
```

The code in Figure 8.9 consists of two functions: the first function *comboBox_SelectedIndexChanged* is an event that is triggered when the value of a *ComboBox* is changed. The example uses the *SelectItem.ToString* method to retrieve the value that the user selected and calls the *popGrdOrders* function. The second function, *popGrdOrders* takes the *CustomerID* as an input parameter, and passes it to the DAL class. The DAL class will return a reference to the *DataSet*. This reference is then specified as the *DataSource* for the *DataGrid* on the form. Notice that the code tests for a null reference to the *DataSet*. If the reference is Null, a Null reference is thrown. The *Clear* method of the *DataSet* removes all *DataRows* in all *DataTables* in the *DataSet*.

# Working with SQL.NET

Working with the *System.Data.SqlClient* namespace is very similar to working with the *System.Data.OleDb* namespace. As a matter of fact, switching back and forth between the two namespaces is quite easy. You can do so by using a simple find and replace operation—and, of course, removing the provider attribute from the connection string. Replace the *OleDb* prefix with *Sql* and compile.

In the examples for Figures 8.5 through 8.9, the data source was MS Access. Let's now switch to SQL Server to demonstrate the *GetOrders* method using a stored procedure. A *stored procedure* is a group of one or more SQL statements that is pseudo-compiled into an execution plan. SQL Server will execute the plan and return the results in one of three ways. Table 8.8 gives a list of these, along with a brief description. All of these are demonstrated later in this section.

**Table 8.8** Stored Procedure Output Options

| Option | Description |
| --- | --- |
| Output parameters | Output parameters can return numeric data, dates, and textual data. A stored procedure can return a maximum of 2100 parameters, including text, ntext, and image data. |
| Return codes | A stored procedure may return a single integer value. These are generally useful for returning the error state or status of the procedure. |
| Result sets | A result set for each *SELECT* statement contained in the stored procedure or any other nested stored procedures. |

## Developing & Deploying…

### Embedded SQL Statements

Embedded SQL or Dynamic SQL is a term given to generating SQL statements at runtime and executing it against the database. For Access, it is the only method. For SQL Server, Oracle, DB2, and so on, it is optional. For SQL Server, the stored procedure is preferred for several reasons. SQL Server can optimize the query plan and cache it for reuse, thus saving the cost of parsing and compiling the statement every time it runs. Also,

**Continued**

you can use a stored procedure to prevent direct access to a table. A table owner can create a stored procedure to select records from the table. You can grant Execute permissions for the stored procedure to a user, however, select permissions are not granted to the user against the owner's table. The user is able to select records using the stored procedure, but they are not able to execute *SELECT* statements directly. This behavior is known as the ownership chain in SQL Server, and it is used by many DBAs to control ad-hoc access to sensitive data. This approach obviously limits the use of Embedded SQL, however, the benefits of speed, reuse, and security gained by the use of stored procedures far outweighs the flexibility gained by Embedded SQL.

## Using Stored Procedures

With ADO.NET, you have a couple of options for calling stored procedures. The obvious method is to create a command object with a *CommandType* of *CommandType.StoredProcedure* similar to the example in Figure 8.10 (Orders*DataSet*\CDalSql.cs on the accompanying CD). The merits of this method are that you can declare parameters and return the values in output parameters. The use of parameters for returning a single row of data is preferred over returning a result set of one row. Output parameters require less overhead both for the server and the client. You can also retrieve return codes by using this method.

**Figure 8.10** *ComandType.StoredProcedure* (OrdersDataSet\CDalSql.cs)

```
public DataSet GetOrders1(string sCustID)
{
    DataSet ds = new DataSet();
    SqlCommand cmd = new SqlCommand();
    SqlParameter param;

    cmd.CommandText = "uspGetOrdersByCustID";
    cmd.CommandType = CommandType.StoredProcedure;
    Param = cmd.Parameters.Add(new SqlParameter("@sCustID", _
    SqlDbType.NChar, 5));

    Param.Direction = ParameterDirection.Input;
```

**Continued**

**Figure 8.10** Continued

```
    Param.value = sCustID;


    try
    {
        if (cn.State == ConnectionState.Closed)
        {
            cn.Open();
        }


        adptr.SelectCommand = cmd;


        adptr.Fill(ds, "Orders");
    }
    catch (Exception e)
    {
        throw e;
    }


    return ds;


}
```

Another method is to set the *CommandType* to *CommandType.Text* and include the *EXEC*(UTE) keyword in the *SelectCommand* property, similar to the example in Figure 8.11 (Orders*DataSet*\CDalSql.cs on the accompanying CD). In this example, you can see that the *CustID* is appended to the SQL statement, which will result in the successful execute and passing of the parameters. Figure 8.12 (Orders*DataSet*\Data\uspGetOrdersByCustID.sql on the CD) contains the definition of the stored procedure. The benefit with this approach is that parameter objects do not have to be created, thus saving some overhead. The downside is that output parameters and return codes are not available.

**Figure 8.11** *CommandType*.Text (OrdersDataSet\CDalSql.cs)

```
public DataSet GetOrders(string sCustID)
{
    DataSet ds = new DataSet();
    string sSQL = "EXEC uspGetOrdersByCustID '" + sCustID + "'";

    try
    {
        if (cn.State == ConnectionState.Closed)
        {
            cn.Open();
        }

        adptr.SelectCommand = new SqlCommand(sSQL, cn);

        adptr.Fill(ds, "Orders");
    }
    catch (Exception e)
    {
        throw e;
    }

    return ds;
}
```

**Figure 8.12** *uspGetOrdersByCustID* Stored Procedure (OrdersDataSet\Data\
uspGetOrdersByCustID.sql)

```
CREATE PROCEDURE uspGetOrdersByCustID(
    @sCustID NCHAR(5)
)
AS
SELECT OrderID
, EmployeeID
```

**Continued**

**Figure 8.12** Continued

```
, OrderDate
, RequiredDate
, ShippedDate
, ShipVia
FROM Orders
WHERE CustomerID = @sCustID
```

As you can see, the code in Figure 8.10 takes fewer lines of code than Figure 8.9, however, it is also important to point out that the stored procedure in Figure 8.11 does not have output parameters defined, nor is a return value defined.

If the data source you are using supports stored procedures, you should take advantage of them. The modularity gained by separating the data access layer and the business layer is enhanced when stored procedures are leveraged in the final solution. The examples in Figures 8.7 through 8.11 demonstrate a possible migration path that might take place in a project that was prototyped using Access and then upgraded to SQL Server—all in all not a lot of changes for a major upgrade in database functionality.

# Working with Odbc.NET

ODBC is an acronym that stands for Open Database Connectivity. Modern relational databases have proprietary APIs that you can use to create data driven applications. These APIs may be cryptic, difficult to use, and may or may not be based on standards. ODBC was envisioned to provide a common programming model that developers could use to create data-driven applications by programming to the ODBC API. Each data provider would then create an ODBC driver that could bridge the gap between the prospective data source and the ODBC API. ODBC is generally thought of as being slower than OLEDB; however, there are many more ODBC drivers available than there are OLEDB drivers.

Microsoft has created an ODBC Managed Provider for .NET. This namespace is designed to work with native ODBC drivers in the same manner that the OLEDB namespace allows developers to work with native OLEDB drivers. Microsoft has made the ODBC namespace available as an add-on to the .NET Framework that needs to be downloaded from the Microsoft Web site. Microsoft has stated that the ODBC drivers for Access, SQL Server, and Oracle will work with the new namespace.

During the setup of the *System.Data.Odbc* namespace, the System.Data
.Odbc.dll is added to the Global Assembly Cache. This will allow a developer to
add a reference to this DLL in the project. In Visual Studio.NET, select **Project
| Add Reference** and select the System.Data.Odbc.dll file. After you have estab-
lished a reference, the *System.Data.Odbc* namespace is ready for use.

The *System.Data.Odbc* namespace is very similar to the *System.Data.OleDb*
and the *System.Data.SqlClient* namespaces. The ease of switching between the
namespaces was demonstrated earlier in the chapter, and much of what was
demonstrated there also applies to the *System.Data.Odbc* namespace. As before, the
obvious difference is that the *Connection*, *Command*, and *DataAdapter* objects are
prefixed with *Odbc*. The *Connection* string is also different. Table 8.9 lists some
examples of connection strings that you can use with the *System.Data.Odbc*
namespace.

**Table 8.9** Sample *Connection* Strings for the *System.Data.Odbc* Namespace

| Connection Strings |
| --- |
| `Driver={Microsoft ODBC for Oracle};Server=<server>;UID=<user>;PWD=<password>` |
| `Driver={Microsoft Access Driver (*.mdb)};DBQ=<path to file>` |
| `Driver={Microsoft Excel Driver (*.xls)};DBQ=<path to file>` |
| `Driver={Microsoft Text Driver (*.txt; *.csv)};DBQ=<path to file>` |
| `DSN=<dsn name>` |

For a DSN connection, the appropriate entries must be made in the Registry
for a successful connection. The ODBC Data Source Administrator in Windows
2000 is used for this purpose.

# Using DSN Connection

Before you can use a DSN connection, you must create it using the ODBC Data
Source Administrator. The application steps the user through the process of creating a the Registry entries used to establish a connection to a particular data
source. The code in Figure 8.13 (Orders*DataSet*\CDalOdbc.cs on the CD) is for

the *CDalOdbc* class, and the *strConnection* method implemented in ODBC. This method is not aware at compile time, whether it will be using a DSN or not. The implementation in Figure 8.14 demonstrates using the method with a DSN.

**Figure 8.13** Data Access Layer for ODBC (OrdersDataSet\CDalOdbc.cs)

```csharp
using System;
using System.Data.Odbc;

namespace OrdersDataSet
{
    public class CDalOdbc
    {
        string strConStr;
        private OdbcConnection cn;
        private OdbcDataAdapter adptr = new OdbcDataAdapter();

        public CDalOdbc(string sConn)
        {
            this.strConnection = sConn;
        }

        public string strConnection
        {
            get
            {
                return strConStr;
            }
            set
            {
                strConStr = value;
                try
                {
                    this.cn = new OdbcConnection(value);
                }
                catch (Exception e)
```

**Continued**

**Figure 8.13** Continued

```
                    {
                        throw e;
                    }
                }
            }


        }
}
```

**Figure 8.14** Using the *CDalOdbc* Class with a DSN

```
string sConn = "DSN=dsn_DotNetSQL";


db = new CDalOleDb(sConn);
```

The DSN used in Figure 8.14 contained the provider definition, path to the file, and any security information necessary to connect to the resource. The rest of the process for using the *System.Data.Odbc* namespace is exactly the same as using the *System.Data.OleDb*, and the *System.Data.SqlClient* namespaces.

# Summary

ADO.NET represents a fundamental change in the way Windows developers will work with data for the foreseeable future. With its rich support for XML, and its demonstrated extensibility, ADO.NET will lead the way for data access.

With the creation of ADO.NET, the architecture of data access has leapt forward with rich support for XML, and is particularly suited to disconnected data manipulation. The recordset object in ADO 2.*x* has been replaced with the *DataReader* and the *DataSet*. The *DataReader* is a read-only, forward-only stream of data. The *DataReader* allows for very fast sequential access to data. The *DataSet* is an in-memory copy of one or more tables from a data source. The *DataSet* has rich support for synchronizing the copy of data in its *DataTable* collection, as well as providing for much of the same functionality that a relational database has to offer, such as relationships, primary keys, and constraints. Because working with data in ADO.NET is connection-less for the most part, the *DataSet* will play an important role in applications that require scrolling access to data. The state management built into the *DataSet* is superb, and it is obvious to see that Microsoft has put a great deal of effort into this object and the related collections.

A *DataSet* contains a collection of *DataTables*. *DataTables* contain a collection of *DataRows*, which contain a collection of *DataColumns*. You can create a *DataSet* manually by adding *DataTables* and *DataRows* at runtime, or you can use the *Fill* method of a *DataAdapter* to dynamically create *DataTables* and *DataRows* by retrieving data from a data source. The *DataSet* does not connect to a data source, as a matter of fact, it is completely disconnected from a data source. A *DataAdapter* represents the connection and command objects that are used to connect to and retrieve data. Implementations of the *DataAdapter* are specific to a Managed Provider. A Managed Provider is a set of classes that are created specifically to connect to a data source, and issue commands against the connection.

The .NET Framework Beta2 ships with the *System.Data.OleDb*, and the *System.Data.SqlClient* Managed Providers. A third was made available as a separate download that creates the *System.Data.Odbc* Managed Provider. The *System.Data.OleDb* provider was created to use the many existing OLE-DB providers that are already available, such as the OLE-DB provider for Oracle, MS Access, and SQL Server, to name a few. The *System.Data.SqlClient* provider was created specifically to take advantage of a lower protocol that is proprietary to SQL Server. This provider is very fast and efficient, but only for connecting to MS SQL Server. The *System.Data.Odbc* provider is similar to the *System.Data.OleDb* provider except that it makes use of existing ODBC drivers.

The Managed Providers inherit interfaces and common objects from the .NET Framework and provide remarkably similar object models. You can use a find and replace operation to switch from one Managed Provider to another. This is made possible by the adherence to a naming convention that involves the use of a prefix that is added to Managed Provider specific objects such as the connection. For example, the *SqlConnection* object has the same interface as the *OleDbConnection* object, which has the same interface as the *OdbcConnection* object.

The command objects are specific to the Managed Providers as well as the connection objects. They are the *OleDbCommand*, *SqlCommand*, and *OdbcCommand*. These commands are used to execute statements that the data source will respond to, such as SQL queries, stored procedures, or functions. These command objects contain a collection of parameters that you can use with either stored procedures or parameterized queries.

# Solutions Fast Track

## Introducing ADO.NET

- ☑ *Recordset* is gone. It was replaced with the *DataSet* and the *DataReader*.

- ☑ Managed Providers are used to create data source–specific objects for connecting to and manipulating data in data sources.

- ☑ ADO.NET contains rich support for XML, and XML is used to transport data between the different layers.

- ☑ The core namespaces are the following:

  - *System.Data*
  - *System.Data.Common*
  - *System.Data.OleDb*
  - *System.Data.SqlClient*
  - *System.Data.SqlTypes*
  - *System.Data.Odbc*

- ☑ *DataSets* are made up of *DataTables*, which are made up of *DataColumns* and *DataRows*.

☑ *DataViews* provide for data binding, as well as search, sort, filter, and navigation of data in *DataTables*.

## Working with *System.Data.OleDb*

☑ The *System.Data.OleDb* ships with the .NET Framework.

☑ A connection string must specify the correct provider attribute.

☑ The *OleDbCommand* object is used to execute a SQL statement.

☑ Use the *ExecuteReader()* method of the *OleDbCommand* object to return an *OleDbDataReader* object to the calling function.

## Working with SQL.NET

☑ The *System.Data.SqlClient* ships with the .NET Framework.

☑ Remove the *Provider* attribute from the connection string.

☑ The SqlClient Managed Provider can only be used to connect to SQL Server 7.0 and higher.

☑ The preferred method of data access is with stored procedures.

☑ Create *SqlConnection* and *SqlCommand* objects for interacting with the SQL Server.

## Working with Odbc.NET

☑ The *System.Data.Odbc* is a separate download from Microsoft.

☑ You can use the *ObdcConnection* in conjunction with a Data Source Name (DSN) or a connection string.

☑ Use *OdbcConnection* and *OdbcCommand* objects to connect to and interact with a data source.

☑ Odbc.NET uses a *Provider* attribute similar to the *OleDbConnection* object, but with a slightly different syntax.

# Frequently Asked Questions

The following Frequently Asked Questions, answered by the authors of this book, are designed to both measure your understanding of the concepts presented in this chapter and to assist you with real-life implementation of these concepts. To have your questions about this chapter answered by the author, browse to **www.syngress.com/solutions** and click on the **"Ask the Author"** form.

**Q:** Which object allows for faster reading of data: the *DataReader* or the *DataSet*?

**A:** As always, testing is the final determination, but generally the *DataReader* is faster than the *DataSet*. The *DataReader* is intended to provide a forward-scrolling source of read-only data that provides access to data one row at a time. If you are returning a great number of rows, the *DataReader* may be a better idea than the *DataSet*. Your testing will determine if the *DataSet* is better for smaller amounts of data.

**Q:** Should I use the OleDb Managed Provider or the SQL Managed Provider?

**A:** If your project is using SQL Server in production, by all means use the SQL Managed provider. The SQL Managed Provider is more efficient and faster than the OleDb libraries—which is about its only advantage. Both objects have the same options and methods—the difference is in the implementation. The OleDb Managed Provider will allow you change the *DataSource* easily without having to change much code.

**Q:** Should I use SQL statements or stored procedures for data access?

**A:** Stored procedures are the preferred method of data access because they allow for another layer of granularity to your application. Most relational databases also precompile and take the opportunity to optimize the query plan of the stored procedure based on index statistics. They do, however, require other specialized skills that may not be available on your team. In general, resort to SQL statements as a last resort or in special instances.

**Q:** When should I use output parameters?

**A:** Output parameters have less overhead than returning data from a stored procedure does. If you are returning a couple of pieces of data, or even an entire row of data, using the output parameters is more efficient. It is, however, a lot more work for both the DBA and the developers. It may come down to your project deadlines, but in general, they are variables in memory that are more efficient than an XML Data Stream.

# Chapter 9

# Working with XML

## Solutions in this chapter:

- **Introduction to XML**

- **Working with XML DOM**

- **Working with XML and Relational Data**

- **Working with XPath and XSL Transformations**

- ☑ **Summary**

- ☑ **Solutions Fast Track**

- ☑ **Frequently Asked Questions**

# Introduction

The popularity of the Internet took off with the advent of the World Wide Web. Suddenly, a world of information was available using a Web browser and dial-up access to the Internet. Without diverse content, however, the World Wide Web would be of little interest.

The wide availability of Hypertext Markup Language (HTML) editors allowed people with little technical knowledge to publish their content on the Web for the world to see. The proliferation of personal Web sites that display family pictures and lists of hobbies is testament to this. HTML is an excellent language for defining the presentation of data, but it is not very useful in describing the data itself. As the Web matured, it became apparent that separation of presentation from content was highly desirable. This separation allowed people such as graphic artists to concentrate on presentation and allowed people such as programmers to concentrate on creating and manipulating data.

Extensible Markup Language (XML) has emerged as the Web standard for representing and transmitting data over the Internet. XML is a generic, platform-independent data description language and as such has gained great popularity in the computer industry, adopted by many of the largest companies in the computer industry. The World Wide Web Consortium (W3C) has produced standards for several XML-related technologies.

Microsoft has realized the importance of XML and has been providing XML support within their products for the past several years. Internet Explorer has continually added new support for XML with each release. XML support is taken to a new level within the .NET Framework. In fact, use of XML is prevalent throughout the .NET Framework including use in configuration files, C# source code comments, and Web services. This chapter teaches you to work with XML and related technologies provided within .NET using C#.

Before we delve into XML support within .NET, we take a brief look at XML and related technologies. You will then be ready to see how .NET provides first-class support for working with XML.

# Introduction to XML

There has been a lot of confusion regarding what XML really is. When XML was first covered in the trade press, there was a tremendous amount of hype surrounding it. XML was touted as the "next big thing" in the computer industry. It was the savior of all things computer-related. It followed in a long line of saviors, such as structured programming, artificial intelligence, case tools, object-oriented programming, design patterns, and so on. Given this coverage in the press, XML had little chance to live up to the expectations placed upon it. XML is, however, an important and viable technology when considered with appropriate expectations.

So what is XML? A very simplified explanation is that it is structured text. If you don't currently know much about XML, you may be thinking, "That's it? What is the big deal?" The simplicity of XML is what makes it a big deal. Text is supported on every computing platform. So, if you can represent your data in text, people on every other computer platform can read your data without need for specialized conversions from one format to another. This makes it easy for a manufacturer to share data with his suppliers, for example.

Let's take a look at a simple example of an XML document:

```
<?xml version="1.0" standalone="yes"?>
  <Employees>
    <Employee EmployeeID="1">
      <FirstName>John</FirstName>
      <MiddleInit>M</MiddleInit>
      <LastName>Smith</LastName>
      <Salaried>true</Salaried>
      <Wage>40000</Wage>
      <Active>false</Active>
    </Employee>
</Employees>
```

The data in an XML document is described by elements and attributes. Elements have a start tag and an end tag, like HTML, enclosed in angle brackets. For instance <Employees> is the start tag and </Employees> is the end tag for the <Employees> element. The "/" character indicates an end tag. The <Employees> element is the first element in the XML document and is known as the *root element*. An element can also have attributes. In this example, *EmployeeID* is an attribute with a value of 1.

Elements can also contain sub-elements. In the example, the <Employee> element is a sub-element of the <Employees> element. This is an important item to note. XML documents are structured in a hierarchical format. An XML document can be known as well-formed. A simplified explanation of a well-formed XML document is that it has one root node, each element must have both start and end tags, and element tags must be nested properly. The following example shows improper nesting:

```
<?xml version="1.0" standalone="yes"?>
  <Employees>
    <Employee EmployeeID="1">
      <FirstName>John</FirstName>
      <MiddleInit>M</MiddleInit>
      <LastName>Smith</LastName>
      <Salaried>true</Salaried>
      <Wage>40000</Wage>
      <Active>false
    </Employee>
    </Active>
</Employees>
```

In this example, the <Active> elements end tag comes after the <Employee> elements end tag. Because the <Employee> element is the parent element of the <Active> element, the <Active> element's end tag should precede it.

You could write your own program to read a well-formed XML document. But, because a well-formed document is a hierarchical representation of data, generic programs have been written to read XML documents. A program that can read an XML document is known as an *XML parser*. Several different types of parsers are available in .NET. Programmer's access XML data read in by a parser using an application programming interface (API) the parser exposes. One popular API is the Document Object Model (DOM), which we describe next.

## Explaining XML DOM

The W3C has standardized an API for accessing XML documents known as XML DOM. The DOM API represents an XML document as a tree of nodes. Because an XML document is hierarchical in structure, you can build a tree of nodes and subnodes to represent an entire XML document. You can get to any arbitrary node by starting at the root node and traversing the child nodes of the root node. If you don't find the node you are looking for, you can traverse the grandchild nodes of the root node. You can continue this process until you find the node you are looking for.

The DOM API provides other services in additional to document traversal. You can find the full W3C XML DOM specification at www.w3.org/DOM. The following list shows some of the capabilities provided by the DOM API:

- Find the root node in an XML document.

- Find a list of elements with a given tag name.

- Get a list of children of a given node.

- Get the parent of a given node.

- Get the tag name of an element.

- Get the data associated with an element.

- Get a list of attributes of an element.

- Get the tag name of an attribute.

- Get the value of an attribute.

- Add, modify, or delete an element in the document.

- Add, modify, or delete an attribute in the document.

- Copy a node in a document (including subnodes).

The DOM API provides a rich set of functionality to programmers as is shown in the previous list. The .NET Framework provides excellent support for the XML DOM API, which you will see later in this chapter. The DOM API is well suited for traversing and modifying an XML document. But, it provides little support for finding an arbitrary element or attribute in a document. Fortunately another XML technology is available to provide this support: XML Path Language (XPath).

# Explaining XPath

XPath is another XML-related technology that has been standardized by the W3C. XPath is a language used to query an XML document for a list of nodes matching a given criteria. An XPath expression can specify both location and a pattern to match. You can also apply Boolean operators, string functions and arithmetic operators to XPath expressions to build extremely complex queries against an XML document. XPath also provides functions to do numeric evaluations, such as summations and rounding. You can find the full W3C XPath specification at www.w3.org/TR/xpath. The following list shows some of the capabilities of the XPath language:

- Find all children of the current node.

- Find all ancestor elements of the current context node with a specific tag.

- Find the last child element of the current node with a specific tag.

- Find the *n*th child element of the current context node with a given attribute.

- Find the first child element with a tag of <tag1> or <tag2>.

- Get all child nodes that do not have an element with a given attribute.

- Get the sum of all child nodes with a numeric element.

- Get the count of all child nodes.

The preceding list just scratches the surface of the capabilities available using XPath. Once again, the .NET Framework provides support for XPath queries against XML DOM documents and read-only XPath documents. You will see examples of this later in this chapter.

## Explaining XSL

According to the W3C, XSL is a catchall phrase that encompasses three different W3C-based specifications. It includes XPath, XSL Transformations (XSLT), and XSL Formatting Objects (XSL-FO). XSL-FO is an XML-based grammar applied to an XML document using stylesheets that affect the presentation of the document. XSL-FO is still a work-in-progress, so in this chapter we focus on XPath and XSLT.

XSLT is an XML-based language for transforming XML documents. XSLT stylesheets applied to an XML document transform the XML to another form. You can use XSLT stylesheets to convert XML documents to other file formats such as HTML, RTF, PDF, etc. XSLT can also be used transform XML to XML. For instance, if a manufacturer creates XML in one format, but his suppliers assume they will receive XML in another format, an XSLT stylesheet can be applied to the XML document to convert it to the format expected by the suppliers. XPath expressions can be used by XSLT stylesheets during the transformation process. You can find more information about XSL at www.w3.org/TR/xslt.

XSLT support is built into the .NET Framework. Later in the chapter, we show examples that apply XSLT stylesheets to XML documents.

# Explaining XML Schemas

As previously mentioned, XML is a good format for exchanging data between diverse groups. However, if groups cannot agree on a specific format for XML that they share, it will be of no help. The data in an XML document itself does not provide the information that defines the structure of an XML document.

Document Type Definitions (DTDs) are one way to describe the structure of an XML document. A DTD specifies the elements and attributes in an XML document. It also indicates the position of elements and the number of times they occur. DTDs are the traditional way the structure of an XML document has been expressed.

If an XML document has a DTD associated with it, an XML parser can read the DTD and determine if the XML document conforms to the DTD. If the XML conforms to the DTD, it is known as a valid XML document. If a document is valid, the receiver of a document knows that the data in it conforms to the structure expected. Not every XML parser performs validation however. Parsers that do perform validation are known as *validating parsers*.

One limitation of DTDs is that they do not give any indication of the data type associated with the elements and attributes in an XML document. For instance, if an XML document has an element with a tag <OrderID>, it is unclear if order ID is a string, numeric, or something else.

XML schemas pick up where DTDs leave off. XML schemas provide all of the same support in defining the structure of an XML document as DTDs. In addition, XML schemas also let you define data types for elements and attributes, specify minimum and maximum values for numerics, specify maximum lengths for strings, and define enumerations.

Very few validating parsers validate against XML schemas at this time. However, the .NET Framework does provide parsers that can validate XML documents against XML Schema Definition (XSD) schemas as well as DTDs. You can find more information about XML schemas at www.w3.org/XML/Schema.

That completes our brief look at XML and related technologies. We are now ready to delve into the XML support provided by the .NET Framework.

# XML Classes in the .NET Framework

Table 9.1 contains a list of the most important classes used to manipulate XML documents in the .NET Framework. You will see many of them used in the examples in the following sections of this chapter.

**Table 9.1** Frequently Used XML Classes in the .NET Framework

| Class Name | Namespace | Description |
| --- | --- | --- |
| *XmlReader* | *System.Xml* | Abstract class for reading an XML document. |
| *XmlTextReader* | *System.Xml* | A nonvalidating *XmlReader*-derived parser that provides forward and read-only access to an XML document. This is the fastest way to read an XML document. |
| *XmlValidatingReader* | *System.Xml* | A validating *XmlReader*-derived parser that validates using both DTDs and XML schemas. |
| *XmlNodeReader* | *System.Xml* | An *XmlReader* for a DOM XML document node set. |
| *XmlWriter* | *System.Xml* | Abstract class for writing an XML document. |
| *XmlTextWriter* | *System.Xml* | An *XmlWriter* implementation that provides forward-only generation of an XML document. This is the fastest way to write an XML document. |
| *XmlDocument* | *System.Xml* | A W3C XML DOM document. |
| *XmlDataDocument* | *System.Xml* | An *XmlDocument* implementation that allows data to be accessed via relational representation or via XML DOM. |
| *XPathDocument* | *System.Xml.XPath* | An XML document class optimized for use with XPath navigation. |
| *XPathNavigator* | *System.Xml.XPath* | Provides XPath navigation over an XML document. |
| *XmlSchema* | *System.Xml.Schema* | W3C XSD schema implementation. |
| *XslTransform* | *System.Xml.Xsl* | W3C XSLT implementation. |

# Working with XML DOM

In the Introduction, you learned that the XML DOM API is used to create, modify, and traverse XML documents. In the .NET Framework, the classes most often used to work with XML DOM documents are contained in the *System.Xml* namespace. Table 9.2 lists the classes in *System.Xml* that you will most likely work with the most when writing C# programs that manipulate XML DOM documents.

**Table 9.2** Frequently Used XML DOM Classes

| Class Name | Description |
| --- | --- |
| *XmlDocument* | A W3C DOM document (note that *XmlDocument* is derived from *XmlNode*). |
| *XmlNode* | A single node in an XML document. Typically an element, text node, CDATA section, processing instruction, or comment. |
| *XmlNodeList* | A list of *XmlNode* objects. Each node in the list may contain child nodes, which in turn may contain their own child nodes. Traversing an *XmlDocument* object walks a tree of *XmlNodeList* objects. |
| *XmlElement* | An element in the document. |
| *XmlAttribute* | An attribute of an element in the document. |

The best way to learn something is by example. So, let's get right into a sample program that exercises the XML DOM support built into the .NET Framework. Imagine a small company whose size may not require the full power of a commercial database to maintain information about employees. Spreadsheets or even flat files are viable alternatives for maintaining company records in this scenario.

Another solution is to use XML documents as a database. The XML DOM sample shows you how you can use the .NET Framework to construct an XML document, save to and load the document from disk, and make updates to the document. This, in effect, uses XML as a database.

The XML DOM sample is a Windows Forms–based program. Figure 9.1 shows the output from the XML DOM sample program. The sample program uses XML files as an employee database. Using the program, you can add, edit, and delete employees from the database. Figure 9.1 shows the one form the program displays for editing employee data. Although the sample program shows a limited amount of employee data, you can easily expand it to include additional information.

**Figure 9.1** The XML DOM Sample Program

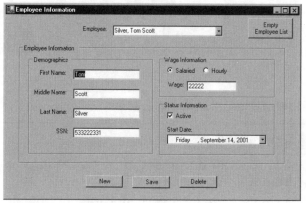

We supply you with a short explanation of program operation and then take a look at the source code. The full source code is on the CD that accompanies this book, in a file named DOMForm.cs in the DOM directory.

When the program starts, it looks for an XML file named employees.xml in the current directory that contains employee information. If the file doesn't exist, you are starting with an empty employee database. If the file exists, it loads the XML file into an XML DOM document. The program traverses the XML document in memory. As it encounters employees, the program adds an entry for each employee in the Employee combo box.

Once the program has finished loading you can begin editing your employee database. Clicking **New** clears the form and allows you to enter a new employee. Clicking **Save** saves the currently displayed employee to the XML document. If the employee displayed on the form is a new employee, it adds the employee to the document. If it is an existing employee, it updates that employee's information. Clicking **Delete** deletes the currently displayed employee from the XML document. Selecting a new employee from the Employee combo box populates the form with that employee's information. The program does not ask you to save any edits made to the current employee displayed on the form prior to displaying the selected employee. Finally, clicking **Empty Employee List** deletes all employees out of the XML document, in effect initializing the database.

One thing to note is that the document on disk is updated every time you click **Save** or **Delete**. This works fine for a small number of employees, but could cause performance problems with a larger number.

Let's take a look at what the employees.xml file looks like after two employees. This will you give an idea of how the fields on-screen relate to the XML file. It is shown in Figure 9.2.

**Figure 9.2** Employees.xml after Adding Two Employees

```
<?xml version="1.0" standalone="yes"?>
<Employees>
  <Employee EmployeeID="1">
    <FirstName>Joe</FirstName>
    <MiddleName>Arthur</MiddleName>
    <LastName>Smith</LastName>
    <Salaried>true</Salaried>
    <Wage>45000</Wage>
    <Active>true</Active>
    <SSN>555-55-5555</SSN>
    <StartDate>2001-09-12</StartDate>
  </Employee>
  <Employee EmployeeID="2">
    <FirstName>Betty</FirstName>
    <MiddleName>Ann</MiddleName>
    <LastName>Butler</LastName>
    <Salaried>false</Salaried>
    <Wage>22.00</Wage>
    <Active>false</Active>
    <SSN>666-66-6666</SSN>
    <StartDate>2001-09-15</StartDate>
  </Employee>
</Employees>
```

At the top of the file, you see the XML declaration. Immediately after that you see the root element, <Employees>. Each time you add a new employee using the New button, a new <Employee> element is added as the last child element of the <Employees> element. An <Employee> element has one attribute, *EmployeeID*. The *EmployeeID* attribute is generated by the program and has no form field associated with it. The rest of the child elements of the <Employee>

element have a one-to-one correspondence with fields on the form. Let's take a look at how we create the XML document.

# Creating an Empty XML DOM Document

When you run the program the first time, it creates an empty XML document. It also creates an empty XML document when you click **Empty Employee List**. Here is the C# code to do this:

```
private void createEmptyXMLDocument()
{
    // Create a new DOM-based XML document
    m_xmlDocument = new XmlDocument();


    // Add the XML declaration
    XmlDeclaration dec =
        m_xmlDocument.CreateXmlDeclaration("1.0", "", "yes");
    m_xmlDocument.PrependChild ( dec );


    // Add the root element
    XmlElement nodeElem =
        m_xmlDocument.CreateElement( TagEmployees );
    m_xmlDocument.AppendChild( nodeElem );
}
```

Here, you can see a new *System.Xml.XmlDocument* object. The *XmlDocument* object is the representation of a W3C XML DOM document. The *XmlDocument* class is derived from the *System.Xml.XmlNode* and is therefore considered a node in the document.

After creating the document, the XML declaration node is created with the *CreateXmlDeclaration* method of the *XmlDocument* class and inserted before the root node of the document using the *PrependChild* method of *XmlNode*. The *PrependChild* method adds a node to the document before the root node of the document. The *CreateXmlDeclaration* method takes three parameters: the version, which must be 1.0; the encoding, which is left blank resulting in the default encoding (UTF-8); and whether the document is a standalone document, which in this case is set to "yes".

Next, the root element of the document object is created using the *CreateElement* method passing the tag of the root element, in our case

"Employees". Finally, the root node is appended to the document using the *AppendChild* method of *XmlDocument*.

Adding the XML declaration and the root element are typical examples of adding to an XML DOM document. Typically you create the type of node you want to add from the *XmlDocument* object. Then you add it to the document by inserting it before or after an existing node. This will normally be done by using one of the following methods of the *XmlNode* class: *AppendChild*, *InsertAfter*, *InsertBefore*, *PrependChild*, or *ReplaceChild*. Here is what the XML document looks like after executing the previous code:

```
<?xml version="1.0" standalone="yes"?>
<Employees />
```

# Adding an Element to the XML Document

You now have an empty XML document. Once you have entered all of the information for an employee on the form and clicked **Save**, a new <Employee> element is added to the XML document. Here is the source code to accomplish this:

```
private void addEmployee( XmlDocument doc, int nEmployeeID,
    string strFirstName, string strMiddleName, string strLastName,
    string strSalaried, string strWage, string strActive,
    string strSSN, string strStartDate )
{
    // Create a new employee element.  Append it as a child of the
    // root element.
    XmlElement nodeParent = doc.DocumentElement;
    XmlElement elemEmployee = doc.CreateElement( TagEmployee );
    elemEmployee.SetAttribute( TagEmployeeID,
        nEmployeeID.ToString() );
    nodeParent.AppendChild( elemEmployee );

    // Add the child elements that make up the employee element
    addTextElement( doc, elemEmployee, TagFirstName,
        strFirstName );

    addTextElement( doc, elemEmployee, TagMiddleName,
```

```
                strMiddleName );


    addTextElement( doc, elemEmployee, TagLastName, strLastName );

    addTextElement( doc, elemEmployee, TagSalaried, strSalaried );

    addTextElement( doc, elemEmployee, TagWage, strWage );

    addTextElement( doc, elemEmployee, TagActive, strActive );

    addTextElement( doc, elemEmployee, TagSSN, strSSN );

    addTextElement( doc, elemEmployee, TagStartDate,

        strStartDate );
}


private XmlElement addTextElement( XmlDocument doc,

    XmlElement nodeParent, string strTag, string strValue )

{

    // Create a new element with tag passed in

      XmlElement nodeElem = doc.CreateElement( strTag );


    // Create a text node using value passed in

      XmlText nodeText = doc.CreateTextNode( strValue );


    // Add the element as a child of parent passed in

      nodeParent.AppendChild( nodeElem );


    // Add the text node as a child of the new element

      nodeElem.AppendChild( nodeText );


    return nodeElem;
}
```

The *addEmployee* method takes the XML document, an employee ID generated by the program, and all of the data on the form as arguments. First, it
retrieves the root node of the document, the <Employees> element using the
*DocumentElement* property of *XmlDocument*. Remember that all <Employee> elements are added as child elements of the root <Employees> element. An empty
<Employee> element is created using the *CreateElement* method. The employee
ID attribute is added to the new element by calling the *SetAttribute* method.

Finally, the empty <Employee> element is appended as the last child element of the <Employees> element via the *AppendChild* method.

## Developing & Deploying…

### DOM Extensions in .NET: The InnerText Property

Microsoft has provided some extensions to the W3C DOM API in the *XmlDocument* class. One of these extensions is the *InnerText* property. You saw code similar to the following when an element with a text node was created:

```
XmlElement elem = doc.CreateElement( "LastName" );

XmlText nodeText = doc.CreateTextNode( "Jones" );

elem.AppendChild( nodeText );
```

The *InnerText* property of the *XmlElement* class is used to create and add text to the text node of an element. This code could have been rewritten as follows:

```
XmlElement elem = doc.CreateElement( "LastName" );

elem.InnerText = "Jones"
```

The *addTextElement* helper method is called to add elements to the <Employee> element that correspond to each field on the form. The method takes the element tag and the string value associated with the element as arguments. The *addTextElement* method performs a familiar set of operations. First, it creates an empty element that uses the tag passed in by calling *CreateElement*. It then creates a new text node that will contain the information associated with one field on the form via the *CreateTextNode* method. The *CreateTextNode* method takes the string data retrieved from the screen as an argument. Then, the new <Employee> element is appended to the <Employees> element, which was passed in as a parameter. Finally, the new text node containing the data from the form is appended to the new <Employee> element by calling *AppendChild*.

Here is what the XML document looks like after adding one new employee:

```
<?xml version="1.0" standalone="yes"?>

<Employees>
```

```xml
    <Employee EmployeeID="1">

      <FirstName>Joe</FirstName>

      <MiddleName>Arthur</MiddleName>

      <LastName>Smith</LastName>

      <Salaried>true</Salaried>

      <Wage>45000</Wage>

      <Active>true</Active>

      <SSN>555-55-5555</SSN>

      <StartDate>2001-09-12</StartDate>

    </Employee>

</Employees>
```

# Updating an Element in the XML Document

Once you create an employee and save it to the document by clicking **Save**, you can update the employee by changing the employee information on-screen and clicking **Save** again. When you click **Save**, the XML document will be updated with the employee information retrieved from the form. Here is the relevant source code to update an employee:

```csharp
private void updateEmployee( XmlDocument doc, int nEmployeeID,
    string strFirstName, string strMiddleName, string strLastName,
    string strSalaried, string strWage, string strActive,
    string strSSN, string strStartDate )
{
    // Find the employee
    XmlElement empElement = findEmployee( m_xmlDocument,
        nEmployeeID.ToString() );
    if ( empElement == null )
        return;

    // Get a list of all the child nodes of the employee
    XmlNodeList nodeList = empElement.ChildNodes;

    // For each element, get the element tag. Based on the tag,
    // set the text data that will be added.
```

```
for ( int i = 0; i < nodeList.Count; i++ )
{
   XmlNode node = nodeList.Item( i );

   if ( node is System.Xml.XmlElement )  // sanity check
   {
      XmlElement element = (XmlElement) node;
      string strTag = element.Name;
      string strData = "";

      if ( strTag == TagFirstName )
         strData = strFirstName;
      else if ( strTag == TagMiddleName )
            strData = strMiddleName;
      else if ( strTag == TagLastName )
            strData = strLastName;
      else if ( strTag == TagWage )
            strData = strWage;
      else if ( strTag == TagSSN )
            strData = strSSN;
      else if ( strTag == TagSalaried )
            strData = strSalaried;
      else if ( strTag == TagActive )
            strData = strActive;
      else if ( strTag == TagStartDate )
            strData = strStartDate;
      else
         continue;

      // Create a new text node with the appropriate data and
      // replace the current text node, effectively updating.
      XmlText nodeText = doc.CreateTextNode( strData );
      element.ReplaceChild( nodeText, element.FirstChild );
   }
```

```
        }
    }


private XmlElement findEmployee( XmlDocument doc,
    string strEmployeeID )
{
    XmlElement nodeFound = null;
    XmlElement root = doc.DocumentElement;

    // Get all employee elements in a document
    XmlNodeList nodeList =
        root.GetElementsByTagName( TagEmployee );

    foreach ( XmlNode nodeEmployee in nodeList )
    {
        if ( nodeEmployee is System.Xml.XmlElement )
        {
            // Get the EmployeeID attribute.  If it matches the one
            // we are looking for, save the node for later removal.
            XmlElement elemEmployee = (XmlElement) nodeEmployee;
            String strIDFound =
                elemEmployee.GetAttribute( "EmployeeID" );

            if ( strIDFound != null && strIDFound == strEmployeeID )
            {
                nodeFound = elemEmployee;
                break;
            }
        }
    }

    return nodeFound;
}
```

The *updateEmployee* method takes the XML document, the employee ID of the employee to update, and the data retrieved from the form as arguments. The first thing it does is call the helper method *findEmployee*, passing the XML document and the employee ID as parameters.

The *findEmployee* method gets a list of all of the <Employee> elements by calling *GetElementsByTagName* on the <Employees> element, passing the tag *Employee*. *GetElementsByTagName* returns an object of type *System.Xml.XmlNodeList*. The list contains all of the elements in the document that have the tag passed in and all of their child nodes. In this case, this means you will get a node list containing all of the <Employee> elements including the child elements such as last name, first name, and so on.

You now have list of all the Employee elements. You need to traverse the list until you find the employee with the employee ID that was passed in to *findEmployee*. The *foreach* syntax of C# is used to iterate through the node list. This is not part of the DOM API, but provides a nice clean shortcut for us. You will see the standard DOM syntax used to iterate through a node list shortly.

The code does a quick sanity check on the nodes in the node list you retrieved by checking the type of the nodes using the code:

```
if ( nodeEmployee is System.Xml.XmlElement )
```

If the node is an element, you get the employee ID by calling *GetAttribute*, passing the tag *EmployeeID*. The ID returned is compared with the ID of the employee you are looking for. If it matches, you found the employee and return it. Otherwise, keep looping through the nodes.

Back in *updateEmployee*, you check to see if you found the <Employee> element. If it was found, you loop through each of the child elements and update the data associated with each element using the data retrieved from the form.

First, you get all of the child nodes of the <Employee> element using the *ChildNodes* property:

```
XmlNodeList nodeList = empElement.ChildNodes;
```

Next, you loop through each node in the node list, doing a quick check to make sure each child is an element. If so, retrieve the tag of the element. This is the more traditional DOM processing that was mentioned before when discussing the *foreach* keyword:

```
for ( int i = 0; i < nodeList.Count; i++ )
{
    XmlNode node = nodeList.Item( i );
```

```
if ( node is System.Xml.XmlElement )   // sanity check
{
    XmlElement element = (XmlElement) node;
    string strTag = element.Name;
```

Finally, based on the tag of the element encountered, a string variable named *strData* is set with the data retrieved from the form corresponding to the tag. A new text node is created containing the data and the current data associated with the element is replaced with the new data using the *ReplaceChild* method of *System.Xml.XmlNode*:

```
    string strData = "";

    if ( strTag == TagFirstName )
        strData = strFirstName;
    // Other cases snipped here

    // Create a new text node with the appropriate data and
    // replace the current text node, effectively updating.
    XmlText nodeText = doc.CreateTextNode( strData );
    element.ReplaceChild( nodeText, element.FirstChild );
}
```

# Deleting an Element in the XML Document

An employee is deleted from the XML document by clicking **Delete** on the form while viewing information for an employee. Deleting an element is relatively straightforward. Here is the relevant code from the sample:

```
private void deleteEmployee( XmlDocument doc,
    string strEmployeeID )
{
    // Find the employee in the XML file
    XmlElement element = findEmployee( m_xmlDocument,
        strEmployeeID );

    // Not found, do nothing
```

```
    if ( element == null )

        return;


    // Remove from the XML document

    XmlElement root = m_xmlDocument.DocumentElement;

    root.RemoveChild( element );

}
```

First, you call *findEmployee* to find the <Employee> element. If the element is found, the root element of the document is retrieved because the <Employee> element is a child of the root element. The *RemoveChild* method of *System.Xml.XmlNode* is called to remove the employee from the document.

# Loading and Saving the XML Document

In the sample, you load and save the XML document to a disk file using the *Load* and *Save* methods of the *XmlDocument* class. Here are examples of this.

```
m_xmlDocument.Load( XMLFileName );

m_xmlDocument.Save( XMLFileName );
```

## Developing & Deploying…

### XML APIs: What About SAX?

Possibly the most frequently asked question regarding XML support in the .NET Framework is if there is support for the Simple API for XML (SAX). SAX is an API that is used to access XML documents like DOM. The advantage of SAX programs over DOM is that DOM parsers typically read the whole XML tree into memory. This can be very slow and just not possible with extremely large XML files. SAX provides a streaming forward-only event-based push model. To write a SAX program, you register a series of callbacks that are called by the parser when events occur, such as the beginning of an element, the end of an element, and so on. SAX itself is not supported in the .NET Framework. The *XmlReader* class implements a forward/read-only pull model that allows you to write SAX-like programs. Instead of registering callbacks, you continually issue *Read* calls to the parser and examine the type of node that is returned, then

Continued

> take some action based on the type of node. In the .NET Framework, *XmlReader*-derived classes offer a very fast streaming model to parse an XML document. So, although it doesn't support SAX per se, the .NET Framework allows you to write programs that use a streaming model like SAX. In fact, if you really wanted to, you could write a SAX parser on top of the *XmlReader* class. It is probably only a matter of time before someone does.

Both the *Load* and *Save* methods have four different overloads to allow maximum flexibility in the underlying data source of the XML document. The *Load* method takes a *Stream*, a *String* (filename), a *TextReader* or an *XmlReader* as an argument. The *Save* method takes a *Stream*, a *String* (filename), a *TextWriter*, or an *XmlWriter* as an argument. This flexibility allows an XML document to be created from several different data sources, including disk files, memory buffers, and Uniform Resource Locators (URLs).

# Working with XML and Relational Data

As you learned in Chapter 8 regarding ADO.NET, the *System.Data.DataSet* class of the .NET Framework is used to manipulate relational data in memory using tables, rows, and columns. The *DataSet* class is disconnected, meaning it does not maintain an active connection to a database. The information in a *DataSet* is held in memory, which can later be written back to a database by getting a connection to the database. Because a *DataSet* does not maintain a connection to a database, other data sources can be used to load a *DataSet*. XML is one such data source. You will see the relationship between XML documents and the *DataSet* class in this section.

The sample program used in the section requires the files employee1.xml, wagehistory.xml, employee.xsd, and wagehistory.xsd to be in the same directory the sample is run from. You can find the files on the CD that accompanies this book in the Relational directory. You may need to copy the files to the directory you run the sample from. The full source code for the sample is in the Relational directory as well. The two files that contain the source code are named RelationalForm.cs and TraversalForm.cs.

Figure 9.3 shows a portion of the employee1.xml file, and Figure 9.4 shows a portion of the wagehistory.xml file. You can see in these figures that an <Employee> element has an attribute named *EmployeeID*, and the <WageChange> element also has an attribute named *EmployeeID*. The *EmployeeID* attribute establishes a parent–child relationship between the two XML documents. Each

<Employee> element in employee1.xml has one or more <WageChange> elements in wagehistory.xml. This relationship is used in the sample program to display all pay raise information for an arbitrary employee.

**Figure 9.3** The <Employee Element> (employee1.xml)

```
<?xml version="1.0" standalone="yes"?>
<Employees>
  <Employee EmployeeID="1">
    <FirstName>John</FirstName>
    <MiddleName>M</MiddleName>
    <LastName>Smith</LastName>
    <Salaried>true</Salaried>
    <Wage>40000</Wage>
    <Active>false</Active>
    <SSN>555-55-55555</SSN>
    <StartDate>1999-04-01</StartDate>
  </Employee>
```

**Figure 9.4** The <Employee Element> (wagehistory.xml)

```
<?xml version="1.0" standalone="yes"?>
<WageHistory>
  <WageChange EmployeeID="1">
    <Date>1999-04-01</Date>
    <Wage>33000</Wage>
  </WageChange>
  <WageChange EmployeeID="2">
    <Date>2001-04-01</Date>
    <Wage>22.75</Wage>
  </WageChange>
```

The sample program performs three separate operations. First, it loads two XML documents without using XML schema files and establishes a relation between the two files. This is shown in Figure 9.3. Second, it loads two XML documents using XML schema files and establishes a relation between the two files. This is shown in Figure 9.4. Finally, it loads the two XML documents using XML schema files and programmatically traverses the documents using the established relation. This is shown in Figure 9.5.

**Figure 9.5** The Relational Sample—Load XML without Schema

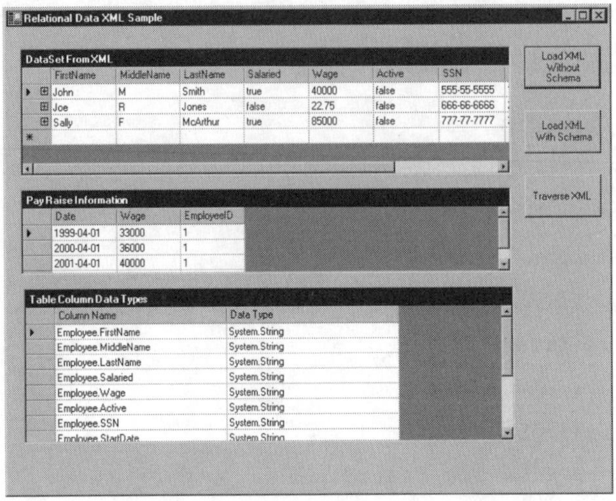

Figure 9.5 shows the sample after you click **Load XML Without Schema**. The program reads the employee1.xml file and the wagehistory.xml files into a *DataSet* class object. This results in an *Employee* table and a *WageChange* table being added to the *DataSet*. A relation between the two tables is established.

The *Employee* table is bound to the top grid and the *WageChange* table is bound to the middle grid. Each grid is of type *System.Windows.Forms.DataGrid* and therefore is a databound control. This means that the grid automatically knows how to display the data in the *Dataset* and understands the relation without having to do any additional programming. You can click on any row in the top grid and the middle grid will be populated with information from the *WageChange* table using the employee in the selected *Employee* table row. No additional work is done to accomplish this.

The bottom grid shows the data type of each column in both the *Employee* table and the *WageChange* table. You can see in Figure 9.5 that the data type for every column is *System.String*. In Figure 9.6, generated after clicking **Load XML With Schema**, some columns have different data types. This shows the effect of using an XSD schema when reading in the XML from disk into the *DataSet* object. The schema file establishes the data type for each element and attribute in the XML document. These data types are carried over to the *DataSet* tables. Note that the grid control recognizes the data types as well. Notice that the *Salaried* and *Active* columns have become check boxes instead of text fields as shown in Figure 9.5.

**Figure 9.6** The Relational Sample—Load XML with Schema

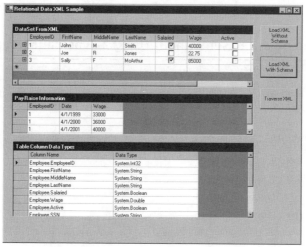

Figure 9.7 shows the results of traversing the *DataSet* manually when you click **Traverse XML**. You can see that the *DataSet* is traversed twice, once using relational calls and once using DOM calls. This is possible when the *DataSet* is contained within an object of the *System.Xml.XmlDataDocument* class. The *XmlDataDocument* class lets you treat the data in the document as a relational *DataSet* or as an XML DOM *XmlDocument*.

**Figure 9.7** The Relational Sample—Traversing XML

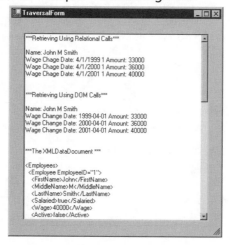

# XML and the *DataSet* Class

Let's take a look at the code that loads the XML documents and sets up the relation when you click **Load XML Without Schema**. Figure 9.5 shows the results of clicking the button. The code that is executed when you click the button is shown in Figure 9.8.

**Figure 9.8** Loading a Dataset without Using a Schema (RelationalForm.cs)

```
/// <summary>
/// Called when Load XML Without Schema button is clicked
/// </summary>
private void button1_Click(object sender, System.EventArgs e)
{
    Cursor currentCursor = Cursor.Current;


    try
    {
        Cursor.Current = Cursors.WaitCursor;


        // Create two new datasets and load them from XML files
        // on disk
        DataSet dsEmployees = new DataSet( "Employees" );
        DataSet dsWageHistory = new DataSet( "WageHistory" );
        loadAndDisplayDatasets( dsEmployees, dsWageHistory );
    }
    catch ( Exception exception )
    {
        MessageBox.Show( exception.Message );
    }
    finally
    {
        Cursor.Current = currentCursor;
    }
}
```

**Continued**

**Figure 9.8** Continued

```
/// <summary>
/// Loads XML files from disk into a dataset and displays the
/// data contained in them on-screen
/// </summary>
/// <param name="dsEmployees">The employees dataset</param>
/// <param name="dsWageHistory">The wage history dataset</param>
private void loadAndDisplayDatasets( DataSet dsEmployees,
    DataSet dsWageHistory )
{
    // Load the dataset from XML files on disk
    dsEmployees.ReadXml( "employee1.xml" );
    dsWageHistory.ReadXml( "wagehistory.xml" );

    // Copy the WageChange table into the Employees dataset
    dsEmployees.Tables.Add(
        dsWageHistory.Tables["WageChange"].Copy() );

    DataTable tblEmp = dsEmployees.Tables["Employee"];
    DataTable tblWageHistory = dsEmployees.Tables["WageChange"];

    // Create a relation between the two tables based on employee
    // ID
    DataRelation relation = new DataRelation(
        "EmpWageHistory",
        new DataColumn[] {tblEmp.Columns["EmployeeID"]},
        new DataColumn[] {tblWageHistory.Columns["EmployeeID"]},
        false);

    dsEmployees.Relations.Add( relation );

    // Bind the dataset to the grid, so we can see it
    m_gridEmployees.SetDataBinding( dsEmployees, "Employee" );
    m_gridRaises.SetDataBinding( dsEmployees,
```

**Continued**

**Figure 9.8** Continued

```
        "Employee.EmpWageHistory" );


    // Save the schema to disk
    dsEmployees.WriteXmlSchema( "employees2.xsd" );


    // Create a third dataset to hold the names of the columns
    // and their datatypes so we can display this information in
    // the third grid to see the effect of using a schema when
    // reading in the XML files.
    DataSet dsDataTypes = new DataSet( "DataTypes" );
    DataTable tblDataTypes = new DataTable( "DataTypes" );
    DataColumn colName = new DataColumn( "Column Name" );
    DataColumn colType = new DataColumn( "Data Type" );


    tblDataTypes.Columns.Add( colName );
    tblDataTypes.Columns.Add( colType );
    dsDataTypes.Tables.Add( tblDataTypes );


    foreach ( DataTable table in dsEmployees.Tables )
    {
        string strTableName = table.TableName;


        foreach ( DataColumn column in table.Columns )
        {
            string strName = strTableName + "." + column.ColumnName;
            string strDataType = column.DataType.ToString();


            DataRow row = tblDataTypes.NewRow();
            row["Column Name"] = strName;
            row["Data Type"] = strDataType;
            tblDataTypes.Rows.Add( row );
        }
    }
```

**Continued**

**Figure 9.8** Continued

```
    // Bind the column and data type information to the grid
    m_gridDataTypes.PreferredColumnWidth = 200;
    m_gridDataTypes.SetDataBinding( dsDataTypes, "DataTypes" );
}
```

The *button1_Click* method is called when you click **Load XML Without Schema**. It creates two empty *DataSet* objects, one for employee information and one for wage history information. It then calls the *loadAndDisplayDatasets* method, passing in the newly created *DataSet* objects.

The *loadAndDisplayDatasets* method is where the real work gets done. First the *DataSet* objects are loaded from XML files on disk by calling the *ReadXml* method of the *DataSet* object. Then the wage history information is copied from the wage history *DataSet* to the employee *DataSet* by the following code:

```
// Copy the WageChange table into the Employees dataset
dsEmployees.Tables.Add( dsWageHistory.Tables["WageChange"].Copy() );
```

This step is necessary because the *ReadXml* method of the *DataSet* class can be called only once to load XML from a disk file. So, you load each file into a separate *DataSet* object and then copy the wage information to the employee *DataSet* object. Now both XML files have been loaded into the *dsEmployees* *DataSet* object. Next, you need to establish a relationship between the employee and wage data information. Here is the code to accomplish this:

```
DataTable tblEmp = dsEmployees.Tables["Employee"];
DataTable tblWageHistory = dsEmployees.Tables["WageChange"];


// Create a relation between the two tables based on employee
// ID
DataRelation relation = new DataRelation(
    "EmpWageHistory",
    new DataColumn[] {tblEmp.Columns["EmployeeID"]},
    new DataColumn[] {tblWageHistory.Columns["EmployeeID"]},
    false);


dsEmployees.Relations.Add( relation );
```

First, create two variables that hold references to the *Employee* table and *WageChange* table in the *dsEmployees DataSet* object. This is done for convenience in passing them to the constructor of the *DataRelation* object.

Next, create the new relation by instantiating a new *System.Data.DataRelation* object. The first parameter of the constructor is the name of the new relation, *EmpWageHistory* in this case. The second parameter indicates the table and column that constitute the parent of the relation. In this case, it is the *EmployeeID* column of the *Employee* table. The third parameter indicates the table and column that constitute the child of the relation. In this case, it is the *EmployeeID* column of the *WageChange* table. The last parameter indicates whether the relation enforces any constraints, such as uniqueness or foreign keys. In this case, the data is read-only, so you will not enforce any constraints.

After the new *DataRelation* is created, you need to add it to the *DataSet* object. You accomplish this by the call to *Relations.Add* method of the *dsEmployees* object.

Finally, you bind the top grid the *Employee* table of the *dsEmployees DataSet*. This results in the employee information shown in the top grid. You bind the middle grid to the new relation that was just created. Wage information is now shown in the middle grid. As an aid in demonstrating the capabilities of the *XmlDataDocument* class, the XML schema currently in use by the *DataSet* is written to a disk file. A *DataSet* always has a schema in use. It is either explicitly specified or is inferred by the *DataSet* class.

The remaining code builds a new *DataSet*, which contains each column name and data type in the two tables in the *dsEmployees DataSet*. It then binds this *DataSet* to the bottom grid, which displays the column name and data type of all tables in the *dsEmployees Dataset* in the bottom grid.

Notice that every column has a data type of *System.String*, as depicted in Figure 9.5. The *DataSet* object will infer a schema for the XML document if one is not provided. The schema that it creates assigns every element and attribute in the XML document a type of *System.String*. For it to do otherwise would be difficult. It had no way of knowing what the data type should be because all data in an XML document is text. This is generally not what you would like. You want the columns in the *DataSet* to represent the actual data type of the information. Fortunately, you can tell the *DataSet* what XSD schema to use when loading an XML document.

# XML Schemas and the *DataSet* Class

You can specify an XML XSD schema file that establishes the data types of elements and attributes loaded into a *DataSet* object. If you use a schema file, the columns in the tables will match the data types supplied by the schema. Here is the code from our sample application that uses a schema. This code is called when you click **Load XML With Schema** (you can see the results of clicking the button in Figure 9.6):

```
/// <summary>
/// Called when Load XML With Schema button is clicked
/// </summary>
private void button2_Click(object sender, System.EventArgs e)
{
    Cursor currentCursor = Cursor.Current;

    try
    {
        Cursor.Current = Cursors.WaitCursor;

        // Create two new datasets and load them from XML files
        // on disk using XML schemas
        DataSet dsEmployees = new DataSet( "Employees" );
        DataSet dsWageHistory = new DataSet( "WageHistory" );

        dsEmployees.ReadXmlSchema( "employee.xsd" );
        dsWageHistory.ReadXmlSchema( "wagehistory.xsd" );
        loadAndDisplayDatasets( dsEmployees, dsWageHistory );
    }
    catch ( Exception exception )
    {
        MessageBox.Show( exception.Message );
    }
    finally
    {
        Cursor.Current = currentCursor;
```

```
        }
    }
```

The only difference from the code that loads the files without a schema are the two calls to the *ReadXmlSchema* method of the *DataSet* class. This is all that is necessary to establish the data types of the table columns in a *DataSet*. Figure 9.9 shows the schema file defined for the *Employees DataSet*, employee.xsd. Figure 9.10 shows the schema file defined for the *WageHistory DataSet*, wagehistory.xsd.

**Figure 9.9** The XML Schema File (employee.xsd)

```
<?xml version="1.0" standalone="yes"?>
<xsd:schema id="Employees" targetNamespace=""
  xmlns="" xmlns:xsd="http://www.w3.org/2001/XMLSchema"
  xmlns:msdata="urn:schemas-microsoft-com:xml-msdata">
  <xsd:element name="Employees" msdata:IsDataSet="true">
    <xsd:complexType>
      <xsd:choice maxOccurs="unbounded">
        <xsd:element name="Employee">
          <xsd:complexType>
            <xsd:sequence>
              <xsd:element name="FirstName" type="xsd:string"
                minOccurs="0" />
              <xsd:element name="MiddleName" type="xsd:string"
                minOccurs="0" />
              <xsd:element name="LastName" type="xsd:string"
                minOccurs="0" />
              <xsd:element name="Salaried" type="xsd:boolean"
                minOccurs="0" />
              <xsd:element name="Wage" type="xsd:double"
                minOccurs="0" />
              <xsd:element name="Active" type="xsd:boolean"
                minOccurs="0" />
              <xsd:element name="SSN" type="xsd:string" minOccurs="0"
/>
              <xsd:element name="StartDate" type="xsd:date"
                minOccurs="0" />
```

**Continued**

**Figure 9.9** Continued

```
         </xsd:sequence>

         <xsd:attribute name="EmployeeID" type="xsd:int" />

      </xsd:complexType>

    </xsd:element>

  </xsd:choice>

  </xsd:complexType>

 </xsd:element>

</xsd:schema>
```

**Figure 9.10** The XML Schema File (wagehistory.xsd)

```
<?xml version="1.0" standalone="yes"?>

<xsd:schema id="Employees" targetNamespace=""

   xmlns="" xmlns:xsd="http://www.w3.org/2001/XMLSchema"

   xmlns:msdata="urn:schemas-microsoft-com:xml-msdata">

  <xsd:element name="Employees" msdata:IsDataSet="true">

    <xsd:complexType>

      <xsd:choice maxOccurs="unbounded">

        <xsd:element name="WageChange">

          <xsd:complexType>

            <xsd:sequence>

              <xsd:element name="Date" type="xsd:date"

                  minOccurs="0" />

              <xsd:element name="Wage" type="xsd:double"

                  minOccurs="0" />

            </xsd:sequence>

            <xsd:attribute name="EmployeeID" type="xsd:int" />

          </xsd:complexType>

        </xsd:element>

      </xsd:choice>

    </xsd:complexType>

  </xsd:element>

</xsd:schema>
```

If you compare the information in the schema files with the output shown in Figure 9.6, you can see that the data types specified in the schema files match the data types displayed in bottom grid control. One example of this is the <Wage> element. In the employees.xsd file, it has a data type of *xsd:double*. In Figure 9.6, the table column *Employee.Wage* is of type *System.Double*.

# Traversing Relations in the *DataSet* Class

Because the grid control is a data bound control, it understands relations defined by a *DataSet* object and can display data based on those relations. So, in the previous examples, you didn't get to see code that actually traverses the parent-child relationship. You will see that in this section. The code that we look at in this section is called when you click **Traverse XML**. You can see the results of clicking the button in Figure 9.7.

The .NET Framework supplies a class *System.Xml.XmlDataDocument*. The *XmlDataDocument* class is interesting because it allows you to access the data in an XML document by using relational methods or by using XML DOM methods. The *XmlDataDocument* class has a *DataSet* object as one of its member variables, which allows you to make relational calls against the *DataSet* member. The *DataDocument* class is derived from the *XmlDocument* class, so you can make XML DOM method calls against it as well. The sample program shows both methods of accessing the document. First, let's take a look at the source code that loads an *XmlDataDocument* instance:

```
/// <summary>
/// Loads two XML documents from disk into a XMLDataDocument and
/// establishes a relation between the two.
/// </summary>
/// <returns>The XMLDataDocument</returns>
private XmlDataDocument loadXML()
{
    // Load the employees XML file
    DataSet dsEmployees = new DataSet( "Employees" );
    dsEmployees.ReadXmlSchema( "employee.xsd" );
    dsEmployees.ReadXml( "employee1.xml" );
    dsEmployees.Tables[0].TableName = "Employee";


    // Load the wage history XML file
```

```
        DataSet dsWageHistory = new DataSet( "WageHistory" );

        dsWageHistory.ReadXmlSchema( "wagehistory.xsd" );

        dsWageHistory.ReadXml( "wagehistory.xml" );

        dsWageHistory.Tables[0].TableName = "WageChange";


        // Copy the WageChange table into the Employees dataset

        dsEmployees.Tables.Add(

            dsWageHistory.Tables["WageChange"].Copy() );


        DataTable tblEmp = dsEmployees.Tables["Employee"];

        DataTable tblWageHistory = dsEmployees.Tables["WageChange"];


        // Create a relation between the two tables based on employee

        // ID

        DataRelation relation = new DataRelation(

            "EmpWageHistory",

            new DataColumn[] {tblEmp.Columns["EmployeeID"]},

            new DataColumn[] {tblWageHistory.Columns["EmployeeID"]},

            false);


        // Set as nested. If an XML document is written to disk it

        // will now contain <WageChange> elements as children of

        // <Employee> elements.

        relation.Nested = true;


        // Add the relation

        dsEmployees.Relations.Add( relation );


        // Instantiate the document

        XmlDataDocument doc = new XmlDataDocument( dsEmployees );

        return doc;

    }
```

Most of this code is similar to the code you saw earlier in Figure 9.8. The two XML files are loaded into separate *DataSet* objects, and then wage information is copied to the employee *DataSet*. The relation is then created and added to the *DataSet*. Finally, a new *XmlDataDocument* object is created whose constructor takes the *DataSet* object we created.

One interesting piece of code is the line that sets the *Nested* property of the relation to *true*. By doing this, you enforce the parent-child relationship. If the *XmlDataDocument* is written to disk, the <WageChange> elements will be children of the associated <Employee> element. If the *Nested* property was set to false (the default), all of the <WageChange> elements would come after the last <Employee> element in the document.

Now let's take a look at the code that traverses the document using relational method calls:

```
/// <summary>
/// Uses relational calls to traverse the XML document and
/// display one employee on-screen.
/// </summary>
/// <param name="doc">The XML document</param>
private void retrieveAsData( XmlDataDocument doc )
{
    string strFirstName;
    string strMiddleName;
    string strLastName;
    string strDate;
    string strWage;

    // Use the Select method to retrieve data relationally
    DataTable tblEmp = doc.DataSet.Tables["Employee"];
    DataRelation relation =
        doc.DataSet.Relations["EmpWageHistory"];
    DataRow[] rows = tblEmp.Select( "EmployeeID = 1" );

    for( int i = 0; i < rows.Length; i ++ )
    {
        // Get the Employee information retrieved
        DataRow rowEmp = rows[i];

        strFirstName = rowEmp[1].ToString();
```

```
    strMiddleName = rowEmp[2].ToString();
    strLastName = rowEmp[3].ToString();


    m_strOutput += "Name: " + strFirstName;
    m_strOutput += " " + strMiddleName;
    m_strOutput += " " + strLastName + "\r\n";


    // Now get the Wage history information, it is a child
    // of the Employee row.
    DataRow[] rowsWage = rowEmp.GetChildRows( relation );
    for( int j = 0; j < rowsWage.Length; j++ )
    {
        DataRow rowWage = rowsWage[j];
        strDate = rowWage[1].ToString();
        strWage = rowWage[2].ToString();


        m_strOutput += "Wage Chage Date: " +
            strDate.Substring( 0, 10);
        m_strOutput += " Amount: " + strWage + "\r\n";
    }

  }

}
```

First, call the *Select* method against the Employee *DataTable* with the following code:

```
DataTable tblEmp = doc.DataSet.Tables["Employee"];
DataRow[] rows = tblEmp.Select( "EmployeeID = 1" );
```

In this case, you will get back one *DataRow* that contains the column information of the employee with *EmployeeID* = 1. We retrieve the first, middle, and last names and get the wage history information by executing the following code:

```
DataRow[] rowsWage = rowEmp.GetChildRows( relation );
```

The relation object was set earlier in the source code as follows:

```
DataRelation relation = doc.DataSet.Relations["EmpWageHistory"];
```

In effect, this code says "find all children of this employee that are defined by the *EmpWageHistory* relation of the *DataSet.*" The *EmpWageHistory* relation establishes a relation between an employee and that employee's wage history using *EmployeeID.* Issuing the call to *GetChildRows* will return all employee wage history rows in *WageChange DataTable* of the employee *XmlDataDocument.DataSet* object. Loop through all of the rows and save the result for later display on-screen.

You've now seen relational calls used to traverse the data in an *XmlDataDocument* object. As mentioned, you can also use DOM calls to traverse the document. Most of the code to traverse the document using DOM calls is very similar to code you saw in the "Working with XML DOM" section of this chapter, so we don't present it here. As previously mentioned, the full source code for the sample is on the CD. The key thing to note is that the output when traversing the document using relational calls is exactly the same when traversing the document using DOM calls. This is shown in Figure 9.7.

The relationship between XML and relational data is very powerful. It allows you to treat data as XML when it is best suited, and as relational database data when that is more appropriate. For instance, let's say that your employee information is contained in a SQL Server database. Suppose you need to transfer some of that employee data to a remote location that does not have access to the SQL Server database. Because the *XmlDataDocument* class contains a *DataSet* member, you can use ADO.NET to retrieve the data into an *XmlDataDocument.* Then, you can write the data contained in the *XmlDataDocument* to an XML file on disk using the *WriteXml* method of the *DataSet* class and transfer that file to the remote location. The remote location can read it back into an *XmlDataDocument* using the *ReadXml* method of the *DataSet* class and then manipulate it using XML DOM calls to generate reports using XSL, for instance. Or it could be written back to a local relational database, possibly Access, and generate reports via Access. Using the information you learned in this chapter and in Chapter 8 about ADO.NET, accomplishing this task becomes quite easy, whereas in the past it may have been quite difficult. By providing the *DataSet* class the ability to read and write XML and providing the *XmlDataDocument* class the ability to use DOM calls as well as relational calls against the *DataSet* member of *XmlDataDocument,* Microsoft has given you the tools to accomplish this.

# Working with XPath and XSL Transformations

In the introduction of this chapter, we introduced XPath. XPath is used to find a set of nodes in an XML document based on a location qualifier and a pattern to match. In the XML DOM, sample you saw that it was tedious to find a specific element. You had to walk the DOM tree in memory until the node was encountered. You couldn't get directly to an element with a given set of characteristics. The XPath language provides this capability.

XSLT also makes use of XPath expression. XSLT is used to transform XML documents from one format to another. The resulting format can be another XML document, HTML, or some other file format. XSLT stylesheets often use XPath statements to locate nodes in an XML document during transformation. In the following sections, you will see examples of XPath used as a generalized query language against XML documents. You will also see XPath used in XSL stylesheets as part of an XSL transformation.

## Working with XPath

The first example you will see of XPath in action uses XPath statements to query against an XML document. The sample requires the file personnel.xml to be in the same directory the sample is run from. You can find the file on the CD in the XPath directory. You may need to copy it to the directory you run the sample from. The full source code for the sample is in the XPath directory as well. The file that contains the source code is named XPathForm.cs. Figure 9.11 shows the XPath Sample program.

**Figure 9.11** The XPath Sample Program

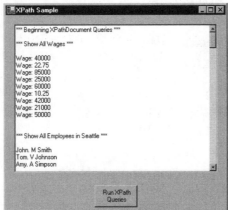

Figure 9.11 shows the program after you click **Run XPath Queries**. When you click the button, the program does a number of queries against the personnel.xml file and writes the results into the listbox on the form. Figure 9.12 shows a portion of the XML contained in the personnel.xml file used to generate the queries.

**Figure 9.12** Generating Queries (personnel.xml)

```xml
<?xml version="1.0" standalone="yes"?>
<Employees>
  <Employee EmployeeID="1">
    <FirstName>John</FirstName>
    <MiddleInit>M</MiddleInit>
    <LastName>Smith</LastName>
    <Salaried>true</Salaried>
    <Wage>40000</Wage>
    <Active>true</Active>
    <Title>Jr. Programmer</Title>
    <Location>
      <Address>103 N.72nd</Address>
      <City>Seattle</City>
      <State>WA</State>
      <Zip>98103</Zip>
    </Location>
  </Employee>
  <Employee EmployeeID="2">
    <FirstName>Joe</FirstName>
    <MiddleInit>R</MiddleInit>
    <LastName>Jones</LastName>
    <Salaried>false</Salaried>
    <Wage>22.75</Wage>
    <Active>true</Active>
    <Title>Graphic Artist</Title>
    <Location>
      <Address>13222 S. 1st Avenue</Address>
      <City>Portland</City>
```

**Continued**

**Figure 9.12** Continued

```
    <State>OR</State>
    <Zip>97206</Zip>
  </Location>
</Employee>
```

Figure 9.13 contains the relevant portions of the source code for the XPath sample. Source code inserted by the Visual Studio.NET designer has been omitted.

**Figure 9.13** Relevant Portions of Source Code (XPathForm.cs)

```
using System;
using System.Drawing;
using System.Collections;
using System.ComponentModel;
using System.Windows.Forms;
using System.Data;
using System.Xml;
using System.Xml.XPath;
using System.IO;


namespace XPath
{
    /// <summary>
    /// Summary description for Form1.
    /// </summary>
    public class Form1 : System.Windows.Forms.Form
    {
        /// <summary>
        /// Required designer variable.
        /// </summary>
        private System.ComponentModel.Container components = null;
        private System.Windows.Forms.TextBox textBox1;
        private System.Windows.Forms.Button button1;
```

**Continued**

## Figure 9.13 Continued

```
private string m_strOutput;

public Form1()
{
    InitializeComponent();
}


/// <summary>
/// The main entry point for the application.
/// </summary>
[STAThread]
static void Main()
{
    Application.Run(new Form1());
}


/// <summary>
/// Called when Run XPath Queries is pressed
/// </summary>
private void button1_Click(object sender, System.EventArgs e)
{
    Cursor currentCursor = Cursor.Current;

    try
    {
        Cursor.Current = Cursors.WaitCursor;

        // Do XPath queries on both XPath Documents and
        // DOM-based XML documents
        doXPathDocumentQueries();
        doXmlDocumentQueries();

        // Show results on-screen
```

**Continued**

**Figure 9.13** Continued

```
            textBox1.Text = m_strOutput;

    }
    catch ( Exception exception )
    {
        MessageBox.Show( exception.Message );
    }
    finally
    {
        Cursor.Current = currentCursor;
    }

}


/// <summary>
/// Do XPath queries against a read-only XPathDocument
/// </summary>
private void doXPathDocumentQueries()
{
    m_strOutput =
        "*** Beginning XPathDocument Queries ***\r\n\r\n";


    // Load the XML document into a read-only XPathDocument
    // and instantiate a navigator for queries.
    XPathDocument doc = new XPathDocument( "personnel.xml" );
    XPathNavigator navigator = doc.CreateNavigator();


    m_strOutput += "*** Show All Wages ***\r\n\r\n";


    // Find all Employee/Wage elements in the document and
    // display the wage information on-screen
    XPathNodeIterator iterator =
        navigator.Select( "descendant::Employee/Wage" );
```

**Continued**

## Figure 9.13 Continued

```
while ( iterator.MoveNext() )
{
    m_strOutput += iterator.Current.Name + ": ";
    m_strOutput += iterator.Current.Value + "\r\n";
}


m_strOutput +=
    "\r\n\r\n*** Show All Employees in Seattle ***\r\n\r\n";


// Find all employees in the Seattle office and display
// their names on-screen
iterator =
    navigator.Select( "//Employee[Location/Zip='98103']" );


while ( iterator.MoveNext() )
{
    XPathNavigator nav2 = iterator.Current;
    nav2.MoveToFirstChild();
    m_strOutput += nav2.Value;                  // First name
    nav2.MoveToNext();
    m_strOutput += ". " + nav2.Value;           // Middle init
    nav2.MoveToNext();
    m_strOutput += " " + nav2.Value + "\r\n"; // Last name
}


m_strOutput +=
    "\r\n\r\n*** Salaried Employee Average Wage ***\r\n\r\n";


// Calculate the average salary for all salaried employees
// in the company and display on-screen
Int32 nAverage =
    (Int32)(Double)navigator.Evaluate(
        "sum(//Employee[Salaried='true']/Wage) div
```

**Continued**

**Figure 9.13** Continued

```
                    count(//Employee[Salaried='true'])" );


        m_strOutput += "Average Salary: $" + nAverage.ToString();
    }


    /// <summary>
    /// Do an XPath queries against a DOM-based XML document and
then
    /// modify the document.
    /// </summary>
    private void doXmlDocumentQueries()
    {
        m_strOutput +=
            "\r\n\r\n*** Beginning XML Document Query ***\r\n\r\n";


        // Load the XML document into a DOM-based XML document
        XmlDocument doc = new XmlDocument();
        doc.Load( "personnel.xml" );


        // Get a list of the Active element nodes for each employee
        // in Portland
        XmlNodeList nodeList =
            doc.SelectNodes(
"//Employee[Location/Zip='97206']/Active");


        foreach ( XmlNode node in nodeList )
        {
            // Mark each Portland employee as inactive
            node.InnerText = "false";
        }


        // Display the modified document on-screen
        StringWriter writerString = new StringWriter();
        XmlTextWriter writer = new XmlTextWriter( writerString );
```

**Continued**

## Figure 9.13 Continued

```
            writer.Formatting = Formatting.Indented;

            doc.WriteTo( writer );

            writer.Flush();

            m_strOutput += writerString.ToString();

        }

    }

}
```

The program runs through two sets of XPath queries against the personnel .xml file. The first set of queries is against XML loaded into an object of type *System.Xml.XPath.XPathDocument*. The *XPathDocument* class has been optimized to work with XPath queries. It supports read-only access to the document. An *XPathNavigator* class object is used to perform queries against an *XPathDocument* document. Here is the code that instantiates and loads an *XPathDocument* with XML from a disk file. An *XPathNavigtor* class object is instantiated to perform XPath queries against the document:

```
XPathDocument doc = new XPathDocument( "personnel.xml" );

XPathNavigator navigator = doc.CreateNavigator();
```

The *Select* method of the *XPathNavigator* class is used to perform a query against the XML document. It takes an XPath statement as an argument. The following query returns all of the <Wage> elements in the XML document:

```
XPathNodeIterator iterator =

    navigator.Select( "descendant::Employee/Wage" );


while ( iterator.MoveNext() )

{

    m_strOutput += iterator.Current.Name + ": ";

    m_strOutput += iterator.Current.Value + "\r\n";

}
```

The *select* statement takes an XPath expression as an argument and returns an *XPathNodeIterator* object, which is used to traverse the node list returned. The *Current* property of *XPathNodeIterator* points to the current position in the node list returned form the *Select* method call. The position is undefined until the first call to the *MoveNext* method. As each <Wage> element is encountered in the returned node list, the element tag and value are saved for later display in the listbox on-screen. The *Name* property of *Current* returns the element tag and the *Value* property of *Current* returns the text contained within the <Wage> element.

## Developing & Deploying...

### XPath Expressions

A brief explanation of XPath statements is in order. XPath expressions use what is termed a *location path*, which is made up of one or more location steps that are separated by a "/" or by a "//". The "/" character indicates an absolute path, and the "//" characters indicate a relative path from the current node. A location step contains an axis and a node test, and it may contain predicates. The axis indicates the direction of the query from the current node. Examples are *child*, *ancestor*, and *descendent*. The node test is either the name of a node in the document, the wildcard character(*), or one of several node tests such as *node()* and *text()*. The predicate is used to filter the node test to pinpoint a specific set of nodes. A predicate is contained within brackets. Here are two examples of XPath expressions:

- In the XPath expression *descendent::Employee/Wage*, *descendent* indicates the axis and *Employee/Wage* indicates the node test. There is no predicate in this case. The expression returns the *Employee/Wage* descendents of the current node.

- In the XPath expression *"//Employee[Location/Zip='98103']*, the "//" indicates the axis, *Employee* indicates the node test and *[Location/Zip='98103']* indicates the predicate. The expression returns the *Employee* elements with a *Location/Zip* element whose value is "98103".

These are relatively simple examples. You can combine extremely complex combinations of axes, node tests, and predicates to create extremely powerful queries against XML documents using XPath.

The second query against the *XPathDocument* returns all the employees in the Seattle office and displays their names. Here is the code to accomplish this:

```
iterator =
   navigator.Select( "//Employee[Location/Zip='98103']" );


while ( iterator.MoveNext() )
{
   XPathNavigator nav2 = iterator.Current;
   nav2.MoveToFirstChild();
   m_strOutput += nav2.Value;                  // First name
   nav2.MoveToNext();
   m_strOutput += ". " + nav2.Value;           // Middle init
   nav2.MoveToNext();
   m_strOutput += " " + nav2.Value + "\r\n";   // Last name
}
```

The only real difference with this query is that you need to use a second instance of *XPathNavigator*. Each node in the node list is an <Employee> element. The second *XPathNavigator* object is needed so that you can maintain your position in the node list of <Employee> elements.

The last query against the *XPathDocument* object does a summary query. It returns a result, not a node list. Here is the code, which calculates the average salary of all salaried employees:

```
Int32 nAverage =
   (Int32)(Double)navigator.Evaluate(
      "sum(//Employee[Salaried='true']/Wage) div
       count(//Employee[Salaried='true'])" );
```

When performing summary queries, the *Evaluate* method is used instead of the *Select* method. It also takes an XPath expression as an argument. You can see from this example that the XPath expressions can get quite complex.

The second set of queries is done against an *XmlDocument* object. As we mentioned earlier, an *XPathDocument* is read-only. So, if you want to use XPath directly against an XML document and update the document, you will need to use an *XmlDocument* object. Here is the relevant code from the sample:

```
XmlDocument doc = new XmlDocument();
doc.Load( "personnel.xml" );


// Get a list of the Active element nodes for each employee
```

```
// in Portland
XmlNodeList nodeList =
    doc.SelectNodes( "//Employee[Location/Zip='97206']/Active");

foreach ( XmlNode node in nodeList )
{
    // Mark each Portland employee as inactive
    node.InnerText = "false";
}
```

This example simulates shutting down the Portland office. The <Active> element is set to false for all employees in the Portland office. First, a new *XmlDocument* object is instantiated and then loaded using the *Load* method. Next, the XPath query against the document is executed using the *SelectNodes* method of the *System.Xml.Node* class. It takes an XPath expression as an argument and returns an *XmlNodeList* object. In this case, it is a node list containing each <Active> element for each employee in the Portland office. The node list is traversed using the *foreach* statement, and the text value associated with the <Active> element is set to false. Assigning the string "false" to the *InnerText* property accomplishes this.

# Working with XSL

The previous section shows how XPath is used as a general query tool. In this section, you will see XSLT used to transform XML documents to a different format. XSL stylesheets will use XPath expressions to select node lists for transformation.

Our sample simulates a real-world scenario. The scenario is that the human resources division of a company named EntegraTech maintains personnel data in an XML file named personnel.xml. Another division of the company maintains a Web site that includes some reports based on personnel information. The Web site uses XSL stylesheets to build HTML Web pages from personnel information contained in XML files. Unfortunately, the Web site stylesheets expect the XML to be in a different format than the format in the personnel.xml file supplied by the HR department. The sample code transforms the XML into the format that the Web site stylesheets expect and then builds one of the HTML reports. XSL stylesheets are used both to transform the XML and to create the HTML.

The sample requires the files personnel.xml, salariedpersonnel.xsl, and salariedreport.xsl to be in the same directory the sample is run from. You can find the files on the CD that accompanies this book, in the XSL directory. You may need to copy the files to the directory you run the sample from. The full source code for the sample is in the XSL directory as well. The file that contains the source code is named XSLForm.cs. Figure 9.14 shows the running program.

**Figure 9.14** The XSL Sample Program

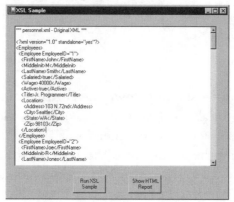

Figure 9.14 shows the program after you click **Run XSL Sample**. When you click the button, it transforms the personnel.xml file by using an XSL stylesheet, displays the original XML file and the transformed XML file in the listbox, and writes the transformed XML to another file on disk. The **Show HTML Report** button then becomes active. Clicking the button runs a second XSLT stylesheet, which creates a HTML document from the newly transformed XML. Internet Explorer is then launched and displays the HTML report. Figure 9.15 shows the report displayed in Internet Explorer.

**Figure 9.15** The EntegraTech HTML Report

You have seen the structure of the personnel.xml file already. Figure 9.16 shows it again for comparison with the format expected by the Web site. Figure 9.17 shows the format of the XML expected by the Web site. Comparing these two will help in understanding what the XSL stylesheet must do.

**Figure 9.16** Partial Contents of the personnel.xml File

```
<Employees>

  <Employee EmployeeID="1">

    <FirstName>John</FirstName>

    <MiddleInit>M</MiddleInit>

    <LastName>Smith</LastName>

    <Salaried>true</Salaried>

    <Wage>40000</Wage>

    <Active>true</Active>

    <Title>Jr. Programmer</Title>

    <Location>

      <Address>103 N.72nd</Address>

      <City>Seattle</City>

      <State>WA</State>

      <Zip>98103</Zip>

    </Location>

  </Employee>
```

**Figure 9.17** XML Format Expected by the Web Site

```
<Salaried>

  <Employee>

    <Name>John M.  Smith</Name>

    <Wage>40000</Wage>

    <Location>98103</Location>

  </Employee>
```

As you can see, the XSL stylesheet needs to combine the <FirstName>, <MiddleInit>, and <LastName> elements into a single <Name> element. It also needs to copy the <Wage> element verbatim. Finally, it needs to copy the contents of the <Zip> element into a <Location> element.

The file salariedpersonnel.xsl is the stylesheet that is used to convert from the first XML representation to the second. It is shown in Figure 9.18.

**Figure 9.18** The Stylesheet (salariedpersonnel.xsl)

```
<xsl:stylesheet version="1.0"
xmlns:xsl="http://www.w3.org/1999/XSL/Transform">


    <xsl:template match="/">
    <Salaried>
        <xsl:apply-templates/>
    </Salaried>
    </xsl:template>


    <xsl:template match="Employees">
      <xsl:apply-templates select="Employee[Salaried='true']"/>
    </xsl:template>


    <xsl:template match="Employee[Salaried='true']">
        <Employee>
          <Name>
            <xsl:value-of select="FirstName"/><xsl:text> </xsl:text>
            <xsl:value-of select="MiddleInit"/><xsl:text>. </xsl:text>
            <xsl:value-of select="LastName"/>
          </Name>
          <Wage>
            <xsl:value-of select="Wage"/>
          </Wage>
          <Location>
            <xsl:value-of select="Location/Zip"/>
          </Location>
        </Employee>
    </xsl:template>


</xsl:stylesheet>
```

An XSL stylesheet uses pattern matching to process an XML document. The XSLT processor begins processing the XML document and looks for statements in the XSL script, called rules, which match nodes encountered in the XML document. Near the top is the rule for the root element of the document:

```
<xsl:template match="/">
<Salaried>
    <xsl:apply-templates/>
</Salaried>
</xsl:template>
```

When the root element of the original XML document is encountered, the previous statements are executed. In this case, a <Salaried> element is created and the child nodes of the root element are processed by the *<xsl:apply-templates/>* statement. When the <Employees> element is encountered, execute the following statements:

```
<xsl:template match="Employees">
  <xsl:apply-templates select="Employee[Salaried='true']"/>
</xsl:template>
```

The *select* attribute of an *<xsl:apply-templates>* statement contains the pattern to match in an XML document. The pattern matching string can be an XPath expression. This is where XPath comes into play in XSL stylesheet processing.

The preceding XSL script statements ignore any <Employee> elements that do not contain a child element <Salaried> with a text node whose value is "true". In effect, you  execute a rule that returns all <Employee> elements that represent salaried employees and ignore all other nodes encountered in the XML document. The following statements process the matching salaried employee elements:

```
<xsl:template match="Employee[Salaried='true']">
    <Employee>
      <Name>
        <xsl:value-of select="FirstName"/><xsl:text> </xsl:text>
        <xsl:value-of select="MiddleInit"/><xsl:text>. </xsl:text>
        <xsl:value-of select="LastName"/>
      </Name>
      <Wage>
        <xsl:value-of select="Wage"/>
```

```
        </Wage>
        <Location>
          <xsl:value-of select="Location/Zip"/>
        </Location>
      </Employee>
   </xsl:template>
```

These statements convert all salaried <Employee> elements in the original XML document to the format required in the new XML document. This is where the meat of the transformation takes place. Let's take a look in Figure 9.19 at the relevant portions of the source code that perform the XSLT transformation.

**Figure 9.19** XML-to-XML Transformation in the Source Code (XSLForm.cs)

```
private void doXMLToXMLTransform()
{
    // Show the original document on-screen
    m_strOutput = "*** personnel.xml - Original XML ***\r\n\r\n";
    showXMLDocument( "personnel.xml" );

    // Load the new document, apply an XSL tranformation to
    // it and save the new document to disk
    XPathDocument docXPath =
        new XPathDocument( "personnel.xml" );

    XslTransform xslTransform = new XslTransform();
    XmlTextWriter writer =
        new XmlTextWriter( "salaried.xml", null );

    xslTransform.Load( "salariedpersonnel.xsl" );
    xslTransform.Transform( docXPath, null, writer );
    writer.Close();

    m_strOutput +=
        "*** salaried.xml - Transformed XML ***\r\n\r\n";

    // Show the transformed document
```

**Continued**

**Figure 9.19** Continued

```
    showXMLDocument( "salaried.xml" );
}


private void showXMLDocument( string strXMLFileName )
{
  XmlDocument docDOM = new XmlDocument();
  docDOM.Load( strXMLFileName );


  StringWriter writerString = new StringWriter();
  XmlTextWriter writer2 = new XmlTextWriter( writerString );
  writer2.Formatting = Formatting.Indented;
  docDOM.WriteTo( writer2 );
  writer2.Flush();
  m_strOutput += writerString.ToString() + "\r\n\r\n";
}
```

In the *doXMLToXMLTransform* method, an *XPathDocument* object is instantiated and loaded with XML contained in the personnel.xml file. Then, an
*XslTransform* object is instantiated. The *XslTransform* object is the engine used to
perform XSLT transformations on XML documents in the .NET Framework.

After the transformation is complete, the results are written to a new XML
file on disk. An *XmlTextWriter* object is created that writes the transformed file to
disk. The file that is created is named salaried.xml, which is the first parameter
passed to the *XmlTextWriter* constructor.

The *Load* method of the *XslTransform* class loads the XSL stylesheet from
disk. Finally, the transform is executed by calling the *Transform* method of the
*XslTransform* class object. The *Transform* method takes the XML document object
and the text writer objects as parameters. The second parameter of the *Transform*
method is used to pass additional runtime arguments that are used in the
stylesheet. Because you have no runtime arguments, it is left null. After the transform is complete, the *XmlTextWriter* object is closed to complete the writing of
the new XML document file to disk.

The *showXMLDocument* method is a helper function that reads an XML
document from disk and formats it with indenting for display purposes. The
*showXMLDocument* method illustrates how the *XmlDocument*, *XmlTextWriter*, and

*StringWriter* classes work together to convert an XML document on disk to an in-memory string.

As you can see, very little source code is necessary to perform the complex task of transforming an XML document to another format. You have now converted the original document to the new format that is needed to generate the HTML reports. Let's take a look in Figure 9.20 at the XSL stylesheet used to transform the converted XML to HTML.

**Figure 9.20** The Stylesheet (salariedreport.xsl)

```
<xsl:stylesheet version="1.0"
xmlns:xsl="http://www.w3.org/1999/XSL/Transform">

    <xsl:template match="/">

        <html>

            <head>

                <title>EntegraTech Salaried Employees</title>

            </head>

            <body bgcolor="#C0C0C0">

                <h1 align="left">EntegraTech Salaried Employees</h1>

                <p></p>

                <xsl:apply-templates />

            </body>

        </html>

    </xsl:template>


    <xsl:template match="Salaried">

        <h2 align="left">Seattle Office Salaried Employees</h2>

        <table border="0" width="100%">

            <xsl:apply-templates select="Employee[Location='98103']" />

        </table>

        <p></p>

        <h2 align="left">Portland Office Salaried Employees</h2>

        <table border="0" width="100%">

            <xsl:apply-templates select="Employee[Location='97206']" />

        </table>

    </xsl:template>
```

**Continued**

**Figure 9.20** Continued

```
<xsl:template match="Employee[Location='98103']">
    <tr>
        <td width="28%">
            <xsl:value-of select="Name" />
        </td>
        <td width="72%">
            $<xsl:value-of select="Wage" />
        </td>
    </tr>
</xsl:template>

<xsl:template match="Employee[Location='97206']">
    <tr>
        <td width="28%">
            <xsl:value-of select="Name" />
        </td>
        <td width="72%">
            $<xsl:value-of select="Wage" />
        </td>
    </tr>
</xsl:template>
</xsl:stylesheet>
```

Briefly, this stylesheet creates an HTML document for display in a Web browser. You can see the familiar pattern matching statements that we saw in the previous stylesheet. This stylesheet creates two HTML tables that display the names of employees and their wages. The first table shows the employees in the Seattle office, and the second shows the employees in Portland. Figure 9.21 shows the C# source code used to perform the transformation from XML to HTML.

**Figure 9.21** XML to HTML Transformation in the Source Code (XSLForm.cs)

```
private void doXMLToHTMLTranformation()
{
    // Load the XML document, apply an XSL transformation to it,
    // resulting in HTML which is written to disk.
    XPathDocument docXPath = new XPathDocument( "salaried.xml" );
    XslTransform xslTransform = new XslTransform();
    XmlTextWriter writer =
        new XmlTextWriter( "salariedreport.html", null );

    xslTransform.Load( "salariedreport.xsl" );
    xslTransform.Transform( docXPath, null, writer );
    writer.Close();
    btnShowHTML.Enabled = true;
}
```

The code looks very similar to the code you saw that performed the XML-to-XML transformation earlier in Figure 9.19 earlier in this section. The only noticeable difference is that the *XmlTextWriter* object now takes the name of the HTML file as a parameter. When the *doXMLToHTMLTransformation* method is complete, a new HTML file exists named salariedreport.html, which contains the report. Here is the source code that launches Internet Explorer and displays the report in the Web browser:

```
private void btnShowHTML_Click_1(object sender,
    System.EventArgs e)
{
    System.Diagnostics.Process.Start("salariedreport.html");
}
```

The *Start* method of the *System.Diagnostics.Process* class executes a program. This overloaded version of the *Start* method takes a document name. If the document type has a file association established with a program on the computer, it will invoke that program. In our case, HTML files are associated with Internet Explorer. So, when the *Start* method is called with an HTML filename as the parameter, Internet Explorer is launched and the HTML file passed in is displayed.

## Debugging...

### XSLT: Debugging Stylesheets

XSLT is a powerful technology for transforming XML documents. The XPath expressions used in XSL stylesheets to match nodes in an XML document can be very complex. It can become difficult to debug what is happening in stylesheet when the output is not what you expect. To aid in debugging problems in XSL stylesheets, it is often helpful to develop the stylesheet in small increments rather than creating the complete stylesheet at one time. Write one rule at a time and run your transformation, verifying that the node list returned is what you expect. When you do encounter output that is not what you expect, you can be relatively sure the problem lies in the last rule you added. This can save you valuable time.

# Summary

XML has emerged as the Web standard for representing and transmitting data over the Internet. The W3C has worked to establish standards for XML and related technologies including XML DOM, XPath, XSL, and XML schemas. XML DOM is an API that is used to create, modify, and traverse XML documents. XPath is a language that is used to query XML documents. XSL translates XML documents from one format to another format. XML schemas define the structure and data types of the nodes in an XML document. All of these technologies are industry standards backed by the W3C.

Microsoft has embraced XML and provides implementations in the .NET Framework for many of the technologies standardized by the W3C. The XML DOM API is fully supported in the .NET Framework by the *XmlDocument* class. The *XmlDocument* class allows you to create XML documents from scratch, persist them to a number of different data stores and read them back into memory from those data stores. Once in memory, an XML document can be traversed and modified including adding, updating, and deleting nodes in the document.

In conjunction with ADO.NET and the XML support in the .NET Framework, the ability to work with data as XML or as relational data is available using C#. The *XmlDataDocument* class is used to read data into a *DataSet* class object from an XML disk file or from a database. Once the *XmlDataDocument* is created, the data is available for access relationally as table and columns or as XML through the DOM API. XML schema support is provided by the .NET Framework to specify the structure and data types of the data in XML documents including the *XmlDataDocument* class. The relationship between the ADO.NET *DataSet* class and the XML API provides a powerful foundation to develop end-to-end applications storing data in databases on both ends of a business process and using XML to transmit the data between.

The .NET Framework supports XPath queries against XML DOM documents or the highly optimized *XPathDocument* class. The *XPathNavigator* class works in conjunction with the *XPathDocument* to issue XPath queries against XML documents in read-only mode. XPath queries can also be issued against the *XmlDocument* class providing a convenient method to locate a specific node in a document and then modify it. XPath queries are also instrumental in XSL transformations. The .NET Framework fully supports XSL transformations as implemented in the *XslTransform* class. XML-to-XML transformations as well as XML to other formats are implemented with a minimum of source code.

Use of XML is found throughout the .NET Framework and is instrumental in the implementation of Web Services, as you will find out in Chapter 11. Because XML is critical to .NET, developers benefit by first class, standards-based support for XML in the .NET Framework. This chapter provided you with the information you need to start taking advantages of that support in your own XML-based applications.

# Solutions Fast Track

## Introduction to XML

- ☑ XML has emerged as the Web standard for representing and transmitting data over the Internet.

- ☑ The W3C has standardized XML and related technologies including XML DOM, XPath, XSL, and XML Schemas.

- ☑ The .NET Framework provides first class support for W3C-backed XML standards.

- ☑ XML is prevalent throughout the .NET Framework including use in configuration files, C# source code comments, and Web Services.

## Working with XML DOM

- ☑ An XML document can be represented as a tree of nodes in memory, which can be traversed and modified using an implementation of the XML DOM API.

- ☑ The *XmlDocument* class is the .NET implementation of XML DOM.

- ☑ The *XmlDocument* class provides the ability to create an XML document, add elements and attributes to a document, update nodes in the document, delete nodes from the document, save the document to persistent storage, and load the document into memory from persistent storage.

# Working with XML and Relational Data

☑ The *DataSet* class is an in-memory representation of relational data using tables, columns, and rows.

☑ The *XmlDataDocument* class has a *DataSet* object as a member variable. XML documents can be read into an *XmlDataDocument* object instance and can then be manipulated using XML DOM method calls or by relational method calls against the *DataSet* member variable.

☑ In conjunction with ADO.NET, the XML support in the .NET Framework can be used to build powerful applications that access data as XML or relational database data when appropriate. The conversion between the two types of data is trivial to implement.

# Working with XPath and XSL Transformations

☑ XPath support is built into the .NET Framework for use as a general-purpose query tool or as part of XSL stylesheets.

☑ XPath queries can be performed against the read-only *XPathDocument* class using the *XPathNavigator* class. The *XmlDocument* class can also be queried using XPath to locate a node in a document, which can then be modified if desired.

☑ XSL Transformations are implemented using the *XslTransform* class of the .NET Framework allowing transformation of XML documents to other formats including XML and HTML.

# Frequently Asked Questions

The following Frequently Asked Questions, answered by the authors of this book, are designed to both measure your understanding of the concepts presented in this chapter and to assist you with real-life implementation of these concepts. To have your questions about this chapter answered by the author, browse to **www.syngress.com/solutions** and click on the **"Ask the Author"** form.

**Q:** What W3C level of support is provided in the XML classes supplied with the .NET Framework?

**A:** The *XmlDataDocument* class supports W3C DOM Core Level 1 and Core Level 2 specifications. The *XmlSchema* class supports W3C XML Schemas for Structures and the XML Schemas for Data Types specifications. The *XslTransform* class supports the XSLT 1.0 specification. See the W3C Web site for details on the specifications at: www.w3c.org.

**Q:** Which set of XML classes should I use to implement my project?

**A:** That depends on your needs and can be difficult to say. Here though are some rules of thumb. If you need fast-forward, read-only access to the data, use one of the *XmlReader*-derived classes, such as *XmlTextReader*. If you need to do extensive updates to the document, use the *XmlDocument* class. If you want fast query capabilities, use the *XPathDocument* class. If you want to read and write from a database and then manipulate the results as XML, use the *XmlDataDocument* class.

**Q:** I have two tables in a *DataSet* and have added a *DataRelation*, which establishes a parent-child relationship. When I write the XML file to disk, the parent-child relationship isn't represented. What is wrong?

**A:** Most likely you did not set the *Nested* property of the *DataRelation* to true. If it is false, the elements associated with the child in the relationship will all appear after the parent elements in the XML file.

**Q:** How do I create an *XmlDocument* instance from a string?

**A:** Here are two methods. One method is to use this:

```
doc.Load( new XmlTextReader( new StringReader( myString ) ) )
```

Another is to write this:

```
doc.InnerXml = myString
```

# Chapter 10

# ASP.NET

## Solutions in this chapter:

- Introducing the ASP.NET Architecture

- Working with Web Forms

- Working with ADO.NET

☑ Summary

☑ Solutions Fast Track

☑ Frequently Asked Questions

# Introduction

ASP.NET is Microsoft's upgrade to Active Server Pages (ASP). ASP.NET architecture is very well woven into the .NET Framework to provide a powerful event-driven programming model. The new feature of *code-behind* allows true separation of code and design. Also, you can write ASP.NET pages in any of the managed languages, and the code is compiled to give high performance.

This chapter acquaints you with writing Web Forms and database-driven Web applications. You will see how you can leverage the use of XML data in the .NET Framework within ASP.NET applications, through "real world" examples (a shopping cart and a message board). We also explain how to e-mail from ASP.NET, which includes an example of a simple e-mail ASP.NET page.

In all the examples, we cover a broad range of new features in ASP.NET. One of these is the capability to have custom validation embedded into the pages from JavaScript (.js) files, which originate from the root on the server; ASP.NET has a whole host of validation controls to use. Also the backbone of the .NET architecture is built on XML. The use of XSL/Transforms on XML data from *DataSets* provide the developer with the ability to create custom content for various clients with minimal program logic overhead. We demonstrate this in the message board example included in this chapter.

ASP.NET is a more robust way to bring applications to the Web. Gone are the endless lines of "spaghetti code" and with it the ambiguous debugging. With ASP.NET, you will be able to create cross-browser, cross-platform applications that you can port across the Web.

# Introducing the ASP.NET Architecture

In the ASP.NET architecture, the .NET Framework works with the OS. A Web client requests a Web Form (ASPX) resource, which is delivered through the Internet Information Server (IIS) combining all additional resources, which may include a database, Web Service, COM component, or a component class. All of these are delivered through a compiled assembly (DLL) from the Web application, which sits in the bin directory within IIS's Web root. See Figure 10.1 for a conceptual overview of the ASP.NET architecture. ASP.NET includes some new file extensions for the different types of pages you can create in your solutions. The new extensions allow ASP.NET to sit alongside ASP 3.0 on the same server with no filename conflicts. Here is a list of the four most commonly used extensions:

- **.aspx**   Used for Web Forms and is the replacement for the standard .asp extension used in ASP 3.0.

- **.ascx**   Used to denote a reusable page components or control.

- **.asmx**   Used to denote a Web Service.

- **.asax**   Used for the Global file and is the replacement for the **.asa** extension.

Each of these page types can have a code-behind page where you can store program logic. Note that using code-behind pages makes your code more modular and helps to hide the program logic from prying eyes, because the code-behind pages are not stored individually on the server but are part of the compiled assembly (DLL).

The corresponding code-behind pages would be .aspx.vb, .ascx.vb, .asmx.vb, and .asax.vb respectively if the project was a VB.NET project, or .aspx.cs, .ascx.cs, .asmx.cs, and .asax.cs respectively if the project was a C# project.

**Figure 10.1** Overview of ASP.NET Architecture

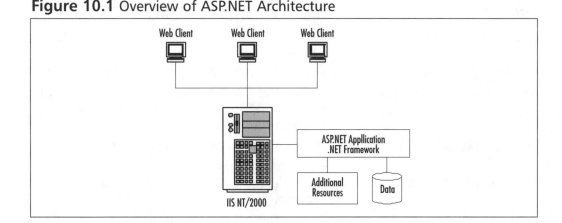

# ASP.NET Server Controls

You can add three main sets of controls to your Web Form (ASPX page): HTML server controls, Web server controls, and validation controls.

- **HTML server controls**   Allow you to work with all the properties of the standard HTML elements within your server-side code (in your code-behind page or in inline server scripting on the ASPX page itself). This will expose them for all server-side processing and for content delivery, which you can provide a specific style sheet to comply with NS

4 or Opera. To provide HTML form elements with the programming power of server-side processing, you must add at least two attributes to the tag in question. The HTML control needs to have the *runat* attribute set to *"server"* (*runat="server"*) and an ID. By doing this, the control is made available to the server for processing instead of being passed as text to the browser. See Table 10.1 for a list of HTML elements that can be easily converted into HTML server controls. The following is an example of a HTML button server control:

```
<INPUT type="button" id="button1"
        value="clickme" runat="server">
```

**Table 10.1** HTML Server Controls

| Server Control | Description |
|---|---|
| *HtmlAnchorControl* | Access the <a> tag in server processing |
| *HtmlButtonControl* | Access the <button> tag in server processing |
| *HtmlFormControl* | Access the <form> tag in server processing |
| *HtmlGenericControl* | Access the <span>, <div>, <body>, <font> tag in server processing |
| *HtmlImageControl* | Access the <img> tag in server processing |
| *HtmlInputButtonControl* | Access the <input type="submit">, <input type="reset">, <input type="button">, tag in server processing |
| *HtmlCheckBoxControl* | Access the <input type="checkbox"> tag in server processing |
| *HtmlInputFileControl* | Access the <input type="file"> tag in server processing |
| *HtmlInputRadioButtonControl* | Access the <input type="radio"> tag in server processing |
| *HtmlSelectControl* | Access the <select> tag in server processing |
| *HtmlTableControl* | Access the <table> tag in server processing |
| *HtmlTableCellControl* | Access the <td>, and <th> tag in server processing |
| *HtmlTableRowControl* | Access the <tr> tag in server processing |
| *HtmlTextAreaControl* | Access the <textarea> tag in server processing |

- **Web server controls** A completely new set of controls designed to interact with the .NET environment by the additional properties and events included, most notably the ability to do a postback. The tags are XML-based, so they all appear in the same manor as XML elements for ease of use. Web server controls are defaulted to render HTML 3.2 for cross browser compliance. Web server controls inherit the *System.Web.UI .Control* namespace, which predefines their attributes. Table 10.2 shows a list of Web server controls. We discuss a number of these in the examples ahead. The following shows a Button Web server control and a Textbox Web server control as they would appear on a Web Form (ASPX page):

```
<asp:button id="button1" runat="server"></asp:button>
<asp:text id="text1" runat="server"></asp:text>
```

**Table 10.2** ASP.NET Web Server Controls

**Web Server Controls**

| | | | | |
|---|---|---|---|---|
| AdRotator | Button | Calendar | CheckBox | CheckBoxList |
| DataGrid | DataList | DropDownList | HyperLink | Image |
| ImageButton | Label | LinkButton | ListBox | Literal |
| Panel | PlaceHolder | RadioButton | RadioButtonList | Repeater |
| Table | TableCell | TableRow | TextBox | XML |

- **Validation controls** You can have customized validation run on the client generated by the server through a JS (external JavaScript) file. Table 10.3 shows a list of validation controls. When working with validation server controls, you must set a couple of attributes. To specify the control to validate, set the *controltovalidate* attribute to the *ID* of the Web server control you want to validate. If you set the *display* attribute to *static*, the validation control will occupy that space permanently. (The position of the control will be held even when the error message is not visible. This works just like setting the Cascading Style Sheet [CSS] attribute *visibility* to *hidden*), but if you set the *display* attribute to *dynamic*, you can have multiple error messages listed in the same space (the position of the control is not held when the error message is not visible. This works like setting the CSS attribute *display* to *none*). Also, the *errormessage* attribute is the error message that will be shown when the validation fails. We use these in the following examples.

**Table 10.3** ASP.NET Validator Controls

| Validator Control | Description |
| --- | --- |
| *CompareValidator* | Compares a value entered into a Web server control against another set value. |
| *CustomValidator* | Can create your own custom validation for specific data. |
| *RangeValidator* | Finds the range between two values on a Web server control. |
| *RegularExpressionValidator* | Uses regular expressions to validate a value entered into a Web server control. |
| *RequiredFieldValidator* | Ensures that all items are supplied data in a Web server control. |
| *ValidationSummary* | Groups the result set of validation control error messages into a summary for viewing. |

## Debugging...

### ASP.NET Server Controls Do Not Display Correctly in Netscape 4.x

A lot has happened over the last few years with Netscape and the open source Mozilla project. Although the newer versions of Mozilla version .094 and above should handle this fine, Netscape still has a significant 4.*x* user base. When we develop Web front-ends for our clients, we strive to ensure at least Netscape 4.72 will display and function correctly.

What's the issue? It seems that most of the examples showing you how to use server controls in Visual Studio.NET have you drag and drop the control to where you want it on the screen. In HTML, this creates span tags with inline style attributes containing "absolute positioning." Those of us that have dealt with cross-browser Dynamic HTML (DHTML) issues know that this can cause problems in Netscape. The solution: Use "FlowLayout" and good old fashioned HTML elements and tricks for positioning. To do this, simply right-click on a page in either Design or HTML view and switch the *pageLayout* property to *FlowLayout*.

# Working with User Controls

If you have some very useful code written in a current Web Form, and you want to reuse that code in another Web Form, you can do that with a user control. This is the same as using a server-side include but with all the programming power of an embedded server control. You can access all the properties of the *User* control within your new Web Form page. This allows you to reuse your code and maintain total control of all the properties in the page.

Making your own custom user control is very easy. Simply take out the code that is between the body tags of your current ASPX page, open a new file in VS.NET, and select **Web User Control** (this will have an .ascx extension), and paste in the code between the form tags of the control page. If you have any code-behind in your ASPX page, you must add that also. This will be placed in the code-behind page for the user control. Look at this example:

```
<DIV style="Z-INDEX: 100; LEFT: 10px; WIDTH: 300px; POSITION: relative;
    TOP: 10px; HEIGHT: 400px">
  <TABLE cellSpacing="1" cellPadding="1" width="300" border="0">
   <TR>
    <TD>From:</TD>
    <TD colspan="2">
      <asp:TextBox id="txtFrom" runat="server" AutoPostBack="False">
      </asp:TextBox>
    </TD>
   </TR>
   <TR>
    <TD>To:</TD>
    <TD colspan="2">
      <asp:TextBox id="txtTo" runat="server" AutoPostBack="False">
      </asp:TextBox>
    </TD>
   </TR>
   <TR>
    <TD>CC:</TD>
    <TD colspan="2">
      <asp:TextBox id="txtCC" runat="server" AutoPostBack="False">
      </asp:TextBox>
```

```
        </TD>
      </TR>
      <TR>
      <TD colspan="3"> </TD>
      </TR>
      <TR>
       <TD colspan="3">Subject:</TD>
      </TR>
      <TR>
       <TD colspan="3">
         <asp:TextBox AutoPostBack="False" id="txtSubject" runat="server"
         Width="288px" Height="24px"></asp:TextBox>
       </TD>
      </TR>
      <TR>
       <TD colspan="3">Message:</TD>
      </TR>
      <TR>
       <TD colspan="3">
         <asp:TextBox id="txtMessage" AutoPostBack="False" Rows="10"
         runat="server" Width="313px" Height="160px"></asp:TextBox>
       </TD>
      </TR>
      <TR>
       <TD colspan="3">
         <asp:Button id="btnEmail" runat="server" Text="Send Email">
         </asp:Button>
       </TD>
      </TR>
    </TABLE>
  </DIV>

<DIV style="Z-INDEX: 101; LEFT: 352px; WIDTH: 264px;
    POSITION: absolute; TOP: 24px; HEIGHT: 400px">
  <TABLE cellSpacing="1" cellPadding="1" width="300" border="0"
```

```
    style="WIDTH: 300px; HEIGHT: 80px">
<TR>
 <TD>
   <asp:RequiredFieldValidator id="rfvTxtfrom" runat="server"
        ControlToValidate="txtFrom"
        Display="Dynamic"
        Font-Name="Verdana"
        Font-Size="10pt">* please provide an e-mail address
   </asp:RequiredFieldValidator>
   <asp:RegularExpressionValidator id="revTxtfrom" runat="server"
        ControlToValidate="txtFrom"
        ValidationExpression="^.*\@.*\..*$"
        Display="static"
        Font-Name="verdana"
        Font-Size="10pt">
     Please enter a valid e-mail address
   </asp:RegularExpressionValidator>
 </TD>
</TR>
<TR>
 <TD>
   <asp:RequiredFieldValidator id="rfvTxtto" runat="server"
        ControlToValidate="txtTo"
        Display="Dynamic"
        Font-Name="Verdana"
        Font-Size="10pt">
    * please provide an e-mail address
   </asp:RequiredFieldValidator>
   <asp:RegularExpressionValidator id="revTxtto" runat="server"
        ControlToValidate="txtTo"
        ValidationExpression="^.*\@.*\..*$"
        Display="static"
        Font-Name="verdana"
        Font-Size="10pt">
  Please enter a valid e-mail address
```

```
        </asp:RegularExpressionValidator>
      </TD>
    </TR>
    <TR>
     <TD>
       <asp:RegularExpressionValidator id="revTxtcc" runat="server"
            ControlToValidate="txtCC"
            ValidationExpression="^.*\@.*\..*$"
            Display="static"
            Font-Name="verdana"
            Font-Size="10pt">
       Please enter a valid e-mail address
       </asp:RegularExpressionValidator>
     </TD>
    </TR>
   </TABLE>
</DIV>
```

Here you have cut out the HTML code from your ASPX page. Now, you need to paste this into your user control page. Here is what it will look like when you have done this (there is a new directive declared called *@Control*):

```
<%@ Control Language="c#" AutoEventWireup="false"
    Codebehind="WebUserControl1.ascx.cs"
    Inherits="simpleMail.WebUserControl1"%>
<TABLE cellSpacing="1" cellPadding="1" width="300" border="0">
  <TR>
    <TD>From:</TD>
    <TD colspan="2">
      <asp:TextBox id="txtFrom" runat="server" AutoPostBack="False">
      </asp:TextBox>
    </TD>
  </TR>
  <TR>
    <TD>To:</TD>
    <TD colspan="2">
```

```
      <asp:TextBox id="txtTo" runat="server" AutoPostBack="False">
      </asp:TextBox>
   </TD>
</TR>
<TR>
   <TD>CC:</TD>
   <TD colspan="2">
      <asp:TextBox id="txtCC" runat="server" AutoPostBack="False">
      </asp:TextBox>
   </TD>
</TR>
<TR>
   <TD colspan="3"> </TD>
</TR>
<TR>
   <TD colspan="3">Subject:</TD>
</TR>
<TR>
   <TD colspan="3">
      <asp:TextBox id="txtSubject" AutoPostBack="False" runat="server"
         Width="288px" Height="24px"></asp:TextBox>
   </TD>
</TR>
<TR>
   <TD colspan="3">Message:</TD>
</TR>
<TR>
   <TD colspan="3">
      <asp:TextBox id="txtMessage" AutoPostBack="False" Rows="10"
    runat="server" Width="313px" Height="160px">
      </asp:TextBox>
   </TD>
</TR>
<tr>
   <td colspan="3">
```

```
        <asp:Button id="btnEmail" runat="server" Text="Send Email">
        </asp:Button>
      </td>
    </tr>
</TABLE>


<DIV style="Z-INDEX: 101; LEFT: 352px; WIDTH: 264px;
      POSITION: absolute; TOP: 24px; HEIGHT: 400px">
    <TABLE cellSpacing="1" cellPadding="1" width="300" border="0"
          style="WIDTH: 300px; HEIGHT: 80px">
      <TR>
        <TD>
          <asp:RequiredFieldValidator id="rfvTxtfrom" runat="server"
              ControlToValidate="txtFrom"
              Display="Dynamic"
              Font-Name="Verdana"
              Font-Size="10pt">
          * please provide an e-mail address
          </asp:RequiredFieldValidator>
          <asp:RegularExpressionValidator id="revTxtfrom" runat="server"
              ControlToValidate="txtFrom"
              ValidationExpression="^.*\@.*\..*$"
              Display="static"
              Font-Name="verdana"
              Font-Size="10pt">
          Please enter a valid e-mail address
          </asp:RegularExpressionValidator>
        </TD>
      </TR>
      <TR>
        <TD>
          <asp:RequiredFieldValidator id="rfvTxtto" runat="server"
              ControlToValidate="txtTo"
              Display="Dynamic"
              Font-Name="Verdana"
```

```
                Font-Size="10pt">
        * please provide an e-mail address
        </asp:RequiredFieldValidator>
        <asp:RegularExpressionValidator id="revTxtto" runat="server"
                ControlToValidate="txtTo"
                ValidationExpression="^.*\@.*\..*$"
                Display="static"
                Font-Name="verdana"
                Font-Size="10pt">
        Please enter a valid e-mail address
        </asp:RegularExpressionValidator>
      </TD>
    </TR>
    <TR>
      <TD>
        <asp:RegularExpressionValidator id="revTxtcc" runat="server"
                ControlToValidate="txtCC"
                ValidationExpression="^.*\@.*\..*$"
                Display="static"
                Font-Name="verdana"
                Font-Size="10pt">
        Please enter a valid e-mail address
        </asp:RegularExpressionValidator>
      </TD>
    </TR>
  </TABLE>
</DIV>
```

Remember that you also need to bring over all the code-behind code as well into the new user control CS page This is what you should have:

```
namespace simpleMail
{
    using System;
    using System.Data;
    using System.Drawing;
```

```
using System.Web;
using System.Web.UI.WebControls;
using System.Web.UI.HtmlControls;
using System.Web.Mail;


/// <summary>
///          Summary description for WebUserControl1.
/// </summary>
public abstract class WebUserControl1 : System.Web.UI.UserControl
{
protected System.Web.UI.WebControls.TextBox txtFrom;
protected System.Web.UI.WebControls.TextBox txtTo;
protected System.Web.UI.WebControls.TextBox txtCC;
protected System.Web.UI.WebControls.TextBox txtSubject;
protected System.Web.UI.WebControls.Button btnEmail;
protected System.Web.UI.WebControls.RequiredFieldValidator fvTxtfrom;
protected System.Web.UI.WebControls.RegularExpressionValidator
    revTxtfrom;
protected System.Web.UI.WebControls.RequiredFieldValidator rfvTxtto;
protected System.Web.UI.WebControls.RegularExpressionValidator revTxtto;
protected System.Web.UI.WebControls.RequiredFieldValidator rfvTxtcc;
protected System.Web.UI.WebControls.RegularExpressionValidator revTxtcc;
protected System.Web.UI.WebControls.TextBox txtMessage;

    public WebUserControl1()
  {
      this.Init += new System.EventHandler(Page_Init);
  }


  private void Page_Load(object sender, System.EventArgs e)
  {
      // Put user code to initialize the page here
  }


  private void Page_Init(object sender, EventArgs e)
  {
```

```
        //
        // CODEGEN: This call is required by the ASP.NET Web Form
        // Designer.
        InitializeComponent();
    }


    #region Web Form Designer generated code
    ///          Required method for Designer support - do not modify
    ///          the contents of this method with the code editor.
    /// </summary>
    private void InitializeComponent()
    {
        this.btnEmail.Click += new
System.EventHandler(this.btnEmail_Click);
        this.Load += new System.EventHandler(this.Page_Load);
    }
    #endregion
    private void btnEmail_Click(object sender, System.EventArgs e)
    {
        MailMessage mail = new MailMessage();
        mail.From = txtFrom.Text;
        mail.To = txtTo.Text;
        mail.Cc = txtCC.Text;
        mail.Subject = txtSubject.Text;
        mail.Body = txtMessage.Text;
        mail.BodyFormat = MailFormat.Text;
        SmtpMail.Send(mail);
    }
}
```

You should build this and make sure you do not have any errors. Next, you need to take your new custom user control and add it to a new Web Form page. This is what it the code should look like:

```
<%@ Page language="c#" Codebehind="WebForm2.aspx.cs"
    AutoEventWireup="false" Inherits="simpleMail.WebForm2" %>
```

```
<%@ Register TagPrefix="simpleEmail" TagName="Email"
    Src="WebUserControl1.ascx" %>
<!DOCTYPE HTML PUBLIC "-//W3C//DTD HTML 4.0 Transitional//EN" >
<html>
  <head>
    <meta name="GENERATOR" Content="Microsoft Visual Studio 7.0">
    <meta name="CODE_LANGUAGE" Content="C#">
    <meta name="vs_defaultClientScript"
        content="JavaScript (ECMAScript)">
    <meta name="vs_targetSchema"
        content="http://schemas.microsoft.com/intellisense/ie5">
  </head>
  <body MS_POSITIONING="GridLayout">
    <form id="WebForm2" method="post" runat="server"  >
        <simpleEmail:Email id="myEmail" runat="server"  />
    </form>
  </body>
</html>
```

This includes a new page directive *@Register* that will register your control based on the information you supply. What you need to supply is the property values: *TagPrefix* is set to *simpleEmail. TagName* is set to *Email*, and, most importantly, the *Src* is set to the path of your user control where it is a relative path in the same directory. Set this Web Form as a start page and run the application—your custom User Control will be there and fully functional.

# Custom Controls

Custom controls are created in much the same way as the user controls, the difference being that they are autonomous from any Web Form and that you can use them anywhere within the application. When applying a custom control, you must use the *@Register* directive along with the *TagPrefix*, but in this example, where the *Src* is used for the user control, you use the *Namespace="CustomCon"* and supply the *Assembly* attribute, as shown here:

```
<%@ Page language="c#"
    Codebehind="WebForm1.aspx.cs"
    AutoEventWireup="false"
```

```
        Inherits="simpleMail.WebForm1"
%><%@ Register

    TagPrefix="simpleEmail"

    Namespace="customCon"

    Assembly="conEamil"

%>
```

**NOTE**

The *@Register* directive must appear after or below the *@Page* directive.

# Understanding the Web.config File

The Web.config file will be placed in the application folder in each Web solution project created. This is an XML file that you can edit with any text editor, and it holds key configuration information for your application. You can also add to this file with custom configuration settings. Let's take a look at one and go over some of the settings within:

```
<?xml version="1.0" encoding="utf-8" ?>
<configuration>
 <system.web>
  <!-- DYNAMIC DEBUG COMPILATION-->
  <compilation
     defaultLanguage="c#"
     debug="true"/>

  <!-- CUSTOM ERROR MESSAGES-->
  <customErrors
     mode="Off"/>

  <!-- AUTHENTICATION-->
  <authentication mode="None" />

  <!-- APPLICATION-LEVEL TRACE LOGGING-->
```

```
<trace
   enabled="false"
   requestLimit="10"
   pageOutput="false"
   traceMode="SortByTime"
   localOnly="true"/>

<!— SESSION STATE SETTINGS—>
<sessionState
   mode="InProc"
   stateConnectionString="tcpip=127.0.0.1:42424"
   sqlConnectionString="data source=127.0.0.1;user id=sa;password="
   cookieless="false"
   timeout="20"/>

<!— PREVENT SOURCE CODE DOWNLOAD—>
<httpHandlers>
   <add verb="*" path="*.vb"
     type="System.Web.HttpNotFoundHandler,System.Web" />
   <add verb="*" path="*.cs"
     type="System.Web.HttpNotFoundHandler,System.Web" />
   <add verb="*" path="*.vbproj"
     type="System.Web.HttpNotFoundHandler,System.Web" />
   <add verb="*" path="*.csproj"
     type="System.Web.HttpNotFoundHandler,System.Web" />
   <add verb="*" path="*.webinfo"
     type="System.Web.HttpNotFoundHandler,System.Web" />
</httpHandlers>

<!— GLOBALIZATION—>
<globalization
   requestEncoding="utf-8"
   responseEncoding="utf-8"/>
</system.web>
</configuration>
```

One of the first settings in the Web.config file is the <compilation> tag. In that tag, you can set the source language of the application and the *debug* property. When you deploy your application, set this property to False to speed up server performance. Also, if you are unable to get debugging working on your server, check to see if the attribute is set to False.

You can turn custom error messages on or off by setting the attribute within the tag. Every time the application is run, the new setting will take effect, much like a Global.asp page would do for an ASP application.

## Using the Global.asax Page

In the upcoming examples, you will set many variables within your Global.asax page. Two of these variables are set in the *Application_Start* and *Session_Start* methods. In this situation, you can use the Global.asax page much the same way as you would use the Global.asa file for your ASP application, the one difference being that you can run the Global.asax file across a Web farm of servers. Both of these methods belong to the *HttpApplication* base class.

You can make changes to the Global.asax file, and when the application starts, the page will be parsed and the settings acted upon. Also, you do not need to have a Global.asax file in your Web application. If you do not supply one, you will not have any supported application settings or session settings.

# Working with Web Forms

Web Forms (ASPX pages) are the replacement for ASP pages in ASP.NET. All controls and UI functionality will be placed within your Web Forms. Web Forms inherit all the methods and properties of the *Page* class, which belongs to the *System.Web.UI* namespace.

## Creating a Simple Web Form

Let's look at some real-world examples of ASP.NET Web applications. We first need to open VS.NET Beta 2 and create a new C# ASP.NET Web application (see Figure 10.2).

Name the project **simpleMail** and have the Location set as **localhost**. By default, one Web Form will be created. You can leave its name as WebForm1.aspx.

In the example, you want to create a form that will send an e-mail. You first need to include the namespace *System.Web.Mail*. This will enable you to use all the *Mail* methods within the SMTP mail service. In the Solutions Explorer window, select **Show all files** from the title bar. Now, you will have a plus sign in front of your ASPX page. Click on the plus sign and select the code-behind page (cs). At the top of the cs page, you will see the *using* directives; this is where you need to add your *using* directive for mail:

```
using System.Web.Mail;
```

**Figure 10.2** Opening a New C# Web Application in VS.NET Beta 2

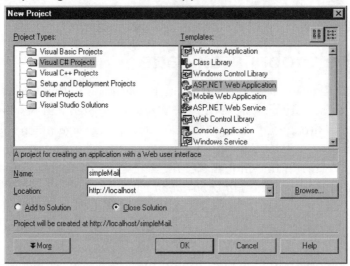

Now you will have all the methods and properties of this class. Let's open the ASPX file and go to HTML view by selecting the **HTML** tab at the bottom of the window. You are going to need some text boxes and a submit button for your form, which you can get by dragging them from the Toolbox. The code should look something like this:

```
<div style="Z-INDEX: 100; LEFT: 10px; WIDTH: 300px; POSITION:
    relative; TOP: 10px; HEIGHT: 400px">
<TABLE cellSpacing="1" cellPadding="1" width="300" border="0">
<TR><TD>From: </TD><TD colspan="2">
<asp:TextBox id="txtFrom" runat="server" ></asp:TextBox>
</TD>
</TR><TR><TD> To:</TD><TD colspan="2">
<asp:TextBox id="txtTo" runat="server" AutoPostBack=
    "False"></asp:TextBox>
</TD></TR><TR><TD>
CC:</TD><TD colspan="2">
```

```
<asp:TextBox id="txtCC" runat="server" ></asp:TextBox>
</TD></TR><TR><TD colspan="3"></TD></TR><TR>
<TD colspan="3">Subject:</TD></TR><TR><TD colspan="3">
<asp:TextBox  id="txtSubject" runat="server" Width="288px"
Height="24px"></asp:TextBox>
</TD></TR><TR>
<TD colspan="3">Message:</TD></TR><TR><TD colspan="3">
<asp:TextBox id="txtMessage" Rows="10" runat="server" Width="313px"
    Height="160px"></asp:TextBox>
</TD></TR><tr><td colspan="3">
<asp:Button id="btnEmail" runat="server" Text="Send Email"></asp:Button>
</td></tr></TABLE>
```

Double-click on the button; this will open up the .aspx.cs page and present you with a method for the *OnClick* event for the button. This is where you will add in your mail function code:

```
MailMessage mail = new MailMessage();
                mail.From = txtFrom.Text;
                mail.To = txtTo.Text;
                mail.Cc = txtCC.Text;
                mail.Subject = txtSubject.Text;
                mail.Body = txtMessage.Text;
                mail.BodyFormat = MailFormat.Text;
                SmtpMail.Send(mail);
```

Here you are setting the values of the separate textboxes equal to the listed mail properties. Lastly, the *Send* method of the *SmtpMail* class is used to send the e-mail message. But how can you make sure that the user will input the correct data? Easy—use *Validation* controls. But first, you must set up an area for them to be displayed outside of the table. Add a <div> tag with a table next to the table for your e-mail form. It should look something like this:

```
<DIV style="Z-INDEX: 101; LEFT: 352px; WIDTH: 264px; POSITION:
absolute;
    TOP: 24px; HEIGHT: 400px">
<TABLE style="WIDTH: 300px; HEIGHT: 80px" cellSpacing="1" cellPadding=
    "1" width="300" border="0">
<TR><TD>
```

```
<asp:RequiredFieldValidator id="rfvTxtfrom" runat="server"
    ControlToValidate="txtFrom" Display="Dynamic" Font-Name="Verdana"
    Font-Size="10pt">* please provide an e-mail address
</asp:RequiredFieldValidator>
<asp:RegularExpressionValidator id="revTxtfrom" runat="server"
    ControlToValidate="txtFrom" ValidationExpression="^.*\@.*\..*$"
    Display="static" Font-Name="verdana" Font-Size="10pt">
Please enter a valid e-mail address
</asp:RegularExpressionValidator>        </TD></TR><TR><TD>
    <asp:RequiredFieldValidator id="rfvTxtto" runat="server"
    ControlToValidate="txtTo" Display="Dynamic" Font-Name="Verdana"
    Font-Size="10pt">* please provide an e-mail address
</asp:RequiredFieldValidator>
<asp:RegularExpressionValidator id="revTxtto" runat="server"
    ControlToValidate="txtTo" ValidationExpression="^.*\@.*\..*$"
    Display="static" Font-Name="verdana" Font-Size="10pt">
Please enter a valid e-mail address
</asp:RegularExpressionValidator>
</TD></TR><TR><TD><asp:RegularExpressionValidator id="revTxtcc"
    runat="server" ControlToValidate="txtCC" ValidationExpression=
    "^.*\@.*\..*$" Display="static" Font-Name="verdana"
    Font-Size="10pt">Please enter a valid e-mail address
</asp:RegularExpressionValidator>
</TD></TR></TABLE></DIV>
```

Here you are using two separate validation controls: *RequiredFieldValidator* verifies that something has been entered, and *RegularExpressionValidator* verifies that the data entered is valid based on the regular expression you have set. Each one of these controls are dragged and dropped into place from the toolbox. Remember that you must supply the *ControlToValidate* attribute with the control you want to validate. Here is the regular expression used in the example to validate the e-mail field:

```
ValidationExpression="^.*\@.*\..*$".
```

To translate, this means from the beginning of the string look for any number of any characters followed by the @ sign, followed by any number of any characters, followed by a period (.), followed by any number of any characters to the end of the string. This will allow for extremely long e-mail addresses that may contain more than one dot (period) before or after the @ sign. This is common for government or public institution mail servers, as well as in some large corporations. See Table 10.4 for a breakdown of the regular expression symbols used in this example.

**Table 10.4** Regular Expression Symbols

| Symbol | Meaning |
| --- | --- |
| ^ | The start of a string. |
| $ | The end of a string. |
| . | Any character. |
| * | Zero or more occurrences of the preceding. |
| \ | Escape used for special characters or when searching for a specific character that has another meaning in regular expression syntax. For example, to search for the period character, you would have to use "\ ." because the period means any character in regular expression syntax. |

Compile the project and run the application by setting the start page and pressing **F5**.

# Building an XML Poll

In this section, you will be building a simple polling page. You will create two polling topics each containing three voting options. The user will click on the radio buttons that reflect their answers to the poll. This data will then be added to an XML document that will act as your data source. You will then post back the updated statistics for the poll. (You can find the files for this example on the CD, see XMLpoll.aspx, XMLpoll.aspx.cs, poll.xml, and stats.xslt.)

1.  Start a new Web application project in VS.NET.

2.  Rename WebForm1.aspx as **XMLpoll.aspx**.

3.  In design mode, right-click on the page and select **Properties**. Change the Page Layout drop-down to **FlowLayout** and click **Apply**. Then click **OK**. This will help with display in Netscape browsers (see the sidebar "ASP.NET Server Controls Do Not Display Correctly in Netscape 4.*x*" earlier in this chapter).

4.  You are now going to create the polling table layout in your Web Form, *XMLpoll*. Choose **Table | Insert | Table**. The Insert Table dialog appears.

5. Select **9** rows and **1** column, clear the *Width* property, and then click **OK**. You can handle the display options later with CSS.

6. In the first cell, type **Programmers Poll**.

7. In the second cell, type **My Focus is on:**.

8. In the third cell, drag **RadioButton** (from the toolbox under Web Forms) into this cell.

9. Next to the radio button (in the same cell), type **Desktop**.

10. Click in the cell, press **Ctrl+A** to select all, and press **Ctrl+C** to copy.

11. Click in the next cell and press **Ctrl+V** to paste.

12. Do this for the next cell, skip one (this cell will contain a subtitle), then do this for the next three.

13. In the cell that you skipped, type in **My Primary Dev Tool is:**.

14. Change the text next to each of the *RadioButton* controls to **Web**, **Mobile**, **VSNET**, **XmlSpy**, and **Other**, respectively.

15. Your page should now look something like the table shown in Figure 10.3.

**Figure 10.3** Adding *RadioButtons* to the *XMLpoll* Web Form

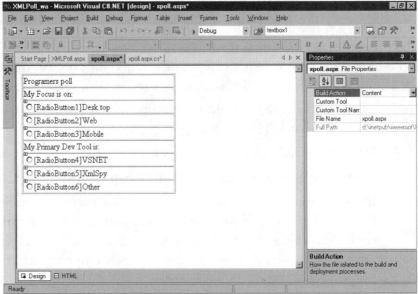

Now you can go into HTML mode and adjust some of your code. Rename your *RadioButton* controls as shown in Table 10.5. Remember, to rename a control, simply view it in HTML mode and change its ID; by default VS.NET will number them consecutively, as shown in the left column of Table 10.5.

**Table 10.5** *RadioButton* Control Name Change

| Current Control Name | Change To: |
| --- | --- |
| *RadioButton1* | *focus_Desktop* |
| *RadioButton2* | *focus_web* |
| *RadioButton3* | *focus_mobile* |
| *RadioButton4* | *IDE_VSNET* |
| *RadioButton5* | *IDE_XmlSpy* |
| *RadioButton6* | *IDE_other* |

In HTML, *RadioButton*s with the same ID are used to create an array so that only one can be selected at a time. The *RadioButton* control requires unique names, hence *focus_Desktop*, *focus_web*, *focus_mobile*, and so on. The *RadioButton* control provides the attribute *GroupName* to generate this HTML *RadioButton* array. So in each of your "focus" *RadioButton* controls, add **GroupName="focus"**, and for each of your "IDE" *RadioButton* controls, add **GroupName="IDE"**. This will create two radio button arrays in your rendered HTML.

Open XMLpoll.aspx.cs. If you can't find this page listed in your Solution Explorer, click the icon for Show All Files, then click the plus sign that appears next to XMLpoll.aspx (see Figure 10.4).

**Figure 10.4** Displaying the Code-Behind File in the Solutions Explorer

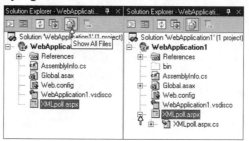

When you drop your first *RadioButton* control on the page, VS.NET adds the following two lines to your code-behind page:

```
using System.Web.UI.WebControls;
using System.Web.UI.HtmlControls;
```

This is the namespace that defines all the properties and methods of all Web controls. As you added each radio button control to the page, VS.NET also added a reference for it within your page class:

```
protected System.Web.UI.WebControls.RadioButton focus_web;
protected System.Web.UI.WebControls.RadioButton focus_Desktop;
protected System.Web.UI.WebControls.RadioButton focus_mobile;
protected System.Web.UI.WebControls.RadioButton IDE_VSNET;
protected System.Web.UI.WebControls.RadioButton IDE_other;
protected System.Web.UI.WebControls.RadioButton IDE_XmlSpy;
```

Now, you can go back to XmlPoll.aspx and view it in design mode:

1. From the toolbar, drag a **Button** control below the table.

2. Either switch back to HTML mode and rename the control **vote** with a *Text* value of **Vote**. Or, from design mode, right-click the **Button** control and select **Properties**.

3. When the properties window opens, change the ID value to **vote** and the *Text* value to **Vote** (see Figure 10.5).

**Figure 10.5** Setting the Button Control's Properties

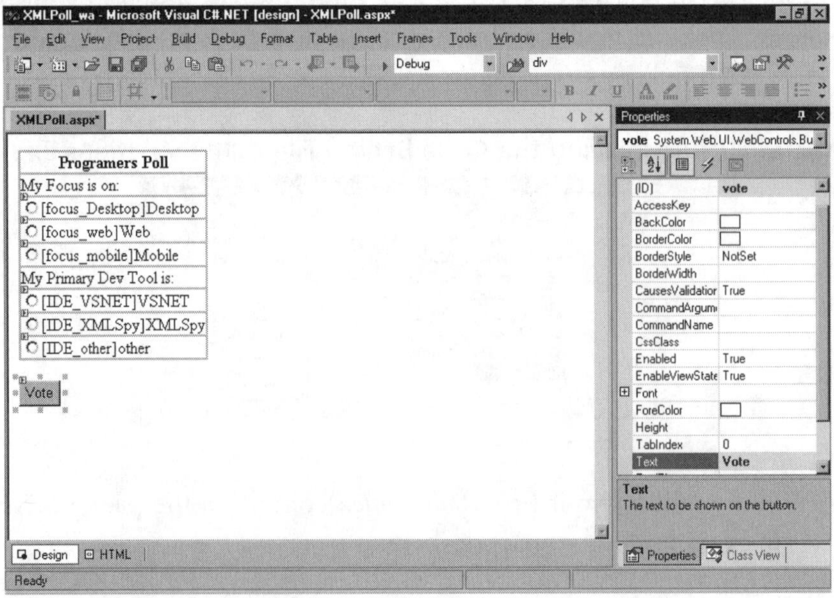

4. Switch to design view.

5. Double-click the **vote** button to add an event handler for the button's *OnClick* event.

Notice that VS.NET has added the following to the page class:

```
protected System.Web.UI.WebControls.Button vote;
```

The following has been added to the *InitializeComponent* method. Its purpose is to register the new event handler. If you remove this line, the *vote_Click* method will never be called:

```
this.vote.Click += new System.EventHandler(this.vote_Click);
```

And, of course, the template for the *Server_Click* method that is an event handler for the button:

```
private void vote_Click(object sender, System.EventArgs e)
{


}
```

In this event handler, create two variables: *focus* and *IDE*. You will use these variables to store the value of the users selections for focus and IDE, respectively:

```
string focus;
string IDE;
```

Test which *RadioButton* in the Focus poll was checked and assign a corresponding value to the focus variable:

```
//get developer focus
if(focus_Desktop.Checked)
{
      focus = "Desktop";
}
else if(focus_web.Checked)
{
      focus = "Web";
}
else if(focus_mobile.Checked)
{
```

```
        focus = "Mobile";
}
else
{
        focus = "not given";
}
```

Do the same for the variable IDE:

```
//get developer tool
if(IDE_VSNET.Checked)
{
        IDE = "VSNET";
}
else if(IDE_XMLSpy.Checked)
{
        IDE = "XMLSpy";
}
else if(IDE_other.Checked)
{
        IDE = "other";
}
else
{
        IDE = "not given";
}
```

Now that you know what was checked, pass that data to a new method that will update your XML data source and display some statistics:

```
updateXPoll( focus, IDE );
```

This completes the code for the *Vote_Click* event. Ahead in this chapter, you will create the *updateXPoll* method, which will update your in-memory XML document. You will then send that data to another method you will create, called *updateFile*, which will overwrite the existing XML data file on the server with your new poll results.

# Creating the *updateXPoll* Method

In the previous section, you handled the click event for the Vote button, which gave you the poll results for the current user. In this section, you are going to take the poll results and add them to your poll data. But, before you write the function *updateXPoll*, let's view the format of the XML data source (see Figure 10.6).

**Figure 10.6** Poll.xml

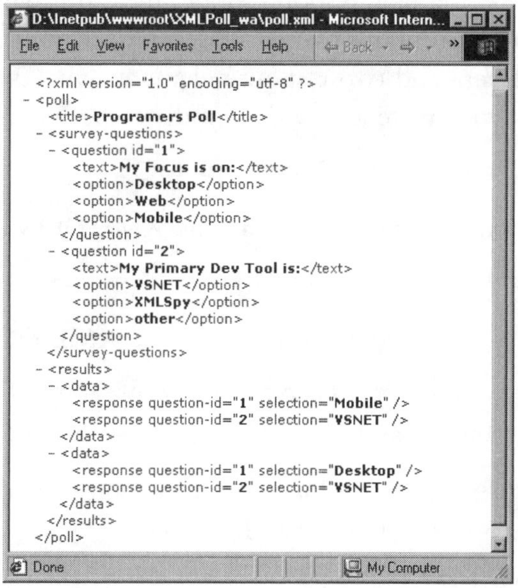

What you want to do in *updateXPoll* is append "data" nodes to the results node. A data node will look like the following:

```
<data>
  <response question-id="1" selection="Mobile"/>
  <response question-id="2" selection="VSNET"/>
</data>
```

First, you need to add support for XML to your page. In the top section to reference the namespaces containing the XML classes, add the following line:

```
using System.Xml;
```

In the *updateXPoll* method, create an instance of the *XmlDocument* object and load poll.xml:

```
XmlDocument xpoll = new XmlDocument();
xpoll.Load( Server.MapPath("poll.xml")  );
```

This creates an in-memory XML DOM instance named *xpoll*. Adding new XML nodes can be a little confusing at first. It is a bottom-up process where you work from the outermost leaf and append branches until they connect to a branch with an ancestor that connects to the main tree. This means that you will create the attributes of the response node first, then assign their values. Next, you will create the response node and append the new attributes to it (you will do the same for the second response node.) Following that, you will create a new data node, then append the new response nodes to it. You will then append the new data node to the appropriate branch node in *xpoll*, the results node.

Create a data element and two response elements with the attributes *question-ID* and *selection*. This will create a new data node in the XML DOM:

```
XmlElement data = xpoll.CreateElement("data");
```

This will create a new response node in the XML DOM:

```
XmlElement response1 = xpoll.CreateElement("response");
```

This will create two new attribute nodes in the XML DOM:

```
XmlAttribute questionID = xpoll.CreateAttribute("question-id");
XmlAttribute selection = xpoll.CreateAttribute("selection");
```

Next, you want to assign the values of the attributes with your user data. For the first question, the values will be as follows:

```
questionID.Value="1";
selection.Value = focus;
```

Now you need to add the attributes to the response node:

```
response1.SetAttributeNode(questionID);
response1.SetAttributeNode(selection);
```

Then do the same for the second response node:

```
XmlElement response2 = xpoll.CreateElement("response");
    questionID = xpoll.CreateAttribute("question-id");
    selection = xpoll.CreateAttribute("selection");
    questionID.Value="2";
    selection.Value = IDE;
    response2.SetAttributeNode(questionID);
    response2.SetAttributeNode(selection);
```

Add them as children to the data element:

```
data.AppendChild( response1 );
data.AppendChild( response2 );
```

Now that you have the data node built, you need to add it as a child to the results node of *xpoll*:

```
xpoll.SelectSingleNode("//results").AppendChild(data );
```

You have successfully added your new poll data to the in-memory version of your *xmlpoll*. Now you need to ensure that you update the file (new data nodes are appended to the results node):

```
updateFile( "poll.xml", xpoll );
```

## Creating the *updateFile* Method

This method will take your in-memory version of *xpoll* and overwrite the existing file. In order to write to a file, you need to add IO support to the page. In the top section, add the following to reference the IO namespace:

```
using System.IO;
```

In this function, you will be using the *File.CreateText* method of the *StreamWriter* object. This method will create a new file at the location and with the name specified. If a file already exists with the same name in that path, it will be overwritten:

```
StreamWriter sr = File.CreateText( Server.MapPath( "poll.xml" ) );
```

Note the use of *Server.MapPath*. The file path is an HTTP relative path. In order for the server to write to the file, it must have the actual path to the file (of the form C:\inetpub\wwwroot\XmlPollApp\poll.xml). *Server.MapPath* converts a relative or virtual path to a file path.

The *OuterXml* method of the *XmlDocument* class returns the contents of the XML document as an XML formatted text string. This is the equivalent of the MSXML parsers *DOMdocument.xml* property. The *StreamWriter.Write* method writes text to the file:

```
sr.Write( xpoll.OuterXml );
```

When it is done, close the file by calling the *Close* method of the *StreamWriter* class:

```
sr.Close();
```

Next time the file is accessed, it will contain the newly added poll data. Next, you will work on displaying the statistics of the current poll data on page load.

# Displaying the Current Poll Statistics

You need to provide the user with some feedback, so you will create a statistics XSL/Transform that will calculate the response percentages and display the results on *Page_load*. So when the user is prompted for the poll, they will also see the current statistics. After submitting their responses, the statistics will be updated and the changes will be reflected to the user.

Let's go back to XmlPoll.aspx and view it in the design mode:

1. From the toolbox under the Web Forms controls section, drag the XML control onto the page next to the Vote button. This will add the necessary references to the code-behind page.

2. Switch to HTML mode and scroll down to the end of the table.

3. Add a <br> tag between the Button control and the XML control. Also, rename the XML control **stats**:

```
<asp:Button id="vote" runat="server" Text="Vote"></asp:Button>
<br>
<asp:Xml id="stats" runat="server"></asp:Xml>
```

The XML control will apply an XSL/Transform to the XML data and display the resulting HTML at this position in the page. The XML control has several properties that you can use to set the XML data source and the XSLT source.

For this example, use the *Document* property, which accepts an *XmlDocument* object, and the *TransformSource* property, which accepts a relative path to a file as its input:

```
doc = new XmlDocument();
doc.Load( Server.MapPath("poll.xml")  );
stats.Document = doc;
stats.TransformSource = "stats.xslt";
```

Recall that *stats* is the name of the XML control. You may be wondering why you didn't use the *DocumentSource* property of the XML control, which works exactly like the *TransformSource* property. The reason for loading poll.xml into an *XmlDocument* object is because you also use it for *updateXPoll*. This way, you load the file only once. Figure 10.7 shows the XSLT used for the transform. You can find this file, called stats.xslt, on the CD.

**Figure 10.7** Stats.xslt

```
File  Edit  View  Favorites  Tools  Help

<?xml version="1.0" encoding="UTF-8" ?>
- <xsl:stylesheet version="1.0" xmlns:xsl="http://www.w3.org/1999/XSL/Transform">
  <xsl:output method="html" />
- <xsl:template match="/">
  - <table class="poll" borderColor="silver" cellSpacing="0" cellPadding="0" border="1">
    - <tr>
        <th colspan="2">Statistics</th>
      </tr>
    - <xsl:for-each select="//question">
        <xsl:variable name="Qid" select="@id" />
      - <tr>
        - <td colspan="2" class="topic">
            <xsl:value-of select="text" />
          </td>
        </tr>
      - <xsl:for-each select="option">
          <xsl:variable name="OP" select="." />
          <!-- count the number of selections that match this option  -->
          <!-- divided by  -->
          <!-- count the number of questions where the ID matches this question
          id  -->
          <xsl:variable name="percent" select="count(//response[@selection = $OP])
            div count(//response[@question-id=$Qid])" />
        - <tr>
          - <td>
              <xsl:value-of select="." />
            </td>
          - <td>
            - <xsl:choose>
              - <xsl:when test="count(//response[@selection = $OP]) = 0">
                  <!-- if there is no response to a poll item show a "-"
                  centered  -->
                  <xsl:attribute name="align">center</xsl:attribute>
                  <xsl:text>-</xsl:text>
                  <xsl:attribute name="align">center</xsl:attribute>
                  <xsl:text>-</xsl:text>
                </xsl:when>
              - <xsl:otherwise>
                  <xsl:value-of select="format-number( $percent, '#.0%')" />
                </xsl:otherwise>
              </xsl:choose>
            </td>
          </tr>
        </xsl:for-each>
      </xsl:for-each>
    - <tr>
      - <td colspan="2">
          Total Respondents:
          <xsl:value-of select="count( //data )" />
        </td>
      </tr>
    </table>
  </xsl:template>
</xsl:stylesheet>
```

All you need to do is add a little CSS and your output will look like Figure 10.8. You can also find the CSS file, called xmlpoll.css, on the CD.

**Figure 10.8** XML Poll

To retrieve a value from a form with method *post*, use the following:

```
Request.Form["name"] or

Request.Form [i]
```

Notice the use of the square brackets when accessing an array or collection. Also, *Response* still works much the same:

```
Response.Write("some string")

Response.End()
```

A new way of writing to the screen in a predefined spot is to use the *Label* control. If you view the source after running the page, you will notice that the *Label* control is actually a handle to a span tag, which can contain a CSS class for font and layout settings (use the *Literal* control if you don't need the span tag wrapper).

You can dynamically write HTML or even JavaScript to the client by assigning the string value to the text attribute of the control. Here, you don't need the span tags so you can use the *Literal* control:

```
MyLiteral.Text = "<script language='javascript'>
                  window.alert(\"Got here\") </script>";
```

# Working with ADO.NET

Up to this point in the chapter, you have built sample applications using Web Forms. In the upcoming applications, you will add data retrieval from an SQL database with ADO.NET. In the next two sample applications—the message board and shopping cart—you  will take a close look at how ADO.NET and SQL interact. You will also get a closer look at the successor to the ADO *Recordset*, the ADO.NET *DataSet*.

# Building a Message Board with SQL

In this section, you are going to build a message board (see Figure 10.9). This application will display a list of all current message boards (Item [1] in Table 10.6). It will allow users to dynamically generate new message board groups (Item [2]) and monitor them (Item [3]). (Users will have the ability to delete messages from message board that they create [4].) Users will also have the ability to post new messages (Item [5]) or respond to any existing message (Item [6]) on any message board (Item [7]). This application will also contain a different interface for the site administrator (Item [8]) who will have the ability to delete any message or response (Item [9]) or even an entire message board (Item [10]). To enable this functionality, you will have to develop several stored procedures and methods. To see a mapping of these requirements to the corresponding pages and methods, see Table 10.6. You can find all the code for this project on the CD—see the page column of Table 10.6 for the filenames. See Figure 10.10 to view all the tables in the database.

**Figure 10.9** Message Board Interface

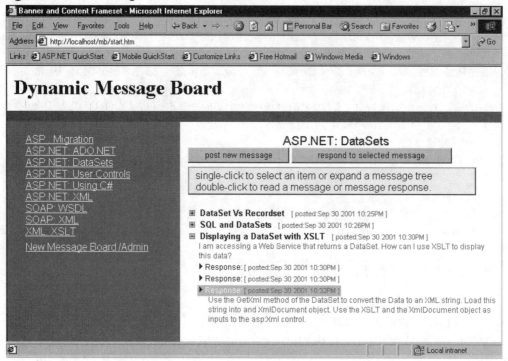

**Table 10.6** Message Board Processes Overview

| Process | Dependency | Function | Page |
|---|---|---|---|
| Display List of Message Boards | Stored Procedure (sproc): *getAllGroups* | Returns list of message boards [1] | BoardList.aspx |
| | XSLT for users | Converts data to HTML [1] | User_group_list.xslt |
| | XSLT for Admin | Converts data to HTML with delete enabled [8] | Admin_group_list.xslt |

**Continued**

**Table 10.6** Continued

| Process | Dependency | Function | Page |
|---------|-----------|----------|------|
| Admin Login | | [8] | BoardList.aspx |
| Moderator Login | Sproc: *LoginModerator* | Returns the mod id of a valid moderator [4] | BoardList.aspx |
| Create New Moderator | Sproc: *NewModerator* | Creates a new moderator and logs them in | CreateMod.aspx |
| Create New Group | Sproc: *AddGroup* | Generates a new message board group [2] | CreateBoard.aspx |
| Delete a Group | Sproc: *delGroup* | Removes message board group and all related messages and responses [10] | DeleteBoard.aspx |
| Display Selected Board | Sproc: *returnAllMess* | Returns all messages and responses for the given group [5] [6] | Board.aspx |
| | XSLT | Convert data into collapsible tree | Message_board_list .xslt |
| Add New Message | Sproc: *AddMessage* | Add a message to given group [5] | Response2message .aspx |
| Add Message Response | Sproc: *AddResponse* | Add a response to a message [6] | Response2message .aspx |
| Delete Message | Sproc: *delMessage* | Removes a message from a group [4] [9] | Board.aspx |
| Delete Response | Sproc: *delResponse* | Removes a response from a message [4] [9] | Board.aspx |

All data interaction between the pages and the SQL database will be handled via ADO.NET methods within a component file (mbdataaccess.cs). You will be using the *SqlClient* classes from the namespace *System.Data.SqlClient*. The SQL Managed Provider, which resides within the *System.Data.SqlClient* namespace, is optimized to work with MS SQL.

**Figure 10.10** Database Diagram

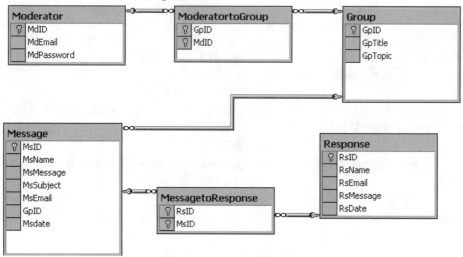

To really optimize the code, you can use stored procedures for all data access. Here is a list of stored procedures that you will need for this example:

- **addGroup** Adds a new message board group into the database.
- **addMessage** Adds a message into the database.
- **addResponse** Adds a response to the database.
- **delGroup** Deletes a message board group from the database.
- **delMessage** Deletes a message from the database and all responses to it.
- **delResponse** Deletes a response from the database.
- **allGroups** Returns all message board groups from the database.
- **returnAllMess** Returns all messages and their associated responses in an XML stream.
- **loginModerator** Logs in a moderator.
- **newModerator** Adds a new moderator:
    1. Open up a new solution in VS.NET.
    2. Add a new folder named **components**.
    3. Right-click the new folder and add a new item.
    4. Select **C# class** and name it **mbdataaccess.cs**.

First, you need a connection to the database. This code will connect to the local SQL Server database:

```
protected string connection = "initial catalog=MessageDb;persist
    security info=False;user id=[user];password=[password];Data
    Source=[server name]; packet size=4096";


public void addMessage(string MsName,string MsMessage, string MsSubject,
    string MsEmail, int GpID)
{
SqlConnection connAddMess = new SqlConnection(this.connection);
```

You can set the connection string on the outside of the class and access for all the functions within the component. Here you are writing the method *addMessage*. Make sure that you have the correct *using* directives:

```
using System;
using System.Data;
using System.Data.SqlClient;
```

You will be accessing the stored procedure *addMessage*, which takes five input parameters:

```
SqlCommand cmdAddMess = new SqlCommand("addMessage",connAddMess);
cmdAddMess.CommandType = CommandType.StoredProcedure;
```

First, create a new variable of type *SqlCommand* (*cmdAddMess*), pass the two parameters for *SqlCommand*, the name of the stored procedure, and the connection you are using for this command. Let's look at the declaration of one of the parameters:

```
SqlParameter prmMsName = new SqlParameter("@MsName",
    SqlDbType.NVarChar, 50);
prmMsName.Direction = ParameterDirection.Input;
cmdAddMess.Parameters.Add(prmMsName);
prmMsName.Value = MsName;
```

You declare a new variable of type *SqlParameter*; pass the name of the parameter used in the stored procedure, the data type, and size. You then set the direction to *Input*. Next, add it to the parameters collection of the *SqlCommand*. Finally, pass the value you have locally to the stored procedure. You must do this for the rest of the input parameters.

What you need to do now is open the connection, run the query using the *ExecuteNonQuery* method of the *SqlCommand* class, and then close the connection:

```
connAddMess.Open();
cmdAddMess.ExecuteNonQuery();
connAddMess.Close();
```

This will add a new record into the message table. You can view the SQL source file to see the stored procedure in any text editor:

```
CREATE    PROCEDURE [addMessage]
        (@MsName         [nvarchar](50),
        @MsMessage       [text],
        @MsSubject       [nvarchar](50),
        @MsEmail         [nvarchar](50),
        @GpID            [int]   )
AS
BEGIN TRANSACTION addMess



        DECLARE @MsDate [datetime]
        SET @MsDate=GETDATE()


 INSERT INTO [MessageDb].[dbo].[Message]
        ( [MsName],
        [MsMessage],
        [MsSubject],
        [MsEmail],
        [GpID],
        [MsDate])


VALUES
        ( @MsName,
        @MsMessage,
        @MsSubject,
        @MsEmail,
        @GpID,
```

```
        @MsDate)
IF @@ERROR <> 0
      BEGIN
              ROLLBACK  TRANSACTION addMess
              RETURN
      END
COMMIT TRANSACTION addMess
```

Most of the stored procedures (sprocs) are similar to the previous SQL script, however, the sprocs for removing messages and message board groups are a little more involved. Look for the MessageDB.sql file on the CD. To set up the database on your machine, run the SQL script in Query Analyzer. The file mbdataaccess.cs contains the following methods:

- *addMessage*
- *addResponse*
- *addGroup*
- *delMessage*
- *delResponse*
- *delGroup*
- *getAllGroups*
- *addMod*
- *loginDbConn (for moderator login)*
- *getAllMess*

The code for these methods is all very similar. Here is the *AddMessage* method:

```
public void addMessage(string MsName,
                       string MsMessage,
                       string MsSubject,
                       string MsEmail, int GpID)
{
SqlConnection connAddMess = new SqlConnection(this.connection);
SqlCommand cmdAddMess = new SqlCommand("addMessage",connAddMess);
cmdAddMess.CommandType = CommandType.StoredProcedure;
```

```
SqlParameter prmMsName = new SqlParameter("@MsName",
                                      SqlDbType.NVarChar, 50);
prmMsName.Direction = ParameterDirection.Input;
cmdAddMess.Parameters.Add(prmMsName);
prmMsName.Value = MsName;

SqlParameter prmMsMessage = new SqlParameter("@MsMessage",
                                      SqlDbType.Text, 500);
prmMsMessage.Direction = ParameterDirection.Input;
cmdAddMess.Parameters.Add(prmMsMessage);
prmMsMessage.Value = MsMessage;

SqlParameter prmMsSubject = new SqlParameter("@MsSubject",
                                      SqlDbType.NVarChar, 50);
prmMsSubject.Direction = ParameterDirection.Input;
cmdAddMess.Parameters.Add(prmMsSubject);
prmMsSubject.Value = MsSubject;

SqlParameter prmMsEmail = new SqlParameter("@MsEmail",
                                      SqlDbType.NVarChar, 50);
prmMsEmail.Direction = ParameterDirection.Input;
cmdAddMess.Parameters.Add(prmMsEmail);
prmMsEmail.Value = MsEmail;

SqlParameter prmGpID = new SqlParameter("@GpID", SqlDbType.Int, 4);
prmGpID.Direction = ParameterDirection.Input;
cmdAddMess.Parameters.Add(prmGpID);
prmGpID.Value = GpID;

connAddMess.Open();
cmdAddMess.ExecuteNonQuery();
connAddMess.Close();
}
```

Now all the data connection code is contained in one file. To access the data, simply create an instance of the *mbdataaccess* component and call its methods. This is exactly like the ASP COM/COM+ scenario, where you create a VB or C++ COM/COM+ object to handle the data source interaction. To see this in action, see the overview of *boardlist* (see Table 10.7).

**Table 10.7** The *boardlist* Overview

| Web Form BoardList.aspx | boardlist.aspx.cs |
|---|---|
| `<head>` | `page_Load` |
| `<Link to stylesheet.css/>` | `{` |
| `<script=javascript src=clientfunctions.js/>` | `    Create and display list of Message Boards.` |
| | `}` |
| `</head>` | |
| `<body>` | `Server_event_handlers` |
| `<form>` | `{` |
| `    <asp:Xml control/>` | `    process logic for login` |
| `    <user login UI />` | `}` |
| `</form>` | |
| `</body>` | |

The form depicted in Figure 10.11 is part of boardList.aspx. It contains the following controls: *Textbox*, *RequiredFieldValidator*, *RegularExpressionValidator*, *CheckBox*, *Label*, and *Button*.

**Figure 10.11** Login interface

The following is an example of using the *RequiredFieldValidator*.

```
<td align="right">
        <asp:RequiredFieldValidator id="reqLogin"
```

```
        ControlToValidate="moderatorLogin"
        runat="server" ErrorMessage="*"/>
    <asp:TextBox id="moderatorLogin" runat="server"/>
</td>
```

This code uses the *RequiredFieldValidator* control to make the *moderatorLogin* textbox a required field in the form. Setting the *RequiredFieldValidator's ControlToValidate* attribute to *moderatorLogin* does this. If the field is left blank, the text contained in the *RequiredFieldValidator's* attribute *ErrorMessage* is displayed in red.

The login is required to be an e-mail address. In order to validate this field, you can use the *RegularExpressionValidator*. This control is placed where you want the error message to appear if the field does not match the regular expression. Here is an example of the *RegularExpressionValidator* control:

```
<asp:RegularExpressionValidator id="rexLogin"
ControlToValidate="moderatorLogin" runat="server"
ErrorMessage="invalid login"
ValidationExpression="^.*\@.*\..*$"/>
```

Notice the attribute *ControlToValidate*, which allows you to place the control anywhere on the page while validating the textbox *moderatorLogin*. The *ErrorMessage* attribute works exactly the same as its counterpart in the *RequiredFieldValidator*. The interesting attribute is *ValidationExpression*. This field holds the regular expressions used to validate the contents of *moderatorLogin*. You can supply your own regular expression, or in VS.NET, you can choose from a list of common validation expressions (for more detail on this, see the E-mail sample application in the "Working with Web Forms" section earlier in this chapter).

# Using VS.NET to Validate Form Input with a Regular Expression

To validate form input with a regular expression using VS.NET, complete the following steps:

1. Open a Web Form in design mode.

2. From the Web Forms toolbox, drag a **textbox** control onto the page.

3. From the Web Forms toolbox, drag a RegularExpressionValidator control onto the page.

4. Right-click on the control and select **Properties**. The Properties window appears (see Figure 10.12).

**Figure 10.12** The VS.NET Properties Window

5. Click in the field next to **ValidationExpression**, a little button with a ellipse on it will appear—click this button. You will be looking at the regular expression editor dialog (see Figure 10.13).

**Figure 10.13** The Regular Expression Editor Dialog

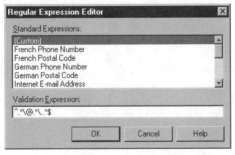

6. Simply select from the list, enter your own, or edit one from the list and click **OK**.

Now, back to the login interface. The validation controls prevent the login submit from occurring until the validation rules are satisfied. Once the rules are met, login is enabled. Remember that the checkbox and textboxes are all server controls. This will give you access to their contents in the server *click* event of the *button* control login.

In VS.NET, the easiest way to generate the code necessary for a server *click* event is to double-click on the server *button* control while viewing it in design mode. This will generate the necessary references and a method template in the corresponding code-behind page.

This reference will be added to the page class. It enables you to access this control's properties and methods in your code:

```
protected System.Web.UI.WebControls.Button login;
```

This will be added to the *InitializeComponent* method. This registers the event handler *login_Click*:

```
this.login.Click += new System.EventHandler(this.login_Click);
```

This event template will be added to the bottom of the page class:

```
private void login_Click(object sender, System.EventArgs e)
{
```

*adminCheckBox* is the check box control. You can check its value here, within the *login_Click* event handler (method):

```
if( adminCheckBox.Checked )
{
```

The site admin is logging in. For simplicity, let's make the admin login static:

```
    if((moderatorLogin.Text =="sa@site.admin") &&
            (moderatorPassword.Text=="password"))
    {
        //login admin
        this.IsAdmin = true;
        Session["IsAdmin"] = true;
        //re-initalize list
        initialize_MessageList();
        adminLabel.Text ="administrator: logged in.";
}
else
{
        adminLabel.Text = "<span style='color:red'>* invalid
```

```
                              admin login *</span>";

  }
```

We cover *Initialize_MessageList* later. What we want to point out here is the *Label* control. This control allows us access to a span tag on the client. This means that you can pass text, or even HTML, to the page by including it in a string assigned to the *Text* property of the *Label* control. A useful property of this control is *CSSclass*. This enables you to assign a Cascading Style Sheet class to the *Label*.

To get a global instance of the *dataaccess* object, add the following code to the variable declaration section at the top of the page class. This is the section where all the controls are instantiated on the server:

```
protected mb.components.mbdataaccess grouplist;
```

This code segment declares a variable *grouplist* of type *mb.components.mbdataaccess* where *mb* is my project namespace (it is the name of my Webproject in VS.NET). *Components* is the folder containing the file mbdataaccess.cs and the namespace that contains the class *mbdataaccess*. *Mbdataaccess* is the class that contains all the data access methods in mbdataaccess.cs.

In the *Page_Load* method, add the following:

```
grouplist = new mb.components.mbdataaccess();
```

This creates an instance of the *mb.components.mbdataaccess* object. The object instance *grouplist* now has access to all the data access methods. You can use it to log in the moderator:

```
string moderatorID =
grouplist.loginDbConn( moderatorLogin.Text, moderatorPassword.Text );
          if( moderatorID !="error")
          {
                  Session["moderatorID"] = int.Parse(moderatorID);
                  adminLabel.Text = "<span
style='color:red'>moderator
                                    logged in</span>";
```

Now that the moderator is logged in, you can add a link so that the moderator can create new message board groups or message boards:

```
              CreateNew.Text =
                  "<span style='width:20px'> </span>
                  <a style='color:white'
```

```
              href='createBoard.aspx?mod="
              + moderatorID + "' target='main'>
              create new group</a>";

          }

      }

}
```

As moderators create new message boards (handled by a relatively simple page you can find on the CD: createBoard.aspx), a list of boards is stored in the database. You can simply retrieve that list on *Page_load*. There are many ASP controls that can display a list, but the one which gives you the most control over the HTML rendering is the XML control. This control has two primary attributes: *xmlsource* and *xsltransform* source. There are multiple properties for these two sources based on the source format: file, string, or DOM. You can set these properties in the method *initialize_Messagelist*. The reason this method is called in the Admin login section is because you will use a different XSLT for admins. The admin XSLT will enable deleting of groups. By using two different XSLTs, you can provide different interfaces with different functionality based on user level.

Because you are going to be using XML, you will need to add the following *using* directive at the top of the code-behind page to reference the namespace containing the XML classes:

```
using System.Xml;
```

Before you can call initialize_MessageList, you must first get the list from the database and convert it to XML. Do this in the *Page_Load* method:

```
listdoc = new XmlDocument();
```

Create a new instance of *XmlDocument listdoc*, which is a global variable declared in the same section as *dataaccess*:

```
listdoc.LoadXml( grouplist.getAllGroups().GetXml() );
```

Using the global *dataaccess* object *grouplist*, call the *getAllGroups* method, which returns a *DataSet* object. You can easily convert the *DataSet* object into an XML-formatted string by calling its *GetXml* method. This is then loaded into the *XmlDocument listdoc*.

*initialize_MessageList* is a very simple method. Note that *xList* is the name of the XML control. This method will cause the data to be transformed and rendered in the HTML where the control is:

```
private void initialize_MessageList()

{

string xsltSource;

if( this.IsAdmin )

{

      xsltSource = "admin_group_list.xslt";

}

else

{

      xsltSource = "user_group_list.xslt";

}

      xList.Document = listdoc;

      xList.TransformSource = xsltSource ;

}
```

## XML and XSLT

Although XSLT is not the primary focus of this book, XMLS and XSLT are very powerful tools to have in your developer's toolbag of skills. This section gives a quick overview of the XML and XSLT file used from this application. Figure 10.14 shows the XML from *getAllBoards*, and Figure 10.15 shows the XSLT from user_group_list.xslt as rendered in IE6.

**Figure 10.14** XML from *getAllBoards*, Rendered in IE6

**Figure 10.15** user_list.xslt

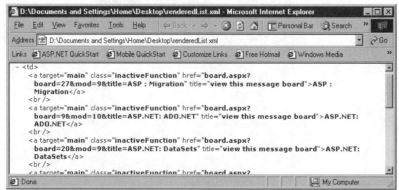

The generated HTML is a series of anchor tags with an embedded query string containing data used by board.aspx to retrieve the correct message board data. Figure 10.16 shows the HTML produced by the transform. Note that the attribute *target="main"* is a reference to the frame in the frameset with *ID="main"*.

**Figure 10.16** XML XSL/Transform Results

Notice that admin_group_list.xslt (see Figure 10.17) is almost identical except for the extra table cell content in front of the original link.

**Figure 10.17** admin_group_list.xslt

In Figure 10.18, you can see the generated HTML. In Figure 10.19, you can see an extra delete image next to the list items. Clicking on this image will pass the board ID to the delete page. The delete page has no UI, it simply verifies that the user is an admin by checking the *Session["IsAdmin"]* value, then passes the board ID to the *delete* method of the *dataaccess* component.

**Figure 10.18** XML XSL/Transform Results for Admin

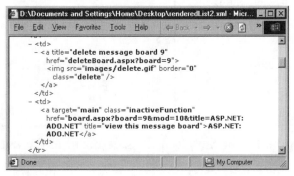

You can use one parameterized XSLT for both user and admin, however, that approach would add complexity to both the XSLT and the code-behind page.

The next page, board.aspx, will display the supplied board XML data based on the type of user. Table 10.8 is an overview of the structure of this page.

**Figure 10.19** boadList.aspx Admin View

**Table 10.8** *Board* Overview

| Web Form board.aspx | board.aspx.cs |
|---|---|
| `<head>` | `page_Load` |
| `<Link to stylesheet.css/>` | `{` |
| `<script=javascript src=` | `    show delete button ?` |
| `    clientfunctions.js/>` | `    show respond to message button ?` |
| `</head>` | `    show group title` |
| `<body>` | `    store board ID in Session["boardID"]` |
| `<form>` | `    get list of messages and responses` |
| `    <button new message/>` | `}` |
| `    <button new response/>` | |
| `  [<button detect selection/>]` | `Server_event_handlers` |
| `      [Moderator \| admin]` | `{` |
| `    <asp:Xml control/>` | `    if delete enabled. Delete responses` |
| `</form>` | `        or messages` |
| `</body>` | `}` |

*Board* receives the ID for the given message board in the query string:

```
int boardID = int.Parse( Request.QueryString["board"]);
```

This is used to load the corresponding messages and responses:

```
DataTable result = dbMethod.getAllMess( boardID );
```

When a user clicks on an item, its ID is stored in a hidden field using client-side JavaScript. The hidden fields in this page are HTML controls:

```
<input type="hidden" id="selection" runat="server" name="selection">
```

Just like the Web controls, the HTML controls have their own namespace. To access this control's properties in your code-behind page, you need to add a variable to the page class that references a corresponding HTML control on the ASPX page:

```
protected System.Web.UI.HtmlControls.HtmlInputHidden selection;
```

## Using the *String Builder* Class

String concatenation is one of the most expensive operations that you can do on the server. Personal experience has shown that almost 80 percent of the CPU can be used while building a large string in a *for* loop while reading through a *Recordset*—let's just say that it's *not* a best practice. For you ASP writers, if you are using JavaScript, use an array and dynamically add to the array, when you are done call array.join('') or array.toString(). For you VBScript writers, the solution is less clear, but dynamic arrays are definitely a headache (best of luck.) So how do you do it with .NET? .NET has a class specifically designed for this: The *StringBuilder* class. In order to use the *StringBuilder* class, you must include a reference to *System.Text*. This is how it would look in our code-behind page:

```
Using System.Text;
.

.

StringBuilder Sb = new StringBuilder();
Sb.Append("stuff to concatenate ");
Sb.Append("more stuff to concatenate");
Response.Write( Sb.toString() );
```

The result would be this:

```
stuff to concatenate more stuff to concatenate
```

In board.aspx.cs, the message and response data is returned as one long XML formatted string split up over multiple rows in a *DataTable*. The following code loops through the columns and rows of the *DataTable* while concatenating one large string. The string is then loaded into an *XmlDocument* object for later processing:

```
#//create an instance of our dataaccess object
      dbMethod = new mb.components.mbdataaccess();
      DataTable result = dbMethod.getAllMess( boardID );
#//create an instance of the string builder object
      StringBuilder xstr = new StringBuilder();


      xstr.Append("<messages>");
      for( int i=0; i < result.Rows.Count; i++)
      {
            for(int j=0; j < result.Columns.Count; j++)
            {
                     xstr.Append( result.Rows[i][j]);
            }
      }
      xstr.Append("</messages>");


#//load the resulting string into the DOM
messagedoc.LoadXml(  xstr.ToString() );
```

The resulting XML should look something like Figure 10.20.

**Figure 10.20** Sample XML Data Result

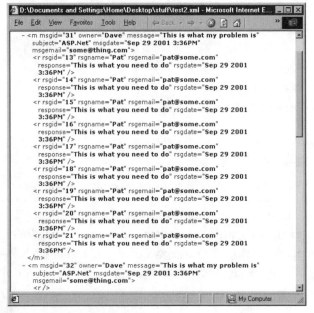

The XML data was created using the MS SQL *FOR XML AUTO* clause. The table column headers become attribute names within an XML element; in this case, the element name chosen by SQL was *m*. Notice also that all responses to any given message become a child element with the name *r*. You could have chosen to convert the attributes into actual elements themselves by using *FOR XML AUTO, ELEMENTS* instead, however, the structure is what matters, and what you have will work fine.

The XSLT for this XML data set is a little longer, but the level of complexity is about the same as those shown earlier in the chapter. The XSLT renders HTML that is tied to the classes in messageBoard.css, along with client-side JavaScripts that enable selection, as well as expand and collapse capabilities. You can find the XSLT, message_board_list.xslt, on the disk. You can find all the code necessary to build this project on the CD.

# Building a Shopping Cart with SQL

In ASP 3.0, the *Session* and *Application* objects suffered from severe limitations, including data loss with server crashes and the inability to maintain state across servers in server gardens and server farms. Unfortunately, some of these limitations still exist in ASP.NET. However, *Session* no longer loses data with server crashes and can work effectively across servers in server gardens and farms (MSDN recommends that developers avoid storing large amounts of data in a single *Session* variable). *Application* is still limited to one process, so it can be a limiting factor when addressing scalability.

So what does it all mean? It means that you have to balance your server resources and make tradeoffs. Using an *Application* variable to store a large static dataset is efficient; from the data server view there is only one read, all subsequent requests for data would come from an in-process object rather than the database. This would also increase page performance for the same reason; however, this does use more IIS resources. On the other hand, the *Application* object does not work across multiple servers; to enable this scenario, you would increase database access, thus the load on the data server. MSDN also recommends using a database to store session information if the site wants to employ personalization or future data mining of persistent data gathered from tracking their users actions while on the site.

Each choice has limits and involves tradeoffs; for the sample application, you will be persisting the data in an *Application*-level variable, and you will be using *Session* variables to maintain state in some instances. You need to be aware, however, that you can use other approaches to solve this problem, including solutions that do not use *Application* or *Session*.

In this section, you will build a shopping cart (see the UI in Figure 10.21). The *SimpleCart* application will contain a catalog of items that can be displayed five at a time (Item [1] in Table 10.9), the user will be able to move forward and back through the catalog (Item [2]). Users will have the ability to select items from the catalog and add it to their shopping carts (Item [3]). Users will also have the ability to view (Item [4]) the contents of their shopping carts, remove items, clear their carts, or check out. To see a mapping of these requirements to the corresponding pages and methods, see Table 10.9. You can find all the code for this project on the CD—see the page column of Table 10.9 for the filenames.

**Figure 10.21** *SimpleCart* UI

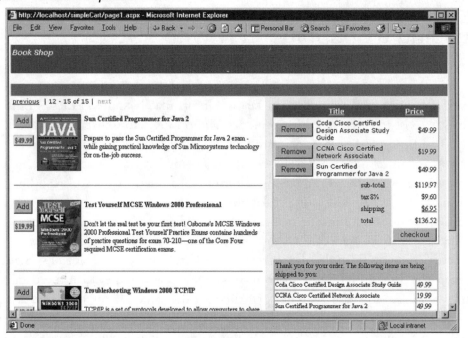

**Table 10.9** *SimpleCart* Processes Overview

| Process | Dependency | Function | Page |
|---|---|---|---|
| Display Catalog | Stored Procedure (sproc): *getAllBooks* | Returns list of all books [1] | Page1.aspx |

**Continued**

**Table 10.9** Continued

| Process | Dependency | Function | Page |
|---|---|---|---|
| | Component class | Handles data interaction with SQL [1] | Dataaccess.cs |
| | Component class | Handles all catalog interaction [1] [2] | Catalog.cs |
| | XSLT for catalog data | Converts data to HTML [1] | Catalog.xslt |
| Display Cart | Component class | Handles all cart interaction [3] | XmlShoppingCart.cs |
| | XSLT for cart data | Converts data to HTML [4] | Cart.xslt |

Notice the simple schema for this project (see Figure 10.22). It also has only one stored procedure that returns all books. You will examine the three components in the following sections:

- dataaccess.cs

- XmlShoppingCart.cs

- catalog.cs

**Figure 10.22** Database Schema for *SimpleCart*

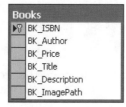

## Creating dataaccess.cs

The dataaccess.cs file is a simple component that contains only one method— *getAllBooks()*. This method contains all the logic necessary to call the stored procedure, retrieve all books, and return a *DataSet*. You can find this file in its entirety on the CD (see dataaccess.cs in the Components folder of the application):

```
using System;
using System.Collections;
using System.ComponentModel;
```

```
using System.Diagnostics;
```

You will need to add these two namespaces to the file to provide data access functionality:

```
using System.Data;
using System.Data.SqlClient;


namespace simpleCart.components
{
        public class dataaccess
        {
```

Set the connection string to connect to the SQL data store:

```
private string connection = "Persist Security Info=False;
        User ID=[user name]; password=[password];
        Initial Catalog=shopDb;Data Source=[server name]";
```

Create the method *getAllBooks*; this method will connect to the database and call the stored procedure *GetAllBooks*:

```
public DataSet getAllBooks()
  {
          SqlConnection conn =
                  new SqlConnection ( this.connection ) ;
          conn.Open ( ) ;
```

Create the command object to reference the stored procedure:

```
SqlCommand   cmd =
     new SqlCommand ( "GetAllBooks" , conn ) ;
cmd.CommandType = CommandType.StoredProcedure;
```

Here you will use the SQL data adapter so that you can retrieve the data returned by *getAllBooks* and store it in a *DataSet*:

```
SqlDataAdapter da = new SqlDataAdapter (cmd) ;
DataSet ds = new DataSet ( ) ;
da.Fill ( ds , "Books" ) ;
```

Next, close the connection to the database and return the resulting *DataSet*:

```
        conn.Close();

        return ds;

    }

  }

}
```

In this section, you created the component that you will use to retrieve the data from the database in a dataset. In the next section, you will create the component that will function as the shopping cart.

## Creating XmlShoppingCart.cs

This component is a wrapper component for XML. It provides add, remove, view, and clear functionality. The only catch is that items added to the cart must be *XmlNodes* from *Catalog* or must adhere to the same document structure. You can find this file in its entirety on the CD (see XmlShoppingCart.cs in the components folder of the application):

```
using System;
```

Add support for XML by including the XML namespace:

```
using System.Xml;


namespace simpleCart.components
{
```

Define the shopping cart class:

```
  public class xmlShoppingCart
  {
      private XmlDocument myCart;
      private string elementType;
```

This initializes the cart. On *page_ load*, the cart can be initialized with an existing *xmlCart* string. This enables client caching of the cart:

```
public void initCart(string dataSource, string elementType)
    {
        this.elementType = elementType;
        myCart = new XmlDocument();
```

```
            if( dataSource != null )
            {
              myCart.LoadXml(dataSource);
            }
            else
            {
              //load default cart root
              myCart.LoadXml("<shopcart-items></shopcart-items>");
            }
        }
```

This method handles adding an item to the cart by importing the node from the *catalog* XML data:

```
public string addItem2Cart( XmlDocument item )
    {
      try
      {
            XmlNode newItem =
            myCart.ImportNode(item.DocumentElement.FirstChild, true);
            myCart.DocumentElement.AppendChild(newItem);
            return "Success";
      }
      catch(Exception e)
      {
            return e.ToString();
      }
    }
```

This method removes an item from the cart based on its ID value using the *removeChild* method of the XML DOM object:

```
public string removeItemFromCart(string idvalue,
                                    string attributename )
    {
        // example: XmlNode curnode =
        //myCart.SelectSingleNode("//Books[isbn='0012-456-789x']");
        string XPathQuery = "//" + this.elementType + "[" +
```

```
                                    attributename + "='" + idvalue + "']";
            XmlNode curnode = myCart.SelectSingleNode(XPathQuery);
            try
            {
                myCart.DocumentElement.RemoveChild( curnode );
                return "Success";
            }
            catch(Exception e)
            {
                return e.ToString();
            }
    }
```

This method empties the cart by removing all the child nodes:

```
public void clearCart()
    {
        XmlElement root = myCart.DocumentElement;
        root.RemoveAll(); //removes all child nodes
    }
```

This method returns the current contents of the cart as an XML DOM object:

```
public XmlDocument getCartDescription()
    {
        return myCart;
    }
```

This method returns the current contents of the cart as an XML formatted string:

```
public string getCartDescriptionString()
    {
        return myCart.OuterXml;
    }
}
}
```

So far, you have built the component that gets the data from the database and the component that handles the cart operations. Next, you will create the object that handles displaying the catalog incrementally: catalog.cs.

# Creating catalog.cs

This is the largest and most complex of the components. On initialize, it loads and stores a *DataSet* object. *Catalog* adds a new table to the *DataSet*, which contains metadata. *Catalog* is able to return the data as *XmlDocuments* by range. You can find this file in its entirety on the CD (see catalog.cs in the Components folder of the application).

This class makes extensive use of *DataSet* operations. You will look at creating *DataRows*, *DataTables*, *DataViews*, and *DataSets*. You will also look at creating new *DataSets* based on the results of filtering your primary dataset:

```
using System;
```

You will need to add the *Data* namespace in order to make use of the *DataSet* and its related object:

```
using System.Data;


namespace simpleCart.components
{
/// <summary>
/// bookCatalog acts as cached datasource.
/// Enables retrieval of data in data ranges
/// </summary>
```

Here you begin creating the catalog object:

```
public class bookCatalog
{
    private DataSet dsAllBooks;

    /// <summary>
    /// Initalizes bookCatalog by reading in a dataset
    /// </summary>
    /// <param name="ds"></param>
```

First, load all the data returned by SQL into your *Catalog* object, this will enable you to filter the data and return the appropriate subset:

```
public void initCatalog(DataSet ds )
{
     dsAllBooks = ds;
    int recordCount = dsAllBooks.Tables[0].Rows.Count;
    try
    {
      dsAllBooks.Tables.Add(
      createSummaryTable(0, recordCount-1, recordCount) );
    }
    catch(Exception e)
    {
        string temp = e.ToString();
        //this fails when attempting to add the table twice
     }
}


    /// <summary>
    /// Creates a table that is added to the DataSet.
    /// This table contains some metadata
    /// about the dataset returned.
    /// </summary>
    /// <param name="startPos"></param>
    /// <param name="range"></param>
    /// <param name="RecordCount"></param>
    /// <returns>Returns a DataTable containing Metadata</returns>
```

This method takes metadata about the entire dataset and adds it to a new *DataTable*: *dtSummary*. This *DataTable* is used by other methods of this object/class:

```
private DataTable createSummaryTable(int startPos, int range,
                                        int RecordCount)
{
```

Create the new table:

```
DataTable dtSummary = new DataTable("Summary");
DataRow drSummary;
```

Add new columns to the table:

```
dtSummary.Columns.Add(
          new DataColumn("RecordCount", typeof(int)));
dtSummary.Columns.Add(
          new DataColumn("FirstItemIndex", typeof(int)));
dtSummary.Columns.Add(
          new DataColumn("LastItemIndex", typeof(int)));
```

Create a new row and add the data to its columns:

```
drSummary = dtSummary.NewRow();
drSummary["RecordCount"]    = RecordCount;
drSummary["FirstItemIndex"] = startPos;
drSummary["LastItemIndex"]  = startPos + range;
```

Add the new row to the new table:

```
dtSummary.Rows.Add( drSummary );
```

Return the new table containing the supplied data:

```
    return dtSummary;

  }


/// <summary>
/// This Method returns the input DataSet
/// </summary>
/// <returns>DataSet containing: DataTable books</returns>
public DataSet catalog()
{
    return dsAllBooks;
}


/// <summary>
/// Specialized interface to catalogRangeByCategory.
```

```
/// This Method returns all the data for only the given book
/// </summary>
/// <param name="book_isbn"></param>
/// <returns>DataSet containing: DataTable books
///& DataTable "Summary"</returns>
public DataSet catalogItemDetails( string book_isbn )
{
    return catalogRangeByCategory( -1, -1, book_isbn);
}


/// <summary>
/// Specialized interface to catalogRangeByCategory.
/// This Method returns all the books within the given range
/// </summary>
/// <param name="startPos"></param>
/// <param name="range"></param>
/// <returns></returns>
public DataSet catalogRange(int startPos, int range)
{
    return catalogRangeByCategory( startPos, range, null);
}
```

This function filters the data by creating a new *DataView*. The resulting data is added to a new table; these new tables along with a new summary table are added to a new *DataSet*. This new *DataSet* is returned to the caller:

```
protected DataSet catalogRangeByCategory(int startPos, int range,
                                         string book_isbn)
{
        DataSet             dsBookRange;
        DataTable           dtBooks;
        DataTable           dtTemp;
        string              strExpr;
        string              strSort;
        DataRow[]           foundRows;
        int                 endPos;
```

```
         int                    RecordCount;
      DataViewRowState recState;
```

Create a local copy of the table *Books*:

```
dtTemp = dsAllBooks.Tables["Books"];
```

Copy the table structure of table *Books* into a new *DataTable* object:

```
dtBooks        = dtTemp.Clone();//create Empty Books Table
```

Create the appropriate data filter:

```
if( book_isbn != null)
{
   //return a single item
   strExpr = "isbn='" + book_isbn + "'";
}
else
{
   strExpr = "";
}
   strSort ="title";
   recState = DataViewRowState.CurrentRows;
```

Filter the data storing the results in an array:

```
foundRows = dtTemp.Select(strExpr, strSort, recState);
```

Grab the appropriate range of the selected data:

```
      RecordCount = foundRows.Length;
      if( (startPos == -1) && (range == -1))
      {
            startPos = 0;
            range = RecordCount;
      }

      if( (startPos + range) > RecordCount)
      {
            endPos = RecordCount;
      }
```

```
        else

        {

                endPos = startPos + range;

        }
```

Fill the new *DataTable* with the selected data subset:

```
        for(int i = startPos; i < endPos; i ++)

        {

                dtBooks.ImportRow( (DataRow)foundRows[i] );

        }
```

Create a new *DataSet* and add the newly filled *DataTable*:

```
        dsBookRange = new DataSet();

        dsBookRange.Tables.Add(dtBooks );
```

Add a summary table to the new *DataSet*:

```
        // add a summary table to the dataset

        dsBookRange.Tables.Add(

                createSummaryTable( startPos, range, RecordCount) );
```

Return the newly created *DataSet*:

```
        return dsBookRange;

    }

  }

}
```

If you look closely at the method *catalogRangeByCategory*, you will get a glimmer of how powerful *DataSets* are. The *DataSet* is the successor to the ADO 2.6 *Recordset* object; it can actually store the entire structure of a multitable relational database and all its data. You can perform query and filter operations on it almost like a real relational database. It is also one of a few data types that can be sent to and from Web Services.

When the data source doesn't change often and is used primarily as read-only, it makes sense to cache the data in a *DataSet* at the application level. What does that mean? The *Application_*Start method within the Global.asax file is executed when the first user accesses the site; the application does not end until roughly 20 minutes after no user accesses the site. This scenario is depicted in

Figure 10.23. The data source is accessed once during the application lifetime. The result is cached as a *DataSet*, and all instances of *simpleCart* that live during the application retrieve their data from the application variable *DataSet*, *Application["catalog"]*.

**Figure 10.23** Application Level Data Caching

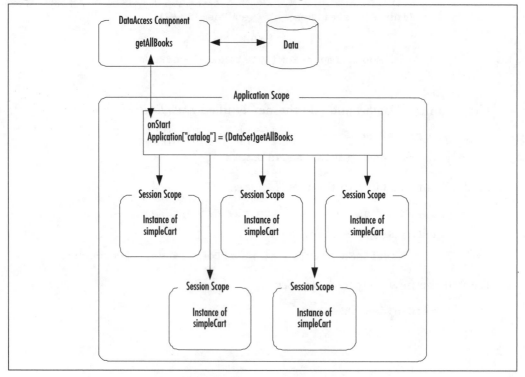

You can set this up in the Global.asax file in the *Application_start* method:

```
protected void Application_Start(Object sender, EventArgs e)
{
        simpleCart.components.dataaccess dbMethod;
        dbMethod = new simpleCart.components.dataaccess();
        Application["catalog"] = dbMethod.getAllBooks();
}
```

Next, you will create the page that will host the controls: page1.aspx. To see an overview of what is accomplished on this page see Table 10.10. You can find the code for this page on the CD (Page1.aspx and Page1.aspx.cs).

**Table 10.10** *Page1* Overview

| Web Form Page1.aspx | Page1.aspx.cs |
|---|---|
| `<head>` | `page_Load( )` |
|    `<client-script functions/>` | `{` |
| `</head>` | `create instance of dataaccess,` |
| `<body>` |     `catalog, and cart` |
| `<form>` | `show catalog` |
|    `<asp:Xml Catalog/>` | `show cart` |
|    `<asp:Xml Cart/>` | `case: add` |
|    `<asp:Label feedback/>` |     `update cart` |
|   `<hidden text server controls/>` |      `show cart` |
| `</form>` | `case: remove` |
| `</body>` |     `update cart` |
| |      `show cart` |
| | `case: checkout` |
| |     `update cart` |
| |      `show cart` |
| | `}` |
| | |
| | `show catalog( )` |
| | `show cart ( )` |

In *Page_Load*, you create instances of catalog and cart:

```
dbMethod = new simpleCart.components.dataaccess();
BookList = new simpleCart.components.bookCatalog();
BookCart = new simpleCart.components.xmlShoppingCart();

showCatalog();              //initialize catalog
showCart();
```

In Page1.aspx, you have a collection of hidden controls:

```
<div style="VISIBILITY: hidden">
    <asp:textbox id="addItem" runat="server" AutoPostBack="True" />
    <asp:TextBox id="removeItem" runat="server" AutoPostBack="True"/>
```

```
<asp:textbox id="firstRecord" runat="server" AutoPostBack="True"/>
<asp:textbox id="lastRecord" runat="server" AutoPostBack="True"/>
<asp:textbox id="direction" runat="server" AutoPostBack="True" />
<asp:textbox id="recordCount" runat="server" AutoPostBack="True"/>
<asp:TextBox id="Ready4Checkout" runat="server"
AutoPostBack="True"/>
</div>
```

*OnLoad* (in the browser), *firstRecord*, *lastRecord*, and *recordCount TextBox* values are populated by client-side JavaScript. As the user makes selections, the other fields are also populated by client-side JavaScript. Table 10.11 shows the relation of user actions on the values of these hidden fields.

**Table 10.11** Effect of Client Events on Hidden Field Values

| User Action | Result |
| --- | --- |
| Click **Add** | *AddItem.value* is set to the books ID.<br>*RemoveItem.value* is cleared.<br>Form is submitted. |
| Click **Next** | *Direction.value* is set to *"next"*.<br>Form is submitted. |
| Click **Previous** | *Direction.value* is set to *"previous"*.<br>Form is submitted. |

In *showCatalog* method, you check the values of these hidden fields to determine what range of data needs to be returned from the catalog object. This data is used as the document source in the XML control—*catalog*:

```
string prevNext  = direction.Text;
      // "previous" or "next"
int totalRecords = int.Parse(recordCount.Text);
      // number of records from previous load
int prevFirst  = int.Parse(firstRecord.Text);
      // first record # from previous load
int prevLast  = int.Parse(lastRecord.Text);
      // last record # from previous load
int range = prevLast - prevFirst;
```

```
switch(prevNext)

{

      case "previous":

      {

            if(prevFirst <= range)

            {

            xstrBooklist = BookList.catalogRange(0,range).GetXml();

            }

            else

            {

            if( range != defaultRange ) range = defaultRange;

                  xstrBooklist = BookList.catalogRange(

                        (prevFirst-range-1), range).GetXml();

            }

      }break;

      case "next":

      {

            if( (prevLast + range) >= totalRecords)

            {

                  int nextRange = totalRecords-prevLast-1;

                  xstrBooklist = BookList.catalogRange(

                        prevLast+1, nextRange).GetXml();

            }

            else

            {

            if( range != defaultRange ) range = defaultRange;

                  xstrBooklist = BookList.catalogRange(

                        prevLast+1, range).GetXml();

            }

      }break;

      default: xstrBooklist =

            BookList.catalogRange(0,this.defaultRange).GetXml();

      break;

}
```

Load the result into an *XmlDocument* object; load the XSL/Transform file; set the properties of the *asp:Xml* control for rendering:

```
catalogContent.LoadXml( xstrBooklist );
catalogDisplay.Load( Server.MapPath("catalog.xslt") );


catalog.Document = catalogContent;
catalog.Transform = catalogDisplay;
```

Figure 10.24 depicts an example of the XML source returned by *BookList*.

**Figure 10.24** *BookList* Sample Data

You can find the XSLT used to transform the data on the CD (look for catalog.xslt) Figures 10.25 and Figure 10.26 show the HTML produced by catalog.xslt.

Figure 10.27 shows a cart containing three books. Note that the structure of the XML is almost identical to that shown in Figure 10.24. This is because *Cart.addItem2Cart* simply copies the node from the XML data source (catalog).

The XSLT for displaying the cart data is a bit more complex than some of the other XSLT shown; it displays the cart data in a table and performs math operations. The filename is cart.xslt—you can find it on the CD.

**Figure 10.25** HTML Produced by catalog.xslt

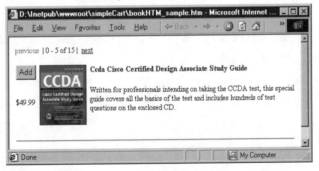

**Figure 10.26** HTML Produced by catalog.xslt and Rendered in IE6

**Figure 10.27** Sample Cart Containing Three Books

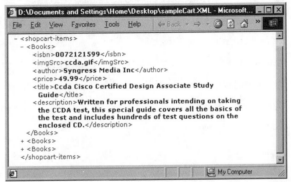

So how does cart work? Recall that you store the selected operation in hidden controls on the page. In *ShowCart*, you initialize the cart to the value of *Session["cart"]*. The first time the page loads, this *Session* variable is null. When you perform any operations, such as *Add*, *Remove*, or *Clear*, you update this *Session* variable so that the cart's state is current:

```
private void Page_Load(object sender, System.EventArgs e)
{
   BookList = new simpleCart.components.bookCatalog();
   BookCart = new simpleCart.components.xmlShoppingCart();

   showCatalog();              //initialize catalog
   showCart();                 //initialize cart

   if( addItem.Text != null && addItem.Text !="" )
   {
      //add item isbn to cart
      XmlDocument newBook = new XmlDocument();
      newBook.LoadXml(
      BookList.catalogItemDetails( (string)addItem.Text ).GetXml() );
      BookCart.addItem2Cart(newBook);
      //update Session variable that holds cart state
      Session["myShoppingCart"] = BookCart.getCartDescriptionString();
      //rewrite cart to page
      showCart();
   }

   if( removeItem.Text != null && removeItem.Text != "" )
   {
      //remove item isbn from cart
      BookCart.removeItemFromCart( removeItem.Text, "isbn" );
      //update Session variable that holds cart state
      Session["myShoppingCart"] = BookCart.getCartDescriptionString();
      //rewrite cart to page
```

```
    showCart();

}


if( Ready4Checkout.Text == "true")

{

    //(1) code to login customer could go here

    //(2) code to process order could go here

    //(3) build the feedback table

    XmlDocument myOrder = BookCart.getCartDescription();


    StringBuilder feedback = new StringBuilder();

    feedback.Append("<table border='1' cellspacing='0'

            bordercolor='silver' width='300px' bgcolor='#ffffff'

            style='margin:3px'>" );

    feedback.Append("<tr><td colspan=2 bgcolor='silver'>

            Thank you for your order. The following items are being

            shipped to you:</td></tr>");

    XmlNodeList Books = myOrder.SelectNodes("//Books");

    for( int i=0; i < Books.Count; i++)

    {

        string title =

            Books.Item(i).SelectSingleNode("title").InnerText;

        string price =

            Books.Item(i).SelectSingleNode("price").InnerText;

         feedback.Append("<tr><td style='font-size:8pt'>");

         feedback.Append(title);

         feedback.Append("</td><td>");

         feedback.Append(price);

         feedback.Append("</td></tr>");

    }


    feedback.Append("</table>");

    lblFeedBack.Text = feedback.ToString();
```

```
    //(4) clear the cart
    BookCart.clearCart(); // empty virtual cart
    showCart();            // reinitialize the cart
    Session["myShoppingCart"] =
            BookCart.getCartDescription().OuterXml;
            // update server variable to prevent refilling of cart
    Ready4Checkout.Text = "false";
    }
}
```

# Summary

In this chapter, you have worked with the ASP.NET architecture, Web Forms, *DataSets*, and *DataConnections* with ADO.NET. You have worked with many of the ASP.NET UI controls, including: *Button*, *TextBox*, *CheckBox*, *RadioButton*, *Label*, and *Xml*. You have worked through examples using the ASP.NET validation controls, including the *asp:RegularExpressionValidator* and the *asp:RequiredFieldValidator*. You have also worked with numerous ASP.NET Server classes, including the following:

- **System.Data Namespace** ADO.NET *DataSets* and *DataTables*, *SqlCommand*, *SqlDataAdapter*

- **System.Web.Mail namespace** *SmtpMail*

- **System.Xml namespace** *XmlDocument*, *XmlAtrribute*, *XmlNode*

- **System.Text namespace** *StringBuilder*

- **System.IO namespace** *StreamWriter*

By examining real-world examples, you can see the potential of ASP.NET and the .NET Framework as viable solutions architecture. ASP.NET will take Web development and Web applications programming to a new level, providing a robust and scalable multideveloper platform.

# Solutions Fast Track

## Introducing the ASP.NET Architecture

- ☑ ASP.NET architecture enables rapid prototyping of cross–platform scalable applications.

- ☑ A Web client requests a Web Form (ASPX) resource that is delivered through IIS combining all additional resources, which may include a database, Web Service, COM component, or a component class. All of these are delivered through a compiled assembly (DLL) from the Web application.

- ☑ Each of the page types (ASPX, ASCX, ASMX, and ASAX) can have a code-behind page where program logic can be stored.

☑ You can set session- and application-level variables within the Global.asax page, in the *Application_Start* and *Session_Start* methods. You can run the Global.asax file across a Web farm of servers.

# Working with Web Forms

☑ Web Forms (ASPX pages) are the replacement for ASP pages in ASP.NET.

☑ All controls and UI functionality will be placed within Web Forms.

☑ Web Forms inherit all the methods and properties of the *Page* class, which belongs to the *System.Web.UI* namespace.

☑ You can add three main sets of controls to your Web Form: HTML server controls, Web server controls, and validation controls.

# Working with ADO.NET

☑ ADO.NET is a worthy successor to ADO 2.6; it contains all the features of its predecessor but with built-in support for XML.

☑ ADO.NET DataSets can cache an entire SQL database structure, including relations and constraints along with data. You can store *DataSet*s at session or application level, reducing the load from the database server.

☑ ADO.NET *DataSet*s are one of the few complex objects that you can pass to and from Web Services because they can be represented as an XML file with an embedded XSD schema.

# Frequently Asked Questions

The following Frequently Asked Questions, answered by the authors of this book, are designed to both measure your understanding of the concepts presented in this chapter and to assist you with real-life implementation of these concepts. To have your questions about this chapter answered by the author, browse to **www.syngress.com/solutions** and click on the **"Ask the Author"** form.

**Q:** How do I set up my project to load only Flow Layout instead of Grid?

**A:** In your Solution Explorer, select the menu option **Properties**; when the solution is highlighted, select **Environment** and then choose **Flow Layout**.

**Q:** Can I set up VS.NET to display in Netscape?

**A:** Yes, in the same Properties window for the solution, select **Script** for Netscape 3.0.

**Q:** When I deploy my ASP.NET project, I do not see any of the .cs code-behind pages, why is that?

**A:** They are compiled into the DLL and stored in the bin directory of the Web root.

**Q:** I want to turn off word complete in my text editor, is that possible?

**A:** Yes—choose **Tools | Options | Text editors | HTML**; you will be able to uncheck that option in the dialog box.

**Q:** Why must I use the SQLClient class when working with SQL as opposed to using the OLEDB class?

**A:** The SQL class has been optimized to work with SQL Server to provide performance gains over the OLE DB.

# Chapter 11

# Web Services

## Solutions in this chapter:

- **The Case for Web Services**
- **Web Service Standards**
- **Working with Web Services**
- **Advanced Web Services**

- ☑ **Summary**
- ☑ **Solutions Fast Track**
- ☑ **Frequently Asked Questions**

# Introduction

The growth of the Internet demands that businesses provide clients with a better, more efficient user experience. Existing technologies have made it very difficult to make applications communicate with each other across businesses. The varied resources used, such as operating systems (OSs), programming languages and object models, pose big challenges to application integrators.

Web Services have been created to solve the interoperability of applications across operating systems, programming languages, and object models. Web Services can achieve this by relying on well supported Internet standards, such as Hypertext Transfer Protocol (HTTP) and Extensible Markup Language (XML).

In this chapter, we tell you why Web Services are an important new development in the area of Internet standards, and what business problems they address. We talk about the Simple Object Access Protocol (SOAP), which lets you exchange data and documents over the Internet in a well-defined way, and related standards to describe and discover Web Services. Finally, we cover techniques for error handling and state management and discuss how Web Services integrate with the Microsoft .NET platform.

# The Case for Web Services

In a broad sense, Web Services may be defined as "Internet-based modular applications that perform specific business tasks and conform to a specific technical format," to quote Mark Colan from IBM. If you accept this definition, you may have very well already developed a number of Web Services. However, the crux of this definition is the "specific technical format." Similar to the way a network becomes more and more useful with the number of systems participating on that network, data interchange between those systems becomes more and more powerful as the interchange conforms to a common format. Everybody can come up with their own protocols to exchange data, and in the past, many people indeed have designed such protocols, but to make distributed application development a reality and have it be truly useful, clearly a common, open, standards-based, universally adopted mechanism needs to be agreed upon. And this is where the more narrow definition of a Web Service comes in: A Web Service is a Web application using the SOAP protocol.

# The Role of SOAP

SOAP stands for *Simple Object Access Protocol*. SOAP was designed with the following three goals in mind:

- It should be optimized to run on the Internet.

- It should be simple and easy to implement.

- It should be based on XML.

SOAP is an open Internet standard. It was originally proposed by IBM, Ariba, and Microsoft, and the W3C has taken on the initiative to develop it further. The current version is SOAP 1.1 (April 2000). You can find the specifications at www.w3.org/TR/SOAP. Work is currently under way on version 1.2 (see the W3C working draft at www.w3.org/TR/soap12), which is, in our opinion, only a minor revision. You can join the authoritative discussion list for SOAP by going to http://discuss.develop.com/soap.html.

SOAP, somewhat contrary to its name, is fundamentally just a protocol that lets two systems—a client and a server—exchange data. Of course, the client system may be, and often is, just another server machine, not a human end user.

Although the SOAP specification was written in such a way as to be implemented on a variety of Internet transport protocols, it is most often used on top of HTTP. In our discussions that follow, when we talk about SOAP and Web Services, we always mean SOAP over HTTP (or Secure HTTP [HTTPS], for that matter).

SOAP supports two message patterns: the first is a simple one-way exchange, where a client issues a request against a server, and will not receive an answer back. We focus in this chapter on the second message pattern, which consists of a request–response interaction, familiar to all Web developers. A client issues an HTTP request for a resource on a server, and the server replies by sending an HTTP response. SOAP adds to that a standard way to pass data back and forth, including a standard way to report errors back to the client. In traditional Web applications, the only thing that's standardized in a Web request is the URL, the HTTP verb (*GET*, *PUT*, and so on), and some of the HTTP headers. Everything else is specific to the application at hand, particularly as it relates to the passing of application-specific data and data structures. A client can, say, *POST* additional information using the form submission mechanism. But imagine that you'd like to post a series of floating point numbers to a server. How would you do that? How would you ensure that the server understands what you're sending it? How would you ensure that the data goes to the right place on the server? SOAP addresses these challenges by defining the following:

- A mechanism to pass simple and structured data between clients and servers using a standard XML syntax
- A mechanism to call objects running remotely on a server

SOAP has two faces. On the one hand, stressing the second item in the preceding list, you can look at it as a remote procedure call (RPC) protocol familiar to anybody who has worked with distributed object models in the past. On the other hand, putting more emphasis on the first item, you can consider it a standardized way to interchange (XML) documents.

However, SOAP being a "simple" protocol, it does not by itself define a number of added-value mechanisms familiar to application developers using not-so-simple protocols (such as Common Object Request Broker Architecture [CORBA] or Component Object Model [COM]/Distributed COM [DCOM]):

- Security
- Transaction management
- Guaranteed delivery

# Why SOAP?

SOAP is not the first attempt at standardizing on an RPC and document interchange mechanism, and it may not be the last one. In the RPC area, previous attempts include CORBA and COM/DCOM, which originated in the client-server world, but both of which now include functionality to work more less well on the Internet, and David Winer's XML-RPC (see www.xmlrpc.com/spec/), which was designed from the ground up to work over the Internet. In the document area, we have seen EDI come (and go?). What makes SOAP important and, quite frankly, remarkable, is that it is supported by *all* major players in the business, including, from the very beginning, IBM and Microsoft, and more recently, Sun Microsystems. The same universal support is true of a number of related standards, such as Web Services Description Language (WSDL) and Universal Description, Discovery, and Integration (UDDI), which we discuss later in this chapter.

As Microsoft developers, we should take notice of the fact that the new Microsoft .NET Framework is currently the *only* system platform that was designed *from the ground up* based on Web Services and SOAP. Web Services on the Microsoft platform are not a mere concept, but they are real, and they are here, today (in Beta, anyway…).

# Why Web Services?

The recent emphasis on Web Services denotes a noteworthy shift in application development: away from insular, monolithical solutions and towards truly distributed, modular, open, interenterprise Internet-based applications. The hope certainly is that Web Services will do to enterprise applications what the World Wide Web did to interactive end user applications. In our opinion, then, Web Services are primarily a technique that allows disparate *server* systems to talk to each other and exchange information, and maybe less a mechanism directly encountered by human end users, for which the Web and the traditional Web browser remains the primary data access point. If you have ever been involved in trying to integrate different systems from different vendor companies, you know how painful an endeavor this can be. Integrating one system with one other system, although often very complex, can usually be done *somehow*, but integrating many systems with many other systems is really beyond the capabilities of any of the current middleware solutions, particularly if done intercompanywide over public networks. SOAP and Web Services offer hope here, because that technique is simple, and because it is a universally accepted standard.

We should all imagine a whole new class of applications appearing on the horizon very soon: massively distributed applications, integrating data from many sources from many different systems all over the world, very fault-tolerant, and accessible at all times from anywhere. One of these new applications is slated to be Microsoft's strategic priority .NET myServices (previously code-named Hailstorm), which, if fully realized, may very well replace their desktop operating systems.

# The World of Web Services

Web Services are useful only if clients can find out what services are available in the first place, where to locate them, and how exactly those services can be called. A number of initiatives are under way driven by the major vendors in the Web Service area to address those application development and business needs. Two of the more important ones, both of which are supported by the Microsoft .NET Framework and fully integrated into Visual Studio.NET Beta 2, are the following:

- **Web Service Description Language (WSDL)**  An XML format to describe how a particular Web Service can be called, what arguments it takes, and so on.

- **Universal Description, Discovery, and Integration (UDDI)**  A directory to publish business entities and the Web Services they offer, and where you can find those services. UDDI is implemented as a Web Service itself.

Additionally, there's DISCO, a mechanism based on XML developed by Microsoft to dynamically discover Web Services running on a particular machine. Putting everything together, a picture of the world of Web Services starts to evolve that may look like Figure 11.1.

**Figure 11.1** Web Service Standards

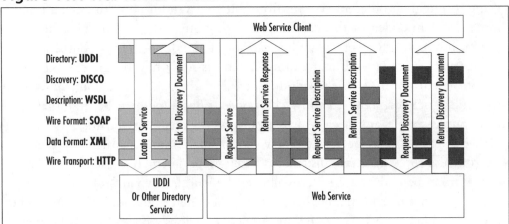

---

> **!** **WARNING**
>
> A variety of groups with Microsoft have implemented the SOAP standard. Apart from the .NET Web Services group, these include, among others, .NET Remoting, Windows XP Message Queue, SOAP Toolkit (Web Services based on COM), and BizTalk Server.
>
> Apparently, these groups all have their own code bases, and the various SOAP implementations differ in their level of support of the standard. For instance, the .NET Remoting group implemented "jagged" and sparse arrays, whereas the .NET Web Services did not. Another difference is the support of MIME-encoded attachments. Be aware then when you're thinking about reusing SOAP code or code designs from one Microsoft product to another that you may have to carefully investigate the details of what exactly is implemented in the various products.

# Web Service Standards

In this section, we cover in detail the various Web Services standards introduced in the previous section: SOAP, the wire transport protocol, WSDL to describe Web Services, DISCO to discover, and UDDI to publish Web Services. You will also write your very first Web Service using the tools provided by Microsoft Visual Studio.NET. By the end of this section, you will have enough knowledge to go ahead and create your own Web Services. The remainder of this chapter then addresses more advanced topics, such as error handling and state management.

## Wiring Up Distributed Objects—The SOAP Protocol

SOAP is the standard used to exchange data over the Internet using Web Services. SOAP is commonly referred to as a *wiring protocol*. As with many other standards, it is often more helpful to see some examples of the standard in action before moving on to reading the standards document. Using Visual Studio.NET, it is very easy to create simple Web Services and see how data is being exchanged. Because SOAP is based on XML and not a binary protocol, such as DCOM, you can inspect the data exchange in detail using a network tunneling tool and see exactly what is going on under the hood.

## Creating Your Very First Web Service

Let's look at a SOAP exchange between a client and a server by way of a few examples. Although Web Services are most interesting when used to couple server computers, our examples are more geared towards end users interacting with a Web Service server; we only do this to keep the examples reasonably simple and self-contained.

As mentioned earlier, we look only at SOAP as implemented over the HTTP protocol. Also, we initially focus on SOAP as an RPC mechanism. In Chapter 11, when we discuss the development of a more comprehensive Web Service, you will encounter SOAP used to interchange complex XML documents.

Let's start by setting up a simple echo Web Service. This service simply returns whatever character string a user submits. Creating a class that echoes its input is fairly straightforward, of course (see Figure 11.2).

**Figure 11.2** Echo Method

```
namespace soapExamples
{
  public class simpleService  {

    public simpleService() {
    }

    public string echo(string input) {
      return input;
    }

  }
}
```

How can you now make this into a Web Service? In other words, what is needed to make this method accessible to everybody in the world who has an Internet connection and knows where to find your method?

It may be hard to believe initially, but all that's needed using the .NET Framework is—apart from an Internet Information Server (IIS) Web server, of course—two tiny little changes:

- Your class *simpleService* needs to inherit from *System.Web.Services.WebService*.

- Your method echo needs to be decorated with the *System.Web.Services.WebMethod* attribute.

See Figure 11.3 for your first fully functioning Web Service. Note that the complete code for the echo Web method is in the directory soapExamples/ on the CD accompanying this book.

**Figure 11.3** Echo Web Method (simpleService.asmx.cs)

```
namespace soapExamples
{
  public class simpleService : System.Web.Services.WebService
  {
    public simpleService() {
```

**Continued**

**Figure 11.3** Continued

```
  }

  protected override void Dispose( bool disposing ) {
  }

  [System.Web.Services.WebMethod]
  public string echo(string input) {
    return input;
  }
 }
}
```

Let's now open up the Visual Studio.NET integrated development environment and create the echo Web Service from scratch, proceeding as follows:

1. Create a new ASP.NET Web Service called *soapExamples*: Go to **File | New | Project**, choose the entry **ASP.NET Web Service** under the **Visual C# Projects** folder, keep the default Location, and enter **soapExamples** as the Name of the project (see Figure 11.4). This will set up a new virtual directory of the same name (see Figure 11.5).

**Figure 11.4** Setting Up a New ASP.NET Web Service

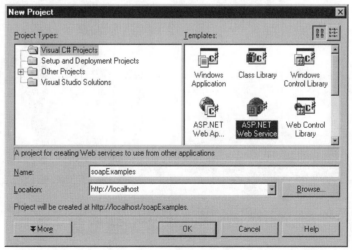

**Figure 11.5** Visual Studio.NET Automatically Sets Up a New Web

2. Visual Studio.NET will then configure the necessary FrontPage server extensions, define an assembly, and create supporting project files for you. Annoyingly, the wizard also creates a default Web Service file called Service1.asmx, which you may remove in the Solution Explorer by right-clicking on the file and selecting **Delete**. Or, you can simply rename that file to **simpleService.asmx** in the Solution Explorer and proceed with Step 4.

3. Now you create your actual Web Service: Right-click on the **soapExamples** project in the Solution Explorer, and choose **Add | Add New Item**. Choose **Web Service** from the list of available templates, and call it **simpleService.asmx** (see Figure 11.6).

**Figure 11.6** Creating a New Web Service

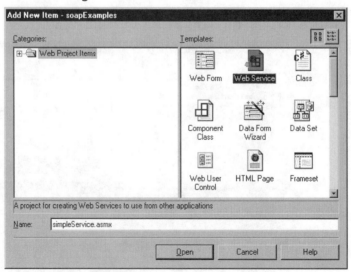

4. Select the Web Service **simpleService.asmx** in the Solution Explorer, and click on the little **View Code** icon to see the code for this Web Service added by the wizard.

5. Replace the code with the code for this class shown in Figure 11.3.

6. The last step is the most remarkable step if you've been used to traditional ASP developing. Compile your project: select **Build | Build** from the User menu, or press **Ctrl+Shift+B**. In other words, ASP.NET applications, such as a Web Service application, are *compiled* applications (and yes, it will create a .NET DLL for you!).

## How Does Visual Studio.NET Organize Your Project?

When you tell Visual Studio.NET to create a new Web Service application, the following process happens, using this section's example of an application called *soapExamples*:

1. A new IIS virtual directory called soapExamples is created in %SystemDrive%\InetPub\wwwroot\. As part of the .NET Framework installation, application mappings were already added to map .NET specific file extensions, such as .aspx, to the .NET DLL aspnet_isapi.dll, located in %SystemRoot%\Microsoft.NET\Framework\v1.0.2914\, which handles .NET-specific Web requests (see Figure 11.7).

**Figure 11.7** Mapping .NET File Extensions

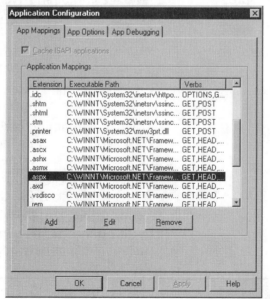

2. The IIS directory is converted to a FrontPage Server Extensions Web, allowing for Visual Studio.NET design support.

3. Under the IIS virtual directory, a variety of standard FrontPage directories are created (see Figure 11.8).

**Figure 11.8** Directory Structure for New ASP.NET Web Service

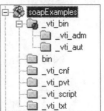

4. The bin directory is created underneath the IIS virtual directory. It will contain the compiled application.

5. A number of files are created and placed in the IIS virtual directory, as described in Table 11.1.

**Table 11.1** Files Created by Visual Studio.NET for *soapExamples* Web Service

| File Name | Description |
| --- | --- |
| soapExamples.csproj | XML file containing project-level settings, such as a list of all files contained in this project. |
| soapExamples.csproj.webinfo | XML file containing Web-related project-level settings, such as the URL to start this application. |
| soapExamples.vsdisco | XML file containing DISCO dynamic discovery information for this Web Service. |
| AssemblyInfo.cs | C# class defining assembly metadata, such as version number information. |
| Web.Config | XML file containing configuration for the Web Service, such as security, session handling, and debug settings. |
| Global.asax | Equivalent to Global.asa file in plain ASP. Points to C# class file Global.asax.cs. |
| Global.asax.cs | C# class file containing instructions on what to do during events generated by ASP.NET, such as when a new application starts or shuts down. |

**Continued**

**Table 11.1** Continued

| File Name | Description |
| --- | --- |
| Global.asax.resx | Resource file to store localization information for Global.asax. Empty by default. |
| Service1.asmx | Sample Web Service file, pointing to C# class file Service1.asmx.cs, created automatically by Visual Studio.NET. |
| Service1.asmx.cs | Sample C# Web Service class file, created automatically by Visual Studio.NET. |
| Service1.asmx.resx | Sample Web Service resource file to store localization information for Service1.asmx. Empty by default. Created automatically by Visual Studio.NET. |

6. A directory called soapExamples is created in %USERPROFILE%\ My Documents\Visual Studio Projects\. Two files are created: soapExamples.sln, a text file containing information as to what projects are contained in the Visual Studio.NET solution, and soapExamples.suo, a binary solution configuration file that cannot be edited directly.

7. A directory called soapExamples is created in %USERPROFILE%\ VSWebCache\ATURTSCHI\. This directory and various subdirectories created underneath it contain the cached version of your Web Service. You should normally not need to make any changes here, although it can happen that the files here get out of synch with the files in the "normal" Web directory underneath InetPub\wwwroot, in which case you may have to manually copy some files around.

Not all of those files can be made visible in Visual Studio.NET. However, you can see many of them by clicking on the **Show All Files** icon in the Solution Explorer (see Figure 11.9).

**Figure 11.9** Showing All Files through Solution Explorer

## Developing & Deploying…

### Separating Design and Code

Microsoft .NET makes a big step forward in neatly separating Web page *design* from Web page *code*. There are actually two files for every Web page: one file that holds all visual elements of a Web page, and another file linked to it that holds the business logic for that page. Web Services are ASP.NET Web applications, and therefore incorporate the same mechanism. Because Web Services don't have a user interface as such, the only content of the Web Service Web page is a directive linking it to the Web Service class that contains all the code to handle Web Service requests.

For the *simpleService* Web Service, the corresponding "front end" file, soapExamples.asmx, looks as follows:

```
<%@ WebService Language="c#" Codebehind="simpleService.asmx.cs"
   Class="soapExamples.simpleService" %>
```

The *Codebehind* attribute points to the Web Service class file, which by default has the same name as the ASMX file, with a file extension appended reflecting the programming language used, in this case .cs for C#.

**Continued**

In order to keeps things "simple," the Visual Studio.NET user interface does not keep those two files apart, which may lead a little bit to confusion. Instead, similar to what you may be used to in the Visual Basic 6 form designer, you switch between design mode (the Web form), and code mode (the underlying code) by clicking the corresponding icons in the Solution Explorer. However, and this may throw you off a bit initially, the files that keep the design and code content really *are* different files; however, Solution Explorer pretends that only one of the files, namely the one containing the page design, exists. You can force Solution Explorer to show you the file containing the page code by clicking the **Show All Files** icon, however even when you then explicitly click the code file, Visual Studio.NET will *still* show you the design page, not the code page.

## Running Your Very First Web Service

Now that you have developed a simple Web Service, you would obviously like to see it in action, if only to check that everything works the way you expect it to work. Because a Web Service at its core really isn't anything else than a very special Web application, you have the usual means of testing and debugging at your disposal. These are running the Web Service through Visual Studio.NET, our preferred integrated development platform, or calling it through a custom client application, such as a simple Visual Basic script. In addition, you have the option of *automatically* generating a client application that calls your Web Service through the Web Reference mechanism. Let's go through each of these three scenarios in detail.

### Testing a Web Service Using Integrated Visual Studio.NET Debugging

If you want to test your Web Service through the debugger that comes with Visual Studio.NET, you first need to check and/or change some settings to enable Visual Studio.NET to debug the application properly:

1. Click on the file **Web.config** in the Solution Explorer. Scan through it and make sure that the *debug* attribute of the *compilation* element is set to True (which is the default). This will cause debug information to be included in the compiled DLL. Obviously, you want to change this setting once you're ready to deploy your application.

2. Go to Solution Explorer and right-click on the **soapExamples** project folder to select its Properties. Under the Configuration Properties folder,

click **Debugging** and make sure that ASP.NET Debugging is enabled, as shown in Figure 11.10.

**Figure 11.10** Enabling ASP.NET Debugging

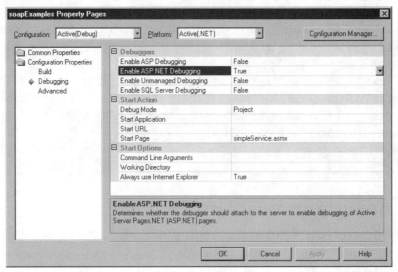

3. Right-click on the file **simpleService.asmx**, which is the file defining your actual Web Service, and select **Set As Start Page**. (Or, you can select this service as the solution Startup Project through the Properties page of the soapExamples solution, as shown in Figure 11.11).

**Figure 11.11** Defining a Startup Project

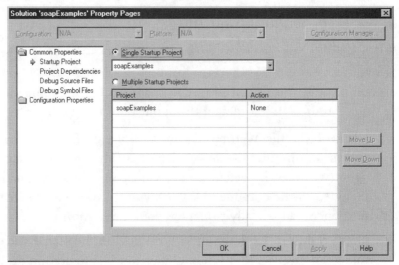

4.  You can now start testing your application by pressing **F5** or by choosing **Debug | Start** through the User menu. As usual, you can set breakpoints anywhere in your code by simply pressing **F9** or selecting **Debug | New Breakpoint** on a line of code through the User menu.

5.  Visual Studio.NET will recompile the application, just to be sure, and launch Internet Explorer (see Figure 11.12).

**Figure 11.12** Starting the Web Service in Debug Mode

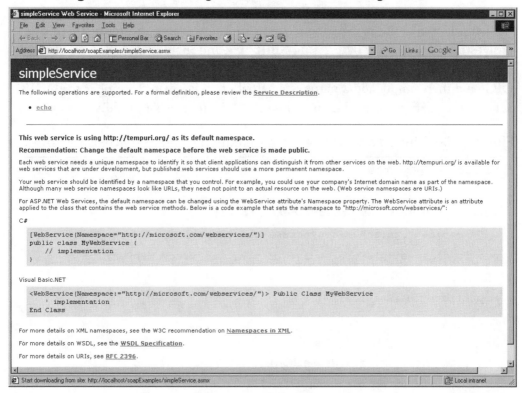

Note the URL convention used by Microsoft .NET. Immediately after the host name (*localhost*) is the name of the application (*soapExamples*), followed by the name of the Web Service (*simpleService*), or rather, the name of the corresponding Web Service definition file, which has the .asmx file extension.

ASP.NET runtime warns you that you are using the default namespace http://tempuri.org. As you have seen in earlier chapters, every .NET class lives in a namespace. Similarly, every Web Service *must* live in a namespace that is exposed globally. This Web Service namespace allows application developers worldwide to distinguish their Web Services from Web Services built by other people. The URL under which a Web Service can be reached, in this case http://localhost/soapExamples/simpleService.asmx, is only an attribute of a *concrete instance* of a Web Service; this Web Service could potentially live on many servers. So, you need to give your Web Service a distinguishing name through the usage of a namespace. By default, ASP.NET will use http://tempuri.org/, but you should really change this. Namespaces are created by using a URI (Uniform Resource Identifier), which really can be anything (see www.faqs.org/rfcs/ rfc2396.html for an explanation of URIs). Common choices include using your DNS entry in order to get a unique name.

Let's then take the namespace related runtime warning in Figure 11.12 seriously; stop the debugger by pressing **Shift+F5**, and include Web Service namespace definitions in the code; urn:schemas-syngress-com-soap seems like a good URI, and then simply add a namespace attribute with that value next to the Web Service class definition, as shown in Figure 11.13 (changes in bold).

**Figure 11.13** Including a Namespace Definition (simpleService.asmx.cs)

```
namespace soapExamples
{
    [System.Web.Services.WebServiceAttribute(
      Namespace="urn:schemas-syngress-com-soap")]
    public class simpleService : System.Web.Services.WebService
    {
      public simpleService() {
      }


      [System.Web.Services.WebMethod]
      public string echo(string input) {
        return input;
      }
    }
}
```

After recompiling and restarting the application, you are presented with a screen as in Figure 11.14.

**Figure 11.14** Web Service in Debug Mode after Namespace Has Been Added

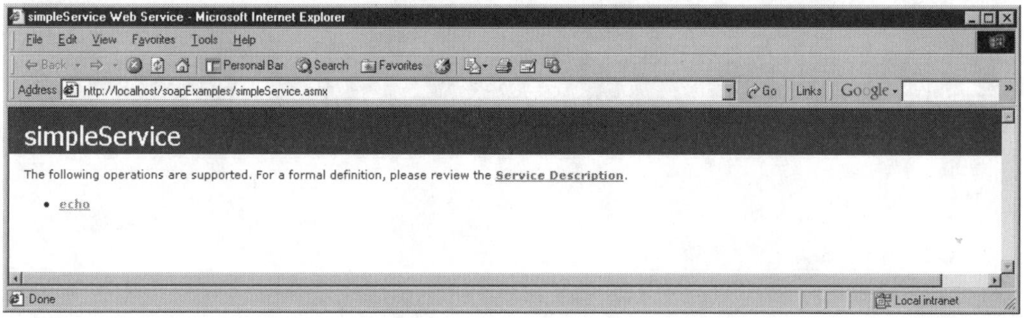

We look at the service description in the next section on WSDL; for now, just click on the **echo** link, which will take you to the welcome screen for the echo Web Service method, as depicted in Figure 11.15.

The URL convention adopted by Microsoft .NET for the Web method welcome screen is to append the name of the exposed Web method through an *op=WebMethodName* URL parameter, in this case *op=echo*. To actually call the Web method, the convention is to just add the name of the Web method to the URL, and to append the name of input parameters as URL parameters to the end, as you'll see in a second.

Enter a value, say "Hello World", in the text box labeled *input*, which by the way, corresponds of course to the only input parameter you have defined for the echo Web method, and click **Invoke**. This then takes you to the output screen, as shown in Figure 11.16.

The input has been echoed in something that clearly looks like XML. As you can see in Figure 11.15, Microsoft offers you *three ways* to call a Web Service:

- Through a straight HTTP GET
- Through a straight HTTP POST
- Through SOAP

Calling a Web Service through an HTTP GET is a simplified way to call a Web Service. Particularly, it allows you to call a Web Service through a Web browser. The only thing you need to do is to append the method name to the URL of the Web Service, and to add the parameters the way you would usually add variables when submitting an HTML form in a Web application:

```
http://localhost/soapExamples/simpleService.asmx/echo?input=Hello+World
```

**Figure 11.15** The *echo* Web Service Method

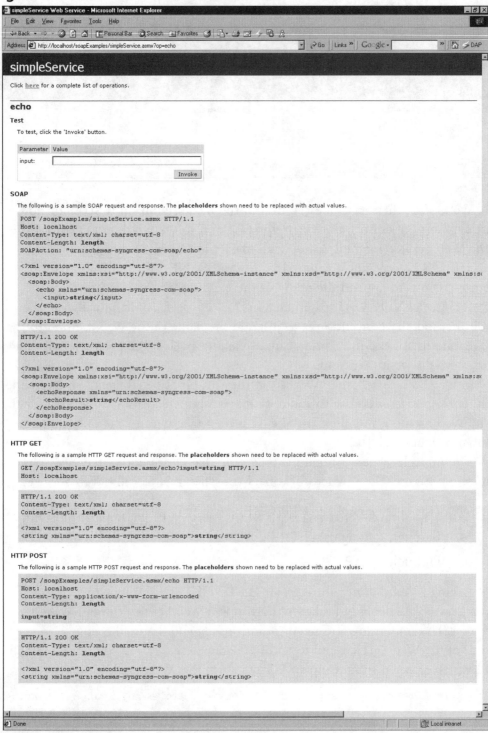

**Figure 11.16** Output of the *echo* Web Method

The result that you get from this call (see the following):

```
<?xml version="1.0" encoding="utf-8" ?>
<string xmlns="urn:schemas-syngress-com-soap">Hello World</string>
```

This is an XML-ish representation of the fact that the return argument is a string, living in the *urn:schemas-syngress-com-soap* namespace, and having a value of "Hello World".

As you can imagine, this technique will work only for the very simplest of Web Services. What if you wanted to pass a complex data type to the Web Service? What if you wanted to pass an XML document to the Web Service?

The *POST* method offered to you by Visual Studio.NET in Figure 11.15 is very similar to the *GET* method, the only difference being that the parameter values are put into the body of the HTTP request, exactly the way you would if you *POST*ed information to a Web application through a form.

This technique of calling Web Services through simple HTTP *GET*s and *POST*s is *not* the standard way of calling Web Services. It is very inflexible, and in fact not supported by most vendors. On the other hand, until such time as SOAP will become universal and supported natively by all client applications, you may find simple *GET*s and *POST*s useful in cases where clients don't yet understand SOAP, but do have XML processing capabilities, as is the case with Macromedia Flash 5.0.

Our suggestion, then, is to forgo convenience, and use the SOAP protocol for calling Web Services from the very start. Unfortunately, this means that you have to do a little bit more work.

## Testing a Web Service Using a Client Script

What do you need to do to call the *echo* Web method through proper SOAP? On the Web Service overview screen, as depicted in Figure 11.17, you can get all the information you need.

**Figure 11.17** The SOAP Section of the Web Service Overview Screen

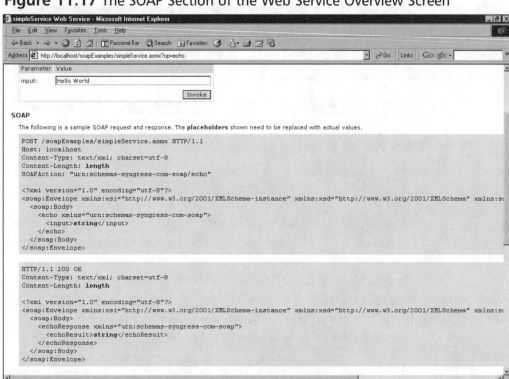

You can make the following observations for the *SOAP request*:

- A SOAP request is issued using an HTTP *POST*.

- The request is *POST*ed to the Web Service ASMX page (http://local-host/soapExamples/simpleService.asmx, in this case).

- SOAP uses an additional HTTP header, called *SOAPAction*, that contains the URI of the Web Service followed by the Web method name (*urn:schemas-syngress-com-soap/echo* in this case).

- The HTTP body of the POST contains an XML document, called the *SOAP envelope*, delimited by an <Envelope> tag.

- The SOAP envelope itself has a <Body> element, and within that element are elements defining the Web method you are calling (<echo>) and what parameters it takes (<input>).

For the *SOAP response*, in turn:

- The SOAP response is a normal HTTP response.

- The HTTP body of the SOAP response contains an XML document, called the *SOAP envelope*, that has the same structure as the SOAP request envelope discussed in the preceding list.

- The SOAP envelope itself has a <Body> element, and within that body element are elements declaring the response from the Web method (the default is adding the word *Response* to the method name (that is, <echoResponse>), along with the return argument (the default is adding the word *Result* to the method name, that is, <echoResult> here).

A detailed discussion of the SOAP protocol is well beyond the scope of this book, however, the basic structure of the SOAP protocol is already apparent:

- Requests are *POST*ed to a server, which in turn issues a response to the client.

- All requests and responses are XML documents, that start with <Envelope> and <Body> elements. Method names show up within the SOAP Body section, and method arguments and return values in turn show up within the method section.

- The server finds the Web class that handles the request through a combination of the URL to the corresponding ASMX file in the HTTP request, the *SOAPAction* header, and the XML element having the name of the Web method to call following immediately after the SOAP *Body* element.

Because Visual Studio.NET does not currently support directly calling a Web method though SOAP (unless you use Web References, which you will do in the next subsection), let's write a little standalone Visual Basic VBS script instead. Simply take the SOAP request shown in Figure 11.17 and *POST* that information to the Web Server using the Microsoft.XMLHTTP ActiveX control, as shown in Figure 11.18.

**Figure 11.18** VBS Script to Test the *echo* Web Method (echo.vbs)

```
myWebService = "http://localhost/soapExamples/simpleService.asmx"
myMethod = "urn:schemas-syngress-com-soap/echo"
```

**Continued**

## Figure 11.18 Continued

```
'** create the SOAP envelope with the request
s = ""
s = s & "<?xml version=""1.0"" encoding=""utf-8""?>" & vbCrLf
s = s & "<soap:Envelope "
s = s & "   xmlns:xsi=""http://www.w3.org/2001/XMLSchema-instance"""
s = s & "   xmlns:xsd=""http://www.w3.org/2001/XMLSchema"""
s = s & "   xmlns:soap=""http://schemas.xmlsoap.org/soap/envelope/"">"
s = s & vbCrLf
s = s & "  <soap:Body>" & vbCrLf
s = s & "    <echo xmlns=""urn:schemas-syngress-com-soap"">" & vbCrLf
s = s & "      <input>Hello World</input>" & vbCrLf
s = s & "    </echo>" & vbCrLf
s = s & "  </soap:Body>" & vbCrLf
s = s & "</soap:Envelope>" & vbCrLf


msgbox(s)


set requestHTTP = CreateObject("Microsoft.XMLHTTP")


msgbox("xmlhttp object created")


requestHTTP.open "POST", myWebService, false
requestHTTP.setrequestheader "Content-Type", "text/xml"
requestHTTP.setrequestheader "SOAPAction", myMethod
requestHTTP.Send s


msgbox("request sent")


set responseDocument = requestHTTP.responseXML


msgbox("http return status code: " & requestHTTP.status)
msgbox(responseDocument.xml)
```

Because this is a simple Visual Basic script file, you can run it by simply double-clicking on it in Windows Explorer, which will start Windows Scripting Host. The script will show us the SOAP request (see Figure 11.19), send it to the server, tell us that it received an HTTP 200 status return code (see Figure 11.20), which means that everything went smoothly, and then display the SOAP response that includes the echoed input parameter (see Figure 11.21).

**Figure 11.19** Sending a SOAP Request

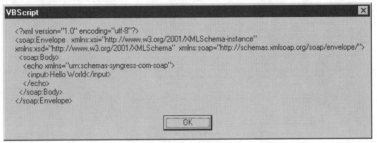

**Figure 11.20** Retrieving a Successful Http Status Code

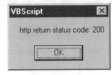

**Figure 11.21** The Successful SOAP Response

The truly amazing fact, however, is that you can run this script, which is not connected in any way to your Visual Studio.NET project, in debug mode. In other words, if you set a breakpoint in one of your project files, start the debugger (by just pressing **F5**), and then go to Windows Explorer or to a command line and run the script in Figure 11.18; execution *will* stop at your breakpoints. See Figure 11.22 for a depiction of the *echo* Web method, paused right before it returns the response back to the client. Notice, for example, the complicated call stack right, which gives you an idea of the heavy lifting that the .NET Framework does for you in order for Web Services to work properly.

**Figure 11.22** Stopping Your Application at a Breakpoint

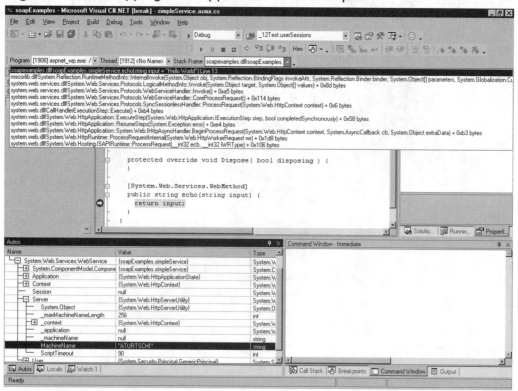

Stop for a moment and consider what you have so far done in this section. Nothing prevents you from taking the Visual Basic script you just created and including it as client-side script in a traditional Web page (other than the fact that your clients will need to use Internet Explorer on a Windows platform, of course). If you do this, you have just created a Web Service client application that runs inside a browser window, making your *echo* service accessible to everybody who has an Internet connection and knows how to find your service.

So far, the only thing you have done is pass a string argument back and forth. The SOAP specification goes a lot further, as you can imagine; it defines a standard for passing a number of basic data types, complex data structures, and XML documents between a SOAP client and a SOAP server. You can also serialize objects and pass them over the wire. You will see examples of this in the section "Working with Web Services," later on in this chapter.

You can find the complete code for the *echo* Web method on the CD accompanying this book in the directory soapExamples/.

## Testing a Web Service Using a Web Reference

Lastly, you can run and test a Web Service application by letting Visual Studio.NET create a .NET client proxy class for you, *automatically*. This proxy class contains one method for each Web method exposed by the Web Service. The tasks of creating the correct SOAP envelope, sending the data over the wire through HTTP, waiting for the response back from the server, and parsing the SOAP response envelope for the return value are all done for you. This may very well end up being your method of choice, because you don't need to worry about the details of the SOAP protocol, but can concentrate on solving the higher-level business problems at hand. However, to do this, you need to create a separate .NET client application, and then let Visual Studio.NET glue the two together by adding a reference to your Web Service server application. In order to do this, however, we need to first talk about how Web Services can be described and discovered by potential clients.

---

### Developing & Deploying…

### Deploying Web Services

How do you deploy a Web Service, such as the *soapExamples* service you just created? The good news is that because Web Services are really just a special kind of an .NET Web application, that is they run under ASP.NET, deploying a Web Service is no different than deploying any other ASP.NET application: You simply create a new IIS virtual directory on the target server, copy all files from your project into the new location, and you're done. Before you do that, though, be sure to compile your Web Service with all debug information removed for better performance (see the section "Testing A Web Service Using Integrated Visual Studio.NET Debugging" earlier in this chapter for details).

However, in the real world, Web Services will likely often act as wrappers around legacy systems, such as database systems or enterprise applications. The difficulty, then, of deploying a Web Service will not be deploying the Web Service as such, but making sure that the Web Service works well together with those legacy systems.

---

# Describing Web Services—WSDL

Because you have programmed the *soapExamples* Web Service that includes the *echo* Web method yourself, you "know" how to access it. Well, at least you remember that the *echo* method takes an input parameter, of type *string*, which you called *input*, and returns as its output another string. And although you may not quite remember how to correctly call this Web method, particularly the gory details of that SOAP envelope, you can always just point your browser to the welcome page (see Figure 11.15) to get more information.

In the world of classic COM, to use an analogy if you are familiar with that framework, classes are described using their interfaces, which in turn were exposed through type libraries. Type libraries are binary files that are created by compiling a file, written in the Interface Definition Language (IDL), that describes the interface of a COM component. It is by enquiring a component type library that a COM client learns how to call a COM server.

In the world of Web Services, the role of a type library is taken by the WSDL description of a Web Service. Not very surprisingly, WSDL is an XML language. Unlike in COM, it does not need to get compiled, which is a very big advantage indeed.

In Microsoft .NET, you can generate the WSDL Web Service description in three ways:

- You can get the WSDL description *dynamically* by calling the Web Service URL appended by the WSDL parameter; in this case, simply http://localhost/soapExamples/simpleService.asmx?WSDL. This is the preferred method, because it always gives you an up-to-date description of the service.

- You can (statically) generate the WSDL description by using the disco.exe tool found at %ProgramFiles%\Microsoft.NET\FrameworkSDK\Bin\. It takes the URL of your Web Service as an argument and writes the information into an XML file. For this example, type **disco http://localhost/soapExamples/simpleService.asmx** on a command line.

- Finally, you can programmatically create WSDL files by using the corresponding classes in the *System.Web.Services.Description* namespace. Note that the documentation sometimes erroneously refers to SDL, an older Web Service description technology that is no longer supported, but rest assured that these classes really do deal with WSDL only.

WSDL is a complex standard that is still undergoing changes, and discussing it in detail is beyond the scope of this book; you can find more information about WSDL, including the actual WSDL specification, which is currently stands at version 1.1, at www.w3.org/TR/wsdl.

However, you can get a cursory understanding of the structure of WSDL by looking at the WSDL description of the *echo* Web method, which you can access by going to http://localhost/soapExamples/simpleService.asmx?WSDL (see Figure 11.23).

**Figure 11.23** WSDL Description for the Echo Web Method

```xml
<?xml version="1.0" encoding="utf-8"?>
<definitions
  targetNamespace="urn:schemas-syngress-com-soap"
  xmlns:s="http://www.w3.org/2001/XMLSchema"
  xmlns:http="http://schemas.xmlsoap.org/wsdl/http/"
  xmlns:mime="http://schemas.xmlsoap.org/wsdl/mime/"
  xmlns:tm="http://microsoft.com/wsdl/mime/textMatching/"
  xmlns:soap="http://schemas.xmlsoap.org/wsdl/soap/"
  xmlns:soapenc="http://schemas.xmlsoap.org/soap/encoding/"
  xmlns:s0="urn:schemas-syngress-com-soap"
  xmlns="http://schemas.xmlsoap.org/wsdl/">
  <types>
    <s:schema attributeFormDefault="qualified"
      elementFormDefault="qualified"
      targetNamespace="urn:schemas-syngress-com-soap">
      <s:element name="echo">
        <s:complexType>
          <s:sequence>
            <s:element minOccurs="1" maxOccurs="1" name="input"
              nillable="true" type="s:string" />
          </s:sequence>
        </s:complexType>
      </s:element>
      <s:element name="echoResponse">
        <s:complexType>
```

*Continued*

## Figure 11.23 Continued

```xml
          <s:sequence>
            <s:element minOccurs="1" maxOccurs="1" name="echoResult"
              nillable="true" type="s:string" />
          </s:sequence>
        </s:complexType>
      </s:element>
      <s:element name="string" nillable="true" type="s:string" />
    </s:schema>
  </types>
  <message name="echoSoapIn">
    <part name="parameters" element="s0:echo" />
  </message>
  <message name="echoSoapOut">
    <part name="parameters" element="s0:echoResponse" />
  </message>
  <message name="echoHttpGetIn">
    <part name="input" type="s:string" />
  </message>
  <message name="echoHttpGetOut">
    <part name="Body" element="s0:string" />
  </message>
  <message name="echoHttpPostIn">
    <part name="input" type="s:string" />
  </message>
  <message name="echoHttpPostOut">
    <part name="Body" element="s0:string" />
  </message>
  <portType name="simpleServiceSoap">
    <operation name="echo">
      <input message="s0:echoSoapIn" />
      <output message="s0:echoSoapOut" />
    </operation>
  </portType>
```

**Continued**

**Figure 11.23** Continued

```
<portType name="simpleServiceHttpGet">
  <operation name="echo">
    <input message="s0:echoHttpGetIn" />
    <output message="s0:echoHttpGetOut" />
  </operation>
</portType>
<portType name="simpleServiceHttpPost">
  <operation name="echo">
    <input message="s0:echoHttpPostIn" />
    <output message="s0:echoHttpPostOut" />
  </operation>
</portType>
<binding name="simpleServiceSoap" type="s0:simpleServiceSoap">
  <soap:binding
    transport="http://schemas.xmlsoap.org/soap/http"
    style="document" />
  <operation name="echo">
    <soap:operation soapAction="urn:schemas-syngress-com-soap/echo"
      style="document" />
    <input>
      <soap:body use="literal" />
    </input>
    <output>
      <soap:body use="literal" />
    </output>
  </operation>
</binding>
<binding name="simpleServiceHttpGet"
  type="s0:simpleServiceHttpGet">
  <http:binding verb="GET" />
  <operation name="echo">
    <http:operation location="/echo" />
    <input>
```

**Continued**

**Figure 11.23** Continued

```
        <http:urlEncoded />
    </input>
    <output>
        <mime:mimeXml part="Body" />
    </output>
  </operation>
</binding>
<binding name="simpleServiceHttpPost"
  type="s0:simpleServiceHttpPost">
  <http:binding verb="POST" />
  <operation name="echo">
    <http:operation location="/echo" />
    <input>
        <mime:content type="application/x-www-form-urlencoded" />
    </input>
    <output>
        <mime:mimeXml part="Body" />
    </output>
  </operation>
</binding>
<service name="simpleService">
  <port name="simpleServiceSoap" binding="s0:simpleServiceSoap">
    <soap:address
        location="http://localhost/soapExamples/simpleService.asmx" />
  </port>
  <port name="simpleServiceHttpGet"
    binding="s0:simpleServiceHttpGet">
    <http:address
        location="http://localhost/soapExamples/simpleService.asmx" />
  </port>
  <port name="simpleServiceHttpPost"
    binding="s0:simpleServiceHttpPost">
    <http:address
```

**Continued**

**Figure 11.23** Continued

```
        location="http://localhost/soapExamples/simpleService.asmx" />
    </port>
  </service>
</definitions>
```

You can see from Figure 11.23 that WSDL has five parts, wrapped in the <definitions> XML element:

- The <types> section defines all data types used by the service. In this case, you have two types, both of *string* type: the *input* parameter, which is the argument passed to the echo Web method, and *echoResponse*, which is the output from *echo* that's returned to the caller.

- The <message> section, which defines input and output parameters of the Web Service. It refers back to the data types defined in the <types> section of the preceding code. In this example are six individual <message> sections. As you have seen earlier, for simple Web Services, .NET defines three access methods—*HTTP GET*, *HTTP POST*, and SOAP. The echo method uses the request–response message pattern, and you see therefore two <message> sections for each of the three access methods: one declaring the input parameter, the other one declaring the output parameter.

- The <portType> section ties the access methods to the messages declared in the <message> section. Because you have three access methods, you see three corresponding <portType> sections.

- The <bindings> section declares the protocols used to access the echo Web method—*HTTP GET*, *HTTP POST*, and SOAP. It also defines the encoding used to send data over the wire; for *HTTP GET* and *POST*, you simply use URL encoding, whereas for SOAP you use the encoding mechanism provided by the SOAP standard. This section also defines the value that has to be used in the *SOAPAction* HTTP header.

- Everything is now tied together in the <service> section: You see your Web Service, *simpleService*, appear, with its only method, *echo*, that has three bindings attached to it, as explained earlier in this list, that can all be accessed at the URL http://localhost/soapExamples/simpleService.asmx.

# Discovering Web Services—DISCO

DISCO, which presumably stands for "discovery", is a mechanism developed by Microsoft for clients to dynamically locate Web Services. More precisely, DISCO guides clients to the WSDL files describing the call syntax of Web Services. DISCO is not supported by anybody outside Microsoft, and it is unclear what future, if any, DISCO has. In practice, DISCO has largely been replaced by UDDI.

DISCO has two parts. Files with the .vsdisco extension contain information where to *dynamically search* for Web Services on the local server. Files with the .disco extension, in turn, contain information about *already found* Web Services on the local server, particularly where the corresponding WSDL information is located. You will now immediately realize the problem with DISCO: It is an insular solution in that you need to know both the name of the server and the DISCO location on that server *before* you can query for Web Services.

Microsoft Visual Studio.NET automatically adds and maintains a file with extension .vsdisco to Web Service projects. It also puts a VSDISCO file into the root directory of the Web server. These VSDISCO files look like the one shown in Figure 11.24.

**Figure 11.24** A Typical DISCO Discovery File

```xml
<?xml version="1.0" ?>
<dynamicDiscovery
   xmlns="urn:schemas-dynamicdiscovery:disco.2000-03-17">
<exclude path="_vti_cnf" />
<exclude path="_vti_pvt" />
<exclude path="_vti_log" />
<exclude path="_vti_script" />
<exclude path="_vti_txt" />
<exclude path="Web References" />
</dynamicDiscovery>
```

When you point a Web browser to such a VSDISCO file, Microsoft .NET starts to dynamically query the server for Web Services in the corresponding virtual directory (and below). If you go to the URL http://localhost/soapExamples/ soapExamples.vsdisco, for example, IIS responds after a while by sending a DISCO file back to you that looks like the one shown in Figure 11.25.

**Figure 11.25** DISCO Information for the *soapExamples* Web Service

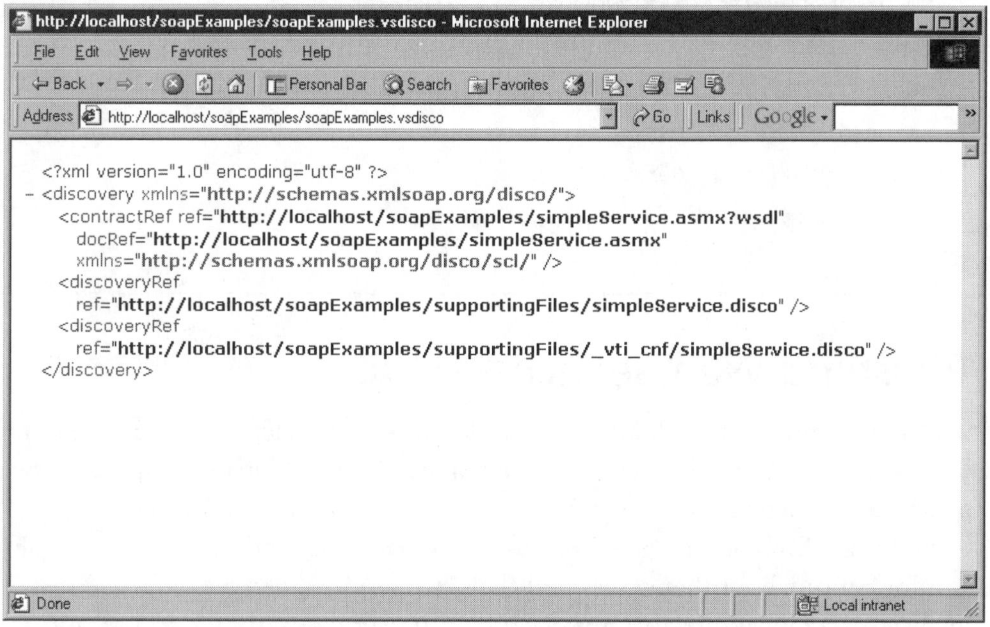

You can also statically generate a DISCO file using the disco.exe tool found at %ProgramFiles%\Microsoft.NET\FrameworkSDK\Bin\. This is the same tool that also outputs the WSDL description. It takes the URL of your Web Service as an argument and writes the information into a file with a .disco extension. Unfortunately, this DISCO file contains slightly different information, but it also directs you to the WSDL description of the service, which is really all that matters (see Figure 11.26).

**Figure 11.26** DISCO Discovery File Containing a Reference to WSDL Description

```
<?xml version="1.0" encoding="utf-8"?>

<discovery

  xmlns:xsi="http://www.w3.org/2001/XMLSchema-instance"

  xmlns:xsd="http://www.w3.org/2001/XMLSchema"

  xmlns="http://schemas.xmlsoap.org/disco/">

  <contractRef

    ref="http://localhost/soapExamples/simpleService.asmx?wsdl"

    docRef="http://localhost/soapExamples/simpleService.asmx"
```

**Continued**

**Figure 11.26** Continued

```
    xmlns="http://schemas.xmlsoap.org/disco/scl/" />
  <soap
    address="http://localhost/soapExamples/simpleService.asmx"
    xmlns:q1="urn:schemas-syngress-com-soap"
    binding="q1:simpleServiceSoap"
    xmlns="http://schemas.xmlsoap.org/disco/soap/" />
</discovery>
```

# Publishing Web Services—UDDI

Fortunately, a more comprehensive way to locate Web Services exists, and that's the Universal Description, Discovery, and Integration (UDDI) initiative, supported by IBM, Microsoft, and a host of other vendors in the field of Web Services.

UDDI is a Web Service *itself*, and it allows businesses and individuals to publish information about themselves and the Web Services they are offering. It is conceived as a global directory service, open to everybody, simple to use, and comprehensive in its scope. You can find the UDDI home page at www.uddi.org.

The three major sponsors of UDDI operate distributed, replicated UDDI services. The access points are as follows:

- **Microsoft**  http://uddi.microsoft.com
- **IBM**  www.ibm.com/services/uddi
- **HP**  http://uddi.hp.com

Visual Studio.NET Beta2 supports UDDI through the possibility to query the UDDI directory and add references to Web Services into client applications. You will see an example of that in the next section.

If you want to programmatically interface with UDDI, you can get the Microsoft UDDI SDK, which consists of a series of both COM and .NET classes to interact with the UDDI registry; you can download it from www.microsoft.com/downloads/release.asp?ReleaseID=30880. Notice, though, that because UDDI is itself a Web Service, you can certainly do everything yourself and interface with it by simply issuing SOAP requests and parsing the SOAP responses from the UDDI server for the information you are looking for.

The industry has put high hopes in UDDI. The functionality of the UDDI registry is still somewhat limited, and the specifications are evolving, but the fact it is so widely supported should encourage you to register yourself, your company, and the Web Services you offer. Best of all, it's free.

# Working with Web Services

In this section, we want to showcase more examples of Web Services, and how the various standards work together. You can find the code of these examples on the CD accompanying this book in the directory soapExamples/. In Chapter 11, we present a fully worked out example of a real-world Web Service based on a three tier architecture.

## Passing Complex Data Types

In this example, you will create a Web method that returns the arithmetic mean of a set of integer valued data points. You can call this method *arithmeticMean* and let it be part of the *simpleService* Web Service started at the beginning of this chapter.

The *arithmeticMean* method takes as argument an integer-valued array of data, called *arrayInput*, and returns a floating point value, as detailed in Figure 11.27.

**Figure 11.27** Web Method to Compute the Arithmetic Mean (simpleService.asmx.cs)

```
01: [SoapDocumentMethodAttribute(Action="arithmeticMean",
02:     RequestNamespace="urn:schemas-syngress-com-soap",
03:     RequestElementName="arithmeticMean",
04:     ResponseNamespace="urn:schemas-syngress-com-soap",
05:     ResponseElementName="arithmeticMeanResponse")]
06: [WebMethod(Description="Computes the " +
07:     "arithmetic means of an array of input parameters")]
08: public float arithmeticMean (int[] arrayInput) {
09:   if ((arrayInput == null) || (arrayInput.Length < 1)) {
10:     throw new Exception("No input data...");
11:   } else {
12:     int sum = 0;
13:     for(int i=0; i<arrayInput.Length; i++) {
14:       sum += arrayInput[i];
15:     }
```

**Continued**

**Figure 11.27** Continued

```
16:      return (float)((float)sum / (float)arrayInput.Length);
17:    }
18: }
```

Note that you've added additional metadata to the method (see Figure 11.27):

- Specify that the *SOAPAction* HTTP header should be the method name, overriding the default, which is the method name, preceded by the namespace of the Web Service class (line 1).

- Specify the namespaces used by SOAP in requests to and responses from this Web method (lines 2 and 4). Namespaces specified at the Web method level overrule namespaces specified at the Web class level. Here, stick with the one you already defined on the class level.

- Set the XML element names used in the SOAP envelope to wrap the method data. As you have seen in the first example of the *echo* Web method, and you don't change this here, by default the method name is used for SOAP requests (line 3), whereas the method name, appended with the string *Response*, is used for SOAP responses (line 5).

- Add a description of the Web method (lines 6 and 7). This shows up, for instance, on the Web Service overview page, as shown in Figure 11.28.

**Figure 11.28** Web Method Descriptions

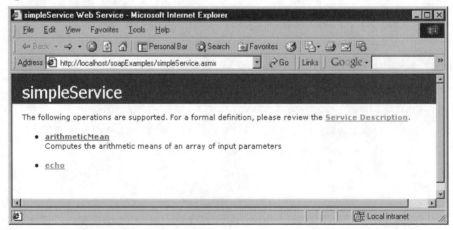

You can start testing the new method by calling it using a simple HTTP *GET*. The individual array input elements are simply appended at the end of the URL—in the example, the numbers 1, 2, and 7:

```
http://localhost/soapExamples/simpleService.asmx/arithmeticMean?
  arrayInput=1&arrayInput=2&arrayInput=7
```

You get the following result:

```
<?xml version="1.0" encoding="utf-8" ?>
<float xmlns="urn:schemas-syngress-com-soap">3.33333325</float>
```

The expected result for the arithmetic mean of 1, 2, and 7 is of course 3.33333333, and not 3.33333325, which shows that you should apparently be more careful when dealing with floating point arithmetic. However, a close inspection of this Web method at runtime using the integrated .NET debugger shows that the correct floating value of 3.333333 is returned from *arithmeticMean*, which seems to indicate that the .NET SOAP serializer adds the strange last two digits to the result before sending it back to the calling client. Hopefully, this behavior will be fixed in the final release.

Calling the method using SOAP, you can go to http://localhost/soapExamples/simpleService.asmx?op=arithmeticMean to figure out the correct syntax of the SOAP request envelope. You can then create a simple Visual Basic script similar to the one in Figure 11.18 (see the file arithmeticMean.vbs on the CD). In Figures 11.29 and Figure 11.30, you can see the SOAP-encoded data being exchanged during a client call to the *arithmeticMean* Web method.

**Figure 11.29** SOAP Request to *arithmeticMean*

```
<?xml version="1.0" encoding="utf-8"?>
<soap:Envelope
  xmlns:xsi="http://www.w3.org/2001/XMLSchema-instance"
  xmlns:xsd="http://www.w3.org/2001/XMLSchema"
  xmlns:soap="http://schemas.xmlsoap.org/soap/envelope/">
  <soap:Body>
    <arithmeticMean xmlns="urn:schemas-syngress-com-soap">
      <arrayInput>
        <int>1</int>
        <int>2</int>
        <int>7</int>
```

Continued

www.syngress.com

**Figure 11.29** Continued

```
        </arrayInput>
    </arithmeticMean>
  </soap:Body>
</soap:Envelope>
```

**Figure 11.30** SOAP Response from *arithmeticMean*

```
<?xml version="1.0"?>
<soap:Envelope
  xmlns:soap="http://schemas.xmlsoap.org/soap/envelope/"
  xmlns:xsi="http://www.w3.org/2001/XMLSchema-instance"
  xmlns:xsd="http://www.w3.org/2001/XMLSchema">
  <soap:Body>
    <arithmeticMeanResponse xmlns="urn:schemas-syngress-com-soap">
      <arithmeticMeanResult>3.33333325</arithmeticMeanResult>
    </arithmeticMeanResponse>
  </soap:Body>
</soap:Envelope>
```

# Error Handling

What happens if something goes wrong? An important part of debugging an application is realizing what can go wrong in the first place. In the case of Web Services, you may frequently encounter three kinds of errors. If you construct the SOAP envelope by hand as opposed to using, say, Web References, your first stab at it will quite likely have some typos—this is the case of a malformed SOAP request. Another frequent error source is that some arguments passed to your Web method are not of the correct type. Finally, something can go wrong during execution of code on the server, and you will need to know how such a server exception is propagated back to the client, in order for you to take appropriate action. The following sections look at those three error scenarios in detail.

## Malformed SOAP Request

Call again the *arithmeticMean* Web method as you did earlier (see Figure 11.29). But this time, change the SOAP envelope in such a way that the XML is no longer valid XML (this shouldn't be too hard). Let's look what happens if you remove the start tag of the last *int* element, as shown in Figure 11.31, line 11.

**Figure 11.31** A Malformed SOAP Request

```
01: <?xml version="1.0" encoding="utf-8"?>
02: <soap:Envelope
03:    xmlns:xsi="http://www.w3.org/2001/XMLSchema-instance"
04:    xmlns:xsd="http://www.w3.org/2001/XMLSchema"
05:    xmlns:soap="http://schemas.xmlsoap.org/soap/envelope/">
06:    <soap:Body>
07:       <arithmeticMean xmlns="urn:schemas-syngress-com-soap">
08:          <arrayInput>
09:             <int>1</int>
10:             <int>2</int>
11:                   7</int>
12:          </arrayInput>
13:       </arithmeticMean>
14:    </soap:Body>
15: </soap:Envelope>
```

You then get a SOAP response that looks like the one shown in Figure 11.32.

**Figure 11.32** SOAP Response Indicating a Malformed Request

```
<?xml version="1.0"?>
<soap:Envelope
   xmlns:soap="http://schemas.xmlsoap.org/soap/envelope/">
   <soap:Body>
     <soap:Fault>
       <faultcode>soap:Client</faultcode>
       <faultstring>System.Web.Services.Protocols.SoapException:
          Server was unable to read request. —&gt; System.Exception:
          There is an error in XML document (7, 21). —&gt;
          System.Xml.XmlException: The 'arrayInput' start tag on line
          '5' does not match the end tag of 'int'. Line 8, position 16.
          at System.Xml.XmlTextReader.ParseTag()
```

*Continued*

**Figure 11.32** Continued

```
        at System.Xml.XmlTextReader.ParseBeginTagExpandCharEntities()
        at System.Xml.XmlTextReader.Read()
        at System.Xml.XmlReader.Skip()
        at System.Xml.Serialization.XmlSerializationReader.
          UnknownNode(Object o)
        at n2499d7d93ffa468fbd8861780677ee41.XmlSerializationReader1.
          Read5_arithmeticMean()
        at System.Xml.Serialization.XmlSerializer.Deserialize
          (XmlReader xmlReader)
        at System.Web.Services.Protocols.SoapServerProtocol.
          ReadParameters()
        at System.Web.Services.Protocols.SoapServerProtocol.
          ReadParameters()
        at System.Web.Services.Protocols.WebServiceHandler.Invoke()
        at System.Web.Services.Protocols.WebServiceHandler.
          CoreProcessRequest()
      </faultstring>
      <detail/>
    </soap:Fault>
  </soap:Body>
</soap:Envelope>
```

What has happened is that the SOAP deserializer on the server noticed that the XML was not valid, threw an exception, and returned a *SOAP Fault*. A SOAP fault is what's returned to the client if an error occurred during program execution on the server. You can check programmatically for a SOAP Fault on the client in two ways:

- SOAP Faults return an HTTP error code 500 (Server error).
- SOAP Faults include the XML element <Fault> in the SOAP return envelope.

Inside the <Fault> element are four standard sections:

- **<faultcode>** Denotes if the error is a client or server error. In the example case of malformed XML, this is a client error. In fact, if you start the debugger in Visual Studio.NET and step through the code as you did in the earlier section on debugging using a client script, you will see that the *arithmeticMean* Web method is never even reached—program execution stops and control is returned to the client during the SOAP deserialization process, before the Web Service class is ever instantiated.

- **<faultstring>** Includes additional information about the error. By default, this contains the call stack at the time the error occurred.

- **<detail>** Where you as an application developer can put additional information about the error. Here, it is empty.

- **<faultactor>** An additional element defined by the SOAP specifications, but not returned by Microsoft .NET in this example.

## Wrong Argument Types

What if you try to pass a float argument to the Web method, that is, if your SOAP request contains the following element?

```
<int>1.1</int>
```

Similar to the malformed XML example earlier, a SOAP Fault is returned by the SOAP deserializer indicating a client fault. This is very powerful—it means that you will rarely have to worry about argument checking, because the .NET runtime environment will do this for you. (You still have to write code on the client to handle this situation appropriately, of course.)

## Exceptions in Server Code

Most often, exceptions will occur during program execution in your Web Service class and objects created by that class on the server. The *arithmeticMean* class, for instance, generates an exception whenever the argument array passed to it is empty.

In Figure 11.33, you see such a SOAP request to *arithmeticMean*: the *arrayInput* argument array containing the integers of which you want to compute the arithmetic mean is empty, and because you did not write your Web method in a robust way, a server error is returned (as shown in Figure 11.34).

**Figure 11.33** SOAP Request to *arithmeticMean*

```
<?xml version="1.0" encoding="utf-8"?>
<soap:Envelope    xmlns:xsi="http://www.w3.org/2001/XMLSchema-instance"
xmlns:xsd="http://www.w3.org/2001/XMLSchema"
```

**Continued**

## Figure 11.33 Continued

```
xmlns:soap="http://schemas.xmlsoap.org/soap/envelope/">
  <soap:Body>
    <arithmeticMean xmlns="urn:schemas-syngress-com-soap">
      <arrayInput/>
    </arithmeticMean>
  </soap:Body>
</soap:Envelope>
```

## Figure 11.34 SOAP Request from *arithmeticMean*

```
<?xml version="1.0"?>
<soap:Envelope xmlns:soap="http://schemas.xmlsoap.org/soap/envelope/">
  <soap:Body>
    <soap:Fault>
      <faultcode>soap:Server</faultcode>
      <faultstring>System.Web.Services.Protocols.SoapException:
        Server was unable to process request.
        --&gt; System.Exception: No input data...
        at soapExamples.simpleService.arithmeticMean
        (Int32[] arrayInput) in
        c:\inetpub\wwwroot\soapexamples\simpleservice.asmx.cs:line 31
      </faultstring>
      <detail/>
    </soap:Fault>
  </soap:Body>
</soap:Envelope>
```

Again, notice how powerful Microsoft .NET is. In the Web class code (Figure 11.27, lines 9 and 10), you just threw a new *System.Exception*, with a custom error message ("No input data…"). .NET then did all the hard work and converted the system error into a SOAP Fault (see Figure 11.34) and even added the error message into the <faultstring> element, even though the formatting is maybe less than perfect. You also see that this time this is a server error (<faultcode>soap:Server</faultcode>), as expected. It turns out that you have fine-grained control over SOAP Faults, and error handling in general.

Finally, note that if you call a Web method through a simple HTTP *GET* (or *POST*) request using a Web browser, depending on the exact request, all you may get could be the bleak browser error page (see Figure 11.35)—another reason to use SOAP from the very beginning!

**Figure 11.35** Not a Very Informative Error Page

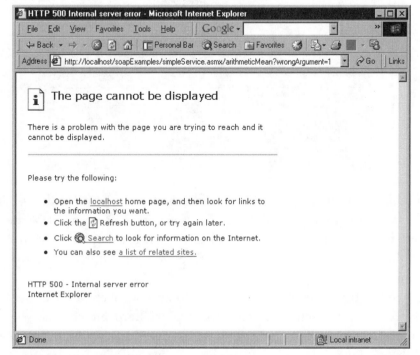

# Writing a SOAP Client Application

Maybe you're a little bit tired by now—manually writing Visual Basic scripts to test your Web Service—and would rather do some pointing and clicking. This is, in fact, possible using Visual Studio.NET, although you lose some control over what's going on by going this route.

Let's then go ahead and create a Windows Forms–based client application for the *echo* Web method of the *simpleService* Web Service. Close the Visual Studio.NET solution you may be working on and create a new C# Windows application by selecting **File | New | Project**, choosing the entry **Windows Application** under the Visual C# Projects folder, and entering **soapExamplesClient** as the Name of the project as shown in Figure 11.36.

**Figure 11.36** Setting Up a New C# Windows Forms Application

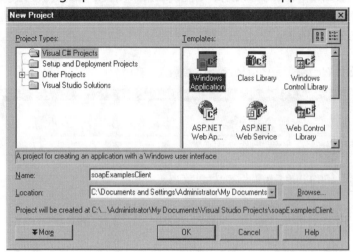

This will set up the necessary project files, and add a new Windows Form called form1.cs. Interestingly, Windows Forms applications do not separate design from code, and you will see references to form elements pop up in your C# code file, even though Visual Studio.NET goes through some efforts trying to "hide" those from you.

You need to teach the client to "know" about your Web Service. Go to the Solution Explorer, right-click the **soapExamplesClient** project, and select **Add Web Reference**. From here you could, for example, query a UDDI registry. Pretend that you didn't know what services are available on your machine, and use the DISCO discovering mechanism exposed under Web References On Local Web Server in the lower-left part of the Add Web Reference window (see Figure 11.37).

After a period of reflection, the DISCO file for your server will appear on the left panel, and the Web Service shows up as Linked Reference Group on the right panel (see Figure 11.38).

Click on the DISCO file, and get to the next window (see Figure 11.39).

You can see the location of the corresponding WSDL file conveniently displayed both within the DISCO file on the left and the listing of Web Services on the right. You can now click **Add Reference** and let Visual Studio.NET contact the Web Service to gather all relevant data about this service through the WSDL mechanism.

**Figure 11.37** The Add Web Reference Window

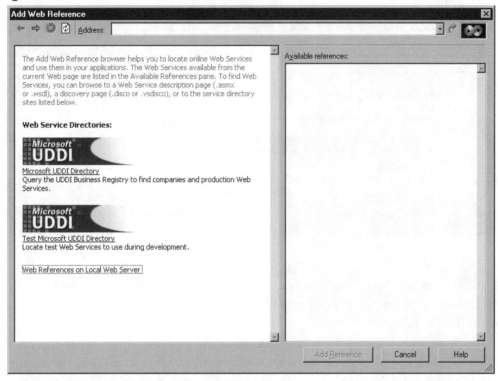

**Figure 11.38** Showing Available Linked Reference Groups through the DISCO Mechanism

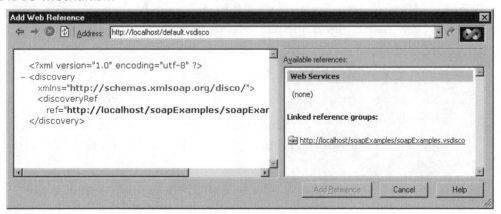

**Figure 11.39** Showing Available Web Services through the DISCO Mechanism

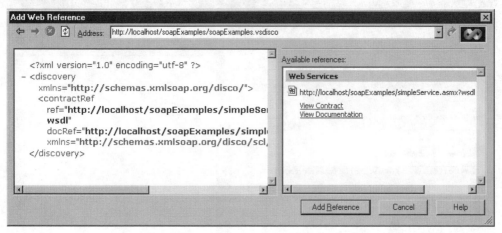

Note that if DISCO fails you, as it has us a few times, just copy and paste the WSDL location (http://localhost/soapExamples/simpleService.asmx?wsdl) directly into the Address input box of the dialog, which is probably the preferred method anyway.

Let's see what Visual Studio.NET has done for you: go to the Solution Explorer, click the **Show All Files** icon to get into expert mode, expand all folders under the Web References folder, select **simpleService.cs**, and click on the **View Code** icon (Microsoft does not make this easy!). What you see is something like Figure 11.40.

What has happened? Visual Studio.NET has generated a *proxy* class for the *simpleService* Web class of the *soapExamples* Web Service. This proxy allows you to do a number of things:

- It has methods to call all methods your referenced Web Service exposes both through synchronous and asynchronous SOAP requests.

- All of the SOAP wire communication, including serializing and deserializing data, is done through the proxy, freeing you from a lot of manual coding.

- It allows you to work with remote Web Services the way you would with local objects, including full IntelliSense support.

**Figure 11.40** A Web Service Proxy

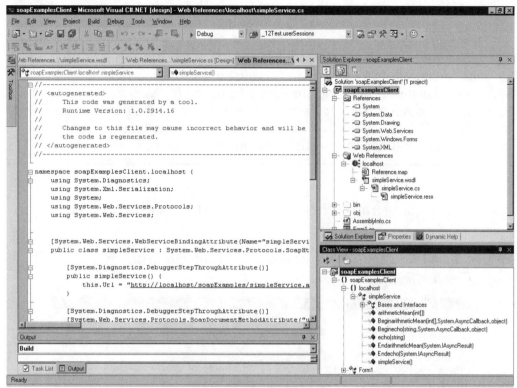

Concretely, it creates the *localhost.simpleService* class, which has the following public methods:

- *echo()* and *arithmeticMean()* to call the corresponding Web methods directly through issuing a (synchronous) SOAP request.

- *Beginecho()* and *BeginarithmeticMean()*, which call the corresponding Web methods through an asynchronous SOAP request. These methods have as an input parameter a reference to a *System.AsyncCallback* delegate which in turn references the callback method to be called when the asynchronous SOAP request has completed.

- Finally, *Endecho()* and *EndarithmeticMean()* are used to return the value of SOAP response after completion of an asynchronous SOAP request.

Note that *simpleService* inherits from the *System.Web.Services.Protocols .SoapHttpClientProtocol* class, where all the heavy lifting occurs to make SOAP calls possible.

---

**W**ARNING

The Web Services proxy that Visual Studio.NET generates for you has some shortcomings in Beta2. For instance, it does not support some of the more standard HTTP codes, such as 302 (Object Moved). In practice, what this means is that if your Web server sends back an HTTP 302 code, the proxy will stop running and throw an exception instead of the correct behavior of following the new URL to the (moved) Web Service. This scenario is not as remote as you might think, because IIS quite frequently sends HTTP 302 codes (see, for example, the "State Information in the Http Header (Cookies)" section later in this chapter).

---

So, let's design a form for the *echo* Web method, like the one shown in Figure 11.41.

**Figure 11.41** Creating a Web Service Client Form (Form1.cs of *soapExamplesClient*)

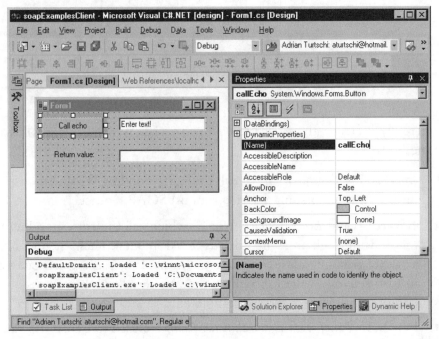

You need to add essentially two lines of code to call the *echo* Web method, as shown in Figure 11.42.

**Figure 11.42** Calling the *echo* Web Method (in Form1.cs of *soapExamplesClient*)

```
private void callEcho_Click(object sender, System.EventArgs e) {
  localhost.simpleService myWebSvc =
    new localhost.simpleService();
  try {
    this.soapReturnEcho.Text =
      myWebSvc.echo(this.enterText.Text);
  } catch (Exception ex) {
    // add error handling here...
  }
}
```

Let Microsoft .NET handle everything else. Running the application, if everything went well, will give you the picture shown in Figure 11.43.

**Figure 11.43** A Happy Web Service Client

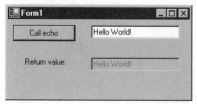

If you want to run this application outside Visual Studio.NET, you will find it at the following location: %USERPROFILE% \Visual Studio Projects\ soapExamplesClient\bin\Debug\.

If you were to analyze HTTP traffic between your Web Service client and server applications using a network monitoring or network tunneling tool, you would see the exact same SOAP envelopes exchanged that you encountered in the earlier section "Testing a Web Service Using a Client Script." For example, TcpTunnelGui, which is an excellent network tunneling tool that ships as part of the Apache SOAP implementation, nicely shows the SOAP exchange as depicted in Figure 11.44.

You can find the complete code for this project on the CD accompanying this book in the directory soapExamplesClient/.

**Figure 11.44** Tunneling the *echo* Web Service to Inspect the SOAP Traffic

```
TCP Tunnel/Monitor: Tunneling localhost:8066 to localhost:80                                    _ □ ×
From localhost:8066                                                           From localhost:80

POST /soapExamples/simpleService.asmx HTTP/1.1              HTTP/1.1 100 Continue
User-Agent: Mozilla/4.0 (compatible; MSIE 6.0; MS Web Services Client Protocol 1.0.2914.'  Server: Microsoft-IIS/5.0
Content-Type: text/xml; charset=utf-8                      Date: Mon, 17 Sep 2001 20:23:19 GMT
SOAPAction: "urn:schemas-syngress-com-soap/echo"
Content-Length: 356                                        HTTP/1.1 200 OK
Expect: 100-continue                                       Server: Microsoft-IIS/5.0
Connection: Keep-Alive                                     Date: Mon, 17 Sep 2001 20:23:19 GMT
Host: localhost                                            Cache-Control: private, max-age=0
                                                           Content-Type: text/xml; charset=utf-8
<?xml version="1.0" encoding="utf-8"?>                     Content-Length: 382
<soap:Envelope xmlns:soap="http://schemas.xmlsoap.org/soap/envelope/" xmlns:xsi="htt
 <soap:Body>                                               <?xml version="1.0" encoding="utf-8"?>
  <echo xmlns="urn:schemas-syngress-com-soap">             <soap:Envelope xmlns:soap="http://schemas.xmlsoap.org/soap/envelope/" xmlns:xsi="htt
   <input>Hello World!</input>                              <soap:Body>
  </echo>                                                    <echoResponse xmlns="urn:schemas-syngress-com-soap">
 </soap:Body>                                                 <echoResult>Hello World!</echoResult>
</soap:Envelope>                                            </echoResponse>
                                                           </soap:Body>
                                                          </soap:Envelope>

                                      Clear

Listening for connections on port 8066 ...
```

# Passing Objects

The *SoapFormatter* class in the *System.Runtime.Serialization.Formatters.Soap* namespace is responsible for serializing and deserializing data according to the SOAP protocol. It is capable of sending and receiving whole objects, in addition to handling simple and complex data types, which you have already seen earlier in this chapter.

As an example, let's construct a simple Web Service that sends performance counter data to a Web client. The *System.Diagnostics* namespace contains the *PerformanceCounter* class, which is perfect for your purposes. You then simply write a Web method that takes as arguments the category, counter, and instance names necessary to instantiate a performance counter object, which you then send as a serialized object over SOAP to potential client applications. Note that valid argument values can be gathered from the Performance Monitor tool that's part of Windows 2000. In Figure 11.45, you see the few lines of code needed to implement such a Web method. Simply add the code to your existing *soapExamples* project.

**Figure 11.45** *getCounterInfo* Web Method (simpleService.asmx.cs)

```
[SoapDocumentMethodAttribute(Action="getCounterInfo",
    RequestNamespace="urn:schemas-syngress-com-soap",
    RequestElementName="getCounterInfo",
    ResponseNamespace="urn:schemas-syngress-com-soap",
    ResponseElementName="getCounterInfoResponse")]
[WebMethod(Description="Returns performance counter information")]
```

**Continued**

**Figure 11.45** Continued

```
public System.Diagnostics.PerformanceCounter getCounterInfo(
  string categoryName, string counterName, string instanceName) {

  System.Diagnostics.PerformanceCounter perfCounter
    = new System.Diagnostics.PerformanceCounter();

  perfCounter.CategoryName = categoryName;
  perfCounter.CounterName = counterName;
  perfCounter.InstanceName = instanceName;

  if (perfCounter.CounterType < 0) {
    // counter is not a valid counter
    throw new Exception("Counter Data Invalid!");
  }

  return perfCounter ;
}
```

As shown, you initiate a new *PerformanceCounter* object using the argument data, check if you have a valid *PerformanceCounter*, and then simply return that object to the calling client. The .NET Framework will then do all the work for you, serializing the object through using a standard format.

If your Web Service client is itself a Microsoft .NET application, you are truly in luck, because the client can then receive the Web Service response as a *PerformanceCounter* object, and not as just an XML document containing SOAP data. Here's how you need to modify the client code:

1. Open again your *soapExamplesClient* client application in Visual Studio.NET.

2. Right-click the **localhost** Web Reference in the Solution Explorer, and select **Update Web Reference**, which will add code to call the **getCounterInfo** Web method you just created to the client proxy (see Figure 11.46).

3. Change the Windows Form a little bit to accommodate the *getCounterInfo* Web method, as in Figure 11.47.

**Figure 11.46** Proxy Code Added for New Performance Counter Web Method (*soapExamplesClient*)

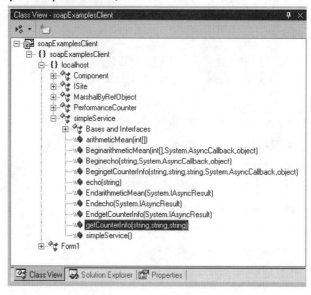

**Figure 11.47** Adding Elements on the Windows Form for the *getCounterInfo* method (Form1.cs in *soapExamplesClient*)

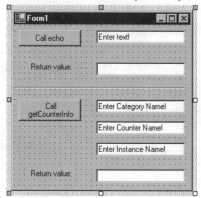

4. Add the necessary code to call the *getCounterInfo* Web method (see Figure 11.48).

**Figure 11.48** Calling the *getCounterInfo* Web Method (Form1.cs in *soapExamplesClient*)

```
private void callGetCounterInfo_Click(
  object sender, System.EventArgs e) {

  localhost.simpleService myWebSvc =
    new localhost.simpleService();
  try {
    this.soapReturnGetCounterInfo.Text =
      myWebSvc.getCounterInfo(
      this.categoryName.Text,
      this.counterName.Text,
      this.instanceName.Text).RawValue.ToString();
  } catch (Exception ex) {
  }
}
```

Note that the *getCounterInfo* Web method returns an object of type *PerformanceCounter*, as IntelliSense correctly tells us (see Figure 11.49).

**Figure 11.49** Microsoft's IntelliSense in Action

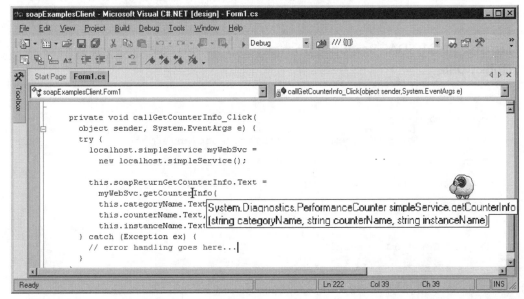

5. After compiling the application, you are now able to expose, say, the size of available physical memory to the world, as depicted in Figure 11.50. Obviously, you should probably now secure this Web Service (see the "Security" section later in this chapter).

**Figure 11.50** Exposing Performance Information through a Web Service

If the Web Service client does not run on the Microsoft .NET platform, however, more work is needed. In this case, as a client application developer, you can either define a class matching the return type and extend the SOAP deserializer to handle that class type correctly, or as a last resort, you can always manually parse the SOAP return envelope for the data you are interested in.

To illustrate what's going on behind the scenes, let's look at the SOAP envelope passed back to the client in the Web Service response (see Figure 11.51).

**Figure 11.51** SOAP Response from *getCounterInfo* Passing Back Serialized Object Data

```
<?xml version="1.0"?>
<soap:Envelope
  xmlns:soap="http://schemas.xmlsoap.org/soap/envelope/"
  xmlns:xsi="http://www.w3.org/2001/XMLSchema-instance"
  xmlns:xsd="http://www.w3.org/2001/XMLSchema">
  <soap:Body>
    <getCounterInfoResponse xmlns="urn:schemas-syngress-com-soap">
      <getCounterInfoResult>
        <Site xsi:nil="true"/>
        <CategoryName>Memory</CategoryName>
```

**Continued**

**Figure 11.51** Continued

```
        <CounterName>Available KBytes</CounterName>
        <RawValue>25080</RawValue>
      </getCounterInfoResult>
    </getCounterInfoResponse>
  </soap:Body>
</soap:Envelope>
```

As you see, the various properties of the *PerformanceCounter* class are serialized as XML elements, with their values being converted to a string format and added as text nodes. If you are sending your objects instantiated from your own classes, you can achieve finer control over how they are being serialized by using the *XmlAttributeAttribute* and *XmlElementAttribute* classes found in the *System.Xml .Serialization* namespace. In the same namespace, you also find classes that let you manipulate the XML namespaces used during the serialization process.

The opposite is also possible: If you already have an XML schema that you would like SOAP to use for data transfer, you can then take advantage of the XML Schema Definition Tool xsd.exe, found in %ProgramFiles%\ Microsoft.NET\FrameworkSDK\Bin\, to generate the corresponding .NET classes to support that schema. However, as you have seen in Chapter 6, there are some restrictions on what kind of objects can be serialized in Beta 2.

# Passing Relational Data

An interesting special case of passing objects over SOAP is passing back data coming from a relational database, such as *DataSets*. The .NET SOAP serializer, which is the piece of code that puts your data in XML format to be sent back inside a SOAP return envelope, can indeed serialize *DataSets* out of the box.

Let's have a look what happens under the hood, by writing a simple Web method that queries Microsoft's Northwind database for all data in the Shippers table and returns a serialized *DataSet* (note that you cannot serialize a *DataTable* using the default serializer). The code is in Figure 11.52, and also on the CD in directory chapter11/rsTest/.

**Figure 11.52** Code to Return a *DataSet* from the Northwind Database (rsTest.asmx.cs)

```
using System;

using System.ComponentModel;

using System.Data;

using System.Data.SqlClient;

using System.Web;

using System.Web.Services;

using System.Web.Services.Protocols;


namespace rsTest

{

  [WebServiceAttribute(Namespace="urn:schemas-syngress-com-soap")]

  public class rsTest : System.Web.Services.WebService

  {

    public rsTest() {

    }


    [SoapDocumentMethodAttribute(Action="returnRS",

        RequestNamespace="urn:schemas-syngress-com-soap:rsTest",

        RequestElementName="returnRS",

        ResponseNamespace="urn:schemas-syngress-com-soap:rsTest",

        ResponseElementName="returnRSResponse")]

    [WebMethod]

    public DataSet returnRS() {

      try {

        string sqlConnectionString =

          "server=(local)\\NetSDK;database=Northwind;User

ID=SA;Password=";

        SqlDataAdapter sqlDataAdapter = new SqlDataAdapter(

            "SELECT * FROM shippers", sqlConnectionString);

        DataSet shippers = new DataSet();

        sqlDataAdapter.Fill(shippers, "shippers");

        return shippers;

      }
```

**Continued**

**Figure 11.52** Continued

```
    catch (Exception e) {
      throw e;
    }
  }
}
}
```

When you now call the Web method *returnRS*, you get the SOAP envelope as in Figure 11.53, which looks complicated indeed! If you study the XML returned in detail, you will notice that the XML contains an XML Schema definition section for the *DataSet* returned, followed by the actual data, which consists of three shipping company records.

**Figure 11.53** SOAP Encoded *DataSet* Returned from Northwind Database

```
<?xml version="1.0" encoding="utf-8"?>
<DataSet xmlns="urn:schemas-syngress-com-soap">
  <xsd:schema id="NewDataSet" targetNamespace=""
    xmlns="" xmlns:xsd="http://www.w3.org/2001/XMLSchema"
    xmlns:msdata="urn:schemas-microsoft-com:xml-msdata">
    <xsd:element name="NewDataSet" msdata:IsDataSet="true">
      <xsd:complexType>
        <xsd:choice maxOccurs="unbounded">
          <xsd:element name="shippers">
            <xsd:complexType>
              <xsd:sequence>
                <xsd:element name="ShipperID"
                  type="xsd:int" minOccurs="0" />
                <xsd:element name="CompanyName"
                  type="xsd:string" minOccurs="0" />
                <xsd:element name="Phone"
                  type="xsd:string" minOccurs="0" />
              </xsd:sequence>
            </xsd:complexType>
          </xsd:element>
```

Continued

## Figure 11.53 Continued

```
        </xsd:choice>
      </xsd:complexType>
    </xsd:element>
  </xsd:schema>
  <diffgr:diffgram
    xmlns:msdata="urn:schemas-microsoft-com:xml-msdata"
    xmlns:diffgr="urn:schemas-microsoft-com:xml-diffgram-v1">
    <NewDataSet xmlns="">
      <shippers diffgr:id="shippers1" msdata:rowOrder="0">
        <ShipperID>1</ShipperID>
        <CompanyName>Speedy Express</CompanyName>
        <Phone>(503) 555-9831</Phone>
      </shippers>
      <shippers diffgr:id="shippers2" msdata:rowOrder="1">
        <ShipperID>2</ShipperID>
        <CompanyName>United Package</CompanyName>
        <Phone>(503) 555-3199</Phone>
      </shippers>
      <shippers diffgr:id="shippers3" msdata:rowOrder="2">
        <ShipperID>3</ShipperID>
        <CompanyName>Federal Shipping</CompanyName>
        <Phone>(503) 555-9931</Phone>
      </shippers>
    </NewDataSet>
  </diffgr:diffgram>
</DataSet>
```

If your client is running Microsoft .NET software, you're in luck: The client will automatically reassemble the SOAP response into a *DataSet* that you can then use to continue processing. However, there are potential (business!) clients on the Internet who do not and never will run on a Microsoft platform. For those, the XML in Figure 11.53 is hard to parse. Theoretically, this should be possible, because the XML does contain the XML Schema definition needed to understand and reassemble the data, but in practice, few people would want to deal with such a monstrosity.

Our advice, then, is to shy away from passing data coming from a database as Microsoft *DataSets*, unless you really, really know that the only clients ever to consume your Web Services will be Microsoft clients, running, preferably, on the .NET platform.

# Passing XML Documents

So far we have focused on using Web Services as an RPC (remote procedure call) mechanism. Although the data being exchanged through SOAP has of course been in the form of XML documents all along, it was the data being exchanged and not the XML document as such that we were interested in so far.

There are cases, however, when you will just want to exchange XML documents between a client and a server; these XML documents could be invoices, tagged magazine articles, your own custom data encoding scheme, and so on. Often, these XML documents being exchanged will have an associated schema against which they will be validated.

The example shown in Figure 11.54 is a simple service that accepts an XML document and returns the same XML document, adding only an XML attribute *dateProcessed* to the XML root element, indicating when the XML was processed. It is part of the *simpleService* Web Service.

**Figure 11.54** *xmlTester* Web Method (simpleService.asmx.cs)

```
01: [SoapDocumentMethodAttribute(Action="xmlTester",
02:      RequestNamespace="urn:schemas-syngress-com-soap",
03:      ResponseNamespace="urn:schemas-syngress-com-soap",
04:      ParameterStyle = SoapParameterStyle.Bare)]
05: [WebMethod(Description="XML echo service that " +
06:      "adds a dateProcessed attribute.")]
07: [return: XmlAnyElement]
08: public XmlElement xmlTester(
09:    [XmlAnyElement]XmlElement inputXML){
10:
11:    inputXML.SetAttribute("dateProcessed",
12:      System.DateTime.Now.ToUniversalTime().ToString("r"));
13:    return inputXML;
14: }
```

Note you've added the instruction:

```
ParameterStyle = SoapParameterStyle.Bare
```

to the *SoapDocumentMethodAttribute* section (Figure 11.54, line 4), specifying that the XML document that is the argument for the *xmlTester* Web method should appear directly beneath the *Body* element of the SOAP request envelope, and that you don't want an intermediate XML element in the SOAP response either.

When you run *xmlTester* through Visual Studio.NET, you will see that this Web method can be called only through SOAP (see Figure 11.55), which makes sense because you can't pass an XML document through a simple HTTP *GET* or HTTP *POST*.

**Figure 11.55** The Overview Page for the *xmlTester* Web Method

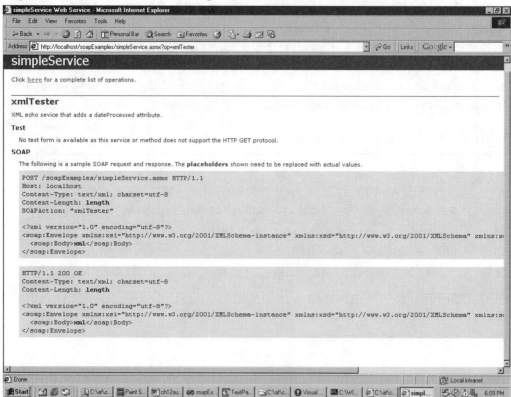

You can test this service by writing a Visual Basic script similar to the ones you created earlier in this chapter (see Figure 11.56). When running this script, you can observe the SOAP data exchange taking place as shown in Figures 11.57

and 11.58. Note the additional attribute *dateProcessed* in Figure 11.58, shown in bold, that was added through the Web *xmlTester* method.

**Figure 11.56** VBS Script to Test the *xmlTester* Web Method (xmlTester.vbs)

```
myWebService = "http://localhost/soapExamples/simpleService.asmx"
myMethod = "xmlTester"


'** create the SOAP envelope with the request
s = ""
s = s & "<?xml version=""1.0"" encoding=""utf-8""?>" & vbCrLf
s = s & "<soap:Envelope "
s = s & "  xmlns:xsi=""http://www.w3.org/2001/XMLSchema-instance"""
s = s & "  xmlns:xsd=""http://www.w3.org/2001/XMLSchema"""
s = s & "  xmlns:soap=""http://schemas.xmlsoap.org/soap/envelope/"">"
s = s & vbCrLf
s = s & "  <soap:Body>" & vbCrLf
s = s & "    <rootElement>" & vbCrLf
s = s & "      <someNode someAttribute=""random"">" & vbCrLf
s = s & "        <someOtherNode>some data</someOtherNode>" & vbCrLf
s = s & "      </someNode>" & vbCrLf
s = s & "    </rootElement>" & vbCrLf
s = s & "  </soap:Body>" & vbCrLf
s = s & "</soap:Envelope>" & vbCrLf


msgbox(s)


set requestHTTP = CreateObject("Microsoft.XMLHTTP")


msgbox("xmlhttp object created")


requestHTTP.open "POST", myWebService, false
requestHTTP.setrequestheader "Content-Type", "text/xml"
requestHTTP.setrequestheader "SOAPAction", myMethod
requestHTTP.Send s
```

*Continued*

**Figure 11.56** Continued

```
msgbox("request sent")


set responseDocument = requestHTTP.responseXML


msgbox("http return status code: " & requestHTTP.status)
msgbox(responseDocument.xml)
```

**Figure 11.57** SOAP Request to *xmlTester* Web Method

```
<?xml version="1.0" encoding="utf-8"?>
<soap:Envelope
  xmlns:xsi="http://www.w3.org/2001/XMLSchema-instance"
  xmlns:xsd="http://www.w3.org/2001/XMLSchema"
  xmlns:soap="http://schemas.xmlsoap.org/soap/envelope/">
  <soap:Body>
    <rootElement>
      <someNode someAttribute="random">
        <someOtherNode>some data</someOtherNode>
      </someNode>
    </rootElement>
  </soap:Body>
</soap:Envelope>
```

**Figure 11.58** SOAP Response from *xmlTester* Web Method

```
<?xml version="1.0"?>
<soap:Envelope
  xmlns:soap="http://schemas.xmlsoap.org/soap/envelope/"
  xmlns:xsi="http://www.w3.org/2001/XMLSchema-instance"
  xmlns:xsd="http://www.w3.org/2001/XMLSchema">
  <soap:Body>
    <rootElement dateProcessed="Tue, 18 Sep 2001 22:15:55 GMT">
      <someNode someAttribute="random">
        <someOtherNode>some data</someOtherNode>
```

**Continued**

**Figure 11.58** Continued

```
        </someNode>
    </rootElement>
  </soap:Body>
</soap:Envelope>
```

Obviously, this is only the very tip of the iceberg. The ability to send generic XML documents back and forth is a powerful feature of SOAP. In passing, we mention that a related standard called *SOAP Messages With Attachments* (www.w3.org/TR/SOAP-attachments) defines a way to pass generic files (binary or text) using SOAP as MIME-encoded attachments. However, the Microsoft .NET Framework does not currently support this standard.

# Working with UDDI

The UDDI registry of Web Services is still in its infancy, and quite frankly, there are not a lot of useful Web Services out there at the time of writing this book. But there are some, and as UDDI seems to be the direction the industry is heading, let's write a simple client application that calls a publicly available third-party Web Service that exposes data about climate conditions of international airports. You can find the complete code for this client application in the directory uddiClient/ in the CD accompanying the book.

You can start by creating a new Windows Forms–based application called *uddiClient*. Query the UDDI registry as follows:

1.  Go to the Solution Explorer, right-click the **uddiClient** project, and select **Add Web Reference**.

2.  Click **Microsoft UDDI Directory** on the left side of the dialog.

3.  Visual Studio.NET will take you to http://uddi.microsoft.com/, and ask you to enter the name of the business publishing the service. Enter **Cape Clear Software**, an early adopter of Web Service technologies (see Figure 11.59).

4.  UDDI will return a page indicating that it has found Web Services published by Cape Clear Software (see Figure 11.60), among them the Airport Weather Check service. Expand that Web Service, and click the **tModel** hyperlink. Note that if you are interested in the internal structure of UDDI, you will usually find the information relevant for you as a developer under the tModel entries.

**Figure 11.59** Searching for a Business in the UDDI Directory

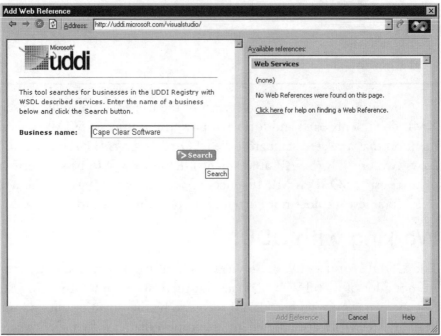

**Figure 11.60** Selecting a Web Service in UDDI

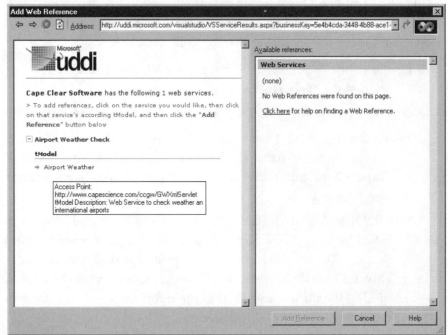

5. The tModel contains a link to the WSDL, which will show up on the left panel of the dialog; the right panel tells you that you have one available (Web) reference (see Figure 11.61).

**Figure 11.61** Displaying the WSDL Description of a Third-Party Web Service in UDDI

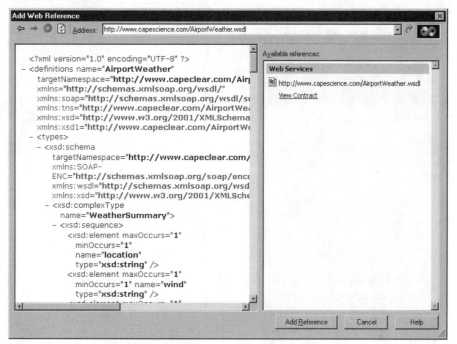

6. Click **Add Reference**. This will create the necessary local client proxy classes to call the AirportWeather Web Service.

If you check what has happened in Visual Studio Class View, you see that a new proxy class com.capescience.www.AirportWeather has been added, with a number of methods returning weather-related information of international airports (see Figure 11.62).

**Figure 11.62** Proxy Classes for the AirportWeather Web Service

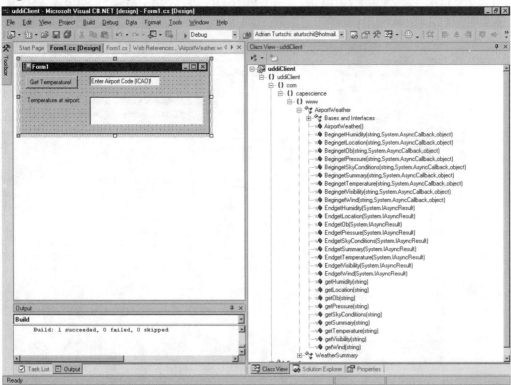

You are just interested in temperature information, maybe, so you can set up a little Windows form to test the service (see Figure 11.62). The code to call the Web Service is shown in Figure 11.63.

**Figure 11.63** Calling the *getTemperature* Web Method (Form1.cs of *uddiClient*)

```
private void getTemperature_Click(
  object sender, System.EventArgs e) {
  try {
    com.capescience.www.AirportWeather airportWeather =
      new com.capescience.www.AirportWeather();
    airportTemperature.Text =
```

**Continued**

**Figure 11.63** Continued

```
    airportWeather.getTemperature(enterAirportCode.Text);
} catch(Exception ex) {
  // error handling goes here...
}
}
```

One question you may be asking is how do we know the *semantics* of this Web method? After all, the code block invoking the *getTemperature* method looks as in Figure 11.64, that is, the argument to the method is named, rather unfortunately, *arg0*.

**Figure 11.64** The *getTemperature* Web Method Definition (AirportWeather.cs of *uddiClient*)

```
public string getTemperature(string arg0) {
    object[] results = this.Invoke("getTemperature", new object[] {
                arg0});
    return ((string)(results[0]));
}
```

Consulting the WSDL description (see file AirportWeather.wsdl) of this method also doesn't help, because the authors did not include any <description> XML elements. The answer, then, is to either contact the business that published this Web Service (UDDI does include such information), or hope that a Web page exists out there describing what the Web Service does and what the parameters *mean*. Luckily, in the case of AirportWeather, such a Web page really exists at www.capescience.com/webservices/airportweather/index.html.

You can now test your application by requesting the current temperature at New York's JFK airport, as shown in Figure 11.65. Unfortunately, the authors of this Web Service want you to use the ICAO rather than the more familiar IATA airport codes, but you can get your favorite airport's code at www.ar-group.com/Airport-Locator.asp.

We note in passing that there's another slight problem with the Web method, in that it returns a string that contains all the relevant information, but that is difficult to parse if all you really want is the temperature information. Returning a complex XML structure might have been a better design decision.

**Figure 11.65** The AirportWeather Web Service in Action

Finally, let's look at the data exchanged on the level of the SOAP protocol, as seen through a TCP tunneling tool: Figure 11.66 shows the SOAP request to find the current temperature at JFK Airport; Figure 11.67 shows the SOAP response with the relevant data in bold (72F).

**Figure 11.66** SOAP Request to Get the Temperature at JFK

```
POST /ccgw/GWXmlServlet HTTP/1.1

User-Agent: Mozilla/4.0

  (compatible; MSIE 6.0; MS Web Services Client Protocol 1.0.2914.16)

Content-Type: text/xml; charset=utf-8

SOAPAction: "capeconnect:AirportWeather:com.capeclear.

  weatherstation.Station#getTemperature"

Content-Length: 630

Expect: 100-continue

Connection: Keep-Alive

Host: localhost


<?xml version="1.0" encoding="utf-8"?>

<soap:Envelope

  xmlns:soap="http://schemas.xmlsoap.org/soap/envelope/"

  xmlns:soapenc="http://schemas.xmlsoap.org/soap/encoding/"

  xmlns:tns="http://tempuri.org/"

  xmlns:types="http://tempuri.org/encodedTypes"

  xmlns:xsi="http://www.w3.org/2001/XMLSchema-instance"

  xmlns:xsd="http://www.w3.org/2001/XMLSchema">

  <soap:Body

    soap:encodingStyle="http://schemas.xmlsoap.org/soap/encoding/">

    <q1:getTemperature xmlns:q1="capeconnect:AirportWeather:com.
```

*Continued*

**Figure 11.66** Continued

```
      capeclear.weatherstation.Station">
        <arg0 xsi:type="xsd:string">KJFK</arg0>
    </q1:getTemperature>
  </soap:Body>
</soap:Envelope>
```

**Figure 11.67** SOAP Response with the Temperature at JFK

```
HTTP/1.0 200 OK
Content-Type: text/xml; charset=UTF-8
Content-Length: 601
SOAPAction: "capeconnect:AirportWeather:com.capeclear.
  weatherstation.Station#getTemperature"
Servlet-Engine: CapeConnect/2.1 (Orcas/4.3; Tomcat Web Server/3.2.1)

<?xml version="1.0"?>
<SOAP-ENV:Envelope
  xmlns:xsd="http://www.w3.org/2001/XMLSchema"
  xmlns:SOAP-ENV="http://schemas.xmlsoap.org/soap/envelope/"
  xmlns:xsi="http://www.w3.org/2001/XMLSchema-instance"
  xmlns:SOAP-ENC="http://schemas.xmlsoap.org/soap/encoding/">
  <SOAP-ENV:Body>
    <cc1:getTemperatureResponse xmlns:cc1="capeconnect:
      AirportWeather:com.capeclear.weatherstation.Station">
      <return  xsi:type="xsd:string">The Temperature at  New York,
        Kennedy International Airport, NY, United States is
        72.0 F (22.2 C)
      </return>
    </cc1:getTemperatureResponse>
  </SOAP-ENV:Body>
</SOAP-ENV:Envelope>
```

## SOAP Headers

Similar to the way the HTTP protocol has a header section that contains general information about the request and a body section that contains specific application data relevant to the request, the SOAP protocol specifies that the SOAP envelope has both a header and a body section. So far, you have only seen examples of SOAP requests (and responses) that had *Body* elements, but no *Header* elements. That's because a SOAP *Body* element is required, whereas a SOAP *Header* element is not. In fact, SOAP headers were designed to give SOAP an extension mechanism.

The SOAP *Header* element appears right underneath the SOAP *Envelope* element, and you're free to define your header name and header value, and what it means to have such a SOAP header present. As an example, you could encode transaction information in a SOAP header. In the "Maintaining State" section to follow, we show you a possible usage of SOAP headers as a mechanism to establish a notion of a client session, and we discuss what classes in the .NET Framework you have to use to handle SOAP headers.

# Advanced Web Services

Web Services were designed to be, above all, simple—simple to implement, and simple to use. Simplicity has its price, however, and there are a variety of features that you won't find in Web Services—features that are part of older, more established data exchange protocols, such as COM/DCOM or CORBA. Such features include state management, security, and transaction processing.

You need to realize that programming on the Internet is different than programming on a private network. Expecting the two to be the same would be wrong. You don't have the same level of control on the Internet that you have on a local area network, and it is clear that data communication on the Internet will mean having less direct control, and allowing for more things to go wrong. You should therefore not expect to be able to implement a complex real-time transactional system involving ten transaction partners using SOAP—at least not today.

Let's look at two problem areas you are likely to encounter when developing real-world Web Services. First, the question of whether to maintain state or not, and if yes, how, and secondly how to handle security.

# Maintaining State

Our suggestion is to not try to introduce state in Web Service applications, at least for the time being. If you consider where state has traditionally been introduced in Web applications, the most prominent area is probably in e-commerce with the usage of so-called shopping carts. Clearly, you should not try to write a Web Service shopping cart application. Another area is security. We discuss security later in the chapter, but good alternatives exist to having explicitly stateful applications in that area as well. In all other areas, introducing state is almost always a bad idea. Considering that Web Services were designed to let distributed systems talk to each other in a *loosely coupled* way, state just doesn't seem to fit the picture quite right from an architectural point of view. Still, you have a variety of options to add state, which we discuss next.

Let's first briefly review the options you have in architecting stateful Web applications.

HTTP, the protocol underlying Web applications, is an inherently stateless protocol. A client issues a request against a server, which in turn issues a response. Every client request is seen by the server as a new request, not connected to any previous request. Technically, the client issues an HTTP request by opening a TCP/IP socket connection to the server, issues a request using the HTTP protocol, gets some data from the server, and then closes the socket. The next HTTP request will be issued using a new TCP/IP socket connection, making it impossible for the server to understand, on the protocol level, that the second request may really be the continuation of the first request. Note that the keep-alive function in HTTP does not change this picture, because it is geared mainly towards making the retrieval of Web pages containing many individual page elements more efficient, but it does not guarantee in any way that a network connection to the server is maintained over any longer period of time.

Introducing state means that you add logic on the server to be able to relate a previous request from a particular client to a subsequent request from the same client. This is being done by introducing information that identifies a particular client to the HTTP request and response data, and developing *application level* code that makes sense of that additional data. Saying that a client establishes a *session* with a server just means that you have application logic that connects several client requests to a logical session using that additional information, even though, because of the nature of the HTTP protocol, there is no physical equivalent to a session (i.e., no ongoing network connection over the lifetime of a client-server interaction).

Looking at the HTTP protocol, there are three places where you may add state information identifying a client:

- The URL against which the request is issued (the first line in an HTTP request)

- The header part of an HTTP request (including cookies)

- The body part of an HTTP request

And the two latter possibilities hold for HTTP responses as well. We look at some examples in the following sections. You can find the code about maintaining state in the directory sessionTest/ on the CD that comes with this book.

## State Information in the URL (URL Mangling)

You can maintain state information by adding a unique client session identifier to the URL. Microsoft's Passport service uses this method to assign and maintain client session authentication information. ASP.NET natively supports this method through a configuration entry in the config.web file. The advantage of this method is that it is very scalable, supports Web farms and Web gardens, can be configured to survive IIS restarts without losing session information, and that you have the option of saving client information on an external SQL Server database. Technically, what happens is that a Web application that is configured to map state information to URLs will redirect a new incoming client request using an HTTP 302 status code (Found) to a new URL that contains a session identifier. Here's how it works:

1. Set the **cookieless** attribute of the **session** element in the web.config ASP.NET configuration file to **True**.

2. Create a new Web method with an attribute **EnableSession** set to **True**, and use the *System.Web.HttpContext.Current.Session* object (or *Web.Service.Session*, which amounts to the same object):

```
[WebMethod(EnableSession=true)]
public string sessionTest__URL() {
  if (Session["HitCounter"] == null) {
    Session["HitCounter"] = 1;
  } else {
    Session["HitCounter"] = ((int) Session["HitCounter"]) + 1;
  }
```

```
        return (Session["HitCounter"].ToString());
    }
```

Let's look what happens on the HTTP protocol level if a client calls this method twice. You can look at the HTTP data exchange by using a TCP tunneling tool. Here we have used TcpTunnelGui, which ships as part of the Apache Project's SOAP implementation, but you can, of course, easily write your own TCP tunnel program using the .NET Framework (do it—it's a great exercise!).

You can call the Web Service through a simple HTTP *GET* request (we ignore some of the irrelevant HTTP headers). In the first call, the client issues an HTTP *GET*:

```
GET /sessionTest/sessionTest.asmx/sessionTest__URL HTTP/1.1
Host: localhost
Connection: Keep-Alive
```

Server issues an HTTP 302 (Moved) to a URL that contains the session identifier:

```
HTTP/1.1 302 Found
Server: Microsoft-IIS/5.0
Date: Wed, 12 Sep 2001 22:14:21 GMT
Location: /sessionTest/(bf33go2yvicwfhbragscdwvu)/
   sessionTest.asmx/sessionTest__URL
Cache-Control: private
Content-Type: text/html; charset=utf-8
Content-Length: 176


<html><head><title>Object moved</title></head><body>
<h2>Object moved to
<a href='/sessionTest/(bf33go2yvicwfhbragscdwvu)/
   sessionTest.asmx/sessionTest__URL'>
here</a>.</h2></body></html>
```

Client reissues an HTTP *GET* for the new URL:

```
GET /sessionTest/(bf33go2yvicwfhbragscdwvu)/
   sessionTest.asmx/sessionTest__URL HTTP/1.1
Host: localhost
```

```
Connection: Keep-Alive
```

Server send back the SOAP response:

```
HTTP/1.1 200 OK
Server: Microsoft-IIS/5.0
Date: Wed, 12 Sep 2001 22:14:21 GMT
Cache-Control: private, max-age=0
Content-Type: text/xml; charset=utf-8
Content-Length: 96


<?xml version="1.0" encoding="utf-8"?>
<string xmlns="urn:schemas-syngress-com-soap">1</string>
```

In the second call, the client issues an HTTP *GET* (using the modified URL):

```
GET /sessionTest/(bf33go2yvicwfhbragscdwvu)/
  sessionTest.asmx/sessionTest__URL HTTP/1.1
Host: localhost
Connection: Keep-Alive
```

The server responds, incrementing the session hit counter:

```
HTTP/1.1 200 OK
Server: Microsoft-IIS/5.0
Date: Wed, 12 Sep 2001 22:14:30 GMT
Cache-Control: private, max-age=0
Content-Type: text/xml; charset=utf-8
Content-Length: 96


<?xml version="1.0" encoding="utf-8"?>
<string xmlns="urn:schemas-syngress-com-soap">2</string>
```

So far, so good. The problem with implementing session state for Web Services this way is that you need to teach your Web Service client application two things:

- They need to follow HTTP 302 messages.
- When issuing a follow-up request, they should either use relative URLs, or they should remember changed URLs through HTTP 302 codes.

Both constraints are hard to implement, and somewhat contrary to the underpinnings of the Web Services philosophy. Basically, you require your Web Service clients to be very smart, as smart, indeed, as a Web browser is. None of the current Web Service clients is currently capable of supporting this functionality, and that includes the .NET Web Service proxy.

# State Information in the Http Header (Cookies)

You can add state information in additional HTTP headers. This is used in two common scenarios:

- **Authentication** The various authentication schemes, such as Basic Authentication, Windows NTLM-based authentication, Kerberos-based authentication, and others, work by sending an additional Authentication header element between client and server. Typically, the client sends credential information to the server, which then verifies the information received, may ask for additional information, and finally answers by returning a session key (which is still sent in the Authentication header field), that is then used by all subsequent client requests to access protected server resources.

- **Cookies** Cookies are pieces of data that are persisted on the client computer. They are stored and received using an additional HTTP header element called *Cookie*.

ASP.NET has improved session handling using cookies; similarly to the "cookieless" session management explained in the preceding section, it now supports cookie-based sessions that scale well, support Web farms and Web gardens, and it can save client information away in a remote database out-of-the-box. Let's look at an example using cookies to store state information:

1. Set the **cookieless** attribute of the **session** element in the web.config ASP.NET configuration file to **False**.

2. Create a new Web method with an attribute **EnableSession** set to **True**, and use the *System.Web.HttpContext.Current.Session object* (or use the *Web.Service.Session* object):

```
[WebMethod(EnableSession=true)]
public string sessionTest__httpHeader() {
   if (Session["HitCounter"] == null) {
     Session["HitCounter"] = 1;
```

```
        } else {
          Session["HitCounter"] = ((int) Session["HitCounter"]) + 1;
        }
        return (Session["HitCounter"].ToString());
    }
```

Let's look what happens on the HTTP protocol level if a client calls this method twice. You can call the Web Service through a simple HTTP GET request (we ignore some of the irrelevant HTTP headers). In the first call, the client issues an HTTP *GET*:

```
GET /sessionTest/sessionTest.asmx/sessionTest__httpHeader HTTP/1.1
Host: localhost
Connection: Keep-Alive
```

The server sends back the SOAP response, including a *Cookie* header requesting the client to set a session cookie:

```
HTTP/1.1 200 OK
Server: Microsoft-IIS/5.0
Date: Thu, 13 Sep 2001 17:58:09 GMT
Transfer-Encoding: chunked
Set-Cookie: ASP.NET_SessionId=znbmf0mqcufv4p45s204wp45; path=/
Cache-Control: private, max-age=0
Content-Type: text/xml; charset=utf-8

<?xml version="1.0" encoding="utf-8"?>
<string xmlns="urn:schemas-syngress-com-soap">1</string>
```

In the second call, the client issues an HTTP *GET*, and sends the session *Cookie* header received form the server in the previous call:

```
GET /sessionTest/sessionTest.asmx/sessionTest__httpHeader HTTP/1.1
Host: localhost
Connection: Keep-Alive
Cookie: ASP.NET_SessionId=znbmf0mqcufv4p45s204wp45
```

The server responds, incrementing the session hit counter (the *Cookie* header is not sent again, because the server retrieved the *Cookie* header in the HTTP request from the client, so it knows that the client honored its cookie request from the first response):

```
HTTP/1.1 200 OK
Server: Microsoft-IIS/5.0
Date: Thu, 13 Sep 2001 17:58:20 GMT
Cache-Control: private, max-age=0
Content-Type: text/xml; charset=utf-8
Content-Length: 96


<?xml version="1.0" encoding="utf-8"?>
<string xmlns="urn:schemas-syngress-com-soap">2</string>
```

However, if you want to encode session state information into cookies, you need to insist that all your Web Service clients are capable of handling cookies correctly. Only very few potential consumers will probably be willing to add that functionality to their client applications because, again, cookies really belong into the domain of Web browsers, and seem strange in a Web Service client application.

On the other hand, you could certainly add session state information in a custom HTTP header (maybe called *webState*?). This would require manually adding code to both the Web Service server to clients to correctly handle that additional header element. Even worse, WSDL, the Web Service description format, has no provisions to support such new, required HTTP headers.

## State Information in the Http Body (SOAP Header)

The last possibility, finally, is to embed state information into the HTTP body itself. This method really only makes sense if you use SOAP to call your Web Service (as opposed to issuing simple HTTP *GET* or *POST* requests).

SOAP indeed does have the option of adding custom SOAP headers into the SOAP envelope. Note that a SOAP header is *not* the same as an HTTP header; it is a header relative to the SOAP message, that is it appears within the HTTP body, inside the SOAP envelope.

There is currently no support for keeping client state information in SOAP headers in ASP.NET, so you need to do everything yourself. Let's try then to re-create a simple hit counter using SOAP headers. You need to implement the following:

- Name your SOAP header element: call it *webState*.

- Create a class that can handle your SOAP header on the server.
- Create a class on the server that records and maintains all client sessions, using a static hash table.

Let's look at the server code (see Figure 11.68).

**Figure 11.68** Implementing a Hit Counter Using SOAP Headers

```
01: using System;
02: using System.Collections;
03: using System.ComponentModel;
04: using System.Data;
05: using System.Diagnostics;
06: using System.Web;
07: using System.Web.Services;
08: using System.Web.Services.Protocols;
09: using System.Runtime.InteropServices;
10:
11: namespace sessionTest {
12:    [WebServiceAttribute(
13:       Namespace="urn:schemas-syngress-com-soap")]
14:    public class sessionTest : System.Web.Services.WebService {
15:      public sessionTest() {
16:      }
17:
18:      protected override void Dispose( bool disposing ) {
19:      }
20:
21:      public class soapHeader : SoapHeader {
22:         public string webState;
23:      }
24:
25:      public soapHeader mySoapHeader;
26:      public static Hashtable userSessions = new Hashtable();
27:
28:      [SoapDocumentMethodAttribute(Action="sessionTest__soapHeader",
```

**Continued**

**Figure 11.68** Continued

```
29:        RequestNamespace=
30:          "urn:schemas-syngress-com-soap:sessionTestst",
31:         RequestElementName="sessionTest__soapHeader",
32:         ResponseNamespace=
33:          "urn:schemas-syngress-com-soap:sessionTestst",
34:         ResponseElementName="sessionTest__soapHeaderResponse")]
35:      [SoapHeader("mySoapHeader",Direction=SoapHeaderDirection.InOut,
36:         Required=true)]
37:      [WebMethod]
38:      public string sessionTest__soapHeader() {
39:        // declare user session hit counter
40:        int hitCounter;
41:        // declare session identifier
42:         string sessionID;
43:
44:         if ((mySoapHeader.webState == null) ||
45:           (mySoapHeader.webState.Trim().Length < 1)){
46:          // create a new random session identifier
47:          sessionID = System.Guid.NewGuid().ToString().ToUpper();
48:         hitCounter = 1;
49:          // create a new user session, and set hit counter to one
50:          userSessions.Add(sessionID, hitCounter);
51:          // return session identifier to user
52:          mySoapHeader.webState = sessionID;
53:        } else {
54:          // valid user session?
55:          sessionID = mySoapHeader.webState.ToString().Trim();
56:          if(userSessions[sessionID] != null) {
57:            // get session hit counter
58:           hitCounter = (int)userSessions[sessionID];
59:           // save away incremented session hit counter
60:           userSessions[sessionID] = ++hitCounter;
61:         } else {
```

**Continued**

**Figure 11.68** Continued

```
62:           // session identifier passed was invalid
63:           // throw error
64:           throw new Exception("Invalid session identifier
passed!");
65:       }
66:     }
67:     // return session counter
68:     return hitCounter.ToString();
69:   }
70:
71:  }
72: }
```

Note the following important elements in the code shown in Figure 11.68:

- It includes a class *soapHeader* (line 21–23), which extends *System.Web.Services.Protocols.SoapHeader*, with a public string variable called *webState* (line 22), which is the SOAP header that should contain your client state identifier. The code calls the corresponding Web Service class instance variable *mySoapHeader* (line 25).

- The code includes a static hash table called *userSessions*, which will contain the collection of all client sessions (line 26).

- It includes the Web method *sessionTest__soapHeader* (line 38) with the attribute *SoapHeader*, (lines 35–36), where you specify that you *require* the *webState* SOAP header, and that this SOAP header is bidirectional. This means that if a client does not send you this SOAP header, the .NET Framework will send a SOAP fault to the client, and you don't need to code for that possibility yourself.

- Because you want to tell your clients what session identifier to use in subsequent requests, you return the new session identifier in the same *webState* SOAP header (line 68).

On the client side, because you require the presence of the *webState* SOAP header, you need to initialize this header before issuing the SOAP request. That is, if you write a client using Web references, your call to the *sessionTest__soapHeader* Web method will look like this:

```
testClient.localhost.sessionTest myClient =

  new sessionTestClient.localhost.sessionTest();

myClient.soapHeaderValue = new testClient.localhost.soapHeader();

string result = myClient.sessionTest__soapHeader();
```

The following code is a sample client server interaction using the SOAP protocol (ignoring HTTP headers). In the first call, the client issues an SOAP request, leaving *the* webState SOAP header empty:

```
<?xml version="1.0" encoding="utf-8"?>

<soap:Envelope xmlns:xsi="http://www.w3.org/2001/XMLSchema-instance"

  xmlns:xsd="http://www.w3.org/2001/XMLSchema"

  xmlns:soap="http://schemas.xmlsoap.org/soap/envelope/">

  <soap:Header>

    <soapHeader xmlns="urn:schemas-syngress-com-soap">

      <webState></webState>

    </soapHeader>

  </soap:Header>

  <soap:Body>

    <sessionTest__soapHeader

      xmlns="urn:schemas-syngress-com-soap:sessionTest">

    </sessionTest__soapHeader>

  </soap:Body>

</soap:Envelope>
```

The server sends back the SOAP response, including the *webState* SOAP header element with the new session identifier:

```
<?xml version="1.0" encoding="utf-8"?>

<soap:Envelope xmlns:soap="http://schemas.xmlsoap.org/soap/envelope/"

  xmlns:xsi="http://www.w3.org/2001/XMLSchema-instance"

  xmlns:xsd="http://www.w3.org/2001/XMLSchema">

  <soap:Header>

    <soapHeader xmlns="urn:schemas-syngress-com-soap">

      <webState>{45D345B6-BE1F-434F-BFD7-D628C756A432}</webState>

    </soapHeader>

  </soap:Header>
```

```
<soap:Body>

  <sessionTest__soapHeaderResponse

    xmlns="urn:schemas-syngress-com-soap:sessionTestst">

    <sessionTest__soapHeaderResult>1</sessionTest__soapHeaderResult>

  </sessionTest__soapHeaderResponse>

</soap:Body>

</soap:Envelope>
```

In the second call, the client issues another SOAP request, and sends the session identifier in the *webState* SOAP header received form the server in the previous response:

```
<?xml version="1.0" encoding="utf-8"?>

<soap:Envelope xmlns:xsi="http://www.w3.org/2001/XMLSchema-instance"

  xmlns:xsd="http://www.w3.org/2001/XMLSchema"

  xmlns:soap="http://schemas.xmlsoap.org/soap/envelope/">

  <soap:Header>

    <soapHeader xmlns="urn:schemas-syngress-com-soap">

      <webState>{45D345B6-BE1F-434F-BFD7-D628C756A432}

      </webState>

    </soapHeader>

  </soap:Header>

  <soap:Body>

    <sessionTest__soapHeader

      xmlns="urn:schemas-syngress-com-soap:sessionTest">

    </sessionTest__soapHeader>

  </soap:Body>

</soap:Envelope>
```

The server responds, incrementing the session hit counter:

```
<?xml version="1.0" encoding="utf-8"?>

<soap:Envelope xmlns:soap="http://schemas.xmlsoap.org/soap/envelope/"

  xmlns:xsi="http://www.w3.org/2001/XMLSchema-instance"

  xmlns:xsd="http://www.w3.org/2001/XMLSchema">

  <soap:Header>

    <soapHeader xmlns="urn:schemas-syngress-com-soap">
```

```
            <webState>{45D345B6-BE1F-434F-BFD7-D628C756A432}</webState>
        </soapHeader>
    </soap:Header>
    <soap:Body>
        <sessionTest__soapHeaderResponse
            xmlns="urn:schemas-syngress-com-soap:sessionTestst">
            <sessionTest__soapHeaderResult>2</sessionTest__soapHeaderResult>
        </sessionTest__soapHeaderResponse>
    </soap:Body>
</soap:Envelope>
```

If you look at the WSDL description of this Web Service, shown in Figure 11.69, notice that it requests the client to send a *webState* SOAP header, and that this header is required. However, as always, the WSDL file does not contain semantic information helping a client to send a correct request. In other words, although it does instruct clients to include this SOAP header, it does not tell them what it means, or how to properly use it. This is a task that you, as a developer, have to do.

Also, note that the WSDL file does not contain HTTP *GET* and HTTP *POST* bindings for this Web Service. This is because those two methods of calling Web Services do not work when SOAP headers are required.

**Figure 11.69** WSDL Description of the *sessionTest__soapHeader* Web Method

```
<?xml version="1.0" encoding="utf-8"?>
<definitions xmlns:s="http://www.w3.org/2001/XMLSchema"
  xmlns:http="http://schemas.xmlsoap.org/wsdl/http/"
  xmlns:mime="http://schemas.xmlsoap.org/wsdl/mime/"
  xmlns:tm="http://microsoft.com/wsdl/mime/textMatching/"
  xmlns:soap="http://schemas.xmlsoap.org/wsdl/soap/"
  xmlns:soapenc="http://schemas.xmlsoap.org/soap/encoding/"
  xmlns:s0="urn:schemas-syngress-com-soap:sessionTest"
  xmlns:s1="urn:schemas-syngress-com-soap"
  targetNamespace="urn:schemas-syngress-com-soap"
  xmlns="http://schemas.xmlsoap.org/wsdl/">

<types>
```

**Continued**

**Figure 11.69** Continued

```
<s:schema attributeFormDefault="qualified"
  elementFormDefault="qualified"
  targetNamespace="urn:schemas-syngress-com-soap:sessionTest">
  <s:element name="sessionTest__soapHeader">
    <s:complexType />
  </s:element>
  <s:element name="sessionTest__soapHeaderResponse">
    <s:complexType>
      <s:sequence>
        <s:element minOccurs="1" maxOccurs="1"
          name="sessionTest__soapHeaderResult"
          nillable="true" type="s:string" />
      </s:sequence>
    </s:complexType>
  </s:element>
</s:schema>
<s:schema attributeFormDefault="qualified"
  elementFormDefault="qualified"
  targetNamespace="urn:schemas-syngress-com-soap">
  <s:element name="soapHeader" type="s1:soapHeader" />
  <s:complexType name="soapHeader">
    <s:sequence>
      <s:element minOccurs="1" maxOccurs="1" name="webState"
        nillable="true" type="s:string" />
    </s:sequence>
  </s:complexType>
  <s:element name="string" nillable="true" type="s:string" />
</s:schema>
</types>
<message name="sessionTest__soapHeaderSoapIn">
  <part name="parameters" element="s0:sessionTest__soapHeader" />
</message>
<message name="sessionTest__soapHeaderSoapOut">
```

**Continued**

**Figure 11.69** Continued

```
    <part name="parameters"
    element="s0:sessionTest__soapHeaderResponse" />
  </message>
  <message name="sessionTest__soapHeadersoapHeader">
    <part name="soapHeader" element="s1:soapHeader" />
  </message>
  <portType name="_sessionTestSoap">
    <operation name="sessionTest__soapHeader">
      <input message="s1:sessionTest__soapHeaderSoapIn" />
      <output message="s1:sessionTest__soapHeaderSoapOut" />
    </operation>
  </portType>
  <binding name="_sessionTestSoap" type="s1:_sessionTestSoap">
    <soap:binding transport="http://schemas.xmlsoap.org/soap/http"
    style="document" />
    <operation name="sessionTest__soapHeader">
      <soap:operation soapAction="sessionTest__soapHeader"
      style="document" />
      <input>
        <soap:body use="literal" />
        <soap:header n1:required="true"
    message="s1:sessionTest__soapHeadersoapHeader" part="soapHeader"
    use="literal" xmlns:n1="http://schemas.xmlsoap.org/wsdl/" />
      </input>
      <output>
        <soap:body use="literal" />
        <soap:header n1:required="true"
    message="s1:sessionTest__soapHeadersoapHeader" part="soapHeader"
    use="literal" xmlns:n1="http://schemas.xmlsoap.org/wsdl/" />
      </output>
    </operation>
  </binding>
  <service name="_sessionTest">
```

**Continued**

**Figure 11.69** Continued

```
   <port name="_sessionTestSoap" binding="s1:_sessionTestSoap">
      <soap:address=location="
        http://localhost/sessionTest/sessionTest.asmx" />
   </port>
  </service>
</definitions>
```

Again, we recommend you think twice (ten times?) before programming stateful Web Services. If you decide to go ahead introducing state, we would advise doing it through SOAP headers, because it seems to be the most natural option you have, and because it is reflected in the WSDL description of your Web Service.

The preceding example should give you a good starting point. However, as you no doubt noticed, the example still needs a bit of work, in particular:

- Although you can add new user sessions, you should have code that is capable of deleting user session information after a certain amount of time (otherwise your memory will eventually fill up to capacity).

- It would be nice to be able to persist user information in a database like MS SQL, the way ASP.NET can do it, and then add a trigger to go off after a specified amount of time cleaning the expired sessions.

- You should add functionality to support Web farms and Web gardens (which, again, ASP.NET does support).

# Security

The SOAP specification does not touch security. You can look at this as a plus, because it keeps the standard small and implementable. RPC protocols that do define security, such as CORBA and COM/DCOM are far more complicated, harder to implement, and don't work well on the Internet. On the other hand, as a developer, you obviously shouldn't ignore security altogether. In the end, you have two possibilities:

- Leverage the security features made available by IIS and ASP.NET.
- Do it yourself.

If you go with the first option, you can secure your Web Services by using the security features of IIS, such as Basic Authentication (probably over SSL), NTLM, or Kerberos-based authentication if you are on an intranet, or authentication-based on Public Key Cryptography (PKC) using client certificates. The latter is particularly interesting for Windows 2000 developers because Active Directory allows you to automatically map client certificates to user accounts if your certificates are issued by a Windows 2000 Certificate Server that's a member of your enterprise domain forest. Note that for this to work, your clients don't need to run on a Windows platform.

Additionally, you can use features provided by ASP.NET on top of what you can do on the HTTP protocol level. ASP.NET allows you to use Microsoft Passport to authenticate users, although you will have to pay licensing fees if you want to go down this route. Note that .NET myServices (previously code-named Hailstorm), Microsoft's own Web Service offering in the making, is based on Passport.

ASP.NET also allows you to grant and deny users of your services every imaginable kind of rights once they have been authenticated (this is called *authorization*).

Yet another interesting option is to use SOAP Digital Signature. Also based on PKC, it enables you to digitally sign the body of a SOAP envelope and to include the signature information in a special SOAP header. This does not actually encrypt the SOAP message, but it does guarantee its integrity, that is, you know that nobody has changed its content as it traveled from one machine to another. See www.w3.org/TR/SOAP-dsig/ for more information.

Security in the context of Web Services is still very much an evolving area and is currently far from well understood. You can find more information in an article that recently appeared in *XML-Journal* ("Securing and Authenticating SOAP Based Web Services," by M. Moore and A. Turtschi, XML-Journal, volume 2, issue 9).

# Summary

Web Services is a new technology designed primarily to facilitate communications between enterprises on the Internet. Web Services are supported by all major software vendors, and are based on Internet standards:

- HTTP as the network protocol (among others)
- XML to encode data
- SOAP as the wire transport protocol
- WSDL to describe Web Service syntax
- UDDI to publish Web Service information

Microsoft's .NET Framework is based on Web Services, and Visual Studio.NET is an excellent platform to develop Web Services. Web Services are different from previous technologies used to create distributed systems, such as COM/DCOM, in that:

- They use open standards.
- They were designed from the ground up to work on the Internet, including working well with corporate firewalls.
- They use a "simple" protocol not requiring multiple round trips to the server.
- They purposefully don't address advanced features such as security or transaction support as part of the protocol specification.

We showed you a variety of examples of Web Services exchanging simple and complex types of data. In addition to using SOAP based Web Services as an RPC (Remote Procedure Call) mechanism, you can use SOAP to exchange any type of XML documents. We explained the basic structure of the SOAP protocol: SOAP exchanges an XML document called a SOAP Envelope, which has two parts:

- The SOAP Header, which is designed to be extended to include application-specific metadata, such as security- or session-related identifiers.
- The SOAP Body, which contains the necessary information to find a class and method on the server to handle the Web Service request, in addition to parameter data that may be necessary to process such a request.

The SOAP specification defines a number of XML encoding schemes for different data types, such as strings, integers, floats, arrays, enumerations, and so on. SOAP also includes a mechanisms for error handling.

We showed you how to call Web Services using standalone Visual Basic scripts, client-side script in a Web browser, and through creating Windows Forms–based applications. Visual Studio.NET includes tools that create client proxies for (remote) Web Services for you, greatly simplifying the effort of developing Web Service client applications.

Finally, we talked about two advanced topics that are not directly part of the Web Services standards, but that are nevertheless important for developers, namely security and state management. We recommend to use standard security mechanisms such as SSL and public key cryptography, and to forgo state management until Web Service clients are more robust.

# Solutions Fast Track

## The Case for Web Services

- ☑ Web Services are a new Internet standard, supported by all major vendors, to facilitate data exchange across system boundaries.

- ☑ Standards include a wire protocol (SOAP), a way to describe services (WSDL), and a way to publish services (UDDI).

## Web Service Standards

- ☑ Web Services are classes that extend *System.Web.Services.WebService*.

- ☑ A method becomes a Web method by decorating it with *[System.Web.Services.WebMethod]*.

- ☑ Visual Studio.NET includes a powerful debugger.

- ☑ Once you are in debug mode, external programs calling your Web Service *will* go through the debugger.

- ☑ Writing a Visual Basic script to call your Web Service through SOAP is a fast, easy way to test your application.

- ☑ Visual Studio.NET tells you the correct format of the SOAP request envelope when you open the Web Service overview page:

    http://serverName/webServiceProjectName/
webServiceName?op=webMethodName.

# Working with Web Services

☑ SOAP can encode arrays, enumerations, and so on. You are rarely directly exposed to the complexities of the underlying protocols because Visual Studio.NET does most of the work for you.

☑ Error handling is seamless. Microsoft .NET lets you work with SOAP errors the way you work with any other exceptions.

☑ Adding a Web reference lets you use remote Web Services the way you would use local objects, including IntelliSense support, hiding all complexities of SOAP from you.

☑ Visual Studio.NET will automatically add client proxy code into your solution.

☑ You add a Web reference by pointing to the WSDL description of the Web Service.

☑ You can find WSDL files through DISCO or UDDI.

☑ SOAP lets you pass instantiated objects between clients and servers. If both the client and the server application run on the .NET platform, the communication is seamless.

☑ You can pass any kind of XML through SOAP. This is particularly relevant for interenterprise and third-party integration applications.

☑ Visual Studio.NET integrates nicely with UDDI. You can find third-party Web Services and add them to your solutions without ever leaving the development environment.

# Advanced Web Services

☑ SOAP itself does not contain a state management mechanism.

☑ Web Services should be stateless, even more so than traditional Web applications.

☑ If you really do need state information, you may want to look into using SOAP headers.

☑ The SOAP protocol does not address security.

☑ Use the mechanisms provided by the underlying network protocols, such as encrypting your network channel (HTTPS) and using Public Key Cryptography (certificates).

# Frequently Asked Questions

The following Frequently Asked Questions, answered by the authors of this book, are designed to both measure your understanding of the concepts presented in this chapter and to assist you with real-life implementation of these concepts. To have your questions about this chapter answered by the author, browse to **www.syngress.com/solutions** and click on the **"Ask the Author"** form.

**Q:** Can I consume Web Services in .NET that have been written in other languages?

**A:** That's the idea! Web Services define a standard to pass data between heterogeneous systems over the Internet. If you are writing a Web Service client in .NET, you don't have to worry what language the Web Service you are consuming has been written in, or on what platform it is running.

**Q:** Can Web Services pass binary data efficiently?

**A:** Yes and no. Web Services are based on XML, and thus the emphasis is maybe more on textual data. You can add binary data as CDATA sections in your XML documents you are sending. However, probably a better way is to add binary data as MIME-encoded attachments to your SOAP calls (see the proposed SOAP Messages With Attachments standard at www.w3.org/TR/SOAP-attachments). Note, though, that .NET Web Services do not currently support attachments out of the box. If you are sending large amounts of binary data, you may want to look into compressing the data you are sending.

**Q:** Is registration to UDDI free?

**A:** Yes, at the moment it is.

**Q:** Where can I find more information about the business case for Web Services, and how Web Services compare with other distributed technologies such as COM/DCOM, CORBA, and EJBs?

**A:** A good starting point is Orchestra Network's white paper at www.orchestranetworks.com/us/solutions/0105_whitepaper.cfm.

**Q:** Where can I find more examples of Web Services?

**A:** Visit Visual Studio.NET's CodeSwap site at www.vscodeswap.com/. XMethods has a large repository of publicly available Web Services at www.xmethods.net/.

**Q:** Where can I find a list of SOAP implementations?

**A:** Paul Kulchenko maintains a list on his Perl::Lite site at www.soaplite.com/#Toolkits.

**Q:** Where can I find more information about how the various implementations of SOAP-based Web Services interoperate?

**A:** XMethods maintains the SOAPBuilders Interoperability Lab at www.xmethods.net/ilab/. You can also find an excellent overview article discussing the various aspects of interoperability at www-106.ibm.com/developerworks/webservices/library/ws-asio/?dwzone=webservices.

# Chapter 12

# Building a Jokes Web Service

## Solutions in this chapter:

- **Motivation and Requirements for the Jokes Web Service**
- **Functional Application Design**
- **Implementing the Jokes Data Repository**
- **Implementing the Jokes Middle Tier**
- **Creating a Client Application**

☑ **Summary**

☑ **Solutions Fast Track**

☑ **Frequently Asked Questions**

# Introduction

In this chapter, we show you—step-by-step—how to build a real-world Web Service, using all the tools and techniques covered in the previous chapters. This Web Service case study will take you through all the important factors to be considered when creating a Web Service application. Together, we create a two-tier Web Service consisting of the following:

- A business logic layer (middle tier) written in C#
- A database backend using SQL Server 2000

We also show you how to access this service through a Windows Forms-based front-end portal application. While developing this application, we cover a range of subjects relevant to real-world Web Service projects. We start off by offering some suggestions for proper Web Service application architecture. We then discuss how to pass structured data from your Web Service to your client application, including basic marshalling and complex object serialization. We talk about namespaces and extended Web Service attributes, and how to properly use them. Further topics include how to secure Web Services, how to generate client proxies, error handling both on the server and on the client, working with Event Logs, and the automatic generation of documentation.

# Motivation and Requirements for the Jokes Web Service

In the case study presented by this chapter, we won't be showing you an ordering application for buying or selling anything, instead we're giving away free content in the form of jokes. Think of our application of the future as a modern version of the venerable Quote Of The Day (*quotd*) Internet service. *Quotd* has been around for almost two decades, used mostly as a TCP/IP test service (see www.faqs.org/rfcs/rfc865.html). It runs on port 17, and all it does is send you an uplifting quote of some wise dead person, before closing the connection again. You can install it as part of the so-called "Simple TCP/IP Services" through **Control Panel | Add/Remove Programs | Add/Remove Windows Components | Networking Services**. Many servers on the Internet still have this service installed, even though it has maybe fallen out of favor in recent years; for an example, simply use Telnet to establish a TCP connection to port 17 of server 209.21.91.3.

Let's try to formulate some design goals for the Jokes Web Service, and see how they compare with what was possible twenty years ago when *quotd* was designed:

- Although we still give away free content, we would like to know who our users are! Hence, there should be some sort of registration process.

- We want to be highly interactive. We are interested in user feedback for particular jokes, and our users should also be able to add content—that is, jokes—of their own. However, too much interactivity can be a dangerous thing, so there should be moderators standing by to remove objectionable content.

- *Quotd* is essentially a 7-bit ASCII service (in fact it's limited to the 94 printable ASCII characters). That's great if you live in the U.S., but even Europeans will already be a little bit annoyed at you, because their accented characters will get lost, and users in Asia won't be able to use the service in their native language. Clearly, we want *our* updated service to fully support Unicode.

- Our service should be universally accessible. *Quotd* is usually blocked by firewalls because it uses a nonstandard port.

To summarize, we would like to develop a Web Service that delivers jokes to registered users, has portal functionality to let users register, and allows them to submit their own jokes. Moreover, we want a mechanism for registered users to rate jokes, say on a scale from 1 to 5. Finally, there should be a class of super users, called moderators, who should be able to administer both users und jokes.

Note that we get support for international users and universal accessibility for free by using Web Services technology:

- Because Web Services are based on XML, we can ensure Unicode support by specifying, say, UTF-8 as our underlying character set (which is the default, anyway). Also, we need to ensure, of course, that our data repository can hold Unicode information.

- Because Web Services usually run on either port 80 (HTTP) or port 443 (HTTPS), firewalls should not be a problem, and clients should be able to establish a connection to our server. However, when designing the service, we also need to ensure that the data we transport through SOAP can easily be read by potential clients, particularly if they run on non-Microsoft systems. We talk about this issue more when we go about sending SQL record data through SOAP.

# Functional Application Design

Coming up with a good application design is critically important for the success of any software application. The first step is to move top-down from goals to design by starting to define (in still very general terms) the functionality exposed by the Jokes service, and then developing a back-end schema that supports that functionality from a data perspective. In a second step, we then create in more detail an object model suitable to implement the services the Jokes application is supposed to provide. At this juncture, it is also appropriate to make decisions about security, state management, and error handling.

# Defining Public Methods

Let's start the application design process by writing down the specific methods we think our Jokes Web Service should offer, and the categories that reflect their function. The application needs methods dealing with user administration:

- **addUser**  Lets a user register to our service.

- **addModerator**  Lets a moderator add an existing user to become a moderator.

- **checkUser**  Verifies that a user has previously registered with the service. Refer to the "State Management" section to see why this is a useful method for the service to expose.

Then, the application needs methods dealing with delivering and managing jokes:

- **addJoke**  Lets a registered user add a joke.

- **getJokes**: Delivers some randomly selected jokes, say up to 10 per request,  to our registered users.

- **addRating**  Lets our users add a rating to a joke, say on a scale of 1–5.

- **getUnmoderated**  Registered moderators can call this method to get the jokes added by the users for moderation.

- **addModerated**  If moderators agree to add a joke to the database, they can use this method.

- **deletedUnmoderated**  If a submitted joke is considered offensive, a moderator should be able to delete it.

# Defining the Database Schema

Let's define the database schema for the Jokes Web Service: The Jokes database supports three basic data entities: users, jokes, and joke ratings. We therefore define the corresponding tables as follows:

- **users**  A table containing user information.

- **jokes**  A table containing joke information.

- **ratings**  A table containing joke rating information.

To keep things simple, all we want to know about our users are their user-names, their passwords, and whether they are moderators or not. We limit both usernames and passwords to 20 Unicode characters. We add a primary key constraint to usernames to speed lookup access and to ensure that usernames are unique.

For the jokes table, we record the username and the actual joke, which we want to be 3,500 Unicode characters or less, keeping SQL Server 2000 limitations on row size in mind. We give each joke a unique identifier though an identity column. Note that we don't relate the users and the jokes table with each other, because users may choose to unsubscribe from the service (but we sure want to keep their jokes!).

Finally, we add a rating column to the ratings table and relate the jokes to the ratings table through a one-to-many relationship on the unique joke identifier. Let's look at a visual representation of our jokes database (see Figure 12.1).

**Figure 12.1** The Jokes Database Tables

**users**

| Column Name | Data Type | Length | Allow Nulls |
|---|---|---|---|
| userName | nvarchar | 20 | |
| password | nvarchar | 20 | |
| isModerator | bit | 1 | |

FK__ratings__jokeID__0425A276

**jokes**

| Column Name | Data Type | Length | Allow Nulls |
|---|---|---|---|
| jokeID | int | 4 | |
| joke | nvarchar | 3500 | |
| userName | nvarchar | 20 | |
| isModerated | bit | 1 | |

**ratings**

| Column Name | Data Type | Length | Allow Nulls |
|---|---|---|---|
| jokeID | int | 4 | |
| rating | tinyint | 1 | |

# Defining the Web Service Architecture

Typically, the actual Web Service layer will be a very small layer of your application. You expose the Web Service methods to your clients, but leave the implementation of those methods to internal implementation classes. The advantage of this architecture is that you can then always change the implementation of your Web Services in the future, while keeping the Web Service interface stable. Nothing is more annoying to consumers of your service (your business clients, that is) than if a change in your server-side code requires them to rewrite their applications. Also, typically, you will already have code on your servers that handles most or all of the business logic required to process client requests; this could be code to access legacy systems or enterprise data. You then simply wrap this already existing code in a lean layer of Web Service access code.

In our example of the Jokes Web Service, we are going to define two Web Services, one to handle the portal aspects of our application, that is managing users and moderators, and a second one dealing with managing and retrieving the actual jokes. We could, of course, collapse these two Web Services easily into one larger service, and there are certainly good arguments for doing so, but keeping the two services apart allows us to architect our application in a nice, symmetric way.

We then define the two corresponding implementation classes, one for user administration, and the other one for handling the jokes. Additionally, we need classes for error management and database access, and a class that allows us to return structured data containing our jokes to clients of our service.

To visualize the architecture, you can use a tool such as Microsoft Visual Modeler. The UML diagram of the class structure looks as follows, ignoring method signature and a few other details, such as destruction methods you don't care about too much at this point (see Figure 12.2).

Let's first look at the details of the *userAdmin* Web Service (see Figure 12.3).

As you can see in the figure, the *userAdmin* class, which exposes the Web Service of the same name, has methods to add a new user, make an existing user become a moderator, and verify that a given user does in fact exist in the system. The class *userAdminImplement* contains implementations of the corresponding methods, and also contains methods that wrap the SQL stored procedures defined in the previous section. Now take a look at the details of the Jokes Web Service in Figure 12.4.

**Figure 12.2** UML Diagram of *jokesService* Middle Tier Architecture

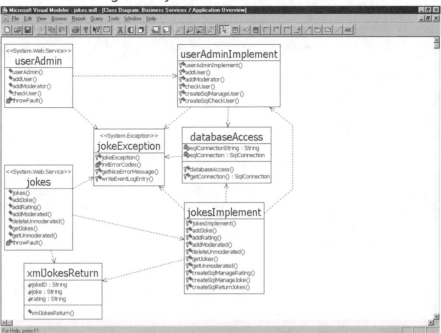

**Figure 12.3** Detailed UML Diagram of *userAdmin* Web Service

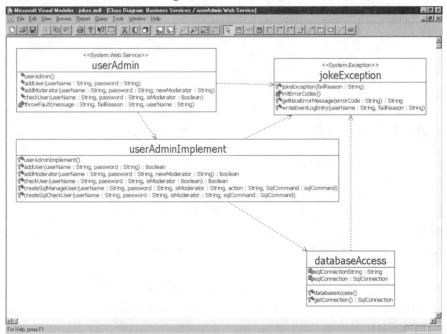

## Figure 12.4 Detailed UML Diagram of the Jokes Web Service

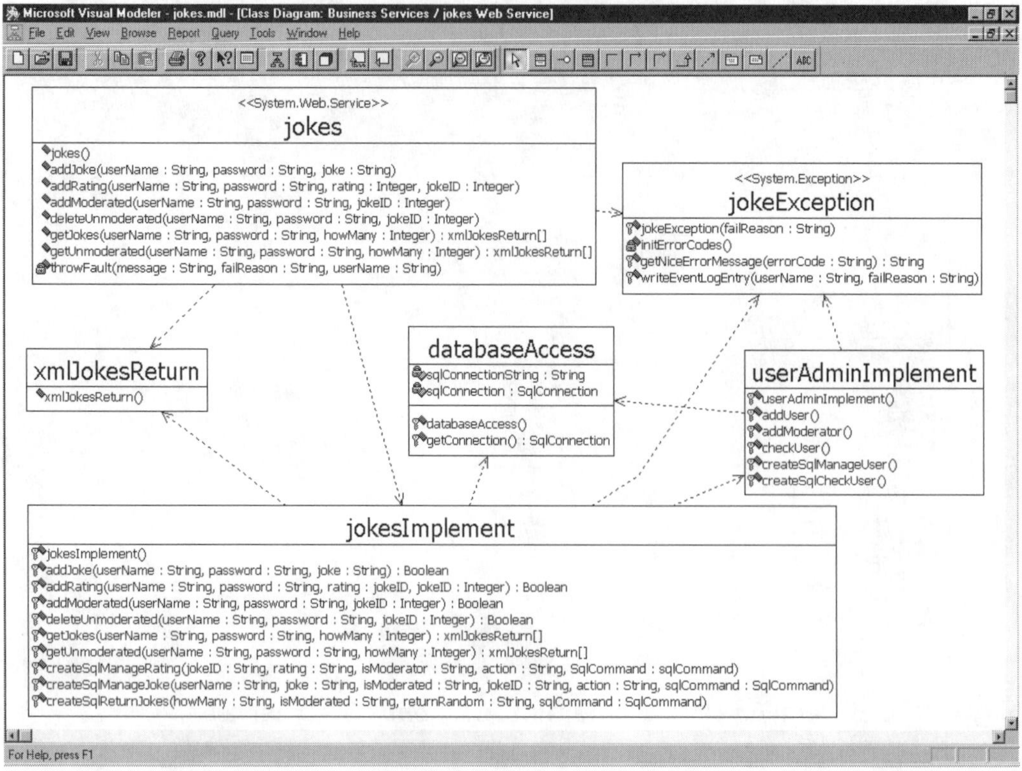

The *jokes* class, which exposes the Web Service of the same name, has methods to add, manage, and retrieve jokes. The class *jokesImplement* contains implementations of the corresponding methods, and also contains methods that wrap the SQL stored procedures defined in the previous section. Before we continue, let's briefly talk about security, state management, and error handling.

# Security Considerations

As discussed in Chapter 11, the Web Service will be wide open to the world. Because you would like to have control over who is accessing your application, the first thing you have to do for each request is to check if the requesting client is a registered user. That's why all of the public methods have *userName* and *password* as arguments. User lookups are done in the *userAdminImplement* class, and therefore the very first thing the *jokesImplement* class does is to call the *userAdminImplement* class to check if the credentials passed match a credential in the database.

Now, you can cheat a little bit and pretend the Web has state. For instance, you can create a client application for the Jokes Web Service that will remember the user's credentials. Using the *checkUser* method in the *userAdmin* class, you can let users log on, and then simply cache the username and password on the client. Although that information still needs to be sent to the server with every single request, at least clients don't need to input it again during the duration of a "session" with the Jokes application.

Obviously, this means that usernames and passwords are sent in clear text over the wire. If this is of concern (it probably should be!), then you need to encrypt either the whole data transfer (by using, for example, a secure channel over HTTPS), or at least the confidential parts of the message (such as the password). We leave this as an exercise for you (you can find more information on securing Web Services in Chapter 11).

## State Management

As we argued in Chapter 11, stateful Web Service applications should almost always be avoided. The only reason for the Jokes Web Service to be stateful would be to support client sessions in order to simplify authentication and authorization to the service. However, a better way to deal with security for this particular application is to store user credentials in the Web Service client, as described in the preceding paragraph.

## Error Handling

For error handling, you would probably like to have more control over what happens during program execution than the standard *System.Exception* class gives you; in particular, you will want to gather enough information so that you can give meaningful, user-friendly error messages to your clients. The *jokeException* class, which extends *System.Exception*, is designed to do exactly that. You will encounter more details on proper error handling as you go about implementing this class.

# Implementing the Jokes Data Repository

Now that the structure of the Jokes Web Service is firmly in place, you can start the work of actual implementation. It is usually a good idea to start with the back end and spend a fair amount of time fleshing out the exact interface to store and retrieve data. You can start off by installing the actual database system. You will then set up the data tables using a SQL installation script before writing all the stored procedures needed to manage the jokes in the database.

---

### WARNING

Later changes in methods exposed by the back end almost always requires major rewrites of the whole application, so it really pays to be very careful when writing your back-end methods.

---

## Installing the Database

The first step in working with a back end is of course to actually have a back end to work with. Because you want to offer dynamic content, a simple flat-file approach probably won't scale very well. Instead, let's use a relational database, such as SQL Server 2000. If you don't have a copy of this server, you're in luck, because the Microsoft .NET SDK Beta2 actually comes with its own copy of Microsoft SQL Server Desktop Engine, a slightly scaled–down version of the full server product, which is more than sufficient for our purposes. To install it, pro–ceed as follows:

1. Open up %ProgramFiles%\Microsoft.NET\Microsoft.NET\ FrameworkSDK\Samples\setup\html\Start.htm.

2. Click **Step 1: Install the .NET Framework Samples Database** and follow the instructions.

3. Verify in the list of services on your computer that the services MSSQL$NetSDK and SQLAgent$NetSDK are up and running.

This will install the SQL Server Desktop Engine, and configure the NetSDK database instance.

Note that SQL Server Desktop Engine does not come with any of the stan–dard GUI client tools. But it does ship with *osql*, a command line utility, which is certainly sufficient for what you are doing. *Osql* is described in detail in the Visual Studio.NET Combined Help Collection, but all you really need to know is how to execute a SQL command script, which is done as follows:

```
osql -S (local)\NetSDK -U sa -P -i myScript.sql
```

However, you can compensate for this lack of user friendliness by using the Server Explorer tool in Visual Studio.NET, which we will get at soon.

First, give yourself a database to work with, which you can fittingly call *jokes*. Run the following SQL script:

```
create database jokes
go
```

Now you can go about setting up the data tables, as defined in Figure 12.5. Also, to bootstrap the system, prepopulate the *users* database with a default moderator, which you can call *admin*, with password *secret*. You can also include a first joke, so that you can show your first user something. See Figure 12.5 for the complete listing of the database installation script.

**Figure 12.5** The Database Installation Script (installJokes.sql)

```
use jokes
go


/* object:  table [dbo].[users] */
create table [dbo].[users] (
  [userName] [nvarchar] (20) not null primary key,
  [password] [nvarchar] (20) not null ,
  [isModerator] [bit] not null
) on [primary]
go


/* object:  table [dbo].[jokes] */
create table [dbo].[jokes] (
  [jokeID] [int] identity(1,1) primary key ,
  [joke] [nvarchar] (3500) not null ,
  [userName] [nvarchar] (20) not null ,
  [isModerated] [bit] not null ,
) on [primary]
go


/* object:  table [dbo].[ratings] */
create table [dbo].[ratings] (
  [jokeID] [int] not null references jokes(jokeID),
```

**Continued**

**Figure 12.5** Continued

```
  [rating] [tinyint] not null,
) on [primary]
go


create  index "jokeID" on [dbo].[ratings](jokeID)
go


/* insert data into users table */
insert into users (userName,password, isModerator) values
  ("admin","secret", 1)
go


/* insert data into jokes table */
insert into jokes (joke,userName, isModerator) values
  ("Have you heard about the new sushi bar that caters exclusively
to lawyers? —It's called, Sosumi.","admin", 1)
go
```

Once you've created your Web Service project, you'll be able to look at the database right through the Visual Studio.NET IDE (from which the database diagram in Figure 12.1 is taken). Also, if you don't like working with SQL command-line scripts, you can create this database through the Visual Studio.NET Server Explorer, but by doing so, you probably open yourself up to errors when setting up your back end manually. Also, you can only write out SQL Create Scripts from Visual Studio.NET if you have the SQL Server client tools installed, which don't come with the SQL Server Desktop Engine—you have to purchase them separately.

## Creating the Stored Procedures

Now that you have defined and implemented the database schema, you need to develop the stored procedures to manage your data, which will be used by the Web Service business components. You need to be able to add, modify, and possibly delete users, jokes, and joke ratings. The Jokes service is so simple that you may be tempted to just hard code the corresponding SQL statements directly in your business components, but of course, you know that is a beginner's mistake, and that you will never get away with doing that in a real-world application. Because this example should show how to write a real application, you should do things the right way and create the corresponding stored procedures.

Right from the start, you want to have a comprehensive error-handling mechanism in place. Therefore, all the stored procedures have a return argument that carries a string-valued return code determined by what's happening during execution of the stored procedures back to the calling function in the middle tier. This return parameter is called, simply enough, *return*. In considering what can possibly go wrong during a stored procedure call, you may come up with the following values shown in Table 12.1.

**Table 12.1** Uniform Stored Procedure Return Codes

| Status/Error Code | User-Friendly Message |
|---|---|
| S_OK | Operation completed successfully. |
| F_ratingInvalid | Joke rating must be between 1 and 5. |
| F_jokeDoesNotExist | Joke selected does not exist in the system. |
| F_unknownAction | Internal error when accessing the database. |
| F_userDoesNotExist | This is not a registered user. |
| F_userExists | Somebody has already registered under this name. |
| F_userInfoWrong | You are not authorized to do this action. Change username or password. |
| F_noJokes | No matching jokes in the system at this moment in time. |

Make a note, then, that you will need a method that's part of the common error-handling procedure used by the middle tier that will translate error codes coming from the database (and elsewhere) into user-friendly messages sent back to the clients of the Web Service.

The errors defined in Table 12.1 are exceptions caught by your code—that's why you are able to return an error code in the first place. Errors may occur over which you have little control, and which cause the stored procedure to abort. In that case, all you can do is catch the exception in the middle tier and return an "unknown system error" back to your clients (maybe adding your apologies).

Secondly, in order to minimize the amount of code, you can employ a mechanism by which you tell the stored procedure what action you want to have done on a table, such as add, modify, or delete. That's why three of the stored procedures have an *action* input parameter indicating the action to perform.

In the upcoming section "Implementing the Jokes Middle Tier," we talk more about security. For now, let's simply assume that all access checks happen *before* program execution reaches a stored procedure, so that at this point you don't need to check on permissions anymore. To make the Jokes Web Service possible, you need to define the following five stored procedures, which are detailed in Tables 12.2, 12.3, 12.4, 12.5, and 12.6.

**Table 12.2** Stored Procedure *sp_manageUser*

| Name | *sp_manageUser* |
| --- | --- |
| Purpose | Allows you to add, modify, or delete a user. |
| Input parameters | *userName*  The username to add, modify, or delete. *password*  The corresponding password. *isModerator*  A Boolean value that tells you if this is a moderator or not. *action*  What to do: add, or modify, or delete. |
| Output parameters | *return*  Status/error code. |
| Returns | Standard SQL numerical return code. |

**Table 12.3** Stored Procedure *sp_checkUser*

| Name | *sp_checkUser* |
| --- | --- |
| Purpose | Allows you to check the user information provided in the arguments against information stored in the database. |
| Input parameters | *userName*  The username to verify. *password*  The corresponding password. *isModerator*  A Boolean value that tells you if this is supposedly a moderator or not. |
| Output parameters | *return*  Status/error code. |
| Returns | Standard SQL numerical return code. |

**Table 12.4** Stored Procedure *sp_manageJoke*

| Name | *sp_manageJoke* |
| --- | --- |
| Purpose | Allows you to add, modify, or delete a joke. |
| Input parameters | *userName*  The username of the registered user (used when adding a joke). |

**Continued**

**Table 12.4** Continued

| Name | sp_manageJoke |
|---|---|
| | *joke*  The actual joke (used when adding a joke). *isModerated*  A Boolean value that tells you if this joke is moderated or not. *jokeID*  The unique identifier of the joke (used when modifying or deleting a joke). *action*  What to do: add, modify, or delete. |
| Output parameters | *return*  Status/error code. |
| Returns | Standard SQL numerical return code. |

**Table 12.5** Stored Procedure *sp_manageRating*

| Name | sp_manageRating |
|---|---|
| Purpose | Allows you to add a rating for a joke. |
| Input parameters | *jokeID*  The unique identifier of the joke. *rating*  The rating, from 1 to 5, the joke gets. *action*  What to do: add or delete. |
| Output parameters | *return*  Status/error code. |
| Returns | Standard SQL numerical return code. |

**Table 12.6** Stored Procedure *sp_returnJokes*

| Name | sp_returnJokes |
|---|---|
| Purpose | Allows you to return jokes. |
| Input parameters | *howMany*  How many jokes you want to return. *isModerated*  A Boolean value that allows you to specify whether you want moderated or unmoderated jokes (or both, if null). *returnRandom*  A Boolean value that allows you to specify whether you want to get randomly selected jokes (for users) or not (for moderators when reviewing unmoderated jokes). |
| Output parameters | *return*  Status/error code. |
| Returns | A record set. |

Some of the stored procedures have what amounts to optional parameters; for example, in order to delete a joke, you need only pass the corresponding unique identifier of the joke to delete, along with the *action* parameter set to *delete* to *sp_manageJoke*. Because T-SQL does not allow you to overload stored procedure calls, you can simply pass null references to the remaining input parameters, and you need to remember to set up your middle tier code accordingly. Figure 12.6 shows the part of the SQL installation script that sets up the stored procedure needed by the Jokes Web Service.

**Figure 12.6** Setting Up the Stored Procedures (installJokes.sql)

```
use jokes
go


/* Create stored procedures */
create procedure sp_manageUser (
  — add, modify, or delete a user
  @@userName nvarchar(20),
  @@password nvarchar(20),
  @@isModerator bit,
  @@action nvarchar(20),        — one of 'add' or 'modify' or 'delete'
    — returns:
    —   'S_OK'                  : success
    —   'F_userExists'         : failed: user already exists
    —   'F_userDoesNotExist': failed: user does not exist
    —   'F_unknownAction'     : action command unrecognized
  @@return nvarchar(20) output
      ) as


  declare @@userCount int
  select @@userCount = count(*) from users where userName = @@userName


  — sanity checks
  if (@@userCount = 0 and ((@@action = 'modify') or
    (@@action = 'delete')))
    begin
```

**Continued**

## Figure 12.6 Continued

```
      select @@return = 'F_userDoesNotExist'

      return

   end


if @@userCount = 1 and @@action = 'add'

   begin

      select @@return = 'F_userExists'

      return

   end


— start
if @@action = 'add'

   begin

      insert into users (userName,password,isModerator)

        values (@@userName,@@password,@@isModerator)

      select @@return = 'S_OK'

      return

   end


if @@action = 'delete'

   begin

      delete from users where userName = @@userName

      select @@return = 'S_OK'

      return

   end


if @@action = 'modify'

   begin

      update users

        set userName = @@userName,

        isModerator = @@isModerator

        where userName = @@userName

      if @@password is not null
```

**Continued**

**Figure 12.6** Continued

```
        update users
            set password = @@password
            where userName = @@userName
        select @@return = 'S_OK'
        return
    end


  — otherwise
  select @@return = 'F_unknownAction'
  return
go


create procedure sp_checkUser (
  — checks user information provided against information in
  — the database
  @@userName nvarchar(20),
  @@password nvarchar(20),
  @@isModerator bit,
    — returns:
    —  'S_OK'              : information matches
    —  'F_userInfoWrong' : information does not match
  @@return nvarchar(20) output
      ) as


declare @@userCount int


  — sanity checks
  if @@userName is null
    begin
      select @@return = 'F_userInfoWrong'
      return
    end
```

**Continued**

## Figure 12.6 Continued

```
— start
if @@password is null and @@isModerator is null
  begin
    select @@userCount = count(*) from users where
      userName = @@userName
    goto checkCount
  end


if @@isModerator is null
  begin
    select @@userCount = count(*) from users where
      userName = @@userName and password = @@password
    goto checkCount
  end


if @@password is null
  begin
    select @@userCount = count(*) from users where
      userName = @@userName and isModerator = @@isModerator
    goto checkCount
  end


select @@userCount = count(*) from users where userName = @@userName
  and password = @@password and isModerator = @@isModerator


checkCount:
if @@userCount = 0
  begin
    select @@return = 'F_userInfoWrong'
    return
  end


select @@return = 'S_OK'
```

**Continued**

**Figure 12.6** Continued

```
  return

go

create procedure sp_manageRating (
  — add a joke rating
  @@jokeID int,
  @@rating tinyint,
  @@action nvarchar(20),       — one of 'add' or 'delete'
    — returns:
    —  'S_OK'                : success
    —  'F_jokeDoesNotExist': failed: joke does not exist
    —  'F_unknownAction'    : action command unrecognized
  @@return nvarchar(20) output
      ) as


— sanity checks on arguments done in middle tier

declare @@jokeCount int

— does the joke even exist?
select @@jokeCount = count(*) from jokes where jokeID = @@jokeID
if @@jokeCount = 0
  begin
    select @@return = 'F_jokeDoesNotExist'
    return
  end

if @@action = 'add'
  begin
    insert into ratings (jokeID,rating) values (@@jokeID,@@rating)
    select @@return = 'S_OK'
    return
```

**Continued**

## Figure 12.6 Continued

```
      end

  if @@action = 'delete'
    begin
       delete from ratings where jokeID = @@jokeID
       select @@return = 'S_OK'
       return
    end


  — otherwise
  select @@return = 'F_unknownAction'
  return
go


create procedure sp_manageJoke (
  — add, modify, or delete a joke
  @@userName nvarchar(20),
  @@joke nvarchar(3500),
  @@isModerated bit,
  @@jokeID int,
  @@action nvarchar(20),      — one of 'add' or 'modify' or 'delete'
      — returns:
      — 'S_OK'                : success
      — 'F_jokeDoesNotExist': failed: joke does not exist
      — 'F_unknownAction'    : action command unrecognized
  @@return nvarchar(20) output
      ) as


  — sanity checks on arguments done in middle tier


  declare @@jokeCount int


  if @@action = 'add'
```

**Continued**

## Figure 12.6 Continued

```
begin
   insert into jokes (userName,joke,isModerated)
     values (@@userName,@@joke,@@isModerated)
   select @@return = 'S_OK'
   return
end


if @@action = 'modify'
   begin
     select @@jokeCount = count(*) from jokes where jokeID = @@jokeID
     if @@jokeCount = 0
       begin
         select @@return = 'F_jokeDoesNotExist'
         return
       end
     if @@isModerated is not null
       update jokes
         set isModerated = @@isModerated
         where jokeID = @@jokeID
     if @@userName is not null
       update jokes
         set userName = @@userName
         where jokeID = @@jokeID
     if @@joke is not null
       update jokes
         set joke = @@joke
         where jokeID = @@jokeID
     select @@return = 'S_OK'
     return
   end


if @@action = 'delete'
   begin
```

**Continued**

**Figure 12.6** Continued

```
        select @@jokeCount = count(*) from jokes where jokeID = @@jokeID
        if @@jokeCount = 0
          begin
            select @@return = 'F_jokeDoesNotExist'
            return
          end
        declare @@dummy nvarchar(40)
        execute sp_manageRating @@jokeID, null, 'delete', @@dummy output
        delete from jokes where jokeID = @@jokeID
        select @@return = 'S_OK'
        return
      end


  — otherwise
  select @@return = 'F_unknownAction'
  return
go

create procedure sp_returnJokes (
  — returns jokes
  @@howMany int,
  @@isModerated bit,
  @@returnRandom bit
    — returns a recordset containing jokeID, joke, and average rating
      ) as

  — sanity checks on arguments done in middle tier

  declare @@jokeCount int
  declare @baseJokeID int
  declare @baseJokeRelPos int
  declare @cmd varchar(1000)
```

**Continued**

## Figure 12.6 Continued

```
— random start position?
— note that in this case, we implicitly assume that
—    * isModerated = 1
—    * howMany <> null
if @@returnRandom = 1
  begin
    select @@jokeCount = count(*) from jokes where isModerated = 1
    if @@jokeCount = 0
      return


    if @@jokeCount < @@howMany
      set @@howMany = @@jokeCount


    — get a random number between 0 and 1
    declare @random decimal(6,3)
    set @random = cast(datepart(ms, getdate()) as decimal(6,3))/1000


    — set a random start position
    set @baseJokeRelPos =
      ((@@jokeCount - @@howMany + 1) * @random) + 1


    — get the corresponding jokeID
    declare jokeTempCursor cursor scroll for select jokeID from
      jokes where isModerated = 1 order by jokeID
    open jokeTempCursor
    fetch absolute @baseJokeRelPos from jokeTempCursor
      into @baseJokeID
    close jokeTempCursor
    deallocate jokeTempCursor
  end


— start building our command
set @cmd = 'select '
```

**Continued**

**Figure 12.6** Continued

```
if @@howMany is not null
   set @cmd = @cmd + 'top ' + cast(@@howMany as varchar(10)) + ' '

set @cmd = @cmd + 'jokes.jokeID, left(ltrim(joke),3500) '
set @cmd = @cmd + ', cast(avg(cast(rating as decimal(5,4)))
   as decimal(2,1)) '
set @cmd = @cmd + 'from jokes left outer join ratings on
   jokes.jokeID = ratings.jokeID '

if @@isModerated is not null
   begin
     if @@isModerated = 1
       begin
         set @cmd = @cmd + 'where isModerated = 1 '
         if @@returnRandom = 1
           set @cmd = @cmd + 'and jokes.jokeID >= ' +
              cast(@baseJokeID as varchar(10)) + ' '
       end
     if @@isModerated = 0
       set @cmd = @cmd + 'where isModerated = 0 '
   end

set @cmd = @cmd + 'group by jokes.jokeID, joke order by jokes.jokeID'

exec (@cmd)
go
```

That completes setting up the back-end infrastructure. You can find the complete installation script in directory SQLSetup/ on the CD accompanying the book.

You are now ready to start up Visual Studio.NET to begin working on the meat of the Web Service, namely the Web Service itself.

# Implementing the Jokes Middle Tier

Now that you have the back-end database system in place, you can go about implementing the actual Web Service that clients will be calling. Of course, you will want to do this work in Visual Studio.NET. Note that you can find the complete code for this project on the CD accompanying this book.

## Setting Up the Visual Studio Project

Start the setup of the Visual Studio project by creating a new ASP.NET Web Service project, called *jokesService*. Go to **File | New | Project**, choose the entry **ASP.NET Web Service** under the Visual C# Projects folder, keep the default Location, and enter **jokesService** as the Name of the project (see Figure 12.7).

**Figure 12.7** Setting Up a New Web Project

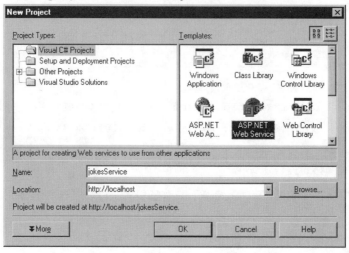

This will set up a new virtual directory of the same name, configure the necessary FrontPage server extensions, define an assembly, and create supporting project files. Rather annoyingly, the ASP.NET Web Service Wizard creates a default Web Service called Service1, which you may want to remove from the project right away (or rename it later when you go about adding Web Services to the project).

Next, check on the database you created earlier: Click on **Server Explorer**, which by default is on the upper left-hand corner of the window. Right-click under **Data Connections**, and enter the connection information for the NetSDK database as follows: under Server, enter **(local)\NetSDK**, the username is **SA**, no password, and the Database you are interested in is **jokes** (see Figure 12.8).

**Figure 12.8** Opening Up a Connection to the Jokes Database

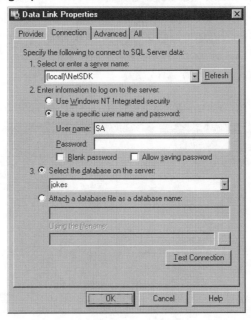

The connection is then added to Server Explorer, and you can go about exploring your database, and, say, look at your *users* table (Figure 12.9).

**Figure 12.9** Exploring the Jokes Database through Visual Studio.NET Server Explorer

Now you are in a position to create the two Web Services: right-click the **jokesService** project in the Solution Explorer and choose **Add | Add New Item**. Choose **Web Service** from the list of available templates, and call it **userAdmin.asmx** (see Figure 12.10). Note that apart from creating the ASMX file, this will also create the corresponding C# class file userAdmin.asmx.cs, and the resource file userAdmin.asmx.resx.

**Figure 12.10** Adding a New Web Service

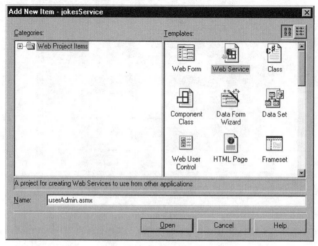

Perform the same step for the second service, called jokes.asmx.

Next, you need to set up the supporting classes. Again, right-click the **jokesService** project in the Solution Explorer, and choose **Add | Add New Item**, but this time select **Class** instead. You need to repeat this procedure five times, for the five C# classes you need:

- userAdminImplement.cs
- JokesImplement.cs
- databaseAccess.cs
- jokeException.cs
- xmlJokesReturn.cs

When looking at the Solution Explorer, and clicking the **Select All Files** icon, your project should now look like the one shown in Figure 12.11.

Lastly, you need to instruct the C# compiler to automatically generate an XML documentation file of your work for you (see the "Making Documentation a Part of Your Everyday Life" sidebar). Go to the Solution Explorer, right–click on the **jokesService** project, and select **Properties**. A dialog will open, as shown in Figure 12.12. Select the **Build** option under the Configuration Properties folder, and enter **jokesService.xml** as the XML Documentation File name.

**Figure 12.11** Overview of All Files Needed for the *jokesService* Web Service

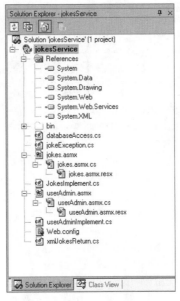

**Figure 12.12** Automatically Generating XML Documentation Output

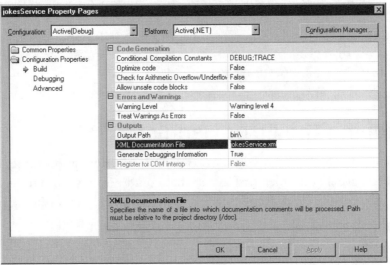

Now you can code away. Note that you can find the complete code for the Jokes Web Service in directory jokesService on the CD that comes with this book.

---

### Developing & Deploying…

## Making Documentation a Part of Your Everyday Life

Documenting your work does not need to be an afterthought—in fact, it should occupy center-stage of your work from the very beginning of a project. The Visual Studio.NET environment supports this philosophy by offering you a set of predefined XML elements allowing you to document your code inside your source files as you are developing it.

This functionality is still rather limited, quite frankly, but it is a start. Among others, there are currently tags defined to describe the function of a class or method (<summary>), and what parameters (<param>) and return values (<return>) a method has. But you are certainly free to add your own set of tags, suitable for your needs. The C# compiler then allows you to extract your XML documentation into a separate XML output file, which you can then use for further processing, for instance to create documentation in HTML format by applying a suitable XSLT style sheet. The compiler validates some of the XML documentation tags for you, such as those describing the method input parameters. You can find more information in the XML Documentation Tutorial that's part of the Visual Studio.NET C# Programmer's Reference.

Because documentation is vitally important for the success of any software project, all of the code for the Jokes Web Service application uses the C# documentation tags liberally.

---

# Developing the Error Handler

Introducing error handling as you start to code is usually a good thing. However, you need to have a good idea first as to what could possibly go wrong. In the "Creating the Stored Procedures" section, we have already identified a number of errors that you can catch at the database level. Because user input data validation checking is done in the business components, you get two more possible exceptions, having to do with invalid ratings (should be between 1 and 5), and requests for "too many" jokes (should be between 1 and 10). Obviously, when you go about creating a client for your Web Service, you will not allow the client application to ask for, say, 10,000 jokes at once. But because your Web Service can certainly be used by "unauthorized" client applications—it is an Internet service, after all—you need to check for user data on the server, and you need to be able to return meaningful information to your clients.

You can then simply set up a hash table *errorCodes* with internal error codes and the corresponding nice messages for end users, and add a method, *getNiceErrorMessage()*, that translates one into the other. The instance variable *failReason* captures the error code and keeps it available as you travel back the call stack after an exception has occurred.

Creating an entry in the server application event log whenever an error does occur is probably a good idea, and that's what the method *writeEventLogEntry()* does. Putting everything together, see Figure 12.13 for the complete code of the *jokeException* class (also on the CD as file jokeException.cs).

**Figure 12.13** Custom Error Handling Class *jokeException* (jokeException.cs)

```
using System;

using System.Collections;

using System.Diagnostics;


namespace jokesService

{

  /// <summary>

  ///    Custom error handling class

  /// </summary>

  /// <remarks>

  ///    Author: Adrian Turtschi; aturtschi@hotmail.com; Sept 2001

  /// </remarks>

  public class jokeException : Exception {

    /// <value>

    /// fail reason error code

    /// </value>

    public string failReason;

    private static Hashtable errorCodes = new Hashtable();

    private static bool isInit = false;
```

**Continued**

**Figure 12.13** Continued

```
/// <summary>
///    Public class constructor.
/// </summary>
/// <param name='failReason'
///    type='string'
///    desc='fail reason error code'>
/// </param>
protected internal jokeException(string failReason) {
  this.failReason = failReason;
}


private static void initErrorCodes() {
  errorCodes.Add("S_OK",
    "Operation completed successfully!");
  errorCodes.Add("F_System",
    "An unknown system error occurred!");
  errorCodes.Add("F_ratingInvalid",
    "Joke rating must be between 1 and 5!");
  errorCodes.Add("F_jokeDoesNotExist",
    "Joke selected does not exist in the system!");
  errorCodes.Add("F_unknownAction" ,
    "Internal error when accessing the database!");
  errorCodes.Add("F_userDoesNotExist",
    "This is not a registered user!");
  errorCodes.Add("F_userExists",
    "Somebody has already registered under this name!");
  errorCodes.Add("F_userInfoWrong",
    "You are not authorized to do this action. Change " +
    "user name or password!");
  errorCodes.Add("F_noJokes",
    "No matching jokes in the system at this moment in time!");
  errorCodes.Add("F_10JokesMax",
```

**Continued**

## Figure 12.13 Continued

```
          "You can only retrieve up to 10 jokes at one time!");
    }


    /// <summary>
    ///    The getNiceErrorMessage method converts an error code into
    ///    a user-friendly error message, returned through a SOAP
fault.
    /// </summary>
    /// <param name='errorCode'
    ///    type='string'
    ///    desc='error code'>
    /// </param>
    /// <returns>a friendly user error message</returns>
    protected internal static string getNiceErrorMessage(
      string errorCode) {
      if (!isInit) {
        // initialize error look up table once and for all
        initErrorCodes();
        isInit = true;
      }
      string temp = errorCodes[errorCode].ToString();
      if(temp.Length < 1) {
        // generic error, if error code unknown...
        return errorCodes["F_System"].ToString();
      } else {
        return temp;
      }
    }


    /// <summary>
    ///    The writeEventLogEntry method writes an error log entry
    ///    into the Application event log
    /// </summary>
```

**Continued**

**Figure 12.13** Continued

```
/// <param name='userName'
///    type='string'
///    desc='name of registered user'>
/// </param>
/// <param name='failReason'
///    type='string'
///    desc='fail reason error code'>
/// </param>
/// <returns>nothing</returns>
protected internal static void writeEventLogEntry(
   string userName, string failReason) {
   //Create the source, if it does not already exist.
   if(!EventLog.SourceExists("jokeService")) {
      EventLog.CreateEventSource("jokeService", "Application");
   }
   //Create an EventLog instance and assign its source.
   EventLog eventLog = new EventLog();
   eventLog.Source = "jokeService";

   //Write an informational entry to the event log.
   eventLog.WriteEntry(userName + ": " + failReason);
   }
  }
}
```

# Developing the Database Access Component

The next task is to write a component that will take care of all back-end data access and offer a single gateway to the database. Externalizing the database connection string is good programming practice, and the .NET Framework offers a good place to put it: the web.config file. Just add the *appSettings* element into the web.config file, as shown in Figure 12.14.

**Figure 12.14** Putting the Database DSN into Web.Config

```
<configuration>

  <appSettings>

    <add key="dsn" value="server=(local)\NetSDK;

      database=Jokes;User ID=SA;Password=" />

  </appSettings>

  <system.web>

      ...standard settings...

  </system.web>

</configuration>
```

The database access class (databaseAccess.cs) is a very simple class that just returns a (closed) SQL connection object to the database. Unfortunately, class constructors are not allowed to return objects, so you can add a single method to do just that, called *getConnection()*. See Figure 12.15 for the complete code for the *databaseAccess* class.

**Figure 12.15** Database Access Class *databaseAccess* (databaseAccess.cs)

```
using System;
using System.Data.SqlClient;


namespace jokesService
{
  /// <summary>
  ///    The databaseAccess sets up the connection to the
  ///    data repository.
  /// </summary>
  /// <remarks>
  ///    Author: Adrian Turtschi; aturtschi@hotmail.com; Sept 2001
  /// </remarks>
  public class databaseAccess {

    private SqlConnection sqlConnection;
```

**Continued**

**Figure 12.15** Continued

```
/// <summary>
///    Public class constructor.
/// </summary>
protected internal databaseAccess() {
  sqlConnection = new SqlConnection(
    ConfigurationSettings.AppSettings["dsn"]);
}


/// <summary>
///    The getConnection method sets up the database connection
/// </summary>
/// <returns>the (closed) SQL connection object</returns>
protected internal SqlConnection getConnection() {
  return sqlConnection;
}
  }
}
```

# Developing the User Administration Service

Now that you have taken care of error handling and database access, you will want to develop the core classes for managing users and jokes. Let's first look at how you will want to manage users: you need to be able to add new users, change existing user information, and check if a user exists in the system, and you also want to be able to promote an existing user to become a moderator.

## Adding New Users

Going through the steps needed to add a new user to the system, you can start by writing the method *addUser()* in *userAdminImplement*, the class that implements user management functionality. The method takes a username and a password as an argument, sets up the necessary infrastructure to call the SQL stored procedure *sp_manageUser()*, gets a connection object from an instance of the class *databaseAccess*, opens the connection, and calls the stored procedure. If everything goes well, the stored procedure will return a status code *S_OK*, and control will go back to the calling Web Service. If an exception occurred, you can create a new custom exception object of type *jokeException*, remember the error code, and throw the exception back to the caller.

The *createSqlManageUser()* method is the method that sets up the call to the stored procedure *sp_manageUser*. It takes a username, a password, and a flag denoting whether the user is a moderator as arguments. Note that all arguments are of type *string*, even the Boolean flag. The reason for this is that some arguments are in fact optional. For instance, when deleting a user, all you need to know is the user's username. You could certainly overload this method to do this, but in the end not a lot would change. Also, because this is an internal method of a class (and is therefore marked as protected internal) implementing functionality exposed by another public class, type consistency is not really an issue. So you can adopt the convention that all arguments to the methods that set up your SQL calls take string arguments, and that an empty string passed will mean that a SQL null value should be passed to the corresponding stored procedure. Note, though, that you can't just pass the keyword *null* to SQL; instead, you have to use *System.DBNull.value*.

You can use the MS SQL Managed Provider created specially for high performance access to MS SQL server database, which is found in the *System.Data.SqlClient* namespace (which you declare in the declaration section of your class).

Figure 12.16 shows the *createSqlManageUser()* method call that sets up the SQL command object for the stored procedure *sp_manageUser*, which deals with adding, updating, and deleting users and managers.

**Figure 12.16** *createSqlManageUser* Method (userAdminImplement.cs)

```
///  <summary>
///     The createSqlManageUser method sets up the SQL command object
///     for the stored procedure sp_manageUser, which deals with
///     adding, updating, and deleting users and managers
///  </summary>
///  <param name='userName'
///     type='string'
///     desc='name of registered user'>
///  </param>
///  <param name='password'
```

**Continued**

## Figure 12.16 Continued

```
///    type='string'
///    desc='password of registered user (zero length if N/A)'>
/// </param>
/// <param name='isModerator'
///    type='string'
///    desc='true/false if this user is a moderator'>
/// </param>
/// <param name='action'
///    type='string'
///    desc='the action the SQL stored procedure should take
///    (see the stored procedure definition for allowed action
///    keywords)'>
/// </param>
/// <param name='sqlCommand'
///    type='SqlCommand'
///    desc='a reference to a SQL command object'>
/// </param>
/// <returns>the prepared SQL command object</returns>
protected internal void createSqlManageUser(
  string userName, string password,
  string isModerator, string action, SqlCommand sqlCommand) {

  sqlCommand.CommandType = CommandType.StoredProcedure;
  sqlCommand.CommandText = "sp_manageUser" ;

  SqlParameter argUserName =
    new SqlParameter("@@userName", SqlDbType.NVarChar, 20);
  argUserName.Value = userName;
  sqlCommand.Parameters.Add(argUserName);

  SqlParameter argPassword =
    new SqlParameter("@@password",SqlDbType.NVarChar, 20);
  if(password.Length > 0) {
```

*Continued*

**Figure 12.16** Continued

```
    argPassword.Value =   password;
  } else {
    argPassword.Value =   DBNull.Value;
  }
  sqlCommand.Parameters.Add(argPassword);


  SqlParameter argIsModerator =
    new SqlParameter("@@isModerator",SqlDbType.Bit);
  argIsModerator.Value =   bool.Parse(isModerator);
  sqlCommand.Parameters.Add(argIsModerator);


  SqlParameter argAction =
    new SqlParameter("@@action",SqlDbType.NVarChar, 20);
  argAction.Value =   action;
  sqlCommand.Parameters.Add(argAction);


  SqlParameter argReturn =
    new SqlParameter("@@return",SqlDbType.NVarChar, 20,
    ParameterDirection.Output, true, 0, 0, "",
    DataRowVersion.Current, "");
  sqlCommand.Parameters.Add(argReturn);
}
```

After the SQL side of adding a new user has been taken care of in method
*createSqlManageUser()*, the implementation of the *addUser()* method is now
straightforward, as shown in Figure 12.17.

**Figure 12.17** *addUser* Method (userAdminImplement.cs)

```
/// <summary>
///     The addUser method adds a new user to the database
/// </summary>
/// <param name='userName'
///     type='string'
```

**Continued**

**Figure 12.17** Continued

```
///    desc='name of new user'>
/// </param>
/// <param name='password'
///    type='string'
///    desc='password of new user'>
/// </param>
/// <returns>true</returns>
protected internal bool addUser(string userName, string password) {
  try {
    string retCode;
    SqlCommand sqlCommand = new SqlCommand();
    createSqlManageUser(
      userName, password, "false", "add", sqlCommand);

    databaseAccess myDatabase = new databaseAccess();
    sqlCommand.Connection = myDatabase.getConnection();
    sqlCommand.Connection.Open();

    sqlCommand.ExecuteNonQuery();
    sqlCommand.Connection.Close();
    retCode = sqlCommand.Parameters["@@return"].Value.ToString();

    // catch problems within the stored procedure
    if (retCode == "S_OK") {
      return true;
    } else {
      throw new jokeException(retCode);
    }
  // catch problems with the database
  } catch (Exception e) {
    throw e;
  }
}
```

Note that the code first inspects the return code set during execution of the stored procedure. If things are not okay, say because the user has already registered previously, you can remember the error code and throw a custom exception of type *jokeException*. If an exception occurred over which you have no control, say because the database is not accessible, you can't do much more than throw an ordinary exception of type *System.Exception*.

## Checking Existing User Information

The next method you will want to add is *checkUser()*, which matches a set of given credentials, consisting of a username, a password, and a flag indicating whether this is a moderator, against the information in the database. You first need to set up the *createSqlCheckUser* method, which wraps the call to the stored procedure *sp_checkUser()*, shown in Figure 12.18 and also part of the CD file userAdminImplement.cs.

**Figure 12.18** *createSqlCheckUser* Method (userAdminImplement.cs)

```
/// <summary>
///    The createSqlCheckUser method sets up the SQL command object
///    for the stored procedure sp_checkUser, which verifies passed
///    user information with user information in the database
/// </summary>
/// <param name='userName'
///    type='string'
///    desc='name of registered user (zero length if N/A)'>
/// </param>
/// <param name='password'
///    type='string'
///    desc='password of registered user (zero length if N/A)'>
/// </param>
/// <param name='isModerator'
///    type='string'
///    desc='true/false if this user is a moderator
///    (zero length if N/A)'>
/// </param>
/// <param name='sqlCommand'
```

**Continued**

**Figure 12.18** Continued

```
///     type='SqlCommand'
///     desc='a reference to a SQL command object'>
/// </param>
/// <returns>the prepared SQL command object</returns>
protected internal void createSqlCheckUser(
  string userName, string password,
  string isModerator, SqlCommand sqlCommand) {

  sqlCommand.CommandType = CommandType.StoredProcedure;
  sqlCommand.CommandText = "sp_checkUser" ;

  SqlParameter argUserName =
    new SqlParameter("@@userName", SqlDbType.NVarChar, 20);
  if(userName.Length > 0) {
    argUserName.Value =  userName;
  } else {
    argUserName.Value =  DBNull.Value;
  }
  sqlCommand.Parameters.Add(argUserName);

  SqlParameter argPassword =
    new SqlParameter("@@password",SqlDbType.NVarChar, 20);
  if(password.Length > 0) {
    argPassword.Value =  password;
  } else {
    argPassword.Value =  DBNull.Value;
  }
  sqlCommand.Parameters.Add(argPassword);

  SqlParameter argIsModerator =
    new SqlParameter("@@isModerator",SqlDbType.Bit);
  if(isModerator.Length > 0) {
    argIsModerator.Value = bool.Parse(isModerator);
```

**Continued**

**Figure 12.18** Continued

```
    } else {
        argIsModerator.Value =  DBNull.Value;
    }
    sqlCommand.Parameters.Add(argIsModerator);


    SqlParameter argReturn =
      new SqlParameter("@@return",SqlDbType.NVarChar, 20,
      ParameterDirection.Output, true, 0, 0, "",
      DataRowVersion.Current, "");
    sqlCommand.Parameters.Add(argReturn);
}
```

Next, you need to implement the actual method, *checkUser()*, that verifies
user's credentials (see Figure 12.19).

**Figure 12.19** *createSqlCheckUser* Method (userAdminImplement.cs)

```
/// <summary>
///    The checkUser method checks if a user or moderator is
///    already defined in the database
/// </summary>
/// <param name='userName'
///    type='string'
///    desc='name of user or moderator'>
/// </param>
/// <param name='password'
///    type='string'
///    desc='password of user or moderator'>
/// </param>
/// <param name='isModerator'
///    type='bool'
///    desc='check for moderator status (if false,
///    we do not check)'>
/// </param>
```

**Continued**

**Figure 12.19** Continued

```
/// <returns>nothing</returns>
protected internal bool checkUser(
  string userName, string password, bool isModerator) {
  string retCode;

  try {
    SqlCommand sqlCommand = new SqlCommand();

    if(isModerator) {
      // check if user is a moderator...
      createSqlCheckUser(userName, password, "true", sqlCommand);
    } else {
      // ... or a registered user
      createSqlCheckUser(userName, password, "", sqlCommand);
    }

    databaseAccess myDatabase = new databaseAccess();
    sqlCommand.Connection = myDatabase.getConnection();
    sqlCommand.Connection.Open();

    sqlCommand.ExecuteNonQuery();
    retCode = sqlCommand.Parameters["@@return"].Value.ToString();

    // catch problems within the stored procedure
    if (retCode == "S_OK") {
      return true;
    } else {
      throw new jokeException(retCode);
    }
    // catch problems with the database
  } catch (Exception e) {
    throw e;
  }
}
```

# Adding Moderators

Lastly, you need to think about adding moderators to the system. You want to let only moderators add moderators, and those new moderators already need to be registered with the system as regular users.

So the *addModerator* method has to have three arguments: the username and password of the moderator adding a new moderator, and the username of the user who should become moderator. You need to first check that the credentials given are indeed the ones of an existing moderator, for which you can use the *checkUser()* method, and then you need to modify the entry in the user table for the new moderator, which consists of simply changing her *isModerator* flag to True.

Even with this simple call, a lot of things can go wrong: the moderator requesting the change may not be a moderator, or the user slated to become a moderator may not exist in the database. Thankfully, you no longer need to worry about these eventualities, because your error-handling system will handle those exceptions automatically. Figure 12.20 shows the code for *addManager()* (which is still part of the CD file userAdminImplement.cs).

**Figure 12.20** *addModerator* Method (userAdminImplement.cs)

```
/// <summary>
///     The addModerator method sets a previously added user to become
///     a moderator
/// </summary>
/// <param name='userName'
///     type='string'
///     desc='name of moderator making the call'>
/// </param>
/// <param name='password'
///     type='string'
///     desc='password of moderator making the call'>
/// </param>
/// <param name='newModerator'
///     type='string'
///     desc='user name of registered user who will become
///     a moderator'>
/// </param>
```

**Continued**

## Figure 12.20 Continued

```
/// <returns>true</returns>
protected internal bool addModerator(
  string userName, string password, string newModerator) {
  string retCode;

  try {
    // check if user is a moderator
    SqlCommand sqlCommand = new SqlCommand();
    createSqlCheckUser(userName, password, "true", sqlCommand);

    databaseAccess myDatabase = new databaseAccess();
    sqlCommand.Connection = myDatabase.getConnection();
    sqlCommand.Connection.Open();

    sqlCommand.ExecuteNonQuery();
    retCode = sqlCommand.Parameters["@@return"].Value.ToString();

    // catch problems within the stored procedure
    if (retCode != "S_OK") {
      sqlCommand.Connection.Close();
      throw new jokeException(retCode);
    }

    // make newModerator a moderator
    sqlCommand.Parameters.Clear();
    createSqlManageUser(
      newModerator, "", "true", "modify", sqlCommand);

    sqlCommand.ExecuteNonQuery();
    sqlCommand.Connection.Close();

    retCode = sqlCommand.Parameters["@@return"].Value.ToString();
```

**Continued**

**Figure 12.20** Continued

```
    // catch problems within the stored procedure
    if (retCode == "S_OK") {
      return true;
    } else {
      throw new jokeException(retCode);
    }
    // catch problems with the database
  } catch (Exception e) {
    throw e;
  }
}
```

# Creating the Public Web Methods—Users

The implementation of the user administration service is now complete, and all that remains to do is to expose this service to the world. To do this, you simply add new (public!) Web methods to the *userAdmin* class, which is found in the file userAdmin.asmx.cs on the CD. First, you need to add some custom initialization code to the *userAdmin* Web Service class, as shown in Figure 12.21.

**Figure 12.21** Code to Set Up the *userAdmin* Web Service (userAdmin.asmx.cs)

```
using System;
using System.Collections;
using System.ComponentModel;
using System.Data;
using System.Diagnostics;
using System.Web;
using System.Web.Services;
using System.Web.Services.Protocols;
using System.Xml;

namespace jokesService {
  /// <summary>
  ///    The userAdmin class provides methods to manage users and
```

**Continued**

**Figure 12.21** Continued

```
///    moderators in the database.
/// </summary>
/// <remarks>
///    Author: Adrian Turtschi; aturtschi@hotmail.com; Sept 2001
/// </remarks>
[WebServiceAttribute(Description="The userAdmin web service " +
    "provides methods to manage users and moderators in the database",
    Namespace="urn:schemas-syngress-com-soap")]
public class userAdmin : System.Web.Services.WebService {
    // SOAP error handling return document structure
    /// <value>error document thrown by SOAP exception</value>
    public XmlDocument soapErrorDoc;
    /// <value>text node with user-friendly error message</value>
    public XmlNode xmlFailReasonNode;

    /// <summary>
    ///    Public class constructor.
    /// </summary>
    public userAdmin() {
        InitializeComponent();
        // initialize SOAP error handling return document
        soapErrorDoc = new System.Xml.XmlDocument();
        xmlFailReasonNode =
            soapErrorDoc.CreateNode(XmlNodeType.Element, "failReason", "");
    }
  }
}
```

The code for the *addUser()* method that adds a new user to the database is shown in Figure 12.22.

**Figure 12.22** addUser Web Method (userAdmin.asmx.cs)

```
01: /// <summary>
02: ///    The addUser method adds a new user to the database
03: /// </summary>
04: /// <param name='userName'
05: ///    type='string'
06: ///    desc='name of new user'>
07: /// </param>
08: /// <param name='password'
09: ///    type='string'
10: ///    desc='password of new user'>
11: /// </param>
12: /// <returns>nothing</returns>
13: [SoapDocumentMethodAttribute(Action="addUser",
14:   RequestNamespace="urn:schemas-syngress-com-soap:userAdmin",
15:   RequestElementName="addUser",
16:   ResponseNamespace="urn:schemas-syngress-com-soap:userAdmin",
17:  ResponseElementName="addUserResponse")]
18: [WebMethod(Description="The addUser method adds a new user to " +
19:    "the database")]
20: public void addUser(string userName, string password) {
21:   userAdminImplement userAdminObj = new userAdminImplement();
22:   try {
23:     userAdminObj.addUser(userName, password);
24:     // catch jokeExceptions
25:   } catch (jokeException e) {
26:     throwFault("Fault occurred", e.failReason, userName);
27:   }
28:   // then, catch general System Exceptions
29:   catch (Exception e) {
30:     throwFault(e.Message, "F_System", userName);
31:   }
32: }
```

Note how simple things suddenly become once you have set the stage correctly: You need just two lines to add a new user to the system. Note two things in Figure 12.22:

- First, some decorations were added to the Web method (which Microsoft calls metadata). They specify the namespaces (lines 14 and 16) and element names (lines 15 and 17) used by the SOAP protocol, as described in Chapter 11.

- Second, if an exception occurs, you call a custom error handler that returns extended error information as part of a SOAP fault (lines 25 and 26).

## Error Handling for the Public Web Methods

If you look at the code that adds users to the system, you'll see that *throwFault* (Figure 12.22, lines 26 and 30) is the name of the method that actually throws a SOAP fault and ends execution of the Web Service method. But it does a whole lot more:

- The (internal) error code is replaced by a user-friendly error message.

- A log entry is written to the *Application* event log.

- The standard SOAP fault XML document is appended with a custom element, called *failReason*, where client applications can find the error message to display to users.

The details of the *throwFault* method are shown in Figure 12.23.

**Figure 12.23** *throwFault* Method (userAdmin.asmx.cs)

```
///  <summary>
///     The throwFault method throws a SOAP fault and ends
///     execution of the Web Service method
///  </summary>
///  <param name='message'
///     type='string'
///     desc='start of text node of faultstring element in
///     SOAP fault message'>
///  </param>
///  <param name='failReason'
```

**Continued**

**Figure 12.23** Continued

```
///    type='string'
///    desc='text node for custom failReason element in SOAP
///    fault message'>
/// </param>
/// <param name='userName'
///    type='string'
///    desc='name of registered user'>
/// </param>
/// <returns>nothing</returns>
private void throwFault(string message, string failReason, string
 userName) {
  xmlFailReasonNode.AppendChild(soapErrorDoc.CreateTextNode(
    jokeException.getNiceErrorMessage(failReason)));
  jokeException.writeEventLogEntry(userName, failReason);
  throw new SoapException(message, SoapException.ServerFaultCode,
    Context.Request.Url.AbsoluteUri,null,
    new System.Xml.XmlNode[]{xmlFailReasonNode});
}
```

For instance, if you try to add a user who is already registered, a SOAP fault will be returned, as pictured in Figure 12.24.

**Figure 12.24** A SOAP Fault Extended by a Custom XML Element

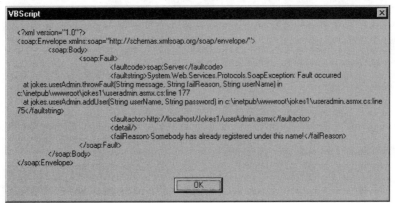

# Creating the Public Web Methods—Administrators

The two other public Web methods of the *userAdmin* Web Service are very similar in their structure to the *addUser* Web method; they are the Web method *addModerator()*, which adds a new moderator to the database, and the Web method *checkUser()*, which checks if a user or moderator is already defined in the database. Those two methods are presented in Figures 12.25 and 12.26, respectively.

**Figure 12.25** *addModerator* Web Method (userAdmin.asmx.cs)

```
///  <summary>
///     The addModerator method adds a new moderator to the database
///  </summary>
///  <param name='userName'
///     type='string'
///     desc='name of moderator'>
///  </param>
///  <param name='password'
///     type='string'
///     desc='password of moderator'>
///  </param>
///  <param name='newModerator'
///     type='string'
///     desc='user name of user who will become a moderator'>
///  </param>
///  <returns>nothing</returns>
[SoapDocumentMethodAttribute(Action="addModerator",
    RequestNamespace="urn:schemas-syngress-com-soap:userAdmin",
    RequestElementName="addModerator",
    ResponseNamespace="urn:schemas-syngress-com-soap:userAdmin",
    ResponseElementName="addModeratorResponse")]
[WebMethod(Description="The addModerator method adds a new " +
    "moderator to the database")]
public void addModerator(
    string userName, string password, string newModerator) {
    userAdminImplement userAdminObj = new userAdminImplement();
    try {
```

*Continued*

**Figure 12.25** Continued

```
      userAdminObj.addModerator(userName, password, newModerator);
      // catch jokeExceptions
   } catch (jokeException e) {
     throwFault("Fault occurred", e.failReason, userName);
   }
      // then, catch general System Exceptions
   catch (Exception e) {
     throwFault(e.Message, "F_System", userName);
   }
}
```

**Figure 12.26** *checkUser* Web Method (userAdmin.asmx.cs)

```
/// <summary>
///    The checkUser method checks if a user or moderator is
///    already defined in the database
/// </summary>
/// <param name='userName'
///    type='string'
///    desc='name of user or moderator'>
/// </param>
/// <param name='password'
///    type='string'
///    desc='password of user or moderator'>
/// </param>
/// <param name='isModerator'
///    type='bool'
///    desc='check for moderator status (if false, we do
///    not check)'>
/// </param>
/// <returns>nothing</returns>
[SoapDocumentMethodAttribute(Action="checkUser",
   RequestNamespace="urn:schemas-syngress-com-soap:userAdmin",
```

**Continued**

**Figure 12.26** Continued

```
    RequestElementName="checkUser",
    ResponseNamespace="urn:schemas-syngress-com-soap:userAdmin",
    ResponseElementName="checkUserResponse")]
[WebMethod(Description="The checkUser method checks if a user " +
    "or moderator is already defined in the database")]
public void checkUser(
    string userName, string password, bool isModerator) {
    userAdminImplement userAdminObj = new userAdminImplement();
    try {
        userAdminObj.checkUser(userName, password, isModerator);
        // catch jokeExceptions
    } catch (jokeException e) {
        throwFault("Fault occurred", e.failReason, userName);
    }
        // then, catch general System Exceptions
    catch (Exception e) {
        throwFault(e.Message, "F_System", userName);
    }
}
```

Et voilà! You're done with your first "real" Web Service: the *userAdmin* Web Service, which is the user administration module for the Jokes application.

## Testing the Public Web Methods

You can immediately check if things work properly by calling it from a Visual Basic script, as described in Chapter 11. The VBS script shown in Figure 12.27 will add a new user.

**Figure 12.27** A Simple Visual Basic Script to Test Adding a New User to the Database

```
myWebService = "http://localhost/Jokes1/userAdmin.asmx"
myMethod = "addUser"


'** create the SOAP envelope with the request
```

**Continued**

**Figure 12.27** Continued

```
myData = ""
myData = myData & "<?xml version=""1.0"" encoding=""utf-8""?>"
myData = myData & "<soap:Envelope xmlns:soap=""http://schemas."
myData = myData & "xmlsoap.org/soap/envelope/"">"
myData = myData & "  <soap:Body>"
myData = myData & "     <addUser xmlns=""urn:schemas-syngress-"
myData = myData & "com-soap:userAdmin"">"
myData = myData & "        <userName>newUser</userName>"
myData = myData & "        <password>newPassword</password>"
myData = myData & "     </addUser>"
myData = myData & "  </soap:Body>"
myData = myData & "</soap:Envelope>"
msgbox(myData)


set requestHTTP = CreateObject("Microsoft.XMLHTTP")


msgbox("xmlhttp object created")


requestHTTP.open "POST", myWebService, false
requestHTTP.setrequestheader "Content-Type", "text/xml"
requestHTTP.setrequestheader "SOAPAction", myMethod
requestHTTP.Send myData


msgbox("request sent")


set responseDocument = requestHTTP.responseXML


msgbox(requestHTTP.status)
msgbox(responseDocument.xml)
```

If things go right, a new user should be added to the database, and a message box depicting a SOAP return envelope should appear, as shown in Figure 12.28.

**Figure 12.28** A Successful Call to Add a New Registered User

# Developing the Jokes Service

The second Web Service to develop is the jokes Web Service. The main feature of this Web Service is that it lets registered users retrieve jokes. Additionally, it contains methods to administer jokes, such as adding and removing jokes, approving jokes submitted by users to be visible to other users, and giving users a way to rate existing jokes. In many respects, things are set up in parallel from what you have already seen in the *userAdmin* Web Service, which is the Web Service to manage user information.

## Best Practices for Returning Highly Structured Data

Compared with the *userAdmin* Web Service you have just developed, the jokes Web Service has one key additional difficulty: how to return joke data. The requirements are as follows:

- Return anywhere from 1 to 10 jokes.
- Along with each joke, return its average user rating and the joke identifier (for future reference, if for example a user wants to rate that joke).

From the stored procedure *sp_getJokes*, you can get a SQL record set. One possibility, then, is to simply return the jokes as "record sets" (the correct term here is objects of type *System.Data.DataSet*). This magic works because the .NET SOAP serializer, which is the piece of code that puts the data in XML format to be sent back inside a SOAP return envelope, can indeed serialize that kind of data out of the box. However, as we discussed in Chapter 11, returning serialized *DataSets* may often not be a good idea because in practice it pretty much forces your clients to run on a Microsoft .NET platform, counter to the idea of Web Services to be an open standard.

What alternatives do you have? Again, our advice is to use a simple structure adapted to the problem at hand. If you want your clients to validate the XML against a DTD or an XML Schema, you can always pass that information as a URL (maybe to another Web Service!), but don't pass that information by default with every call to the client. In your case, you simply pass a structure that looks essentially like everything above starting from the *NewDataSet* element; that is, you want an XML element delineating rows of data, and additional XML elements delineating the fields of data within each row of data.

This is done very simply by creating a custom C# class, the *xmlJokesReturn* class, which is designed to hold a single row of data, as shown in Figure 12.29. Of course, if you prefer, you could achieve the same thing by using a structure.

**Figure 12.29** The *xmlJokesReturn* Class That Holds the Jokes (xmlJokesReturn.cs)

```csharp
using System;

namespace jokesService
{
  /// <summary>
  ///    The xmlJokesReturn class is the return type of all public
  ///    methods returning joke data.
  /// </summary>
  /// <remarks>
  ///    Author: Adrian Turtschi; aturtschi@hotmail.com; Sept 2001
  /// </remarks>
  public class xmlJokesReturn {
    /// <value>ID of joke returned</value>
    public string jokeID;
    /// <value>the actual joke</value>
    public string joke;
    /// <value>average rating of the joke (can be empty)</value>
    public string rating;

    /// <summary>
    ///    Public class constructor.
```

**Continued**

**Figure 12.29** Continued

```
///  </summary>
    public xmlJokesReturn() {

    }
  }
}
```

Because you may return more than one row of data, of course, you can simply set up the *getJokes* Web method to return an array of objects of type *xmlJokesReturn*. The SOAP serializer does the rest automatically. In Figure 12.30, you can see the definition of the *getJokes* Web method (note that we haven't talked about the corresponding implementation method yet).

**Figure 12.30** *getJokes* Web method (jokes.asmx.cs)

```
[WebMethod]
public xmlJokesReturn[] getJokes(
    string userName, string password, int howMany) {
    jokesImplement jokesObj = new jokesImplement();
    try {
      xmlJokesReturn[] myJokes =
        jokesObj.getJokes(userName, password, howMany);
      return myJokes;
    }
    // error handler omitted
```

The SOAP object serializer does what it is supposed to do, that is it returns a serialized array of *xmlJokesReturn* objects, and you retrieve a SOAP envelope on the client that may look like the one in Figure 12.31, containing two jokes.

**Figure 12.31** SOAP Response Envelope Containing Two Jokes as Serialized *xmlJokesReturn* Objects

```
<?xml version="1.0" encoding="utf-8"?>
<soap:Envelope xmlns:soap="http://schemas.xmlsoap.org/soap/envelope/"
   xmlns:xsi="http://www.w3.org/2001/XMLSchema-instance"
   xmlns:xsd="http://www.w3.org/2001/XMLSchema">
```

**Continued**

**Figure 12.31** Continued

```
<soap:Body>
   <getJokesResponse xmlns="urn:schemas-syngress-com-soap:jokes">
     <jokeData>
       <jokeID>1</jokeID>
       <joke>this is the first joke</joke>
       <rating>3.5</rating>
     </jokeData>
     <jokeData>
       <jokeID>2</jokeID>
       <joke>this is the second joke</joke>
       <rating />
     </jokeData>
   </getJokesResponse>
  </soap:Body>
</soap:Envelope>
```

# Setting Up Internal Methods to Wrap the Stored Procedure Calls

Similar to the way you proceeded when developing the *userAdmin* Web Service, you want to create internal methods to wrap calls to the stored procedures that interface with the jokes in the database. You have three stored procedures that deal with jokes:

- *sp_manageJoke*
- *sp_manageRating*
- *sp_returnJokes*

The corresponding wrapping methods, part of file JokesImplement.cs, are shown in detail in Figure 12.32 (*createSqlManageJoke*), Figure 12.33 (*createSqlManageRating*), and Figure 12.34 (*createSqlReturnJokes*).

**Figure 12.32** *createSqlManageJoke* Method (JokesImplement.cs)

```
/// <summary>
///    The createSqlManageJoke method sets up the SQL command object
///    for the stored procedure sp_manageJoke, which deals with
///    adding, updating, and deleting jokes
/// </summary>
/// <param name='userName'
///    type='string'
///    desc='name of registered user (zero length if N/A)'>
/// </param>
/// <param name='joke'
///    type='string'
///    desc='the joke (zero length if N/A)'>
/// </param>
/// <param name='isModerated'
///    type='string'
///    desc='true/false if this is/is not a moderated joke
///    (zero length if N/A)'>
/// </param>
/// <param name='jokeID'
///    type='string'
///    desc='the joke ID for the joke (zero length if N/A)'>
/// </param>
/// <param name='action'
///    type='string'
///    desc='the action the SQL stored procedure should take
///    (see the stored procedure definition for allowed action
///    keywords)'>
/// </param>
/// <param name='sqlCommand'
///    type='SqlCommand'
///    desc='a reference to a SQL command object'>
/// </param>
/// <returns>the prepared SQL command object</returns>
```

**Continued**

**Figure 12.32** Continued

```
protected internal void createSqlManageJoke(
  string userName, string joke, string isModerated,
  string jokeID, string action, SqlCommand sqlCommand) {

  sqlCommand.CommandType = CommandType.StoredProcedure;
  sqlCommand.CommandText = "sp_manageJoke" ;

  SqlParameter argUserName =
    new SqlParameter("@@userName", SqlDbType.NVarChar, 20);
  if(userName.Length > 0) {
    argUserName.Value =  userName;
  } else {
    argUserName.Value =  DBNull.Value;
  }
  sqlCommand.Parameters.Add(argUserName);

  SqlParameter argJoke =
    new SqlParameter("@@joke",SqlDbType.NVarChar, 3500);
  if(joke.Length > 0) {
    argJoke.Value =  joke;
  } else {
    argJoke.Value =  DBNull.Value;
  }
  sqlCommand.Parameters.Add(argJoke);

  SqlParameter argIsModerated =
    new SqlParameter("@@isModerated",SqlDbType.Bit);
  if(isModerated.Length > 0) {
    argIsModerated.Value = bool.Parse(isModerated);
  } else {
    argIsModerated.Value =  DBNull.Value;
  }
  sqlCommand.Parameters.Add(argIsModerated);
```

**Continued**

**Figure 12.32** Continued

```
SqlParameter argJokeID =
  new SqlParameter("@@jokeID",SqlDbType.Int);
if(jokeID.Length > 0) {
  argJokeID.Value =  Int32.Parse(jokeID);
} else {
  argJokeID.Value =  DBNull.Value;
}
sqlCommand.Parameters.Add(argJokeID);

SqlParameter argAction =
  new SqlParameter("@@action",SqlDbType.NVarChar, 20);
argAction.Value =  action;
sqlCommand.Parameters.Add(argAction);

SqlParameter argReturn =
  new SqlParameter("@@return",SqlDbType.NVarChar, 20,
  ParameterDirection.Output, true, 0, 0, "",
  DataRowVersion.Current, "");
sqlCommand.Parameters.Add(argReturn);
}
```

**Figure 12.33** *createSqlManageRating* Method (JokesImplement.cs)

```
/// <summary>
///    The createSqlManageRating method sets up the SQL command
///    object for the stored procedure sp_manageRating, which
///    deals with adding and deleting user joke ratings
/// </summary>
/// <param name='jokeID'
///    type='string'
///    desc='the joke ID for the joke we would like to rate'>
/// </param>
```

**Continued**

## Figure 12.33 Continued

```
/// <param name='rating'
///    type='string'
///    desc='the user rating for the joke (1-5)'>
/// </param>
/// <param name='action'
///    type='string'
///    desc='the action the SQL stored procedure should take
///    (see the stored procedure definition for allowed action
///    keywords)'>
/// </param>
/// <param name='sqlCommand'
///    type='SqlCommand'
///    desc='a reference to a SQL command object'>
/// </param>
/// <returns>the prepared SQL command object</returns>
protected internal void createSqlManageRating(
  string jokeID, string rating, string action,
  SqlCommand sqlCommand) {

  sqlCommand.CommandType = CommandType.StoredProcedure;
  sqlCommand.CommandText = "sp_manageRating" ;

  SqlParameter argJokeID =
    new SqlParameter("@@jokeID", SqlDbType.Int);
  argJokeID.Value =  Int32.Parse(jokeID);
  sqlCommand.Parameters.Add(argJokeID);

  SqlParameter argRating =
    new SqlParameter("@@rating",SqlDbType.TinyInt);
  argRating.Value =  Int32.Parse(rating);
  sqlCommand.Parameters.Add(argRating);

  SqlParameter argAction =
```

**Continued**

**Figure 12.33** Continued

```
   new SqlParameter("@@action",SqlDbType.NVarChar, 20);
argAction.Value =  action;
sqlCommand.Parameters.Add(argAction);


SqlParameter argReturn =
   new SqlParameter("@@return",SqlDbType.NVarChar, 20,
   ParameterDirection.Output, true, 0, 0, "",
   DataRowVersion.Current, "");
sqlCommand.Parameters.Add(argReturn);
}
```

**Figure 12.34** *createSqlReturnJokes* Method (JokesImplement.cs)

```
/// <summary>
///    The createSqlReturnJokes method sets up the SQL command object
///    for the stored procedure sp_returnJokes, which returns jokes
/// </summary>
/// <param name='howMany'
///    type='string'
///    desc='how many jokes we would like (zero length if N/A)'>
/// </param>
/// <param name='isModerated'
///    type='string'
///    desc='true/false if we are interested in (not) moderated
///    jokes (zero length if N/A)'>
/// </param>
/// <param name='returnRandom'
///    type='string'
///    desc='true/false if we are interested getting random jokes
///    (actually, only the starting position is random, from there
///    on we retrieve jokes in sequential order for practical
///    reasons)'>
/// </param>
```

**Continued**

## Figure 12.34 Continued

```
/// <param name='sqlCommand'
///    type='SqlCommand'
///    desc='a reference to a SQL command object'>
/// </param>
/// <returns>the prepared SQL command object</returns>
protected internal void createSqlReturnJokes(
  string howMany, string isModerated, string returnRandom,
  SqlCommand sqlCommand) {

  sqlCommand.CommandType = CommandType.StoredProcedure;
  sqlCommand.CommandText = "sp_returnJokes" ;

  SqlParameter argHowMany =
    new SqlParameter("@@howMany", SqlDbType.Int);
  if(howMany.Length > 0) {
    argHowMany.Value =  Int32.Parse(howMany);
  } else {
    argHowMany.Value =  DBNull.Value;
  }
  sqlCommand.Parameters.Add(argHowMany);

  SqlParameter argIsModerated =
    new SqlParameter("@@isModerated",SqlDbType.Bit);
  if(isModerated.Length > 0) {
    argIsModerated.Value =  bool.Parse(isModerated);
  } else {
    argIsModerated.Value =  DBNull.Value;
  }
  sqlCommand.Parameters.Add(argIsModerated);

  SqlParameter argReturnRandom =
    new SqlParameter("@@returnRandom",SqlDbType.Bit);
  argReturnRandom.Value =  bool.Parse(returnRandom);
```

**Continued**

**Figure 12.34** Continued

```
    sqlCommand.Parameters.Add(argReturnRandom);
}
```

# Setting Up Internal Methods to Manage Jokes and Ratings

Now that you can call the stored procedures that deal with jokes in the database, you want to implement the business logic that deals with jokes. You have four methods that either add or delete jokes and ratings:

- **addJoke()**  Checks that user is registered, and then adds the passed joke as an unmoderated joke to the system.

- **addRating()**  Checks that user is registered, and then adds the passed rating to the joke having the passed joke identifier to the system.

- **addModerated()**  Checks that user is a moderator, and then changes the isModerated flag of the joke having the passed joke identifier to the system.

- **deleteUnmoderated()**  Checks that user is a moderator, and then removes the joke having the passed joke identifier, along with all its user ratings, from the system.

Figure 12.35 shows the business logic for the *addJoke* method, and Figures 12.36, 12.37, and 12.38 deal with the *addRating*, *addModerated*, and *deleteUnmoderated* methods, respectively.

**Figure 12.35** *addJoke* Method (JokesImplement.cs)

```
///  <summary>
///     The addJoke method lets registered users add a joke
///  </summary>
///  <param name='userName'
///     type='string'
///     desc='name of registered user'>
///  </param>
///  <param name='password'
```

**Continued**

**Figure 12.35** Continued

```
///    type='string'
///    desc='password of registered user'>
/// </param>
/// <param name='joke'
///    type='string'
///    desc='the joke we are adding'>
/// </param>
/// <returns>true</returns>
protected internal bool addJoke(
  string userName, string password, string joke) {
  string retCode;

  try {
    // check if user is registered
    userAdminImplement myUser = new userAdminImplement();
    SqlCommand sqlCommand = new SqlCommand();

    myUser.createSqlCheckUser(userName, password, "", sqlCommand);

    databaseAccess myDatabase = new databaseAccess();
    sqlCommand.Connection = myDatabase.getConnection();
    sqlCommand.Connection.Open();

    sqlCommand.ExecuteNonQuery();
    retCode = sqlCommand.Parameters["@@return"].Value.ToString();

    // exit, if user not registered
    if (retCode != "S_OK") {
      sqlCommand.Connection.Close();
      throw new jokeException(retCode);
    }

    // add the joke (unmoderated, at this point)
```

**Continued**

**Figure 12.35** Continued

```
    sqlCommand.Parameters.Clear();
    createSqlManageJoke(
      userName, joke, "false", "", "add", sqlCommand);


    sqlCommand.ExecuteNonQuery();
    sqlCommand.Connection.Close();


    retCode = sqlCommand.Parameters["@@return"].Value.ToString();


    // catch problems within the stored procedure
    if (retCode == "S_OK") {
      return true;
    } else {
      throw new jokeException(retCode);
    }
    // catch problems with the database
  } catch (Exception e) {
    throw e;
  }
}
```

**Figure 12.36** *addRating* Method (JokesImplement.cs)

```
/// <summary>
///    The addRating method lets registered users rate a joke
/// </summary>
/// <param name='userName'
///    type='string'
///    desc='name of registered user'>
/// </param>
/// <param name='password'
///    type='string'
///    desc='password of registered user'>
```

**Continued**

## Figure 12.36 Continued

```
/// </param>
/// <param name='rating'
///    type='int'
///    desc='the rating of the joke to rate (1-5)'>
/// </param>
/// <param name='jokeID'
///    type='int'
///    desc='the ID of the joke to rate'>
/// </param>
/// <returns>true</returns>
protected internal bool addRating(
   string userName, string password, int rating, int jokeID) {
   string retCode;

   try {
     // check if user is registered
     userAdminImplement myUser = new userAdminImplement();
     SqlCommand sqlCommand = new SqlCommand();

     myUser.createSqlCheckUser(userName, password, "", sqlCommand);

     databaseAccess myDatabase = new databaseAccess();
     sqlCommand.Connection = myDatabase.getConnection();
     sqlCommand.Connection.Open();

     sqlCommand.ExecuteNonQuery();
     retCode = sqlCommand.Parameters["@@return"].Value.ToString();

     // exit, if user not registered
     if (retCode != "S_OK") {
       sqlCommand.Connection.Close();
       throw new jokeException(retCode);
     }
```

**Continued**

**Figure 12.36** Continued

```
    // add the joke rating
    sqlCommand.Parameters.Clear();
    createSqlManageRating(
      jokeID.ToString(), rating.ToString(), "add", sqlCommand);

    sqlCommand.ExecuteNonQuery();
    sqlCommand.Connection.Close();

    retCode = sqlCommand.Parameters["@@return"].Value.ToString();

    // catch problems within the stored procedure
    if (retCode == "S_OK") {
      return true;
    } else {
      throw new jokeException(retCode);
    }
    // catch problems with the database
  } catch (Exception e) {
    throw e;
  }
}
```

**Figure 12.37** *addModerated* Method (JokesImplement.cs)

```
/// <summary>
///    The addModerated method sets a previously submitted joke
///    to become a moderated joke
///    (for moderators only)
/// </summary>
/// <param name='userName'
///    type='string'
///    desc='name of moderator'>
```

**Continued**

## Figure 12.37 Continued

```
/// </param>
/// <param name='password'
///    type='string'
///    desc='password of moderator'>
/// </param>
/// <param name='jokeID'
///    type='int'
///    desc='joke ID of joke'>
/// </param>
/// <returns>an XML representation (xmlJokesReturn)
/// of a single joke</returns>
protected internal bool addModerated(
  string userName, string password, int jokeID) {
  string retCode;

  try {
    // check if user is a moderator
    userAdminImplement myUser = new userAdminImplement();
    SqlCommand sqlCommand = new SqlCommand();

    myUser.createSqlCheckUser(
      userName, password, "true", sqlCommand);

    databaseAccess myDatabase = new databaseAccess();
    sqlCommand.Connection = myDatabase.getConnection();
    sqlCommand.Connection.Open();

    sqlCommand.ExecuteNonQuery();
    retCode = sqlCommand.Parameters["@@return"].Value.ToString();

    // exit, if user not a moderator
    if (retCode != "S_OK") {
      sqlCommand.Connection.Close();
```

**Continued**

**Figure 12.37** Continued

```
      throw new jokeException(retCode);
   }


   // make the joke a moderated one
   sqlCommand.Parameters.Clear();
   createSqlManageJoke(userName, "", "true", jokeID.ToString(),
      "modify", sqlCommand);


   sqlCommand.ExecuteNonQuery();
   sqlCommand.Connection.Close();


   retCode = sqlCommand.Parameters["@@return"].Value.ToString();


   // catch problems within the stored procedure
   if (retCode == "S_OK") {
      return true;
   } else {
      throw new jokeException(retCode);
   }
   // catch problems with the database
} catch (Exception e) {
   throw e;
}
}
```

**Figure 12.38** *deleteUnmoderated* Method (JokesImplement.cs)

```
/// <summary>
///    The deleteUnmoderated method deletes a previously
///    submitted joke (unmoderated) joke
///    (for moderators only)
/// </summary>
/// <param name='userName'
```

**Continued**

**Figure 12.38** Continued

```
///    type='string'
///    desc='name of moderator'>
/// </param>
/// <param name='password'
///    type='string'
///    desc='password of moderator'>
/// </param>
/// <param name='jokeID'
///    type='int'
///    desc='joke ID of joke'>
/// </param>
/// <returns>true</returns>
protected internal bool deleteUnmoderated(
  string userName, string password, int jokeID) {
  string retCode;

  try {
    // check if user is a moderator
    userAdminImplement myUser = new userAdminImplement();
    SqlCommand sqlCommand = new SqlCommand();

    myUser.createSqlCheckUser(
      userName, password, "true", sqlCommand);

    databaseAccess myDatabase = new databaseAccess();
    sqlCommand.Connection = myDatabase.getConnection();
    sqlCommand.Connection.Open();

    sqlCommand.ExecuteNonQuery();

    retCode = sqlCommand.Parameters["@@return"].Value.ToString();

    // exit, if user not a moderator
```

*Continued*

**Figure 12.38** Continued

```
if (retCode != "S_OK") {
  sqlCommand.Connection.Close();
  throw new jokeException(retCode);
}

// delete the joke
sqlCommand.Parameters.Clear();
createSqlManageJoke(
  userName, "", "", jokeID.ToString(), "delete", sqlCommand);

sqlCommand.ExecuteNonQuery();
sqlCommand.Connection.Close();

retCode = sqlCommand.Parameters["@@return"].Value.ToString();

// catch problems within the stored procedure
if (retCode == "S_OK") {
  return true;
} else {
  throw new jokeException(retCode);
}
// catch problems with the database
} catch (Exception e) {
  throw e;
}
}
```

# Setting Up Internal Methods to Return Jokes

Finally, you have two methods that return joke data:

- **getJokes()**  Check that user is registered, and then return one or more
  moderated jokes, depending on an argument passed

■ **getUnmoderated()** Check that user is a moderator, and then return one or more moderated jokes, depending on an argument passed

As mentioned earlier, you should forgo returning *DataSets*, and return instead an array of type *xmlJokesReturn*. Figure 12.39 shows the code for the *getJokes* method, and Figure 12.40 details the method *getUnmoderated*.

**Figure 12.39** *getJokes* Method (JokesImplement.cs)

```
/// <summary>
///    The getJokes method returns howMany new jokes from
///    the database
/// </summary>
/// <param name='userName'
///    type='string'
///    desc='name of registered user'>
/// </param>
/// <param name='password'
///    type='string'
///    desc='password of registered user'>
/// </param>
/// <param name='howMany'
///    type='int'
///    desc='number of jokes to return (1-10)'>
/// </param>
/// <returns>an XML representation (xmlJokesReturn) of a
///    single joke</returns>
protected internal xmlJokesReturn[] getJokes(
  string userName, string password, int howMany) {
  string retCode;

  try {
    // check if user is registered
    userAdminImplement myUser = new userAdminImplement();
    SqlCommand sqlCommand = new SqlCommand();
```

**Continued**

## Figure 12.39 Continued

```
    myUser.createSqlCheckUser(userName, password, "", sqlCommand);

    databaseAccess myDatabase = new databaseAccess();
    sqlCommand.Connection = myDatabase.getConnection();
    sqlCommand.Connection.Open();

    sqlCommand.ExecuteNonQuery();

    retCode = sqlCommand.Parameters["@@return"].Value.ToString();

    // exit, if user not registered
    if (retCode != "S_OK") {
      sqlCommand.Connection.Close();
      throw new jokeException(retCode);
    }

    // retrieve a random joke

    // maximum is 10 jokes
    if((howMany < 1) || (howMany > 10)) {
      throw new jokeException("F_10JokesMax");
    }

    sqlCommand.Parameters.Clear();
    createSqlReturnJokes(
      howMany.ToString(), "true", "true", sqlCommand);

    sqlCommand.ExecuteNonQuery();

    sqlCommand.Connection.Close();

    SqlDataAdapter sqlDataAdapter = new SqlDataAdapter(sqlCommand);
    DataTable dataTable = new DataTable("sqlReturn");
```

**Continued**

**Figure 12.39** Continued

```
      sqlDataAdapter.Fill(dataTable);


      // convert SQL table into xmlJokesReturn class
      int rowCount = dataTable.Rows.Count;
      xmlJokesReturn[] myJokes = new xmlJokesReturn[rowCount];
      for(int i = 0; i < rowCount; i++) {
        myJokes[i] = new xmlJokesReturn();
        myJokes[i].jokeID = dataTable.Rows[i][0].ToString();
        myJokes[i].joke   = dataTable.Rows[i][1].ToString();
        myJokes[i].rating = dataTable.Rows[i][2].ToString();
      }
      // catch problems within the stored procedure
      if(rowCount > 0) {
        return myJokes;
      } else {
        throw new jokeException("F_noJokes");
      }
      // catch problems with the database
    } catch (Exception e) {
      throw e;
    }
}
```

**Figure 12.40** *getUnmoderated* Method (JokesImplement.cs)

```
/// <summary>
///    The getUnmoderated method retrieves howMany jokes from
///    the database
///    (for moderators only)
/// </summary>
/// <param name='userName'
///    type='string'
///    desc='name of moderator'>
```

**Continued**

**Figure 12.40** Continued

```
/// </param>
/// <param name='password'
///    type='string'
///    desc='password of moderator'>
/// </param>
/// <param name='howMany'
///    type='int'
///    desc='number of jokes to return'>
/// </param>
/// <returns>an XML representation (xmlJokesReturn)
/// of a single joke</returns>
protected internal xmlJokesReturn[] getUnmoderated(
  string userName, string password, int howMany) {
  string retCode;

  try {
    // check if user is a moderator
    userAdminImplement myUser = new userAdminImplement();
    SqlCommand sqlCommand = new SqlCommand();

    myUser.createSqlCheckUser(
      userName, password, "true", sqlCommand);

    databaseAccess myDatabase = new databaseAccess();
    sqlCommand.Connection = myDatabase.getConnection();
    sqlCommand.Connection.Open();

    sqlCommand.ExecuteNonQuery();

    retCode = sqlCommand.Parameters["@@return"].Value.ToString();

    // exit, if user not a moderator
    if (retCode != "S_OK") {
```

*Continued*

**Figure 12.40** Continued

```
    sqlCommand.Connection.Close();

    throw new jokeException(retCode);

}


// retrieve the first <howMany> unmoderated jokes


// maximum is 10 jokes
if((howMany < 1) || (howMany > 10)) {

    throw new jokeException("F_10JokesMax");

}


sqlCommand.Parameters.Clear();
createSqlReturnJokes(

    howMany.ToString(), "false", "false", sqlCommand);


sqlCommand.ExecuteNonQuery();


sqlCommand.Connection.Close();


SqlDataAdapter sqlDataAdapter = new SqlDataAdapter(sqlCommand);
DataTable dataTable = new DataTable("sqlReturn");
sqlDataAdapter.Fill(dataTable);


// convert SQL table into xmlJokesReturn class
int rowCount = dataTable.Rows.Count;
xmlJokesReturn[] myJokes = new xmlJokesReturn[rowCount];
for(int i = 0; i < rowCount; i++) {

    myJokes[i] = new xmlJokesReturn();

    myJokes[i].jokeID = dataTable.Rows[i][0].ToString();

    myJokes[i].joke   = dataTable.Rows[i][1].ToString();

    myJokes[i].rating = dataTable.Rows[i][2].ToString();

}
// catch problems within the stored procedure
```

**Continued**

**Figure 12.40** Continued

```
if(rowCount > 0) {
   return myJokes;
} else {
   throw new jokeException("F_noJokes");
}
// catch problems with the database
} catch (Exception e) {
throw e;
}
}
```

## Creating the Public Web Methods

You are now finished with the internal methods, and you can now go about implementing the public Web methods for the jokes Web Service. Remember that you put all of those Web methods in the *jokes* class (the file on the CD is jokes.asmx.cs). Figures 12.41 through 12.46 detail the code for those public Web methods.

**Figure 12.41** *addJoke* Web Method (jokes.asmx.cs)

```
/// <summary>
///    The addJoke method adds a new joke to the database
/// </summary>
/// <param name='userName'
///    type='string'
///    desc='name of registered user'>
/// </param>
/// <param name='password'
///    type='string'
///    desc='password of registered user'>
/// </param>
/// <param name='joke'
///    type='string'
///    desc='the joke'>
```

**Continued**

**Figure 12.41** Continued

```
///   </param>
///   <returns>nothing</returns>
[SoapDocumentMethodAttribute(Action="addJoke",
    RequestNamespace="urn:schemas-syngress-com-soap:jokes",
    RequestElementName="addJoke",
    ResponseNamespace="urn:schemas-syngress-com-soap:jokes",
    ResponseElementName="addJokeResponse")]
[WebMethod(Description="The addJoke method adds a new joke " +
    "to the database")]
public void addJoke(
  string userName, string password, string joke) {
  jokesImplement jokesObj = new jokesImplement();
  try {
    jokesObj.addJoke(userName, password, joke);
  // catch jokeExceptions
  } catch (jokeException e) {
    throwFault("Fault occurred", e.failReason, userName);
  }
    // then, catch general System Exceptions
  catch (Exception e) {
    throwFault(e.Message, "F_System", userName);
  }
}
```

**Figure 12.42** *getJokes* Web Method (jokes.asmx.cs)

```
///   <summary>
///     The getJokes method gets howMany (moderated) jokes
///     from the database
///   </summary>
///   <param name='userName'
///     type='string'
///     desc='name of registered user'>
```

**Continued**

**Figure 12.42** Continued

```
/// </param>
/// <param name='password'
///    type='string'
///    desc='password of registered user'>
/// </param>
/// <param name='howMany'
///    type='int'
///    desc='how many jokes we would like'>
/// </param>
/// <returns>an XML representation (xmlJokesReturn)
/// of howMany jokes</returns>
[SoapDocumentMethodAttribute(Action="getJokes",
   RequestNamespace="urn:schemas-syngress-com-soap:jokes",
   RequestElementName="getJokes",
   ResponseNamespace="urn:schemas-syngress-com-soap:jokes",
   ResponseElementName="getJokesResponse")]
[WebMethod(Description="The getJokes method gets <howMany> " +
   "(moderated) jokes from the database")]
[return: XmlElementAttribute("jokeData", IsNullable=false)]
public xmlJokesReturn[] getJokes(
   string userName, string password, int howMany) {
   jokesImplement jokesObj = new jokesImplement();
   try {
     xmlJokesReturn[] myJokes =
       jokesObj.getJokes(userName, password, howMany);
     return myJokes;
   // catch jokeExceptions
   } catch (jokeException e) {
     throwFault("Fault occurred", e.failReason, userName);
     return null;  // code never reached, but needed by compiler
   }
     // then, catch general System Exceptions
   catch (Exception e) {
```

**Continued**

**Figure 12.42** Continued

```
    throwFault(e.Message, "F_System", userName);
    return null;  // code never reached, but needed by compiler
  }
}
```

**Figure 12.43** *addRating* Web Method (jokes.asmx.cs)

```
/// <summary>
///    The addRating method lets a user add a rating
///    for a joke to the database
/// </summary>
/// <param name='userName'
///    type='string'
///    desc='name of registered user'>
/// </param>
/// <param name='password'
///    type='string'
///    desc='password of registered user'>
/// </param>
/// <param name='rating'
///    type='int'
///    desc='rating of the joke (1-5)'>
/// </param>
/// <param name='jokeID'
///    type='int'
///    desc='ID of the joke'>
/// </param>
/// <returns>nothing</returns>
[SoapDocumentMethodAttribute(Action="addRating",
    RequestNamespace="urn:schemas-syngress-com-soap:jokes",
    RequestElementName="addRating",
    ResponseNamespace="urn:schemas-syngress-com-soap:jokes",
    ResponseElementName="addRatingResponse")]
```

**Continued**

**Figure 12.43** Continued

```
[WebMethod(Description="The addRating method lets a user add a " +
    "rating for a joke to the database")]
public void addRating(
    string userName, string password, int rating, int jokeID) {
    jokesImplement jokesObj = new jokesImplement();
    try {
        if((rating < 1) && (rating > 5)) {
            throwFault("Fault occurred", "F_ratingInvalid", userName);
        } else {
            jokesObj.addRating(userName, password, rating, jokeID);
        }
        // catch jokeExceptions
    } catch (jokeException e) {
        throwFault("Fault occurred", e.failReason, userName);
    }
        // then, catch general System Exceptions
    catch (Exception e) {
        throwFault(e.Message, "F_System", userName);
    }
}
```

**Figure 12.44** *getUnmoderated* Web Method (jokes.asmx.cs)

```
/// <summary>
///    The getUnmoderated method lets a moderator retrieve
///    howMany unmoderated jokes from the database
/// </summary>
/// <param name='userName'
///    type='string'
///    desc='name of moderator'>
/// </param>
/// <param name='password'
///    type='string'
```

**Continued**

## Figure 12.44 Continued

```
///    desc='password of moderator'>
/// </param>
/// <param name='howMany'
///    type='int'
///    desc='how many jokes we would like'>
/// </param>
/// <returns>an XML representation (xmlJokesReturn)
/// of howMany jokes</returns>
[SoapDocumentMethodAttribute(Action="getUnmoderated",
    RequestNamespace="urn:schemas-syngress-com-soap:jokes",
    RequestElementName="getUnmoderated",
    ResponseNamespace="urn:schemas-syngress-com-soap:jokes",
    ResponseElementName="getUnmoderatedResponse")]
[WebMethod(Description="The getUnmoderated method lets a " +
    "moderator retrieve <howMany> unmoderated jokes from " +
    "the database")]
[return: XmlElementAttribute("jokeData", IsNullable=false)]
public xmlJokesReturn[] getUnmoderated(
  string userName, string password, int howMany) {
  jokesImplement jokesObj = new jokesImplement();
  try {
    xmlJokesReturn[] myJokes =
      jokesObj.getUnmoderated(userName, password, howMany);
    return myJokes;
    // catch jokeExceptions
  } catch (jokeException e) {
    throwFault("Fault occurred", e.failReason, userName);
    return null;  // code never reached, but needed by compiler
  }
    // then, catch general System Exceptions
  catch (Exception e) {
    throwFault(e.Message, "F_System", userName);
    return null;  // code never reached, but needed by compiler
```

Continued

**Figure 12.44** Continued

```
    }
}
```

**Figure 12.45** *addModerated* Web Method (jokes.asmx.cs)

```
/// <summary>
///    The addModerated method lets a moderator set a joke to be
///    'moderated', i.e. accessible to regular users
/// </summary>
/// <param name='userName'
///    type='string'
///    desc='name of moderator'>
/// </param>
/// <param name='password'
///    type='string'
///    desc='password of moderator'>
/// </param>
/// <param name='jokeID'
///    type='int'
///    desc='ID of joke'>
/// </param>
/// <returns>nothing</returns>
[SoapDocumentMethodAttribute(Action="addModerated",
    RequestNamespace="urn:schemas-syngress-com-soap:jokes",
    RequestElementName="addModerated",
    ResponseNamespace="urn:schemas-syngress-com-soap:jokes",
    ResponseElementName="addModeratedResponse")]
[WebMethod(Description="The addModerated method lets a " +
    "moderator set a joke to be 'moderated', i.e. accessible " +
    "to regular users")]
public void addModerated(
    string userName, string password, int jokeID) {
    jokesImplement jokesObj = new jokesImplement();
```

**Continued**

**Figure 12.45** Continued

```
try {
   jokesObj.addModerated(userName, password, jokeID);
   // catch jokeExceptions
} catch (jokeException e) {
   throwFault("Fault occurred", e.failReason, userName);
}
   // then, catch general System Exceptions
catch (Exception e) {
   throwFault(e.Message, "F_System", userName);
}
}
```

**Figure 12.46** *deleteUnmoderated* Web Method (jokes.asmx.cs)

```
/// <summary>
///    The deleteUnmoderated method lets a moderator delete a
///    (unmoderated) joke from the database
/// </summary>
/// <param name='userName'
///    type='string'
///    desc='name of moderator'>
/// </param>
/// <param name='password'
///    type='string'
///    desc='password of moderator'>
/// </param>
/// <param name='jokeID'
///    type='int'
///    desc='ID of joke'>
/// </param>
/// <returns>nothing</returns>
[SoapDocumentMethodAttribute(Action="deleteUnmoderated",
   RequestNamespace="urn:schemas-syngress-com-soap:jokes",
```

Continued

## Figure 12.46 Continued

```
   RequestElementName="deleteUnmoderated",
   ResponseNamespace="urn:schemas-syngress-com-soap:jokes",
   ResponseElementName="deleteUnmoderatedResponse")]
[WebMethod(Description="The deleteUnmoderated method lets a " +
   "moderator delete a (unmoderated) joke from the database")]
public void deleteUnmoderated(
   string userName, string password, int jokeID) {
   jokesImplement jokesObj = new jokesImplement();
   try {
     jokesObj.deleteUnmoderated(userName, password, jokeID);
   // catch jokeExceptions
   } catch (jokeException e) {
     throwFault("Fault occurred", e.failReason, userName);
   }
     // then, catch general System Exceptions
   catch (Exception e) {
     throwFault(e.Message, "F_System", userName);
   }
}
```

And you need to either add the same error-handling routine, *throwFault*, as you did for the *userAdmin* Web Service, or you simply reference that method (in which case you need to modify its access scope).

This completes the Web Service section of the jokes Web Service. As mentioned before, you can find the complete code for the Jokes Web Service in the directory jokesService on the CD accompanying this book.

Let's quickly review what you have done so far. You have implemented two out of three tiers of a complex Web application that delivers jokes to users using Web Services technology. You have set up a database back-end system to hold user and joke information, you have created business logic components to manage users and jokes, and you have implemented a data access mechanism using Web Services. Although you could now go ahead and publish your Web Service in a UDDI registry and wait for clients out there to consume your Web Service, you should make an additional step and build a portal application that lets users interface with the jokes application through Windows forms.

## Developing & Deploying…

## Creating Human Readable Documentation

As you set up the Web Service project, you instructed the C# compiler to automatically create an XML documentation output file (see Figure 12.12). If you now have a look at that file, you'll see something similar to Figure 12.47.

**Figure 12.47** XML Documentation Generated by the C# Compiler

```xml
<?xml version="1.0" ?>
- <doc>
  - <assembly>
      <name>jokesService</name>
    </assembly>
  - <members>
    - <member name="T:jokesService.databaseAccess">
        <summary>The databaseAccess sets up the connection to the data
          repository.</summary>
        <remarks>Author: Adrian Turtschi; aturtschi@hotmail.com; Sept
          2001</remarks>
      </member>
    - <member name="M:jokesService.databaseAccess.#ctor">
        <summary>Public class constructor.</summary>
      </member>
    - <member name="M:jokesService.databaseAccess.getConnection">
        <summary>The getConnection method sets up the database
          connection</summary>
        <returns>the (closed) SQL connection object</returns>
      </member>
    - <member name="T:jokesService.jokeException">
        <summary>Custom error handling class</summary>
        <remarks>Author: Adrian Turtschi; aturtschi@hotmail.com; Sept
          2001</remarks>
      </member>
    - <member name="F:jokesService.jokeException.failReason">
        <value>fail reason error code</value>
      </member>
    - <member name="M:jokesService.jokeException.#ctor(System.String)">
```

Although all comments appear as they should, this document needs some improvement to be truly useful for human consumption. Unfortunately, the Beta2 does not contain style sheets to work with the ML documentation files.

However, Dan Vallejo was kind enough to make an XSLT style sheet (www.conted.bcc.ctc.edu/users/danval/CSharp/CSharp_Code_Files/doc.xsl) publicly available on his C# Web site at www.conted.bcc.ctc.edu/users/danval/ that generates a nice looking HTML documentation file. Although

**Continued**

not quite as functionally rich as the documentation generated by, say, the *javadoc* tool in the Java world, it is a first step in the right direction. The XSLT file was originally conceived by Anders Hejlsberg. We use it by permission of the author.

After applying that style sheet, your documentation will look similar to Figure 12.48.

**Figure 12.48** HTML Documentation after Applying a Style Sheet

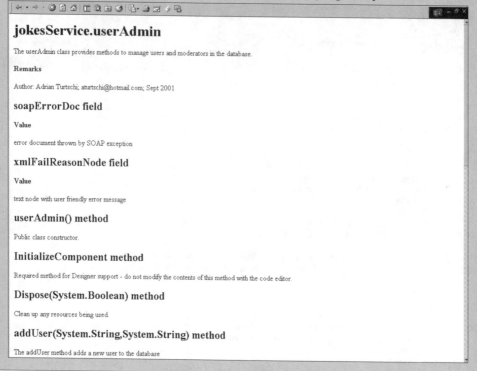

# Creating a Client Application

Let's go ahead and develop a simple Windows Forms–based client for the Jokes Web Service. The complete code for this application is on the CD in the directory jokesClient. Start by opening up Visual Studio.NET. Go to **File | New | Project**, choose the entry **Windows Application** under the **Visual C# Projects** folder, keep the default Location, and enter **jokesClient** as the **Name** of the project, as indicated in Figure 12.49. This will set up a new form and create supporting project files.

**Figure 12.49** Creating the *jokesService* Client as a Windows Forms Application

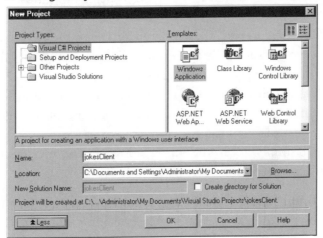

Next, add a reference to the Jokes Web Server. Right-click on the **jokesClient** project in the Solutions Explorer and select **Add Web Reference**. At the **Address** input box, enter **http://localhost/Jokes1/userAdmin.asmx**, as shown in Figure 12.50.

**Figure 12.50** Adding a Web Reference to the Web Service

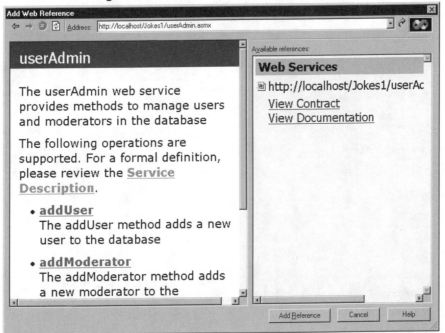

Once you verify that everything is fine, click **Add Reference**. Do the same for the Jokes Web Service, which is at the URL http://localhost/jokesService/jokes.asmx.

As described in Chapter 11, these references create the necessary proxy classes for your client to access the Jokes application. Keep in mind that those references are static, and as you change the Web Service public Web methods, you need to manually refresh the Web references. (You don't need to do this if you change the internal implementation classes, which was, after all, one of the reason you created them in the first place.)

The rest is just simply an exercise in Windows Forms programming. Things to keep in mind are the following:

- Even though Web Services are stateless, you can let your users "log on" by asking for their credentials once, checking them against the user database with the *checkUser* Web method, and then caching them locally on the client.

- The Web Service throws SOAP exceptions if things go wrong. You can extract a user-friendly message by looking at the *failReason* custom XML element in the SOAP exception return envelope.

Look at Figures 12.51, 12.52, and 12.53 to see how the client application looks.

**Figure 12.51** The Web Service Client at Startup

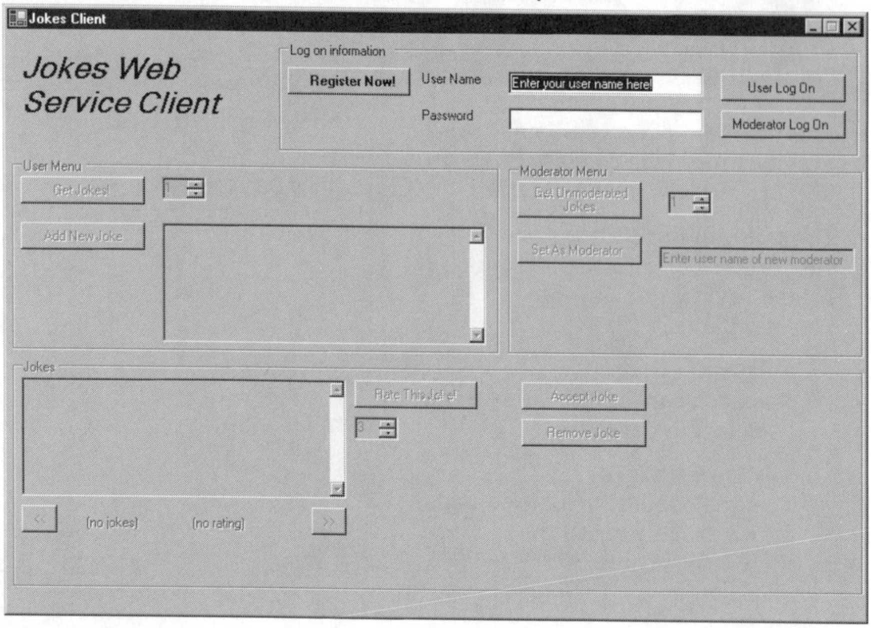

**Figure 12.52** The Web Service Client after Logging On as a User, Retrieving Some Jokes, and Adding a User Joke Rating

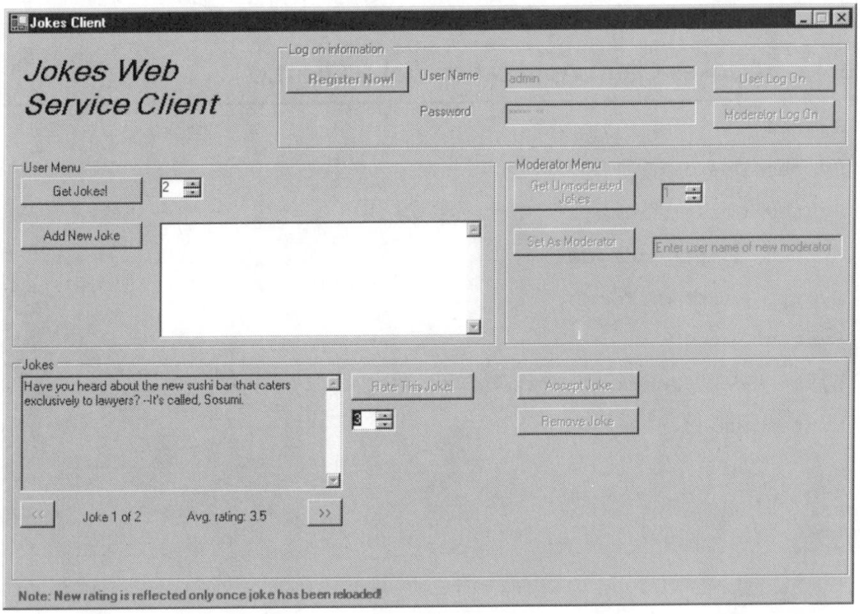

**Figure 12.53** The Web Service Client after Logging On as a Moderator, Retrieving One Unmoderated Joke, and Accepting It to Become Moderated

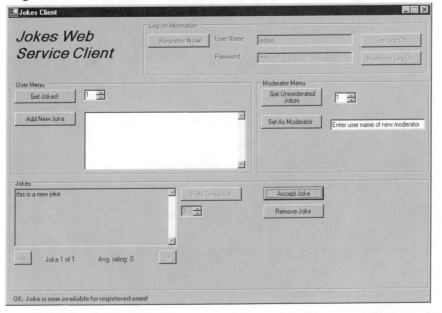

Figure 12.54 shows the code for the Jokes Client, ignoring code generated through the form designer. For the complete code, see the file jokesClient.cs on the CD.

**Figure 12.54** Jokes Client Application (jokesClient.cs)

```
using System;

using System.Drawing;

using System.Collections;

using System.ComponentModel;

using System.Windows.Forms;

using System.Data;

using System.Web.Services.Protocols;

using System.Xml;


namespace jokesClient
{
  /// <summary>
  ///    Form f_jokeClient.
  /// </summary>
  /// <remarks>
  ///    Author: Adrian Turtschi; aturtschi@hotmail.com; Sept 2001
  /// </remarks>
  public class f_jokeClient : System.Windows.Forms.Form
  {
    // placeholders for Web Service objects
    private userAdmin.userAdmin userAdminObj ;
    private jokes.jokes jokesObj;
    // remember if objects have been created
    private bool userAdminObjCreated = false;
    private bool jokesObjCreated = false;

    // remember username and password, and moderator status
    private string userName = "";
    private string password = "";
    private bool isModerator = false;
```

Continued

**Figure 12.54** Continued

```
// hold jokes

private jokes.xmlJokesReturn[] myJokes;

private int jokesReturned = 0;

private int currentJoke = 0;

// are we looking at moderated jokes or not?

private bool moderatedJokes = false;



// IGNORE setting up of form elements

public f_jokeClient() {

  InitializeComponent();

}


public void InitializeComponent() {

  // IGNORE

}


protected override void Dispose( bool disposing ) {

  if( disposing )

  {

    if (components != null)

    {

      components.Dispose();

    }

  }

  base.Dispose( disposing );

}



[STAThread]

static void Main() {

  Application.Run(new f_jokeClient());
```

**Continued**

**Figure 12.54** Continued

```
    }

private void displayJoke(
   string joke, int jokeNumber, int totalJokes, decimal rating,
   bool moderatedJokes) {
   this.l_statusMessage.Text = "";

   if(totalJokes == 0) {
      this.gb_jokes.Enabled = false;
      this.tb_jokesJoke.Text = "";
      this.nud_jokesRating.Value = 3;
      this.l_jokesNumber.Text = "(no jokes)";
      this.l_jokesRating.Text = "(no rating)";
      return;
   }

   if(totalJokes > 0) {
      this.gb_jokes.Enabled = true;
      if (!moderatedJokes) {
         this.b_jokesAddModerated.Enabled = true;
         this.b_jokesRemove.Enabled = true;
         this.nud_jokesRating.Enabled = false;
         this.b_jokesAddRating.Enabled = false;
      } else {
         this.b_jokesAddModerated.Enabled = false;
         this.b_jokesRemove.Enabled = false;
         this.nud_jokesRating.Enabled = true;
         this.b_jokesAddRating.Enabled = true;
      }
   }

   if(totalJokes > 1) {
      if(jokeNumber == 1) {
```

**Continued**

**Figure 12.54** Continued

```
            this.b_jokesNext.Enabled = true;
            this.b_jokesPrev.Enabled = false;
        } else {
          if(jokeNumber == totalJokes) {
              this.b_jokesNext.Enabled = false;
              this.b_jokesPrev.Enabled = true;
          } else {
              this.b_jokesNext.Enabled = true;
              this.b_jokesPrev.Enabled = true;
          }
        }
      } else {
        this.b_jokesNext.Enabled = false;
        this.b_jokesPrev.Enabled = false;
      }


      this.tb_jokesJoke.Text = joke;
      this.l_jokesNumber.Text = "Joke " + jokeNumber.ToString()
        + " of " + totalJokes.ToString();
      this.l_jokesRating.Text = "Avg. rating: " + rating.ToString();
  }


  private void logon(bool isModerator, bool register) {
    string userName = this.tb_logonUserName.Text;
    string password = this.tb_logonPassword.Text;
    if((userName.Length > 0) && (password.Length > 0)
        && (userName.Length <= 20) && (password.Length <= 20)) {
      if(!this.userAdminObjCreated) {
        this.userAdminObj = new userAdmin.userAdmin();
        this.userAdminObjCreated = true;
      }
      try {
        // register new user?
```

**Figure 12.54** Continued

```
if(register) {
  // Call our Web Service method addUser
  this.userAdminObj.addUser(userName, password);
} else {
  // Call our Web Service method checkUser
  this.userAdminObj.checkUser(
    userName.Substring(0,Math.Min(userName.Length, 20)),
    password.Substring(0,Math.Min(password.Length, 20)),
    isModerator);
}
// OK
this.userName = userName;
this.password = password;
this.isModerator = isModerator;
if(isModerator) {
  this.gb_moderatorMenu.Enabled = true;
} else {
  this.gb_moderatorMenu.Enabled = false;
}
this.gb_userMenu.Enabled = true;
this.gb_userInfo.Enabled = false;
this.l_statusMessage.Text = "";
displayJoke("", 0, 0, 0, this.isModerator);
if(register) {
  this.l_statusMessage.Text = "OK: you have successfully " +
    "registered with the system!";
}
} catch (SoapException ex) {
XmlNode[] customErrorMsgs = ex.OtherElements;
if(customErrorMsgs.Length > 0) {
  XmlNode customErrorMsg = customErrorMsgs[0];
  if (customErrorMsg.InnerText.Length > 0) {
    this.l_statusMessage.Text = "Error: " +
```

**Continued**

**Figure 12.54** Continued

```
                    customErrorMsg.InnerText;
            return;
        }
    }
} catch (Exception ex) {
    this.l_statusMessage.Text = "Error: " + ex.Message;
}
}
}


private void getJokes(int howMany, bool moderatedJokes) {
    try {
        if(!this.jokesObjCreated) {
            this.jokesObj = new jokes.jokes();
            this.jokesObjCreated = true;
        }
        // Call our Web Service method getJokes
        if(moderatedJokes) {
            myJokes = this.jokesObj.getJokes(
                userName, password, howMany);
        } else {
            myJokes = this.jokesObj.getUnmoderated(
                userName, password, howMany);
        }
        // OK
        this.jokesReturned = myJokes.Length;
        if(this.jokesReturned == 0) {
            displayJoke("", 0, 0, 0, this.isModerator);
        } else {
            this.currentJoke = 1;
            displayJoke(
                myJokes[this.currentJoke - 1].joke,
                this.currentJoke,
```

*Continued*

**Figure 12.54 Continued**

```csharp
            this.jokesReturned,
            // need leading zero in case NULL is returned from
            // the database, i.e. joke unrated (which
            // will come back as zero length string)
            Decimal.Parse(
              "0" + myJokes[this.currentJoke - 1].rating),
              moderatedJokes);
        }
    } catch (SoapException ex) {
      XmlNode[] customErrorMsgs = ex.OtherElements;
      if(customErrorMsgs.Length > 0) {
        XmlNode customErrorMsg = customErrorMsgs[0];
        if (customErrorMsg.InnerText.Length > 0) {
          this.l_statusMessage.Text =
            "Error: " + customErrorMsg.InnerText;
          return;
        }
      }
    } catch (Exception ex) {
      this.l_statusMessage.Text = "Error: " + ex.Message;
    }
  }


private void b_logonUserLogOn_Click(
  object sender, System.EventArgs e) {
  logon(false, false);
}


private void b_logonModeratorLogOn_Click(
  object sender, System.EventArgs e) {
  logon(true, false);
}
```

**Continued**

**Figure 12.54** Continued

```
private void b_logonRegisterNow_Click(
  object sender, System.EventArgs e) {
  logon(false, true);
}


private void b_moderatorMakeModerator_Click(
  object sender, System.EventArgs e) {
  displayJoke("", 0, 0, 0, this.isModerator);
  string newModeratorUserName =
    this.tb_moderatorNewModeratorUserName.Text;
  if(newModeratorUserName.Length > 0) {
    newModeratorUserName = newModeratorUserName.Substring(
      0,Math.Min(newModeratorUserName.Length, 20));
    if(!this.userAdminObjCreated) {
      this.userAdminObj = new userAdmin.userAdmin();
      this.userAdminObjCreated = true;
    }
    try {
        // Call our Web Service method addModerator
        this.userAdminObj.addModerator(
          this.userName, this.password, newModeratorUserName);
      // OK
      this.l_statusMessage.Text =
        "OK: " + newModeratorUserName + " is now a moderator";
    } catch (SoapException ex) {
      XmlNode[] customErrorMsgs = ex.OtherElements;
      if(customErrorMsgs.Length > 0) {
        XmlNode customErrorMsg = customErrorMsgs[0];
        if (customErrorMsg.InnerText.Length > 0) {
          this.l_statusMessage.Text =
            "Error: " + customErrorMsg.InnerText;
          return;
        }
```

*Continued*

**Figure 12.54** Continued

```
        }
      } catch (Exception ex) {
        this.l_statusMessage.Text = "Error: " + ex.Message;
      }
    }
  }


private void b_userGetJokes_Click(
  object sender, System.EventArgs e) {
  displayJoke("", 0, 0, 0, this.isModerator);
  this.moderatedJokes = true;
  getJokes((int)this.nud_userHowMany.Value, this.moderatedJokes);
}


private void b_moderatorGetUnmoderated_Click(
  object sender, System.EventArgs e) {
  displayJoke("", 0, 0, 0, this.isModerator);
  this.moderatedJokes = false;
  getJokes(
    (int)this.nud_moderatorHowMany.Value, this.moderatedJokes);
}


private void b_jokesPrev_Click(object sender, System.EventArgs e) {
  // displayJoke() ONLY enables this button if there are jokes
  // to display, so we don't need a sanity check here.
  this.currentJoke = this.currentJoke - 1;
  displayJoke(
    myJokes[this.currentJoke - 1].joke,
    this.currentJoke,
    this.jokesReturned,
    Decimal.Parse("0" + myJokes[this.currentJoke - 1].rating),
    this.moderatedJokes);
}
```

**Continued**

## Figure 12.54 Continued

```csharp
private void b_jokesNext_Click(object sender, System.EventArgs e) {
  // displayJoke() ONLY enables this button if there are jokes
  // to display, so we don't need a sanity check here.
  this.currentJoke = this.currentJoke + 1;
  displayJoke(
    myJokes[this.currentJoke - 1].joke,
    this.currentJoke,
    this.jokesReturned,
    Decimal.Parse("0" + myJokes[this.currentJoke - 1].rating),
    this.moderatedJokes);
}


private void b_jokesAddRating_Click(
  object sender, System.EventArgs e) {
  try {
    if(!this.jokesObjCreated) {
      this.jokesObj = new jokes.jokes();
      this.jokesObjCreated = true;
    }
    // Call our Web Service method addRating
    this.jokesObj.addRating(
      userName,
      password,
      (int)this.nud_jokesRating.Value,
      Int32.Parse(this.myJokes[this.currentJoke-1].jokeID));
    // OK
    // try to tell user not to rate the joke again...
    this.b_jokesAddRating.Enabled = false;
    this.l_statusMessage.Text = "Note: New rating is " +
      "reflected only once joke has been reloaded!";
  } catch (SoapException ex) {
    XmlNode[] customErrorMsgs = ex.OtherElements;
```

**Continued**

## Figure 12.54 Continued

```
            if(customErrorMsgs.Length > 0) {
              XmlNode customErrorMsg = customErrorMsgs[0];
              if (customErrorMsg.InnerText.Length > 0) {
                this.l_statusMessage.Text =
                  "Error: " + customErrorMsg.InnerText;
                return;
              }
            }
          } catch (Exception ex) {
            this.l_statusMessage.Text = "Error: " + ex.Message;
          }
        }


      private void b_jokesAddModerated_Click(object sender,
    System.EventArgs e) {
        try {
          if(!this.jokesObjCreated) {
            this.jokesObj = new jokes.jokes();
            this.jokesObjCreated = true;
          }
          // Call our Web Service method addRating
          this.jokesObj.addModerated(
            userName,
            password,
            Int32.Parse(this.myJokes[this.currentJoke-1].jokeID));
          // OK
          this.l_statusMessage.Text =
            "OK: Joke is now available for registered users!";
        } catch (SoapException ex) {
          XmlNode[] customErrorMsgs = ex.OtherElements;
          if(customErrorMsgs.Length > 0) {
            XmlNode customErrorMsg = customErrorMsgs[0];
            if (customErrorMsg.InnerText.Length > 0) {
```

**Continued**

**Figure 12.54** Continued

```csharp
        this.l_statusMessage.Text =
          "Error: " + customErrorMsg.InnerText;

        return;
      }
    }
  } catch (Exception ex) {
    this.l_statusMessage.Text = "Error: " + ex.Message;
  }
}


private void b_jokesRemove_Click(
  object sender, System.EventArgs e) {
  try {
    if(!this.jokesObjCreated) {
      this.jokesObj = new jokes.jokes();
      this.jokesObjCreated = true;;
    }
    // Call our Web Service method addRating
    this.jokesObj.deleteUnmoderated(
      userName,
      password,
      Int32.Parse(this.myJokes[this.currentJoke-1].jokeID));
    // OK
    this.l_statusMessage.Text = "OK: Joke has been removed!";
  } catch (SoapException ex) {
    XmlNode[] customErrorMsgs = ex.OtherElements;
    if(customErrorMsgs.Length > 0) {
      XmlNode customErrorMsg = customErrorMsgs[0];
      if (customErrorMsg.InnerText.Length > 0) {
        this.l_statusMessage.Text =
          "Error: " + customErrorMsg.InnerText;
        return;
      }
```

**Continued**

**Figure 12.54** Continued

```
      }
  } catch (Exception ex) {
    this.l_statusMessage.Text = "Error: " + ex.Message;
  }
}


private void b_userAddJoke_Click(
  object sender, System.EventArgs e) {
  displayJoke("", 0, 0, 0, this.isModerator);
  string newJoke = this.tb_userJoke.Text;
  if(newJoke.Length > 0) {
    newJoke = newJoke.Substring(
      0,Math.Min(newJoke.Length, 3500));
    try {
      if(!this.jokesObjCreated) {
        this.jokesObj = new jokes.jokes();
        this.jokesObjCreated = true;
      }
      // Call our Web Service method addRating
      this.jokesObj.addJoke(
        userName,
        password,
        newJoke);
      // OK
      this.l_statusMessage.Text = "OK: Joke has been " +
        "submitted for consideration to the system!";
      this.tb_userJoke.Text = "";
    } catch (SoapException ex) {
      XmlNode[] customErrorMsgs = ex.OtherElements;
      if(customErrorMsgs.Length > 0) {
        XmlNode customErrorMsg = customErrorMsgs[0];
        if (customErrorMsg.InnerText.Length > 0) {
          this.l_statusMessage.Text =
```

**Continued**

**Figure 12.54** Continued

```
"Error: " + customErrorMsg.InnerText;

                return;

            }

        }

    } catch (Exception ex) {

        this.l_statusMessage.Text = "Error: " + ex.Message;

    }

}

}

}
```

# Some Ideas to Improve the Jokes Web Service

If you like the idea of the Jokes application, you may want to think about expanding it a little bit. It would be nice, for example, to get to know the users and to have a logging and reporting subsystem to identify who submits jokes, and which jokes are the most popular. Another idea would be to add additional *metadata* to the jokes. For instance, you could add joke categories, such as language categories, or categories that describe the joke subject matter. Along those lines, you may want to have an additional Web Service that lets moderators manage those categories and add new ones. You could also delve into the internationalization classes that the .NET Framework has built in and localize status and error messages. Let us know what interesting ideas you came up with!

# Summary

In this chapter, we have set out to develop a real-world Web Service application, namely a service that delivers jokes to the Internet community. We started out by gathering requirements, such that we want to know our users, that our users should be able to submit their own jokes and rate other user's jokes, and that there should be an administrative module in place to manage both users and jokes.

Our choice of developing this application as a Web Service was reinforced by the fact that Web Services make our application universally accessible, even for users behind corporate firewalls, and that Web Services give us support for non-English languages for free because they are based on XML and Unicode.

We started out our design by using a visual modeling tool in order to get a clear road map for our back-end and middle-tier application architecture. We designed the various components of our application in such a way that we had a clear separation between a thin Web Service "front end" layer, and implementation classes where the business logic of our application sits. We abstracted access to the Microsoft SQL Server database by providing for wrapper methods for the SQL stored procedures and by creating a separate data access class. We also designed a security and error-handling mechanism, and we made the first steps in implementing an application logging system based on interaction with the machine Event Log.

Once we had the database schema and the middle tier object model firmly in place, we started implementing the various pieces in a methodical way, starting at the back end. Because the various layers of our application are clearly separated, it would have been possible to create our project in a team of developers, say one person writing the back end infrastructure, one person writing the business logic, and a third person writing the actual Web Service itself.

Apart from encountering a very methodical way towards application development in general, we have seen a number of best practices in the area of Web Services:

- Don't put a lot of business logic into your Web Service classes! Have implementation classes do the heavy lifting. This way, you also don't limit yourself to Web Services as the only way to access your application; there may be instances where you want Internet users to access your application through Web Services, whereas it may be better for intranet users to use COM/DCOM or .NET Remoting.

- Put special emphasis on how the XML should look like between Web Service client and server. But don't limit yourself to the best case, rather decide from the very start how error information should be communicated to the client, particularly if the error can be corrected by the client. The SOAP Fault mechanism is a good start, but it has the disadvantage that it is an all-or-nothing mechanism. You may want to think about a scheme where the server can communicate to the client that *part* of the information it received was all right, but not all of it.

- There are alternatives to sending relation data through SOAP using .NET DataSets. If you think your clients will not all be running on Microsoft's .NET platform, you may want to create an alternative (and simpler!) schema to bring such data to your clients.

- Because of inherent limitations of state management in Web Services, there are currently probably few alternatives other than sending user authentication information to the server with every single Web Service request.

- Pay special attention to add documentation comments in your code throughout the project from the very start. You can then utilize the .NET feature to automatically generate project documentation files in XML format for you. You can use those files to generate your API documentation as a set of, say, HTML pages.

Lastly, we developed a client application based on Windows Forms to use our service.

# Solutions Fast Track

## Motivations and Requirements for the Jokes Web Service

☑ Internet-based applications must be *universally accessible*; on a technical level, which means they should work well with corporate firewalls, and on a user level, they have to support an international audience. You can achieve both by employing Web Service technology.

# Functional Application Design

☑ Security, state management, and error handling are critical elements of application architecture that need to be considered first.

# Implementing the Jokes Data Repository

☑ Visual Studio.NET includes a fully working copy of Microsoft's SQL Server Desktop Engine.

☑ Visual Studio.NET's Server Explorer lets you interface with data repositories such as Microsoft SQL Server, including both reading and writing database schemas and data.

☑ Starting the application development process by implementing the back end first is usually a good idea.

# Implementing the Jokes Middle Tier

☑ Visual Studio.NET continues in the tradition of the Visual Studio product line in being a very comfortable and efficient environment for application development.

☑ It is often a good idea to extend the *System.Exception* class to add custom error-handling mechanisms, such as additional logging functionality.

☑ When throwing a new exception in a Web Service context, the .NET runtime will automatically send a SOAP Fault back to the client application.

☑ The .NET Framework allows you to extend SOAP Faults to include custom XML elements, such as user-friendly status or error information.

☑ Web Service security can either be implemented using the standard ASP.NET security mechanisms, or using a custom authentication and authorization scheme. We have chosen the latter method and implemented a stateless security system for the Jokes Web Service.

# Creating a Client Application

☑ Web Service clients that run on the .NET Framework can be very easily created through employing Web References.

☑ Caching user credentials on the client is one way to address state management and security.

# Frequently Asked Questions

The following Frequently Asked Questions, answered by the authors of this book, are designed to both measure your understanding of the concepts presented in this chapter and to assist you with real-life implementation of these concepts. To have your questions about this chapter answered by the author, browse to **www.syngress.com/solutions** and click on the **"Ask the Author"** form.

**Q:** My back end data repository is not Microsoft SQL Server. How do I go about accessing my data?

**A:** One solution is to use the data access classes provided in the *System.Data.OleDb* namespace, which allow you to open data connections to essentially all the data sources that have OLEDB providers, such as Microsoft Office files or Oracle databases. However, because the .NET Framework is still very new, you may run into problems if you stray too far from the main-stream. For instance, those classes don't currently work well with Microsoft's own Exchange 2000 Web Storage System, particularly if you are dealing with multivalued fields. Your last recourse is to use straight OLEDB or straight ADO through the .NET COM Interoperability layer.

**Q:** How do I deploy the Jokes Web Service?

**A:** Deploying an ASP.NET application is as easy as creating a new IIS virtual directory on a production machine and copying all the application files into the new location. Be sure, though, to compile your application in Release mode.

**Q:** Do I need .NET on the client to use the Jokes application?

**A:** No, not at all. Although the client application we created in this chapter does in fact run only on a machine that has the .NET Framework installed, this is not a prerequisite. Any client that allows you to call a Web Service will do; specifically, all you need is a client that can send data over HTTP—so you can certainly go ahead and write a client that runs in a Web browser, as we did in Chapter 11.

# Index